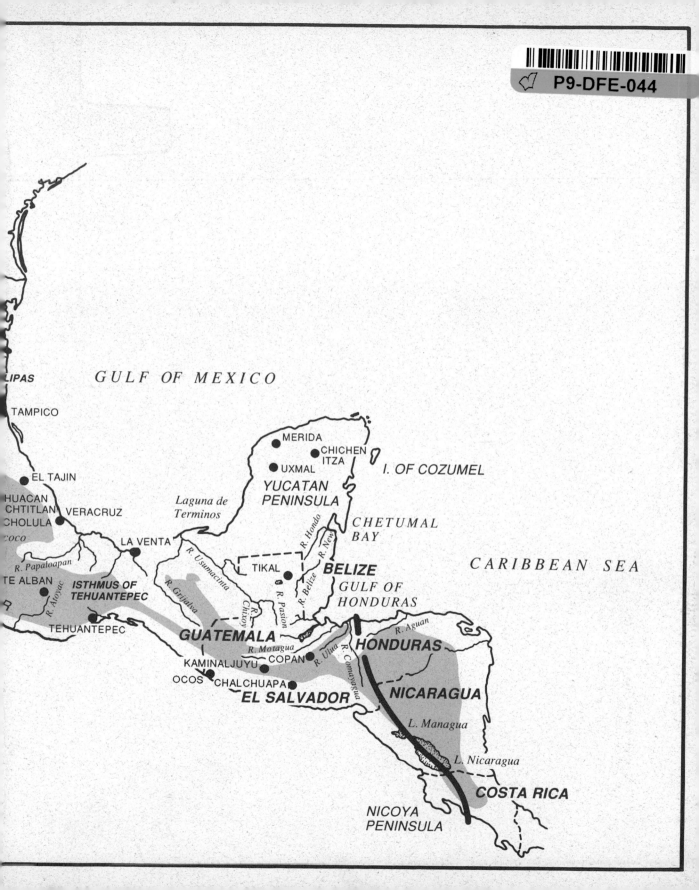

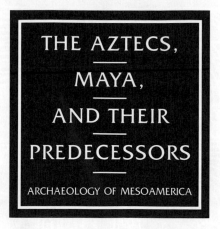

THE AZTECS,
MAYA,
AND THEIR
PREDECESSORS

ARCHAEOLOGY OF MESOAMERICA

THIRD EDITION

THE AZTECS,

MAYA,

AND THEIR

PREDECESSORS

ARCHAEOLOGY OF MESOAMERICA

THIRD EDITION

Murial Porter Weaver

ACADEMIC PRESS

San Diego New York Boston London Sydney Tokyo Toronto

Find Us on the Web! http://www.apnet.com

Academic Press
A Division of Harcourt Brace & Company
525 B Street, Suite 1900, San Diego, California 92101-4495

United Kingdom Edition published by
Academic Press Limited
24–28 Oval Road, London NW1 7DX

Library of Congress Cataloging-in-Publication Data

Weaver, Muriel Porter,
    The Aztecs, Maya, and their predecessors :   archaeology of mesoamerica /
    Muriel Porter Weaver.   -- 3rd ed.
        p.   cm.
    Includes index.
    ISBN 0-12-739065-0
    1. Indians of Mexico--Antiquities.   2. Indians of Central America- Antiqui-
ties.   3. Mexico--Antiquities.   4. Central America-Antiquities.   I. Title.
    F121.W42   1993
    972.01–dc20   92-15524
                                                                        CIP

Printed in the United States of America
99 00 01 02 EB 7 6 5 4 3

FOR HAROLD

CONTENTS

LIST OF ILLUSTRATIONS   xi
PREFACE   xvii

CHAPTER 1

Introduction: Humans Find Mesoamerica   1

A Geographic Area of Cultural Unity   1
Early Human Evidence   7
Summary   12

CHAPTER 2

Humans Become Farmers   13

Tehuacán Valley   15
Basin of Mexico   18
Tamaulipas   21
Oaxaca, Southern Mexico, and Coastal Sites   21
Summary   23

Setting the Mesoamerican Pattern and the Role of the Olmec   25

West Mexico   26
Central Highlands   28
Guerrero   46
Oaxaca   48
The Olmec   52
Great Preclassic Ceramic Traditions   71
Summary   74

Monuments, Wealth, and Complex Societies   77

The Basin of Mexico   78
Teotihuacan   79
West Mexico   93
Tlaxcala and Puebla   97
Oaxaca   98
The Maya Region   108
The Southeast Periphery   112
The Southeastern Highlands   114
Southern Maya Lowlands   120
Tikal   123
Belize   135
The Northern Region from the Gulf to the Caribbean   137
Summary   139

CHAPTER 5

Códices, Calendrics, and Maya Writing   141

Books, Calendrics, and Writing   141
The Códices   142
Other Early Maya Books   144
Time-Keeping: The Calendar Round   145
The Maya "Zero," Numbers, and Counting   148
The Maya Long Count (Initial Series)   148
Deciphering Maya Hieroglyphs   152
A Roster of Early Mesoamerican Dates   157

CHAPTER 6

Teotihuacan and Its Neighbors: The Maya Kings and a New Order   161

Teotihuacan   162
Puebla-Tlaxcala   205
Xochicalco   213
The Ñuíñe   217
Oaxaca   218
El Tajín and the Ball Game   223
Central and Southern Veracruz   229
El Salvador   231
Guatemala Valley   232
The Lowland Maya: A.D. 300–1200   237
Tikal   249
Belize   268
Copán   273
Quiriguá   292
The Southeast Periphery   297
The West   303
The Usumacinta Sites   309
The "Collapse" in the Southern Lowlands   333
Southern Campeche and Central Yucatán   335
Northern Yucatán   344
The Putún (Chontal-Maya) and the Itzá   353
Summary   379

CHAPTER 7

Tula and the Toltecs   383

Tollan, Tula, and the Toltecs   383
The Postclassic in Oaxaca   413
Chichén Itzá and the Toltecs   420

CHAPTER 8

Final Scenes: The Maya, the Tarascans, and the Aztecs   425

The Maya   425
The Tarascans   434
The Aztecs   438
Summary   479

CHAPTER 9

Mesoamerica in Perspective   481

The Southern Classic Lowland Maya   483
Teotihuacan   484
The Maya of Northern Yucatán   485
The Mexica   485
The Tarascans   486

GLOSSARY   489
REFERENCES   495
AUTHOR INDEX   537
SUBJECT INDEX   545

LIST OF ILLUSTRATIONS

COVER

Scribe (God N) from Structure 9N-82, Sepulturas, Copán. In one hand he holds a writing tool and in the other a shell fragment to serve as his ink or paint pot. (Photographed by Justin Kerr [No. 2870]).

FRONTISPIECE

Stone mosaic figure from the north façade of the House of the Bacabs, Copán, Honduras. Drawing is from a photograph by William L. Fash.

CHAPTER HEADINGS

CHAPTER 1   Entering the New World packing a tumpline (from Codex Mendoza).   1

CHAPTER 2   Cultivating a corn field (from Codex Florentino).   13

CHAPTER 3   Olmec figure from stone relief carving at Chalcatzingo (from Piña Chan, 1955a).   25

CHAPTER 4   Exchange of conversation (adapted from Codex Mendoza).   77

CHAPTER 5   Glyph with numbers depicting the day 9 Coatl (serpent) (from Codex Telleriano-Remensis, 1889).   141

CHAPTER 6   Stucco detail of a head from the Palace complex, Palenque (from drawing by Maudslay, Marquina, 1951).   161

CHAPTER 7   Glyph 4 Acatl, Toltec year sign (from Acosta, 1957).   383

CHAPTER 8   Portrait of Cuauhtémoc, last Aztec monarch (from Codex Matritense).   425

CHAPTER 9   Arrival of the Spaniards (from Codex Vaticanus A).   481

END OF TEXT   Mummy bundle (from Codex Magliabecciano).   487

FIGURES

FIGURE 1.1   Riverine-estuary environment on the southern Isthmus of Tehuantepec near Juchitán.   5

FIGURE 1.2   Jaguar, Chiapas, Mexico.   5

FIGURE 1.3   Tropical forest, Petén, Guatemala.   6

FIGURE 1.4   View from Mil Cumbres toward the Balsas Depression.   7

FIGURE 1.5   Early American projectile points.   9

FIGURE 1.6   Tools found with Iztapan mammoths.   9

FIGURE 1.7   Reconstruction of Tepexpan "man."   10

FIGURE 1.8   Sacrum of extinct llama carved to resemble the head of an animal, Tequixquiac, Mexico.   11

FIGURE 2.1   Comparison of early and modern dent corn.   14

FIGURE 2.2   Cornfield with beans growing up the stalks near San Miguel de Milagro, Tlaxcala.   15

FIGURE 2.3   Amaranth (ancient *huauhtli*) in florescence in Tlaxcala.   17

FIGURE 2.4   Early tools of stone, bone, and clay.   19

FIGURE 2.5   Prickly pear cactus bearing fruit.   22

FIGURE 3.1   Shaft-and-chamber tomb, El Opeño, Michoacán.   28

FIGURE 3.2   Black trifid vessel, Gualupita, Morelos (?).   29

FIGURE 3.3   Clay female figurine, recovered from a hearth at Zohapilco, Tlapacoya.   30

FIGURE 3.4   Preclassic pottery forms.   32

FIGURE 3.5   Bottle-shaped food storage/rubbish pit at Tlatilco.   34

FIGURE 3.6   Graves at Tlatilco cemetery.   35

FIGURE 3.7   Preclassic figures and figurines.   36

FIGURE 3.8   Preclassic miscellaneous objects.   37

FIGURE 3.9   Preclassic ceramics: special forms and decorations.   38

FIGURE 3.10   Gray ware figurine from Las Bocas, Puebla.   42

FIGURE 3.11   Hollow seated baby figure from Las Bocas, Puebla.   43

FIGURE 3.12   Hollow clay figure wearing a jaguar (?) pelt, Atlihuayán, Morelos.   44

FIGURE 3.13   Hollow white-slipped, Olmec-style "baby-face" fragment. Teopantecuanitlán, Guerrero.   47

FIGURE 3.14   Riverine-estuary, Isthmus of Tehuantepec near Juchitán.   52

FIGURE 3.15   Monumental Preclassic stone sculpture.   59

FIGURE 3.16   Small stone sculptures.   60

FIGURE 3.17   Ceremonial precinct of La Venta.   63

FIGURE 4.1   Pyramid at Cuicuilco, Valley of Mexico.   78

FIGURE 4.2   Goblet with pedestal base, decorated in *al fresco* technique, Tlapacoya.   79

FIGURE 4.3   White-on-red cylindrical tripod with very small supports, Valley of Mexico.   79

FIGURE 4.4   Pyramid of the Sun, Teotihuacan.   81

FIGURE 4.5   The Street of the Dead marked by the Pyramid of the Moon at its northern end.   84

FIGURE 4.6   The Ciudadela.   85

FIGURE 4.7   Architecture at Teotihuacan.   86

FIGURE 4.8   Carved façade of the Feathered-Serpent (Quetzalcoatl) Pyramid.   88

FIGURE 4.9   West Mexico ceramics.   95

FIGURE 4.10   A sacrificed victim, "Danzante," one of bas-relief slabs forming a public gallery.   100

FIGURE 4.11   Danzante No. 6.   101

FIGURE 4.12   Stela 12 and 13, Monte Albán.   101

FIGURE 4.13   Bat mask of polished jade pieces.   103

FIGURE 4.14   Civic-ceremonial center of Monte Albán.   105

FIGURE 4.15   Stela 21, Izapa, Chiapas, Mexico.   110

FIGURE 4.16   Tripod jar decorated in Usulután resist technique, Cobán, Guatemala.   115

FIGURE 4.17   Mound E-III-3, Tomb 1, Kaminaljuyú.   117

FIGURE 4.18   Pyramid E-VII-sub. Uaxactún, Guatemala.   122

FIGURE 4.19   The corbeled arch.   124

FIGURE 4.20   The Hauberg Stela.   130

FIGURE 5.1   The Dresden Codex, page 50.   143

FIGURE 5.2   The twenty Maya day signs.   146

FIGURE 5.3   The eighteen Maya months.   147

FIGURE 5.4   Maya numerals.   149

FIGURE 5.5   Maya calendrical hieroglyphs.   150

FIGURE 5.6   Example of a Long Count date: Monument 6, Quirigua.   151

FIGURE 5.7   Event and family glyphs.   154

FIGURE 5.8   A Classic Maya vase bearing glyphs of a Primary Standard Sequence.   156

FIGURE 5.9   Stone stelae with Long Count dates.   157–159

FIGURE 6.1   Plan of Tlamimilolpa Compound.   165

FIGURE 6.2   Quetzalpapálotl (Quetzal-butterfly) Palace, Teotihuacan.   166

FIGURE 6.3   Classic Teotihuacan artifacts: pottery and stone.   169

FIGURE 6.4   Atetelco palace reconstruction of the White Patio.   171

FIGURE 6.5   Tepantitla mural; sketch of ball game and ball court marker.   173

FIGURE 6.6   Painted figure wearing the tassel headdress proceeded by a compound sign.   175

FIGURE 6.7   Notational signs of Teotihuacan.   178

FIGURE 6.8   Votive pyramid at La Quemada.   190

FIGURE 6.9   Talud-tablero style construction at Tingambato, Michoacán.   195

FIGURE 6.10   Large platform supporting a series of rooms. Tingambato.   196

FIGURE 6.11   The Guachimontón Complex, Teuchitlán, Mexico. Pattern of circular architecture.   197

FIGURE 6.12   West Mexican metallurgy.   201

FIGURE 6.13   Cacaxtla, Tlaxcala: the site.   208

FIGURE 6.14   Cacaxtla battle mural.   209

FIGURE 6.15   The woman on a pillar of the Venus Temple, Cacaxtla.   211

FIGURE 6.16   The man with scorpion tail on a pillar of the Venus Temple, Cacaxtla.   212

FIGURE 6.17   Main pyramid at Xochicalco, Morelos.   214

FIGURE 6.18   Detail of sculptured relief of the Xochicalco pyramid.   214

FIGURE 6.19   Three stelae at Xochicalco constituting a set.   216

FIGURE 6.20   Xochicalco ball court with stone rings in lateral walls.   217

FIGURE 6.21   System IV building complex, Monte Albán.   220

FIGURE 6.22   Monte Albán urns.   222

FIGURE 6.23   Pyramid of the Niches, El Tajín. Veracruz.   224

FIGURE 6.24   Relief carving of the south ball court showing sacrificial scene, El Tajín.   225

FIGURE 6.25   Ball game artifacts.   228

FIGURE 6.26   Classic Gulf coast figurines and mirror.   230

FIGURE 6.27   Classic Period pottery.   235

FIGURE 6.28   *Cacao* growing in the Río Grijalva delta region of Tabasco.   245

FIGURE 6.29   Classic Period architecture including variations of talud-tablero style.   251

FIGURE 6.30   Front and lateral faces of Stela 31, Tikal.   254

FIGURE 6.31   Plan of the North Acropolis, Tikal.   257

FIGURE 6.32   View of the North Acropolis from Temple 1.   258

FIGURE 6.33   Detail of hieroglyphs from Stela 26, the Red Stela.   260

FIGURE 6.34   Temple I, Tikal, Guatemala.   261

FIGURE 6.35   Temple II, Tikal, Guatemala.   262

FIGURE 6.36   Plan of central Tikal.   264

FIGURE 6.37   Copán: ceremonial precinct and acropolis.   275

FIGURE 6.38   Ball game scene on polychrome Maya vase.   277

FIGURE 6.39   Ball court A-III at Copán.   277

FIGURE 6.40   Entrance to the sanctuary of Temple 22, Copán.   281

FIGURE 6.41   Detail of entrance to Temple 22, Copán. Skull of the Underworld.   281

FIGURE 6.42   The Great Plaza of Copán.   282

FIGURE 6.43   Stela depicting Ruler XVIII-Jog.   282

FIGURE 6.44   The hieroglyphic stairway at Copán.   284

FIGURE 6.45   The executioner god. Reviewing Stand, Temple 11, Copán.   287

FIGURE 6.46   Altar Q, Copán.   288

FIGURE 6.47   Scribe (God N) from Structure 9N-82, Sepulturas, Copán.   289

FIGURE 6.48   Detail of Stela C, portraying Ruler Cauac Sky, Quiriguá.   294

FIGURE 6.49   Late Classic zoomorph sculpture, Quiriguá, Guatemala.   296

FIGURE 6.50   Miscellaneous Classic Maya artifacts.   298

FIGURE 6.51   Ruler 3, Dos Pilas, Petexbatún, Guatemala.   306

FIGURE 6.52   Fine Classic Maya pottery.   308

FIGURE 6.53   Entrance to the ruins of Bonampak, Chiapas.   311

FIGURE 6.54   Wall painting showing part of the Bonampak band.   312

FIGURE 6.55   Continuation of the celebration begun in Figure 6.54.   313

FIGURE 6.56   Building 19 at Yaxchilán, Chiapas.   314

FIGURE 6.57   Bloodletting on Lintel 14, Temple 20, Yaxchilán.   315

FIGURE 6.58   The Yaxchilán Plaza with the sacred ceiba tree.   316

FIGURE 6.59   Lintel 15, Temple 21, Yaxchilán.   317

FIGURE 6.60   The great Temple 33, commissioned by Bird-Jaguar.   318

FIGURE 6.61   The Usumacinta River below Yaxchilán.   319

FIGURE 6.62   *Temescal* at Piedras Negras.   319

FIGURE 6.63   Pacal's Tomb, Temple of the Inscriptions, Palenque, Chiapas.   324–325

FIGURE 6.64   Views and details of Palenque.   327–329

FIGURE 6.65   Ruins of Comalcalco, Tabasco.   331

FIGURE 6.66   Comparison of Maya temples, northern and southern lowlands.   336

FIGURE 6.67   Architecture of central Yucatán.   338–342

FIGURE 6.68   Las Monjas (the Nunnery) at Uxmal, Yucatán.   346

FIGURE 6.69   El Adivino (the House of the Magician) pyramid at Uxmal, Yucatán.   347

FIGURE 6.70   Detail of the façade of the Governor's Palace at Uxmal.   348

FIGURE 6.71   The arch over the *sacbé* at Kabah, Yucatán.   349

FIGURE 6.72   The Codz Poop structure at Kabah, Yucatán.   350

FIGURE 6.73   The Xlopah Cenote at Dzibilchaltún, Yucatán.   351

FIGURE 6.74   The Temple of the Seven Dolls, Dzibilchaltún, Yucatán.   352

FIGURE 6.75   A non-Maya stela at Seibal, Guatemala.   358

FIGURE 6.76   Temple A-3, Seibal, commissioned to celebrate a period-ending date.   359

FIGURE 6.77   Jaina figurines.   362

FIGURE 6.78   Nohoch Mul pyramid (Structure 1) at Cobá, Yucatán.   363

FIGURE 6.79   Las Monjas (the Nunnery) at Chichén Itzá.   366

FIGURE 6.80   Plan of Chichén Itzá.   367

FIGURE 6.81   Round structure known as the Caracol at Chichén Itzá.   368

FIGURE 6.82   Temple to Kukulcán, the feathered-serpent, at Chichén Itzá.   368

FIGURE 6.83   Group of the thousand columns adjacent to the Temple of the Warriors, Chichén Itzá.   369

FIGURE 6.84   The Temple of the Warriors, containing the interior Temple of the Chacmool, murals, and Atlantean figures.   370

FIGURE 6.85   A low dance platform located in front of the Temple of the Warriors.   370

FIGURE 6.86   The giant of all Mesoamerican ball courts.   371

FIGURE 6.87   View out the ball court toward the Temple of the Warriors and the Temple of Kukulcán.   372

FIGURE 6.88   The Sacred Cenote of Chichén Itzá.   373

FIGURE 6.89   One of the numerous *chacmool* figures of Chichén Itzá.   375

FIGURE 7.1   Aerial view of Tula Grande in 1957 before reconstruction.   391

FIGURE 7.2   South side of Pyramid B, Tula Grande after reconstruction.   391

FIGURE 7.3   Atlantean figures, Tula Grande.   392

FIGURE 7.4   Side view of Atlantean figures.   393

FIGURE 7.5   Detail of Tula Grande.   394–396

FIGURE 7.6   Main structures of Tula Grande.   398

FIGURE 7.7   *Chacmool*, Tula.   400

FIGURE 7.8   El Corral Temple.   401

FIGURE 7.9   House groups of the Canal Locality.   403

FIGURE 7.10   Toltec Period pottery (line drawings).   404

FIGURE 7.11   Toltec Period pottery
               (photographs). 407

FIGURE 7.12   The great pyramid at Cholula,
               Puebla. 412

FIGURE 7.13   Huastec stone stela, Castillo de Teayo,
               Veracruz. 414

FIGURE 7.14   Huastec priest (?) performing
               autosacrifice. 415

FIGURE 7.15   Palace structure at Mitla, Oaxaca. 416

FIGURE 7.16   Various calendrical hieroglyphs. 419

FIGURE 7.17   Comparative features: Tula and Chichén
               Itzá. 421

FIGURE 7.18   Comparison of benches from Tula and
               Chichén Itzá. 422

FIGURE 8.1   Maya deities. 426

FIGURE 8.2   View of Tulum, Quintana Roo. 429

FIGURE 8.3   Diving God, Tulum. 430

FIGURE 8.4   View of Flores (Tayasal), Petén,
               Guatemala. 432

FIGURE 8.5   The five *yácatas* of Tzintzuntzan,
               Michoacán. 437

FIGURE 8.6   Tarascan "teapot" vessel,
               Tzintzuntzan. 438

FIGURE 8.7   Aztec kings. 441

FIGURE 8.8   Model of the ceremonial precinct of
               Tenochtitlán. 446

FIGURE 8.9   Details of the Great Temple precinct,
               Tenochtitlán. 447–449

FIGURE 8.10   Aztec treasures. 450

FIGURE 8.11   Monolith of a dismembered
               Coyolxauhqui, Great Temple,
               Tenochtitlán. 451

FIGURE 8.12   Early *chacmool* figure from the Great
               Temple, approximately A.D. 1350. 452

FIGURE 8.13   Pyramid of Tenayuca,
               Tlalnepantla. 453

FIGURE 8.14   Restored pyramid of Santa Cecilia at
               Tenayuca. 453

FIGURE 8.15   General view of Teotenango. 454

FIGURE 8.16   Aztec numerals. 455

FIGURE 8.17   The twenty Aztec day-signs. 456

FIGURE 8.18   The eighteen Aztec months. 456

FIGURE 8.19   Aztec picture writing. 458

FIGURE 8.20   Xipe Totec, Tlalpan, Valley of
               Mexico. 459

FIGURE 8.21   Chalchihuítlicue, Aztec water
               goddess. 459

FIGURE 8.22   Portion of polychromed *chacmool* at
               entrance to shrine of Tlaloc, Great
               Temple of Tenochtitlán. 461

FIGURE 8.23   Page from the Codex Borgia, example of
               Mixteca-Puebla style painting. 462

FIGURE 8.24   Postclassic adornments. 463

FIGURE 8.25   Ceramics of the Postclassic period. 464

FIGURE 8.26   Aztec deities. 466

FIGURE 8.27   *Chinampa* at Mixquic, Valley of
               Mexico. 470

FIGURE 8.28   Prominent commercial goods. 474

FIGURE 8.29   Music makers. 476

MAPS

MAP 1.1   Mesoamerica. 2

MAP 1.2   Mesoamerica: linguistic groups. 3

MAP 2.1   Early humans and the Preclassic Basin of
           Mexico. 20

MAP 3.1   West Mexico. 27

MAP 3.2   The Preclassic Period. 41

MAP 4.1   Oaxaca Valleys. 99

MAP 6.1   Simplified map of civic-ceremonial center
           of Teotihuacan. 163

MAP 6.2   Highland resources. 184

MAP 6.3   Classic Mesoamerica west of the Isthmus
           of Tehuantepec. 188

MAP 6.4   The Teuchitlán tradition of western
           Mexico. 198

MAP 6.5   The Classic Maya. 247

MAP 6.6   Belize, eastern Guatemala and
           southwestern Campeche. 269

MAP 6.7   The southern periphery. 299

MAP 6.8   The conquered realm of Dos Pilas. 304

MAP 7.1   Tula during the Tollan phase. 387

MAP 8.1   The Postclassic Maya. 427

MAP 8.2   The Tarascans. 435

MAP 8.3   The Basin of Mexico A.D. 1519. 443

MAP 8.4   Extent of the Aztec state in
           A.D. 1519. 478

PREFACE

How naive I was to embark on this third edition! I had earmarked certain sections of the text for revision but felt that much of the rest could stand. Wrong! Once I started putting it all together I realized how very productive archaeologists have been during the last ten years; now, precious little remains of the second edition. New approaches, theories, areas of investigation, sites, and a new generation of researchers have challenged ideas embedded for fifty years.

Belize, once scarcely noticed by archaeologists, now contributes to every time frame with both coastal and inland sites. Recent investigations on the southeastern edge of Mesoamerica have given greater perspective to Quiriguá and Copán, as well as a better understanding of local cultures in Honduras and relationships with lower Central America. The epigraphers have put real kings and nobility into the palaces of the Maya heartland, while the excavations at Dos Pilas provide one example of Classic Maya "collapse."

As for earlier Olmec culture, we now see some roots of the San Lorenzo Olmec, and La Venta has come alive with urban residents and its own early history. We observe a possibly older Olmec manifestation in Guerrero, and the questions remain: who were these people and what inspired their monuments? Teotihuacan stunned the scientific world by revealing mass sacrifices in the very center of a site we thought we knew. The continuing enigma of a Mexican–Maya relationship is rekindled by the Maya influence in Cacaxtla murals in highland Mexico. We know much more about

Tula, but the Toltecs can still stir debate. West Mexico plays an interesting role in early development and provides a different model of an independent Mesoamerican state.

Is nothing left untouched? No, indeed. By demolishing a number of city blocks in the heart of Mexico's capital, the Great Temple of the Aztecs has been uncovered, revealing how various kings added construction, the massive offerings contributed by members of the empire, and the devastation wrought in the final days of the Spanish Conquest.

This book is conceived as a general introduction to the archaeology of Meso-america. Integrating all the aspects of this area in a single volume has meant concentrating on the broad picture at the expense of smaller sites and discussion. When possible I have tried to guide the reader to alternative literature and opinions. This work represents the current status of our knowledge, but we must allow for flexibility and expect inevitable changes.

Although I am still unhappy with the terms Preclassic, Classic, and Postclassic, I find nothing more suitable. Their usage has continued and is embedded in the archaeological literature. Readers should note that I have taken liberties by stretching these labels and adapting the time frames according to region. Chapter 4, for example, deals with the special years 300 B.C.–A.D. 300, combining a variety of labels (late Preclassic, Terminal Preclassic, Proto-Classic, and even Early Classic in part). For the Classic Period in central Mexico, I have kept A.D. 300–900 B.C., which includes the Epi-Classic. For the Maya, I run the Classic Period until A.D. 1200 to accommodate Chichén Itzá. The reader can follow the sequence of any particular site by consulting the Subject Index.

A general map and a basic chronology appear again on the front and back end-papers, with additional sectional maps in the text. The Glossary lists terms and names commonly used in Mesoamerican literature. I hope that the text stimulates and invites further reading.

Volumes composed of multiple articles, often resulting from conferences or symposiums, have become a popular way to present ideas of a particular theme or temporal period. A list of the most frequently cited articles appears on pages 495–497 (Section II). When these articles appear in the reference list (Section III), only the editor's name and the date of publication appear. Readers should refer to Section II for the complete citation. This "editors list" is, I believe, useful in itself and I have been able to include more references because of this shortened method.

Finally, I would like to thank those individuals and institutions that have been so helpful to me in preparation of this edition by providing comments, reprints, photographs, line drawings, news, and advice. My debt is great and my list long, but I would like to extend my appreciation to the following: Wendy Ashmore, Carolyn Baus, Elizabeth Boone, Warwick Bray, George Cowgill, Arthur Demarest, Richard Diehl, William Fash, Roberto García Moll, Arturo Gómez-Pompa, John Graham, Dan Healan, Marie-Areti Hers, Doris Heyden, Dorothy Hosler, Christopher Jones, Julie Jones, Justin Kerr, James C. Langley, Jack Lissack, Richard MacNeish, Linda Manzanilla, Eduardo Matos Moctezuma, Lorraine Matys, Curt Muser, Ben Nelson, Christine Niederberger, Bertina Olmeda Vera, Esther Pasztory, Román Pina Chan,

Evelyn Rattray, Kent Reilly III, Arturo Romano, William Rust III, Linda Schele, Paul Schmidt, Felipe Solís, George Stuart, Karl Taube, Paul Tolstoy, and Phil Weigand.

I also thank the following institutions for permitting reproductions of their photographs: The British Museum, London; the Dallas Art Museum, Dallas, Texas; Dumbarton Oaks, Washington, D.C.; the Fine Arts Museums of San Francisco; the Instituto Nacional de Antropología e Historia, Mexico; the Metropolitan Museum of Art in New York City; Museum of the American Indian, Heye Foundation in New York City; the National Museum of Anthropology, Mexico; Peabody Museum of Harvard University, Cambridge, Massachusetts; and the University Museum of the University of Pennsylvania.

None of the above are responsible for any of this volume's flaws and shortcomings; these are mine alone.

The research, done largely at the Robert Goldwater Library of the Metropolitan Museum of Arts in New York City, was made particularly enjoyable by the assistance of Ross Day and Peter Blank.

What brought the book to fruition was the enthusiasm of Charles Arthur and Rick Roehrich of Academic Press in San Diego and my good fortune to have Eileen Favorite as production editor, with a final polish by Gayle Early, and Alli Spooner as art coordinator. I thank them all.

My husband Harold has again sustained me during the preparation of this book, and I am most grateful for his continued forbearance.

Williamsburg, Virginia
January, 1993

CHAPTER 1

Introduction: Humans Find Mesoamerica

A GEOGRAPHIC AREA OF CULTURAL UNITY

Mesoamerica is a term coined by Paul Kirchhoff in 1943 to refer to a geographical region in the Western Hemisphere that shared a basic cultural unity at the time of the Spanish Conquest in 1521. The boundaries were drawn up largely on the basis of ethnographic and linguistic data and have been adapted to archaeology as well.

The area of Mesoamerica generally includes central and southern Mexico with the Yucatán Peninsula, Guatemala, El Salvador, and parts of Honduras, Nicaragua, and northern Costa Rica (Map 1.1). The northern border roughly separates hunters and gatherers from their more sophisticated neighbors to the south. The southern limits are less sharply defined culturally.

The people of Mesoamerica shared a number of traits that characterize this area. The most oustanding are ball courts with rings, particular farming techniques, códices (books made of amate paper or deerskin), hieroglyphic writing, human sacrifice, position numerals, stepped pyramids, and a year of 18 months of 20 days plus 5 extra days. More general features would include stratification of society with merchants, warriors, artisans, farmers, an elite leadership, along with market systems, urbanism and complex religious, economic, and political structures. We will find great regional diversity in the distribution of these features, and at the same time intense interaction

MESOAMERICA

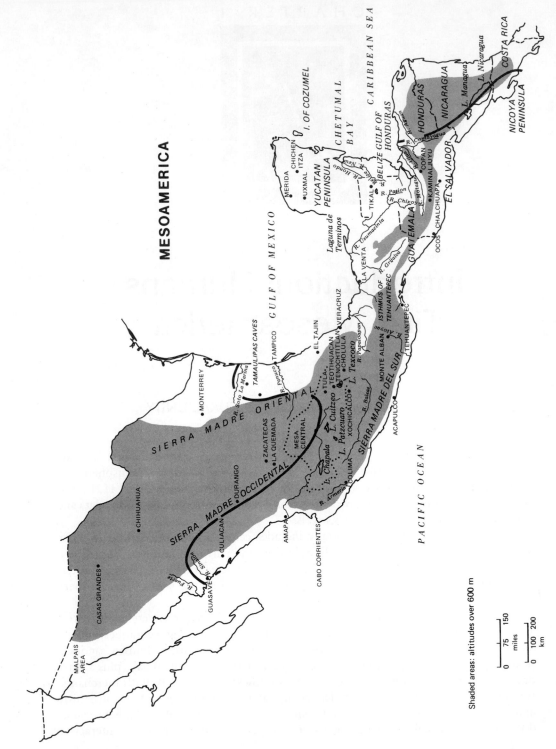

Shaded areas: altitudes over 600 m

MAP 1.1 Mesoamerica.

among centers locally and over great distances through trade and communication. Religion, astronomy, mythology, and a fatalistic cosmology were all bound together in a philosophy that directed the course of humans' lives. This book is concerned with the development of a unique civilization that grew up in Mesoamerica beginning with the time it was first settled until the arrival of the Europeans in the sixteenth century.

We do not know who these Mesoamericans were. We only know what they called themselves at the time of the Conquest. In Pre-Columbian times a great variety of languages were spoken. Prior to 4000 B.C., all languages in Mesoamerica may have been related but soon after that the great Uto-Aztecan strain can be distinguished. This group in turn split into many subdivisions, Náhua being the most important, and its close relative Náhuatl became the language of the Aztecs. It is still spoken today by many rural groups in central Mexico. It is a beautiful and melodious language and became one of the literary tongues of ancient America used for recording epic poems, proverbs, flowery rhetoric, and hymns to the gods. (See Map 1.2.)

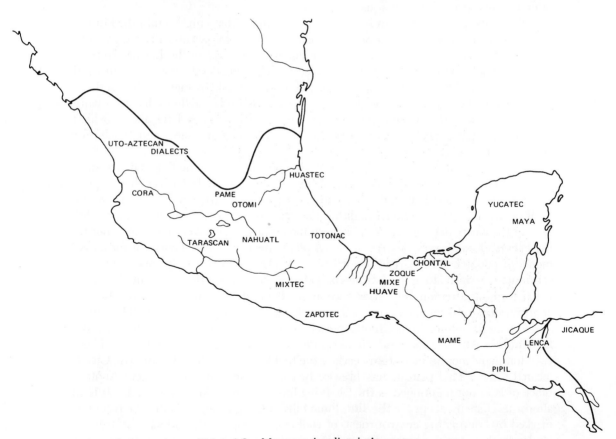

MAP 1.2   Mesoamerica: linguistic groups.

Another large group was made up of Macro-Mayan speakers who spread throughout the southern lowlands of the Gulf Coast and the eastern highlands. This same area spun off the Yucatecans to Yucatán and the Cholans to the Petén around 900–800 B.C. Other great migrations took place at a much later time from central Mexico to El Salvador. Today the vast majority of Mesoamerican inhabitants speak only Spanish, but a minority is still bilingual, speaking an additional autochthonous Indian language.

The map of Mesoamerica is shaped like an irregular bow with the knot in the center forming the Isthmus of Tehuantepec, a narrow corridor of land uniting western Mesoamerica with the Maya area to the east. In the western sector, two great mountain systems ran like backbones down each coastline until interrupted by an east–west chain of volcanoes. These mountain systems enclose the central highland plateau of the Mesa Central that has always been a focus of social, political, and economic forces. At one time the waters here drained off to the southeast, but volcanoes rose up cutting off this flow and formed a large inland basin with no outlet, today's Valley of Mexico. Five shallow lakes were created in the basin floor that, being swampy at the shoreline, offered many attractions for aquatic life.

The principal river system in the east is the Pánuco that empties into the Gulf of Mexico near Tampico. In the opposite direction, the Basin of Toluca is the gateway to all western Mexico and gives rise to the mighty waterway of the Lerma-Santiago that eventually pours into the Pacific Ocean. The great volcanoes soar upward 4000 m to over 5000 m. To them the people owe the fresh springs on the southern escarpments, the cinder cones, wide lava flows, ash falls, and mud flows that eventually enriched the soils that would improve agricultural yields. They have also provided the volcanic glassy rock, obsidian, for human tools, and andesites and basalts for construction work.

South of this volcanic chain, the land falls off sharply into the Balsas depression, an area dominated by two enormous drainage systems, the Balsas River that empties into the Pacific and the slower, more tranquil Papaloapan, that winds eastward to the Gulf of Mexico. The southern highland plateau of Oaxaca is the only relatively flat land in the entire depression. The western mountains, Sierra Madre del Sur, border the Pacific Ocean leaving a strip of coastal plain offering a natural corridor for movements of peoples. The narrow coastal plain, backed by a wet hilly piedmont area, continues eastward along the Isthmus of Tehuantepec and southward through Guatemala, forming a region known as Soconusco. Beyond this, the mountains rise and continue down the Pacific Coast of Guatemala, crossing into northeastern Honduras. The mountains of northern Chiapas present a high and difficult terrain and form the highlands of Alta Verapaz and the Sierra de Santa Cruz (see Figures 1.1–1.4). These two dominant mountain systems enclose the highland area where Guatemala City is located today. This plateau has likewise benefited from volcanic activity. Another block of land not mentioned is the low-lying limestone peninsula of Yucatán. It is an almost level shelf except for the little Puuc hills of Campeche. This diverse terrain is marked by contrasting environments of cool tropical highlands and varying tropical lowlands; there are also areas of near-desert conditions such as those near the northern frontiers of Mesoamerica.

FIGURE 1.1   Riverine-estuary environment on the southern Isthmus of Tehuantepec near Juchitán. (Courtesy of Robert and Judith Zeitlin.)

FIGURE 1.2   The lowland jaguar, prominent in Mesoamerican iconography from very early times, became a symbol of classic Maya royalty. (Chiapas, Mexico. Photographed by Lorraine Matys.)

FIGURE 1.3   Tropical forest, Petén, Guatemala. (Courtesy of the University Museum, University of Pennsylvania.)

In the cool highlands of Mexico and Guatemala, white-tailed deer and rabbit were probably the most common game animals. Peccaries, coyotes, bats, raccoons, and a great variety of rodents and small mammals were typical of the entire area. Especially common in the tropical lowlands were howler, marmoset, and spider monkeys and tapirs, ocelots, jaguars, and opossums. Turtles, lizards, iguanas, crocodiles, and many varieties of snakes were common reptiles. Birds included ducks, geese, swans, teals, and coots, that were often a valuable addition to the diet. Owls lived at all elevations; vultures and birds of prey were important as scavengers. Lakes and streams as well as the two lengthy coastlines afforded abundant fish, mollusks, and crustaceans; deep shell middens attest to their importance as a basic food supply (West, 1964).

When human beings settled in Mesoamerica, they could live at an elevation of 2400 m, at sea level, or at intermediate points. They had a wide choice of dwelling sites: alluvial plains, terraces, caves, valleys, and inland basins. They could choose to live near a lake, spring, or river, in areas of abundant rainfall, or choose a dry, semiarid climate, lush tropical forest, savannas, deciduous forests, or barren desertlike terrain. These offered very different opportunities for exploitation and, as we shall see, they chose them all.

FIGURE 1.4   View from Mil Cumbres toward the Balsas Depression. (Photographed by the author.)

EARLY HUMAN EVIDENCE

Physical anthropologists tell us that humans first entered the New World via the Bering Strait of Alaska. There are many points on which anthropologists differ, but they agree that humans originated in the Old World and were a fully developed species, *Homo sapiens*, when they came to the Americas. All are in accord with this second statement, but questions have arisen concerning the first.

We have long been taught that where the bison, the woolly mammoth, and the tundra-loving musk ox wandered, humans followed. During the height of the Wisconsin glaciation, which was marked by two major advances of the ice separated by a relatively ice-free interval ending approximately 25,000 years ago, the water was locked up into great ice sheets, and the sea level was lowered at least 90 m and possibly as much as 300 m. This created the massive Bering Land Bridge connecting what is now Siberia and Alaska, a 1000-km-wide strip of land that would have permitted easy access to America from Asia (Jennings, 1968).

When did humans first cross over into the Americas? Was this their route? The event is not easily estimated chronologically for the land bridge must have opened and closed at different times. We do not believe that humans arrived in one migration as a single homogeneous population. But they have surely inhabited the Western Hemisphere for at least 15,000 years, and some specialists feel justified in extending this to 40,000. Most of the absolute dates for their presence here fall between 12,000 and 6000 B.C., but a few are considerably older.

Now it seems that the Bering Land Bridge may not be the only acceptable theory to explain human entry in the New World (Dixon, 1985). The scenario above is challenged on the following points.

The Clovis projectile point (see Figure 1.5) is widely accepted as the earliest evidence of human occupation and is "well dated" to 9500–9000 B.C. But similar Alaskan points are 1000 years *younger* than those found further south in the Americas. Geologists and botanists have also found that the land bridge did not offer good grazing and was characterized by sand dunes and high winds not attractive to either animals or humans. In southcentral Chile a site has been found that is 13,000 years of age with stone tools and a footprint of a child. Highland Peru may have human remains of the same age (MacNeish, 1970). Current research has at least reopened the question of how humans reached the Americas, suggesting that transoceanic voyages across the Pacific Ocean from Asia were entirely possible (Dixon, 1985).

The best evidence of early humans is derived from four sources: (1) stratigraphy; (2) reliable and consistent C-14 dates; (3) evidence from other disciplines lending chronological and geological support; and (4) artifacts made by humans in a primary stratigraphic context (Fagan, 1987).

The Clovis Culture in the Great Plains of the United States is documented by dozens of sites where stone artifacts are found in direct association with Ice Age mammals and carbon dated to 9500–9000 B.C. (Dixon, 1985). Clovis points were projectiles that could be attached to wooden spears. This particular style of point (Figure 1.5) was made by careful percussion and pressure flaking to form a channel extending part way up the shaft from the base, on one or both sides. It inspired the later Folsom point (Figure 1.5). Many of these tools have been found at "kill" sites. Another type was shaped like a willow leaf and was pointed at both ends. This Cascade point had a wide distribution in Meso- and South America.

As regards Mesoamerica, our knowledge of the early Paleo-Indian is based on fragments of skeletal remains and tools made to kill and dismember big-game animals. Many "kill" sites are known in North America where groups of men drove the animals over cliffs, or perhaps into swampy lake shores where their movements were restricted by the deep mire and they could be killed by projectile points and butchered.

In Mesoamerica some very early finds have been reported but in many cases are doubtful and may be poorly documented (see discussion in Fagan, 1987). Claims for "unifacial flaked-stone technologies" or "chopper-tool industries" have not stood up to rigorous scientific scrutiny. Our most reliable record begins with the Iztapan mammoths with carbon dates around 7270 B.C.

Iztapan Mammoths

The remains of two imperial mammoths (*Mammuthus imperator*) discovered at Santa Isabel Iztapan in 1948 provided undisputed evidence that these beasts were pursued by men and driven into the swampy edge of old Lake Texcoco where they were killed and dismembered (Aveleyra, 1956). A surprising variety of tools was

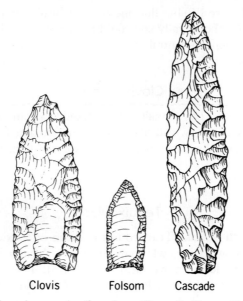

Clovis   Folsom   Cascade

FIGURE 1.5 Early American projectile points. (From *Prehistory of North America (1968)* by J. D. Jennings. Copyright by McGraw Hill, Inc. Used with permission of McGraw-Hill Book Company.)

found: obsidian side-scrapers, flint blades, a fragment of a bifacial knife, three projectile points, and prismatic knives of obsidian, all of which are common in later archaeological horizons (Fig. 1.6). The mammoths are dated around 7700–7300 B.C. (Johnson and MacNeish, 1972).

Tepexpan "Man"

Actually a woman 25–30 years of age, the Tepexpan "Man" was interred on the former northwestern shore of Lake Texcoco. No more than 5 ft. 5 in. tall, the unfortunate creature was found face down with her legs flexed. There were no

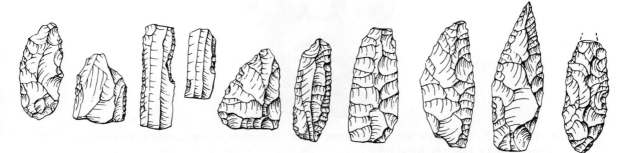

FIGURE 1.6 Tools found with Iztapan mammoths. (From Aveleyra, 1964.)

associated artifacts (Figure 1.7) but fluorine analysis bears out a date coeval with that of the mammoths. Morphologically she could fit in the normal range of variation of present Indian populations of central Mexico.

Clovis Points

At a hunting campsite, Los Tapiales, in highland Guatemala, the base of a Clovis point, bifaces, burins, scrapers, and blades were found, dated at 8760 B.C. Another complete Clovis point of obsidian was picked up west of Guatemala City (M. Coe., 1988).

Tequixquiac

This is a site north of Lake Texcoco in the Basin of Mexico. Scrapers, uniface pressure-flaked blades, and bone awls were recovered. A carved sacrum of a camelid was fashioned to resemble an animal head (Figure 1.8). There were no associations but its estimated antiguity is Upper Pleistocene (?) (Aveleyra, 1950).

Tlapacoya

This is a Basin of Mexico site. Tools of andesite, obsidian, basalt, and quartz were found with hearths in a living area dated at 19,000 B.C. (?) (Tolstoy, 1980).

FIGURE 1.7   Reconstruction of Tepexpan "Man." (Courtesy of the Instituto Nacional de Antropología e Historia, Mexico.)

FIGURE 1.8 Sacrum of extinct llama, carved to resemble the head of an animal. Tequixquiac, Mexico. Width: 7 inches. Courtesy of the Instituto Nacional de Antropología e Historia, Mexico.

Valsequillo

South of Puebla, abundant Pleistocene fossils make this a promising site for possibly very old remains dated at 28,000 B.C. (?) (Tolstoy, 1980).

Richmond Hill

In Belize, thousands of crude flint tools cover the surface along with remains of early hunters and gatherers who also exploited marine resources. No dates are available but the site is suggestive of great antiquity (Coe, 1988).

After 7000 B.C. the big-game hunting gave way to a generalized pattern known as the Desert Tradition in western North America. This did not take place uniformly, but the new way of life in Mesoamerica seems like a southern extension of this pattern. It is characterized by hunting techniques and tools (choppers, scrapers, gouges, mortars, and *manos*), that were made to exploit the smaller fauna that replaced the big-game animals. People lived in extended family groups of probably no more than 25–30 individuals. Few material possessions were needed and basketry and milling stones predominate in the archaeological record (Jennings, 1968).

We call this a period of incipient agriculture, and it lasted approximately from 7000 to 2000 B.C. The beginning of this period conforms very closely to the pattern of traits just listed. During these 5000 years, Mesoamerica gradually pulled ahead of her neighbors until by 2000 B.C. a year-round sedentary village life was possible. From this time on we can begin to see the emergence of the distinctive Mesoamerican culture.

The shift from a hunting-and-gathering existence to a sedentary life sustained mainly by agriculture is one of the most exciting accomplishments in the history of humankind. Cultivation of plants did not, however, "produce" a sedentary way of life, for this could be sustained in certain regions by harvesting and collecting wild food, trapping and hunting game, or exploiting marine and freshwater environments. Apparently it took humans a long time to rely predominantly on domesticated plants. But the eventual dependence on agriculture seems to have led to the development of a high, complex civilization.

SUMMARY

Mesoamerica is defined as a geographical region that includes central and southern Mexico with the peninsula of Yucatán, Guatemala, El Salvador, and parts of Honduras, Nicaragua, and northern Costa Rica. The northern boundary separated hunters and gatherers from farming communities to the south, but fluctuated greatly with changes in environmental conditions, dipping south in times of desiccation. Mesoamericans at the time of the Spanish Conquest possessed certain traits that were absent or rare among their neighbors. Some of these were hieroglyphic writing, a complex calendar, particular farming techniques and human sacrifice, books of bark paper or deer skin called códices, a knowledge of the movements of the planets, and a rubber ball game played on courts.

The time and place of humans' entry into the Western Hemisphere is still debated, although a passage from Siberia to Alaska over the Bering Land Bridge has long been postulated. The paucity of stone tools marking their presence in North America, and the finding of early artifacts in South America is raising the possibility of crossings by boat from Asia in the Southern Hemisphere. A preferred date for humans' entry is around 15,000 years ago, but some scholars support 40,000.

The earliest reliable indication of their presence in Mesoamerica is the remains of two mammoths discovered at Iztapan in the Basin of Mexico that had been butchered by projectile points, blades, and knives around 7500 B.C. The skeleton of a woman (the Tepexpan "Man") nearby is of equal age. Two Clovis projectile points are reported from Guatemala and there are numerous finds of scattered Pleistocene tools across Mesoamerica.

The Big-Game Hunting Tradition gave way to a Desert Tradition by 7000 B.C. that produced a variety of tools to exploit smaller fauna. Baskets and milling stones mark the beginning of incipient agriculture, and we find humans leading a more settled life by 2000 B.C.

CHAPTER 2

Humans Become Farmers

The origins of New World agriculture have long been a subject of interest, debate, and speculation. It seems clear that agriculture was developed independently in the New World because the principal crops, maize, squash, beans, and manioc, form an inventory differing greatly from the Old World staples of wheat, barley, and rye. Distinctive patterns of cultivation and technology further reinforce a belief in independent origins. This much seems clear, but in trying to answer questions of when, where, and how agriculture arose in the Americas, opinions vary.

For a long time little progress was made in this field. Data on primitive agriculture in Mesoamerica lagged far behind information on pottery types and ceremonial centers. But in the 1950s and 1960s, a concerted effort was made to locate an area where corn might have been first domesticated. Maize was selected because it eventually became the basic crop of much of the New World.

A truly domesticated plant is one that can no longer disperse its seeds by itself, but has become dependent on humans. Once this happens, the food value is greatly increased. Domestication must have entailed a long period of experimentation and mutation, and eventually a conscious selection by humans improved the species. The search was initiated by looking for the ancestor of maize. Two wild grasses were considered: *teosinte* and *tripsacum*. *Teocinte* is maize's (*Zea mays*) closest relative and is a widespread grass native to semiarid subtropical regions of Mesoamerica. *Tripsacum* is a wild grass also, but was eventually ruled out as the possible wild ancestor of maize because of its dispersal pattern (Beadle, 1977). Richard MacNeish set about investigating likely dry caves in northern Mexico, Chiapas, Honduras, and Guatemala and was finally rewarded when caves in the Tehuacán Valley in highland Mexico yielded some corn samples that preserved all parts of the plant including the cobs (MacNeish, 1981). The early cobs were only 1.9–2.5 cm in length (Figure 2.1).

This corn was already fully domesticated and cultivated by 5000–3400 B.C. (Coxcatlán phase), and must have undergone many years of experimentation. At present the area favored for domestication of maize is thought to be the Balsas region in the state of Guerrero, where it was developed from *teocinte*. *Teocinte* is a successful wild plant that could disperse its own seeds without being dependent on humans for survival. Here in this wetter, low- to mid-altitude environment, maize would have undergone many mutations prior to 5000 B.C. Large populations of Balsas *teocinte* are still found today in this region of west Mexico and from here, as domesticated maize, it would have spread quickly to much of Mesoamerica, reaching Tehuacán by 5000 B.C. (MacNeish, 1981), La Venta, Veracruz by 2250–1750 B.C. (Rust III and Leyden, n.d;), Oaxaca caves by 4000–3000 B.C. (Flannery, 1983a), Honduras around 5000–3000 B.C. (Rue, 1989), and South America well before 3000 B.C. The Valdivia culture of Ecuador (3200–2500 B.C.) has charred maize and a kernal of maize that had become embedded in the soft clay of a pot prior to firing. Maize had reached Ecuador and Peru by 5000 B.C. (Pearsall and Piperno, 1990) but never attained the importance in the Peruvian highlands that it did in Mexico and existed in the south only as a secondary crop (Burger and van der Merwe, 1990).

Although corn became Mesoamerica's most important domesticated plant, its

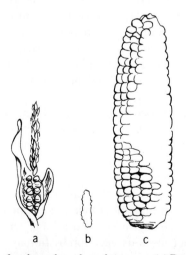

FIGURE 2.1 Comparison of early and modern dent corn. (a) Reconstruction of early ancestral corn (?); (b) Coxcatlán phase corn cob, Tehuacán Valley; (c) modern corn. (From Mangelsdorf, et al., 1967. Copyright by Andover Foundation for Archaeological Research. Courtesy of Richard S. MacNeish.)

cultivation was preceded by that of avocados, chili peppers, squash, and beans, which were undoubtedly more useful for food until maize was produced with enlarged cobs. *Teosinte* had grown for thousands of years alongside beans and squash. This was a highly successful planting arrangement whereby the beans and squash climb up the corn stalks in the shade of its leaves (Figure 2.2). When avocados were added to the diet, Mesoamerica had its common staples by 1300 B.C. (Flannery, 1983a). Maize supplied the carbohydrates, squash and beans were sources of plant protein, and avocados provided the fats and oils.

TEHUACÁN VALLEY

There are several well-documented excavations with evidence of early cultivated plants and settlements during these years. The most extensive is that of the Tehuacán Archaeological Botanical project directed by Richard MacNeish from 1960 to 1965.

FIGURE 2.2 Cornfield with beans growing up the stalks near San Miguel de Milagro, Tlaxcala. (Photographed by the author.)

This was a project that utilized botanists, geologists, geographers, ethnographers, and specialists in irrigation and human and animal remains. The results have given us a long stratified sequence of cultural evolution from an early hunting-and-gathering economy to a fully agricultural village life (MacNeish, 1967, 1981).

The Tehuacán Valley is located in southeastern Puebla at an elevation of 1400 m (see Map 3.2). Long and narrow, it is almost completely surrounded by high mountains that help create an extremely hot and dry environment with rainfall limited to 2 months of the year. Although this is a desert environment, a close scrutiny of the vicinity reveals that humans had several microenvironments to exploit. The lower elevations and alluvial valley floors provided caves for shelter and enough rainfall for primitive agriculture; there were gentle slopes to the west and higher still were the thorn and pine forests. These several ecological niches enabled humans to survive seasonal variations in food supplies and therefore furnished ideal conditions for the establishment of farming communities.

Of the many archaeological sites, 7 caves or rock shelters were excavated, and 5 others that were located out in the open. In addition to plant and animal remains, foodstuffs, feces, and other perishables such as nets, baskets, and woven cloth were found. Utensils made of stone, wood, and ceramics were also recovered.

Three phases, El Riego, Coxcatlán, and Abejas, represent this period of incipient agriculture. They are preceded by Ajuereado, a phase during which humans were still nomadic hunters and collectors. A brief summary of these phases in the Tehuacán Valley will give a good idea of the gradual change to sedentary life in this setting.

Ajuereado (10,000–7600 B.C.)

Nomadic microbands engaged in hunting, collecting, and trapping, moving their camps several times a year. Now-extinct species of horses and antelope were hunted, but small game—rabbits, gophers, rats, turtles, and birds—provided most of the meat. The enormous quantity of rabbit bones suggests communal drives. Tools include chipped flint knives and projectile points, choppers, scrapers, and crude prismatic blades. There are no ground stones or evidence of weaving, burials, or agriculture.

El Riego (7000–5000 B.C.)

Microbands (4–8 people each) occupied seasonal camps, but joined others in the spring to form temporary macrobands, and thus the population increased over the former Ajuereado hunters and collectors. MacNeish (1967) suggests that these people may have been organized into patrilineal bands and believes there may have been shamans who, as part-time practitioners, were heeded in matters of ritual and cere-mony. These people subsisted primarily by gathering plants and hunting deer and cottontail rabbits. Chili peppers (*Capsicum* sp.) and avocados provide the first evidence of domesticated plants, followed by squash (*Cucurbita mixta*) toward the end of this period. Remains of amaranth (*Amaranthaceae*) a fast-growing bushy weed well known for its brilliant red foliage, have been found, but this plant may have been collected in its wild form rather than cultivated. Although greatly in demand later for use in ceremony and ritual, amaranth was utilized by the El Riego peoples for the food value of its black shiny seeds (Figure 2.3). Tiny maize cobs may have been sucked or chewed but could not have been important as food. The evidence for cotton is not conclusive. Flint knapping continued, but the important innovation in tools was the manufacture of ground-stone and pecked-stone implements, mortars, pestles, and milling stones. The first evidence of weaving and woodworking occurred during this phase. El Riego remains have evidence of ritual burials, offerings, and cremation or human sacrifice. Skulls were found in baskets and the multiple burial of a man, woman, and child suggests that they did not all die a natural death.

Coxcatlán (5000–3400 B.C.)

By now macrobands had become semisedentary, perhaps splitting into small camps only in the dry season, the most difficult time for survival. Occupied sites are fewer but larger leading to speculation about the subsistence economy. Although still largely collectors and hunters, agriculture advanced significantly: the bottle gourd,

FIGURE 2.3 Amaranth (ancient *huauhtli*) in florescence in Tlaxcala. (Photographed by the author.)

crookneck squash (*Cucurbita moschata*), and the common bean (*Phaseolus vulgaris*) were added to the group of cultigens. Domesticated maize is common, followed toward the end of the period by white and black sapotes (*Casimiro edulis* and *Diospyros digyna*) that produced an edible fruit. These plants are not native to the valley. They had been brought in from a wetter region and must have been carefully watered. Tool changes were slight but a new tanged projectile point, more delicate blades, and end-scrapers and choppers were developed. True *metates* and *manos* are found.

Abejas (3400–2300 B.C.)

Some outstanding changes in settlement patterns occurred in this period. Some macroband settlements were located along river terraces, where groups of pit houses have been found. These could have been occupied year-round. Caves were still used by hunting macrobands in the dry season. Corn was improving and two new domesticated beans appeared, the jack and tepary bean (*Canavalia sp.* and *Phaseolus acutifolius*). Another possible domesticate was the pumpkin (*Cucurbita pepo*), and cotton was widely used. Remains of dogs have been found, the earliest reported from Mesoamerica. They soon became a favorite food.

The older techniques of tool manufacture were continued and new additions include the long prismatic obsidian blade, stone bowls, and oval *metates*. (Figure 2.4) The hunting of large animals such as deer, puma, and peccaries gradually gave way to trapping or collecting smaller game animals like rodents, foxes, skunks, turtles, lizards, and birds. This explains the decline in arrow points, projectile points, and the *atlatl* in favor of the slip noose, snares, and nets.

These three phases in the Tehuacán Valley, El Riego, Coxcatlán, and Abejas, serve to illustrate the gradual transition toward sedentary life in a semiarid environment in highland Mexico.

BASIN OF MEXICO

The southern part of the Basin of Mexico offers an entirely different paleoecological environment from that of semiarid valleys. Prior to the excavations at Tlapacoya in 1969, early settlements had been found only in xerophytic settings where life was difficult and particularly exacting. Pollen spectrum analyses have helped reconstruct the rich biotic scene in the Basin of Mexico that has been so drastically altered by humans. Between the seventh and fourth millennium B.C., Lake Chalco, a sweetwater lake, offered good riparian soils rich in peaty components (Map 2.1). Forests of pines, oaks, and alders covered large areas, whereas at higher levels there were fir, willow, and poplar. Lake Chalco was never very deep but was ideal for freshwater mollusks, turtles, and fish, while the swampy shoreline was covered with cattail, reeds, water lentils, and a variety of aquatic plants. Plant remains include amaranth seeds and *teosinte* (*Zea mays?*), the latter still a minor food item. White-tailed deer, rabbit, dog or coyote, small rodents, and fish and turtles are all present. Between November and

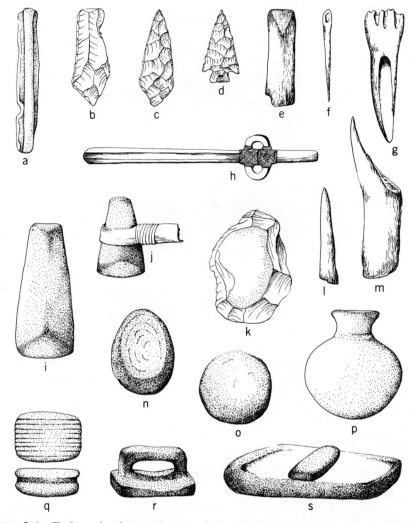

FIGURE 2.4 Early tools of stone, bone, and clay (a) obsidian blade; (b) burrin; (c) knife; (d) projectile point; (e) bone polisher; (f) needle; (g) bone auger; (h) *atlatl;* (i) chisel; (j) hafted axe; (k) scraper; (l) bone stone-flaker; (m) bone perforator; (n) hammer stone; (o) stone ball; (p) pottery olla; (q) stone barkbeater; (r) stone polisher; (s) *metate* and *mano.* (Adapted from Piña Chan, 1955.)

May, migratory birds flocked into the Chalco region for the winter. The inventory includes Canadian geese, ducks, pintails, mallards, teals, and the American coot. This was an optimal ecological area in which to live.

The ancient volcano of Tlapacoya formed an island in Lake Chalco (now drained), but when the lake waters receded, the island became a peninsula. Zohapilco is a

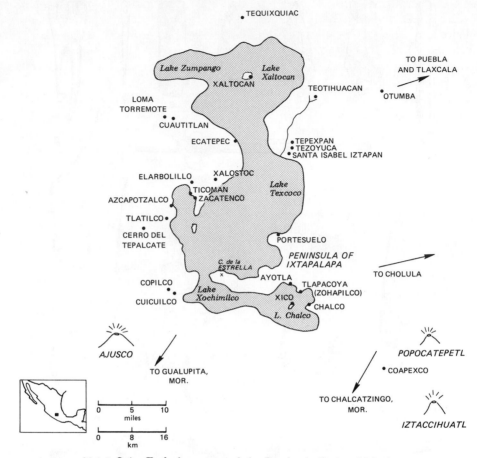

MAP 2.1 Early humans and the Preclassic Basin of Mexico.

site on the much-eroded hill of Tlapacoya. Christine Niederberger (1987) opened a stratigraphic trench (50 m long × 1 m wide) designed to cut across the greatest number of lake and shoreline occupation levels possible. Later extensions were opened at various points. Her excavated material has provided our best information on preceramic settlements in the Basin of Mexico.

Zohapilco

The two earliest levels of occupation at Zohapilco have been called Playa 1 and 2 (5500–3500 B.C.) in which permanent villages were located along the lake shore. Turtles and fish provided the most food, supplemented by wild fruits and small game from the forests. It was the great variety of food resources year-round such as waterfowl and freshwater fish that made permanent settlement possible.

Other evidence consists of hearths, charcoal, and fire-cracked andesite rocks. Nearby were traces of tool production: flakes, chips of andesite, basalt, obsidian, and chalcedony debitages. Andesite, the most abundant, was available locally and made into heavy biface tools. Gray obsidian was locally and made into heavy biface tools. Gray obsidian was brought in from Otumba in the northeastern part of the Basin of Mexico for making prismatic blades and projectile points.

This exceptional combination of factors made permanent settlement possible at a very early time. The long transition to sedentary life outlined by MacNeish for the Tehuacán Valley was not necessary in the Basin of Mexico. People were living well at Tlapacoya by the sixth millennium B.C. However, prior to 3000 B.C. great volcanic eruptions devastated this area and covered the southern sector of the basin with a thick white pumice. Not until plant life was once more restored and a new biotic balance was achieved was the lacustrine region resettled. The new phase of development (Zohapilco phase) is one of the earliest of the Preclassic Period (Niederberger 1976).

TAMAULIPAS

The Infiernillo complex of southwestern Tamaulipas, an earlier excavation by MacNeish, is known from similarly well-preserved remains from dry caves in an arid mesquite desert scarred by deep canyons. This site is contemporary with El Riego at Tehuacán; in both regions the people were primarily meat eaters during the early phases. Projectile points, flake choppers, and scrapers were recovered along with baskets, net bags, and twilled and plaited mats (MacNeish, 1958).

Wood was used for making fire tongs and fire drills; sticks were peeled and whittled to desired shapes to serve various purposes in traps, snares, rods, and *atlatls*. Darts were the most prominent weapon.

Fibers from the yucca and agave (maguey) plants provided the material from which the bags and mats were made. The fibers were softened and twisted into strings and woven into a great variety of these articles. Abundant bag and net containers provided means of carrying and storing wild foodstuffs such as nuts, seeds, and fruits, and the gourd was an excellent receptacle. By comparison, bone and antler tools are relatively scarce, but a few were fashioned into needles, punches, and awls.

Among the wild plants utilized were agave, *Opuntia* (prickly pear cactus) (Figure 2.5), and the runner bean, while domesticates included the bottle gourd, chili pepper, and possibly the pumpkin. Maize does not appear until after 3000 B.C., and thereafter the percentage of domesticated plants greatly increases.

OAXACA, SOUTHERN MEXICO, AND COASTAL SITES

Also belonging to this incipient agricultural period are the remains from caves and rock shelters near Mitla in the state of Oaxaca (Flannery *et al.*, 1981; Flannery and Spores, 1983). The oldest remains from preceramic levels show that deer and cottontail rabbits were hunted. The tools include flint projectile points and the usual

FIGURE 2.5   Prickly pear cactus bearing fruit. Planted in a tight row, it provides an excellent defense. (Photographed by the author.)

assortment of choppers, scrapers, and knives. These remains correspond to the El Riego and Coxcatlán phases of Tehuacán. The Guilá Naquitz cave (ca. 8000–6700 B.C.) 5 km northwest of Mitla, and 300 m above the valley floor, has preseved dried remains of acorns, maguey, prickly pear, and organ-cactus fruit, whereas toward the end of the period, squash seeds and small black beans marked the beginning of agriculture. These people trapped small game and cooked over hearths kindled with fire drills.

   Another cave, Cueva Blanca (3000–2800 B.C.) was located near the lower forest limits, but its exposure to rain made preservation poor. It yielded only remains of deer and mud turtles, and abundant tools but no sign of plant domestication.

   An open-air preceramic campsite (Gheo-Shih), was found on an alluvial fan that was occupied in the summer as well as the fall, by a larger number of people. Two rows of boulders (20-m long × 7-m wide) marked off an area that was free of artifacts and "swept clean" as a possible public area or "dance ground" (?). Tools for hunting and butchering and drilled stone ornaments (mostly pendants) were concentrated in another area. The lack of plant remains here is attributed to the shallow depth and probable leaching of the soil. Pollen of *teocinte* was present, and maize could have been cultivated along the flood plain. The estimated date is 5000–4000 B.C.

In the state of Chiapas, the Santa Marta rock shelter near Ocozocautla has yielded preceramic remains with estimated dates of 7000–4300 B.C. These remains underlie Preclassic deposits from the cave floors (MacNeish and Peterson, 1962). The tool inventory of points, knives, and scrapers is similar to that at Tamaulipas. There is no evidence of the beginnings of agriculture here. These people seem to have eaten mostly wild foods. A nearby rock shelter at Comitán likewise has yielded preceramic tools but no plants, while on the Pacific Coast in the Chantuto zone, the lower levels indicate that many shellfish were collected. Three large middens were accumulated over 1000 years from 3000 to 2000 B.C. This concentration of debris is enormous, mostly of clam shells. There are a few stone artifacts, animal bones, and lots of charcoal. This could represent seasonal exploitation by inland peoples, but the vast accumulations suggest intensive occupation. The finding of a house floor tends to favor permanence, but periodic influxes of people may have come in to collect clams, fish, and maybe shrimp (Stark and Voorhies, 1978). Obsidian is present from the very earliest levels, indicating early contact with highland peoples.

The earliest remains near Acapulco, Guerrero, and Matanchén, Nayarit, are evidence of this same coastal lifestyle further west. A very large midden on the coast of Nayarit at Matanchén contains material dated at 2000 B.C.

On the Gulf Coast side, there are sites in southern and central Veracruz that are preceramic and belong to this period. A good sequence for this area is at Santa Luisa on the Tecolutla River, Veracruz (Wilkerson, 1975, 1980) (see Map 3.2). The surface architecture has been largely destroyed but large middens are of particular interest. A preceramic phase (Palo Hueco; 4000–2400 B.C.) represents a simpler version of its contemporary Abejas phase at Tehuacán with a little different subsistence base. People here lived by hunting, fishing, and collecting, but a riverine orientation predominated. There is no trace of agriculture. The few tools include cracked sandstone cobbles, shells, and only one projectile point. Local limestone was procured from the El Paraiso Mountains near Querétaro.

SUMMARY

There were multiple origins of New World plant domestication and many regions shared their knowledge and stimulated each other. Although maize was not the first cultigen in Mesoamerica (preceded by squash, avocado, chili peppers, and amaranth in Tehuacán; pumpkins, bottle gourds, and beans in Tamaulipas), it was the most important as it became the staple of Mesoamerica. A likely area for its domestication from *teocinte* is the Balsas region of Guerrero prior to 5000 B.C. Thereafter it appears as a domesticate in the Tehuacán Valley, in Oaxaca, on the Gulf Coast and Honduras, reaching South America by 3000 B.C.

The domestication of plants was a slow process, supplementing the diet of the hunter and collector to gradually dominate the subsistence economy. There was no sudden or rapid process, no "revolution." This transition required about 5000 years.

A fine stratified sequence of the transition to a fully agricultural village life is that of the semiarid Tehuacán Valley. Over the mountains to the west, the forests and lakes of the Basin of Mexico offered a richer environment with such a variety of lacustrine plants, game, and migratory birds that permanent settlements were possible at Tlapacoya around 5000 B.C. Another excellent sequence from a preceramic hunting life to incipient agriculture comes from caves and rock shelters of Oaxaca. A number of riverine and coastal sites (La Venta, Santa Luisa in Veracruz, the Santa Marta rock shelter in Chiapas and other sites in Guerrero and Nayarit) were inhabited by people leading similar lives by hunting, fishing, and collecting.

The archaeological record shows that as population increased, so did the percentages of cultigens in the diets of these incipient farmers. As each region incorporated agriculture into its economy, new techniques of exploitation were developed, and irrigation, terracing, flood controls, and drainage devices appeared that would lead to increased food production. These in turn permitted humans to farm new land and produce a surplus.

Although our knowledge of life during this period is based on very few sites as yet, there is evidence that by 2000 B.C. maize was widespread. Certainly by 1500 B.C. farming villages were common. One of the most fascinating phases in the development of Mesoamerica was beginning.

CHAPTER 3

Setting the Mesoamerican Pattern and the Role of the Olmec

This chapter covers the years between 2500–300 B.C., usually considered Early and Middle Preclassic. In these years the basic pattern of Mesoamerica was formulated, one that was to lead directly to the great civilizations to follow.

At the beginning of this long span of time, hunting, gathering, and fishing still formed the most important economic activity, but gradually they came to occupy a position second to farming.

We will see the growth of hamlets and a great increase in population; the appearance of pottery, domestic and public architecture, special industries and crafts, ranking and social stratification, and the first rudimentary steps toward hieroglyphic writing. As cultigens increased, farmers responded with innovations in land use and methods of water control. Intersite communication was lively whether through exchange of ideas, plants, products, or resources, for evidence of sharing or imitating is there. This interaction was a vital force in stimulating and unifying beliefs in the regional cultures that developed.

The most outstanding event during these years is the Olmec civilization of southern Veracruz that reached its cultural peak between 1100–600 B.C. There were few Mesoamericans then, and probably fewer today, that have not heard of these people who carved the great colossal stone heads, for they are as popular a topic of conversation as the "collapse" of the Maya. It is a long stretch in time and evolution from the domestication of plants to these sophisticated Olmec.

There are great gaps in our knowledge of these years, but we have particularly good information for central highland Mexico, Oaxaca, and the Gulf Coast. I will concentrate on these regions after a brief look at developments in west Mexico. Then, after examining the Olmec civilization, one may well ask, Who were the Olmec and from where did they come? We certainly do not have all the answers, but I think we have some good clues provided by the region east of the Isthmus.

WEST MEXICO

From west Mexico we have news of an early preceramic site that may have been typical of cultures from Panama to the United States border. This is the Matanchén Complex known from a large midden on Matanchén Bay, Nayarit, and is dated around 2000 B.C. The site covers 3600 m with debris 7 m deep and may be the result of seasonal activity. The small sample of artifacts includes obsidian flakes for opening shellfish, cobble hammerstones, choppers, and a few remains of fish, turtle, and bird bones. Mountjoy believes this to have been a food-extracting station with the preparation of food done elsewhere (Meighan, 1974; Mountjoy, 1978).

Shaft-and-Chamber Tombs   The most distinctive feature of Preclassic west Mexican cultures is the hundreds of shaft-and-chamber tombs that occur in a great arc from north of Ixtlán del Río, Nayarit, through Jalisco to Colima (Map 3.1). Chronologically they range from approximately 1500 B.C. to A.D. 400. Apart from skeletal remains they usually contain conch-shell trumpets and pottery, including large hollow ceramic sculptures. The tombs, often beehive-shaped, consist of a vertical shaft usually 4–6 m deep that leads to one or more side chambers. The deepest tombs are often placed in a row along a high ridge with the entrance facing west into the setting sun.

Although abundant, most have been ransacked, but several unlooted tombs were excavated years ago near Jacona at El Opeño, Michoacán (Noguera, 1942) (Figure 3.1). Two others have more recently been opened by the Mexican archaeologist Arturo Oliveros (1974) in highland Michoacán. One tomb was 4.45 m deep and was entered through a shaft with four steps. The chamber, sealed by three stone slabs, contained skeletal remains of 10 individuals, pottery, and figurines that had been buried long after the tomb was constructed. The second tomb had not been reused and contained two adult male skeletons. Some of the pottery was of local style with negative painting and geometric designs. The rest was similar in form and decoration to ceramics of Tlatilco in the Basin of Mexico and to eastern Morelos. A few sherds resemble Capacha pottery (Kelly, 1980). Sixteen figurines of C and D types were piled in the interior passageway of one tomb. Some of these represent ball-players, with knee pads and a bat (?) in hand. Others of kaolin clay had been broken prior to interment. A basalt *yuguito* like examples from Tlatilco (see Figure 3.8d), Tlapacoya, and Guerrero, a greenstone pectoral carved with a St. Andrews cross, obsidian projectile points and

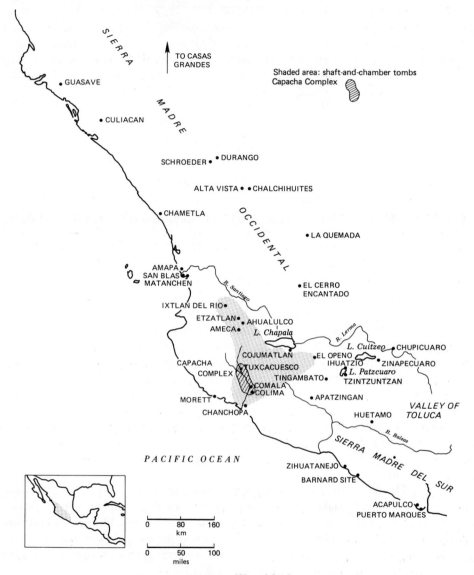

MAP 3.1 West Mexico.

tools, probably used in chopping the tomb out of the *tepetate*, were left inside the burial chamber. A C-14 date for this tomb is 1500 B.C., roughly coeval with Capacha.

Capacha In 1970, while pursuing her long involvement with the archaeology of Colima, Isabel Kelly identified a distinctive ceramic assemblage that she named the Capacha phase (Kelly, 1978, 1980). This is the earliest Colima material known, and consists largely of ceramics from graves disturbed and smashed by looters. Shaft tombs were probably a Capacha trait also.

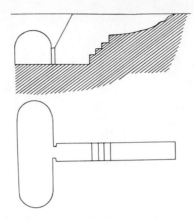

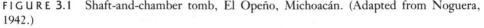

FIGURE 3.1   Shaft-and-chamber tomb, El Opeño, Michoacán. (Adapted from Noguera, 1942.)

Capacha ceramics occur inland at elevations ranging from 186 to 800 m and stretch from Colima into Jalisco (see Map 3.1). As yet there is no information on living sites, possible mounds, or the economy of these people. Characteristic is a huge open-mouthed olla with cinctured body, that the local farmers call a *bule*. Kelly's largest specimen, for example, measures 38 cm in height by a rim diameter of 36 cm. Many are undecorated but some have several navel-like depressions with radiating incised lines. Other forms include *tecomates*, small wide-mouthed ollas, animal effigies, and miniature vessels. One stirrup-spout was found, but more common is a curious trifid form (Figure 3.2). There are no shallow flat-based bowls, and no supports or bottles. This material is known only from graves and we have one C-14 date of 1450 B.C.

A lot of similar pottery vessels that included several stirrup-spouts, undoubtedly also from looted graves, was reported in an area near Apulco, Jalisco (Greengo and Meighan, 1976).

The El Opeño tomb material together with other isolated finds, several trifids from central coastal Sinaloa, and a stirrup-spout from Baja California indicate that this complex was not restricted to a local Colima community. The trifids and constricted body forms are close to many Tlatilco and Morelos shapes and share the stirrup-spouted vessel. The latter is well known in northwestern South America, an area famous for its shaft tombs. (See Figure 3.9i.)

CENTRAL HIGHLANDS

Many settled villages had been established by this time and at Tehuacán pottery appears around 2300 B.C. in the Purrón phase. Vessel forms are *tecomates* and the flat-bottomed bowl with outslanting walls. This phase is one of the least well defined in the long Tehuacan sequence and has been dated partly by comparison with a pottery

FIGURE 3.2   Black trifid vessel, Gualupita, Morelos (?). Form and decoration are distinctive features of the Capacha complex, Colima, but this is an unusually elegant example. Height: 29 cm. (Courtesy of the Museum of the American Indian, Heye Foundation, N.Y. [13/3034].)

called "pox." Found at Puerto Marquez near Acapulco on the Pacific Coast (C. F. Brush, 1969), this is a fiber-tempered ware very similar to that of Purrón and thought to be of equal antiquity (2300 B.C.). *Tecomates* were also present, but the distinguishing feature is the pitted surface on the sherds giving rise to the term "pox pottery."

Other possibly early material is reported from Las Bocas (Caballo Pintado) near Izúcar de Matamoros in southern Puebla, where Piña Chan found coarse-tempered pottery rather like Tehuacán's Purrón and Ajalpan phases (Piña Chan, personal communication).

The Basin of Mexico

Around 2500 B.C. life began to renew itself and the plant equilibrium was gradually restored at Tlapacoya. In this Zohapilco phase (Niederberger, 1976, 1987), farming was well established. Grains of *Zea* pollen have been recovered that are much larger and three times as numerous as in earlier years. Squash, peppers, amaranth, and chayotes formed part of the diet as well as fish, snakes, and migratory birds. Basalt tools were well finished and polished. Obsidian, mostly gray, was brought in from Otumba and prismatic blades were more regular in form. There is a notable increase and better quality of grinding tools. This is still a preceramic phase with the exception of a clay figurine recovered from a hearth (Figure 3.3). Made from local clay and fired, it represents a pregnant female with four depressions for eyes, and is devoid of mouth or arms. The associated charcoal produced a date of 2300 B.C.

Other material from the Basin of Mexico that may be as early as 1900 B.C. is that from the Tlalpan phase at Cuicuilco (Heizer and Bennyhoff, 1972). The thin burnished pottery bears some resemblance to the later Ixtapaluca phase ware from Tlapacoya.

The Basin of Mexico has probably been more thoroughly surveyed, sampled, dug, and generally disturbed than any other area of Mexico. Archaeologically it has benefited by public interest, funding, and accessibility, but from the time of the Conquest in 1521, it has suffered alterations and interference with the lakes, forests, and subsequent erosion, and by building one of the largest cities of the world today on top of the ancient Aztec capital.

Fortunately Franz Boas and Manuel Gamio started stratigraphic work at the beginning of the century, and George Vaillant from the American Museum of Natural History began to dig in the 1920s and 1930s. By 1944 he had published a sequence of Preclassic development for the area that forms the basis of our chronology today (Vaillant, 1930, 1931, 1935). Only now, after 25 more years of probing, erring, and revising, do we have a sequence for this complex region that affords reasonable cross-correlations with other parts of Mesoamerica. The presentation that follows is a simplified version of events based on Piña Chan's excavations at Tlatilco (1958), Niederberger's work at Tlapacoya (1976, 1987), and Tolstoy's work at Coapexco, Tlatilco, and various other Basin sites (Tolstoy, 1975, 1980, 1989a; Tolstoy *et al.*, 1977; Tolstoy and Paradis, 1971; Tolstoy and Fish, 1975). These are the earliest known sedentary communities in the Basin.

FIGURE 3.3   Clay female figurine, recovered from hearth at Zohapilco, Tlapacoya. Height: 2 1/4 in. Dated at 2300 B.C. (Courtesy of Christine Niederberger.)

Ixtapaluca

Preclassic events after 1500 B.C. fall into three large divisions: Ixtapaluca, Zaca-tenco, and Ticomán (see Map 2.1). Subphases provide finer details, but here only the broader outlines will be attempted.

Nevada   The earliest full ceramic phase from the Basin of Mexico is Nevada, estimated to have begun about 1360 B.C. This material correlates with Tierras Largas in Oaxaca and Ocós on the coast of Chiapas and Guatemala. It is known only from a small sample of a farming community at Tlapacoya that made andesite tools and sophisticated pottery. The latter is thin and well polished with forms that include semispherical bowls, ollas, plates, and low-walled, flat-bottomed vessels. Decoration was by fine channeling, zoned thumbnail impression, rocker-stamping, and red slip with or without bands of specular hematite.

Ayotla   From 1200 to 1100 B.C., a number of changes took place in the Basin of Mexico. There was a flood of new features in iconography, ritual, ceramics, and tools that reflect contact with neighboring valleys, west Mexico, and the Gulf Coast. The resemblances to the Gulf Coast in the Basin of Mexico refer specifically to the Olmec pottery and figurines found at San Lorenzo Tenochtitlán at this time. The Gulf Coast Olmec are represented in well-burnished, flat-based dishes that may be rocker-stamped in zoned motifs, excised, incised white wares with exterior incision; differen-tially fired white wares, red-on-buff painted designs sometimes combined with resist technique. The cylinder and *tecomate* form is included, along with certain decorative techniques of burnishing and rubbing cinnabar or ochre in carved or incised areas. Specific motifs include the paw-wing, flame-brows, cleft-head, and St. Andrews cross (see Figure 3.9a,h).

A culturally distinctive element is found at Tlatilco in addition to the Olmec. This consists of tall-necked bottles, some with mid-body constrictions, stirrup-spouts, whistling jars, and a great variety of effigy vessels. This group is closely related to eastern Morelos and has remote affiliations with west Mexico (Jalisco and Colima).

All the above are found in conjunction with local assemblages.

The contemporary sites of Coapexco and Tlatilco offer a stimulating comparison of villages in the Basin at this time.

Coapexco   This unusual site actually predates Ayotla. It is not a valley site, but is perched at an elevation of 2600 m on the flanks of Iztaccíhuatl, an altitude higher than any settlement either before or after its brief occupation (1200–1100 B.C.). This was a community where an estimated 30 houses occupied about 44 ha and the population is estimated at 1000. House sites were found to have hearths, storage, and/ or refuse pits. The larger house with the fancier or more unusual ceramics and the finest *manos* and *metates* surely occupied a higher status than a smaller house that did its grinding on a slab of stone with cobbles. Pottery was found as refuse scatters from individual households and shallow trenching to sterile soil, on house floors and roof

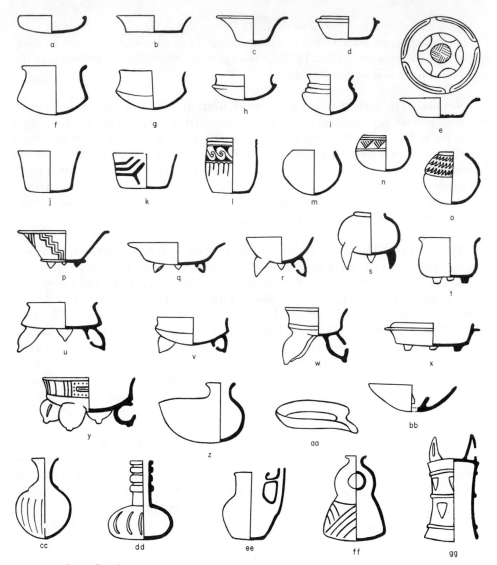

FIGURE 3.4 Preclassic pottery forms (exceptions: t and x are marble). (a) Simple bowl, La Venta; (b) flat-bottomed bowl with flaring walls, La Venta; (c) black-brown bowl with flat rim, Miraflores, Kaminaljuyú; (d) rim-flanged bowl, Chicanel; (e) "grater bowl" with double-line break, Tlapacoya; (f) black-ware composite silhouette, Zacatenco; (g) black ware, composite silhouette, Zacatenco; (h) basal-flange gray ware, Monte Albán I; (i) thin black ware, Zacatenco; (j) deep bowl, Tlatilco; (k) deep bowl, excised decoration, Tlatilco; (l) black-brown, fine-line incised ware, Miraflores, Kaminaljuyú; (m) *tecomate*, Tehuacán Valley; (n) incised *tecomate*, Tlatilco; (o) rocker-stamped *tecomate*, Tlatilco; (p) fine red incised tripod, Miraflores, Kaminal- juyú; (q) composite silhouette tripod, Zacatenco; (r) tripod bowl, Ticomán; (s) *tecomate* tripod, Ocós, La Victoria; (t) marble tripod bowl, Miraflores, Kaminaljuyú; (u) gray-ware tripod bowl,

falls, and then seriated. The Olmec features were not limited to ceramics, but seen in projectile points, blades, and grinding utensils as well as ritual objects (figurines, iron ore mirror, and stamps).

In this small community, Coapexco had relatively little obsidian, but it was a real surprise to find that 5 different obsidian sources were represented. Over half of all the blades recovered came from Zinapécuaro and Altotonga, sites located at considerable distances (250 and 190 km, respectively). These are considered exotic sources and at Coapexco are "grossly overrepresented" (Tolstoy, 1989a). Sixty percent of the non-blade obsidian was from Otumba. There was surely some economic enterprise going on, perhaps set up to mine, manufacture, and market blades in the area from Puebla to Michoacán (Boksenbaum *et al.*, 1987; Tolstoy, 1989a).

Tlatilco   Tlatilco is located 65 km away on the western shore of Lake Texcoco. (see Map 2.1). After a brief season in 1943, excavations here were resumed by INAH in 1947, at a time when the area was being stripped of clay for making sun-dried bricks. Now it has all disappeared under modern Mexico City, but when Coapexco was importing goods or hosting outsiders (?), and marketing prismatic blades, Tlatilco was a simple farming community. The residents dug deep, triangular, bottle-shaped pits into the earth to store their food but when these were found, they were filled with general household debris, pottery and figurine fragments, burned pieces of walls from huts, animal bone, ash, and charcoal (Figure 3.5).

An estimated 500 graves are said to have been taken out, of which 375 have been documented (Figure 3.6). Some burials had few or no offerings, but others were lavishly supplied with pottery vessels, figurines, masks, tools, and ornaments (Figures 3.7 and 3.8). A great range of vessels include those found at Coapexco as well as other non-Olmec wares.

The Ayotla subphase is represented at Coapexco, Tlatilco, Tlapacoya, and El Terremote. El Terremote is less well known, but was located on an island on the edge of Lake Chalco-Xochimilco, 1 km southwest of today's town of Tlaltenco. It shares much Ayotla material with these other sites. The history of El Terremote is one of exploiting the lake resources. Abundant tools such as needles, punches, and spatulas have been found that were needed to produce the baskets, *petates*, rope, bags, and nets

---

Monte Albán I; (v) composite silhouette tripod, Ticomán; (w) gray-ware tripod bowl, Monte Albán I; (x) marble vessel, flanged tripod, Miraflores, Kaminaljuyú; (y) tetrapod, mammiform shaped supports, incised, Holmul I; (z) shoe-shaped vessel, Monte Albán (aa) spouted tray, Tlatilco; (bb) burner bowl with three inner horns, central vent, Chiapa de Corzo; (cc) gadrooned bottle, Tlatilco; (dd) reconstructed bottle, La Venta; (ee) gray-ware vessel with spout, Monte Albán II; (ff) black-brown grooved stirrup-spout bottle, Tlatilco; (gg) incense burner, Las Charcas type. (From the following sources: a, b, dd, Drucker, 1952; c, t, x, Shook and Kidder, 1952; d, Smith and Gifford, 1965; e, Weaver, 1967; f, g, i, q, Vaillant, 1930; h, u, w, z, ee, Caso and Bernal, 1965; j, k, n, cc, ff, Porter, 1953; l, p, gg, Rands and Smith, 1965; m, MacNeish, 1962; o, aa, Piña Chan, 1955b; r, v, Vaillant, 1931; s, Coe, 1988; y, Marquina, 1951; bb, Lowe and Mason, 1965.)

FIGURE 3.5   Bottle-shaped food storage/rubbish pit at Tlatilco. (Courtesy Arturo Romano.)

that were used on the lake. Eventually it became one of the most important centers in the Late Preclassic period (Serra Puche, 1988). The Olmec attributes at all these sites are most abundant at the outset in Ayotla, and begin to fade after 1100 B.C. either by being absorbed or replaced. Coapexco had a life span of only 100 years whether due to some failing of the obsidian industry, or more likely by moving down to the valley when some fertile agricultural land became available.

Manantial   Around 1100 B.C. a number of other features are found at Tlatilco that are shared with Tlapacoya and Chalcatzingo in eastern Morelos: long-necked bottles, the stirrup-spout, masks, and certain effigies. The stirrup-spout is a distinctive form found in the early Capacha complex of Colima (Kelly, 1980). It has a curious distribution appearing in the middle Preclassic in Honduras (see page 70). Grove has called these features the Tlatilco tradition (or Río Cuautla or Amacuzac style) in Morelos where they occur in the long Barranca phase. (See Figure 3.9.)

A decoration known as the double-line-break is also found in these sites and has a widespread and long history. It consists of two incised lines that encircle the interior rim of a vessel, where the lower line turns to join the upper one (Figure 3.4e). It is very common in the Manantial subphase of Ixtapaluca, but becomes even more widespread in Zacatenco. It is found at San Miguel Amuco, Guerrero, at 1500 B.C., the earliest occurrence on record (Tolstoy and Fish, 1975).

FIGURE 3.6   Graves at Tlatilco cemetery. (Courtesy of Arturo Romano.)

After determining the chronology of Tlatilco's remains, Tolstoy was far from finished. He was also able to see ranking in the quality and quantity of offerings. With Johanna Faulhaber's study of the skeletal material in hand, sex, age, and orientations of graves could be plotted. Partial results seem to indicate that the graves may represent two social groups; statistically the women received more vessels with Olmec motifs than did the men, and Olmec materials do not denote a higher status. Further implications may yet be drawn from the orientation of skeletons, depth of graves, and/or design motifs as possible insignia of kin or residential groups.

The inventory is not restricted to these particular sites. Large hollow ceramic figures, for example, are found in contemporaneous Ixtapaluca subphases in Puebla and Morelos and may be San Lorenzo products. These exceptional hollow white-slipped sculptures are often called dolls, made realistically with spread chubby legs and baby faces (see Figure 3.11). Of the tools, small pointed-stem projectile points and *metates* without supports are typical of all related sites. Oaxaca gray ware and pottery from the Gulf Coast have been identified as imports in the Basin: iron ore,

FIGURE 3.7 Preclassic figures and figurines.
a. Ball player with traces of red and yellow paint. Tlatilco, Burial 129. Height: 16.5 cm.
b. Olmec-style figurine with traces of red paint wearing a hematite mirror on the chest. Tlatilco, Burial 172. Height: 5.5 cm.
c. Figurine pendant, perforated from ear to ear. Slipped in white with red headdress. Isolated find in cemetery. Tlatilco. Height: 4.25 cm.
d. Hollow figure, Gualulpita, Morelos. Height: 33 cm. (Photograph courtesy of the Museum of the American Indian, Heye Foundation, N.Y. [22/1351].)
e. K-type figurine. Red and yellow paint. Tlatilco, Burial 177. Height: 7.2 cm.
f. D1-type figurine. Red, yellow, and white paint. Tlatilco, Burial 60. Height: 11.5 cm.
(Photographs courtesy of Arturo Romano unless otherwise noted.)

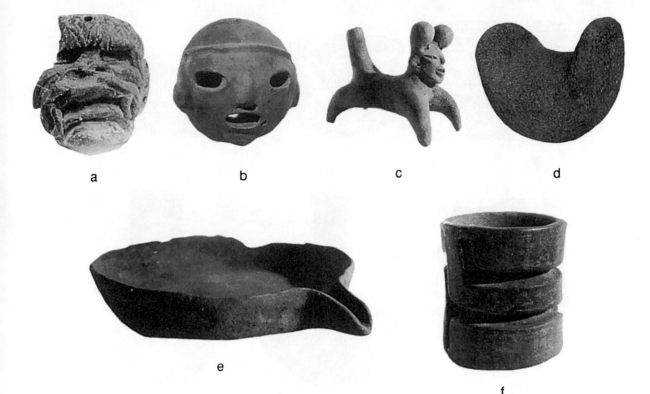

a   b   c   d

e   f

FIGURE 3.8 Preclassic miscellaneous objects.
a. Rough mask, isolated object in Tlatilco cemetery. Height: 7 cm.
b. Mask. Tlatilco, Burial 79. Height: 13 cm.
c. Effigy whistle from 1944 season at Tlatilco. Length: 14 cm.
d. U-shaped stone (yuguito), isolated find. Length: 15.5 cm.
e. spouted tray with remains of red paint. Tlatilco, Burial 2. Maximum length: 17 cm.
f. Hollow cylindrical roller stamp. Purchase. Height: 7 cm. (Photographs courtesy of Arturo Romano.)

pyrite, and a small amount of jade at Tlatilco are others. There are as yet no indications of ceremonial structures, but some construction took place at Tlapacoya where cut pieces of *tepetate* and flooring of red earth are reported.

The beauty of the hand-modeled figurines of Tlatilco and Tlapacoya are among the most spectacular objects of Mesoamerica (Piña Chan, 1958; Porter, 1953; Niederberger, 1987). Mothers hold babies or dogs, while men are depicted as ball-players, shamans, musicians, or acrobats. The dwarfs, hunchbacks, and monstrosities with two heads or one head and three eyes are no doubt related to mythological or shamanistic beliefs. Preclassic figurines are always hand modeled. Thereafter, though produced by molds, some kind of small solid figurine was continuously made in central Mexico even after the Conquest into Colonial times. Figurines are usually found associated

FIGURE 3.9 Preclassic ceramics: special forms and decorations. These vessels, found at Tlatilco, Tlapacoya, and Chalcatcingo, were selected for similarites to ceramics outside the Mexican central highlands. Those more typical of the Basin of Mexico are seen in Figure 3.4. **a.** Black bowl, excised decoration (Calzadas Carved) with traces of red. Tlatilco, Burial 21. Rim diameter: 13 cm.

with household debris, but at Tlatilco, they were often placed in burials where as many as 60 were found in a single grave. Following the earliest Zacatenco phase, this practice was discontinued.

In general the Zacatenco period seems less affluent with life a little harder and much less exciting.

Zacatenco

The beginning of the Zacatenco phase is marked by a real population explosion in the Basin of Mexico. Larger settlements continued to be made in the southern part of the valley, but people moved around to form small hamlets, even choosing more arid regions such as the Teotihuacan Valley, Cuautitlán, and Texcoco. Others took up residence in the piedmont areas. Some distinction can be seen between large and small villages, but no one center dominated (Sanders *et al.*, 1979).

The population at Tlapacoya was very dense in the early years of Zacatenco. Inhabitants erected buildings with well-cut blocks of *tepetate* sometimes combined with undressed stones held together with clay. But gradually the momentum lessened and by 500 B.C. much of the population moved elsewhere. Many features of Tlatilco now disappear along with any lingering trace of the Olmec.

The most important ceramic change is the great increase in white paste wares accompanied by incised sunburst decorations on the interior of bowls and the incised double-line-break on the rim. This forms a cluster of traits that is a reliable middle Preclassic marker with a broad-based distribution from the Basin of Mexico to coastal Guatemala, including Guerrero and the Huasteca.

Other Zacatenco ceramic features are dark bay wares in olla and composite-silhouette forms, annular bases, *comals*, and pinched bowls and oval shapes. White-on-red painted wares come in late, and at the very end of the period a red-on-black appears (see Figure 3.4).

Despite the population boom, there is a general drabness of Zacatenco remains not found earlier. Burials contain fewer and simpler offerings; imports are negligible. More arid land was farmed and small-scale irrigation experiments were conducted on the floor of the valley by 700 B.C.

---

b. Brown and red zoned bowl. Tlatilco, Burial 146. Rim diameter: 12 cm.
c. Flat bowl with rocker-stamped decoration. Isolated find. Tlatilco. Rim diameter: 26 cm.
d. Excised (Calzadas Carved) decorated fish resting on its tail. Tlatilco, Burial 53. Height: 15 cm.
e. Long-necked bottle with gadrooning. Tlatilco, Burial 90. Height: 19 cm.
f. Bottle with differential firing. Tlatilco, Burial 162. Height: 20 cm.
g. Brown bottle with modeled swivel decoration. Tlatilco, Burial 61. Height: 18 cm.
h. Flat bowl with St. Andrews cross in excised decoration, (Calzadas Carved). Tlatilco, Burial 198. Rim diameter: 19 cm.
i. Black stirrup-spout with incised and thumb-impressed decoration. Tlatilco, Burial 90. Height: 13.5 cm. (Photographs courtesy of Arturo Romano.)

Ticomán

The Ticomán phase is distinguished by further growth in population (90,000) and the first civic-ceremonial architecture at Cuicuilco. This settlement had grown from a tiny hamlet founded about the same time as Coapexco. Around 400 B.C. these people constructed an oval truncated cone of adobe. The main pyramid was built in four stages and soon after was altered and enlarged, resulting in a round temple platform (80 m in diameter). This was faced with stone and 2 ramps lead up to double altars at the summit, 27 m above ground. (See figure 4.1). Eleven additional mound structures have been found at Peña Pobre, 1 km to the east. This was a bustling hub of activity with Cuicuilco dominating the southern Basin of Mexico in the late Preclassic. Its population is believed to have reached 20,000 concentrated in an area of 400 ha, the peak of its expansion.

El Terremote and Tlapacoya were important regional centers. Between 650 and 300 B.C. nearly two thirds of the total Basin resided around Lake Chalco-Xochimilco (Sanders *et al.*, 1979). After 300 B.C. the Chalco region still attracted new settlements but the Basin as a whole underwent sociopolitical changes. Groups settled for the first time on the eastern saline lakeshore of Texcoco in the marshes, presumably to exploit the lake, for this was not agricultural land.

Large nucleated villages, such as Loma Terremote near Cuauhtitlán, with an estimated population of about 2500 people represented a radical change in social structure and developed a more varied economy than seen earlier. Sanders *et al.*, 1979 suggest that such communities with powerful lineage heads could have collaborated in the procurement and redistribution of materials such as obsidian. In order to increase their control and be nearer the sources of obsidian, they may have been drawn to the Teotihuacan Valley.

Puebla-Tlaxcala

It seems that throughout the entire Preclassic period, Puebla-Tlaxcala was a cultural jump ahead of its neighbors. This may be explained in terms of its more favorable environment and geographic location. There is much more agricultural land available, much less risk of frost, at least for a shorter time, and it receives about 25% more rainfall than the Basin of Mexico (Sanders *et al.*, 1979). It is not a closed interior basin but gives rise to the headwaters of the Atoyac River and many minor streams leading eastward to the Gulf lowlands. Strategically Puebla-Tlaxcala is much better situated for dealing with Oaxaca, the southern and eastern lowlands, and the Maya region; in fact across it lay the major routes of communication in Classic and Postclassic periods and probably Preclassic as well. (Map 3.2).

Nineteen different sites have been located belonging to the Tzompantepec phase by the year 1600 B.C.. Although sites are scattered, people made similar pottery, placed their houses on terraces near agricultural fields, and practiced some kind of ritual. The Puebla Valley consistently follows a regional variant of the larger Puebla-

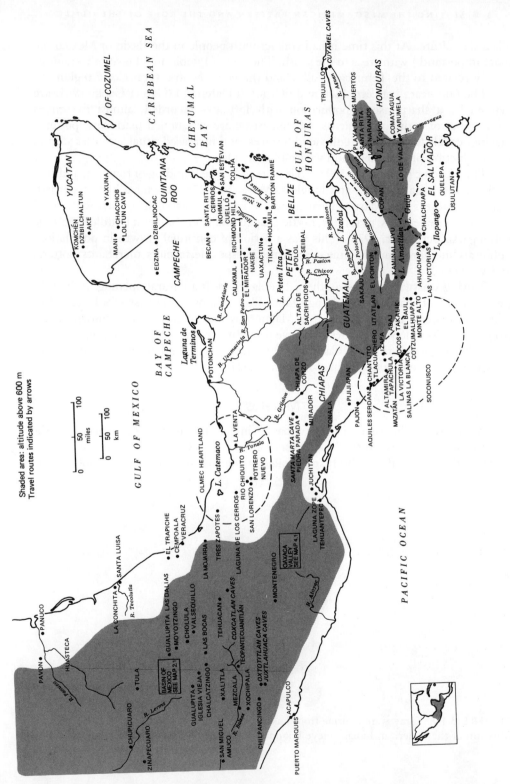

MAP 3.2 The Preclassic period.

Tlaxcala culture. At this time it had contact with people in the Basin of Mexico but more importantly with areas to the south. The rest of Puebla and Tlaxcala were more closely related to the Tehuacán Valley and the north-central Gulf Coast region.

The 600 years between 1200 and 600 B.C. (Tlatempa) (García Cook, 1981) are marked by a sharp rise in population with 150 sites recorded, almost five times the number of earlier settlements. Characteristic are ceremonial platforms, pottery-making, canals for irrigating cultivated terraces, and increased ritual activities seen in the production of figurines and incense-burner lids.

The Texoloc phase (800–300 B.C.) is marked by the founding of towns in addition to the earlier small villages and hamlets. More than 275 sites have been recorded. Moyotzingo near San Martín Texmelucan, Puebla, is just such a town with small platform house remains, pyramids, bottle-shaped pits, and abundant middle Preclassic pottery (Aufdermauer, 1973). This was a period of continual growth in population, public architecture, and full-time specialists: craftspeople, farmers, merchants, potters, and weavers.

Bearing westward across southern Puebla, there is a natural opening in the hills leading to Las Bocas, a site yielding Olmec-like remains at the base of a large hill or cliff at the eastern edge of the Izúcar de Matamoros Valley. Las Bocas is known largely from the spoils of looting parties that have brought out beautiful Olmec hollow baby-faced figures, white-rimmed black ware, spouted trays, and black-excised pottery with the paw-wing motif (Figures 3.10 and 3.11).

Morelos

Across the valley, one of the few passes in the mountains affords access to the central Morelos plains. At the Morelos end of the pass is Chalcatzingo whose location parallels that of Las Bocas. Both are situated at the base of a tall cliff and both would

FIGURE 3.10   Gray ware figurine from Las Bocas, Puebla. Height: 3 in. (Courtesy of the Museum of the American Indian, Heye Foundation, N.Y. [23/5495].)

FIGURE 3.11 Hollow seated baby figure from Las Bocas, Puebla. Height: 34 in. (Courtesy of the Metropolitan Museum of Art. The Michael C. Rockefeller Memorial Collection. Bequest of Nelson A. Rockefeller, 1979. [1979.206.1134].)

have been well situated to monitor any traffic. Chalcatzingo could have controlled access to three routes: south to Guerrero, north to the Basin of Mexico, and southeast to Oaxaca and the Gulf Coast. (see Map 3.2.)

At an altitude of 1370 m, Morelos enjoys a temperate year-round climate. Open forests of pine and oak, numerous streams, and abundant summer rainfall make the Morelos valleys favorable habitation sites. However, to our knowledge the earliest human remains date only from 1500 B.C. Early macrobands may not have been drawn to this area as some seasons offer little to collect and others have an overabundance. Year-round occupation may have presented difficulties (Hirth, 1987).

Chalcatzingo

The site is located in the Amatzinac River valley about 100 km southeast of Mexico City where farmers had fine bottom land for agriculture in the south. The north offered diverse vegetation zones for exploitation, while the central zone had deep fertile soil and a spring from which canals could channel the water for irrigation. Remains here fall into three Preclassic phases: Amate, Barranca, and Cantera (Grove, 1981, 1987, 1989; Angulo, 1987; Guillén and Grove, 1984, 1987; Hirth, 1987). The culmination of the Preclassic in Morelos belongs to the Cantera phase. In general the development follows that of the Basin of Mexico, with the addition of a surprising corpus of monumental art.

Amate (1500–1100 B.C.) About 10 small farming settlements were made in the Amatzinac Valley at this time. All were hamlets with the exception of a small village, Chalcatzingo, taking its name from the tall cliff behind it. This site offered a spring and good agricultural land. An earthen structure 2 m in height was erected faced with stone on the lowest level. A stone pavement forming a public area probably extended south of this mound. An additional stone-faced platform is yet to be explored. Ceramics with flat-based bowls and cylindrical forms are related to Tierras Largas in Oaxaca and early phases of Ixtapaluca in the Basin of Mexico. Unfortunately most of the pottery is known only from fill and disturbed areas, not from graves or stratified deposits (Fig. 3.12). Although contemporary with San Lorenzo in Veracruz, no specific relationship with the Olmec site is found.

Barranca (1100–700 B.C.) During these years a large portion of Chalcatzingo was terraced and the village moved up while still maintaining the public area and small stone-faced structure of Amate. Small hamlets grew up within 5 km of Chalcatzingo but none of them had public architecture. Thus Chalcatzingo was already becoming a major regional center. Water was so plentiful that dams were built to divert the excess. Aside from the massive terracing, a central plaza was laid out adjacent to an area of bas-reliefs and a large mound was raised (70 m long × 40 m wide × 4 m high). Ceramics of this phase correlate very nicely with the Manantial subphase of the Basin of Mexico, sharing form, decoration, and general inventory of remains. Bottles reach their peak of popularity, as well as cylindrical bowls, kaolin ware, excised Olmec designs, stirrup-spouts and white wares with the double-line-break. Here again contact has been postulated with west Mexico (Green and Lowe, 1967; Kelly, 1974; Grove, 1971) to account for some of these intrusive features.

Probably some of the famous Olmec-style bas-reliefs on rock exposures and boulders above the early village area belong to this phase. One of the best known is El Rey (Monument 1) showing an elite figure seated amid swirls of mist or smoke in the jaws of a mythological earth monster (the maw of the Underworld). The rain clouds above are shown with a triple raindrop motif taken as a sign of rulership (Grove, 1989). As the *axis mundi* he has the ability to ensure rain and the harmony of nature.

FIGURE 3.12   Hollow clay figure wearing a jaguar (?) pelt. Atlihuayán, Morelos. Height: 23 cm. (Courtesy of the Museo Nacional de Antropología, Mexico.)

Monument 12 is another outstanding sculpture, depicting a wonderful helmeted figure dubbed "the flying Olmec." He appears flying through the sky with birds. He is ceremonially dressed and holds a torch in his outstretched hand, probably heading for the open portal to the supernatural world. Flying Olmec figures are not uncommon (Reilly III, n.d.). The monuments in this area are mythicoreligious in theme.

Cantera (700–500 B.C.)   This is the apogee of Chalcatzingo at which time it controlled the entire valley with 49 sites and a population of 1429–3623, three times the size of Barranca. Now Chalcatzingo was one of the largest sites in central Mexico along with Cuicuilco.

On Terrace 25 a sunken patio was outlined by a low stone wall. Placed on the south side was a table-top altar (Monument 22) built of 20 large stone slabs. It is reminiscent of La Venta, lacking the latter's niche containing a figure. On the front face are the eyes of an earth monster, resembling that of the Oxtotitlán mural. The altar had been dismantled and rebuilt in antiquity. Grove (1989) believes it dates to the Cantera phase. A number of monumental sculptures are found near the central platforms and may be related to rulership or historial themes. Monument 21, for example, depicts a woman who must have been of some importance. This monument might commemorate a marriage (?). It had once stood in front of a stone-faced platform on Terrace 15. There are other examples of such sculptures placed in similar positions. Many were intentionally mutilated, particularly the head or headdress, in order to destroy the identity, perhaps along with any residual supernatural power. Grove considers these monuments to be political in nature and believes them to date to the Cantera phase. The dating of stone monuments is recognized as difficult and uncertain and is usually done by stylistic comparisons with other sites, in this case La Venta (see comments in Grove, 1989 and Tolstoy, 1989b).

In general the non-elite material is in the central Mexican tradition. The clay figurines correspond to those of the Basin of Mexico, of which nearly half of those found may represent attempts at portraiture (rulers?) as some series suggest (Grove and Gillespie, 1984).

Outside central Mexico, contacts are found with the Gulf Coast, Oaxaca, and Izapa. Unusual features are *comal*-like plates that first appeared in the Barranca phase, the presence of a polychrome ware with abstract designs in red, black, orange, and sometimes brown, on a white-slipped base color. This is the earliest appearance of the 3-pronged ceramic brazier or stove in highland Mexico.

The great economic prosperity in the Amatzinac Valley was fomented by its commercial activities. Chalcatzingo is what Hirth (1987) calls a gateway community, located at the convergence of natural corridors of communication. The Amatzinac Valley was a source of kaolin, cotton, lime, and hematite. Obsidian and salt could be obtained from the Basin of Mexico; jadeite, magnetite, hematite and other minerals came from Guerrero. Chalcatzingo undoubtedly moved agricultural produce, but its greatest wealth was probably derived from handling scarce exotic products destined for the elite.

In the late Preclassic, Chalcatzingo gradually declined and its surrounding clusters disappeared, a situation that resembles events in Puebla-Tlaxcala and the Basin of Mexico when a single large community was replaced by small politically autonomous centers. Rather than a period of cultural decadence or stagnation, it was a period of readjustment in Morelos. Grove (1989) suggests that Chalcatzingo was so closely tied to the Gulf Coast, that when the Olmec Centers declined, the role of a gateway community such as Chalcatzingo was no longer needed. It seems that trade alone is not enough "to generate the prolonged and steady development of complex society" (Hirth, 1987).

GUERRERO

The state of Guerrero has not been exactly ignored by scholars but is admittedly one of the least known archaeological areas in Mexico. The rugged terrain dominated by the Sierra Madre Occidental and the great Río Balsas matched by a reputedly cool reception to outsiders, has not encouraged penetration beyond the one highway crossing the state from Mexico City to Acapulco. However nothing has kept portable art treasures, often with Olmec features, from reaching private hands and local markets. All manner of objects of greenstone, jadeite, serpentine, and onyx so fascinated the artist Miguel Covarrubias that he became convinced this was the birthplace of the Olmec culture. Still debated, his ideas are again being reviewed.

In 1967 an Olmec sandstone stela at San Miguel Amuco (see Map 3.2) near Coyuca in the middle Balsas area was discovered. This is a full standing figure wearing a cape and holding in his arm a bundle of reeds (?) greatly resembling the later Aztec year symbol, the *xiuhmolpilli* (Grove and Paradis, 1971).

Teopantecuanitlán (Tlacozotitlán) (see Map 3.2.)

In 1984 news reached archaelogical circles that an "Olmec ceremonial center" had been discovered near the confluence of the Amacuzac and Balsas rivers. INAH immediately dispatched Guadalupe Martínez Donjuan and Christine Niederberger to investigate. What they found was the first large-scale stone architecture of any Olmec site, two ball courts and a stone-lined aqueduct that brought water from a dammed spring into the center of the site. Names for the site were coined, the first meaning "The Place of the Temple of the Jaguars" (Martínez Donjuan, 1986).

The site was undoubtedly selected because of a natural formation for a dam. This permitted a great increase in agriculture by irrigation. The extent of the site is estimated at 160 ha embracing the ceremonial or public structures, two ball courts, and an extensive residential zone.

Three stages of construction based on C-14 dates, have been outlined by Martínez Donjuan (1986): (1) 1400–900 B.C. was a time of earthen construction; (2) following 900 B.C. travertine block walls were added, monoliths carved, and an elaborate stone-lined drain was put in place; (3) 800–600 B.C. a large (not colossal) stone head was carved.

A pyramid (Mound 3) was faced with a curious arrangement of stone blocks, creating "bar and dot" and "V" designs. There is also a sunken stone enclosure (one of the earliest constructions) with interior walls of carefully cut travertine blocks. Four upside down T-shaped monoliths were set on top of the walls, representing baby-faced supernaturals that hold a torch in each hand. The largest monolith measures 2.20 m × 1.50 m and weighs 3 tons. There are still older adobe constructions beneath the enclosure with balustrades decorated with sculptured "were-jaguars" with flame eyebrows.

Associated with a domestic unit and a small adobe and boulder platform were ceramics and artifacts corresponding to many other areas dating to 1000–700 B.C. Ceramics include white-slipped, flat-based bowls or dishes with outslanting straight walls decorated with the double-line-break, the "star" motif on the inner bottom, and thin-walled, white-slipped *tecomates* with the cleft-head mythical Olmec. Hollow, highly polished baby figures with remains of red pigment are also present (Figure 3.13). Notable was a workshop of the Pacific Coast species of *Pinctada mazatlanica* and other marine shells involved in a long-distance exchange network (Niederberger, 1986, 1987).

By following the Cuautla-Amacuzac river combination from Chalcatzingo one could reach Teopantecuanitlán and the Balsas River, a natural thoroughfare to the Pacific Ocean. Chalcatzingo must have been the closest neighbor, ally, or market center of Teopantecuanitlán and their estimated dates are compatible. The general configuration of the sunken stone enclosure parallels that at Chalcatzingo and we can expect other resemblances as the material is studied (Grove, 1989).

Guerrero was the land of tin, copper, silver, gold, and precious stones, and a probable source of jade, the most prized of exotic materials. Most Mesoamerican "jade" comes from the Motagua River Valley in Guatemala but Guerrero has small

FIGURE 3.13 Hollow white-slipped, Olmec-style "baby-face" fragment. From Sitio 5, Teopantecuanitlán, Guerrero. Length: 5.2 cm. (Courtesy of Christine Niederberger.)

but numerous deposits that were undoubtedly exploited. One boulder of 15–29 g was found along the Atoyac River (A. Langenscheidt, personal communication).

We suspect that even in early times the immense delta of the Balsas River was an exciting port, offering shelter to ocean-going crafts as well as being the terminal of the vast interior communication line to the highlands.

Other Sites   From Chilpanzingo north to Xalita is sometimes known as the Mezcala area where many small stone carvings have been found. It is also the area of Xochipala, an important source of figurines that have appeared in private collections and are often cited for their Olmec traits. Paul Schmidt of UNAM has excavated in the area and recorded about 90 sites near the modern town of Xochipala (Schmidt, 1990). In general the pottery shares the Zacatenco trends of white-slipped bowls with the double-line-break, followed by polished composite silhouette incised bowls, but nothing specifically Olmec. The Xochipala figurines are difficult to date as they only appear in graves that for the most part have been disturbed. Those in collections are very naturalistic in gestures and movements (Griffin, 1972; Gay, 1982). The Xochipala figurines do form a distinctive group and although difficult to date, perhaps late Preclassic-Early Classic would be a reasonable estimate.

About 65 km southeast of Chilpanzingo are two caves with paintings located only a few miles apart, both located high above the river valley. The Juxtlahuaca paintings are about 1 km inside the mountain and were painted in black, green, red, and yellow. A standing figure wears an elaborate headdress and tunic. His arms and legs are covered with a jaguar skin and he has a jaguar tail. He holds out a ropelike object and a knife pointed toward a smaller crouching figure, probably a captive. This scene takes place in the Underworld.

At the second cave, Oxtotitlán (see Map 3.2) about 12 km to the north, there are a series of polychrome paintings on a cliff above a series of shallow caves. The best preserved, over a cave (an Underworld entrance) depicts a ruler seated on an earth-monster throne, as the center of the cosmos, symbolized by his pectoral of crossed bands. He is dressed in feathers and wears a bird mask (Reilly III, 1990). The iconographers see correspondences between this ruler and the bas-relief of El Rey at Chalcatzingo. Paintings, like monumental stone carvings, are difficult to date, but Coe (1977) places the Juxtlahuaca caves around 1000 B.C. and the Oxtotitlán murals slightly later (800 B.C.), contemporaneous with La Venta. Both caves are considered Olmec in style and lie approximately 55 km directly south of Teopantecuanitlán.

OAXACA

An area we will often refer to in chapters ahead is the Valley of Oaxaca, situated in the southern highlands of Mexico at an average elevation of 1500 m. Blessed by a warm, temperate, semiarid climate and drained by the Atoyac River and its tributary the Salado or Tlacolula River, the area has one of the longest most informative cultural sequences in Mesoamerica. Three valleys converge at the modern city of Oaxaca: Etla

Valley to the north, Tlacolula to the east, and Zaachila or the Valle Grande to the south. (See Map 4.1.)

The earliest formative material known comes from the valley of Etla, northwest of the city of Oaxaca, where there is a concentration of early sites. Here, soon after 1900 B.C. (?) people lived in settled communities on the high alluvial flood plain. Since the water table is only 3 m below the surface, this land could be farmed by "pot irrigation," a technique in which water was hauled up from wells in the fields and distributed around plants.

Much of the source material presented here is contained in two volumes, Flannery (1976) and Flannery and Marcus (1983), both composed of articles by scholars in their specialized fields of interest. In this section I will focus on the Zapotecs of the Etla or northwestern arm of the Oaxaca Valley, the scene of greatest activity.

Espiridión Phase (1900–1400 B.C.)   Ceramics that appear at this time are the earliest known from Oaxaca. Sherds were recovered from a small wattle-and-daub house (post holes) in the area of San José Mogote in the central Etla Valley. The pottery has no paint, slip, or decoration and is very similar to the ollas with short flaring necks and flaring-wall bowls of Purrón in Tehuacán. Espiridión lacks Purrón's *tecomate* forms, but produced a thin, irregularly fired hemispherical bowl. At this time potters were experimenting and not every village was producing pottery. Both known samples are small: Espiridión, 262 sherds; Purrón, 127. Every form at both sites could be derived from parts of a bottle gourd. An estimated time would fall between 1900 and 1400 B.C. (Marcus, 1983a)

Tierras Largas Phase (1400–1150 B.C.)   At this time Etla, the most densely occupied valley, had 5 small hamlets and a small village, San José Mogote, with an estimated population of 147. These people lived in wattle-and-daub houses with associated storage pits, drainage ditches, ovens, and refuse pits similar to other pits in highland Mexico, Chiapas, and highland Guatemala. Here they were dug into soft, decomposed rock and, when sealed with a flat stone, could store grain efficiently.

At San José Mogote, a one-room building was raised on a crushed rock foundation and plastered within and without with lime stucco. A step or altar was placed against the south wall and a storage pit in the center of the room. This became a standard pattern for public buildings with an orientation of 8° west of true north.

Pottery was well made and trimmed in red stripes, bands, or chevrons. *Tecomates* and flat-based, outleaning-wall bowls are minor ingredients but characteristically decorated with zoned rocker-stamping. Ceramics in general are like those of the Ajalpan phase at Tehuacán (Flannery, 1983b).

San José Phase (1150–850 B.C.)   This phase is contemporaneous with San Lorenzo in Veracruz. Contact is seen between the two regions in Olmec pottery designs among the dozen or more sites known. Population increased dramatically to 700 and including nearby settlements, occupied about 70 ha. The central core area of

20 ha included residences, a one-room public building, evidence of social stratification, craft specialization, pooling, and redistribution of obsidian.

After 900 B.C. the demand for prismatic blades increased to the point that a few high-status families may have acted as a central agency that received, pooled, and redistributed obsidian to other families. Status was marked by where you lived, what sacred ritual objects you possessed, what ornaments you wore, and what access you had to exotic raw materials.

The village of San José Mogote grew to 10 times the size of any others, with the elite settling near the public buildings. Four residential wards (roughly corresponding to the 4 cardinal points) have been found to specialize in certain activities such as jade, tool manufacture, basketry, and sewing in one household; another produced magnetite mirrors and work in shell; another specialized in pearl oysters and freshwater mussel shells from the Pacific, as well as manufacturing all the stone celts.

Pottery was generally similar to that found elsewhere in the lowlands and central highland Mexico (differentially fired wares, excised designs, Olmec motifs, rocker-stamping, figurines of C and D types). The Olmec motifs seem to be associated with two major descent groups of lineages: the were-jaguar (earth) and the fire-serpent (lightning). The association of these motifs with particular residential wards suggests that affiliation with these groups was inherited. In graves, men were given most of these vessels.

This was a time of great interregional exchange of ritual items over great distances. A Oaxaca excised gray ware found its way to Tlapacoya and also to San Lorenzo. Deposits of magnetite and ilmentite in the Oaxaca Valley were exploited to make small iron-ore mirrors that were traded to San Lorenzo and Morelos. These may have been worn on the chest as an elite badge of distinction. At least some are thus found on clay figurines.

In turn, Oaxaca received wares from the Gulf Coast, Ocós in Guatemala, and later from Morelos. Sting-ray spines used for bloodletting, sharks teeth, turtle-shell drums, conch-shell trumpets, and armadillo shells were all part of the lowland imported ritual inventory.

Guadalupe Phase (850–700 B.C.)   Public architecture increased in the Etla Valley where at Huitzo an adobe public platform was raised 1.3 m high and 11.5 m long, which once supported a lime-plastered wattle-and-daub building. The traditional orientation of 8° west of true north was preserved.

Contact with the Gulf Coast falls off rapidly at this time, coinciding with the demise of San Lorenzo.

Ceramics no longer use the fire-serpent and were-jaguar motifs, but the former will still be seen in the day-sign for earthquake, and the second associated with the Rain God, Cocijo, who becomes the most powerful supernatural at Monte Albán. Thus the people of the were-jaguar (earth) association emerge as the elite (Marcus, 1989).

The ubiquitous double-line-break in pottery reaches its peak, and among the figurines, the Basin of Mexico's type A (with its well-defined eye with punched pupil) predominates. This style has a very general distribution throughout lowland sites and as far east as the Petén. Burials sometimes paired a man and a woman and a secondary burial might be added later to a grave of a primary adult male. This might be a family member or a sign of political association (?) (Marcus, 1989).

Rosario Phase (700–500 B.C.) In these years, San José Mogote reached its apogee with a population reaching 1300–1400 and a downtown area covering 40 ha. We now find 18–20 villages, public buildings mounted on large stone masonry platforms, monumental stone carving, human sacrifice, and evidence of the 260-day calendar.

Some sacrificial victims were found in foundations of buildings, but the most dramatic display is a carved stone (Monument 3) set on the threshold of a public building precisely where one would tread. This stone is carved with a sprawling figure, the first of such slabs we will find at Monte Albán, called the "danzantes." A day-sign, 1-Earthquake, is carved in glyphs between the figure's feet. These glyphs are the first-known evidence of the 260-day calendar in Mesoamerica and perhaps mark the beginning of the custom of naming an individual for the date of his birth.

There were now numerous small chiefdoms in the Oaxaca Valley. Each contained a village with some public buildings that served as the local civic-ceremonial center for a series of nearby hamlets. At San José Mogote a leading family preempted a locality that had been the largest public structure on 15 m high ground. A similar situation is recorded at Huitzo.

Population and activity declined sharply with the founding of Monte Albán in 500 B.C., but its roots are clearly seen in the Rosario phase at San José Mogote. After little activity in Monte Albán I, this center underwent a great renaissance in Monte Albán II when it became a secondary administrative center of the capital. The rebuilding produced almost a replica of Monte Albán with a main plaza almost as large. An I-shaped ball court was built with a duplication of style and measurements of the later one at Monte Albán.

Oaxaca conforms in many ways to the general pattern of Formative development in Mesoamerica with farming and pottery-making communities. Distinctive innovations include the early emergence of ceramics, evidence of the 260-day calendar, human sacrifice, and significant steps in sociopolitical organization. How much of this is due to a greater availability of information only time and future excavations will tell. At present Oaxaca is on the leading edge of the emergence of the great civilizations to follow.

Laguna Zope

Located 1 km west of Juchitán, Oaxaca, Laguna Zope was positioned on crossroads of travel across the Isthmus (See Map 3.2). A long sequence of remains here reach back to at least 1500 B.C. This was a large Preclassic settlement on a narrow strip of coastal plain with good water and agricultural land. (Figure 3.14). Ocós ceramics are well represented (Zeitlan, 1978).

FIGURE 3.14   Riverine-estuary environment on the southern Isthmus of Tehuantepec near Juchitán. (Courtesy of Robert and Judith Zeitlin.)

From 1100–800 B.C. population increased and maintained a close relationship to Soconusco. As San Lorenzo reached its peak on the Gulf coast, at Laguna Zope we find Olmec designs and forms superimposed on the pre-existing ceramic complex. Guadalupe Victoria, Zaragoza, and El Chayal provided the obsidian. The contacts we have noted between the Gulf Coast and San José Mogote may well have passed this way.

As growth continued after 800 B.C. ceramics were typical of the middle Preclassic, and after 400 B.C. the waxy orange wares of the Maya lowlands are found. Laguna Zope marks the northern limit of a cloudy Usulután resist ware that we will see often in the pages ahead.

THE OLMEC

Olmec studies began in 1939 when Matthew W. Stirling was sent by the Smithsonian Institution of Washington, D.C. and the National Geographic Society to investigate colossal heads at Tres Zapotes, Veracruz. From then until 1970, work concentrated on the major sites of San Lorenzo and La Venta in southern Veracruz and Tabasco. The area was soon considered to be the hearth of the Olmec culture, the "mother-culture," from where certain art styles and iconographic features were thought to have spread over a wide peripheral area. Various theories were proposed to account for this diffusion: religious beliefs, colonization, an empire, trade, and/or an exchange network of exotic goods. After some time a number of artifacts were called Olmec that may not be found in the Gulf Coast heartland or were obviously intrusive there (see Map 3.2). So we still find ourselves in the position of trying to define what is meant by Olmec.

Nonetheless, the mother-culture concept is not without some merit and is still widely accepted, although now both the idea and the place have been challenged. Other areas to take its place have been proposed such as central highland Mexico or Oaxaca. Guerrero and the Pacific piedmont region of Chiapas and Guatemala are other contenders. Or perhaps there was not a single area but a number of interacting regional developments. At a conference held in 1983 at the School of American Research to present these views, no consensus was reached. Tolstoy, Lowe, and M. D. Coe upheld the traditional Gulf Coast view, while Marcus, Grove, Demarest, and Sharer argued for diverse interaction among Preclassic centers, many of which were independent of involvement with the Gulf Coast Olmec (Sharer and Grove, 1989).

The issue is an important one, calling into question the very base from which following Mesoamerican civilizations would emerge.

I cannot hope to do more than present a general summary of what is known at the moment to be followed by the most pervasive interpretations to date. The main cultural developments as we know them come from the major sites of San Lorenzo and La Venta, but there are others such as Potrero Nuevo, Río Chiquito, Laguna de los Cerros, and Tres Zapotes. To avoid polemics, I will refer to the Gulf Coast region as the heartland of the Olmec, and try to point out what may or may not be attributed to Olmec influence in other areas.

Today we have a good idea of the material culture and layout of La Venta and San Lorenzo. Interpretations continue and since 1970, the focus has passed to studying connections of these heartland Olmec with their neighbors. Risking oversimplification, I will mention only a few basic references, including conferences, each of which offers further detailed reading material: Benson (1981); M. D. Coe (1965a,1981b); Coe and Diehl (1980a,b); Drucker et al., (1959); Stirling (1943); Drucker (1943, 1952, 1981); Covarrubias (1946a,b,1957); Sharer and Grove (1989); Reilly III (n.d.); Rust III and Sharer (1988); González (1988); Lowe (1977, 1989); Lee (1989); Tolstoy (1989a,b); Demarest (1989).

The Olmec heartland is most simply defined as the broad coastal plain of the Gulf Coast between the Papaloapan River, Veracruz, and the Tonalá River in Tabasco (See Map 3.2).

For many years La Venta was envisioned as an odd little ceremonial center occupied by a few priestly elite who held ritual celebrations for the populace that lived beyond the outlying swamps and would come in periodically for special ceremonies or to market.

From 1985 to 1988 the Proyecto Arqueológico La Venta under auspices of INAH conducted extensive investigations directed by Rebecca González, University of California, Berkeley, aided by William Rust, University of Pennsylvania. The work was supported by the National Science Foundation together with both universities. The results have completely altered former concepts of La Venta (Rust III and Sharer, 1988; González, 1988). This project has revealed that La Venta was a large cosmopolitan center with residential areas associated with public-civic-religious centers and an extensive sustaining population on small "islands" on high land along the rivers. Moreover the area had a long period of earlier settlement.

To early peoples, Mesoamerica did not have western and eastern sectors astride the Isthmus of Tehuantepec. Instead they saw low flood plains with streams, lagoons, estuaries, and a row of rivers flowing north to the Gulf of Mexico: the Papaloapan, Tonalá, the Great Grijalva, and Usumacinta. By following some like the Grijalva to the south, one could find smaller tributaries that led to a great fertile strip of land we call Soconusco on the Pacific coast of Chiapas. On the Gulf side were early settlers along the old Río Barí, while on the Pacific side lived the Mokaya. Both groups lived much as their earlier ancestors did at Palo Hueco and Chantuto (hunting, gathering, and collecting) with one exception. Now they both planted maize. Settlements gradually increased in size and number until there were villages, some larger than others, and some with prominent citizens. Inevitably as they moved around, by approximately 1500 B.C., these groups made contact with each other. I will begin with the Río Barí folk on the Gulf Coast of La Venta in Tabasco.

Life on the Levees at La Venta (2250–1150 B.C.)

One day in 1986, William Rust sat down to analyze aerial photographs and discerned two channels of an old silted-in river (Río Barí) that once flowed north of La Venta to empty into the Gulf of Mexico. This led to the discovery that maize (*Zea mays*) was an imported domesticate and was being planted along the levees in 2250 B.C. by ceramic-using villagers (Rust III and Leyden, n.d.).

These early peoples lived along the river levees and subsisted on a diet of mollusks, fish, turtles, and food from mangrove resources in addition to maize. Maize is known to have been brought down to the tropical lowlands from semiarid highlands between 5000 and 2000 B.C., reported now at numerous sites underlying complex societies in coastal and riverine tropical environments. Manioc could have been an important cultigen but no evidence of it has been found. This is a hot, humid, tropical region, of no help in preserving remains of bone and perishables. But it is a rich agricultural area that offered an almost inexhaustible food supply: fish, aquatic birds, dogs, toads (an hallucinogen?), and crocodiles. There are few early signs of hunting, and the environment was probably never exploited to its fullest capacity.

On the San Andrés levee along the ancient river course inhabitants in 1750–1400 B.C. were making brushed, grit-tempered pottery found with many remains of brackish water mollusks, capped by a sterile layer of alluvium. The next layer (1400–1150 B.C.) yielded thin, neckless rim sherds, grinding stones of imported basalt, mollusk shells, and charred palm nuts.

We are just now beginning to have information on housing, burials, and settlement patterns for the La Venta area. Just how simple villages were transformed into the complex hierarchies that we find by 1150 B.C. is only inferred. But it is possible that competition for the best land on the levees for farming, for living, and facilities for trade and transport could have led to Olmec social stratification (Carneiro, 1970).

Soconusco, the Mokaya, and the Olmec

A coastal strip of Chiapas east of the Isthmus of Tehauntepec is called Soconusco, perhaps the finest cacao growing region of Mesoamerica (See Map 3.2). The most productive agricultural land is toward the east where the plain is 20–30 km wide and lies between coastal estuaries and lagoons on the south and the Sierra Madre de Chiapas on the north. It is here in the region of Mazatán (See Map 3.2) that permanent villages were settled around 1800 B.C., presumably based on agriculture and making very early pottery (Barra phase). These inhabitants have been called Mokaya, which is a Mixe-Zoque term for corn people, and they are believed to have been proto-Mixe-Zoque speakers (Clark and Blake, 1989; Blake, 1991; Clark, 1991).

A short Locona phase follows before the major phase of Ocós begins in 1500 B.C. lasting to 1325 B.C. The development we see among the Mokaya is possibly typical of village growth during these years.

The size of settlements varied from 400 to 1000 inhabitants, implying the presence of a leader or chiefdom-type control. Clark and Blake (1989) speculate that some people felt the urge to accumulate goods, create a personal following, and become noticed in the community. It could have begun by simply bestowing a gift on an individual, arousing feelings of respect or loyalty as well as indebtedness and allegiance. A large center would be the result of a natural desire to be handy and close to the political activity. Thus small villages gathered around a large center that attracted people. Some specialization was seen in fishing, salt extraction, and pottery making. In Mazatán the population explosion took place after the social changes. There was no true population pressure. The population increased as competition for prestige and privilege attracted followers whose loyalty and steadfastness were carefully nurtured.

Pottery-making in this Mazatán region had a special role. Cord-marked pottery is rare in Mesoamerica but characteristic of northern North America and common in the Old World. This was a ware decorated by wrapping a fine cord around a paddle and pressing it against the unfired clay vessel, leaving an imprint. The fine quality of Locona ceramics differs greatly from that of Tehuacán and Oaxaca and has led to suggestions of a South American origin. Not only is the quality fine, but several unusual features of Ocós ceramics are shared with South America. For example, an unusual decoration using thin stripes of iridescent paint gave almost a metallic luster to the finish. This is found in Ecuador in sites of comparable age and has led to speculation regarding intercontinental travel at this time (M. D. Coe, 1960; Lathrep, 1975; Meggers et al., 1965). Rocker-stamping is another decoration shared with the Andean region and not uncommon in Mesoamerica at this time. There is little doubt of contacts between this area and South America, as well as that already noted with west Mexico. Clark and Blake feel, however, that we need not look abroad for the origin of pottery-making. Pottery here, as in Oaxaca, highland Mexico, and on the Gulf Coast could be a local achievement, the forms reflecting copies of earlier containers made of wood or gourds. In this case *tecomate* forms may have been produced to store or serve liquids and have an elegant simplicity surely designed for ritual or display. None show evidence of cooking. This enterprise was motivated by political competition for prestigious goods.

In general it seems that Ocós pottery evolved out of Barra and Locona, but is more sophisticated and has many new shapes and decorations such as effigy bowls, thick-walled *tecomates*, plates with vertical walls, incense burners with pedestal bases, tripod supports on bowls and *tecomates*, grooved rims, flanges, and complex silhouette vessels. Human figurines were made with thin faces, large noses and mouths, and rudimentary arms, but heavy thighs and hips. Ocós sites are known along the upper Grijalva River, but are most common along the Pacific littoral. They are typically small, located along rivers.

Regarding agriculture, *metates* and *manos* were present, but few in number. Maize productivity was low and the cobs measure only 4–5 cm in length. The Mokaya still fished, hunted, and gathered food. Corn as a newly adopted crop may have been considered very special, a treat to be brought out on occasions. Perhaps its success in this area was due precisely to its use in ritual and made into an alcoholic drink. Eventually the *tecomate* form was replaced by deep plates and dishes implying more feasting than ritual drinking (Clark, 1991).

Ranking was well established as seen at Paso de la Amada, for example, where a dwelling raised above ground level contained remains of fine pottery and ornaments: clay earspools, jade beads, and mica. There were few burials but a child, age 11, was covered with red pigment and wore a mica mirror on its forehead. Mirrors are also seen on clay figurines. Male figurines are fat, wear animal masks, aprons, and sometimes mirrors as pendants. An active contact with highland Guatemala was maintained to bring in three different kinds of obsidian.

According to linguistic history, some Mokaya groups may have passed across the Isthmus to Tabasco and Veracruz from coastal Chiapas about this time. They would have come in contact with proto-Maya speakers on the Gulf Coast and many Otomanguean speakers (a large linguistic group inhabiting Oaxaca and Puebla). A long-recognized split is believed to have taken place around 1600 B.C., resulting in some Maya speakers moving north to become the group we know as Huastecs. While the Mixe took hold on the Olmec heartland, the Mokaya retained their own Mixe-Zoque language. Because the Gulf people stayed in contact with their neighbors culturally and commerically (Maya to the north and south, and Otomanguean groups of Oaxaca, Puebla, and Guerrero), the Olmec culture emerged as the first truly mestizo culture of Mesoamerica (Clark and Blake, 1989).

The language of the Olmec has been much discussed since Jiménez Moreno (1942) first suggested that the earliest inhabitants spoke a Maya language, perhaps Huastec, but lived among speakers of other tongues. Both Maya and Mixe-Zoque languages have been suggested as the language of the Olmec (Diehl, 1989; Justeson, 1986) and a Mixe-speaking mestizo culture would seem to meet with general approval.

The Mokaya are a good example of these early phases (Barra-Ocós, sometimes called early Olmec) with ceramics closely associated with a "Greater Isthmian Tradition," (see page 71). This tradition shows great cultural continuity ultimately evolving out of Barra and Ocós, and is linked to the Mixe-Zoque peoples.

With this perspective I return to the Olmec heartland to examine the great San Lorenzo phase and the flowering of the Olmec civilization.

San Lorenzo

This site lies about 100 km southwest of La Venta and about 60 km from the coast up the Coatzacoalcos River in Veracruz. The remains of San Lorenzo Tenochtitlán span the years 1450–400 B.C., the peak falling between 1150 and 900 B.C.

The privileged location of San Lorenzo close to both highland and lowland forest habitats, while being on high land near the fertile flood plain at the confluence of the Coatzacoalcos and Chiquito Rivers, gave these people many economic advantages at the outset. Before long they managed to dominate their neighbors and became powerful enough to assemble an impressive labor force for an ambitious earth-moving program.

The first three phases at San Lorenzo are considered "pre-Olmec" (Ojochí, Bajío, and Chicharras), but the remains conform to the Greater Isthmian Tradition. Ojochí (1500–1350 B.C.) is known largely from ceramics of this tradition: flat-bottomed bowls, thin *tecomates*, red rims, rocker-stamping, differentially black-and-white fired wares, zoned decorations, a variety of slips, burnishing, and figurines. This ties in nicely with Ocós, lacking the more elaborate features such as hematite mirrors and the unusual ceramics. The first modest construction began after 1350 B.C. (Bajío phase) by leveling terraces and building low platforms atop the ridges of the plateau.

After 1250 B.C. (Chicharras phase) a source of basalt was located at Cerro Cintepec, 70 km away in the Tuxtla Mountains, and quarrying began. Stones had to be dragged to the nearest stream, floated out to sea, and rafted up the Coatzacoalcos River—no small undertaking even though the river probably flowed closer than it does today. Craftsmen turned out well-made two-legged *metates* and sculptors began to work on basalt.

Long-necked bottles are strangely abundant at San Lorenzo and neighboring sites. These are not part of the Isthmian Tradition but closely resemble those of Tlatilco and Chalcatzingo. The history of these bottles is an enigma, and they shortly disappear at San Lorenzo around 1150 B.C. when the full ceramic complex we know as Olmec appears.

In these early stages the Olmec consolidated their power structure and managed to command wide support to sustain their elite. The society centered around the administration of a social organization and formalized ritual. The site of San Lorenzo became in a way, a gigantic artifact. Situated on a plateau 50 m above the surrounding savannas, artificial ridges were added, created by hauling up baskets of fill. When completed, the ridges reached out like fingers in some planned pattern. There are many mounds atop the plateau, the main cluster being aligned along a north–south axis oriented at 8° west of true north, with rectangular courts surrounded by pyramids. Structures are made of earth and colored clays. There was no stone available locally, and although the Olmec did not hesitate to move huge chunks of basalt for their monuments, these were not used in construction.

The Olmec are most famous for their monumental stone carving. Colossal heads, altars (or thrones), 3-dimensional figures, and stela were all carved in a distinctive style (Figure 3.15). The basalt heads are very uniform. They represent a human head, often with infantile features, wide, thick lips, and a close-fitting cap. Because the features do not contain any supernatural elements, and each headgear is distinctive, they are believed to be portraits of Olmec rulers. The heads are complete monuments in themselves, some measuring 3 m in height and weighing up to 20 tons. Although sometimes found deep in ravines, originally they were prominently displayed on the platforms and courts on the plateau. The time and effort spent in moving these huge stones is staggering. M.D. Coe estimates that to drag Monument 20 to where it was found (presumably with ropes), would have required hundreds of men. The stone was quarried and probably sculpted at the base of the mountains since no debitage or basalt workshops were found at San Lorenzo itself. The heads were carved from large smooth boulders that occur naturally on the surface and required minimal basic shaping (Drucker, 1981).

Another special feature of San Lorenzo are the buried drains, one of which is 170 m long with three branches. It was composed of neatly shaped sections of basalt with lids. Some were connected to stone sculptures arranged around a system of artificial ponds and fountains that could have been purely functional or used in ritual.

The cultural peak at San Lorenzo was reached between 1150–900 B.C. During these years contacts were established with highland central Mexico, Guerrero, and Oaxaca and with Chiapas peoples. Such materials as mica, schist, serpentine, and iron ore were sought out to be used in ritual. The exact nature of the relationship with other centers has been the subject of much dicussion. Very specific San Lorenzo objects that moved abroad at this time were two ceramic types (Calzadas Carved and Limón Incised) and the large, hollow, white-slipped baby figure. Other ceramics, small figurines, polished stone figures, stamps, and whistles have left almost a continuous trail through these areas (Figure 3.16). As typical of Mixe-speakers, obsidian was brought down from central Mexico and Guatemala (Tajumulco and El Chayal) (Lee Jr., 1989). Oaxaca shared this network.

The Central Depression of Chiapas sites of Mirador and Plumajillo were areas of possible Olmec colonization in order to procure or control the production of high-

---

FIGURE 3.15   Monumental Preclassic stone sculpture.
a. Stela 2. La Venta, Tabasco. Height: 2.46 m. (Courtesy of the Instituto Nacional de Antropología e Historía. Mexico.)
b. Carved stone altar (throne ?). From La Venta, Tabasco. Height: 1.53 m. (Courtesy of the Instituto Nacional de Antropología e Historía, Mexico.)
c. Monument 34. San Lorenzo. This unusual figure probably represents a ball player with ratcheted disk shoulder sockets. On his chest hangs a large concave mirror. (Courtesy of Michael D. Coe.)

a

b

c

d

e

d. Colossal stone head, Monument 1. San Lorenzo. Height: 2.74 m. (Courtesy of Michael D. Coe.)

e. Colossal stone head in profile (note ear). Recarved. Monument 23. Abaj Takalik, Guatemala. Height: 1.85 m. (Courtesy of John A. Graham.)

a   b   c   d

FIGURE 3.16   Small stone sculptures.
a. Stone seated figure with child. Tabasco? Height: 11.3 cm. (Courtesy of The Metropolitan Museum of Art. The Michael C. Rockefeller Memorial Collection. Bequest of Nelson A. Rockefeller, 1979. [1979.206.940].)
b. Black stone carving representing a kneeling Olmec figure with hollow in top of the head. Incense burner? Height: 24.8 cm. (Courtesy of the Museum of the American Indian, Heye Foundation, N.Y. [15/3560].)
c. Stone votive axe with human figure carved on one side. Veracruz. Height: 29 cm. (Courtesy of the Museum of the American Indian, Heye Foundation, N.Y. [16/3400].)
d. A supernatural being. San Lorenzo, Veracruz. Height: 1.0 m. (Courtesy of Michael D. Coe.)

grade iron-ore cubes, curiously drilled with multiple subconical holes (Lee, Jr., 1989). A number of cubes of hematite, ilmenite, and magnetite have been found in San Lorenzo-phase contexts as well as a mirror fragment. The use of the cubes (approximately 4 cm) is unknown (weights, beads, amulets?) A magnetic hematite grooved bar at San Lorenzo may have been the "world's first lodestone compass" (Coe and Diehl, 1980a). This would have enabled the Olmecs to properly orient their sites, tombs, and offerings so as to live with the desired balance and in harmony with their cosmic world. Surely lapidaries would have noticed that, in grinding the magnetite, ilmenite, or hematite for mirrors, magnetic properties of the resulting dust would have made a "peculiar" pattern. This would explain the divinatory-mirror tradition that grew up in Mesoamerica (Carlson, 1981). Mirrors are found in ritual contexts, associated with high-status individuals, worn as a pendant with possible divinatory power, or on the forehead, perhaps to light the way to the Underworld.

San Isidro, Mirador, and Miramar might be considered as way stations along an

Olmec route between the Gulf Coast, Soconusco, and highland Guatemala. Outstanding Olmec stone carvings are known from coastal Chiapas around Pijijiapan where Olmec-style life-size reliefs are carved on three huge granite boulders (Navarrete, 1974). The figures carry no weapons or burdens, implying civic personnel rather than warriors or merchants.

Further east was the homeland of the Mokaya who were still living in simple chiefdom societies. The Olmec in San Lorenzo by now had developed a far more complex political system. As they ventured outside their homeland, it was natural that they would come to Soconusco. The Mokaya first began to copy the Gulf Coast ceramics, including the designs and figurines. Finally they adopted all the Olmec ceramic complex as well as household utensils. The entire Mazatán zone was reorganized politically and economically to become "Olmecized" (Cuadros and Jocotal phases). Changes are seen primarily in politics, ritual, and ranking. New Olmec centers in Mazatán produced monolithic sculptures that represent Olmec-type leaders, perhaps local or heartland personnel sent to supervise and administer the region. Clark and Blake (1989) visualize an exchange network operating from El Salvador to Veracruz.

Back at San Lorenzo, most of the monuments were carved prior to 900 B.C. Thereafter changes are seen. Activity seems to have centered on commercial or exchange relationships rather than carving monuments. In the Nacaste phase (900–700 B.C.), Olmec civilization at San Lorenzo came to an end. Monuments were savagely mutilated; faces were smashed, heads knocked off. Axe marks indicate the trials of energy expended. The systematic destruction of monuments and their methodical concealment and burial may have been done by the Olmec themselves. The Nacaste invaders, whoever they were, replaced the old ceramics with new types; figurines stare out of strange, large punched eyes, non-Olmec in design typical of Chiapas and Guatemala.

The succeeding phase, Palangana (600–400 B.C.) introduces different pottery suggestive of further contact with coastal communities and with Maya peoples to the east. It was at this time that two long parallel mounds were erected that are thought to have been a ball court (Coe and Diehl, 1980a). The game was certainly known, for clay figurines depict the players in their sporting attire and Monument 34 (see Figure 3.15) is thought to represent a decapitated ball player.

All activity on the ridge seems to have ceased around 400 B.C. and San Lorenzo, although reoccupied in Postclassic years, never regained the prominence attained by the early Olmec.

San Lorenzo is only one of a number of sites. Río Chiquito and Potrero Nuevo were minor satellites of San Lorenzo having mounds around plazas, colossal heads, and carved monuments. Laguna de los Cerros, in today's sugar cane country 35 km south of Lake Catemaco, is a huge archaeological zone with clay and earthen structures, plazas also aligned at 8° west of true north. Small sculptures of torsos, Olmec reliefs on a huge rectangular block, and small Olmec figurines and carved stone drains are typical.

La Venta: The Site

La Venta, Tabasco, is actually situated on a salt dome 12 km from the Gulf Coast surrounded by freshwater swampland (see Map 3.2). At this time, things were well under way at La Venta itself as the greatest construction took place from 1150 to 800 B.C. This was a time when the Río Barí levees were 4 m high and the river reached its maximum height enabling heavy stone materials to be rafted in, passing within 2 km of Complex A (Rust III and Sharer, 1988).

When La Venta reached its apogee in 800–500 B.C. (middle Preclassic), it had already become a stratified society with a major ceremonial core, with the imports it needed for ritual and domestic use. Maize was well established as a basic part of the diet, and there is a pronounced increase in eating dogs, deer, and crocodiles, apparently by high-status families (Rust III and Leyden, n.d.).

The well-known ceremonial center (Complexes C and A) (Figure 3.17) formed but a small part of the extensive site located in the midst of a swampy network of rivers. The general orientation was along a north–south axis (actually 8° west of true north, as in the Etla Valley of Oaxaca). When the airstrip was put in, it severely damaged the western area of the site, overrunning part of Complex A. Northwest of Complex A beyond the airstrip, Stirling found three of La Venta's four colossal heads set in a row facing north (Stirling, 1943), not their original location. Some kind of a circular civic or public building was also reported from this area (González, 1988).

The ceremonial area is at the northern end of the central axis. To the south of it was a large open court where many monuments have been found. Beyond that is an enormous area designated as Group D composed of at least 20 structures. Along the east side of this main axis is the Stirling Acropolis, an immense platform (325 m long × 260 m wide and 7 m high) supporting four small structures, two of which are circular. Of particular interest is the news that residential areas have been located directly northeast of the ceremonial center (Rust III and Sharer, 1988).

The Ceremonial Center

Complex C   The main feature in this group is a huge platform supporting an earthen mound 32 m high. It is so badly eroded that it has been described as having various forms including a fluted cone imitating a mountain. It has also been described as having a form similar to Tikal's Pyramid 5C-54 and Uaxactún's Pyramid E-VII-sub, that is, a radial pyramid with inset corners. According to the most recent investigations, the latter is the most likely (González, 1988). The rest of the complex consists of two long low mounds on each side of the center axis with a small mound (A-3) in the center. To the north is the broad court enclosed by upright basalt columns of Complex A.

Complex A   Here Drucker found 14 sculptures and more than 50 offerings, 5 mosaic and massive serpentine offerings, 10 mounds, and platforms distributed around two courts. The north court was limited on 2 sides by a wall of basalt columns, with

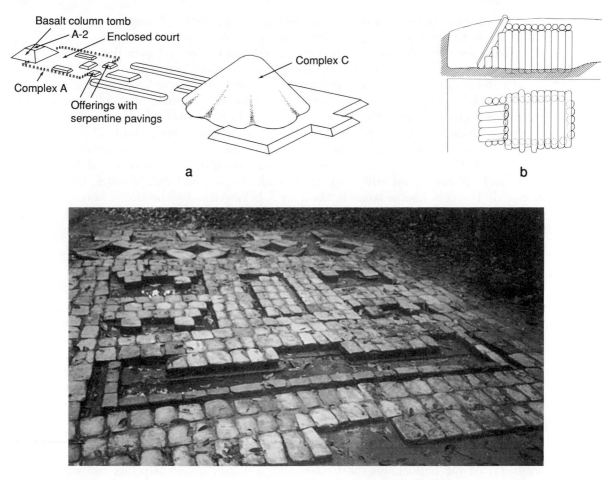

FIGURE 3.17 Ceremonial precinct of La Venta. a, Complexes A, and C; b, basalt columned tomb; c, serpentine mosaic pavement. (Photographed by the author.)

the north end marked by Mound A-2. The southern entrance to the court was partially restricted by two platform mounds, and a third located in the center. Complex A underwent 4 phases of construction and on each occasion new offerings were buried and Mound A-2 was enlarged. In the second phase, massive deposits of serpentine ("28 courses" of rough blocks weighing 1000 tons) (Drucker *et al.*, 1959) were laid down on either side of the south entrance to the court. Above each, a mosaic pavement of 485 blocks of serpentine formed a mask with diamond-shaped fringe appendages. Spaces were filled with orange, purple, and red clays. Higher still in the fill, a cache was arranged in a cruciform pattern. On one side the cache consisted of 20 celts and a hematite mirror. The other cache had 6 serpentine axes. Finally, platform mounds were raised over both groups of layered offerings. Comparable offerings were also found under a third platform in the center during the third construction phase. At this time a series of clay floors (red, purple, and pink) were laid over the entire complex, raising the ground level to the top of the three platforms.

The fourth and last phase of activity was associated with Mound A-2, at which time the basalt columned walls were added to the court. Now there was only one layer of polished serpentine blocks, but to put them in place a pit was dug through the top of Mound A-2 to a depth of 4.8 m below the surface of the ground. Then a sandstone sarcophagus (Monument 6) was placed directly over the buried pavement at ground level. The sarcophagus contained jade jewelry but no bones. It was beautifully carved to represent a great earth monster/crocodile, floating on bands of water, legs extended. The only human bones in Complex A belonged to two juveniles, heavily coated with cinnabar paint and buried in a tomb of 44 basalt columns (see Figure 3.17) located 3 m north of the sarcophagus. With the deceased were some of the most beautifully crafted Olmec objects known: ear flares, perforators, figurines, beads, a large shark's tooth, frog, and clam shell, all of jade. The latter was a 10-in. pendant that contained a small chrystalline hematite mirror. (The famous Offering No. 4 forming a scene with 16 jade figures and 6 jade celts, was not found here, but in the extreme northeast corner of the court near the basalt columned wall).

The final act was to cover the entire complex with a foot of thick red clay and with this, activity at Complex A ended.

Nothing like these massive offerings and the Underworld of Complex A has been found elsewhere in Mesoamerica, but the architectural layout is paralleled in formal centers in Chiapas (Lee, Jr., 1989). No one doubted that this enclosure was sacred and of great importance to the Olmec, but its significance was puzzling. A likely interpretation is offered here (Reilly III, n.d.), based on the Maya world view.

The Maya had worked out the organization of their universe in a very detailed and precise fashion. They "knew" for example that the world was composed of 3 levels: (1) At the bottom was the Underworld, a watery abode of plants and sea creatures, the place of the dead and certain lords of darkness and evil. Human beings lived on a terrestrial, middle level (2), where the world floated on a primordial sea symbolized by a great earth monster. The heavens above (3) were inhabited by deities and birds, and was the final resting place of ancestors after their rebirth in the Underworld. These three realms were linked by a great world tree with roots in the Underworld, the trunk in the Middle World, and spreading branches in the Heavens where a mythological celestial bird perched on the top. The middle level was often pictured as a crocodile, or it might also take the form of a mountain, or a ruler wearing proper cosmic symbols. The Underworld could only be entered by special portals opened by the bloodletting act, followed by sinking into water, or passing through the maw of the earth monster, a cave, or special locales (Schele and Miller, 1986). With this Maya cosmos in mind, the interpretation of Complex A is more readily understood (Reilly III, n.d.).

When one entered the enclosed court, he or she was passing through the portals to the Underworld. The court itself was constructed as a sacred landscape and the portal to the water below could be entered via the massive offerings of masks and pavements. The deeply buried serpentine layers represent the waters of the Underworld. Above them are the mosaic pavements where the earth monster/crocodile on the sarcophagus floats on the lily-covered surface of the terrestial world of living human beings. The location of Offering No. 3 under the middle platform would permit any ritual activity in the court to initiate communication with the Underworld and any ancestors who might be there.

This is a very simple version of Reilly's interpretation. There are many symbols and iconographic details I have not dwelt on that have Underworld connotations. The placement of the serpentine blocks however, directly under the earth monster illustrates that the Olmec shared the same cosmic view of the world as the Maya. The presence of an underwater landscape with representations of fish, shells, amphibians, and shark teeth confirms this premise. It may be that the Olmec ceramic motifs bearing symbols of fish, waterfowl, and watery associations, when placed in graves elsewhere, signify that the occupant had already reached the watery environment of the Underworld. This concept of the cosmic world was probably not limited to the Maya or to the tropical lowlands but was very widespread in the Preclassic Period.

Tres Zapotes with its two colossal heads is the site that inspired Stirling to excavate and "discover" the Olmec. Its long history is estimated to date from 1000 to 50 B.C. It probably marks the northern limit of Ocós-related sherds. Tres Zapotes is best known for its Stela C of Olmec derivation, having an early Long Count date of 31 B.C. At this time resemblances are found with carvings of Izapa. Flat-bottomed bowls and differentially fired wares were still produced, but the trend was now toward bowls with wide, everted rims and grooved and modeled decorations of Izapa and some Petén sites. The composite silhouette bowls are distinctly late in flavor.

Olmec Civilization

Looking now at our two sequences in the Olmec heartland, we see that during San Lorenzo's prime years (1150–900 B.C.), La Venta was beginning to build and was carving colossal heads. But by 900 B.C. San Lorenzo was finished and La Venta continued on to reach its apogee 100 years later in 800 B.C.

Both sites carved colossal heads, and huge table-top altars or thrones, as well as U-shaped stone drains. One 16-m-wide pond existed at La Venta and there are probably more. Constructions at both sites were oriented at 8° west of true north. One La Venta-style offering of 7 serpentine celts was found at San Lorenzo under Monument 21. The exotic minerals, iron ore, hematite, and magnetite are also found at both sites. Enough evidence has now accumulated to show that these centers partially overlapped in time and were closely related, each with stratified societies under strong leadership. Only large populations under highly centralized control could have managed their ambitious undertakings. Were these two centers friendly? No evidence suggests that they were not. Did La Venta have a part in the final destruction of San Lorenzo? Probably not, for the new occupants of the San Lorenzo ridge used very different ceramics and effectively replaced any remaining Olmec traditions.

After 800 B.C.(?) La Venta carved no more colossal heads but carved monuments that were flatter, or slablike and less bulky than those of San Lorenzo. Notable late changes at La Venta include introduction of massive offerings, jade, basalt columns, bilateral symmetry in Complex A, and a cessation of the large white-slipped hollow baby figures.

The sculptures of these sites provide considerable information about the Olmec, even without the benefit of hieroglyphs. Drucker (1981) believes the strong centralized authority to be a hereditary elite. Ranking is evident not only in offerings but in the manner of dress and ornamentation of the sculptured figures. Scenes are depicted involving animals, supernaturals, and Olmec themselves with non-Olmec both at La Venta and San Lorenzo. In one case (Monument 19, La Venta), a visitor is seen arriving at La Venta bearing gifts. Altar 4 (La Venta) and Monument 14 (San Lorenzo) both show a scene with a principal figure holding a rope tied to a lesser figure, evidence of subjugation or a captive. Autosacrifice and bloodletting were practiced as seen in the presence of perforators, sting-ray spines, and perhaps the large shark's tooth. Among the Maya, the bloodletting act opened the portal to the Underworld where water was blood (Schele and Miller, 1986:304).

The religion of the Olmec is one that is difficult to understand. Opinions are based on the relief carvings and decorations (incised, excised, or painted) on smaller artifacts, celts, and ceramics. Many abstract symbols occur repeatedly such as fangs, eyebrows, scrolls, a step motif, U-element, a cleft on top of the head, brackets, dots, and St. Andrews cross. Of the numerous interpretations, the most widely accepted is that of Joralemon (1976) that he himself has modified with time. His basic concepts of Olmec art I find very helpful: (1) the art represents creatures that are biologically impossible; (2) an iconographic symbol may combine several images; (3) there is a tendency toward abstraction or abbreviation (e.g. "flame-eyebrows" and "hand-wing-paw" for the Olmec dragon); and (4) images may be shown in frontal and profile variants. Creatures that commonly appear are the jaguar, crocodile, eagle, shark, feathered-serpent, a bearded face, and most common of all, a supernatural with a "knobbed frontal band and waved side-ornaments on the side of the head" (Coe, 1989), often thought to be a rain god. There is some kind of a maize deity and other curious supernaturals, often with a cleft on the top of the head.

Attempts have been made to derive the later pantheon of Mesoamerican deities from the early Olmec supernaturals. Specific evolution of identities is risky, but good bets for continuity are the maize and feathered-serpent entities, recognizing that form, interpretations, and meaning may vary considerably from one region to the next over time.

Today few would disagree that Olmec society was authoritarian with absolute power in the hands of royal kings. This was not an egalitarian social system, but one in which semidivine kings had their portraits immortalized on huge colossal stone heads and altars. This birthright was constantly reaffirmed in art as a means to reinforce royal power.

Some needed materials could be found locally, such as basalt, bitumen, and red hematite, but a great variety of artifacts and materials were imported, particularly toward the end of the phase. Iron-ore mirrors, schist, serpentine, mica, and small sandstone slabs for lapidary working were all imported and valued as prestigious goods and used in ritual. The procurement of all these items and many more would involve various exchange networks, accounting for Olmec "presence" in the different areas cited. The mechanisms of operation are not known, but probably elite items were exchanged only with the elite of other groups. Obsidian would have circulated in another network with a wider distribution and was procured from four different sources as early as Ojochí at San Lorenzo. During the middle Preclassic La Venta used obsidian from San Martin Jilotepeque like the centers in the Chiapas Central Depression and the Maya lowlands. What could the Olmec have offered in return? Possibly crocodile meat and pelts along with perishables of a tropical environment. San Lorenzo might have traded the large, hollow, white-slipped baby figures and the excised (heavily carved) or incised ceramics with iconographic Olmec markings (such motifs as crossed bands, jaguar-paw-wing, flame-eyebrows, and fire-serpent jaws) (Coe, 1981). A scroll design known as *ilhuitl* restricted to a particular incised ware is considered very diagnostic of the San Lorenzo phase, and was also traded. The Olmec probably gave to other elites the promise of power and prestige gained from associating with royalty. "Trade" may have begun as a simple gift exchange that grew into a steady relationship.

The Olmec civilization is the most complex known during these early and middle Preclassic years, exhibiting a more dynamic and sociopolitical organization than we have seen elsewhere in western Mesoamerica.

In summary, the Gulf Coast Olmec culture is very prominent in the Basin of Mexico at the four main sites known. In eastern Morelos, this influence is found in ceramics as well as on rock carvings and stone monuments. Oaxaca too reflects a strong connection with the Gulf Coast in ceramics and ritual artifacts. In each case the Olmec complex is combined with local assemblages already in existence (with the possible exception of Coapexco). In this broad area the intrusive traits that appear together as a complex represent a close contact between people, probably the elite.

There is no indication that one center dominated another. The highest ranking Olmec communities are thought to be San Lorenzo and La Venta, followed by Laguna de los Cerros and Tres Zapotes. All four were probably independent polities making their own arrangements with other communities. There is no evidence of conquest or of an Olmec "empire."

The Olmec and the Rise of Chiefdoms in Soconusco

The early and middle Preclassic developments in Chiapas and Guatemala are particularly helpful in understanding the evolution of Maya civilization and the role of the Olmec. Work in this area has progressed at a rapid pace. The following ideas should be considered speculative, as many concepts will surely be refined and altered.

The middle Grijalva region of Chiapas was geographically close to the Olmec heartland and there is convincing evidence that the Olmec were in contact with inhabitants at San Isidro and actively exploited the iron-ore deposits around Mirador, Plumajillo, and adjacent sites. They may have procured similar minerals from the Oaxaca Valley as well. Probably the most important site in Chiapas is Chiapade Corzo, located in the Tuxtla Gutierrez, an area with a dry tropical climate. Shortly before 600 B.C. a new architectural pattern similar to La Venta's Complex A is found that involved arranging one (or more) tall earthen mound(s), a long structure, and an acropolis-type platform in a pattern facing a court that may form a solstice observatory (Lowe, 1978). This formal arrangement spread rapidly across central and southern Chiapas and was accompanied by the appearance of new ceramic types. Characteristic were highly polished reddish-orange slips with flat-bottomed, flaring-wall bowls and composite silhouette shapes, many with cloudy resist designs on the waxy surface. This pottery represents an intrusion of the Maya Lowland Tradition (see page 71). Toward the end of the period several ball courts appear.

The most abundant Olmec remains are found in a string of centers along the Pacific Coast of Chiapas (see Map 3.2). Near Tonalá, stone carvings at Tzutzuculi are late Olmec in date, flanking the stairway of a pyramid. Continuing along the coast, life-sized reliefs in Olmec style were carved on three huge granite boulders at Pijijiapan (Navarrett, 1974).

The greatest activity took place in the Mazatán zone and beyond the Mexican-Guatemalan border to El Mesak at a number of sites that include Paso de la Amada, Salinas la Blanca, Ocós, La Victoria, La Blanca, Izapa, Abaj Takalik, and El Jobo. In the Mazatán zone of the Mokaya, complex societies had emerged in this littoral zone several centuries prior to the Olmec (Clark, 1991). Very simple chiefdoms were already in place here by 1650 B.C. and strong interactions with the Olmec heartland were operating by 1000 B.C. Within a century, Clark believes the Mazatán people were living under the Olmec hegemony. The earliest contact had been made by exchange, followed by Olmec artifacts being copied by Mokaya potters, and eventually the dynamic Olmec themselves came in and incorporated the Mazatán zone into the first Mesoamerican state with a multi-ethnic composition. This is seen in the relocation of large settlements around a new ceremonial center where monolithic sculptures of leaders were placed representing local or Olmec chiefs (Clark and Blake, 1989).

Were this the case, it should come as no surprise to find that Olmec artifacts reached other settlements further east. The nature and extent of the contact is yet to be determined.

Some sites are located toward the backwaters of estuaries where villagers could travel by canoe and at the same time be within walking distance of mixed tropical forest lands. One village, Salinas la Blanca, was located on the edge of a mangrove swamp where the banks had been artificially raised by alternating layers of clay with domestic refuse. A typical house was formed by a foundation dug into this base and a hard-packed clay floor placed on top. Posts set close together with interstices chinked with clay formed the walls. Hearths dug into the courtyard contained small roasting stones and remains of crabs and mollusks that had been opened by the heat (Flannery, 1976).

Prior to 900 B.C. societies had no centralized authority and operated with a more or less egalitarian political system with self-sufficient households. But afterward population on the coast reached a peak of density not to be attained again until late in the Classic Period. Villages were not necessarily larger, but certainly more numerous. La Blanca became a major center with four public buildings and a huge domestic area with 40 residential housemounds. Mound 1, 25 m high, was nearly as tall as the great pyramid at La Venta. Carved figures on the stone sculptures may be attempts at portraiture. Elite households contained ceramics with typical Olmec form and designs. This was probably the seat of a chiefdom with a four-tiered settlement hierarchy that participated in an Olmec sphere of interaction (Love, 1991).

The same transition to middle Preclassic is found further down the coast at a modest village called El Mesak that lived by hunting, collecting, farming, and exploiting the marine resources and salt. Surprisingly the remains here contained a variety of Olmec-type artifacts: ceramics, jade, a baby-faced figure fragment, and figurines. Did an elite society emerge at El Mesak? Perhaps these intrusive features were simply added to El Mesak as it became a way station on the coastal trade route to procure jade and obsidian from the highland Motagua River basin. It may have acquired the goods without the necessity of maintaining an elite or going beyond a simple exchange function. The Olmec connection might have been with Chalcatzingo or Oaxaca rather than with the Olmec heartland (Pye and Demarest, 1991). A takeover by the Olmec is not suggested.

Abaj Takalik

Northeast of El Mesak is Abaj Takalik (see Map 3.2), a large site at 600 m elevation where the heavy tropical forest vegetation has been replaced by sugar cane and coffee plantations. The site consists of many earthen mounds grouped around plazas and courts on wide terraces cut back into the hillside. This was a major center of Olmec art where monuments and massive ceremonial construction indicate the presence of powerful and independent chiefdoms.

Among the large corpus of stone carvings are incised boulders, high- and low-relief, and full-round sculptures. Two monuments (Mon. 16/17) proved to form one giant columnar head that had been broken and the parts reerected as separate monuments. A parallel situation was noted at La Venta where Monuments 25/26 have likewise been found to form a single stela (González, 1988).

In another case at Abaj Takalik, a colossal head of andesite (Monument 23, Figure 3.15) was recarved in antiquity, altering the original nose and lips to create a niche figure. The head is 1.84 m high, within the range of colossal Olmec heads in the heartland.

There has been considerable debate as to the dating of the Abaj Takalik monuments. As at most sites, they are seldom found in their original setting. Monuments are often moved around, reset, and, in the case of Monument 23, recarved. In addition, some of the early sculptures at this site were reerected in later contexts with Izapa and proto-Maya-style monuments. Graham (1989) proposes that this area is the hearth from which the Olmec civilization began, having moved from here to the Gulf Coast. Present evidence cannot disprove this theory, although the general feeling is that they belong to the middle Preclassic Period when the major Olmec activity took place in this area. Again, stone carvings are dated largely on stylistic interpretations.

Izapa

Izapa is located in hilly country 20 miles inland on the Pacific coastal plain of Chiapas east of Tapachula. This site yielded pottery affiliated with Chiapa de Corzo, some Olmec styles, as well as those of Soconusco. Early material is represented by sherds from Mound 30A, a massive, stepped pyramid faced with uncut stone, that in its final stages is estimated to have been 9 m in height. It was built some time between 900 and 600 B.C. when major transformations and ceramic changes took place throughout this region. Platforms and plazas are oriented on a north–south axis that was just the beginning of the enormous center Izapa was to become in the late Preclassic.

Chalchuapa

If one were leaving La Blanca or El Mesak to reach the Motagua River, he would logically continue east along the coast and follow the Río Paz inland to Chalchuapa, El Salvador. At 700 m elevation this is a good transitional stopover to the high country.

The greatest early development at Chalchuapa took place nearby in the El Trapiche Group. No architecture or monumental art belongs to the early Preclassic, but during the middle Preclassic, a huge conical structure (22 m high x a 60-m base diameter) was erected in one construction effort. This was a tremendous earthen mound (Structure E3-1-1) often compared to Structure C-1 at La Venta, although this latter may not be conical in shape after all (see page 63). The general ceramic assemblage is similar to other middle Preclassic complexes of the southeast with little of Olmec derivation.

Beyond Chalchuapa, further traces of the Olmec are limited to a large jaguar altar found at Quelepa (see page 112) and some interesting remains in Honduras.

Honduras

The Cuyamel Caves in eastern Honduras (see Map 3.2) (Healy, 1974) were used as a depository for secondary burials over many years. More than 50 ceramic vessels are intact or restorable. The predominant form is the long-necked bottle well known from Tlatilco and Morelos in central Mexico. Gadrooning, cinctured forms, double bottles, composite bottles, and flat-bottomed bowls with flaring walls make up the inventory. The same bottle form was found along with a vessel bearing Olmec motifs in the Quebrada Sesemil caves near Copán excavated by Gordon in 1898.

Until recently the cave pottery was the only Preclassic material known in the Copán Valley. But in 1983 a middle Preclassic cemetery was discovered underlying a late Classic residential complex known as Group 9N-8. At least 12 individuals were found covered by stones and associated with two vessels bearing Olmec motifs. Another group of more than 20 fragmented or secondary graves were discovered a short distance to the north. Among them, a young adult skull was found with 300 jade beads, 8 greenstone celts, and 2 more Olmec-style vessels. The rest of the pottery from these graves was either local or similar to the Xe Complex (see page 72). Although the sample is small, Fash (1985) believes the Olmec designs on the two burial groups may indicate the presence of descent groups as in Oaxaca. The splendid quality of the jade offerings in the north group is some indication of wealth and status differences.

This middle Preclassic assemblage at Copán probably represents some kind of cultural lag from the San Lorenzo and La Venta Preclassic phases to which it would normally belong. These items as well as the cave materials suggest evidence of indirect Olmec symbolism, derived from Chalchuapa or coastal Guatemala, and are considered middle Preclassic in date.

The development of the Olmec civilization and the extent of its remains tell only part of the Preclassic story. Some of the lowlands were unsettled or not securely dated prior to 900 or 800 B.C. but thereafter, development took place very rapidly. The central portion of the Yucatán Peninsula was either unpopulated or sparsely settled during the early period. Small groups had been scattered all through the area for hundreds of years, but are known largely from their hunting and fishing tools. Therefore it was astounding to find a remarkable development around 600 B.C. in the northern Petén at the site of Nakbé, mentioned along with the Swasey Complex in Belize that shares similar ceramics (see page 73).

The Loltún Cave in northern Yucatán had yielded deep deposits with flint and bone tools associated with very ancient extinct fauna (González, 1987), but sedentary villages in the north make their appearance along with pottery around 600 B.C. In the northeast, we do not find permanent settlements until around 400 B.C. or later. Although some early maize pollen was recovered from Lake Petenxil in the central Petén, no trace of early farmers has been found in that area.

GREAT PRECLASSIC CERAMIC TRADITIONS

Much of what we know of the earliest settlements and their increasing complexity has been learned from the ceramic record. Villages produced pots like those of their neighbors. Common forms and styles of decoration would spread over contiguous areas that undoubtedly corresponded to linguistic and ethnic affiliations. A number of years ago Gareth Lowe recognized that a certain continuity of ceramics in the area of southern Veracruz, western Tabasco, and Chiapas corresponded to the Olmec civilization and Mixe-Zoque speakers. These ceramics became known as the Greater Isthmian Tradition. A second ceramic pattern with distinctive firing techniques, forms, paste, slips, and decorations was also identified that surely belonged to people of different ethnic and linguistic affiliation that lived in the highlands of northern Guatemala—the Maya. Their ceramics are known as the Maya Lowland Tradition.

The Greater Isthmian Tradition is the older of the two dating back to at least 1800 B.C., while the second (Maya Lowland) cannot clearly be identified until around 600 B.C. By tracing these two traditions a general picture emerges of the interregional Maya relationships, many of which endured for hundreds of years if not until the Spanish Conquest. This knowledge has been compiled over many years of research by archaeologists, ceramicists, as well as linguists. My presentation of these traditions is based largely on Lowe (1977) and Andrews V (1990).

The Isthmian Tradition is what we have seen throughout much of the lowland Preclassic so far. The earliest manifestations date to Barra and Ocós phases on the coast of Guatemala and Chiapas, including *tecomate* forms, the flat-bottomed bowls with vertical walls, some white-on-red paint, iridescent paint, cord-making, rocker-stamping, and black wares. Surface smudging and differential firing was early and the technique of oxidation was gradually diagnostic of middle Preclassic ceramics. It was this tradition that is found at San Lorenzo by 1400 B.C. and at La Venta around 1200 B.C.

Around 600 B.C. a ceramic complex called Xe was identified at the Pasión River sites of Altar de Sacrificios and Seibal that belonged to non-Maya peoples that migrated to the southern Petén, an area that seems to have been very sparsely inhabited previously. Numerous traits link Xe to very early material (1000–800 B.C.) in northern Guatemalan highlands sites of the Salamá Valley and to contemporaneous material from Sakajut (Sharer and Sedat, 1987). Both of these have earlier roots leading back to Ocós on the Pacific Coast. Xe ceramics most likely did not enter the southern Petén from the Tabasco-Veracruz lowlands by way of the Usumacinta River, but from eastern Chiapas and via the highlands to descend to the Petén via the river systems. Xe pottery on the Pasión is of middle Preclassic date, ultimately derived from the Isthmian group.

We move now to northern Belize where Xe ceramics are also found. A great amount of recent work has changed our view of early life in this region. This is an ecological frontier lying between the northeast edge of the central rain forest of the Yucatán Peninsula and the dry karstic plain of the north. Major rivers flow in depressions between parellel ridges of limestone, while swamps and lagoons are found along the shallow edges of Chetumal Bay. On one of these ridges at a site called Cuello, Norman Hammond and his team found early stratified deposits with pottery, remains of architecture, and burials known as the Swasey Complex.

Cuello

Cuello was an early village that had a courtyard and public buildings by the middle Preclassic Period (800–450 B.C.). The Swasey ceramics include bottles, fine slips in red, brown, and black, and resist decoration. Seven burials were accompanied by offerings of pottery, shell-bead bracelets, two jadeite beads, and powdered hematite. Material for flint and chert tools was available from nearly Colhá, but the fragments of *mano* and *metate* of quartzite must have been brought down from the Maya mountains and the jadeite from the Motagua River valley.

The ceramics can be correlated with early phases at Tikal, Barton Ramie, as well as Altar de Sacrificios and Seibal. The Xe Complex appears here along with very different ceramics of glossy reds and blacks or thin orange-to-buff. The latter are early examples of Swasey ceramics leading to Mamom, the first pottery of the Maya lowlands.

The origins of the Swasey are unknown but were probably the result of an expansion out of the Guatemalan highlands around 700–600 B.C. The Xe Complex was either replaced or assimilated by the Maya Mamom ceramics. They are too different for one to have been ancestral to the other.

The polished orange wares of Mamom also spread into the Isthmian region bearing clear ties to the Usulután resist pottery of western El Salvador. Mamom wares eventually spread to northwestern Yucatán. Reasons for the movement of peoples into the lowlands is not known, but they finally covered the lowlands from the tropical rain forests to the drier forests and plains of the north. The major route north seems to have been along the western edge of the Yucatán Peninsula in a pattern we will see repeated in years ahead. Mamom-type pottery forms part of the early Nabanché phase at Komchén, a site adjoining Dzibilchaltún. A later intrusion from south to north took place via central Yucatán to the Chenes area into Quintana Roo after 400 B.C. Southwest of Cuello, some precocious Maya chose to settle on the northern edge of the Petén at a site we call Nakbé.

Nakbé

When the site of Nakbé (Map 3.2) was excavated in 1988 (Hansen 1991), we realized that the roots of Maya civilization were deeper than previously suspected. Nakbé flourished from 600 to 400 B.C. at which time stone temples were built 65 feet high with others estimated at 150 feet. Ceramics were typical of Mamom leading into the following Chicanel (proto-Classic) phase. Obsidian and *Strombus* shells were notable highland and lowland imports. Human incisors inlaid with jade disks were a sign of high rank. With a dry season 4 months of the year, water conservation was a major concern. A drainage ditch to channel water suggests that the public buildings may have helped to collect a supply. This was already a sophisticated society.

The raised platforms and pyramids signify a massive construction effort. The first temple (Structure 1) was undecorated but in its final remodeling, a 3-temple complex on the summit was approached by a central stairway of 13 steps (levels of the Underworld?) These were flanked by 6 large stucco panels and grotesque monster masks of mythological deities. Public structures were seemingly dedicated to gods rather than to individual rulers (Sharer, 1992).

One important discovery was a fragmented 11-ft. stela (400 B.C.?) carved with 2 figures on each side, that may illustrate a mythical scene of the Hero Twins (see page 239). Another was an incised rim sherd with the earliest inscribed Maya hieroglyph known. Interpretations link it to sculptures of Izapa and the stucco masks of Uaxactún and Cerros (Demarest, 1984c).

By 300 B.C. Nakbé ceased to be of any importance, eclipsed by neighboring El

Mirador only a few kilometers to the northwest. It offered a better water supply and a more defensible location that may have been critical in a world of growing militarism.

SUMMARY

The Olmec and ceramics have inevitably dominated this chapter. During these years, slips, paste, form, and decorations of pottery have provided the best insights into relationships between regions, movement of peoples, and structure of society (lineage, social, and political organization). The Gulf Coast Olmec may not be responsible (or credited?) with all that has been attributed to them, but there is little doubt of their powerful influence on central Mexico and their early/middle Preclassic neighbors.

What features can we consider Olmec? The San Lorenzo phase is the best example remembering that intrusive features have been incorporated into its culture. La Venta is surely Olmec, but is more eclectic in nature.

Origins are admittedly difficult. No one believes the colossal heads were passed around, but who inspired and who copied? It seems reasonable to speak of a San Lorenzo Olmec and a La Venta Olmec based on our current knowledge of assemblages at those two sites, without implying origins for all components.

The recent news of very early settlers along the Río Barí has given a whole new perspective to the La Venta region and to the site of La Venta itself. This was not an empty center with widely scattered groups off in the hinterland. They had been planting maize since 2250 B.C. and by 1200 B.C. the area was alive with people unloading huge blocks of basalt off river rafts close to the center of town. The elaborate La Venta we see emerged from many years of local development that will surely be further elucidated in current studies.

West and further inland, San Lorenzo's early years (prior to 1200 B.C.) are firmly tied to early cultures of coastal Chiapas. The Mokaya of Mazatán had developed a chiefdom level of complexity by 1650 B.C. and these Mixe-Zoque peoples spread across Chiapas to Tabasco where they mingled with others. In early years San Lorenzo developed a lasting relationship with its Isthmian neighbors. Perhaps inspired by the more precocious Mokaya, the mestizo community that grew up at San Lorenzo produced a very special Olmec civilization with hereditary rulers and an elite society held in place by the populace convinced of the ruler's supernatural powers that required adherence to certain ritual. It worked for close to 500 years, carving colossal stone heads, altars (thrones), working magic with iron-ore mirrors and minerals from Chiapas and Oaxaca, obsidian from highland Mexico and Guatemala. They carved and incised certain abstract symbolic designs on pottery called San Lorenzo Calzadas Carved and Limon Incised and exported large, white-slipped, hollow baby-dolls to highland Mexico. Olmec ideology moved along with exchange relationships that were developed with the elite in other societies.

La Venta overlapped with the late years at San Lorenzo, the latter failing just as La Venta gathered momentum toward its apogee in 800 B.C. Early on, La Venta, following the example set by San Lorenzo, carved colossal heads, altars, stone drains, used hematite mirrors, and oriented structures 8° west of true north. Later on La Venta shared Maya-like features that include a predilection for jade, Mamom ceramics, an architectural layout, and possibly constructed its great pyramid with a radial pattern. La Venta in the middle Preclassic years maintains some of the Isthmian ceramics and continued the relationship with central Mexico, although in the Basin of Mexico Olmec features begin to fade. At Chalcatzingo, sculptured human figures on stelae replaced the older mythological scenes carved on the cliffs.

San José Mogote reflects strong Olmec influence a bit later than central Mexico. Olmec motifs were associated with lineages, apparently prestigious signs of rank. Was their meaning the same as among the Olmec? We cannot tell. The first evidence of the 260-day calendar, construction of public buildings, elite residences, and well-developed specializations in stone, ceramics, and shell make this one of the earliest complex societies in Mesoamerica.

The relationship of the Olmec with other societies has been the subject of much debate. Suggestions include: aggression, trade, proselytizing, intermarriage alliances, colonization, and various of these combinations. Exchange or trade at the elite level is usually felt to be the initial means of contact that carried with it associations of wealth, ranking, and no doubt ideology. Did these areas become part of an Olmec hegemony? It is possible in some cases, such as the Mokaya. A close trading network among elites and emulation of Olmec style rulership and resulting prestige may have been the unifying force. There is no sign of coercion or aggressive takeover.

As to bottles, the truly long-necked bottles are practically limited to Tlatilco, Tlapacoya, Chalcatzingo, pre-Olmec San Lorenzo, caves in eastern Honduras, and at the Maya site of Copán. These are not Olmec although found along with Olmec-style pottery outside the heartland. They are also not west Mexican (Kelly, personal communication), but they are often erroneously lumped with the west Mexican stirrup-spout and Capacha's trifid form. The source and inspiration for these very distinctive vessels remain unresolved. Also attracting attention is the presence of bark-beaters at La Victoria (800 B.C.) and at Chalchuapa (400 B.C.), a reminder of the similar paper-making process and technologies of southeast Asia (Tolstoy, 1986, 1991).

In summary, the Gulf Coast Olmec exercised a strong influence on and maintained a close relationship with Guerrero, Central Mexico, and Oaxaca during the early Preclassic, with particular ties to Chalcatzingo in the middle years. East of the Isthmus there was a strong Olmec presence in the Central Depression of Chiapas and along the Chiapas Coast culminating in a possible Olmec statehood in the Mazatán zone. La Blanca was a major regional chiefdom with extensive public architecture and residential chiefdom with extensive public architecture and residential zones. The Olmec were surely active at Abaj Takalik, believed to be a powerful center with a proliferation of Olmec stone carvings. This is close to the edge of the Olmec world.

We will find many portable Olmec objects in other areas and in later periods. These may be imitations or heirlooms, retained and passed along as amulets or treasures. No one, past or present, is likely to discard an Olmec art form.

Many elements of Olmec symbolism and iconography persisted and had a lasting effect on Mesoamerica, with or without a Gulf Coast connection. Whether or not ultimately identified with the Olmec, the origins of writing and perhaps the calendar may have their roots in this coastal region or neighboring areas. We will be talking about the Olmec into Aztec times.

The Southern Lowlands

The identification of separate ceramic traditions (based on techniques of production, form, paste, decoration) has helped to understand the movement of peoples during these years. The Greater Isthmian Tradition is found in southern Veracruz, western Tabasco and Chiapas, associated with the Olmec and Mixe-Zoque speakers. Pottery of the Maya Lowland Tradition was produced by people in the highlands of northern Guatemala that moved into the southern lowlands. Their pottery is known as Mamom. Xe ceramics is a particular style found at Seibal and Cuello that became absorbed or eclipsed by the lowland tradition.

Nakbé, a surprising development in the Petén near El Mirador, flourished from 1000 to 450 B.C. with Mamom ceramics, monumental construction with stone temples, and panels with great monster masks and enormous sculpted birds. A sherd was recovered with the earliest known inscribed Maya hieroglyph. This is a unique development in middle Preclassic years providing a kind of prototype for the southern Maya lowlands. Activity at Nakbé ended by 300 B.C., as El Mirador rose to take its place.

West Mexico

Not to be forgotten is west Mexico where elements of the Capacha complex, the stirrup-spouted vessel form, and shaft-and-chamber-tombs support an early maritime contact with South America around 1500 B.C.

Monuments, Wealth, and Complex Societies

The years from 500/300 B.C–A.D. 300 are in many ways the most productive in Mesoamerica. This was the time when evolutionary forces that had been building since 2000 B.C. came to visible fruition. We may not find the largest cities, the most elaborate stone carvings, monuments, tombs, or perhaps the most beautiful paintings on pots and murals, but we will see the emergence of these features plus two outstanding innovations: the use of a calendar and writing.

As we approach the beginning of the Christian era, dramatic changes become apparent in the manner of living with new ideas that transformed simple institutions into innovative patterns of energy and power, bringing in a more complex sociopolitical society.

This is one of the most outstanding periods of change in Mesoamerican history. The terms Preclassic, Terminal Preclassic, Epi-Olmec, and Protoclassic, all refer in some way to these years that will be the subject of this chapter. The exact time frame will be dealt with loosely, in some areas embracing fewer years, in others more, as dictated by the archaeological record. Some regions continued their Preclassic existence with few alterations, but in central highland Mexico, Oaxaca, the coastal lowlands, and Maya regions, the changes are dramatic.

I will resume the story in highland central Mexico at Teotihuacan with the Patlachique Phase and follow the emergence of this gigantic urban center and its neighbors until A.D. 300.

77

THE BASIN OF MEXICO

By the final Preclassic phase, two huge centers equal in rank had emerged: Cuicuilco (Figure 4.1) to the south and Teotihuacan to the northeast. Not only did each of these dominate its immediate area and attract population but they must have competed with each other for land, resources, and services. The other regional centers were infinitely smaller and possibly already under domination of one of the big two.

Some hints of conflict or competition between Teotihuacan and Cuicuilco can be detected in massive stone retaining walls on the southeastern corner of Lake Texcoco and by an increasing number of hilltop sites. The chronology of the latter, Tezoyuca centers, is still unclear but they belong to this somewhat unsettled Terminal Preclassic period. Thirteen such hilltop centers of approximately 300–600 people have been identified and all have some modest public architecture in an isolated steep-sided setting which looks good for defense (Sanders *et al.*, 1979). Chronologically they may represent a short phase between Ticomán and Patlachique, or they may be contemporaneous with the latter. At this time valley peoples were subjected to various pressures or influences from the east and northwest that resulted in cultural diversification. Population continued to increase, and if the Texcocan region reflects the prevailing settlement pattern, the great majority of people lived in large concentrated centers characterized by ceremonial or public works. Tlapacoya had by this time ceased to be of any importance. Temesco on the eastern lakeshore and the remains at Cerro del Tepalcate (literally "potsherd hill") high above Tlatilco, probably relate to this period, which basically continues the Cuicuilco tradition (Figures 4.2 and 4.3).

FIGURE 4.1   Pyramid at Cuicuilco, Valley of Mexico. (Courtesy of the Instituto Nacional de Antropología e Historia, Mexico.)

FIGURE 4.2 Goblet or vessel with pedestal base, decorated in *al fresco* technique, polychrome. Tlapacoya, Late Preclassic. Height: 19 cm. (Courtesy of Museo Nacional de Antropología, Mexico.)

One source of new influence was Chupícuaro, a late Preclassic site on the Lerma River, some 128 kilometers northwest of the valley (See page 96).

Despite its early leadership, Cuicuilco was doomed, but the end was not quite as sudden as once thought. The first volcanic eruption of nearby Xitli occurred in the Patlachique subphase around 50 B.C. and reduced the great center to a small community, leaving Teotihuacan as the only major center. The ash and lava of a second eruption effectively put an end to activities in the southwestern region of the valley.

TEOTIHUACAN

The history of archaeological investigations at Teotihuacan dates back to the late 1800s with the early work of Désiré Charnay and Leopoldo Batres. The latter began his disastrous explorations resulting in the destruction of parts of monuments and loss

FIGURE 4.3 White-on-red cylindrical tripod with very small supports. Valley of Mexico. Late Preclassic. Height: 18 cm. (Courtesy of Museo Nacional de Antropología, Mexico.)

of data. The list of serious scientists who have focused their studies on Teotihuacan since then is too voluminous to be included here, but a fine account of investigators and their activities is to be found in Rattray (1987a).

In the early 1960s the Mexican Government initiated the Teotihuacan Project directed by Ignacio Bernal and Jorge Acosta to "explore and reconstruct the ceremonial center of Teotihuacan." Since that time the Teotihuacan Valley has been humming with archaeologists and scientists in related fields. The publications of the Basin of Mexico Survey Project headed by William Sanders, Jeffrey Parsons, and Robert Santley (1979) and the Teotihuacan Mapping Project of René Millon, Bruce Drewitt, and George Cowgill (1973) are indispensable for an understanding of this remarkable site. Other basic publications are Berrin, 1988; Cabrera Castro, 1990a,b; Cabrera Castro *et al.*, 1991; Cowgill, 1983; Langley, 1986; 1991; Manzanilla, 1990; R. Millon 1973, 1981, 1988a,b; Pasztory, 1988a, 1988b, 1990, n.d.a; Sanders, 1981; Séjourné, 1966; Sugiyama, 1989a; and Taube (1992).

Founding of the City

Although some small villages were settled in the Valley of Teotihuacan (25 miles northeast of Mexico City) as early as 900 B.C., this northern region had no major Preclassic centers and was culturally marginal to the more active peoples around the lakes in the Basin of Mexico. By 300 B.C., however, settlements had begun to diversify and there were a few signs of occupational centers and obsidian workshops. Of the two main regional centers, Teotihuacan in the north and Cuicuilco in the south (See Map 2.1), Teotihuacan soon outdistanced its southern rival. Realistically, Cuicuilco had little to develop; there were no resources at hand. The area was relatively well watered but had killing frosts (Hirth, 1984). In any event, any competition was settled by the volcanic eruptions, and nothing was to challenge the dominance of Teotihuacan for nearly 600 years.

Although Teotihuacan drew most of its population from the Basin of Mexico, perhaps others were attracted to the new settlement from Tlaxcala, just over the mountains to the east. A drop in population there is noted about this time, and more specifically the Tlaxcalans had been erecting a civic-ceremonial architecture from 300 B.C. that was to become a hallmark of Teotihuacan: the talud-tablero style (see Figure 4.7). They had also made great advances in agricultural technology. Terracing, canals, irrigation, and dams have all been documented. García Cook (1981) suggests that many skilled technicians and laborers moved over the mountains to the Basin of Mexico where they would have been welcomed at Teotihuacan.

This was a culture that would become unique in many ways, not just an elaboration of the earlier Olmec and Valley of Mexico traditions. Someone or some group had very precise plans and goals in mind when they led the way to Teotihuacan.

Not always do we know exactly why specific sites are selected for settlement, but in the case of Teotihuacan we have some good clues. The earliest settlements were made about 1 km west of the Temple of the Moon at Oztoyahualco (the Old City).

The finest springs were not here, but to the southwest near Cuanalán, so water was not the main attraction. One answer was caves.

Natural caves are closely related to religion and mythology in Mesoamerica. Creation myths tell of the human race being spawned from the center of the earth, the sun and moon emerging from caves. Caves were also an entrance to the Underworld, providing access to the womb of the earth, an area of fertility appropriate for spirits or hidden treasure.

Recent studies have revealed a network of caves and tunnels that run precisely from Oztoyahualco in a southeasterly direction to continue under the Pyramids of the Moon and the Sun. A team of scientists (Barba *et al.*, 1990) conducted a magnetic survey (600 readings!) confirmed by gravimetric profiles and five electrical resistivity profiles to obtain the precise location of the tunnels. Some caves have collapsed and are seen on the surface as depressions. This presumed network of tunnels and caves is found only in the northern part of the valley as the southern region of Teotihuacan's ceremonial center presents an entirely different geologic formation and was not built over caves or swamps.

The earliest villages were located in the north, many with three temples grouped around a small plaza; these three-temple complexes were usually associated with caves (Barba *et al.*, 1990; Pasztory, n.d.b) and commonly viewed as an entrance to the Underworld.

Among the thousands of visitors that climb to the summit of the Pyramid of the Sun (Figure 4.4) few realize that almost directly beneath them is a cave over 100 m in length, roofed with basalt slabs, having walls undecorated but still plastered with

FIGURE 4.4 Pyramid of the Sun. The earliest major structure at Teotihuacan. Constructed over a sacred cave. (Courtesy of Compañía Mexicana Aerofoto, S.A.)

mud. This was a natural formation enlarged by the Teotihuacanos to branch into four small chambers, and used throughout the Tzacualli period (A.D. 1–150). It never had a natural spring, but water was artificially channeled to flow through a covered stone drain for ritual purposes (R. Millon, 1981).

A simple shrine constructed with a nucleus faced with adobe bricks, uncut stone, and cobble like that from Cuicuilco, was constructed outside over the four small chambers of the tunnel. Then the Pyramid of the Sun, the first major structure built at Teotihuacan, was raised directly over this sacred place. Doris Heyden (1981) has compared this cave to the legendary Chicomoztoc or Seven Caves that according to Aztec mythology spawned these people of the sun. This concept could apply to Teotihuacan, which was considered to be the *axis mundi* or "the place where the world began." For some reason the entrance to the cave was sealed off by the Teotihuacanos. This may have taken place when the political center of the city was moved south to the Ciudadela, for this must have somehow affected the religious dogma. Hundreds of years later, the site (cave/pyramid) was still considered sacred, for among the Aztecs, it was known as "Moctezuma's Oracle."

The Underworld was one sacred realm but another was the heavens. The city was planned in a landscape almost ringed with mountains. Cerro Gordo was selected to be at the high northern end of a great central avenue that slopes gently to the south. This was the spine of the great ceremonial center of Teotihuacan that was oriented in a roughly north–south direction. Astronomer Anthony Aveni and his associates (1978) have located twenty cross-circles pecked into rocks at various points around the city. Some of these circles line up with a north–south direction and other cosmic phenomena. Similar cross-circles have been found at other sites. In the Petén jungle city of Uaxactún, a cross-circle relates the location of buildings to solstices and equinoxes and the northern site of Alta Vista is set precisely on the Tropic of Cancer (see page 192). The Teotihuacanos consciously chose 15° 25′ east of true north, perhaps having to do with the setting point of the Pleiades at that time in history. Apparently orientation was a choice made by each city influenced by its geography as well as religious interests.

According to mythology the world was in darkness, so the gods gathered at Teotihuacan to create a fifth sun. At the proper moment a rich god failed to throw himself into the fire, so a lowly, poor god unhesitatingly jumped in and was consumed to become the Sun. Deeply humiliated, the rich god then threw himself into the flames and became the Moon (Sahagún, 1950–1982, Book 7).

Thus Teotihuacan was very sacred, "the place where the sun was born," a privileged place where one lived in hallowed space protected and blessed by the gods. As R. Millon (1981) points out, religion and deities were the driving force behind the construction and maintenance of Teotihuacan. This inspirational force was already strong in Patlachique years.

As a practical matter, the proximity of obsidian resources would have attracted residents to the growing city. An early obsidian industry had become a complex commercial operation during the Patlachique phase. By Tzacualli, a network was already exploiting several different obsidian sources and provided for production and redistribution of finished products. This coincides with the dramatic increase of population and urban development at Teotihuacan. An estimated 2% of the population was working full time at this trade (Charlton, 1978). Potters would have also moved along with any new settlement, for their products were in demand in every household. They continued the Cuicuilco-style ceramics with similar shapes and a flat-base dish. There was some resist-painting, but most pottery was a plain, dark-colored burnished ware.

The earliest documented evidence we have of irrigation took place during the Tzacualli and Miccaotli phases (A.D. 1–200) on the western edge of the settlement. Here a network of small flood water canals irrigated productive farm land. The canals were simple earthen ditches, U-shaped in cross section and dug into the soil or bedrock. The source of water was probably the Barranca de Cerro Colorado flowing to the northwest. Apparently use was greatly curtailed and most of the canals had to be abandoned when the area was settled by Zapotec immigrants after A.D. 200, presumably with the approval of the Teotihuacan authorities (Nichols et al., 1991).

By A.D. 150, the end of the Tzacualli phase, the city had covered an area over 20 km, nearly as large as it was ever to grow. People had swarmed into the city, swelling the population to perhaps around 80,000. Workers toiled as never before, and soon the Pyramid of the Sun and the first structures of the Pyramid of the Moon were completed. By A.D. 1–100 the basic layout of a metropolis in quadrants was in place with East–West Avenues meeting the Street of the Dead near its center, the Ciudadela, 2.2 km south of the Pyramid of the Moon (Figure 4.5). What did this city look like?

The discussion that follows will deal with streets, residences, and temples and it will be helpful to follow their locations within the city as we go along (See Map 6.1, p. 163).

The Pyramid of the Moon guards the northern end of the central axis, the Street of the Dead. Directly in front of the pyramid and its *adosada* (a frontal platform) is a great plaza flanked by three pyramids on either side.

A series of five such 3-temple groupings form a rough line starting near the old city of Oztoyahualco, associated with the presumed course of the tunnels. It is possible that there was access to the tunnels from the plazas of these 3-temple complexes (Barba et al., 1990), but this has not yet been investigated, nor do we know that kind of ceremonies were performed in these complexes. They form, however, part of the earliest settlements of the city. R. Millon (1981) counts more than 20 of these complexes. Most were located in the northern portion of the city, perhaps representing twenty social groups (clans, ethnic units?) that might have formed some kind of alliance to found the city. This area has scarcely been touched by the archaeologists but sizable mounds are visible.

The Plaza of the Columns is by itself a rather typical 3-temple complex with extra small pyramids in addition to its three main ones (G. L. Cowgill, personal communication). The Moon Pyramid together with two small pyramids to the southwest and southeast might have formed a 3-temple complex, and possibly the Sun Pyramid may have formed another with small pyramids that face each other on the north and south sides of the Sun's Plaza.

Off the southwest corner of the Moon Plaza is the sumptuous residential Palace

FIGURE 4.5   The Street of the Dead marked by the Pyramid of the Moon at its northern end. A prominent *adosada* is seen in front of the staircase, and three pyramids on either ide of the Moon Plaza. At the lower right is the Pyramid of the Sun. (Courtesy of Compañía Mexicana Aerofoto, S.A.)

of Quetzalpapálotl (Quetzalbutterfly, See Figure 6.2), erected later in the history of the city with some restoration by Jorge Acosta.

The Pyramid of the Sun with its cave, located further down the great avenue on the east side, faces west (See Figures 4.4 and 4.5). Tunnels have revealed that the first structure (Tzacualli in date) was almost as large as what we see today and may have been capped by two temples. To have built such an enormous structure so quickly at such an early date is evidence not only of the presence of a powerful religious/political leader but also of a strong supportive community. (The largest pyramid at Cuicuilco was 65 feet high, whereas the Pyramid of the Sun soared magestically to a height of 215 feet!)

Continuing south along the Street of the Dead the sides are lined with civic and religious buildings. Narrow, alleylike streets lead off into residential areas which are crowded in between the more important religious edifices.

Nearly 2 km to the south, the Street of the Dead is straddled by a group of structures called the Calle de los Muertos Complex (Street of the Dead Complex). Although only partially excavated this was a special macrocomplex, consisting of many temples, residential clusters, platforms, and some open spaces. Its very prominent location on the main axis was not as accessible as one might imagine. Entrance was somewhat restricted, or at least slowed down, by a freestanding wall and the necessity of climbing stairs over transverse platforms that formed part of the complex as well as dividing the Street of the Dead at this point. But a resident privileged to live here would have enjoyed some of the finest buildings of the city. The apartments of the Viking Group, for example, were constructed of top-quality building materials and finished with splendid floors, lined with layer upon layer of mica. One wonders what kind of furnishings would have completed the decor. These apartments must have been designed for and occupied by very high-ranking personnel (Cowgill, 1983).

The Ciudadela

Crossing the barranca of the San Juan River and heading south, we reach the center of the ancient city, a monumental structure known as the Ciudadela (Citadel). This gigantic rectangular construction of platforms sustains 15 pyramids and encloses a plaza that alone approximates 4.4 ha (11 acres). Two residential palaces and one of the most celebrated buildings in Mesoamerica, the so-called Temple of Quetzalcoatl (Feathered Serpent) are located toward the back (Figure 4.6).

This marks a major shift away from the earlier 3-temple complex. Here again on the east side (often mentioned as ritually important), a whole new center of pyramids,

FIGURE 4.6 The Ciudadela. This gigantic quadrangle is entered by way of the stairs leading up from the Street of the Dead. The Feathered-Serpent Pyramid is seen as a mound to the back of the large plaza, with the stepped *adosada* marking the western face. Two palaces flank the Feathered-Serpent Pyramid, barely visible here. (Courtesy of Compañía Mexicana S.A.)

palaces, temples, and a gigantic plaza were combined and somewhat restricted by platforms, with an equally enormous area across the street believed to be the city's marketplace. This area was the heart of the city, where administrative, political and economic functions had been brought together.

The Ciudadela is "architecturally unlike anything else in the city" (Cowgill, 1983). Its talud-tablero architecture is a distinctive feature (Figure 4.7) that dominated Teotihuacan. It consists of a rectangular body (the tablero) with recessed inset, which rests on an outward-sloping basal element (the talud). Elsewhere the relative proportions might vary, but at Teotihuacan the tablero was always larger than the talud. The tablero usually served as a panel for painted or sculptured motifs but at times the talud was decorated as well. This talud-tablero combination is repeated throughout the city on pyramids, platforms, shrines, and altars, but nowhere is it more pervasive than at the Ciudadela. The repetition of this terraced profile emphasizes its privileged form which was restricted to religious structures and probably conveyed a message. We will find this form and variations of it in many areas of Mesoamerica. Its origin is yet to be determined but it was surely a trademark of this period, and nowhere as prevalent as here.

The gigantic structure of the Ciudadela is approximately 400 m long × 400 m wide, limited by a wide platform on the north, east, and south sides. The north and south platforms each support four small pyramids on top and the eastern side, three. These eleven pyramids are connected by a wall. A wide staircase on the west affords access to a slightly lower platform with four pyramids and provides entrance to the entire compound.

One enters this enormous complex from the Street of the Dead, mounting a broad

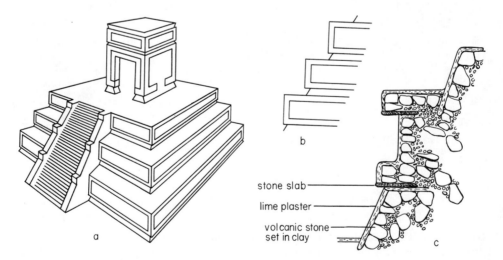

stone slab
lime plaster
volcanic stone
set in clay

FIGURE 4.7 Architecture at Teotihuacan. a, Reconstruction of a Teotihuacan pyramid and temple based on an excavated stone model; b, profile of a talud-tablero style; c, talud-tablero contruction. (Based on Salazar, 1966; Acosta, 1964.)

staircase to gaze down upon an immense interior plaza. This could have served well for large celebrations, parades, or affairs of state, and was probably an impressive state symbol of power! According to estimates, as many as 100,000 standing individuals could have been comfortably accommodated (Cowgill, 1983)

The Feathered-Serpent (Quetzalcoatl) Pyramid

Toward the back is the famous so-called Temple of Quetzalcoatl tucked behind a structure, the plataforma *adosada* built against its west face. This *adosada* restricts the view of the Quetzalcoatl Pyramid and may have been deliberately constructed to lessen any residual impact of a former ruler and to display control over the military (R. Millon, 1981). Traces of remaining murals suggest its possible dedication to a deity known as the Great Goddess (See p. 172). With the passing of time, the *adosada* had inadvertently protected the famous stone carvings of the older structure it shields from view. These represent some of the finest stone carvings in the city and probably covered all four sides of the older temple.

The Quetzalcoatl Pyramid is a 7-tiered structure of typical talud-tablero construction built in a single operation. The façade of this spectacular pyramid is elaborately carved with two serpent heads, one (Quetzalcoatl) is complete with an undulating feathered serpent body, laced with shells and marine motifs (Figure 4.8). Pasztory (1988a) points out that the Feathered Serpent, although prominent here, is more often utilized at Teotihuacan in border designs and is not as important a deity as the Great Goddess or the Storm God.

The other head represents an ancestral form of the Aztec fire serpent, Xiuhcoatl. Here it functions as an emblem of war. These two serpents pass through a façade of circular mirrors. Mirrors were considered to be a kind of supernatural passageway into which mortals could look but not pass. The Feathered Serpent emerges from a mirror rimmed with feathers. The other serpent head covers his mirror completely.

Taube (1992) traces this latter creature through Zapotec and Maya representations and demonstrates a continuity up to its Aztec manifestations. This War Serpent is far more common in the Classic period than the more easily recognized Feathered Serpent. In fact, the only place where it has been identified at Teotihuacan is on the Quetzalcoatl Pyramid.

He is a strange-looking creature with no body or lower jaw, but has large, slightly curved teeth. Placed above the large, round eyes are a pair of rings (frequently mistaken as eyes of Tlaloc) that are protective goggles often worn by Teotihuacan warriors. What appears to be a head is actually a helmet worn as a mask. The "skin" is made up of tiny mosaic platelets, probably made of shell. At the back under the mouth is a nose bar pendant worn by the individual wearing the mask (see also Langley, 1986; Sugiyama, 1989a).

Representations abroad leave little doubt of this serpent's association with war. The headdress or helmet is worn by rulers at Lamanai, Tikal, Copán, Piedras Negras, and Bonampak, among others, in what seems to be a conscious identification with Teotihuacan and specifically with the Temple of Quetzalcoatl. "It is possible that the

FIGURE 4.8 Carved facade of the Feathered-Serpent (Quetzalcoatl) Pyramid. Serpents, shells, and marine motifs decorate both talud and tablero. The serpent head of one feathered serpent is framed by feathers. The squarish head with paired rings may represent the War Serpent. (Courtesy of Instituto Nacional de Antropología e Historia, Mexico.)

alternating serpent heads, Quetzalcoatl and the War Serpent, refer to dual aspects of rulership, the feathered serpent with fertility and the interior affairs of the state and the War Serpent with military conquest and empire" (Taube, 1992). Militarism, religion, and power are all themes supported by the recent excavations of the Quetzalcoatl Pyramid. (For an alternative interpretation of this temple, see López Austin *et al.*, 1991).

Why was this pyramid singled out for such an elaborate façade and why, after perhaps 200 years, was the front of it nearly obscured by a large *adosada?* It was time to investigate. (For a detailed description of the excavations at the Feathered–Serpent Pyramid, see Cabrera Castro *et al.*, 1990, 1991; Sugiyama, 1989b.)

Burials In 1983–1984 Cabrera Castro and Sugiyama, under the auspices of INAH, dug along the southern edge of the pyramid. In a long 8-m pit, Burial 190 was found, containing skeletons of 18 males, 169 obsidian projectile points, and over

4000 pieces of worked shell, probably from the war helmet that would have made a hard, tough, and relatively light protective covering (Taube, 1992). There were also a number of imitation human jaws (maxillae) with teeth carved of shell, and a few real maxillae and mandibles (Cabrera Castro *et al.*, 1991). Several had slate disks at the lower back, resembling the large mirrors (*tezcacuitlapilli*) associated with shields worn by the carved stone warriors of Tula. These were not only protective devices in battle but could guard against any danger from supernaturals.

The position of the skeletons strongly suggests that these individuals had been seated, with backs to the pyramid and hands tied behind them. The associated artifacts left little doubt that these were sacrificed warriors perhaps positioned to guard and protect the pyramid that rose behind them.

Two smaller pits each containing one grave were found a short distance to the east and west of Burial 190. The east one, Burial 153, was a female with 1606 small, worked shells. The one to the west, Burial 203, contained 9 large, bifacial, obsidian projectile points, greenstone beads, earspools, and a "butterfly" nose pendant.

In 1986, the north side of the pyramid yielded a similar pattern of multiple graves and associated materials. Several examples of human sacrifice had been reported previously from Teotihuacan, but never before had anything comparable to these multiple graves of sacrificed individuals been found. And this is just the beginning.

In 1988–1989 excavations were expanded to investigate other remaining areas and to tunnel into the heart of the pyramid. The east side produced more sacrificial victims of males, younger and similarly positioned with comparable militaristic paraphernalia. One individual may prove to be of different origin or status, to judge from his very pronounced cranial deformation and a collar of nine real, human maxillae.

Tunneling into the center of the Feathered-Serpent Pyramid was very complicated and risky because of the construction, but it yielded a great deal of information. The 1988–1989 tunnel excavated by Saburo Sugiyama under the direction of George Cowgill and Rubén Cabrera Castro, entered from the center of the south edge of the pyramid and encountered two walled burial chambers containing eight skeletons (Burial 2) and a third longer chamber (18 m × 1.5 m) that held 18 skeletons (Burial 4). In each case the head had been located toward the center of the pyramid. Burial 4 was far richer than Burial 2, having slate disks, shell beads, animal bones, and human maxillae.

The INAH tunnel continued toward the center until it came upon an earlier excavation by looters. In their tunnel, the looters missed the center, rummaged through a large burial pit (Burial 12), and continued west where they thoroughly ransacked Burial 13 in a large pit. Despite the destruction, the INAH group was still able to extract valuable information. They believe Burial 12 had contained a number of sacrificed individuals. Burial 13 had been sacked and the pit subsequently refilled, but had been a very rich multiple grave. One complete skeleton on the west edge of the pit had been overlooked. This robust fellow had been uncomfortably positioned "face-and-belly down with the knees tucked under the chest," but he was protected (physically and/or symbolically) by stones. His grave goods denoted high status: large greenstone earspools, 21 large greenstone beads, a greenstone nose pendant with bifurcated tongue, and a large obsidian eccentric with a point in the form of a serpent's head.

In the fill was a carved wooden baton 58 cm in length, well preserved. One end is appropriately carved on both sides with the head of a feathered serpent. This might have belonged to the unusual occupant of Burial 13, for surely this baton was a special insignia of someone in authority, suggestive of the badge of office (manikin scepter) of the Maya (See page 491).

Suspecting that the center of the pyramid had not been disturbed, Sugiyama and his team enthusiastically renewed their digging to be rewarded with a multiple burial of 20 individuals with the richest offerings found to date at Teotihuacan, placed in the exact center of the pyramidal base.

These skeletons (Burial 14) were so close together that some overlapped others and all had been placed directly on the hard *tepetate* floor and covered with stones and mud. Most or all were males, but it was impossible to determine a proper distribution of goods. All heads pointed to the easternmost individual. He seemed special in no other way, and his arms and hands were behind his back as if they had been tied just like nine others in the group. Offerings (Cabrera Castro *et al.*, 1991) were too numerous to list here (over 3400 shell items alone) but followed the same type grave-good assemblage already noted. Unusual was the finding of nine groups of objects, seemingly arranged in sets located with the burial. A "set," for example, might include 1 figurine, 2 earspools, beads, a few shells, and about 8 bifacial obsidian knives. Originally these may have been placed in bags, which upon disintegration appeared as organic material around and under them. Finally, the tunnels were all filled in with the same debris that had been taken out.

Reviewing these finds, postholes, and fragments of walls and floors had indicated that an earlier structure once existed, but the Feathered-Serpent Pyramid was placed directly on the *tepetate*. It was built entirely in one stage of construction, in the Miccaotli phase or very early in the Tlamimilolpa phase (Cabrera Castro *et al.*, 1991). This is further confirmed by the homogeneous nature of the fill and surrounding material.

Remains of a supreme leader (head of state or high-ranking individual) have never been found at Teotihuacan, and this pyramid was a logical location for such a tomb. These excavations have not resolved the issue of a supreme leader's whereabouts. It is possible that a major tomb could have been looted, missed, or never existed. As we will see, the Teotihuacanos did not exalt rulers or publicize dynasties or personalities as did the Olmec, Zapotecs, and Maya. We do not yet know the significance of the Ciudadela and why the Feathered-Serpent Pyramid was built. Perhaps we are mistaken in envisioning the typical rulership of an exalted individual.

The astounding exidence of mass sacrifice of around 200 individuals revealed by these remarkable excavations came as a startling surprise. Many questions now flood the mind. Why, when, and how did these people meet their death? Who were they? Does this mean conquest? Where might there be further evidence?

Sugiyama (1989b) believes that a great dedication ceremony was held upon completion of the construction of the Feathered-Serpent Pyramid and that human sacrifice formed an important part of the ritual. It would have been an impressive display of power and wealth, an awesome scene to witness, at the same time serving as an effective means of maintaining control over the populace.

We still do not know who the sacrificial victims were: foreigners or high-ranking or distinguished personnel? These questions are yet to be answered but the possibility of foreigners is almost ruled out (Cabrera Castro *et al.*, 1991). The victims seem like other central Mexicans, at least non-Maya. They may even be local Teotihuacanos, a defeated faction, loyal retainers, and/or willing volunteers. With their backs to the pyramid those on the exterior look more like defenders than attackers. Perhaps the warriors were members of a military society who by offering their lives in sacrifice expected to gain prestige and a privileged status after death. There are many questions left unanswered but the extent of human sacrifice and evidence of militarism has led to a reappraisal of many aspects of Teotihuacan.

Other Ciudadela Structures Flanking the north and south sides of the Quetzalcoatl Pyramid are twin palaces. These North and South Palaces were nearly identical, each with several apartments grouped around a central courtyard and accessed only via the Ciudadela Plaza.

The inauguration ceremonies of the Quetzalcoatl Pyramid and temple are thought to have taken place no later than the end of Miccaotli or Early Tlamimilolpa phases. By this time the Teotihuacanos were seasoned builders and must have developed a strong political system and a high-ranking elite in the stratified society. Affairs of state do not always run smoothly and surely there were times of stress, conflicts, or disputes in the hierarchy. Basing my ideas on Cowgill (1983) and R. Millon (1981), I suggest the following scenario to account for the radical changes represented by the unusual arrangement and facilities of the Ciudadela.

Suppose that by the time the Ciudadela was built a consolidation of political power in the emerging state had gained the upper hand over the prevailing religious faction, and this new central authority physically moved to the Ciudadela. The head of state might have taken his power and his court to reside in the residential North and South Palaces. The spacious quarters there would surely have housed no lesser figures.

Perhaps the early ruler, possibly buried in the center of the Pyramid of the Sun, had been a tyrant and despot. The new faction initiated a change that moved the religious offices south and built the Ciudadela and the Feathered-Serpent Pyramid. A collective leadership was thereafter institutionalized that proved to be extraordinarily effective. It would have needed strong ideological support, some kind of economic power base, and administrative know-how, logically provided by the military. This would imply a governing system that exercised effective control that apparently remained unchallenged for centuries. This is highly speculative but some such dramatic alteration in the administrative and religious organization of Teotihuacan would logically account for the unique pattern and composition of the Ciudadela.

Returning to a few more details of the construction, adjoining its north side is a long, free-standing wall that encloses an 80-m-wide area running the length of the building. This formed a large quadrangle that was used for special activities apparently closely monitored by state authorities, as it could only be reached by two staircases from within the Ciudadela. It contained two semicircular structures, a possible *temescal* (sweat bath), the first reported in the city, some living quarters, and a ceramic workshop that during later years produced incense burners, figurines, and adornos.

The main structures of the Ciudadela that we see today were built toward the end of Miccaotli or early Tlamimilolpa phases, but archaeologists have discovered remains of earlier structures predating today's ruins. One example is a shrine of some sort erected in what is now the main plaza. This structure (Str. 1B′) was rebuilt perhaps as many as seven times, spanning the entire history of Teotihuacan (Cabrera Castro, 1990b). In one phase the red floors were painted with a scroll and geometric motifs all in red. On a superimposed enlargement, a staircase and balustrade were painted in concentric circles of black and green on a red background. Both talud and tablero of a still later structure were found to be decorated with an elaborate cross design in red, green, and black, which may have had some calendrical significance. Thirty-one or -two such crosses encircled the structure. Today the last renovation stands as a plain talud-tablero structure (1B′) in the plaza with no outward sign of its colorful background.

The great platforms were constructed during Miccaotli and probably the Quetzalcoatl Pyramid as well, its *adosada* being added possibly two centuries later (Cabrera Castro *et al.*, 1991). We are not certain exactly when the East Avenue was added, as both East and West Avenues may not have been part of the original city planning. During the Early Tlamimilolpa period, some renovating was done in the residential palaces, but beyond that no major architectural changes are apparent until Metepec (A.D. 650–750), a curious situation in view of the Mesoamerican penchant for periodic rebuilding. There seems to have been a lessening of day-to-day living in the Ciudadela during these prime years which is hard to explain. A possible explanation is that the head of state and his retinue moved out. Perhaps the newly finished apartments in the Viking Group were more desirable with their rather dramatic central location and elegant mica floors taking precedence over the smaller rooms in the North and South Palaces. In any event, the Ciudadela was never abandoned. It continued to serve as a state symbol of power and maintained its function as a great center for public display of authority, pomp, and circumstance.

The Great Compound

Directly west across the Street of the Dead from the Ciudadela and occupying an area roughly equivalent, is another huge area identified by R. Millon (1973) as a possible marketplace (The Great Compound). This is entered at street level from the east, via the Street of the Dead, or from West Avenue, and is formed by an enormous plaza flanked by wide platforms on the north and south sides sustaining 27 apartment compounds. These are thought to have taken care of the city's bureaucracy, perhaps representing local and regional economic interests. Today it has been taken over by a huge parking lot, museum, restaurant, and tourist shops.

Beyond the Great Compound and the Ciudadela, the Street of the Dead continues south for approximately another 3 km, but aside from some sizable platforms to the south, no major structures have been reported like those found to the north. Thus the area from the Moon Pyramid south to the Ciudadela along the Street of the Dead embraced the main civic and religious structures of Teotihuacan. Although many more buildings were added thereafter, the heart of the great metropolis was in place by A.D. 300.

The discussion will return often to Teotihuacan because this metropolis played a major role in the future of Mesoamerica. Now we will leave the Teotihuacanos comfortably gathered in their great city while we look at some of their neighbors and then turn to Oaxaca and points south.

WEST MEXICO

Colima

After the early Capacha material there is a gap in our knowledge of this west coast region until approximately 500 B.C.–A.D. 100, a phase known by archaeologists as Ortices. Our information on these years comes from tombs excavated by Isabel Kelly in the Ortices district and one at Chanchopa near Tecomán. The Ortices phase is characterized by small solid figurines and fine quality cream to gray wares with shadow-striping, a decorative technique that appears to be the forerunner of *blanco levantado* in the region of Guanajuato, Querétaro, and Hidalgo. Tombs were dug during this phase but often reopened, cleared out, and reused in the following Comala phase, which includes the best known Colima pottery: beautiful red vessels, black-on-red decorated pots, engraved monochrome vessels, and an almost infinite number of large, hollow human and animal effigy figures.

A promising Colima site is Morett, on the Jalisco border, where an early phase is dated from 300 B.C.–A.D. 300 (Meighan, 1972). There are no mounds or structures here, but it is known from a midden some 3 m in depth that yielded remains of tripods and tetrapod vessels decorated in negative painting and a zoned-hatchure decoration, as well as a white-on-red pottery, conforming to the general feeling of Preclassic Mesoamerica. Nothing specific relates it to the early Ocós horizon, and Meighan sees more affiliation with Conchas of Guatemala, Playa de los Muertos in Honduras, and even Ecuador, where Chorrera and Tejar phases share many of these features. He believes some kind of relationship existed between these areas prior to the Christian era.

Jalisco

One of the few sites with architecture at this time is Etzatlán, Jalisco, excavated by Phil Weigand (1974). Extensive surveying yielded 438 sites that have been grouped into (1) hunting stations and kill sites; (2) small simple villages with a central mound or altar with 3–6 outlying mounds and temples; (3) larger sites with more complex mounds and tombs with elaborate offerings; and (4) Ahualulco, a large and most impressive site with eight separate circular constructions, each with a huge central mound. These belong to the Arenal phase (?B.C.–A.D. 200), where each mound circle may represent a lineage. The smaller centers suggest an occupation by several lineages of more or less equal rank. Ahualulco is a curious site located on high ground surrounded by valleys and old lake beds. Tombs were found in the central mounds containing typical shaft-tomb pottery.

Reusing tombs was a common practice complicating their study as contents were moved about and mixed up. Kelly (1978) relates that in clearing out one Colima tomb for reuse, its contents were dumped into the shaft of another. In other cases, shafts remained open for deposition of rubbish. A famous Ezatlán tomb from this region of Jalisco may have been used three times.

What we believe to be the total contents of this tomb came to rest in the Los Angeles County Museum. They consist of nine articulated skeletons and jumbled bones of three others without skulls. The nine deceased were accompanied by 17 hollow polychrome figurines ranging in height from 27.5 to 51.5 cm, 40 polychrome dishes and bowls, several rectangular ceramic boxes with lids, shell and obsidian ornaments, and conch-shell trumpets. The trumpets proved to be of both Caribbean and Pacific Coast origin. It is not uncommon to find Caribbean trumpets in the shaft tombs. This one yielded a C-14 date of 266 B.C.; the west coast shell from this tomb is dated at A.D. 254. (Dates refer to the death of the mollusks, not to their placement in the tomb). This particular tomb had been reopened and used three times over a period of 200 years.

Another shaft tomb from Tequilita in the southern temperate highlands of Nayarit yielded a date around A.D. 100. In west Mexico during these changing times, people were greatly preoccupied with the disposal of the dead and dug these curious tombs that in themselves are far more characteristic of northwestern South America than Mesoamerica and may be the result of direct contact by sea (see page 200).

A great variety of hollow and solid figurines as well as effigy vessels are known to come from Colima, Jalisco, and Nayarit where they are found in shaft tombs. The large hollow Colima figures (Figure 4.9), often of highly polished red or brown clay, portray adults and children in a variety of activities in a somewhat different style. Particularly charming are small figures forming scenes of people grouped around a house or temple. Musicians beat drums, shake rattles, and play flutes while others dance and do acrobatics. This gaiety and frivolity is in marked contrast to the later macabre sobriety of altiplano art. The Colima modeled pottery flutes are among

---

FIGURE 4.9   West Mexico Ceramics.
a. Red and black on buff polychrome tripod effigy bowl. Chupícuaro, Guanajuato. Length: 23 cm. (Courtesy of the UCLA Museum of Cultural History collections. Gift of Miss Natalie Wood [X69W-159].)
b. "Spider-leg" red-on-buff tripod. Chupícuaro, Guanajuato. Burial 123. Height: 29 cm. (Photographed by the author.)

a   b   c   d

e   f   g   h

c. Figurine with thin slab skirt. Cuitzeo, Michoacán. Height: 4 cm. (Courtesy of the Museum of the American Indian, Heye Foundation, N.Y. [23/9352].)

d. Chupícuaro figurine of local style. Height: 8 cm. (Courtesy of the UCLA Museum of Cultural History collection. Gift of Miss Natalie Wood [X69W-422].)

e. H-4 type figurine widely traded. Chupícuaro, Guanajuato. Height: 8 cm. (Courtesy of the UCLA Museum of Cultural History collections. Gift of Miss Natalie Wood [X69@-3991].)

f. Polychrome figure of a woman holding a jar. Nayarit, Mexico. Height: 27 cm. (Courtesy of the Museum of the American Indian, Heye Foundation, N.Y. [23/2275].)

g. Large red-ware hollow dog. Colima. Length: 43 cm. (Courtesy of the Museum of the American Indian, Heye Foundation, N.Y. [23/8366].)

h. Effigy figure from Buena Vista, Colima. Height: 22 cm. (Courtesy of the Museum of the American Indian, Heye Foundation, N.Y. [22/5100].)

Mesoamerica's finest. The red dogs (Figure 4.9g) are believed to have been made for interment in order to carry the soul of the deceased across a river, one of the obstacles to be overcome before reaching paradise. These figures have been the subject of study by Peter Furst, who believes they are related to shamanism (Furst, 1965).

Not all the ceramic sculptures come from tombs. At Cerro Encantado in northeast Jalisco, the same complex is found in graves. Bell (1972) relates these remains to those of Chupícuaro and to Chalchihuites sites in the north around A.D. 100–250.

Chupícuaro, Guanajuato

On the banks of the Lerma River in the southern part of the state of Guanajuato lay the village of Chupícuaro, in an area that shares motifs and pottery styles with west, northern, and central Mexico. Thousands of complete pottery vessels from this region have stocked museums and private collections around the world. The site itself is now covered by a lake created by the completion of the Solís Dam in 1949. Prior to inundation, extensive excavations undertaken by INAH in 1946 uncovered nearly 400 richly stocked graves, a veritable cemetery located along the top of a hill at the confluence of the Lerma River and a small tributary. The only remains of construction were stone alignments somewhat similar to those on the Cerro del Tepalcate and burned clay fragments presumably from floors (Porter, 1956). Burials were placed at random among rectangular mud-packed basins (*tlecuil*) filled with fine ash. We imagine that fires were lit in the basins while interment took place.

Pottery was either a black-brown unpainted ware typical of Ticomán (composite silhouette, mammiform, or plain tripod shapes) or elaborately polychromed in combinations of red and black or brown on buff, with lesser amounts of red-on-buff bichrome. Designs are exclusively geometric with variety provided by form: simple and composite silhouette bowls, with and without supports, oval, elongated, and kidney shapes, shallow bowls with great long spider-leg supports (see Figure 4.9b), and human-faced effigy vessels. Stirrup-spouted vessels are known from private collections in the area, but not from the INAH excavations. Hand-modeled figurines were abundant, not only the well-known slant-eyed (H-4) type, but several other well-defined local styles (see Figure 4.9c,d). Figurines were found carefully placed in graves and many fragments recovered from the surrounding earth.

Musical instruments, clay ocarinas, flutes, whistles, and rattles, were interred with children. Dogs were carefully buried and sometimes they too were given offerings.

Warfare was much in evidence with extra skulls placed in graves, brain cases neatly cut horizontally, painted red and perforated for suspension, stacked on the knees of one skeleton. Decapitation was widespread in Mesoamerica and there are many early examples among the Zapotecs, the coastal lowlands, and southern Maya region. The custom increased in the Classic Period when it was intimately associated with the ball-game cult and is well documented for the Postclassic Period. It must have been an important part of ceremonial life of Preclassic peoples related to warfare, personal achievement, and/or ancestor worship (Moser, 1973).

The use of black and brown paint in the ceramics may indicate a chronological difference, but evidence is slim, and all the pottery is securely tied to the Late Preclassic period. Florance (1985) suggests that Chupícuaro could represent a militaristic expansion from Cuicuilco out of the Basin of Mexico via the Lerma River. Chupícuaro-style ceramics and figurines are found both in the Valley of Mexico and in Tlaxcala (García Cook, 1981). The distinctive polychromed geometric style has been found in a wide area along the Bajio and in the states of San Luis Potosí, Querétaro, as far north as Zacatecas, and west to Jalisco (Braniff, 1974). This was an area of dispersed villages and the Chupícuaro wares occur with local and regional variations. It is not yet clear how to account for the popularity and spread of this style but after A.D. 300 there was no sign of further activity at its major production center on the Lerma River (Porter Weaver, 1969).

TLAXCALA AND PUEBLA

The four hundred years between 300 B.C. and A.D. 100 (Tezoquipan phase) saw the cultural peak of Tlaxcalan development and a consolidation of the technological and ideological processes. Villages were now transformed into a dozen regional centers or cities and into more than 40 towns. The technological advances and urban aspects are illustrated by the large, planned ceremonial centers with streets, plazas, drains, ball courts, common use of stucco, talud-tablero architecture, and complete hydraulic systems of terrace cultivation, irrigation canals, dikes, and ridged fields. Institutionalized religion was a major concern and the government is believed to have been a theocracy (García Cook, 1981).

Three colonies from west Mexico may have settled in the northwestern part of the state of Puebla at this time, one of which is represented by Gualupita las Dalias, located on a hill surrounded on three sides by deep barrancas. The very position suggests a defensive location, borne out by lookout posts and an entrance point that could have been easily guarded. About 17 structures have been located, of which 3 are pyramids, and the rest are low, residential platforms. A series of bottle-shaped pits were found containing rubbish as at Tlatilco. Among the inventory of remains are solid earspools, *malacates*, and quantities of clay figurines types H-3 and H-4 along with pottery decorated by resist painting or polychromed, at times with mammiform supports, or cut-out pedestal bases.

These remains could be those of colonists from the area around Chupícuaro, Guanajuato or neighboring Michoacán. The presence of similar material has already been noted at Cuicuilco and Tezoyuca sites in the Basin of Mexico.

Contacts in general between Tlaxcala, Puebla, and the Basin of Mexico were strong during these years. Just as ceremonial architecture had started in the Basin of Mexico, so at Cholula a small pyramid was built 17 m in height and decorated with creatures resembling mythical insects painted red, black, and yellow. Meanwhile, the Tlaxcalans were working closely with Basin of Mexico masons, demonstrating their technique of stuccoing and building in the talud-tablero style. The two areas shared some figurines and ceramics. As these were largely domestic effects, it is not surprising to find that some Teotihuacanos may have moved into the western and northern part of Tlaxcala (García Cook, 1981).

OAXACA

We return now to Oaxaca where two ethnic peoples of Otomanguean tongue, the Mixtecs and Zapotecs, were growing apart, each developing special features while maintaining an unmistakable Oaxaca flavor. We have seen that the Mixtecs and Zapotecs probably shared an early common egalitarian band-level society but by the Preclassic had already begun to develop their own lifestyles. This may have been the result of regional adaptations to different environments. The Zapotecs settled in the valleys of Oaxaca where they could farm, taking advantage of floodwaters, dig wells, and irrigate with small canals. The Mixtecs found that the Nochixtlán Valley in the highlands, the Mixteca Alta, was suitable for dry farming. The Mixteca Baja to the west and Mixteca de la Costa were of lesser prominence (see Map 6.3).

In this chapter, I have included Oaxaca material from 500 B.C. to A.D. 200, which combines the usual Middle and late Preclassic Periods (Monte Albán I and II) in order to highlight the founding of the Zapotec capital and its evolution to statehood and subsequent expansion.

The Zapotecs

By 500 B.C. the early egalitarian chiefdoms had become autonomous communities with ascribed social statuses. Such a community might consist of a relatively large village with smaller satellite hamlets. San José Mogote was the outstanding community of 62 ha that had participated in an exchange network with the Gulf Coast Olmec (see page 50). Many features such as the 260-day calendar, ceremonial bloodletting, human and animal sacrifice, formalized religious art, and ritual were well established by this time.

Monte Albán   Around 500 B.C. the settlement of Monte Albán was founded by one such aggressive confederacy to serve as an administrative center for the Oaxaca valleys. It is hard to know how this decision was reached. It could have been a deliberate decision to form a capital (Blanton et al., 1981), or several resident groups of separate descent may have settled in distinct areas. These could have been people who developed differences with their neighbors and moved off, an explanation that would justify building early defenses. Whatever the initial reasons for settlement, the endeavor successfully spawned a major center that was to dominate the Oaxacan region until Toltec times.

The choice of the site for this capital, Monte Albán (Flannery and Marcus, 1983b), may at first glance seem inappropriate: a hilltop never before occupied, offering no agricultural potential, a scarcity of water, and perched 400 meters above the valley floor not easily accessible for commercial activities or a casual visit. The choice was actually rather astute in many ways. The hilltop, removed from competing rivalries of the valley communities, was on neutral ground, strategically and diplomatically situated in the center of the three valleys with wonderful visibility in all directions (Map 4.1) Perhaps the precocious San José Mogote was an instigator in the move and

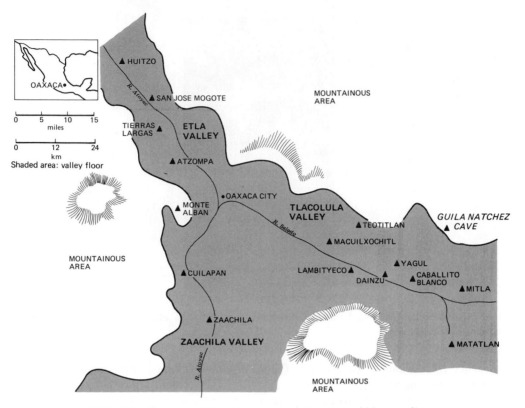

MAP 4.1 Oaxaca valleys. Note strategic location of Monte Albán.

gathered support from other high-ranking communities to found the capital. It is surely not a coincidence that as Monte Albán was populated, San José Mogote was abandoned. Once well established, a professional Zapotec ruling class emerged and any old ties to a former village withered away (Marcus, 1983c).

In this early Monte Albán I period, people moved closer to the piedmont area, a rather risky venture for farmers for little water was available. However, wattle-and-daub houses were soon replaced with more durable adobe construction. The pottery griddle (*comal*) makes its appearance on the hilltop and a market system aided the distribution of local resources. By 350 B.C. population increased and piedmont settlements were growing in number (Kowalewski, 1980).

Few buildings of this time (i.e., prior to 200 B.C.) are to be seen today as most are covered by later construction, but the famous "Danzantes" belong here. These are human figures carved in low relief on large stone slabs bearing the same Olmec cast as the single figure found at San José Mogote. The slabs here were set into the southern section of the platform of building L, a structure toward the southwest corner of the hilltop. The "Danzantes" form a huge gallery along the eastern side of the building displaying low reliefs of captives and sacrificed victims (Figure 4.10). They were

FIGURE 4.10 A sacrificed victim, "Danzante," one of bas-relief slabs forming a public gallery. Photo by author.

arranged in four superimposed rows. On the bottom, the most visible place, the best carvings with finest details were placed. These so-called "Danzantes" represent nude male figures (nudity itself being a humiliation for Mesoamerican peoples), with rubbery lifeless limbs, half-closed eyes, and drooping mouths sagging open in death. Sex organs are depicted in elaborate flowery designs, possibly representing blood flowing from castration or from ritual penis bloodletting with sting-ray spines. Name glyphs often accompany a figure as on the threshold stone at San José Mogote. Piña Chan (personal communication) suggests that the two glyphs behind the head of Danzante No. 6 (Figure 4.11) might be read as "the collector of tribute of birds of prey," such as eagles or falcons. (The lower glyphs represent an *atlatl* or spearthrower; the square with dots could indicate tribute, and the head, that of a bird of prey (Piña Chan, 1990).

Unfortunately, some Danzantes have been moved about, many reused in subsequent construction, and Building L was partially destroyed in antiquity, so the sequences and exact location of each slab cannot be accurately re-created. An estimated 300 such slabs were carved, a truly tremendous display of military power. This graphic scene of so many captives and slain prisoners would have given any potential insurgent cause for reflection. Two stelae (Nos. 12 and 13) were found at the southern end of the Danzantes building and together contain one of the earliest texts (Figure 4.12). Although all the glyphs are not understood, names and/or dates are clearly recorded (Marcus, 1983b).

North of the Danzantes an early construction was raised with a sloping talus of

FIGURE 4.11 Danzante No. 6 Glyphs may be read as "collector of tribute of birds of prey" (?). (Courtesy of Piña Chan.)

FIGURE 4.12 Stela 12 and 13 from the southern end of Building L, the Danzantes gallery, constituting a single text. Included are a year sign, possible day-sign, and noncalendrical glyphs of unknown meaning. The order of reading is not clear, across both stones as a double column or each read independently. Height: approx. 1.20 m. (Photographed by the author.)

huge stones and a pair of rubble masonry columns, similar to what we will see at neighboring Monte Negro. This was later covered over by a complex to be known as System IV.

Prestigious deceased were placed in simple rectangular stone tombs roofed over with slabs of stone. Much of the pottery of this period comes from such tombs or from valley sites. A fine-paste gray ware is typical of Monte Albán and makes up 76% of vessels from Period I and II tombs. Very small vessels with fine polish and slip were characteristic. Forms include wide, everted rims, bridged spouts, stucco decoration, flanges, and mammiform supports. Also from Monte Albán I is a flat-based bowl with fine combed incision on the interior base. By Monte Albán II, cylindrical forms and tetrapods became popular. Hand-modeled figurines are known, but were not produced in quantity. The pottery is not unlike some found in Chiapas at this time (Tolstoy, 1980).

The success of this hilltop settlement was remarkable. Estimates of the early population that resided in three different wards or barrios ranges from 3600 to 7200 and by 200 B.C. reached 10,000–17,000 inhabitants (Blanton and Kowalewski, 1981). This was not the result of any intrusive group but grew out of the local valley culture seen in antecedents of ceramics and architecture. Much of this conforms to other Preclassic development in Mesoamerica.

Statehood   Just how the Zapotec state emerged is not entirely clear, but its origins are probably to be found in its unique topographical and ecological base (Sanders and Nichols, 1988).

Flannery and Marcus (1983b) base their evidence for Zapotec statehood on the presence of four features: (1) centralized government in the hands of a professional non-kin-based ruling class; (2) an ability to wage war, draft soldiers, levy taxes, and collect tribute; (3) public works by professionals including religious structures tended by specialists (priests); and (4) a four-tiered administrative hierarchy. Tolstoy (1980) would add one more criterion: the existence of a city of over 10,000 inhabitants. Most scholars now agree that by 200 B.C., preceding Teotihuacan by approximately 500 years, a Zapotec state centered at Monte Albán was a reality.

Massive construction projects had been initiated around 300 B.C. and the Danzante gallery continued to grow. The large defensive wall (3 km in length, 3–4 m in height) now surrounded much of the northern, northwestern, and western boundaries of the city (Blanton, 1983a). Gray pottery production greatly increased and a massive labor force began to level the Main Plaza and pave it with white stucco. Any natural outcrops encountered were incorporated into foundations for buildings; System IV was constructed and spaces were filled in with small temples, thus avoiding an asymmetrical plan. The first stages of the ball court were built at this time in Period II (200 B.C.– A.D. 100). The completed Main Plaza looks well organized and balanced.

The demand for stone masonry tombs increased and some were constructed with corbeled roofs. Why this style and slab masonry construction was not widely applied elsewhere remains a mystery.

Near the east side of Building H, centrally located in the Main Plaza, a multiple grave of five young adults placed on a flagstone floor contained some of Monte Albán's finest offerings; jade necklaces, earspools, masks and pectorals of jade, pearls, and shells. The most spectacular piece was a jade bat mask worn as a pectoral (Figure 4.13). Its 25 separate pieces of beautifully polished dark green jade fitted neatly together to form a human face disguised as a bat, with eyes and teeth of shell. It seems odd that such finery would not have warranted a tomb, but nothing is known of these people, or from whence they came (Flannery, 1983d).

Mound X, northeast of the Main Plaza, provides evidence of a state religion, seen in a two-room temple. This, combined with the cessation of hand-modeled figurines, is taken as an indication of transferring the major business of prayer and ritual from the individual household to the hands of the more reliable and knowledgeable priests. The outer chamber of the temple, flanked by single columns, leads one step down to a smaller and narrower inner sanctuary entered between another pair of large columns. Certain architectural features in Mound X, such as this chamber combined with an outer room or porch, have counterparts at Teotihuacan. There this architectural

FIGURE 4.13   Bat mask of polished jade pieces; Burial XIV-10 in Building H. Monte Albán II. Height: 17 cm. (Courtesy of the Museo Nacional de Antropología, Mexico.)

feature is commonly found in palaces or residences grouped around courtyards or patios.

Conquests   Looking again at the Main Plaza of Monte Albán, there is a small building in front of the South Platform built in the odd shape of an arrowhead (Figure 4.14). This is Building J, where the Zapotecs continued to publicize their military victories with fewer monuments than the Danzantes but with more specific information. Building J, dating from Monte Albán II (200 B.C.–A.D. 300), has approximately 50 carved slabs that are set into the lower wall of the building. These comprise a glyphic record of Zapotec conquests and are decorated with reliefs of sacrificed captives. Not all glyphs can be "read" but Marcus (1983b) believes that four refer to areas conquered within 140 m of Monte Albán and may delineate the boundaries of the Zapotec state at this time. We know for example that one toponym, identified as Cuicatlán, was a fortified mountain town on the northern border between Oaxaca and the Tehuacán Valley (see below). Tututepec was near the Pacific coast; Miahuitlán and Ocelotepec lie south of Monte Albán midway to the coast (see Map 8.4). In some cases a glyph may represent not only a conquest but also the tribute it must pay (See Fig. 4.11).

A Zapotec conquest did not necessarily mean territorial occupation. One tactic used was to distribute prestigious goods of some strategic or economic value among the highest ranking members of a settlement. In return the Zapotecs would demand agricultural surpluses and strict allegiance to the state. This was a kind of advantageous exchange arrangement that guaranteed the cooperation of local authorities while reinforcing the political integration at Monte Albán (Zeitlin, 1990).

Cuicatlán Cañada and Zapotec Expansion   The conquest of the Cuicatlán Cañada may be an exception, but serves as a heartless example of Zapotec imperialism in the hinterland. Located at a warm, frost-free altitude of 500–700 m, a thousand meters lower than Oaxaca Valley, this region produced *tierra caliente* products coveted by the elite bureaucracy at Monte Albán. Furthermore, all north–south traffic to Tehuacán and central highland Mexico had to traverse a natural pass in these mountains, a crucial control point. The Cuicatlán Cañada must have been a high priority for conquest by Monte Albán's rulers.

Its outright conquest is well documented by Redmond (1983) and Spencer (1982), providing evidence that villages were devastated, some relocated, frontier garrisons set up that housed Monte Albán overlords; hierarchical settlements were reduced to simple villages and the local inhabitants terrorized by public skull racks displaying heads of slain warriors. No longer did prestigious imports arrive from Monte Albán. The local culture was stripped of its own architecture, ritual, traditions, and language. Thus what had begun as a reciprocal exchange program with the Zapotecs had been replaced by outright exploitation after conquest. The Cuicatlán Cañada, reduced to tributary status, so remained until the early Classic Period.

Because of the nature of the Zapotec expansion it is not possible to define the extent of the state. Miahuatlán and Tututepec both yield Zapotec pottery, but Ocelotepec

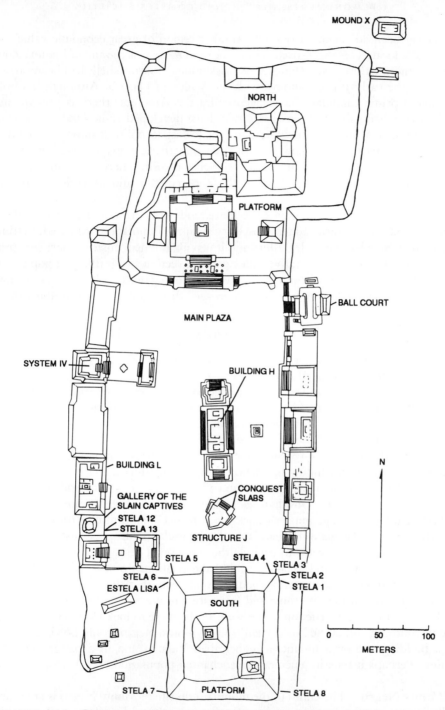

FIGURE 4.14 Civic-ceremonial center of Monte Albán. (Courtesy of Scientific American, Joyce Marcus, 1980.)

has not yet been adequately explored. Another region of great economic value and strategically located on a well-used communication route was the site of Laguna Zope on the southern Isthmus (see Map 3.2). A brisk trade in marine shells had been carried on here in the early Preclassic days with the Valley of Oaxaca. Although it would seem like a prime candidate for a takeover by the Zapotecs, there is no evidence that this ever happened. Laguna Zope may have developed some kind of a special relationship with Monte Albán, while managing to keep its political autonomy (Zeitlin, 1990), or perhaps was somehow incorporated into the Zapotec realm, but by less brutal means not yet detected in the archaeological record. There is still much we do not understand about the operations of the Zapotec state and its varied system of exploiting the hinterlands.

These aggressive ventures into the hinterlands (Flannery and Marcus, 1983a; Spencer, 1982) did not mean added prosperity at home. Population decreased. Settling the piedmont area had proved a failure and it was abandoned. Instead there is a great rise in the number of administrative valley centers, seen in a reshuffling of population and duties. This should not be interpreted as a weakening of the political organization. Indeed Oaxaca was about to enter a "golden age" that would last about 400 years.

The Mixteca

Yucuita   What caused the ups and downs of Yucuita's fortunes is not completely understood. This is another hilltop center located at the very northern end of the fertile Nochixtlán Valley in the Mixteca Alta (Winter, 1982). It seems to have been a large village from 1400 to 1200 B.C., but at the end of this period the population declined and Yucuita was hardly more than a ranch. After 500 B.C. a great development took place paralleling the rise of Monte Albán. Yucuita grew to a center of 3000 inhabitants with a large civic-ceremonial center and satellite communities. Residences were very simple but the hilltop flourished with large platforms and buildings, patios with staircases, drains, and passageways and a large rectangular nonresidential building, presumably a temple. Obsidian, jade, and marine shell were traded in, but by the first century B.C. Yucuita was once more in decline. Building projects ended abruptly, residential areas were abandoned, and population dropped just as construction had begun on stone walls to encircle the ceremonial center.

Yucuita peaked around 200–1 B.C. and the relationship with Monte Albán is unclear. Architecture and material goods may indicate that the resident population here belonged to a different ethnic and linguistic group. Some kind of conflict may well have led to the construction of the wall. If one were to look from Yucuita to the extreme southern end of the Nochixtlán Valley, Monte Negro would be visible. This was a budding site on a mountain higher than Yucuita and in a better defensive position. Perhaps it took in Yucuita's disenchanted population.

Monte Negro   The climb to the mountaintop site of Monte Negro is steep and hardly convenient for farmers working the flat agricultural land below. But for the archaeologist it offers the great advantage of not having been built over by later Classic peoples, thus preserving the plan and architecture of a late Preclassic civic-ceremonial site. For many years Monte Negro was thought to be a model for, or forerunner of, Monte Albán, but it is now dated at 200 B.C., so this order must be reversed (Flannery, 1983c).

The hilltop is covered with artificial terraces, and the entire site is so small it could fit in the Main Plaza of Monte Albán. No structure is more than six meters in height.

Buildings are grouped along a linear L-shaped plan like Yucuita, an arrangement not found among the Zapotecs who built around plazas. The construction, although rough, using undressed blocks of stone in irregular rows, is distinctive with its columns made of drumlike stones or rubble, placed on stone platforms, patios, and porticos. Columns supported roofs of the finest homes and rooms facing stone-paved open patios had columns in the corners. Walls were constructed of adobe or wattle-and-daub over stone foundations. Some residences were connected with a temple or public building via a private covered passageway.

Elite members of society deformed their heads, inlaid their teeth with bits of pyrite and wore jade earspools, all marks of elegance. Upon death they were buried in adobe tombs sunk in the platforms, accompanied by goods befitting their rank.

This is Mixteca Alta country, but Monte Negro has both Mixtec and Zapotec features. Many ties can be found with the Oaxaca Valley including architectural features of San José Mogote. The gray fine-paste pottery of Monte Albán is more abundant here than at Yucuita. Mixteca features include the L-shaped site layout, temples of one chamber, and the design of ball courts.

Despite some differences, Zapotecs and Mixtecs were both Oaxaca cultures that chose defensible mountaintops for their ritual and administrative centers. They were very different from Teotihuacan with its concentration of workshops, huge residential compounds, marketplace (?), and grid layout.

Valley Sites

Dainzú   Dainzú, about 20 km southwest of Oaxaca City in the Tlacolula Valley, has proved to be an extensive site. Of particular interest is a large pyramidal platform into which were set two superimposed rows of bas-relief sculptures that bear some resemblance to Monte Albán's Danzantes executed in local style. Two figures are humanized jaguars. Among the others, at least 47 represent ball-players decked out in wide pants, knee guards, visored helmets, gauntlets, and holding a ball in the right hand. Some are shown with yokes (see Figure 6.25a,d) around the waist (Bernal, 1973). If these figures accurately depict the game, the rules at this time (500–100 B.C.) surely differed from the Postclassic sport, for that game was played without hands.

Yagul and Caballito Blanco   Yagul and Caballito Blanco are only two of many other mesatop sites in the Oaxaca Valley that should be mentioned in this early period. Yagul is known for a special pottery urn found in tombs or graves, typically decorated with an Olmec-like face. The neighboring site of Caballito Blanco, only 300 m away, is best known for an arrowhead-shaped structure like Building J at Monte Albán. The pottery here is also of interest. The gray ware bowl with interior combed decoration mentioned at Monte Albán and widely distributed in the Mixteca Alta is found here in great abundance. Another distinctive ceramic feature is a white-rimmed black ware on which the white may be painted.

These two sites are probably related in some way, but there are no buildings at Yagul and only three small, low platforms at Caballito Blanco (Paddock, 1983a).

THE MAYA REGION

The Maya present a different situation. West of the Isthmus we have seen Teotihuacan rise to power and dominate the central highlands, while in Oaxaca an independent Zapotec state emerged with a capital at Monte Albán. These developments have no counterpart in the Maya region where a series of small kingdoms developed but never united to form a centralized state. The Maya thrived under a succession of regional centers, none of which ever prevailed over more than close neighbors for a short time.

Crossing the Isthmus of Tehuantepec, we will refer to several Maya regions: the Pacific Coastal Plain and Piedmont areas, the Southeast Periphery, the Southeastern Highlands, the Southern Lowlands to the north extending into part of Belize, and the Northern Region across the peninsula of Yucatán from the Gulf Coast to the Caribbean (see Maps 6.5 and 6.6). During the 500/600 years prior to A.D. 300 each of these geographical areas developed distinctive characteristics, many of which continue on through the Classic and even into Postclassic years.

In the region spanning from Abaj Takalik east to Chalchuapa, El Salvador, the inhabitants maintained their earlier centers on the old Olmec trade route and prospered. The elite segment of society grew in status and prestige, and regional centers became the focus for both ceremonial and economic activities. Elaborate stone monuments were carved depicting narrative scenes with human and animal figures. Carved stelae recorded historical events accompanied by dates in the Long Count system and were set up in public places.

One of the most important centers was a large site called Kaminaljuyú in the Guatemala Valley. Kaminaljuyú occupied a prominent and powerful position, since it not only controlled a large obsidian resource at El Chayal, but was strategically perched between the Pacific slope communities to the south and the Maya lowlands to the north. The people of the upper Chixoy and Salamá valleys in the northern highlands along with Kaminaljuyú were important in these interrelationships.

Although the greatest development after A.D. 300 is concentrated in the northern lowlands, Maya civilization owes a cultural debt to its southern highland neighbors. This may comprise the stela-altar complex, the Long Count calendar, hieroglyphic writing, and the distinctive Maya sculptural style. There is even early evidence of dynastic rulership (Sharer and Sedat, 1987).

The Maya of these two areas (the southeastern highlands and southern lowlands) developed a stimulating relationship. The southern lowland Maya realized that the highlanders' carved stelae provided a fine medium for their public propaganda. By A.D. 300 the institution of kingship was firmly established and used the stelae format. The nobility has worked out an elaborate scheme to provide for royal succession that was to continue throughout the history of the southern lowland Maya.

We will see competition and skirmishes between regional centers or kingdoms, but not between these larger areas mentioned above. Warfare at this time was largely a local exercise and as yet there was no organized polity aspiring to carve out a territorial domain. Meanwhile, interactions between highlands and lowlands, coastal and interior communities fostered exchange of resource materials and exotic goods.

What we know as Maya civilization gradually emerged out of its earlier Preclassic base. Our present inventory of Long Count dates and the beginning of writing suggests a lowland Isthmian priority in this field. Although archaeologists have learned how elusive the subject of origins can be, the Gulf Coast region or Oaxaca offer the most likely possibilities in this field.

We will now examine a number of regional centers to gain some perspective of the whole region. The following sites are selected for their content, environmental setting, and not least of all, because they are examples about which we know the most at the moment. I do not attempt to give a full account of these sites, but only to point out the salient features in relation to the emergent Maya civilization. First of all, we will discuss a very special site known as Izapa (Quirarte, 1973).

The Pacific Coastal Plain and Piedmont Areas

Izapa   South of the Isthmus in the rich cacao-growing region of the Pacific coastal plain where earlier Preclassic peoples erected the massive Mound 30A, the site of Izapa underwent an extraordinary building boom accompanied by the erection of elaborately carved stone monuments (Lowe *et al.*, 1982). Although Izapa expanded to include 80 temple/pyramids around courts and plazas, it is the remarkable stone-carving style that was widely copied and is found as far north as Veracruz and in much of the Maya region.

This art style is manifested in a complex religious iconography that is portrayed on many of the 250 stone altars, stelae, and boulders (Figure 4.15). Some motifs are familiar such as the Olmec St. Andrews cross, the U-shaped design, and a long-lipped deity believed to be derived from the were-jaguar. The art here is full of motion. Combined animal-and-human figures fly, paddle canoes, descend from the sky, and wrestle. Some are busily decapitating a victim while others burn incense. Izapan figures are free to move between earth, sky, and heaven. Above all, these combined human, bird, jaguar, crocodile-serpent figures are narrations. Some tell stories of the Popul Vuh (Schele and Freidel, 1990). Art is narrative, mythic, and pictorial but is not accompanied by hieroglyphic texts. It is possible however, that the institution of kingship was already present at this time, because its symbol, the diadem of the Jester God, is depicted on Stela 5 (250 B.C.–A.D. 115) (Schele and Freidel, 1990).

Parsons (1988) sees Izapa-like resemblances reaching Tres Zapotes, Veracruz, on Stelae A, C, and D, where Long Count dates were already being recorded (see page

FIGURE 4.15   Stela 21. Izapa, Chiapas, Mexico. Decapitation scene. Height: 1.78 m. (Courtesy of the Instituto Nacional de Antropología, Mexico.)

157). Another stela, Monument 2 at El Mesón, Veracruz, is decorated with Izapa-style dragons in profile, flanking a mask. In the opposite direction, the Izapa style spread through the highlands to Kaminaljuyú, and through the lowlands reaching Belize.

Abaj Takalik   Much work has been done at the large site of Abaj Takalik with its Olmec background, and the site is well known for its great tradition of sculptured monuments, some of which bear dates. The creation of an archaeological park will now allow large-scale architecture to be exhibited along with groups of Maya-style sculptures. Despite the large size of the site, numerous mounds built around plazas and courts, Abaj Takalik is best known for its abundant monumental sculptures. The early ones exhibit many Olmec features, and by late Preclassic time a very sophisticalted level of stone carving had been achieved (Graham and Benson, 1990; Graham, 1979, 1989).

A number of the famous sculptured "pot-bellied" boulders have been recovered over the years at this site. These have a very wide distribution including neighboring Monte Alto, Kaminaljuyú in the highlands, Sin Cabezas, Bilbao, and Santa Leticia in El Salvador. Two examples are known from Copán, Honduras. Pot-bellies are huge natural boulders that have been incised or grooved to depict fat human figures sometimes with avian features with heavy flat noses and cheeks, thick lips, and limbs that wrap around the stone. They are nude with only ear ornaments and segmented collars for adornment (Miles, 1965). Animal figures may also be represented. Dating has been hard to determine and most scholars feel that they were carved after 500 B.C. The excavations at Santa Leticia, El Salvador have been very helpful in this regard as they were found *in situ*, in terraces of late Preclassic date (Demarest, 1986).

Among monuments considered unequivocally Maya is Altar 12, a handsome boulder sculpture (Graham and Benson, 1990). This is a huge slab of stone that Graham believes was not originally intended for its later use as an altar. It is an unmodified slab, with a Maya portrait figure carved in low relief flanked on each side by four glyphs. This might be of Cycle 6 date.

El Baúl   At El Baúl, halfway between the Valley of Guatemala and the Pacific, another stela with glyphs, some of which are numerals, was associated with late Preclassic pottery of the Arenal phase. The hieroglyphs are badly eroded, but it furnishes further evidence of the early recording of Long Count dates. Stela 1 at El Baúl has a baktun 7 coefficient (see Figure 5.9c) thus reading 7.19.15.7.11 or A.D. 36 in our calendar.

Monte Alto   Monte Alto, a site in close contact with Kaminaljuyú, is only 40 km from the Pacific coast on the fertile alluvial plain, ecologically transitional between the rain forest and savanna zone. There are a number of badly weathered earthen mounds spaced in two rows enclosing a plaza, but again the most outstanding feature is its curious boulder sculptures. Two are colossal human heads, and three are round human figures with wrap-around limbs and closed eyes; they are nude, sexless, and bald. Another boulder has a carving of a jaguar-monster mask. Opinions on dating may vary but all agree on Preclassic production.

Santa Leticia, El Salvador   The archaeology at Santa Leticia on El Salvador's northern border only goes back to 500 B.C., a fact hard to understand with its magnificent setting at 1400 m overlooking the coastal plain and inland basins, and offering rich volcanic soil provided by three towering volcanic peaks. Today this is coffee-growing country, some of the finest in Central America. In the ancient past, this was not on a commercial route and offered no special resource, but in relative isolation provided a dramatic setting for a religious center (Demarest, 1986).

Clusters of houses are associated with storage pits and middens, and three earthen mounds probably served as substructures for wattle-and-daub temples. Ceramics, artifacts, and refuse from bell-shaped pits permit cross-dating to Chalchuapa and Kaminaljuyú. Pot-bellies weighing 7–12 tons each were set in a north–south line in stone basins in a terrace and fit into a time span from 400 B.C. to A.D. 100. "Jaguar heads" such as are found on the coastal plain, together with the "pot-bellies" form a close tie to the rather distant "sister center" of Monte Alto. Obsidian was brought down from Ixtepeque and in smaller amounts from El Chayal.

Santa Leticia is believed to have participated in an ideological network linked to major chiefdoms at Chalchuapa, Kaminaljuyú, Izapa, and Abaj Takalik. These were all larger centers where people would have gathered from the surrounding areas to socialize, exchange goods, or attend special events (Demarest, 1986).

THE SOUTHEAST PERIPHERY

East of Chalchuapa the far southeast was quietly emerging from a less complicated background. The limits of this region are not clearly defined but in general eastern El Salvador, Guatemala and Honduras, and parts of Nicaragua and Costa Rica are included (Sharer, 1989b). This area was not peripheral to Mesoamerica during the Preclassic years, and prior to A.D. 300 the burial offerings and ritual indicate that a number of settlements became nucleated communities with ceremonial architecture and stratified societies. Gradually, smaller centers appeared all along the Sula-Ulua-Comayagua corridor. The stimulation for this development was due in part to the spread of the Izalco Usulután pottery.

This is a large region and our knowledge is still spotty. Ceramic remains have been the basis of most archaeological interpretation. With the small sample of material at hand, the tendency to stress the external relationships is understandable, but at times this has obscured the local sociopolitical development. We are now beginning to understand some of the processes that brought about these changes in the Late Preclassic. First a few highlights from the major sites.

Quelepa   Quelepa is a well-known major settlement in eastern El Salvador where residential mounds and pyramids are grouped along the north bank of the Esteban River. A large platform terrace and several ceramic caches constitute most of the Preclassic material from 500 B.C.–A.D. 115. Of the pottery, 60% is Usulután. A famous jaguar altar was discovered in 1926, carved with a feline face and two lateral heads. It is a monumental carved basin 3 m × 85 cm in height and is often cited as Olmec-derived influence (Andrews V, 1977).

Los Naranjos   Los Naranjos on the northern shore of Lake Yojoa exhibits the greatest complexity of its area (Baudez and Becquelin, 1973). During the Eden I phase (400–100 B.C.) several large mounds were erected. One stepped platform supported four structures and was aligned to the cardinal directions. The core was built entirely of earth faced with undressed limestone blocks. The earlier ditch was now enlarged, enclosing not only the main buildings but a sizable area of agricultural land.

Naco   Naco (Urban, 1986) is marked by a strong local tradition with ceramic ties to Chalchuapa and Los Naranjos, also having a very large percentage of Usulután ware. Structures were placed according to natural elevations rather than fronting on plazas. Construction was of rounded river cobbles, flat rock slabs, and perishable superstructures. An interesting feature is the paving of raised walkways uniting some structures. One well-preserved platform of cobble terraces gives the appearance of a stairway running the length of the building. Low cobble walls on the top outlined a cruciform-shaped room paved with flat stone slabs.

Also in the Sula Plain, the site of Río Pelo consists of a group of mounds along the mountainous east ridge. Pelo II (150 B.C.–A.D. 150) is the major component. Over a dozen structures are loosely arranged around two open areas, but they were not all built simultaneously. Río Pelo was probably a ceremonial center with a dispersed residential pattern. There is no sign of differentiation here and the material culture was almost entirely pottery and chipped stone (Wonderley, 1991).

Copán At Copán there were indications in the middle Preclassic burials that these inhabitants were already interacting with western areas of Mesoamerica as to ritual and perhaps engaging in economic activities as well. So it is surprising that there are few signs of further complexity in the Late Preclassic (Chabij phase). The small sampling of ceramics comes from the bottomlands south of the Acropolis. There are also two notable decapitated pot-bellied sculptures that had been used as foundations for Stelae 4 and 5 (Baudez, 1986). These correspond to others of the southern highlands, forming part of a widespread southeastern sculptural tradition. So, despite an apparent drop in population and activity at Copán, ties with the southern highlands continued (W. L. Fash, 1991b; Sharer, 1989b).

This assorted information of various scattered sites is gradually leading to a better understanding of the area, as we now find uniting factors that give the whole region cohesion. For example, construction was largely earthen and cobbled with a linear layout of settlements that were adapted to the natural elevations of the terrain. The great unifying factor was the surprising consistency in ceramics. This led Andrews V (1977) to name this phenomenon the Uapala Ceramic Sphere, comprising a uniform ceramic complex that spread throughout the region. It was dominated by Usulután ware, with other characteristics consisting of a red-slipped group, *tecomates, comals*, single and composite silhouette bowls with four nubbin feet, and some fine whitish-paste figurines. This ceramic sphere would include Eden I phase at Los Naranjos, Chabij at Copán and in the Comayagua Valley, Yarumela III and Lo de Vaca, and the Ulua Bichrome phase on the Sulu Plain (Wonderley, 1991; see also Baudez, 1986, who finds greater diversity than this ceramic sphere suggests).

The success of Usulután ware was probably due to its distinctive pleasing appearance, and it spread naturally through trade, not by migrations or special introduction. The demand was such that El Salvador's elite grew wealthy and powerful. Trading partners and distribution must have been set up with local hierarchies in the southeast. It is easy to imagine that the local chiefs would have likewise grown in prestige, adopting ideas and customs through contacts with their counterparts in an interregional exchange.

This scenario in the Late Preclassic is a hypothesis outlined by Schortman and

Urban (1991) as a possible explanation for the developments seen in the far southeast. The pattern of prosperity in El Salvador did not transfer to the far southeastern chiefs however, and great nucleated centers did not arise. In this region where earthen platforms were of ceremonial nature, construction did not require a large concentrated labor force, or great skill, or even a need for much supervision or administration. Communities were widely dispersed and not easily controlled or taxed. Grave offerings in the south do not compare to elite burials of Chalchuapa or those we will see at Kaminaljuyú, for how were these local readers to accumulate wealth? As a result a number of smallish societies developed some degree of complexity but did not approach that of their highland neighbors.

When Mt. Ilopango erupted, this entire interregional trade network disintegrated. The local leadership was discredited, its stability threatened, perhaps raising doubts about any new ideology. Rulers may have even lost the right to govern. Ashmore (1987) believes the old monuments were revived and continued in use, but there is some doubt. Many Late Preclassic monumental sites were abandoned, accompanied by the associated social and ritual complex.

THE SOUTHEASTERN HIGHLANDS

Chalcuapa

The two most important southeastern highland centers at this time were Chalchuapa and Kaminaljuyú. The late Preclassic remains at Chalchuapa show a continuous and gradual development out of earlier years, but no further construction took place until after 400 B.C. This new development was closely related to activity in highland Guatemala as seen in the distribution and composition of architecture, monumental stone carving, and early steps toward writing and recording of dates.

The old El Trapiche E3-1 pyramid was rebuilt and enlarged to enormous proportions; a new summit platform was added with access ramps of adobe. A tremendous earth-moving crew was engaged to level and create a large artificial plaza with a complex of ceremonial platforms distributed like those of highland Guatemala.

It is at this time that roots of the Classic Maya script are found in texts of stone monuments in the highlands and Pacific coastal plain. In this regard Chalchuapa has two noteworthy monuments. The first is Monument 10, marked by a series of pits on a stone not otherwise defaced. At first glance the deep pits may not seem very significant, except that a number of similar depressions, pits, or dots have been reported from numerous sites from Chalcatzingo, Mexico, to highland Guatemala that suggest some kind of notational tradition (Sharer, 1985; 1989a,b).

The second, Chalchuapa Monument 1, is a Maya stela of andesite (80.5 cm in height × 64 cm width) that had been deliberately defaced and covered over by Structure E3-1. Dated to 100 B.C.–A.D. 200, it depicts a seated figure in profile wearing a large feathered headdress with the right arm extended forward, holding some object that has been obliterated. A series of 8 hieroglyphic panels above are so battered as to be undecipherable, but one calendrical glyph (uinal) was saved from destruction.

As a regional center, Chalchuapa continued to grow and form an important focus for trade serving the southern Maya and lower Central America. A lucrative exchange had grown up around a pottery known as Usulután that became the most characteristic ware in southern Mesoamerica at this time defining the southern periphery (Demarest and Sharer, 1982). It was produced by the ton!

The name refers to a very distinctive resist decoration in which a series of wavelike lines were applied after the vessel had been fired to a light buff color. A second firing removed the resist substance, exposing the original cream slip, while the rest of the vessel turned orange or brown. The decoration produced by this laborious process was very fashionable. At times the lines were carefully made with a multiple brush, but at others, dots, cloudy blotches, and simple lines were the result of careless or less skillful potters (Figure 4.16).

The style was first manufactured in western El Salvador in the early Preclassic where a good sequence of its development has been found (Demarest and Sharer, 1982). Usulután vessels have a continuous range in El Salvador, western Honduras, Guatemala, and even neighboring Nicaragua. There are a few examples from Mexico, the northern limit being Laguna Zope on the Oaxaca coast (Zeitlin, 1978). A multiple-line Usulután, called Izalco, is of late Preclassic date and persisted into Classic times in the extreme southern regions of Mesoamerica (Andrews V, 1977) and is found as far south as the Nicoya Peninsula. Demarest and Sharer do not think the wide distribution of this ware involves migrations of people, but is simply the result of a pottery that was esthetically pleasing. It was so popular that imitations were made, and have been found in quantity at the distant site of El Mirador, Guatemala (Demarest, 1984a).

These were fine, productive years in Chalchuapa. Its inhabitants had created a complex regional center with a smooth functioning and efficient social and political system. Population rapidly increased, and just as a budding civilization was gathering momentum, rumblings were heard from the throat of Mt. Ilopango, 75 km to the east. The volcanic eruption of A.D. 250 was so devastating that pumice covered the entire valley and much of the southern lowlands. Given time, life would begin again, but

FIGURE 4.16 Tripod jar decorated in Usulután resist technique. Cobán, Guatemala. Height: 9 cm. (Courtesy Museum of the American Indian, Heye Foundation, N.Y. [9/9473].)

for most Chalchuapan families, their homes and belongings disappeared under the ash.

Where was one to go? Probably to the nearest kinfolk or to the closest similar environment with economic opportunities. In this case the most likely region would have been southeastern Guatemala or the highlands of western El Salvador out of the ash-buried basins (Demarest, 1986).

Kaminaljuyú

Returning to the site of Kaminaljuyú in the Valley of Guatemala, this now became the most powerful center of the highlands, attracting people from the highlands and lowlands as well as from the Pacific slopes. Sculptors at Kaminaljuyú were influenced by religious concepts and ideas from these different regions and we see this reflected in the eclectic iconography. Although Kaminaljuyú became the most powerful center, this does not imply control over any great domain. It no doubt enjoyed its role as community leader and may well have exercised control over the nearby El Chayal obsidian source, but there is nothing to indicate any aggressive political action.

From 400 B.C. to A.D. 100, religious architecture got off to a good start. Temple/pyramids, which in some cases also served as burial mounds, were arranged along both sides of a long rectangular plaza or avenue. Religion was the driving motivation, and all nearby peoples must have contributed heavily in time and muscle, to the necessary labor force. Apparently there was no fear of outsiders, as the sacred or civic centers were located on open valley floors without visible means of protection. Sanders and Michels (1969) suggest that these centers may have been utilized largely for ritual burials of chiefs.

A brief look at the Miraflores phase serves to exemplify the peak of development in this area. Huge earthen mounds were brightly painted, and two or more staircases led to a hutlike temple on top. But these mounds were not built to their final height of 18 m all at once. One such mound may contain as many as seven interior structures. The custom of enlarging a pyramid periodically is a common feature of Mesoamerica. Thus the oldest structure will be the smallest and form the initial interior core of a later pyramid. This was the case at Miraflores, but prior to one of these periodic enlargements, the builders dug through the top of the existing pyramid and excavated a rectangular-stepped opening to be used as a tomb (Figure 4.17). The corners were carefully braced by wooden uprights, and then the privileged deceased, covered with red paint, was carefully extended on a litter in the center.

In the case of Tomb 2 in Mound E-111-3, both adults and children were offered in sacrifice, along with more than 300 objects to accompany the distinguished corpse in afterlife. These objects were items of great luxury, such as jade beads, mosaics, and masks; beautifully carved vessels of soapstone, fuchsite, and chloite schist; stingray spines (used in bloodletting); stuccoed gourds; sheets of mica; fine implements of obsidian and basalt; bone; quartz crystals; fish teeth; and quantities of fine pottery vessels. The contents complete, the tomb was then roofed over with crossbeams and rush mats, the flooring restored above, and construction of a new grander pyramid

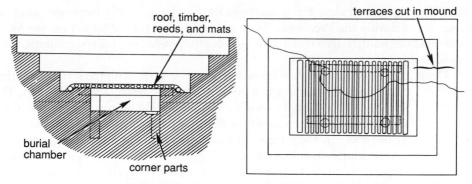

FIGURE 4.17   Mound E-III-3, Tomb 1. Kaminaljuyú. (Adapted from Shook and Kidder, 1952.)

accomplished by covering the entire mound according to plan. (Shook and Kidder, 1952).

Two such tombs were found, both occupying prominent positions in pyramidal structures. Mound E-III-3 is the largest and best-known structure of the Miraflores people. Actually it forms part of a small compact group of nine mounds that were arranged around a plaza. Two other such groups of public buildings have also been identified that contain similar though smaller constructions. Each of these has a high, terraced temple platform and a low, sprawling platform presumed to be the substructure of an elite residence. These buildings constituted what must have been the administrative center adjacent to which the local population lived in a tightly knit group. In turn, these groupings of administrative centers, each with some local residents, were well spaced. Sanders estimates the total population around 5000 (Sanders, 1977).

Kaminaljuyú was kept well supplied with consumer goods. Usulután ware was much in style during these years. Although clay figurines, stamps, and whistles were made in abundance by the Miraflores people, none was found among the numerous articles in the tombs. One can only assume that these were not considered prestigious and were produced only for household use.

The possible significance of toads as a hallucinogenic medium was mentioned earlier in relation to the Gulf Coast Olmec. Another possibility is that they were associated with the ball-game complex (Rose cited in Parsons, 1981). We again encounter the toad or frog represented on stone mortars and pottery bowls among the contents of Tomb 1 at Miraflores. Stone sculpture at Kaminaljuyú reflects the result of a long history of monumental carving shared with the Pacific slopes. The pot-bellies are also found here. The sexless figure commonly represented is fat, heavy-shouldered, and usually clasps his flexed knees. These at Kaminaljuyú were deliberately smashed and suffered heavy damage.

Perhaps slightly later in time belong pedestal sculptures that depict jaguars, monkeys, birds, opossums, armadillos, and some human figures that cap a long square shaft. They are found almost exclusively in the highlands, being most numerous at Kaminaljuyú during the Preclassic. They probably form part of an indigenous local tradition of the southeastern region that includes the pot-bellies, pillars, columns, and pegged sculptures.

The peak of stone sculpture is exemplified by two great sculpted stelae from the Miraflores phase, both of which exhibit some features of Izapa (Miles, 1965; M. D. Coe, 1988; Stirling, 1943). Stela 11 shows a single standing human figure, attired in a cape and bearing four different varieties of the dragon mask. Standing on a platform and observed from above by the sky god, he carries in his left hand a kind of ceremonial hatchet and an eccentric flint like one found in the Miraflores tombs. The most important sculpture is Stela 10, made of black asphalt, which unfortunately was deliberately smashed and mutilated before being buried with Stela 11. It depicts an anthropomorphic jaguar, a human figure, and possibly a god. Below a pair of out-stretched arms is a long hieroglyphic text which cannot be read, looks non-Maya, and is unrelated to any known script. Its estimated date is 100 B.C.–A.D. 200 (Sharer, 1989a). Other sculptures attributed to this period are tenoned or silhouette figures. These stones have a projection at the back that permits them to be embedded in walls or floors.

The glory and luxury evident at Kaminaljuyú signify a high degree of social stratification with wealth, power, and prestige in the hands of an elite few. The trend toward standardization of ritual material and the exclusion of certain artifacts such as figurines from the rich tombs suggest that religion was becoming formalized and rigidly patterned.

Although formal structured ball courts of Preclassic date have been few (Cerros, San Lorenzo?, Chiapas, Oaxaca), the list is growing and the game has been well known from the early Preclassic. Carved slabs representing ball players (Bernal, 1973) are found at Dainzu, and many clay figurines in ball game attire are familiar (see Figures 3.7 and 6.25a). At Kaminaljuyú a composite ball-game marker was found with a burial in the lower levels of the C-II-4 Acropolis along with Arenal phase ceramics. This marker consists of a stone shaft surmounted by a round ring topped by a perforated triangle (Parsons, 1988). Similar objects found at Tikal (Fialko, 1987), at Teothiuacan (Aveleyra, 1963), and at Arcelia (Cepeda, 1970) in the state of Guerrero are thought to be semiportable ball-game markers. The ring of the Kaminaljuyú example is carved with dragon heads in Miraflores styles.

By the succeeding Santa Clara phase (A.D. 300) the great building boom was over; population declined and people fell on hard times.

Salamá Valley Sites

The Salamá Valley is particularly well situated for communication between the southern region and the lowlands. A number of overland trails led to river drainage systems whereby one could travel from the major site of El Portón in the Salamá

Valley over the mountain passes to Kaminaljuyú, to the southern lowlands, or west to Chiapas and the Grijalva drainage basin. Building materials (wood and clay for adobe), schist for *manos* and *metates*, sand and volcanic ash for tempering pottery, and even salt were easily available. Above all jade and obsidian were highland resources within reach (Sharer and Sedat, 1987).

El Portón is located at the head of the Salamá Valley near San Jeronimo, Baja Verapaz, and is the most important of more than a dozen sites in the valley. In the Middle/Late Preclassic period, platforms with adobe-plastered superstructures were raised, and by 400 B.C. El Portón had become the dominant ritual center, possibly with tombs analogous to those of the Miraflores people at Kaminaljuyú.

A major discovery was Monument 1 found in a pit but which had originally stood in front of a low platform with a plain altar. The estimated date of the monument is 400 B.C. This would make it one of the earliest Maya glyphic inscriptions on record. It bears a horizontal row of irregular hieroglyphs that may be an ancient text. Significant features are the single-column format and the absence of day-signs. Only one side of the 2.3-m-high slab of schist was carved, and it had been badly eroded or defaced (?). Aside from these markings, there is a possible dragon mask suggestive of Izapa while other motifs have similarities to Abaj Takalik and Kaminaljuyú. Perhaps this monument can be considered an "ancestral form of Maya writing" (Sharer, 1989a).

Another notable find was a stone-lined crypt containing an adult male (Burial 6) elaborately interred in a mortuary structure. This elite individual, a headman or shaman (?), was buried with jade, shell, and three trophy heads. Twelve retainers had been sacrificed to accompany him.

The architecture, elite goods and crypt, stela-altar combination, and early writing are evidence of a stratified community owing its prosperity to a strategic location affording participation in a large interregional exchange of network.

Another site, Los Mangales, was well positioned on the north edge of the valley where it could control traffic heading north and east. This was a specialized elite mortuary center probably eclipsed by the growth of El Portón. Dates at this site go back to 500 B.C. Belonging to the late Preclassic, however, are two burial chambers of considerable interest. The chambers contained two monuments (Nos. 11 and 14) that had been reused as lintels. Monument 13, a small schist "stela," is the more elaborate and pecked into one face is a horizontal bar with two dots suggesting the numeral 7. Underneath are some other markings and two vertical columns of dots. Monument 14 has a single bar, one dot, and perhaps a second. The burial chamber held an elite individual, additional human skulls, and other artifacts. Ceramics date the material to 500–200 B.C., but because the monuments had been reused as lintels, they are presumably earlier.

A boulder known as Monument 21 on the south side of this valley has engraved and grooved markings that may be an attempt to record numerals in the bar and dot system. These markings might be overlooked were it not that the dots are connected by grooves in a pattern similar to Altar 1 at Chalcatzingo, Morelos. Fragments of pottery at the base of the boulder are of a date around 500–200 B.C. (Sharer, 1989a).

Sakajut, Alta Verapaz

Sakajut in the Cobán region of Alta Verapaz is precisely the point from which native peddlers leave today following the old footpaths north to the Petén and east to the Polochic Valley. It is 4 days travel on foot to Guatemala City and a week or less to the Petén. It probably took no longer in Preclassic days. Close to sources of jade, quetzal feathers, and obsidian, Sakajut functioned as a gateway to the lowlands from the larger centers of El Portón and Kaminaljuyú. Early Xe ceramics reflect interaction with the southern Maya region as well as with the lowlands to the north, but the earliest architecture is of Middle to Late Preclassic date (500–200 B.C. (Sharer and Sedat, 1987). Preclassic remains include five mounds grouped around a plaza across a small river from another similar grouping of eight mounds.

La Lagunita, Upper Chixoy Valley

Another highland–lowland route was to follow the Río Negro to the Río Chixoy and hence to the Pasión River area. La Lagunita at 1200 m elevation, lies 15 km north of Zacualpa and is known from excavation in the 1970s by Alain Ichon (see Sharer, 1989b). The stone monuments here, with the exception of a fragment of an Olmec-derived head, can be related to the Izapa and Kaminaljuyú traditions, although there are indications that La Lagunita was occupied earlier. An important discovery was a tomb (No. 44) that contained a carved stone sarcophagus with a plain yoke. Most extraordinary was the entry chamber stacked with pottery, jade, and other artifacts, while on the staircase itself were 16 greenstone figures arranged as in Cache 4 at La Venta (Sharer, 1989b). The latter contained 16 figurines placed upright in a group surrounding a central figure (Drucker et al., 1959).

The southeastern highlands show great uniformity in the sharing of many details of ceramics, sculpture, and iconography, and concerted efforts have been made to discover some linguistic or ethnic relationship between these peoples. As yet no agreement has been reached. However they expressed themselves verbally, archaeologically it has been shown that there was continual communication and interaction among these groups. Pottery and obsidian moved great distances; close parallels are found in the pot-bellied sculptured monuments, ceremonial complexes, details of 3-pronged censers (Demarest and Sharer, 1986), and figurine styles, believed to reflect household ritual. It is only one step further to speculate that some political understandings were achieved between the two powerful centers in control: Kaminaljuyú and Chalchuapa.

SOUTHERN MAYA LOWLANDS

We will touch here on the major pattern that developed in the central Petén region and Belize that moved the Maya dramatically toward the culmination of the Classic period. These years (300 B.C.–A.D. 300) are sometimes known as Chicanel, a ceramic phase that followed Mamom. Chicanel wares are uniform and standardized with variety achieved by adding wide, everted rims and flanges. Usulután ware was very characteristic as were ceramics with a waxy finish. Toward the end of the period polychrome ceramics appear. Pottery has been and continues to be important in archaeological studies, but will not receive much more attention here as we focus on small kingdoms and the emergence of kingship. This was a period of multicenters, and of general instability.

Improved agricultural techniques were bearing fruit, long distance trade seems to have accelerated, and the growth of a complex, ranked, elite society suddenly replaced the earlier rather egalitarian scene of village communities. Formerly everyone had equal access to imports to judge from the distribution of burial goods, but this was now to change.

The Maya of the southern lowlands developed indigenous patterns simultaneously with the highland and Pacific coast Maya. Many basic religious concepts were shared and both Izapa and the carved monuments of the southeastern highlands were inspirational. The lowlanders did not copy highlanders' art but used art in a different way. Their style was to build massive monumental constructions, some with vaulted stone architecture, at times decorated with huge stucco masks to display a new social order.

In this period (300 B.C.–A.D. 300) art is publicly displayed and massive building programs ensued. Many people moved closer to newly formed centers or raised enormous structures over older remains. This was evidence of a new social system, a reorganization of society in which an elite institution of kingship took charge to interpret and manipulate the prevailing ideology for political ends. The transformation was so complete that the new system was seen as the divinely ordered natural world, uniting all humankind into one elaborate social arrangement that would last for hundreds of years. By A.D. 300 the institution of kingship was firmly in place and was to continue throughout the classic history of the southern lowland Maya.

We will see that this new world order was not restricted to certain environments, resources, or circumscribed areas. The timing, presentation, and ideological expectations fit the needs of the moment. We will see the erection and abandonment of some of the most enormous structures ever built in the Americas. And by A.D. 300 a Maya king records the beginning of a long dynastic history.

Uaxactún

A discussion of the southern lowland Maya area logically begins with Uaxactún in the northeast Petén. It was here that the earliest excavation by the Carnegie Institution of Washington in 1926–1937 set up the basic chronological sequence (based on ceramics, calendrical inscriptions, and architectural development) that has been followed ever since. By extension this chronology has been applied to all Mesoamerica.

The main site is laid out on five low hills surrounded by house platforms. Of particular importance is an arrangement of observatory structures often referred to as the E-Group layout, which is a pattern to be found at many centers. The west building of Group E served as the observation point to sight points at which the sun rose and set on the solstices and equinoxes on three temples aligned on a large platform on the east side of a plaza. These sightings signaled the longest and shortest days of the year (and in some areas meant the initiation of wet and dry seasons).

This E-Group layout has been reported from three sites in the Lake Petén zone (Tayasal, Cenote, and Paxcaman) Chase, 1985b). The earliest example is that at Cenote, possibly predating the one at Uaxactún, and is unusual in that burials were found in the largest building. At the same time the stela cult and tetrapod ceramics appear.

As at many sites, the early structures are often overlaid by later ones and this was true at Uaxactún. Beneath the astronomical observatory of the E-Group lay the well-known E-VII-sub pyramid excavated by the Ricketsons of the Carnegie Institution in the 1920s (Figure 4.18). For many years this pyramid was considered a curious maverick, but is now viewed as representative of its day. This beautiful white stuccoed structure, preserved intact by its later superimposed observatory, measures only 8 m in height and displays 16 giant masks flanking staircases that lead up the middle of all four sides. The pictorial imagery depicts the same celestial cycle of the Sun and Venus to be seen at Cerros, interpreted by Schele and Freidel (1990) as an expression of kingship. The summit once supported a simple pole and thatched-roof temple and the entire radial structure was set in the center of its own plaza.

In the South Plaza a small acropolis (Group H) with six temples lay unseen for years, buried under Early Classic structures. This complex is entered from the west via a short staircase and a small building that acts as a gateway into a central court, such as we will also find at Cerros, Belize. The stairs are flanked by stucco anthropo-

FIGURE 4.18   Pyramid E-VII-sub. Uaxactún, Guatemala. (Model, Neg. No. 125974). (Courtesy of the Department of Library Services, American Museum of Natural History, New York.)

morphic jaguar masks while portraits of the ruler himself are set into the walls of the temple above the entrance (Valdés, 1988).

This practice is a portent of the Classic Period in which we will find royal portraits not so much at entrances to buildings, but sculpted on stelae to stand in front of temples.

The acropolis contains the greatest number of monumental masks of this period. Those on one of low, plastered pyramids (H-sub-3) have a textual format similar to that of Cerros. Here the theme is the sacred mountain monster, Witz, who, rising from a watery habitat in the lower tier, reappears in upper masks with a Vision Serpent emerging from its head (Schele and Freidel, 1990).

We will return to Uaxactún in the Early Classic Period at the time of a conflict with Tikal in the fourth century, after which Uaxactún never fully recovers its early prestige.

TIKAL

The dense Petén jungle could never completely hide the imposing ruins of Tikal and, as often happens, word of them was brought to the outside world by Europeans in the 1800s. The scientific background for field work at Tikal was laid first by the Englishman, Alfred P. Maudslay (1889-1902), and his wonderful photographs and plans made around 1881–1882. Then a German, Teobert Maler (1908-1910), did pioneering work for the Peabody Museum of Harvard University in 1895 and 1904, drawing and photographing everything he could find. A few years later Alfred M. Tozzer was sent down on a special expedition to record further information for the museum and his month at Tikal resulted in a fine joint report with Maler. Thereafter Sylvanus G. Morley, who was primarily interested in recording inscriptions of the Petén monuments, conducted excavations from 1926 to 1937 at the neighboring site of Uaxactún, a half-day's journey by foot from Tikal (Morley, 1937-1938).

By 1956, archaeologists decided that Tikal could wait no longer. The University Museum of the University of Pennsylvania got together with the Guatemalan Government to begin the Tikal Project of explorations with Edwin M. Shook (1957) as its first Field Director. Later it was William R. Coe who saw the Tikal explorations through the final field seasons and publication of the Tikal reports (W. R. Coe, 1956b, 1988, 1990). The entire project hinged on the Guatemalan Government putting in an airstrip, which it did in 1950. All was ready to go in 1956.

The aims of the Project included not only the archaeological excavations, but provided for establishment of a field laboratory, the study of plant, animal, and bird life, and geology and climate of the forest. This turned out to be the most extensive project of its kind ever undertaken, lasting from 1956–1970. While work still continues under the Guatemalans, the government has created a 576-km national park surrounding the site.

Results of the excavations will take years to prepare. Thirty-nine reports are planned. Some of these have already appeared (Numbers 1–13, 19, 31, 33A, and the six volumes of No. 14). Many articles and publications of various kinds, including a dozen dissertations, are available replete with beautiful illustrations and drawings. I have liberally culled from writings by W. R. Coe, 1965a, 1965b, 1975, 1990; Coe and McGinn, 1963; Coggins, 1979a; Schele and Freidel, 1990; Jones, 1984, 1989; Jones and Satterthwaite, 1982; Haviland, 1967; Miller, 1985a; Puleston, 1971, 1979; and Schele and Miller, 1986.

Tikal is special, not only because it has been the object of 14 years of intensive scientific exploration, but because its history embraces the full range of lowland Maya civilization in the south from its modest beginnings to its demise in the ninth century as a major political/dynastic power.

Many details of the art, architecture, and ceramics we have already seen in Belize, the highlands of Guatemala, and on the Pacific Coast, for Tikal was, after all, a product of its earlier Preclassic past with outside stimulation from contacts with far-flung areas. But Tikal adapted what it took and gave it new meaning. Astounding is the apparent will and power to constantly build, demolish, and rebuild, increase size, remodel, or extend as demonstrated in the dramatic construction projects. These changes necessitated full-time specialists, for how could a farmer work even part-time at such massive projects? His crops requiring constant care and vigilance, he helped sustain the laborers, stone masons, sculptors, and painters as well as the elite and nobility who presumably planned, organized, and gave the orders for building programs, and arranged for distant trade relationships to bring in the jade, shells, stingray spines, and other exotic goods that their status and ritual required.

The new building program involved the use of stone masonry architecture, and a special style was developed using so-called apron moldings (a sloping tier with inset corners) for platforms and pyramids that was to become the preferred lowland style. Another innovation was the corbel or "false" arch initially used for roofing tombs (Figure 4.19). Much is made of this type for several reasons. It was the most sophisticated arch known in New World architecture and we believe it was developed by the Maya for their tombs. Later it was used to support roofs of temples, palaces, stairways, and passageways. It is called "false because it lacks the central keystone that can

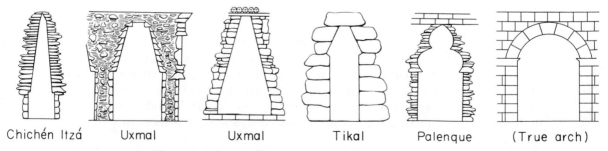

Chichén Itzá   Uxmal   Uxmal   Tikal   Palenque   (True arch)

FIGURE 4.19   The corbeled arch. (Reprinted from Pollock, *Handbook of the Middle American Indians* (1965). Fig. 17. By permission of the University of Texas Press.)

support an enormous weight and permit wide doorways and graceful curves. The corbel arch results in dark, narrow rooms and necessitates thick, massive walls. It is built up from the top of a column or wall, each successive stone jutting slightly out over the one below, eventually closing the gap with a capstone. The corbel vault is always associated with fine Classic Maya architecture.

Tikal expanded from a simple village in 300 B.C. to a huge center recording its dynastic history by A.D. 300.

North Acropolis

The scene is the North Acropolis and the Mundo Perdido (Lost World) Complex, as these are the areas of Tikal that have yielded the bulk of Preclassic remains (see Figures 6.31 and 6.36). The Great Plaza was the ceremonial and geographical center of Tikal, bounded on one side by the North Terrace behind which rises the North Acropolis. The latter is comprised of a series of superimposed rectangular platforms, each connecting to the North Terrace below via one or more stairways. The platforms are neatly faced with plastered masonry walls. To give the reader some idea of the complexity involved, I might point out that by A.D. 700 the flooring of the North Terrace was the eighth to be laid down, of which the first six are of Preclassic date. The 20 plaster floors in the Acropolis gradually raised the last one 10 m over the first. I will not attempt to describe the corresponding series of shrines and temples that were painstakingly erected on each level, only to be subsequently demolished or altered. At Tikal solid foundations were laid of stone and mortar with plastered masonry surfaces. Broad platforms paved with thick graveled and plastered floors surrounded them. The practice of building and renovating directly over earlier structures provides a fine opportunity to detect long sequences of construction. Changes and new constructions can be dated by associated inscriptions, ceramic remains, caches, placement of monuments, and burials. The extensive excavation of the North Acropolis and Great Plaza studied in this context has provided much of the chronological ordering to be related here (Jones, 1989).

The earliest construction of the North Acropolis dates from the Chuen phase (250–100 B.C.).

Building 5D-14   This structure began with a masonry platform (Structure 5D-14) that was subsequently enlarged three times, the final version enclosing three rooms on top, probably roofed with thatch supported by four poles at the corners. This building was burned and refloored. The skeletons of an infant and two adults protected by inverted plates were found in the construction. In an area of destroyed floors a pit cut into the bedrock contained a necklace of shell pendants as well as imported jade and shell beads. Another pit contained disarticulated remains of an adult along with sting-ray spines for self-sacrifice or bloodletting. By the next stage of construction, block masonry was used to form the characteristic apron moldings.

Within a short time a much larger and sophisticated platform 7 1/2 ft. high with multiple stairways supporting a number of stone temples was built, covering all the earlier construction. Keeping the same style with fine apron moldings, but adding stairways, this platform was beautifully designed and neatly plastered, a tribute to the authorities in power, designers, and architects. Nonetheless, before long it too was demolished to make room for another newer North Acropolis platform, nearly doubling the size of the old with the main temples situated toward the north end. This pattern of periodic renovation, demolishing, and rebuilding was to be repeated throughout the history of Tikal (Jones, 1991).

Perhaps the most remarkable and important building of the North Acropolis (Structure 5D-sub-1-1st) was discovered by Ed Shook in 1960. Built about 50 B.C. the pyramidal base was a 2-level platform with a central inset stairway leading to two broad rooms at the summit. The apron moldings were so cleverly integrated as to make an intricate, harmonious structure. Two large jaguar masks flanked the upper stairway and the entire upper façade was finished in a modeled stucco design painted in cream, black, red, and pink. One would approach this stunning construction by passing through a gateway building to the south, after ascending a long staircase from the North Terrace below. These stairs were flanked with stuccoed, polychromed masks.

Burial 166   To the northwest in another cluster of structures within the Acropolis complex, a bright red-orange building (Sub 10) attracted attention. Directly in center front the earliest Tikal cache was found, consisting of a few shell and jade beads. This custom of placing an offering in front of a temple was to become a common practice. Tunneling deeper, Burial 166 had been placed in a vaulted stone masonry tomb in the bottom of a deep cut under the Acropolis platform before Structure Sub 10 was started (W. R. Coe, 1965a,b). To everyone's surprise, the lavish remains in the tomb belonged to a woman, surely of noble status to have been given such a privileged resting place. She had been fully extended on her back and a dismembered skeleton placed beneath her lower legs. The skull of the less fortunate individual was found nearby in a pot.

One wonders who the woman might have been. (If only she had lived in the next century her name and home town might have been recorded in hieroglyphs). Her chamber was littered with exotic goods: 20 pottery vessels, some had held food, others powdered cinnabar, a special import. Jade beads from the highlands, sting-ray spines, and shell from the east coast were treasured objects of the elite. She was further honored by decorating the red plastered walls of the tomb. On the walls six human figures had been outlined in black. The plaster, crudely applied, had flaked and crumbled in places, but enough remained to show some seated figures in profile. Fragments of others show heads with elaborate plumed headdresses and earspools in a style seen at Kaminaljuyú suggestive of Izapa. These figures might represent relatives or ancestors of the deceased.

Burial 167   Other paintings of this period were found in a shrine built about 25 years later. These were produced upon the death of a prominent dignitary that called for another splendid tomb. A new shrinelike building, almost a twin of the main

Acropolis structure, was chosen for this grave (Burial 167). In this case, most of an older shrine had tumbled so a burial chamber could be put right in the middle of the floor. A vaulted chamber was cut out and the deceased, an elegant noble, was installed with all his appropriate wealth. A huge bowl on his chest contained remains of another adult, probably his wife, while an infant lay on its back in another large bowl on his chest. The walls of this tomb were plastered in mud and unpainted. However, the new shrine that was raised directly above it made up for any shortcomings. It was elegantly painted with a series of polychrome frescoes at the four corners of the exterior walls. Although badly damaged when found (perhaps in antiquity), human figures can be seen in fancy dress with grotesque faces, painted in colors of black, red, and yellow over pink. There is even a hint of the hieroglyphic day sign *akbal* tucked in a headdress. The iconography also bears similarities to the Izapan sculptural style of the Guatemalan highlands.

Burial 85   When another high-ranking individual died around A.D. 76, where was he to be interred? The most prestigious location was surely center front of the sacred temple of the most important building of the North Acropolis, Structure 5D-sub-1-1st. The deceased is known only as Burial 85. His skeleton (minus his skull and thigh bones) was tied in a bundle soaked in red cinnabar along with his bloodletting instruments. A greenstone mask with inlaid shell eyes and teeth had probably been sewn to the top of the bundle to replace the skull (?). The 3-pointed headdress on the mask symbolizes royalty, so this was a king! His skull and thigh bones were nowhere to be found, so may have been kept aside to be treasured by his survivors.

Note the presence of sting-ray spines used in bloodletting in these elite graves. Although this was a ritual necessary for all major events that seem to have occurred with some frequency, the health of the nobility does not appear to have been affected. Remains of the elite indicate that they were taller in stature and of more robust constitution than the general populace, probably an indication of better nutrition and the exalted life they led (Haviland, 1967).

In these first centuries A.D. the entire North Acropolis underwent one more of its many renovations. The great East and West Plazas were leveled and paved. The fine tombs and earlier buildings were covered over by new construction. The Acropolis platform now covered nearly two acres facing south across a large open gathering place to a multi-roomed structure on the other side. The well-used path that led into the city may have ended at the East Plaza for as yet there were no paved causeways (Jones, 1991). A new ceramic complex (Cimi) makes its appearance at this point, introducing elegant forms with mammiform feet and polychrome pottery. These ceramics were produced in a gorgeous range of colors, and were (then as now) the most highly prized of all Maya pottery. What inspired this decorated ware is not known.

The earliest figure named at Tikal is a person called Yax-Moch-Xoc. We know he is not the first ruler, but was considered by his descendants to be the founder of the first royal dynasty that ruled this city. Since he left no monuments of his own, his reign is reconstructed from other inscriptions as lasting from A.D. 219 to 238

(Schele and Freidel, 1990). Approximately sixty years later, Tikal's first historic king, Jaguar Paw I (Scroll-Ahau-Jaguar) is depicted on Stela 29 with a Long Count date of 8.12.14.8.15 (A.D. 292). (See Figure 5.9b.) We believe his tomb has been identified southwest of the Main Plaza in an area called the Mundo Perdido.

Mundo Perdido

In the transitional period from Preclassic to Classic, the North Acropolis was apparently not used for royal interments (W. R. Coe, 1965b; Jones, 1991). The site for royal burials seems to have shifted to a ceremonial area known as the Mundo Perdido (Lost World) Complex located southwest of the Great Plaza (See Figure 6.36.) This complex was occupied from the middle Preclassic to the Terminal Classic and excavations in the 1980s have contributed greatly to our knowledge of Tikal history (see Fialko, 1987; Laporte 1987a,b; Laporte and Fialko, 1990).

The first buildings erected were a radial pyramid known as 5C-54, and a rectangular platform to the east between 600 and 500 B.C. The pyramid is thought to be a prototype of the Group E Complex at Uaxactún that was built as an astronomical observatory. The pyramid (5C-54) grew through Tzec and Chuen phases adding elements of talud-tablero construction and monumental masks. A causeway was constructed leading in from the area of the North Acropolis. More masks were added in Cauac (100 B.C.–A.D. 250) when the whole complex underwent a massive expansion and three temples were raised on the East Platform (Laporte, 1987a; Laporte and Vega de Zea, 1988). By A.D. 300 the 5C-54 pyramid had tableros of "great dimension" and new structures had been placed in the northeast corner, old structures remodeled, and a new South Plaza was added along with associated buildings. The final version of the Main Pyramid (5C-54) consisted of 10 terraces and reached a height of 31 m, the tallest structure in all Tikal in the year A.D. 378 (Early Classic). At this time the plan of the East Platform closely resembled a corresponding structure in Group E at Uaxactún supporting three temples.

A significant feature of the Mundo Perdido Complex is the fact that all enlargements were made according to its ritual nature and conformed to the completion of ritual cycles. The orientation of the main structures (Pyramid 5C-54 and the East Platform 5D-84 with its three temples) was placed along a general east–west axis. Caches and burials were regularly and ceremonially aligned with this established axis.

Royalty

Usually Group E layouts do not have residences or burials (Coggins, 1983). Mundo Perdido is the exception as it was the location chosen to inter members of the Jaguar Paw dynasty.

The first royal tomb was found on the east–west axis of Structure 5D-86 (one of the three temples on the East Platform, 5D-86), and was notable for its elaborate construction (vaulting with stone slabs) and sumptuous offerings. Unfortunately, the osteological remains were badly fragmented and many of the burial goods had been removed in the course of construction. It seems possible that this was the tomb of Tikal's first historic king, Jaguar Paw I (Scroll-Ahau-Jaguar), pictured on Stela 29 who reigned from A.D. 278 to 317 (Jones, 1991; Laporte and Fialko, 1990). This stela dated at A.D. 292 (See Figure 5.9b) was found in an area near Temple III, not far from the causeway to Mundo Perdido. A version of the Tikal emblem glyph, one of the earliest on record, appears in the twisted rope in front of his earflare (Schele and Freidel, 1990). His dynastic ancestor floats overhead and kingship symbols are plentiful denoting his rank and power. One of these is a "disembodied" head emerging from a double-headed serpent bar. Schele and Freidel (1990:142) point to this as a symbol of kingship derived from the ancient colossal heads of the Olmec. The stela may have originally been placed on a small radial platform located at the base of the stairs. This platform partially covered a mass grave of 16–17 individuals probably sacrificed in ritual or dedication ceremonies.

Jaguar Paw II, also known as Moon Zero Bird, would logically be the next ruling king whose inauguration is recorded on the Leyden Plaque of A.D. 320. He may be the Jaguar Paw referred to on Stela 31 at A.D. 317. A chamber with a vaulted roof suitable for a ruler was found under the stairs of Structure 5D-86, but it was empty. Either it was never used or had been cleaned out at an early time. Perhaps contemporaneous is a frieze on the back wall of the temple depicting five nude captives with their hands tied together. A similar scene is recorded at Río Azul that would be roughly contemporaneous. There is no evidence that the frieze and unused tomb belonged to Jaguar Paw II, but it is a reasonable supposition.

Six elite burials were placed in the other East Platform, temples at the same time. These were not intrusive but had been made during the renovation. Offerings were similar and of high quality. The largest was Burial PNT-019 placed in the central east–west axis of the main temple. This is believed to be the tomb of the ruler represented on Stela 39, Jaguar Paw III (also known as Jaguar Paw Skull I) who ruled about A.D. 360–378. Among the contents of the tomb was a jade mask incised with the *kin* and *akbal* hieroglyphs, symbols of this dynasty, worn by the ruler on Stela 39.

This stela was found redeposited in the temple above. The individuals in the other five burials may have been prominent members of the Jaguar Paw lineage or close relatives who were sacrificed upon or soon after his death. Jaguar Paw III seems to be the last of this lineage to be buried at Mundo Perdido. Of this ruler we have not only his tomb and Stela 39 but also the legacy of an important residential palace of the Central Acropolis. A carved blackware vessel in its dedicatory cache bears an inscribed text that reads "his house, Jaguar Paw, Ruler of Tikal, 9th Ruler" (Jones, 1991).

Following his death in A.D. 378 we will find dramatic changes in politics, ritual, and calendrical activity at Tikal. Was there a struggle or competition for control of Tikal? There are only hints of military activities— captives depicted on monuments and on the frieze, but no other signs of conflict. All we know at present is that there are no further signs of this dynasty at Mundo Perdido and it may have relocated at nearby Uolantun where the Jaguar Paw iconography appears on Stela 1.

If Jaguar Paw III was indeed the ninth ruler, we are missing some of his predecessors.

They may be among the early elite buried in the North Acropolis that have not yet been identified.

There is however, an early Long Count date inscribed on the Hauberg Stela, unfortunately of unknown provenance, but probably from the Petén region. This is a small stela only 86.8 cm in height with a Long Count date of A.D. 199, which provides the first hieroglyphic text with a named ruler (Figure 4.20). A standing figure (Bac T'ul) is shown in the act of bloodletting, while a Vision Serpent looks down on his head from above. The text tells us that 52 days before his accession, he performed the bloodletting ritual, selected to be depicted here on the stela as the most important event heralding his approaching reign. The inclusion of the Vision Serpent in the scene sanctifies his accession and demonstrates his power (Schele and Miller, 1986).

From this time on we will see the practice of using stelae instead of architecture for recording events and displaying propaganda. It is also a good example of the Maya writing system in which hieroglyphs are combined with a pictorial image of an event

FIGURE 4.20   The Hauberg stela. Small stela, beautifully executed, Petén style. Unknown provenance. A.D. 199. (Photographed by Justin Kerr, 1968. No. 152.)

that are meant to be "read" together. The Hauberg Stela does not give a clue as to where Bac T'ul reigned but we may well find another stela that provides some details of his life and family. It is reasonable to expect to find other hieroglyphic texts of this date as well as earlier ones, for the workmanship and style of the Hauberg Stela reflect many years of sculpting experience.

We are already into the historic period with Jaguar Paw III, to whom we will return later. By now, the North Acropolis was approaching its final layout. The builders already had grandiose plans for the rest of the city as the Great Plaza and North Terrace were laid down in such proportions that no subsequent enlargement was necessary.

What did Tikal look like around A.D. 300? The North Acropolis was huge, incorporating at least 100 buildings. The Great Plaza and North Terrace were as large as they would be in A.D. 700. Tikal was ruled by lords so powerful that they had a huge labor force at their command. It was a period of great pomp and prosperity.

As Tikal and Uaxactún increased their wealth and power we move on to see the activity that had been taking place in the north in a very dramatic form at El Mirador.

El Mirador

Until 1978 no one suspected that the magnitude of a site deep in the Petén jungle would so alter our conception of the early Maya. But such a site was El Mirador where excavations revealed not only the most massive architectural undertaking in the Maya area, but placed its cultural peak in the years around 400 B.C.–A.D.100. This meant that El Mirador had been built, peaked, and declined several hundred years before the traditional "Classic" period in Mesoamerica. Archaeologists began to review their evolutionary concepts of Maya civilization.

El Mirador is located on the northeastern edge of Guatemala near the Mexican border of Campeche and 105 km northwest of Tikal. Here the Maya turned 16 km of Petén swampland and low hills into the most massive concentration of civic and religious buildings in the Maya area (Matheny, 1987; Demarest, 1984a,b,c; Fowler Jr., et al., 1989; Sharer, 1992). The construction is grouped in complexes with large empty spaces in between. Gigantic pyramids, temples, terraces of earthen constructions with superimposed plazas, elegant elite residences, and courtyards were constructed under direction of a strong political hierarchy. There are also reservoirs, causeways, and more modest residences. The city was built over an outcrop of limestone, a resource that facilitated construction and was the only natural resource in the region aside from wood.

The site had been known since 1930 and visited later by Ian Graham who took notes and sketches, but not until 1978 did excavations begin, sponsored by the New World Archaeological Foundation, The National Science Foundation, and the National Geographic Society, which were directed by Ray Matheny and Bruce Dahlin until 1982. Thereafter work was continued by the Harvard University Project and the University of Pennsylvania led by codirectors Arthur Demarest and Robert Sharer and their assistants. The work was made possible by the close collaboration of the Instituto Nacional de Antropología e Historía of Guatemala.

El Mirador seems to have eclipsed its early neighbor Nakbé at the beginning of the late Preclassic Period, perhaps because it had a better supply of water as well as being more easily defended. It was placed so as to be protected on the north and west sides by an escarpment. With a major wall constructed to the east and south, El Mirador was well fortified.

Its monumentality is staggering. Basically the center is divided into a western complex, El Tigre, and Danta to the east. Dominating the western part of the city with a base of 18,000 m, El Tigre Pyramid is the equivalent of 12 stories in height, rising 55 m over the jungle floor to support three structures on top. The tallest of these raises El Tigre to a total height of 18 stories. The stairway is flanked by large composite stucco masks of a humanized head with earflares, jaguar paws, and knotted bundles. These are all symbols believed to relate to rulership, purposely placed and designed to convey a message. This was a form of communication that can be considered an early or proto-writing system that was also used at Tikal, Uaxactún, Cerros, and Lamanai.

The main center or sacred precinct, El Tigre, is composed of an acropolis with temples, terraces, and courts. This performed the usual function of serving as a theater for public pageantry, ritual, and ceremonies. The entire center is interconnected by a system of low walls and elevated causeways. The latter extended out more than 20 km to small settlements such as Nakbé and Tintal and could also have served to monitor or control traffic in and out of the city as needed.

The privileged elite had homes near the temples and public buildings. These were carefully built using cut stone and mortar, beautifully stuccoed, and designed with wide doorways and steps between levels of rooms furnished with sitting benches, sleeping platforms, and a window in the principle room.

The other main group is the Danta Complex on the eastern edge of the site. Wide terraces covered another immense area with the east side supporting the huge Danta Temple built on a natural rise. Here as at Cerros the stairways are flanked with gigantic masks whose iconography dealt with the celestial cycle of the sun. A stone-paved causeway runs for 1 km in an east–west direction leading to a gate in a wall that provides entrance into the western or ceremonial part of the site.

How did these people live and what brought them to choose such a seemingly remote location for their enormous building program? The answers are not all in. El Mirador is as large, certainly more complex, and more densely populated than any of its contemporaries. There is no lake, river, or coastal feature that often dictate the choice of settlement. In fact, water is scarce and rainfall irregular. Agriculture must have been risky and there is no sign that the *bajos* here were used in any sort of *chinampa* arrangement. The economic base is uncertain. It is hard to visualize the sizeable labor force that was required for the buildings program and even harder to imagine how a ruler acquired the political power to bring it about. The peak of construction was probably reached around A.D. 1 when fortifications were built, along with three causeways on the west side.

There are no corbeled arches, no hieroglyphs. Most stelae and altars are left plain. The exception is Stela 2 depicting a standing figure on the front and some sort of dragon on the back. On the basis of stylistic comparison with Kaminaljuyú sculpture, Parsons (1988) dates this stela around 50 B.C. Ceramics show that Mamom wares were typical of the early remains and these continued into the Chicanel period with red and orange jars and bowls, largely monochrome. An imitation Usulután ware is more common than the real thing, but a few examples of the latter do occur in late deposits, probably representing imports from highland Guatemala. An important pottery sherd from a pit in the east plaza of El Tigre has an incised decoration with a symbol also found on Kaminaljuyú stelae and at Abaj Takalik. Mathews suggests it is an early form of the *ahau* (or lord) glyph. If not genuine writing it may be an antecedent (Demarest, 1984b; Fowler, Jr., *et al.*, 1989). Carbon from the pit yielded a date of 250–310 B.C. Some decorated pottery is similar to that at Becán and wares from northern Yucatán.

Red pigment was brought in from Belize and shells from the Caribbean, Pacific, and Gulf coasts, Volcanic ash was used for tempering ceramics. Obsidian figures prominently from the Guatemalan highlands source of El Chayal (Fowler, Jr., *et al.*, 1989) and some green obsidian projectile points were recovered from El Tigre. Prismatic blades was the predominating obsidian industry, confined largely to the elite, suggesting a control of its distribution. No obvious trade route is apparent, but a well-established network somehow moved goods into El Mirador from these areas. As commodities, El Mirador could only offer flint and limestone, easily obtainable elsewhere in the lowlands. Perhaps it provided a welcome way station or redistribution node for trans-Petén commerce in the vast forested area and functioned much as the later ninth century trade network through central Petén (Morley *et al.*, 1983).

By A.D. 300 El Mirador slipped into a gradual decline. Early Classic remains show some fine construction and opulent residences built directly over Late Preclassic structures. There was continued occupation and El Mirador's decline was less traumatic than once supposed. A small population occupied the area in Classic times and minor construction was accomplished, but the diminished late Classic population left only decadent remains of poor quality.

What caused the retrenchment is unclear. A severe drought would certainly have wrought a problem but no catastrophe is apparent. Perhaps the aggressive neighbor Calakmul to the north had a hand in the demise of the great center (Schele and Freidel, 1990:440). In any event we begin to see that cultural growth among the Maya was never a smooth, steady evolution but seemed to go through periods of growth and decline (Willey, 1977a,b). This pattern is repeated with one center after another enjoying a brief cultural peak to be followed by decline or abandonment.

Calakmul   Calakmul is an enormous site equal in area to El Mirador (Folan, Jr. 1990). Located north of El Mirador over the Guatemalan border in the Mexican state of Campeche, this too is a swampy region, often under water in the rainy season. Calakmul is best known for its abundance of Classic inscribed stelae and its participation in the Classic wars of the Petén. But earlier remains span these years from the Middle Preclassic to Terminal Classic.

Calakmul may be the "snake site" or Site Q, a kingdom named in the inscriptions. Or the snake-head emblem glyph might refer instead to El Perú, a Petén site west of Tikal (see Schele and Freidel, 1990; Culbert, 1991a).

Calakmul stretches out along the western edge of a great depression or *bajo* of 24 km in length by 8 km in width. It is built over and around a large natural hill 35 m high surrounded by arroyos, *bajos*, and canals, In many ways it resembles the site of Cerros in Belize, only here everything is magnified.

A canal system encircles the core section of town. A 6-m-high wall, 2 m thick still stands for more than a kilometer along the northern limits. The date of this construction is uncertain but it may be contemporaneous with the moat at Becán, A.D. 100-250. Adams (1981) points out a line of military features formed by Becán, Oxpemul, Calakmul, and El Mirador extending in a rough northeast–southwest line (See Map 6.6). Is this a coincidence? Possibly. Somehow southwest of the "line" centers are much less important. The Calakmul wall could have been designed to discourage intruders from Laguna de los Términos on the Gulf coast.

Folan postulates that El Mirador and Calakmul could have grown up side by side, developing into an early Maya regional state embracing a territory of more than 10,000 km. Folan visualizes a moiety-type social organization that both united and separated Calakmul and El Mirador. It is true that both Structure 2 at Calakmul and El Tigre at Mirador depict the same ancestral deities. When El Mirador failed, perhaps Calakmul assumed its prominent position (Folan, Jr. 1990). Another likely possibility was Tikal (Culbert, 1988a).

Río Azul

The settlement of Río Azul in northeastern Guatemala (Map 6.6) took place around 1000 B.C. but was rather undistinguished until the late Preclassic. In 1983 the site received urgent attention after some extraordinary painted tombs had been opened by looters. After five years of excavations (1983–1988) directed by Richard E. W. Adams, we now know that large and small housemound clusters were strung out along 5 km of the east bank of the Río Azul. Around A.D. 250 two major temples were constructed, not around a plaza with other monumental buildings, but in two areas of rather humble dwellings. In addition, there is a small hilltop settlement accompanied by considerable landscaping, leveling, and stair construction.

Although no elaborately decorated structures have been reported, the archaeological evidence shows a familiar pattern of a wealthy elite emerging from local families "reinforced by ancestor worship ceremonialism" (Adams, 1990). Later we will see that the location of Río Azul, being equidistant from Tikal and El Mirador on a river route to Belize, was not to be overlooked by the commercial and military interests of Classic predators.

BELIZE

Belize is on the leading edge of Mesoamerican recent developments. Once thought to be a remote region marginal to the core of Maya civilization, Belize is now providing some vital evidence concerning early growth, revealing details of Classic Maya history, and altering traditional views on the renowned Maya "collapse."

Belize is basically divided in half by the Belize River, separating the southern area of high hills, steep slopes, and short seasonal rivers from the north, a much flatter, but undulating surface with long year-round rivers. In general, most of the known archaeological sites lie between the northern Río Hondo and New Rivers: Projects of Cerros, Río Hondo, and Corozal. Further south are Lamanai and Altun Há and sites of the middle Belize Valley. (Willey *et al.*, 1965). The far south has received less attention but work at Caracol, Lubaantún, and Pusilhá is closing the gap.

The people of Belize kept up with current trends and events in the hinterlands. At Cuello the old Platform 34 was renovated and enlarged. Archaeologically the early Mamom ceramics of Belize were superseded by the latest Chicanel-styles. There are strong ties between sites in northern Petén and northern Belize.

Diane and Arlen Chase (1989) point to Maya ideology to explain the growth of Maya civilization, as opposed to other suggestions based on long-distance trade (Sanders and Price, 1968) or exchange based on resources of differing ecological niches (Rathje, 1971; Andrews, 1984). The Maya visualized a world floating in water (Schele and Freidel, 1990; Reilly III, n.d.; Chase and Chase, 1989). The important bloodletting ritual required instruments such as sharks' teeth, sting-ray spines, and other marine products. The procurement of these items would have stimulated inland–coastal trade. It follows that Belize with easily navigable rivers and its great barrier reef could provide these necessities. Cerros and Santa Rita Corozal at the mouth of the New River and Chetumal Bay were positioned to handle this trade. It may have been preferable to live at sites like these, with access to marine products but away from the open sea that might be a portal to the Underworld.

Cerros

Cerros grew from early beginnings near a lagoon where a stone platform is all that remains of an ancient docking facility. A simple village of perhaps 30 dwellings was so successful in procuring marine-estuary resources and fostering exchange that an elite emerged that was able to organize a labor force that developed raised-field agriculture, built an extensive water-control system, and engaged in massive monumental construction. Cerros at 50 B.C. had adopted the social innovation spreading throughout the Maya lowlands: the institution of kingship (Cliff, 1988).

In the course of two generations, the labor of fishermen, farmers, stonemasons, and the spiritual guidance of religious leaders created stone-faced temple/pyramids decorated with a pictorial imagery to glorify and enhance the power of a king. The buildings at Cerros have a rather scattered arrangement, roughly north–south. Pyramids are accompanied by plazas. This urban renewal began around 50 B.C. at which time a small temple, now known as Structure 5C, was built over the old village at the water's edge. Its pyramid was built of rubble faced with smooth stone blocks. Massive modeled stucco masks were placed in four panels to the right and left of a staircase on the two levels and painted in red, pink, black, and yellow on a cream-colored background. The two lower masks depict the Jaguar Sun God, so placed that the rising sun emerges from the sea in the east, and sets into the sea on the west. The upper masks are believed to represent Venus as the Morning and Evening Star. The temple was therefore a kind of model of the sun's daily path.

A long staircase extended south from the center of the pyramid giving it a T-shaped plan. This was designed as a public stage, low enough that as the king gradually mounted this path of power into the sacred world, he was in full view of the community.

At the same time, the iconography portrays a subtle message. The Maya first established kingship by honoring their gods and then declared the king to be their direct descendant and spiritual manifestation. Kingship is portrayed at Cerros as three points on the crown of the upper masks of gods. In glyphic writing this sign of kingship is a glyph for *ahau*, "lord," a person of authority from whose ranks a king was chosen. At Cerros there are no hieroglyphs but this early art was designed to be "read." Although not everyone would understand all the imagery, some part of it would have been recognized and appreciated by the community (Schele and Freidel, 1990).

Kingship was the result of cooperation between all the people of the community who had labored long and hard to create it. It was a new social phenomenon which took root in Maya society and is manifested at other sites of this period such as Lamanai, El Mirador, Tikal, and Uaxactún.

At Cerros, Temple 5C was but the beginning. A new temple/acropolis (Structure 6) followed, three times larger and more complex in plan. Here a gigantic plaza was raised, 48 ft. above ground level in front of a pyramid where bloodletting and sacrifice would be seen only by the elite accommodated by the plaza. A staircase then led from here to a taller, more complex temple. Imagery was similar to that of the early temple (Structure 5C) but unfortunately the masks are badly eroded and difficult to read.

Below the summit of Structure 6, a rich cache was found containing royal jades and jewels, mosaic hematite mirrors, red spiny oyster shells, and drinking cups. These treasures were probably buried by a ruler as a link to his predecessor, presumably his ancestor, and also to dedicate the new edifice. This is the kind of act we will see repeated as a common practice among Maya royalty.

Finally, Structure 4, the largest of all, measuring 60 m at the base and 22 m high, was erected. This building held a mortuary chamber at the top, constructed with an early corbel-vaulted roof. Other temples and platforms were subsequently added, along with two ball courts where ritual war and sacrifice were enacted.

The ball courts were constructed between 400 and 150 B.C., very early for the southern Maya lowlands. They were not associated with elite residences, but help define the north–south axis of the central layout. The southern one was built with inclined benches facing the plastered floor of the playing alley, and probably had central markers. The southern court was built with massive end-zone structures (Scarborough *et al.*, 1982).

For reasons unknown, no ruler was ever buried in the mortuary chamber prepared for him in Building 4, nor was any offering placed at the summit. By A.D. 50, kingship was over at Cerros. Why it failed is not known, but the end was abrupt and once over, the elite returned to the countryside. The remaining populace, after burning and smashing what they could, resumed their former life of fishing and farming (Schele and Freidel, 1990). Across Chetumal Bay, Santa Rita Corozal would grow to take Cerro's place.

Elsewhere in Belize

Although many Preclassic sites in Belize are still imperfectly known, some are outstanding for special features. By A.D. 250, Santa Rita Corozal was a vibrant center with a stratified society and had replaced Cerros in the coastal–inland trading system. At Kuhunlich, a well-preserved stuccoed pyramid shows evidence of kingship and royalty with huge masks of the Sun God and other deities. To the southeast at Altun Há, Structure C-13 started out as a small platform in the late Preclassic times and was enlarged by a superimposed construction during the Classic Period. This single building seems to have served the ritual needs of the entire community for a long time (Pendergast, 1979–1982). At Lamanai, Pendergast (1981) has found great wealth and enormous buildings, one of which is similar to E-VII-sub of Uaxactún, indicating kingship. A few exotic items have been found on Moho Cay and sites on Colson point further south. Barton Ramie and Mountain Cow are sites well known for early studies of settlement patterns.

One of the most beautiful jade objects known is from Pomona, a small site in Stann Creek Valley in central Belize. Now in the British Museum and known as the Pomona earflare, it measures 18 cm in diameter with a large central hole and wide obverse flare. Certainly too large to have been worn, it may have been mounted on a headdress or simply treasured as an object of very high status. It is carved with four deity heads in a familiar cosmogram and is undoubtedly a sacred ritual object (see Hammond, 1987; Justeson *et al.*, 1988). Suggested dates range from the first century B.C. to A.D. 250.

At the site of Holmul (eastern Petén) early vaulted chambers were built underground, preceding the use of the corbel arch for rooms, the sequence seen at Tikal.

THE NORTHERN REGION FROM THE GULF TO THE CARIBBEAN

The central region of Yucatán was a scene of growing conflict. Whether domains were expanding or competing for land or control of resources and exchange monopolies is not clear. Amid Campeche's swampy *bajos* the ruling authority at Becán gave the order to construct an enormous ditch. This famous moat or dry ditch was 16 m in width × 5.3 m deep with a circumference of 1.9 km. The inner parapet formed a vertical wall of 5 m, so from the bottom of the moat, any intruder was confronted with a combined obstacle of nearly 11 m in height. Seven causeways or natural limestone bridges led across the great ditch to Becán itself. This is the most outstanding defensive system of the Maya on record, and the labor required for its construction is staggering to contemplate (Webster, 1976).

If one were to travel from Laguna de los Términos on the Gulf Coast, to Chetumal Bay on the east coast, Becán would lie on the shortest route (See Map 6.5). At the time of its great ditch it was already an important society with a civic-ceremonial center. This included a good-sized 14-m-high platform along with smaller buildings. Stone masonry and stucco were used in construction but there are no vaulted tombs or rooms, and no elaborate façade decorations. The fame of Becán lies in its fortifications. One wonders what relations it might have had with the precocious Calakmul only 60 km to the south.

As Becán is remembered for its defenses, so Edzná to the northwest is noted for an extensive hydraulic system of 22 km of canals, moats, and artificial ponds. There is a large pyramid and entire Preclassic settlement just west of a later palace structure. The large canal that extends out from the palace possibly to the Champotón River was begun very early and greatly improved in the late Preclassic. The water-filled moat also served defensive purposes as at Becán.

Edzná today is easily reached by road that connects to the main highway between Champotón and Mérida. This is a site best known for its late Classic palace structure of five stories, but the cultural peak of Edzná was actually reached in the late Preclassic Period. Thereafter, as is true of a number of sites in Yucatán, the activity diminished after A.D. 300 (Matheny *et al.*, 1983).

Only in the last few decades have we become aware that the northern Maya lowlands were equally active in late Preclassic years. It is now clear that northern Yucatán paralleled the southern regions in growth of large centers and building massive architectural aggregations and complex centers by 300 B.C.

The major development took place on the northern plains where Dzibilchaltún outstripped every other site. Buildings were erected in great number and size. A single acropolis with a heavily stuccoed block masonry building (Structure 450) was raised facing a large courtyard enclosed by walls. Façades were not carved or decorated. Nor do we find them at nearby Komchén where an earlier temple-platform was now greatly enlarged. Fortunately Komchén was never covered by later constructions which greatly facilitates its exploration.

The quantity of jade and exotic luxury goods from this area indicates the presence of an elite that probably owes its wealth to the local salt industry. Long-distance merchants could have arrived either by land or sea. Ball (1977a,b) thinks that the sudden prosperity of northern Yucatán could also have been brought on by population pressure that led to competition for limited agricultural land. Whatever the cause, the economic boom was short lived at Dzibilchaltún, for like Edzná, it fell on hard times by A.D. 250. Its bankruptcy at this time was not general, however, for some centers continued on unaffected. Perhaps a monopoly of exotic products built on coastal traffic was undercut by an overland route through the central region (Freidel, 1978).

Yucatán sites are both scattered and numerous. At Yaxuná, a pyramid over 18 m high with a base of 61 × 12 m was built of cut stone masonry and undoubtedly sustained a temple on top, although no remains of it have survived. Dzibilnocác raised stone walls in addition to a pyramid. Chicanel-type pottery associated with it is covered with the waxy slip so common in the Petén. At the same time, a northern plain opaque ware was circulating (Nelson, 1973). Pottery throughout this area was mainly a variation of Chicanel regional styles.

What of royal symbols and kings? At present the best evidence of kingship is found southeast of Mérida at Acanceh, where a massive four-sided pyramid is decorated with a monumental stucco mask as at Cerros. And the well-known bas-relief of Loltún Cave in the Puuc region is now thought to represent a Maya king in full regalia wearing an early variant of the 3-pointed headdress (E. Gonzalez L., 1987; Freidel and Schele, 1988). Dating has been uncertain until recently, but Schele and Freidel (1990) feel confident it can be considered late Preclassic.

SUMMARY

The years between 300 B.C. and A.D. 300 mark the coming together of the main features that characterize Mesoamerican civilization. In Chapter 3 we saw the basic pattern formed: a strong ruler in one place, an early hieroglyph in another, monumental construction at certain sites. During the 600 years prior to A.D. 300, all the ingredients are blended together. A multitude of sites appear in the Maya region. West of the Isthmus, Teotihuacan is the greatest power in the central highlands; in Oaxaca it is Monte Albán.

In general it was a time of great prosperity and growth. It is marked by a great number of regional centers with lively interaction between highlands and lowlands seen in exchange of resources and exotic goods. Societies are ranked and stratified; power and authority reflect a strong ideology, permitting the assemblage of great labor forces. Wealth is much in evidence in lavish graves, caches and offerings, tomb construction, palaces, and fine residences. Sites are oriented according to cosmological planning. Formal ball courts begin to appear (Cerros and in Chiapas) but the game had been known from very early Preclassic times. Dainzú depicts ball-players on bas-reliefs and a ball-game marker at Kaminaljuyú will soon have a counterpart at the Mundo Perdido. Fortifications, mostly walls and moats, indicate competition and conflict (El Mirador, Calakmul, Tikal, Becán, Edzná, Monte Albán, Puebla-Tlaxcala); capture and sacrifice of victims is portrayed most often in art, but at Teotihuacan actual graves of sacrificed warriors were found. Warfare was a matter of raids and skirmishes at this time.

By A.D. 300 Long Count dates are known from Tres Zapotes, La Mojarra, Abaj Takalik, El Baúl, and from Tikal's Stela 29 and the Hauberg stela. The matter of calendrics and writing becomes more complex from now on. A simple explanation of the calendar, methods of time-keeping, hieroglyphic writing, and the recording of events are the subject of Chapter 5.

SPECIFICS OF CHAPTER 4

By A.D. 300 Teotihuacan is a city of about 80,000 and controlled the entire Basin of Mexico.

Monte Albán achieves statehood by A.D. 200.

The corbeled vault appears in southern lowland Maya construction.

In northern highland Guatemala, a number of sites (Los Mangales, El Portón, La Lagunita, Sakajut) exhibit stone-carvings with proto-writing.

The volcanic eruption of Mt. Ilopango ends the prosperous economic boom at Chalchuapa and the Zapotitán Valley.

E-Group arrangements are constructed in the Lake Petén zone, Uaxactún, and Mundo Perdido.

Tikal expands to become a huge center constantly remodeling. Main focus is the North Acropolis with elite burials.

The Mundo Perdido is an important ceremonial complex with graves of the Jaguar Paw dynasty.

The institution of kingship may have begun earlier at Nakbé (?) but is prominent at this time in the iconography of temple/pyramids faced with large stucco masks (El Mirador, Cerros, Lamanai, Uaxactún, Tikal).

Talud-tablero style construction (Mundo Perdido, Puebla-Tlaxcala, Teotihuacan).

CHAPTER 5

Códices, Calendrics, and Maya Writing

BOOKS, CALENDRICS, AND WRITING

We will pause here in our march through history to highlight those features that set Mesoamerica apart from all other American cultures: calendrics and writing, elements considered essential to all high cultures.

The passing of time was recognized by all Mesoamericans for the movements of the celestial bodies guided humans' lives, dictated agricultural activities of planting and harvesting, and influenced the scheduling of important ceremonial and ritual events and various anniversaries. They also provided the basis for prognosticating the future, for Mesoamericans were astrologers as well as astronomers.

Glyphs were carved on vertically set shafts of stone called stelae, on stone altars, stairways, benches, and lintels. Occasionally some inscriptions are found carved on shell, bone, or semiprecious stones. Others were worked in stucco or painted on pottery, on the walls of temples and tombs, and in the books called códices, a kind of picture album.

Maya hieroglyphs may occur singly, in groups, arranged in a row or in multi-rows forming long texts. Some convey information about the calendar, cycles of time, the role of the sun, moon, and planets along with presiding deities. Other inscriptions reveal names of people and places, information about genealogies, conflicts, ritual, and religious practices.

In this chapter we will first examine the books and methods of time-keeping that were shared by all Mesoamericans and continue thereafter with the development of hieroglyphic decipherment in the Maya area.

THE CÓDICES

Of the thousands of códices that must have existed, precious few have survived to the present day. Many must have been destroyed by climatic conditions of changing degrees of humidity and temperature, and we know that others were purposely burned by the Spaniards in an effort to destroy all vestiges of the native religion.

Códices were made by gluing together pieces of bark paper to form a long strip and then folded like a screen. Bark paper (or more accurately cloth) served not only for making the códices but also for ceremonial clothing, flags, and banners and various ritual purposes. Appearing on central Mexican tribute lists, bark paper was cherished and there is abundant evidence that scribes who wrote the códices were highly regarded by society. The paper was prepared from the inner bark of a variety of trees. First pounded, the fibers were then separated by soaking in lime water or boiled with ashes, and then beaten to form a smooth surface. Once dry, the paper was whitewashed with a thin coat of limestone or gypsum-based paste at which point the page was ready to be painted. This process and technology is the same used in southeast Asia about 2500 years ago, and is one of a number of items believed by some to have been transferred to Mesoamerican by sea (Tolstoy, 1991). Sometimes deer skin was used, but demand often exceeded supply and the bark of the amate or fig tree was more commonly used.

The códices in existence today are located in museums and libraries of Mexico and Europe and date from late Postclassic days into Colonial times. The majority come from either highland central Mexico or the Mixteca region of Puebla and Oaxaca. The latter are the most numerous and in addition to calendrics, they provide information about ritual, religion, genealogies, and some aspects of daily life (see page 419). Maya códices deal almost exclusively with astronomy and ritual.

Maya Códices

Only four pre-Conquest Maya códices are known at present of Postclassic date, and one recently discovered ceramic codex dates to the Classic period.

The Dresden Codex (Figure 5.1) is the finest and most useful of the four books. It somehow made its way from coastal Yucatán to Vienna around 1519 and has remained abroad ever since, being presently located in Dresden, Germany. Made of amate paper, it is 39 pages in length, painted on both sides with tabulations of the planet Venus for consultation, and contains astronomical and astrological information

FIGURE 5.1   Codex Dresden, page 50, dealing with astronomical matters. Deities above, a warrior in the center, and an individual wounded by a spear through his shield in the right-hand corner. (From Códices Maya, edited by J.A. Villacorta, 1930.)

as well as prophesies. Opinions vary as to its age, ranging from A.D. 1250–1345 (Lee, Jr., 1985).

A second codex known as the Codex Tro-Cortesiano, now in Madrid, is not complete, nor is it as finely executed as the Codex Dresden. Much of it is not understood and it probably contains some errors. Also drawn on amate paper, it is 56 pages long.

The third codex, Codex Peresiano (Paris) dates from the period of Mayapán's supremacy in Yucatán (A.D. 1200). It deals with predictions and prophesies and gives a sequence of 20-year periods (katuns) and prescribes certain ceremonies. Since some of the drawings resemble the art of Tulum and Mayapán, it may be of east coast origin (?)

In 1971 a fourth codex known as the Grolier Codex surfaced in Mexico City. Its history is somewhat sketchy, but it is said to have been found by looters in a dry cave in the northern part of the state of Chiapas, perhaps near Palenque. It had been placed in a wooden box along with a mosaic mask. Its romantic appearance raised doubts concerning its authenticity but it is widely accepted today and is dated at A.D. 1230. It contains an almanac based on the planet Venus and depicts gods and daily ritual. The pages have deteriorated but the original may have consisted of about 20 pages. The deity figures are beautifully drawn in a Toltec-Mixtec style (Coe, 1973).

Remains of another codex were recovered in 1987 under extraordinary preservation conditions at the site of Cerén, San Salvador. It was found where it had been left on a bench in a communal building when the Laguna Caldera volcano erupted in A.D. 600. Tests reveal it had been sized with kaolinite and painted with cinnabar and iron pigments, but the text itself could not be recovered.

It was a surprise to find a "pottery codex" that recently came to light in a private collection. Known as the Wright Codex, it is a rectangular vessel, 10 in. high, and is probably of Guatemalan origin. Each of the four sides represents the page of a codex with rows of hieroglyphs and mythological figures. This is the earliest codex known (A.D. 600–900) and judging from the high quality of workmanship, writing must have been developed long before this time (Marilyn Goldstein, personal communication).

OTHER EARLY MAYA BOOKS

Although not códices, other valuable sources of information on ancient Maya life are preserved in the books of the Chilam Balam, which were compiled in the Colonial Period after the Indians had learned to write with the Spanish alphabet (Roys 1933). The word Chilam is derived from the name of a famous Maya prophet living around the end of the fourteenth century. Various communities wrote down their own traditions and after the Conquest these hieroglyphic texts were transcribed into the Yucatec language using Spanish script. Best known of these books are the Chilam Balam of the three towns of Chumayel, Tzimín, and Maní. The books contain prophecies and bring out the importance of cyclical events, the anxieties associated with the onset of a recurring unlucky katun.

The Popol Vuh, literally "Book of the Community" of the highland Maya, is a treasured collection of documents on mythology, astronomy, history, and religion, and contains the legends of the Quiché and Cakchiquel people. The original Quiché manuscripts have never been found, but are believed to have consisted of pictorial writings or paintings. An anonymous transcription was made in the Quiché language about 1554, and modern versions are based on this document (Recinos, 1950; Tedlock, 1985).

TIME-KEEPING: THE CALENDAR ROUND

The Calendar Round was known and observed by all Mesoamericans as their basic time-keeping system. The primary unit of time was the day. Neither the Maya nor any other Mesoamerican group broke time down further into hours, minutes, or seconds. Two recurring cycles of time (a 260-day cycle and a solar year of 365 days) ran simultaneously. Together they make up a period of 52 years called the Calendar Round.

The 260-day cycle (Sacred Round: Maya Tzokin; Aztec Tonalpohualli), a kind of ritual almanac with very ancient roots, was primarily religious and divinatory in purpose and was consulted for guidance in daily affairs. This cycle was composed of 20 named days (Figure 5.2) which ran consecutively, combined with recurring numbers from 1 to 13. In order for the exact combination of name and number to come around again, 260 days (20 × 13) would have to pass. This cycle is not based on any natural phenomenon and we do not know how to account for its invention. Even today this march of days is observed among some groups of southern Mexico and highland Guatemala who consult a priest for his reading of the sacred almanac.

The other cycle resembled our solar year of 365 days (Maya Haab; Aztec Xíhuitl). This was made up of 18 named months (Figure 5.3) of 20 days each (18 × 20 = 360), plus 5 additional days of apprehension and bad luck at the end of the year (Maya Uayeb; Aztec Nemontemi). Days were numbered from 0–19. These two cycles ran concurrently like intermeshed cogwheels, and to return to any given date, 52 years (18,980 days) would have to pass.

It is generally believed that the calendar evolved prior to a writing system, although we have a rich corpus of early hieroglyphs that do not bear numerals or dates. Its place of origin is also unknown, but it may have been a lowland environment since fauna represented in the glyphic names include creatures such as crocodile, monkey, and jaguar.

Most Mesoamericans were satisfied to locate a date within this 52-year period of the Calendar Round. But the Maya worked out a distance calendar that permitted them to record dates in the ancient past, or into the future. To accomplish this, they found they needed a symbol for completion, a "zero."

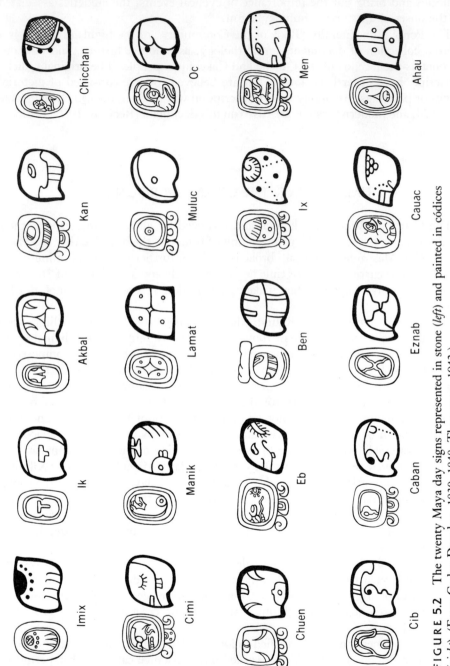

FIGURE 5.2 The twenty Maya day signs represented in stone (*left*) and painted in códices (*right*). (From Codex Dresden, 1830–1848; Thompson, 1942.)

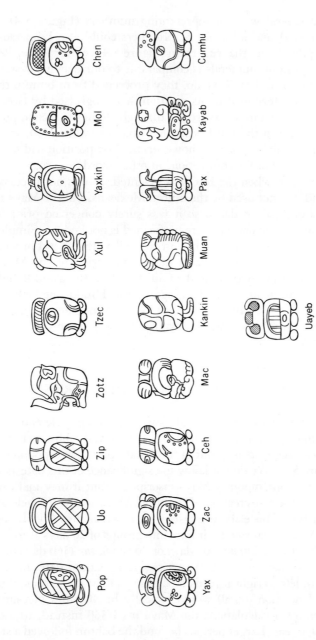

FIGURE 5.3 The eighteen Maya months with five remaining days (Uayeb). (From Morley, 1915.)

147

THE MAYA "ZERO," NUMBERS, AND COUNTING

The Maya had several ways of representing numbers (Figure 5.4). The most common was a dot for 1 and a bar for 5. Numbers could also be personalized by glyphs representing the deities that rule them (Figure 5.4, center; Jones, 1984). Their vigesimal system of position numerals is comparable to our decimal system. Instead of progressing from right to left as we do, they proceeded from bottom to top. The value of each unit was determined by its position that progressed by twenties. That is, the first position included numbers from 1 through 19; in the second position each unit had the value of 20; in the third position a unit was worth 400, and so on. In order to write a number higher than 19, however, the first position had to be filled by either a number or a symbol for completion, in other words a zero.

We do not know just when the zero was invented. It was not necessary for the Calendar Round and was not used by the central Mexicans, but the Maya needed the concept to record Long Count dates, so it was surely conceived prior to the first century B.C. How actual calculations were performed is not known. Simple additions and subtractions may have been scratched in the soil with the aid of some kind of counter. The invention of the zero was a major innovation of the Maya. To our knowledge it was invented only twice in the Old World, in India and Babylonia. The Maya zero may have been in use as long ago as the Hindu one, whose origin is estimated around 500 B.C. We have no recorded Long Count dates of that age, but the fully developed calendrical system was known by the second century A.D. and surely had long antecedents.

THE MAYA LONG COUNT (INITIAL SERIES)

Most peoples were satisfied with calculating the 52-year cycle and being able to place a date accurately within that span of time. The Maya however, related each Calendar Round to a fixed starting point in the distant past, corresponding to August 13, 3114 B.C. (Figure 5.5). We do not know the significance of this date as it is earlier by centuries than any contemporary Maya inscription, but it may mark some event in mythology such as the last creation of the three Maya worlds (Schele and Miller, 1986; Hammond, 1988). This elaborate system is known as the Maya Long Count or Initial Series. The Maya organized their time into groups of 20 days as follows: *baktun* (144,000 days or 20 katuns); *katun* (7200 days or 20 tuns); *tun* (360 days or 18 uinals); uinal (20 days or kins); *kin* (one day). We write a Long Count date, for example, as 9.14.8.0.0, and from left to right it reads 9 baktuns, 14 katuns, 8 tuns, 0 uinals, and 0 kins. The second position (uinal) would logically be 400 in a vigesimal system, but for use in calendrical calculations the Maya used 360 instead, to more closely approximate the solar year. Larger periods beyond the baktun followed a strict vigesimal system.

The most common stela inscription shows a large introductory glyph representing the patron deity of the current month, typically heading two vertical rows of hiero-

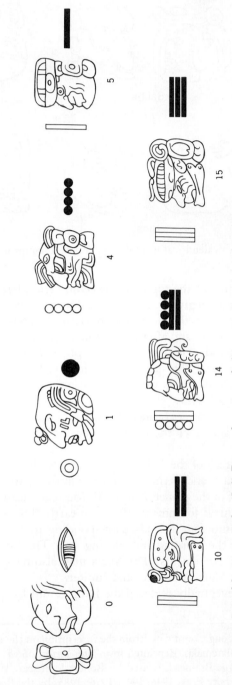

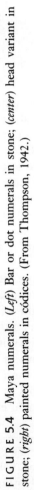

FIGURE 5.4 Maya numerals. (*Left*) Bar or dot numerals in stone; (*center*) head variant in stone; (*right*) painted numerals in códices. (From Thompson, 1942.)

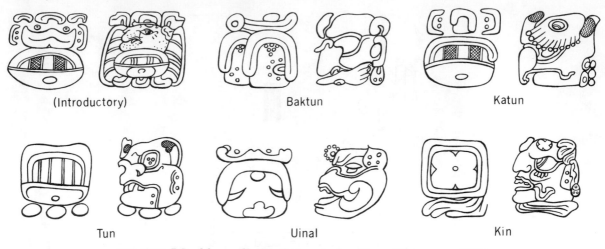

(Introductory)   Baktun   Katun

Tun   Uinal   Kin

FIGURE 5.5   Maya calendrical hieroglyphs. (From Thompson, 1942.)

glyphs (Figure 5.6). Beginning at the top and proceeding from left to right are the baktun, katun, tun, uinal, and kin glyphs, each prefixed by a coefficient. Immediately following is a glyph that represents the sacred round day in the 260-day cycle reached by the recorded Long Count date, and after approximately 8 more glyphs, the corresponding month glyph is found. The intervening glyphs tell us which of the Nine Lords of the Night presides over the specified day involved and the length of the current lunar month (29 or 30 days), as well as indicating the phase of the moon on the date reached by the Long Count.

A secondary series may sometimes be included within a text. These glyphs record distance numbers, that is, announce the exact number of days and 360-day years between two dates.

In addition to keeping track of the 365-day year, the 260-day cycle, the phase of the moon, the presiding deity, and perhaps distance numbers, the Maya were also interested in the movements of the planet Venus. All Mesoamericans considered this planet to be sinister and a threat to humans' affairs on earth. The Maya divided the Venus cycle of 584 days into four periods corresponding to the appearance and disappearances of Venus as the morning and evening star. The Dresden Codex has lengthy tabulations of these movements. The Maya may also have understood and observed the movements of Mars, Mercury, and Jupiter.

The Maya of Yucatán eventually replaced the Long Count by a shorter system.

FIGURE 5.6   Example of a Long Count date, from the inscription on the east side of Monument 6 (Stela E), Quiriguá, Guatemala. (Reprinted from *The Ancient Maya, Fourth Edition*, by Sylvanus G. Morley and George Brainerd; revised by Robert J. Sharer. With permission of the publishers, Stanford University Press 1946, 1947, 1956, 1983, by the Board of Trustees of the Leland Stanford Junior University.)

INITIAL SERIES
Stela E, Quiriguá

This abbreviated system (Short Count) started from the end of katun 13 Ahau and used only tuns and katuns. A 13-katun period was the time span of greatest concern. Prophecies, most of which were unlucky, were associated with each katun. The Maya believed that in recurring cycles, events were expected to repeat themselves, leading to a fatalistic attitude.

DECIPHERING MAYA HIEROGLYPHS

Aside from calendrics, what can be said about all the remaining hieroglyphs that are found scattered between dates and form long texts of their own? These are often accompanied by scenes of elaborately attired figures engaged in some activity.

The decipherment of these hieroglyphs does not consist of studying a list of signs with a meaning for each. It is the combination of pictorial imagery with hieroglyphic decipherment that gives a pattern "inherent in Maya art" (Schele and Miller, 1986). These patterns in imagery follow certain rules as do the hieroglyphs. This is the "key to understanding Classic Maya art." A primary pattern used to construct Maya history is provided by the dates on the stone monuments. Usually the dates recorded are found to be contemporary with the images of people portrayed. One must consider the pictorial scene together with the hieroglyphs to understand the "embedded text" the artist intended to reveal. The art is always meaningful. The verb or activity may well be provided by the image, as, for example, cases where the scene depicts bloodletting, accession to power, or publicizing a victory. Events showing sacrifice, ritual, or a ball game illuminate and complete the text. Although attempts at establishing a phonetic relationship in the glyphs had been discouraged for years, finally linguists found that by linking the ancient inscriptions with a spoken language (Chol or Yucatec), some signs represented whole words and others made a single syllabic sound: consonant plus vowel. Thus Maya writing is seen as fully functional.

How did the breakthrough come about? The story extends across continents, nationalities, and languages, gathering enthusiastic participants of various backgrounds. The decipherment made in the last few years has outstripped and upstaged all other fields of investigation.

Nearly 100 years have passed since Alfred Maudslay struggled into Copán, his team of mules hauling 4 tons of plaster of paris, with the determination to make molds from the stelae. Eventually the molds reached England, casts were made, and from them the drawings that set Ernst Forstmann in Dresden, Germany on his way to understanding the Maya calendar. Forstmann as royal librarian, had the Dresden Codex at hand, which, together with the drawings of the Copán stelae, enabled him to work out the Maya Long Count dating system. Equally dedicated to the study of the ancient Maya was Sylvanus G. Morley, who combed the jungles searching for new inscriptions. His enthusiasm kindled the interest of the Carnegie Institution of Washington and led to the extensive program of excavation and restoration at Chichén Itzá and Copán. All subsequent studies of Maya glyphs are based on the early works of pioneer scholars in this field such as Paul Schellhas, Teobert Maler, Herbert J.

Spinden, John E. Teeple, Herman Beyer, Thomas Barthel, and more recently J. Eric Thompson.

A prominent figure in this story was the first bishop of Yucatán, Diego de Landa, who was recalled to Spain in 1568 to answer charges concerning his strict methods of administration. He wrote his famous Relación de las Cosas de Yucatán as part of his legal defense. His crime of burning the Maya books is somewhat lessened because in his Relación he unknowingly provided us with a partial key to decipherment. Apparently he had asked his Maya informant to write signs corresponding to the Spanish alphabet. When this was studied it was hard to see that the 27 signs Landa called an alphabet corresponded in any way to the hieroglyphs on the monuments or the signs in the códices. Scholars became discouraged from looking for any phonetic approach and decided that the Maya hieroglyphs were largely ideographs and required no knowledge of the ancient Maya language. Therefore throughout the 1930s and 1940s studies concentrated on deciphering dates and calendrical information while the remaining inscriptions were largely ignored.

It was a young Soviet epigrapher, Yuri Knorosov (1958, 1967) who renewed efforts to discover phoneticism and began publishing articles in 1952. It was important to determine which of the 28 Maya tongues spoken today would be closest to the Maya of 800–1000 years ago. The most helpful proved to be Chol and Yucatec for, despite many changes that have taken place, both the ancient and modern languages follow specific word orders.

Knorosov finally saw that by combining the signs (consonant plus vowel), words were formed phonetically. This was the clue that, together with work going on in the west, brought results. In 1958 in Mexico City, Heinrich Berlin, working independently, identified what he called emblem glyphs that could stand for the name of a center, region, or possibly a dynasty (Berlin, 1958). We now have emblem glyphs for Copán, Quiriguá, Tikal, Naranjo, Piedras Negras, Palenque, Seibal, Dos Pilas, Bonampak, and many others.

Only two years later, Tatiana Proskouriakoff of the Carnegie Institution of Washington, well known for her beautiful drawings and reconstructions of Maya architecture and sculpture, completed a third major step toward decipherment. In noting dates on the Piedras Negras stelae that were still grouped before a temple/pyramid, she realized that all dates fell easily into the life span of a single individual. Her curiosity thoroughly aroused, she embarked on a complete study of 35 monuments at Piedras Negras and others at Yaxchilán and Naranjo (Proskouriakoff, 1960, 1961). She found that the recorded dates marked historical events in the lives of rulers and their families (Figure 5.7). Between Knorosov, Berlin, and Proskouriakoff, a revolution in Maya decipherment was initiated. Their studies convincingly demonstrated that ideographs and signs for consonant-vowel combinations made up the writing system and that the texts dealt with dynastic history, rulers, and actual events in their lives, rather than simply mythical narratives and calendrical notations.

In 1973 the first Palenque Round Table Conference was held at that site in Chiapas, Mexico, drawing together a wealth of dedicated Mayanists. A young Australian, Peter Mathews, attempted to work out the dynastic history of Palenque following

| Birth | Accession | Father | Capture | War (?) | Death |

FIGURE 5.7   Event and family glyphs. (Redrawn with permission from Jones, 1984.)

Proskouriakoff's model. Before the conference ended, with the inspired collaboration of Linda Schele and Floyd Lounsbury, Palenque's history unfolded with details of names, dates, and events. The floodgates of decipherment had opened.

About one-third of the signs still cannot be deciphered and the two-thirds that can be read only give us a partial view of the Maya world, the view of elite members of society. This information was carefully orchestrated by Maya rulers to legitimize their reign, to advertise their ancestral lineage, and sanctify their divine power and actions. Included in the inscriptions are family names, events such as birth, marriage, death, and accession to power, along with conquests and ritual behavior. You will find little information about craftspersons, farmers, traders, living conditions, and daily life.

It is beyond the scope of a general book such as this to explain the intricacies of deciphering Maya hieroglyphs, but what follows are some of the basic principles involved and examples of texts that have been "read" [see Jones (1984), Kelley (1976), Kerr (1989, 1990, 1992), and Stuart and Houston (1989)].

The great bulk of hieroglyphic texts are carved in stone, but the Maya also used other media such as wood or stucco. A second body of texts were incised, painted, or carved on ceramic vessels, lintels, shell, obsidian, jade, or even objects of clothing. Probably only a small fraction of Maya society could read and interpret the hiero-glyphs. Certainly scribes and educated elite were literate. Traders, merchants, and artisans must have had some rudimentary knowledge. Simple pictorial signs would have been understood by the general public and were visibly displayed.

Stone-Carved Texts

We have already seen the calendrical information inscribed on stelae and lintels and how the glyphs are usually arranged. A consistent pattern is followed in presenting historical data that is usually found after the calendrical material. This may include (1) a date; (2) an event glyph (for example, the date mentioned might mark the end of a katun); (3) name and title of a ruler. (A variety of information may be included here. Glyphs may tell the ruler's position in the dynasty. The father's death may be recorded. Considerable space is sometimes devoted to a parentage statement naming parents and children. The name or title of a ruler may be very descriptive, for example "Cauac Sky of Quiriguá," or "Bird Jaguar, Captor of Jeweled Skull." The king of

Yaxchilán sometimes referred to himself as "He of the Twenty Captives," emphasizing his prowess in war); (4) a distance number may follow, giving number of days that passed between events; (5) day and month date leading to another event; (6) event glyph, for example, when the ruler ascended his throne; and (7) ruler performs a particular ritual such as bloodletting.

This, or parts of it, is the kind of information that may be found in a historical text. These are often accompanied by a scene illustrating the event mentioned. The ruler may be depicted letting blood, having a vision, sitting on a throne, or standing on a captive. It was a matter of primary importance to establish one's position in a dynasty by naming one's ancestors, thus legitimizing the claim to the throne. A polity could increase its power by conquest or marriage thus acquiring more power by forging an alliance.

Another reason for commissioning a text was to celebrate the conquest of a foreign ruler. Lords and nobility are distinguished by their elegant attire, whereas captives are stripped bare and often shown crouching under the feet of a tall conqueror. Another humiliating posture is for a victim to have his hands tied together or showing the conqueror grabbing the victim by his hair, a universal way of portraying capture in Mesoamerica. If, however, the captive was of high rank, he might be adorned for sacrifice and publicly displayed. A frequent scene is that of ball-playing, a sport and a ritual associated with sacrifice.

Some rituals are portrayed in scenes accompanied by texts, the most common being bloodletting and incense burning. These were personal rites performed as offerings to the gods in return for divine favors and to ensure their continued benevolence. As a major celebration or anniversary approached, it was important to have divine sanctification either prior to or after the happening. And to be certain that the populace was aware of a ruler's devotion and adherence to prescribed ritual, he commissioned his act of bloodletting to be recorded in stone.

Ceramic Texts

For many years Maya vases have been treasured for their beautiful figure-painted scenes that are often accompanied by a row of hieroglyphs banding the rim. The fantastic figures of humans and animals cavorting about were once thought to portray imaginary mythical scenes, and the hieroglyphs purely decorative. Now we know that many scenes portray myths that eventually were written down and became the creation legends of the Quiché Maya known as the Popol Vuh. Some figures have been identified as the Hero Twins, Hunahpu and Xbalanque, and illustrate their adventures in Xibalbá, the Maya Underworld. Many other figures depict Xibalbá gods. Coe (1989) noted that groups of hieroglyphs were repetitious and occurred in a fixed sequence on ceramic vessels. He figured out that the text acts as a kind of vessel identification tag that is called the Primary Standard Sequence (PSS). After an introductory glyph, a short text follows, telling what the vessel was used for—usually drinking (in the case of a vase), the manner of decoration (painting), the contents (cacao or atole), name of the owner or person for whom the vessel was made, and sometimes the artist's signature. Names and titles may follow (Figure 5.8). This practice is not strictly confined to ceramics. It has also been found on a lintel at Yaxchilán and painted on a skirt in the Bonampak murals (Stuart, 1989).

Cylindrical vases were drinking cups or goblets; dishes and bowls bear a different sign. If a Calendar Round date is present, it probably refers to the production of the vessel, not the scene depicted. Unfortunately there is no clue as to where the vessel was made that would be of great interest. Vessels known to have been made by the same artist have been found at various cities in the southern lowlands, so we know that pottery moved considerable distances.

Of particular interest is the artist's signature, revealing the high esteem granted to scribes among the Maya. This is apparent at Copán, where life-sized 3-dimensional figures of scribes decorate a building in the Sepulturas Compound. In the world of art, it is the subject that matters, and artists do not usually receive public recognition.

Some of the fantastic animals and supernatural beings are also named. This type text is usually composed of three to five glyphs. The first two will name the subject, followed by an emblem glyph and a title. Animals named include monkeys, jaguars, turkeys, toads, serpents, deer, and peccaries (Kerr and Spero, 1989).

Hieroglyphs on ceramic vessels comprise the largest body of glyphs other than those of the stone monuments, and the Primary Standard Sequence has added another dimension to decipherment. "Tagging" vessels seems to be limited to the 150 years prior to A.D. 950. Thereafter the practice was discontinued.

FIGURE 5.8 Roll-out photograph of a Classic Maya vase bearing glyphs of a Primary Standard Sequence, indicating it was used for drinking cacao. (From Kerr, 1989. Photo No. 1837 by Justin Kerr, 1983.)

A ROSTER OF EARLY MESOAMERICAN DATES

The Maya carried the calendar to its greatest elaboration but in our present record, their neighbors have earlier antecedents that may be the roots of all calendrics and writing. The data listed below are a current roster of the earliest known dates.

OAXACA

San José Mogote.   Earliest evidence known of the 260-day cycle. Stone slab with "1 Earthquake" glyph. 600 B.C.?

VERACRUZ

Tres Zapotes.   Stela C, Long Count date of 31 B.C. One of earliest dated monuments in the New World. Bar-and-dot notation, noncalendrical text is inscribed above the date.

La Mojarra.   Stela 1, two Long Count dates of A.D. 143 and A.D. 156 (see below).

San Andrés Tuxtla.   Tuxtla Statuette, Long Count date of A.D. 162 ? Portable greenstone figure.

CHIAPAS

Chiapa de Corzo.   Stela 2, Long Count date of 36 B.C. Badly damaged. A baktun 7 is reconstructed. Bar-and-dot notation is arranged horizontally using position values.

GUATEMALA, PACIFIC SLOPES

El Baúl.   Stela 1 dated A.D. 36. Partialy eroded hieroglyphic text accompanied by a standing figure. Dating assumes a baktun 7.

FIGURE 5.9   Stone stelae with Long Count dates.

a. Stela C (rear view) from Tres Zapotes, Veracruz, one of the earliest dated monuments in the New World, 31 B.C. (*Left*) Lower part of stela with partial inscription. (Courtesy of Museo Nacional de Antropología, Mexico.) (*Right*) Drawing of completed Initial Series date, following recovery of upper part of stela in 1972. (Courtesy of Michael C. Coe.)

b. Stela 29, Tikal, Guatemala (*left*) with a drawing of the inscription (*right*). This is the earliest securely dated lowland Maya inscribed monument, dated at A.D. 292. Height: 1.33 m. (Courtesy of Christopher Jones and the University Museum, University of Pennsylvania.)

c. Stela 1, El Baul, Guatemala, which bears a partially eroded hieroglyphic text. Assuming a 7 baktun, the date corresponds to A.D. 36 in our calendar. Height: 1.80 m. (Courtesy of the Peabody Museum of Archaeology and Ethnology, Harvard University, copyright by the President and Fellows of Harvard College.)

d. Stela C, Copán, with double figures and lateral hieroglyphic texts. The figures are bearded and the entire monument was painted red. The Long Count date (9.17.12.0.0) corresponds to A.D. 782. Height: 3.52 m. (Photographed by the author.)

e. Stela 5, Abaj Takalik, bearing Long Count date A.D. 126. Height: 2.11 m. (Courtesy of John A. Graham.)

f. Stela 1, La Mojarra, Veracruz. An elegant dignitary with unusually long hieroglyphic text. Height: 2.20 m. (Drawing courtesy of George Stuart.)

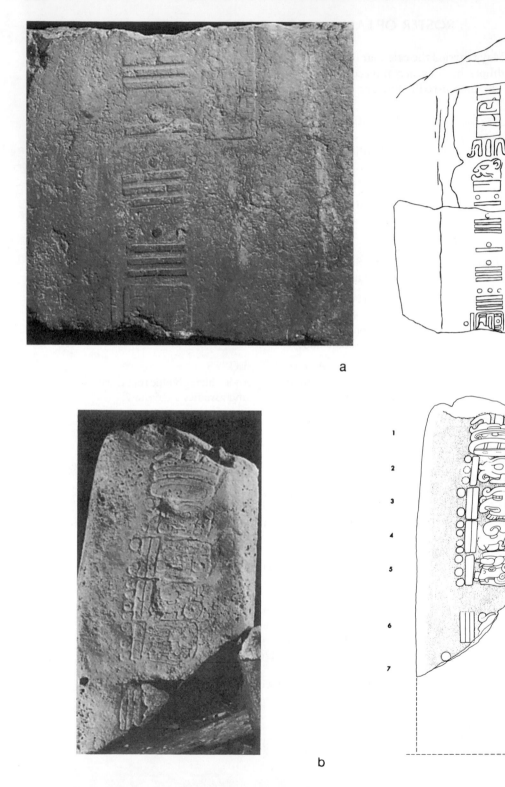

a

b

c

d

e

f

Abaj Takalik.	Stela 5, Long Count date of A.D. 126.

GUATEMALA HIGHLANDS

El Portón.	Monument 1, estimated date 400 B.C. Monument is associated with a platform construction dated 500–100 B.C. Monument 1 has a vertical glyph column, some of which are numerals.
Los Mangales.	Salamá Valley. Monuments 13 and 14. Dated on basis of ceramic associations at 500–200 B.C. Monument 13. Single vertical column of pecked motifs, a bar with two dots (number 7?). Monument 14, possible number 7, bar-and-dot notation.
Kaminaljuyú.	Stelae 10 and 11, considered early but cannot be deciphered.

EL SALVADOR

Chalchuapa.	Monument 1, Maya stela dated to 100 B.C.–A.D. 200. Damaged hieroglyphic text.

SOUTHERN MAYA LOWLANDS

Hauberg stela.	A.D. 199. The earliest known Long Count date from the southern Maya lowlands. A named Maya ruler accompanies text with bloodletting scene.
Pomona, Belize.	An early text on jadeite earflare. Estimated date, A.D. 100–250?
Tikal.	Stela 29, A.D. 292. The earliest known Long Count date with secure provenience in the southern lowlands. The portrait believed to depict Ruler Jaguar Paw I.

La Mojarra, Veracruz

A "new" dated text surfaced (literally) in 1986 (Winfield Capitaine, 1988). La Mojarra Stela 1, as it is now known, was hauled out of 6 feet of water from the Acula River in southeastern Veracruz where it had been found by a fisherman (Map 3.3). This stela is a 4-ton, roughly trapezoidal-shaped slab of basalt, with one side completely carved with an unusually long hieroglyphic inscription and an elaborately attired figure (Figure 5.9f). The monument is in remarkably good condition, although the lower part of the figure is damaged. Barthel and von Winning (1989) speculate that the stela could have accidentally tumbled into the river as it was being transshipped from or to La Mojarra. It bears two Long Count dates of A.D. 143 and A.D. 156. The closest resemblances to the writing are found on the Tuxtla Statuette and the language is thought to be Mixe-Zoque.

CHAPTER 6

Teotihuacan and Its Neighbors: The Maya Kings and a New Order

The cultural achievements in Mesoamerica immediately prior to A.D. 900 were so remarkable that these years have long been called the Classic Period. It used to be defined as beginning with the earliest recorded Long Count dates from the Petén and ending with their cessation. Now, however, the Classic Period has blurred those boundaries and only serves as a general label.

It now embraces the first nine centuries of the Christian Era in western Mesoamerica. For the Maya region east of the Isthmus of Tehuantepec, the upper limits may be extended to A.D. 1200 as I have done. Where one draws the line between phases and how the years are divided up varies with one's point of view. A Protoclassic phase, for example, may be useful in some areas but meaningless in others. I have included the Protoclassic years in the previous chapter, and now with Teotihuacan, already a well-established urban center of 80,000 inhabitants, we will examine its greatest years from A.D. 300–900, including its demise.

The Classic Period is one in which we find the integration of many small communities into urban developments. I have considered a concentration of 10,000 people as a city, or urbanism. Accompanying this we may expect to find a class-structured society, occupational specialization, and the concentration of capital wealth. This broad definition of a city permits the inclusion of a great variety of settlements.

In this period skilled architects throughout Mesoamerica directed the erection of pyramids, temples, multi-room palaces, and stone masonry ball courts. Each region developed its own style and ornamentation. The vaulted or corbeled arch was a distinctive feature of the lowland Maya, where sculptors were in constant demand for executing stone carvings, decorating façades, and carving altars, stelae, tablets, and inscriptions. Artists painted scenes on walls of tombs and palaces with iconographic messages. Ceramicists specialized in elaborate decorative techniques and distinctive wares were widely exchanged and imitated. From small clay figurines to painted murals, everything was executed with meaning. Advanced knowledge of calendrics and astronomy permitted prediction of cosmic events that scheduled ritual, warfare, and daily activities. Signs and glyphs were used as a form of communication and Maya texts recorded dates and personal histories as kingship became institutionalized.

It is easy for a student of Mesoamerica to find herself or himself overwhelmed by a glimpse of these Classic years. In attempting to avoid a bewildering "laundry list" of sites, I will focus on two outstanding areas of spectacular development, central highland Mexico and the Maya lowlands, and go into less detail with their peripheral neighbors. In the first part of this chapter I look at the events in the Basin of Mexico, examining Teotihuacan and her neighbors, and then turn south to the Classic Maya.

TEOTIHUACAN

We have seen Teotihuacan emerge from the earlier Preclassic development in the Basin of Mexico and become a well-established city by A.D. 300. Nothing was to challenge its leadership and power for the next 500 years. We are still learning about this city, so what follows is in no sense definitive, but only how we see it at this time. It was a remarkable, complex city and a close look at these years provides a data base to which scholars will repeatedly turn.

Urban Living: Housing Arrangements

It is not hard for us to visualize Teotihuacan, as it was a city in our sense of the word: busy, crowded, bustling with commercial and religious activities, and laid out in a grid pattern with multi-family dwellings (Map 6.1). The only open areas were those in the Street of the Dead and in the Great Compound. The main axis, the Street of the Dead, was the civic-ceremonial center of town with the most elegant residential section located towards the northern end. Middle-class housing was slightly removed from the main thoroughfares and the outskirts of the city were the least desirable as living quarters. The city had to house not only craftspersons and skilled workmen, but also a considerable number of religious personnel, some of whom, if not all, must have been full-time practitioners to judge from the size and number of temples under their supervision. The civic officials and administrators also needed appropriate housing. Two-thirds of the population were farmers, living in the city and traveling every day to their outlying fields. Their homes were the least well constructed and used more adobe than stone. Much wood was used in general construction which made the city easy prey to the final conflagration. Finer housing was of stone, roofed over with wooden beams.

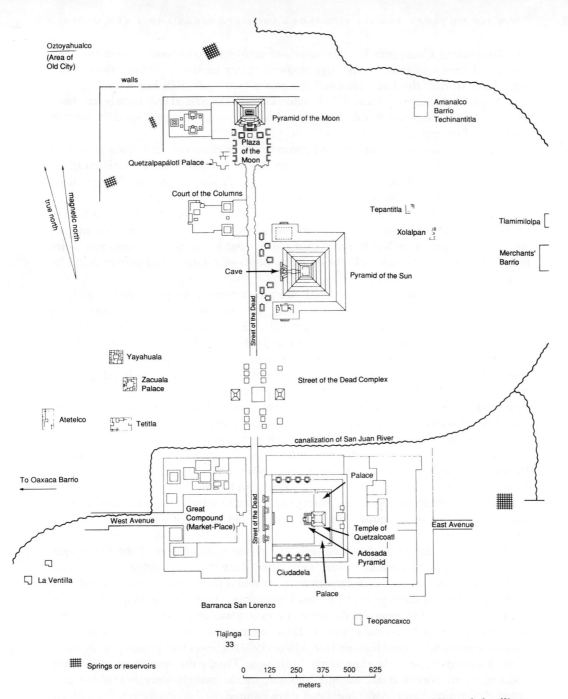

MAP 6.1 Simplified map of civic-ceremonial center of Teotihuacan. Additional dwellings filled in many spaces between constructions shown. From Pyramid of Moon to Great Compound: 2000 m. (Information from Millon, 1973; Millon, Drewett and Cowgill, 1973; Berrin, 1988; Widmer, 1987).

Apartment Compounds   Thousands of apartment compounds were the standard residential unit built for the large majority of city residents (Millon, 1981). Most were built during the Late Tlamimilolpa phase (A.D. 300–400) but were begun in A.D. 200 and continued until A.D. 550. Residents of each compound may have been related kin, an arrangement that would have been advantageous for a craft specialization or commercial enterprise.

The compounds vary in size and construction and do not look mass produced by the state, but their compact arrangement would have facilitated administration, taxation, and general supervision or social control. A single compound might have housed multi-family groups of 60–100 individuals.

A compound was constructed in a single operation, well planned in advance. Just as we install plumbing and electrical wiring before finishing walls and flooring, so stone-lined drains were laid to carry excess water out to the street or into reservoirs for storage. Once this network was in place, floors of concrete and plaster could be laid.

This was a one-story structure, encased by high stone walls, plastered but without windows. Inside were rooms, porticos, patios, and passageways forming apartments that had access to a centrally located courtyard with at least one temple. The architectural pattern of 50–100 rooms was quite standardized in the 2000 structures of this type that have been identified. Remains of storage wares, cooking utensils, and debris leave little doubt as to the purpose of some rooms. Cooking was probably done on 3-pronged ceramic stoves placed directly on the plastered floor. According to excavated compounds, each had its own temple or shrine, drainage, and some sort of sanitary facilities, all enclosed within the wall, providing privacy.

The residential compound of Tlamimilolpa (Figure 6.1) was probably a lower-class dwelling and is a relatively large compound. It was located 1.2 km east of the Pyramid of the Sun in a sparsely built up section of the city. It covered an area of 3500 m with an estimated 176 rooms, 21 patios, and 5 larger courts, plus numerous alleys. Although the sunlight of Teotihuacan is dazzling today, during Classic times the small interior rooms must have been gloomy and conditions crowded.

Palaces   A step up in the social scale and closer to the Street of the Dead were other residential compounds, Tetitla, Tepantitla, Zacuala, and Xolalpan, which have been partially excavated and are famous for their mural paintings. These are composed of clusters of rooms arranged around small open patios with central altars. Rainwater drained into a kind of cistern in the patio and excess was conducted from there to the outside by an interior drainage system. There were no windows but small patios and courts admitted additional light and air. Miller (1973) believes that painting and murals were designed at the same time as the buildings. Thus patios and wall space were planned in advance and accordingly allotted, so the murals were not added as a decorative afterthought. Most buildings were painted.

The Palace of Zacuala offered a special attraction, for there the Teotihuacanos played a game of chance. We do not know the name of their game, but among the later Aztecs it was called *patolli*. This was played on a flat surface and the pattern of

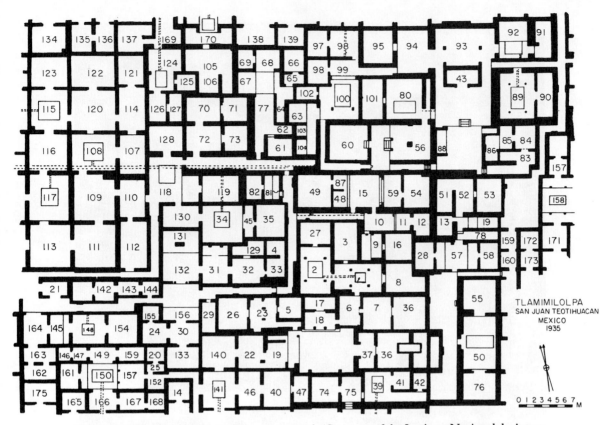

FIGURE 6.1 Plan of Tlamimilolpa compound. (Courtesy of the Instituto Nacional de Antropología e Historia, Mexico.)

the board was scratched on the floor of Zacuala. This is the earliest known example of this game in Mesoamerica (see discussion, page 399).

Tetitla was apparently a dwelling of higher status than its neighbors, and even when luxury goods began to be scarce elsewhere, Tetitla's fortunes remained undiminished. La Ventilla to the south and Xolalpan housed the less privileged. Tepantitla was rather special with larger and more spacious rooms.

The most sumptuous establishments were built close to the main street. A good example is furnished by the restored Quetzalpapálotl Palace (Acosta, 1964; Figure 6.2), located at the southwest corner of the Plaza of the Moon. It is a curious combination of public rooms and residential quarters. One enters the elegant palace by way of a wide stairway and porches leading to a magnificent court. This is bordered by a gallery with sculptured piers carved to represent owls in frontal view, originally painted in red and green, with inlaid obsidian eyes. Other piers are carved with the profile of a quetzal bird. The owl is a common war emblem and its association with the quetzal

FIGURE 6.2   Quetzalpapálotl (Quetzal-butterfly) Palace, Teotihuacan. (Courtesy of the Instituto Nacional de Antropología e Historia Mexico.)

here may well have a meaning related to a lineage and warrior cult (Kubler, 1967). This structure postdates A.D. 500. Behind the court and public rooms are living quarters, a jumble of rooms resembling those in other apartmentlike dwellings.

The Calle de los Muertos Complex straddling the Street of the Dead between the Ciudadela and the Pyramid of the Sun has already been mentioned. This huge complex embraced patios, passageways, temples, and fine residential quarters. The Viking Group sector is composed of unusually large rooms and its residents enjoyed the curious distinction of having mica floors (Armillas, 1944). This Street of the Dead Complex might have accommodated as many as 800–1600 people (Cowgill, 1983).

Tlajinga 33   On the southern outskirts of the city lay Tlajinga, a single compound of 2200 m, which probably formed part of a larger complex. On the edges of the metropolis, the boundaries of compounds such as this were less well defined and Tlajinga's architectural history is one of adding rooms and moving walls as its fortunes improved. In the Early Xolalpan phase, Tlajinga 33 became a craft center specializing in lapidary work and jewelry production using slate, onyx, greenstones, and maybe frescoing tripod vessels. Apparently this led to greater wealth and its status rose accordingly. A dramatic shift from lapidaries to potters led to a complete reorganization of site architecture in Late Xolalpan and Metepec. Construction was upgraded to building with concrete and masonry walls; concrete courtyards replaced the cobbles. Tlajinga was a single compound, now forming part of a larger barrio of ceramic specialization. As full-time potters, they no longer had surplus grain to raise their own dogs and turkey for food and therefore bought what they needed at the market (Widmer, 1987).

This is an interesting example of changing form and function of a residential complex. A surface survey would have given only a hint of the history of Tlajinga 33.

Maquixco Bajo   Life in the rural villages would have been similar, for we think it was controlled directly by the city authorities. The small community of Maquixco Bajo, excavated by the Teotihuacan Valley Project in 1961–1972, furnishes an example of a planned rural settlement of middle Classic date (Sanders *et al.*, 1979). Located on the edge of an alluvial plain only 2 km west of Teotihuacan and occupying 8 ha, it probably accommodated 140–150 families, roughly 500–600 people.

Housing consisted of either individual households or apartmentlike compounds of 10–12 nuclear families. Farming was the principal occupation and possibly sap was extracted from the maguey plant and made into pulque to bring in extra money. The unusual number of obsidian scrapers can best account for this activity. The stucco work was so far superior that it might represent a specialization. Otherwise there was little variety and life looks monotonous indeed. Basic staples were provided locally but there was not much in the way of crafts, no innovations, nor were any seemingly encouraged, for access to raw materials was controlled. The picture presented is one of little flexibility or variety, for each family bought the same pots and products at the Teotihuacan market.

The head of the community may have been more politician than religious leader to judge from the local temple/pyramid and unimpressive paraphernalia associated with it. For important ceremonies, one surely went into the city to participate in its pageantry. Meanwhile, household artifacts suggest it was important to observe daily household ritual where the individual could most effectively communicate with the gods on a personal basis. Typical are broken clay figurines, incense burners, *candeleros*, and some fine tripod vessels, all found among debris. Larger houses had special rooms presumably for storing such objects.

This highly structured arrangement for living would have had a profound influence on the nature of Teotihuacan society, dictating daily life and social and political organization. The compounds did not have Preclassic antecedents, nor did they outlast the life of the city. They were a special feature of Teotihuacan, reflecting its desire for privacy, and are probably a key to understanding the functioning of the city (Pasztory, n.d.a).

Fine Arts and Religion

Religion was seemingly the key factor in the integration of Teotihuacan society. One has only to see the Street of the Dead with more than 100 temples, shrines, altars, and quantities of smaller temple mounds to realize how religion dominated the lives of these people. Teotihuacanos may have regarded this as the holiest place on earth, the "center of the cosmos," the place "where time began" (Millon, 1981). The monumental architecture provided for massive ritual celebrations and gatherings of thousands.

Teotihuacan artisans turned out beautiful pottery in great variety but preferred polished monochromes to the multicolored vessels of their ancestors and Maya contemporaries. Having developed from the local Preclassic tradition, many ceramic features continued.

Small clay figurines are one example. These are found largely in household contexts. After the Late Tlamimilolpa phase, around A.D. 400, they were turned out by molds (see Figure 6.3a). The "portrait" figurine (a misnomer), is a very stylized

---

FIGURE 6.3   Classic Teotihuacan artifacts: pottery and stone.
a. Pottery mold for producing figurine heads. Classic period. Height: 10 cm. (Courtesy of the Museum of the American Indian, Heye Foundation, N.Y. [22/9145].)
b. Mold-made figurine made for articulation. Teotihuacan culture. Height: 25 cm. (Courtesy of the Museum of the American Indian, Heye Foundation, N.Y. [24/6664].)
c. Black-brown vessel with excised and incised decoration. Teotihuacan. Late Tlamimilolpa phase. Height: 20 cm. (Courtesy of the Museo Nacional de Antropología, Mexico.)
d. Large orange jar with stamped decoration. Teotihuacan. Metepec phase. Height: 20 cm. (Courtesy of the Museo Nacional de Antropología, Mexico.)
e. Thin Orange effigy vessel: early Classic Teotihuacan. Toluca, Stat of Mexico. Height: 31 cm. (Courtesy of the Museo Nacional de Antropología, Mexico.)
f. *Incensario* typical of middle Classic Teotihuacan with hourglass-shaped base and ornate lid. Height: 60 cm. (Courtesy of the Instituto Nacional de Antropología e Historia, Mexico.)
g. Green-stone mask. Teotihuacan type. Santiago Tlatelolco. Height: 27 cm. (Courtesy of the Museum of the American Indian, Heye Foundation, N.Y. [2/6607].)
h. Stone figure with incisions and cavities for inlays. Teotihuacan. Height: 30 cm. (Courtesy of the Museum of the American Indian, Heye Foundation, N.Y. [10/7462].)
i. Stone representation of the Storm God with bifurcated serpent tongue. Teotihuacan, subterranean structures. Height: approximately 80 cm. (Courtesy of the Museo Nacional de Antropología, Mexico.)
j. Life-size ceramic sculpture representing Xipe Totec, who holds a jaguar-paw vessel of Monte Albán-type in his right hand. Teotihuacan culture. Height: 122 cm. (Courtesy of the Museo Nacional de Antropología, Mexico.)

a

b

c

d

e

f

g

j

h

i

mass-produced figure in strange postures and gestures. There is usually a depression in the top of the head over a triangular-shaped face. Articulated figurines with movable limbs were another innovation (Figure 6.3b). Although many fragments have been recovered, complete figures are rare. What meaning these figurines had and what the Teotihuacanos did with them is a mystery. Not gods or spirits, they are representative of local village tradition.

During the Tlamimilolpa phase, contact was close with Gulf Coast cultures, and toward A.D. 450 Maya influence can also be recognized. Outside contacts are evident in both form and style of ceramics as well as in the mural paintings. The Tajín-scroll, applique ornamentation, and the first plano-relief decoration appear on vases and are more fully elaborated in the phases that follow. The lidded cylindrical tripod, Teotihuacan's single most distinguished pot, became popular at this time. It was decorated by painting, plano-relief, fresco, incising, or simply burnished. Thin Orange pottery, a fine paste ware, is found all over the city, commercially produced in southern Puebla (see page 181). Another orange pottery, San Martin Orange, was a popular utility ware, mass produced to make deep cooking vessels and large amphorae. The production of the latter was a chief livelihood of the Tlajinga 33 potters in the Xolalpan period (Widmer, 1987). There were other ceramic specialities such as coarse matte censers, 3-pronged burners (stoves), and *candeleros* that, along with figurines, were produced in the western sector of the city.

Numerous masks of green stone, serpentine, onyx, and obsidian, sometimes incrusted with turquoise mosaic or having inlaid eyes of cut shell and obsidian, are attributed to Classic Teotihuacan. Oddly enough, not one of these has been found *in situ* and it is therefore impossible to date them with any accuracy, or in some cases to be certain of their authenticity. Thin clay masks found in the household rubbish of Yayahuala and Tetitla are believed by Séjourné (1966) to have been tied to the wrapped and bundled deceased before cremation.

Murals   There are different interpretations of Teotihuacan mural art, and paintings have been the subject of considerable study (Kubler, 1984; Miller, 1973; C. Millon, 1966, 1973, 1988; Pasztory, 1976a, 1988a; Séjourné, 1966). The art of Teotihuacan that is profoundly religious and mythological in nature (Millon, 1981) introduced new forms and media. It was in mural painting that the Teotihuacanos excelled. And it is from murals that we learn most about the art, religion, society, foreign affairs, and writing of this unique Mesoamerican culture.

Murals are found in palaces, public buildings and in private dwellings (Figure 6.4). The earliest murals date from the Tlamimilolpa period and decorate small buildings along the Street of the Dead with motifs of plants, birds, fish, jaguars, and serpents, but no human figures. By Xolalpan days, murals began to cover walls in the apartment compounds, a trend that was to continue until the collapse of the city. This is the most abstract art style in Mesoamerica, highly religious but without any portraits; no ruler or prominent figure can be identified (Millon, 1981). Figures are all identical; humans are seen in profile, deities in frontal position. There are no narrative scenes; no one is pictured as a slave, a ruler, or a sacrificed victim (Pasztory, n.d.a). Eventually art became more complex and culminated in the late Techinantitla murals.

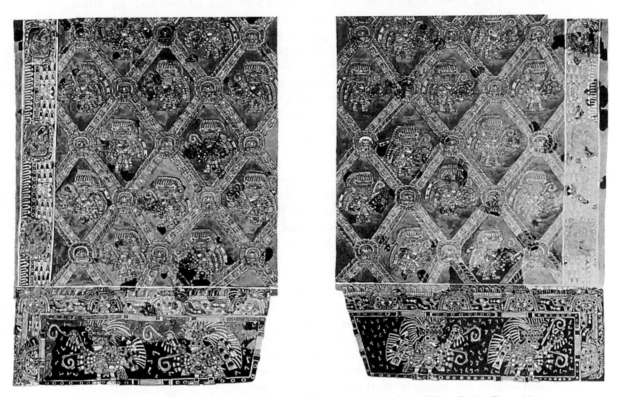

FIGURE 6.4   Atetelco mural, Teotihuacan. Reconstruction of the White Patio. Repetitious designs illustrate use of patterns. Figures are sometimes cut off in a corner like unmatched wallpaper. (Courtesy of the Instituto Nacional de Antropolotgía e Historia, Mexico.)

Apparently the Ciudadela apartments were never decorated with murals nor were the residences along the Street of the Dead. This is curious, owing to their high quality of artifacts and elegance in other respects. The palatial complexes of the Sun and the Jaguars (near the Sun and Moon pyramids, respectively) had the greatest concentrations of mural paintings (Pasztory, 1988a). Residences at Zacuala, Tetitla, Tepantitla, Atetelco, and Teopancaxco all contain painted murals.

The quality of the workmanship as well as the subject matter may vary even in the same house. Pasztory thinks the mural painters may have constituted a kind of guild. Walls were prepared by first applying a thin layer of clay over which another layer of lime mixed with fine quartz and sand was spread. A red wash was then applied and figures were outlined in black or red. Blues and greens were added last of all and were the first to flake off. A final burnish was achieved by rubbing the whole surface with a hard stone (Pasztory, 1976a).

In general, the art style is very austere and monotonous in its overwhelming liturgic and abstract character, with the notable exception of the murals of the Tlalocan patio at Tepantitla, that depict little figures dancing, singing, and frolicking about

(Figure 6.5b). In this scene a ball game in progress is of some interest since no formal courts have been found. In the painting, the limits of the court are marked by end-markers or posts, and the game is being played using a bat, a different form of the usual Mesoamerican game (Figure 6.5b). A composite stela from La Ventilla is believed to be such a marker (Aveleyra, 1963; Figure, 6.5c). Somewhat similar markers have been excavated at Kaminaljuyú, Tikal, and in the state of Guerrero.

There were different ways in which the ball game was played and the rules changed over time (see page 226). It is believed to have been an innovation of early Gulf Coast people and its presence at Teotihuacan reflects this contact.

Deities   Some of the female representations are now seen to be different aspects of the Great Goddess, a term coined by Esther Pasztory (n.d.a) and Clara Millon (1988). This deity's most imposing example is the gigantic (22 ton) block figure known for years as a water goddess found near the Plaza of the Moon. Although she is Teotihuacan's most important deity, she is not easily identified in the murals until one knows what to look for. She has a dual personality; for example, she is life giving as a nourisher of life and vitality, shown in watery settings with flower and marine creatures (Tepantitla). But she also has a terrifying evil aspect (Tetitla and Techinan-titla), depicted with bared teeth, fangs, and clawed hands, associated with heart sacrifice. Her face is usually hidden by a mask or not shown at all. Her most common attributes are a nose bar, a bird in her headdress, and a red and yellow zigzag band (Pasztory, 1988a). Hands are often present even if the face does not show. There is nothing feminine or sexual in her appearance, but as the supreme deity of the city, she is a cut above factions and politics. Perhaps she might be best understood when compared to our image of Justice or our Statue of Liberty, a supreme symbol of positive values and principles (Pasztory, n.d.a). The Great Goddess exemplifies the religious system of Teotihuacan, believed to be remote, impersonal. The Teotihua-canos were well aware of the ancient Olmec monuments, the conquests of Monte Albán, the great pride of the Maya dynasties, and their publicized history. But you find no named individuals at Teotihuacan until Metepec when cracks in the system begin to appear. Teotihuacan art was abstract and had to be a conscious rejection of the other Mesoamerican traditions. The Great Goddess is first identified around A.D. 200 by a headdress, but gradually became more visible and is well represented in the Techinantitla murals (Berrin, 1988). However grand her role in the ideology of Classic Teotihuacan, neither she nor the ideology survive the ultimate collapse of the city.

As to other deities, Kubler cautions against identifying Teotihuacan figures with those of the Postclassic Aztec. This has been partly ameliorated by referring to another prominent deity as the Storm God rather than Tlaloc. The latter is a Náhuatl term for the Aztec Rain God with goggle eyes, handle-bar mustache, and fangs. Storm God is more suitable for the Teotihuacan figure because although rain related, he is closely associated with thunder and lightning. Moreover, a goggled figure is not a very helpful criterion because although all Storm Gods have goggles or rings, these may also accompany other deities and even secular figures (Langley, 1986).

The Storm God appears with many attributes and in many different aspects depending on his role and on the circumstances of his appearance (C. Millon, 1973;

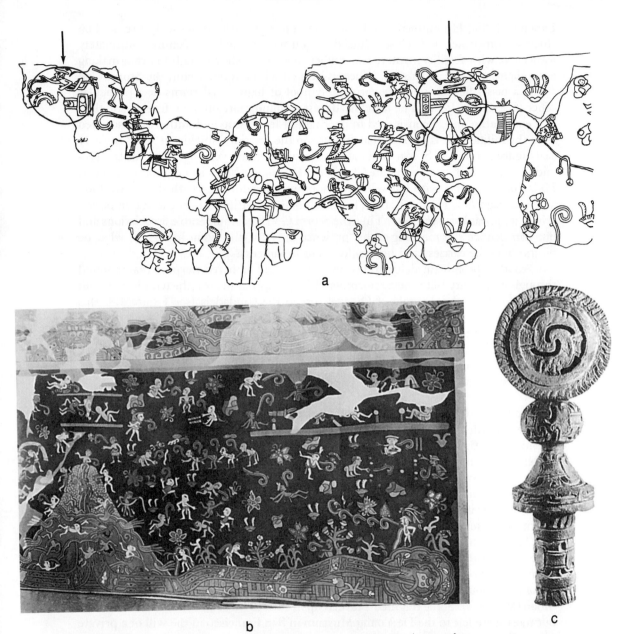

FIGURE 6.5 Tepantitla mural; sketch of ball game and ball court marker.
a. Sketch of ball game in progress. End markers are noted. (Courtesy of Esther Pasztory.)
b. "Tlalocan" mural paintings from Tepantitla. (Courtesy of the Instituto Nacional de Antropología e Historia, Mexico.)
c. Composite stela used as ball court marker. Volute carving in Tajín-style. La Ventilla, Teotihuacan. Height: 211 cm. (Courtesy of the Instituto Nacional de Antropología e Historia, Mexico.)

Langley, 1986). His emblem can be seen on pottery vessels, stone sculpture, and on shields. Sometimes he is closely linked to rain with crocodilian features, intimately associated with fertility, water, water lilies, and often shown with his rain-making equipment, a vessel and a staff. When associated with a warrior cult, the Storm God wears a tassel headdress representing a symbol of high social status or a particular office (C. Millon, 1973). The tassel headdress is found more often on foreign soil than at Teotihuacan and is considered to be a sign of leadership and authority associated with the military. It is his face that appears on the warriors' shields on Tikal Stela 31 (see Figure 6.30). The Storm God may also wear a familiar year-sign with the trapeze-and-ray symbol often seen in Late Classic and Postclassic Maya iconography. At Tula, Hidalgo, two stelae with bas-relief warriors wear headdresses with the Storm God and year-sign (see Figure 7.5b). This combination continues into the Aztec period where it appears on a *chacmool*. Thus the Storm God has innumerable associations and one can deduce the meaning of his presence only by observing his attire; what he wears, what he carries, and his headdress or ornaments.

Another prominent deity at Teotihuacan is the Feathered Serpent that is found throughout the city but is best remembered for his appearance on the temple/pyramid named for him, the Temple of Quetzalcoatl in the Ciudadela (see Figure 4.8, this volume). This was his greatest monument and may have been associated with resident rulers during the Miccaotli years.

Another deity familiar from Preclassic days is the Old Man God, a crouching figure holding a brasier on his head. He is usually known by the later Aztec name, Huehuéteotl.

Techinantitla Murals.   Gradually a trend toward painting in tones of red and the use of borders became widespread. For many years signs of militarism were easily overlooked in the murals but after the discovery of the sacrificed captives and warriors at the Temple of Quetzalcoatl, we have become keenly aware of the fact that warfare was a deep-rooted tradition. To recognize a martial scene one needs to learn how darts, *atlatls*, and knives are represented. It is only after A.D. 500 that the trend toward individual glorification and warfare becomes more apparent in carved reliefs, Metepec figurines, pottery, murals, and sculpture (Kubler, 1967; Millon, 1966).

The Techinantitla murals revealed in the 1970s substantially enlarged our knowledge of Teotithuacan. These invaluable murals, so often cited, had been crudely wrenched out of walls and brutally looted in the early 1960s from a civic or residential 1-story compound called Amanalco, approximately 500 m east of the Pyramid of the Moon (Map. 6.1). Some fragments turned up in various museums in the United States but most were left to the De Young Museum in San Francisco in the will of a private estate (Berrin, 1988).

One carefully restored section shows a wonderful 9-m procession of human figures. Eight of the figures are accompanied by a name glyph and all are wearing the militant tassel headdress. Footprints form upper and lower borders (Figure 6.6). Some of the most interesting are rows of flowering plants and trees with glyphic signs just above the base of each plant. There are 12 signs on 31 trees that have different flowers and leaves, perhaps indicating botanical names or toponyms.

FIGURE 6.6   Painted figure wearing the tassel headdress, symbol of power and leadership. It is proceeded by a compound sign, a possible patronym. Techinantitla mural, Teotihuacan. (Courtesy of the Fine Arts Museums of San Francisco, bequest of Harold J. Wagner, 1985-104.5. Tracing by Saburo Sugiyama from original mural.)

The rooms were apparently filled with marching tasseled figures with military insignia: body armor, martial coyote imagery, and heart sacrifice. Some Storm God murals in an unlooted anteroom are still preserved in places up to a height of 6 ft. Fortunately, when the building fell into disuse and collapsed, its debris sealed ceramics that have aided in dating the remains.

The murals are securely dated toward the end of the Xolalpan phase and Metepec, a time frame spanning the years A.D. 600–750. It seems clear that they belong to the last construction phase, and were left to fall into ruin (R. Millon, 1988b). Fortunately, this was not one of the buildings destroyed in the final conflagration.

We do not know how the military was organized at Teotihuacan, but it seems likely that the Amanalco area represents a military barrio of some sort. R. Millon (1988b) believes this complex could have housed personnel while the main structure might have been a public building. Its temple is larger than any known from apartment compounds. The series of structures making up this complex might have had some relation to ritual or special events at the Temple of the Moon, given its proximity. Future excavations will surely provide some of these answers.

By now it is apparent that Teotihuacan presents a very unusual living pattern and one that we will not find again in subsequent polities. There was an emphasis on privacy and anonymity. Strong leaders were certainly present, but so self-effacing that they are neither represented nor named. Hiding was part of it, behind masks, embedded texts. They would have shunned the self-glorification of the Maya. Pasztory (n.d.a) suggests that Teotihuacan may represent an experiment in living, a kind of utopia run not for kings or an elite aristocracy, but for the people, grouped in their lineages in their compounds. This "new order" that they were willing and ready to defend explains other features such as the continuity of maintaining traditional house-hold objects like the clay figurines and the Old Man God.

A natural corollary follows in which this tendency toward privacy led to isolating themselves and probably did not encourage outsiders. It would have been a city preoccupied with itself and relatively uninterested in the rest of the world, choosing to reject many customs of their contemporaries. Did they feel morally superior? One question Pasztory (n.d.a; 1990) raises: If the Teotihuacanos were so disinterested, why were they such travelers? We might also ask, were they only merchants, and not colonists? Are we seeing only down-the-line traded objects and imitations?

Visual Communication: "Writing"

At a time when Teotihuacan had grown to a huge city embracing 125,000 people with all the accompanying social, religious, economic, and political complexities urbanism brings, together with distant interaction with foreigners, is it possible that the Teotihuacanos did not have some kind of a system of record-keeping and written communication? We now believe that they did, but are just beginning to understand how to recognize and interpret their signs.

Early investigators in this field at Teotihuacan were Eduard Seler and Herman Beyer, but the first real steps were taken by Alfonso Caso, who worked on calendrical systems and symbols in Mesoamerica and specifically the art of Teotihuacan. More recent scholars have been Laurette Séjourné (1966); Hasso von Winning (1987); George Kubler (1967); Clara Millon (1973); Esther Pasztory (1976a, 1988a,b); and Janet Berlo (1983, 1989). Various approaches have been taken by them in studying Teotihuacan iconography, for this is the rich field of symbolic compositions. In this case, stone sculpture and carvings are not the prime iconographic medium, but mural paintings, ceramic decoration, and figurines. Various approaches have been made and many signs catalogued but it proved difficult to understand how the signs were used since there were few linear texts of the kind familiar in advanced writing systems.

Finally the magnetism of Teotihuacan converted a Canadian diplomat, James C. Langley, to archaeology, and he has given us the most comprehensive study of Teotihuacan "writing" to date (Langley, 1986, 1991). He began from a different premise, convinced that some system existed if only we could recognize it. He started by looking at abstract decorations and motifs. In the absence of clearly hieroglyphic signs, he looked for symbolic motifs that were extraneous to the pictorial contexts in which they appeared. These are to be found in the attire, ornaments, and attributes of human and zoomorphic figures, in the natural world of trees, birds, flowers, and butterflies, as well as in abstract decoration in mural painting, stucco-painted and champleve pottery vessels, and mold-made figurines. Since they seem to supplement the pictorial imagery with which they are associated, he calls them notational signs. After an exhaustive search through archaeological collections in Mexico, the United States, and western Europe, he compiled a compendium of 228 notational signs used in the time frame of approximately A.D. 400–700. Often the linguistic context is provided by the pictorial imagery. This is what Berlo (1989) calls an embedded text, but sometimes the imagery is entirely abstract. Signs were found to occur in isolation, in simple compounds, or grouped in clusters. Some signs are repeated often with variations. I have selected a few of these to illustrate how they may appear in these different media.

The tassel headdress (Figure 6.6) was one of the first signs to be recognized as a symbol, that Clara Millon (1973) distinguished from the ordinary decorative tassel, that is, one worn as a normal item of apparel. She identified it as a badge of office, or of a particular group, a symbol of power and leadership. But when worn by the Storm God it is particularly associated with warfare. The Techinantitla murals have now provided ample evidence of the tassel as a notational sign. For example, it is sometimes found placed at the feet of some of the human figures (Figure 6.6). These cannot be "read" in the conventional way but Millon believes they may name the person, his family, or perhaps an association. This is particularly startling as being contrary to the customary impersonal spirit of Teotihuacan art.

In one 2-part notation, the tassel is placed directly over a coyote head, thus forming a "compound," a set of glyphs forming a column as was the style in Oaxaca and among the Maya. Four signs stacked in a column are a good example of a more complex arrangement forming a "core cluster" (Figure 6.7j). This group of glyphs appears in the exact same order and location on two other examples on the lid of incense burners (Langley, 1986).

Another distinctive sign, particularly important in regard to Teotihuacan is the reptile's eye (Langley's RE glyph) distinguished by a volute immediately above an inverted U element (Figure 6.7g). This sign has been shown to have convincing martial connections, as does the coyote head. Both the reptile's eye and the half star (a Venus symbol; Figure 6.7b), are prominent signs at Cacaxtla.

Although the residential murals (Tepantitla, Tetitla, Zacuala, and Teopanaxco) provide other information about Teotihuacan, the Techinantitla murals have given us the greatest corpus of notational signs and examples of "writing" to date. It is likely that glyphic notation was accelerating during late years at Teotihuacan (Metepec) when these murals were painted.

Did these Teotihuacanos have a calendar? The day-signs and numerals that are found at Teotihuacan are all on portable objects. Both the bar-and-dot and dot-only systems coexisted. These two numeral systems of highland Mexico eventually became dot-only and the use of the bar was eliminated for reasons we do not know. At present

FIGURE 6.7   Notational signs of Teotihuacan. (a) RM; (b) Half Star; (c) Trapeze Ray; (d) Feathered eye; (e) Four-way Hatching; (f) Kan Cross; (g) RE; (h) Trilobe; (i) two-part notation (tassel with coyote head beneath); (j) Core cluster detail of a right lateral tablet on an *incensario*; (k) Storm God insignia on a pottery vessel. (Photographs courtesy of James C. Langley.)

there is no positive evidence of the Mesoamerican calendar at Teotihuacan (Langley, 1991). The Teotihuacanos certainly had the opportunity to see it in operation among the Zapotecs of Monte Albán and the Maya. This is not surprising in view of extensive interaction among Mesoamerican peoples during this period even though they maintained very distinctive independent polities. Both Zapotecs and Maya as well as central Mexicans incorporated some Teotihuacan glyphs into their inscriptions.

Did a Teotihuacan's postulated rejection of many features of contemporary societies extend to time-keeping? Of this we cannot be certain, but we do know that numerous signs were shared with the major centers of Classic Mesoamerica. Examples include the Kan Cross, Quincunz, Bow/Knot, Footprint, and Four-way Hatching. All have some representations of human and zoomorphic heads, flowers, and sound scrolls. Langley (1991) lists the following signs as being unique or closely associated with Teotihuacan: trispiral and trilobal signs, human and feathered eyes, nose pendants, Storm God imagery, trapeze-and-ray, and reptile eye. These may occur in various combinations in compounds and clusters.

A major obstacle to the understanding of the writing sytem at Teotihuacan is our ignorance of the spoken language. This hampers any attempt at phonetic and other linguistic analysis. Various suggestions have been advanced as to the ancient language including Mixe-Zoquean, Totonac, Náhuatl, and even Maya but no agreement has been reached among the linguists. Náhuatl is the language most often mentioned as a possibility, but it is doubtful that these speakers arrived in the Valley of Mexico before the final days of Teotihuacan (Kaufman, 1976:113).

Langley (1986:174) writes, "The conventionalization of signs, their arrangement in sequences of various kinds and in abstract symbolic compositions completely disassociated from any pictorial imagery, are all suggestive of texts such as might be expected in an emergent writing system. Although no texts of a conventional kind have been discovered, perhaps we can think of Teotihuacan as having a well-developed protowriting."

Although the glyphs cannot yet be read in linguistic terms, we have come a long way toward understanding the significance of many notational signs and see that their presence in paintings, on sculptured reliefs, and on pottery was designed to transmit personal information and display attributes of power. It is now well established that writing as visual communication was used at Classic Teotihuacan and was continued and further elaborated by the successor states of Xochicalco and Cacaxtla.

In simple terms this is a brief view of the recent studies of Teotihuacan writing. Analysis of glyphic signs is continuing along lines of this notational beginning, hoping eventually to be able to interpret glyphic meanings that can be tested in different contexts for similar semantic values. This day lies in the future, probably awaiting some signal as to linguistic affiliation.

Earning a Living

The subsistence economy was based on the cultivation of maize, squash, and amaranth, and supplemented by a variety of other cultigens; essentially it was the same diet established in Preclassic times. Dogs were probably eaten as well as turkeys, but hunting even of white-tailed deer does not seem to have been very important, and the daily food supply depended heavily on local crop production. For a flourishing urban center, with commercial interests and a complex sociopolitical structure, an agricultural surplus was a paramount necessity. Members of the religious hierarchy were surely not expected to till the soil in addition to tending the temples and seeing to daily demands of the populace. Likewise, specialized artisans devoted the greater portion of their time to their trades.

Fortunately Teotihuacan was blessed with a dozen or more large permanent springs. Eventually the tributaries of the San Juan River were harnessed farther north, and this river was canalized and led along the eastern confines of the city past Tlamimilolpa and the Merchants' Barrio, then westward, traversing the city center just north of the Ciudadela and Great Compound to flow out the southwestern region (Map 6.1). Four reservoirs, wells, and small canals helped distribute water to the city. These hydraulic systems enabled Teotihuacan farmers to produce their staples within about 15 km of the city limits. Sanders *et al.* (1979) calculate that during the Classic period 9700 ha of land were under permanent irrigation that could easily maintain the enormous population of city dwellers. Additional foods would have come in from other areas in the Basin. We think in terms of supporting a city of 125,000–200,000 (Millon, 1981).

It is now felt that not only did Teotihuacan control the entire Basin, but that certain areas were carefully colonized to exploit specific resources. Thus the southern regions of Chalco-Xochimilco, Ixtapalapa, and southern Texcoco were settled by people who hunted deer and provided the oak and pine timber for building. Others exploited the lake by fishing and taking waterfowl. The most substantial rural settlements were concentrated in the west-central region of Tacuba, Tenayuca, Cuauhtitlán, and Temascalapa to the east, where multi-family dwellings like those of Teotihuacan were erected. Ecatepec seems to have been a salt-producing station. Special stone, earth, and various clays were in demand for building and pottery-making. Maguey fibers were always needed for clothing and cordage. The lake shore provided reeds from which baskets and mats were woven. Farmers everywhere raised staples. The settlement at Zumpango in the extreme northwestern corner of the Basin may have been located to extract lime in the Río Salado drainage. Extensive lime quarries have been located that could have met the demands of the builders and masons of the great metropolis. Thus the Basin itself could have supplied most of the necessary basics and was viewed as a giant resource area for the maintenance of the city.

Commerce   A city of this magnitude would have required any number of skills, because clothing, household furnishings, and luxury objects for ceremony and trade, such as fine stone masks and exquisitely decorated tripod vessels with lids, were manufactured here and either sold in the marketplace or exported in all directions.

A very specialized workshop was excavated by INAH at the northwest corner of the Ciudadela (Munera, 1989). It was as if the five o'clock whistle blew and workers put down their tools and walked out leaving half-finished products behind. In this case the products were ritual objects, the fancy hourglass incense burners so characteristic of the Metepec phase (Figure 6.3f). These were mass produced from A.D.650 to 750, and each household may have kept one as an everyday altar or shrine.

The workshop was well organized, most activity taking place in an open patio where the raw material, clay, was received. Tempering was added and the clay then worked to the desirable texture. When ready, parts of the incense burner would be molded. Firing was done close by in open hearth ovens and then the various parts were assembled and finishing touches added. The final products were stored in the north palace of the Temple of Quetzalcoatl within the Ciudadela to await distribution.

Although the burners appear very similar, there was a great variety of ornamentation. In the center was usually a hieratic face richly adorned. Tlaloc, a plumed-serpent deity, Huehuéteotl, and Xipe Totec were other favorites. Many animals, birds, and plants were also used as motifs along with elements of marine and aquatic life. Butterflies were common, sometimes represented by just a wing or antenna. The censers were another source of glyphic signs such as the Reptile Eye, Turquoise, and Speech Scroll. Munera (1989) believes these signs conveyed a message.

Other specialized workshops produced domestic pottery (see Tlajinga 33, p. 167), clay figurines, both hand- and mold-made, lapidary work in shell, jade, and serpentine, ground stone and basalt tools, and slate ornaments. Leather and wood workers, feather workers, paper makers, weavers, and basketmakers must have also had their own shops, but being of perishable materials, their products have not been preserved. Builders were needed for construction, cutting stone, making concrete for walls, floors, and ceilings. Lime was important for plastering and needed in large quantities, as walls had to be covered in preparation for paintings.

Thin Orange   Thin Orange pottery is a distinctive fine-paste ware that was Teotihuacan's most important commercial ware and the most abundant in surface collections. The origin of this unusual clay has been sought for many years. The precise source is now thought to be in the Tepexi region of the State of Puebla. Rattray (1990) has found seven or eight nucleated settlements with pottery-making workshops along the Río Carnero where both Thin Orange pottery for export and coarser wares for local consumption were produced. This fine clay was made into a variety of bowls, jars, and effigy vessels and taken to Teotihuacan for distribution. Thick, coarse Thin Orange amphorae were also produced having three handles, measuring 75 cm in height by 40 cm at the shoulder. As utilitarian vessels, they could have carried resins to Teotihuacan and, once emptied, might have served as storage jars, or been reused to export a product such as pulque (Lackey, 1986). Although Thin Orange is one of Teotihuacan's most important exports, Rattray found no evidence of a Teotihuacan presence in Tepexi. Thin Orange was abundant in the Classic period at highland sites such as Cholula, but rare in Oaxaca, and almost unknown in Morelos sites. It is also present in the Prado phase at Tula, Hidalgo. The ware was in such demand that cost and distance were apparently of little concern. Loaded on the backs of *tamemes*, these bearers could have made deliveries via Calpulalpan to the southern coastal lowlands for distribution. Just what the arrangement was between Teotihuacan and Tepexi we do not know but Teotihuacan may have had exclusive rights. Probably these loads were tribute payments exacted by the city. The operation came to a swift end when Teotihuacan collapsed. By A.D. 800 a Thin Orange pot had become an heirloom.

The constant movement of raw materials and finished products entailed much going and coming of people who earned their living backpacking tumplines. All routes led to the marketplace, the commercial heart of the city. The Great Compound across the Street of the Dead from the Ciudadela possibly served this purpose (Millon *et al.*, 1973). A market complex such as this was vital to the proper functioning of the city. A well-organized market served as a necessary and perfect vehicle for the distribution and exchange of goods. Here one could find raw materials and luxury goods that might include magnetite, hematite, marine shell, chert, cotton, feathers, and rubber (Kolb, 1986).

Obsidian   We have seen how Teotihuacan housed and fed its urban population but what was the basis of its commercial "empire" that brought such great prosperity? One answer is probably obsidian.

The study of obsidian permits us not only to appraise the tools into which it was made, but to see the functioning of a particular exchange network. This black volcanic glass found only in highland areas of volcanism, is formed by rapid cooling of igneous ejecta and has the advantages of being durable, datable by modern techniques, and easily transported. With practice it can produce a sharp cutting edge valued by Mesoamericans since slaughtering the Iztapan mammoth. Although obsidian looks black, when a thin flake or transparent edge is held to the light, it shows a color (usually green or gray) and it may be streaked, cloudy, or have spots. Another variety is reddish brown in color from an as yet unidentified source that was exploited on a small scale in Classic times.

By trace analysis studies, 25 sources in highland Guatemala and Mexico have been identified and it is now possible to locate the source system of many obsidian artifacts. In some cases where the source system is very extensive (100 km) it is difficult to identify the precise quarry site therein (Cobean *et al.*, 1991). The great hill of obsidian near Pachuca, Hidalgo is the only known source of green obsidian and was the most desirable for several reasons. It is found in veins which can be mined in large quantities. The matrix is cleaner with fewer flaws and fractures which made it well suited for making prismatic blades (Santley *et al.*, 1986), the favorite knife of Mesoamericans. Gray, with 15 known sources, is far more common and of lesser grade. Guadalupe Victoria's obsidian in eastern Puebla was of rather poor quality, being unusually brittle and hard to work, and consequently in less demand.

Obsidian has been mentioned with some frequency as being one of the earliest traded goods, but it is during the Classic Period that what had begun in Preclassic times as an exchange system was transformed into a major industry (Sanders and Santley, 1983; Santley, 1989).

In the case of Teotihuacan, bear in mind that sources of green and gray obsidian were only 50 and 22 km away. In the Late Preclassic Period (Patlachique), the Old City of Teotihuacan used large quantities of points and knives of gray obsidian. By the Tlamimilolpa phase numerous workshops near the Great Compound produced exclusively green blades, a successful commercial enterprise. Whether or not Teotihuacan had direct control over the mines is debatable but the workshops in the city suggest procurement, production, and exchange activities (R. Millon, 1988a). As the city began to decline, the quantity of gray obsidian greatly increased and the green became scarcer, implying a breakdown in an out-of-town enterprise at Tepeapulco. This establishment, closely associated with Teotihuacan, reflected its fortunes and thus did not operate again on a large scale until later Toltec times.

The Tepeapulco network operated an obsidian industry and is believed to date from the Preclassic Period. With the exception of a hiatus after the fall of Teotihuacan, it remained a major commercial enterprise until the Conquest and even into the Colonial Period (Charlton, 1978). The beginning of the line was the extraction of the raw material in the form of cores and blanks from the source areas of Cerro de las Navajas (Pachuca), Barranca de los Estetes (Otumba), Paredón, and Tulancingo, from where they were taken via footpaths to Tepeapulco (Map 6.3). Workshop areas have been identified there by the heavy concentrations of obsidian in the form of unused, retouched flakes, broken tools, and the near absence of cores. From Tepeapulco, the final products could be taken via a natural exit in the terrain to Tulancingo in the Meztitlán Valley that afforded the most direct route to central Veracruz and the important center of El Tajín.

The efficient operation of this network and its strict control by Teotihuacan operation reveals a degree of sophistication previously undetected. It is interesting to note that although the city had some obsidian workshops within its confines, the main industrial center for this craft was located away from the urban development.

Outsiders in the City

Xolalpan and Metepec phases provide ample evidence of nonlocal traits at Teotihuacan. From Veracruz came the cult of the ball game, recorded in the Tepantitla murals, the Ventilla ball court marker, stone yokes, and figurines. A particular double-scroll style, a hallmark of El Tajín, is prominently displayed on pottery and on the ball court marker. In the murals we see evidence of relationships with Oaxaca, the Gulf Coast, and both highland and lowland Maya areas. The "Pinturas Realistas" (Tepantitla) show a "long-nosed deity," certainly a stranger to Teotihuacan. These paintings portray foreigners such as Mayoid peoples with distinctive slanted eyes, body paint, masks, and dress. The bands of glyphs placed in a row are clearly Maya inspired. Maya pottery and iconography is in evidence but no Maya colony or settlement at Teotihuacan has ever been found. There are, however, two interesting areas in which foreigners lived in the city. One is the Merchants' Barrio.

Merchants' Barrio   What is known as the Merchants' Barrio is an area in the extreme northeastern sector of Teotihuacan near the modern town of San Francisco Mazapan. This lies just south of the residential compound of Tlamimilolpa and straddles the barranca of the San Juan River. The inhabitants may or may not have been merchants, but the neighborhood was named for the unusually high concentra-

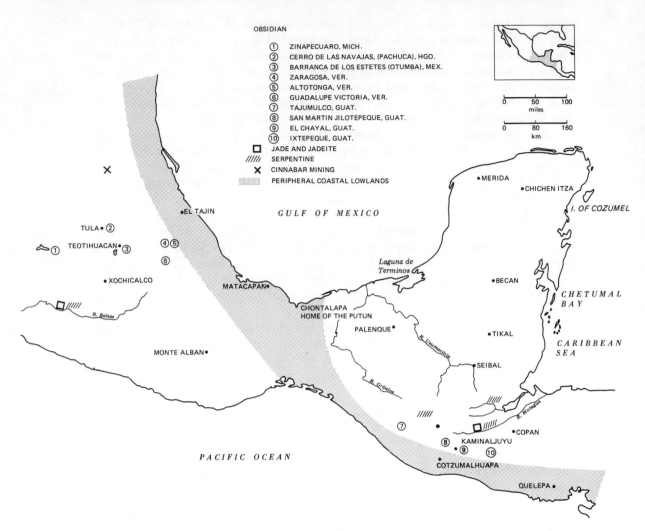

OBSIDIAN

① ZINAPECUARO, MICH.
② CERRO DE LAS NAVAJAS, (PACHUCA), HGO.
③ BARRANCA DE LOS ESTETES (OTUMBA), MEX.
④ ZARAGOSA, VER.
⑤ ALTOTONGA, VER.
⑥ GUADALUPE VICTORIA, VER.
⑦ TAJUMULCO, GUAT.
⑧ SAN MARTIN JILOTEPEQUE, GUAT.
⑨ EL CHAYAL, GUAT.
⑩ IXTEPEQUE, GUAT.
☐ JADE AND JADEITE
///// SERPENTINE
✕ CINNABAR MINING
▨ PERIPHERAL COASTAL LOWLANDS

M A P 6.2   Highland resources.

tions of foreign pottery found here (R. Millon, 1988a; Rattray, 1987b, 1989). This proved to be an area where Gulf Coast people and lowland Maya first settled in the late Tlamimilolpa period (A.D. 200–400) and by early Xolalpan (A.D. 400–500) had increased their numbers. As yet we have no data on population estimates but approximately 18 circular constructions (7–10 m in diameter) accessed by ramps were found associated with burials. Some of these constructions might have been living quarters (?) but most were for storage; others were designed for ceremonial purposes. There was one standard Teotihuacan apartment compound. Although stone was eventually used for construction, the quality of the work was inferior to that of Tlamimilolpa.

These intruders brought with them their own fine paste pottery that made up

15% of the ceramic assemblages with the southern Veracruz region predominating. Maya imports were largely from northern Belize, the Yucatán Peninsula, and coastal sites rather than from highland Guatemala (Ball, 1983).

Burials were often found under altars centered in patios, frequently associated with fine paste wares of orange, cream, and gray foreign wares. In one pit, 41 secondary graves of men, women, and children included small pieces of jade, shell beads, and weaving instruments. Some obsidian workshops produced prismatic blades and bifacial points. The variety and number of bone instruments suggest a weaving industry. Undoubtedly, lowland ceramics were not the only imports, and perishable goods such as cacao would also have made the trip to the highlands. Cotton would have been another import and feathers were needed for warrior outfits and priestly attire.

Changes were made in late Xolalpan. A group of rectangular rooms were built with large, rough stones which covered two earlier circular structures. In other areas square platforms bordered large patios with a central shrine. A great number of thick Fine Orange amphorae were brought in from Puebla probably filled with some kind of liquid.

This barrio was distinct from Tlamimilolpa. The latter yielded great quantities of domestic and ceremonial pottery typical of Teotihuacan and few imports. In the Merchants' Barrio there was little local domestic ware but toward the end of Xolalpan, local censers, miniatures, and figurines became popular. These inhabitants were outsiders with different customs of burial, and styles of architecture and ceramics. The *comal*, for example, so typical of Teotihuacan, was absent in the Merchants' Barrio. Although the most abundant foreign pottery is from the Tuxtlas region of Veracruz, R. Millon (1988a) does not believe these were Teotihuacanos from Matacapan where you find rectilinear domestic architecture. Teotihuacanos would have lived elsewhere in the city. From the burials it is also clear that these were resident families, not just traders, but the other foreigners in the city were more permanently established.

The Oaxaca Barrio   Crossing the Street of the Dead to the western sector of the city is an area known as Tlailotlacan, more commonly referred to as the Oaxaca Barrio (Map 6.1). Here we find another foreign settlement where the first inhabitants arrived in late Tlamimilolpa about A.D. 300 and continued to thrive throughout the great Xolalpan period, perhaps outlasting the eastern Merchants' Barrio (Spence, 1989).

This enclave presents a somewhat different situation from that just seen. Here some Oaxaqueños arrived, built an adobe platform, and by the following Xolalpan period seem to have adapted to life at Teotihuacan. They lived in Teotihuacan-style apartments, built a talud-tablero-style temple, and used local pottery. The extent of their quarters was small, perhaps 6 to 7 apartment complexes with patios, shrines, platforms, rooms, and storage areas.

Archaeologists were amazed to find tombs modeled after those of Monte Albán with stairs, antechambers, and inner chambers in which the deceased and offerings were placed. In at least one case the typical Monte Albán urn with Zapotec glyphs was placed in the niche over the chamber entrance. Commoners were given extended graves and women were buried as well as men, not the practice among Teotihuacanos. Oaxaca-type urns, incense burners, and ritual vessels were included in offerings along with typical Teotihuacan vessels and Thin Orange ware.

Even more surprising was finding abundant domestic pottery and household objects still made in Oaxaca-style several hundred years after the initial settlement of the barrio. This is noteworthy because the presence of these objects reflects not only respect, taste, and pride in things Oaxacan, but a conscious effort to see that each generation would grow up with an intimate and constant contact with an ancestral culture it had not experienced. More often ethnic goods are produced for public display and acclamation.

What was the role of this community and what was their incentive to preserve this ethnic identity? Spence (1989) suggests that it may have benefited from maintaining close ties with other groups of Zapotec affiliation. Several such settlements existed near Tula where Teotihuacan controlled a major lime extraction industry (see page 387). The Tlailotlacan people residing at Teotihuacan may have controlled or administered this project.

This makes two groups of foreigners that resided in the city and there may have been others. The Oaxaqueños give the impression of sedentary residents who traded on their ethnic affiliation and mixed well with the Teotihuacanos while overseeing some profitable mercantile operation. An arrangement such as this would reinforce the ethnic identity of the Zapotecs, and help maintain the language and perhaps endogamy as well.

Nearest Neighbors

Thus far we have been concerned with the growth and socioeconomic organization of the city. It is now time to examine the extent of Teotihuacan's contacts with other areas. So powerful did Teotihuacan become that it is tempting to speak of an empire. This is not really applicable as "empire" implies more complete control than the evidence warrants at the present time. Teotihuacan's domain would have included the Basin of Mexico, probably eastern Morelos, and an area across the north (see below) but beyond that her fame was probably spread by merchants instrumental in building contacts and diplomatic relationships. Teotihuacan's products were in great demand, especially finished obsidian tools, fine quality pottery, figurines, and minor crafts. Its predilection for talud-tablero architecture may have been imitated in some areas, but it may have an earlier history at Tikal and the style was very widespread. The greatest and most lasting impact of Teotihuacan was made in the field of art and iconography.

In order to support and maintain this enormous capital, a very successful and ambitious economic program was called for. Already Teotihuacan depended on the entire Basin of Mexico. Eastern Morelos with its fine cotton and rich agricultural products loomed as a desirable objective. As Teotihuacan increased in size and power, this eastern area of Morelos was incorporated into its tributary domain. Agriculture was intensified and rural settlements were encouraged under a system of hierarchical order: small settlements reporting to the next larger ones in a coordinated network. In this way, the sustaining hinterland of Teotihuacan was organized around one nucleated administrative center and dispersed rural hamlets. The important crop was undoubtedly cotton.

Adjacent to the Basin of Mexico to the north was a wide band of land stretching across southeastern Hidalgo and northern Tlaxcala. This area was important for provisioning the city and for communicating with other regions. A number of settlements sprang up, leaving telltale remains of Thin Orange pottery, Teotihuacan figurines, and objects of household use. Chingú, near Tula, is an example of one such settlement, founded around the fourth century. This was a kind of provisional center located near fine lime deposits. The demands of urban construction called for great quantities of lime and the role of Chingú was to administer and handle the transfer of this commodity. By A.D. 600, however, the retrenchment of Teotihuacan brought this enterprise to an end and Chingú was abandoned.

The North

To the far north, Teotihuacan sent out colonists to exploit mineral resources. During this Classic Period, the frontier of Mesoamerica was pushed northward, for during these years rainfall was more plentiful and farmers extended their cultivation accordingly. Along the eastern foothills of the Sierra Madre Occidental lay a corridorlike area inhabited by sedentary farmers that extended north through the states of Zacatecas and Durango to the southern boundary of Chihuahua. This narrow strip of cultivation, limited on the west by the juniper, pine, and oak forests of the foothills and by the great interior desert plateau on the east, has been found to have a great number of archaeological remains consisting of fortresses combined with religious centers. The fortified settlements are usually situated on hilltops with village-farming communities occupying terraces and the alluvial plains in the valleys below. These remains scattered east of the Sierra Madre Occidental and north of the great Santiago River system belong to the Chalchihuites culture.

This culture is known from a number of sites that are found from La Quemada and Alta Vista in Zacatecas as far north as Zape in northern Durango (Map 6.3). Alta Vista was a major center of the so-called Suchil Branch of Chalchihuites sites. The Schroeder site was the best known of a later branch known as Guadiana in Durango. This is a great northern peripheral region of high cultural development and is believed to be the possible hearth of many cultural and militaristic traits that later became associated with Postclassic cultures of central Mexico. These may include Coyotlatelco and *blanco levantado* pottery, smoking pipes, Tezcatlipoca ceremonialism, the *tzompantli* (skull rack), and the sculpture known as *chacmool*. Characteristic of the region are square sunken courts, columned structures, orthongonal site layout, and, in some places, extensive causeways corresponding to the *sacbeob* of the Maya.

Leopoldo Batres and Manuel Gamio were the earliest investigators, but perhaps the name that most frequently comes to mind is that of Pedro Armillas (1969), having

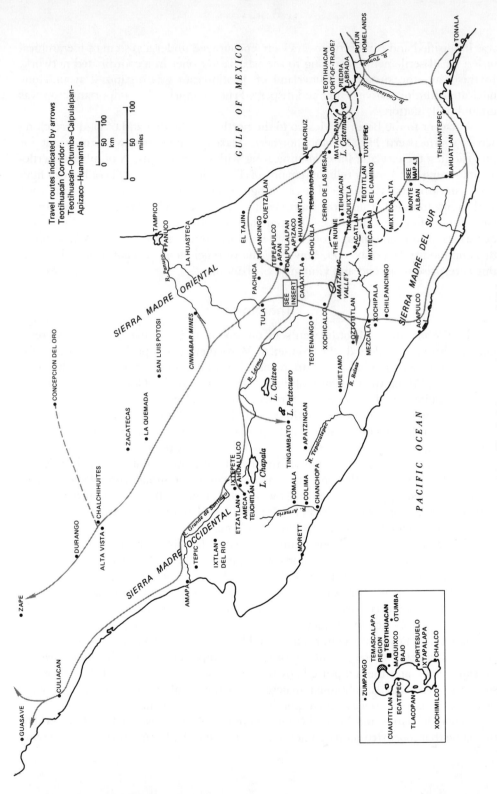

MAP 6.3 Classic Mesoamerica west of Tehuantepec.

worked in 1951–1952 at La Quemada. Since then no one has contributed more to this northern frontier than J. Charles Kelley and Phil C. Weigand.

The term Chalchihuites was coined many years ago by J. Alden Mason to include this wide area. More recently, Kelley (1990a) prefers to restrict the culture to the Suchil branch in Zacatecas and the Guadiana branch in Durango. Trombold (1990), Nelson (n.d.), and Hers (1989) also include La Quemada in this culture. Both arrangements have their justification and supporters, and there are overlaps on many points. Although La Quemada was not a mining center as was Alta Vista, I include it here in the sense of a broad Chalchuihuites tradition.

La Quemada La Quemada is a familiar name in Mesoamerica but belongs to a site few people have seen, regrettably myself included. It is popularly known as a site fortified against the northern hordes of Chichimecs and rumored to have been founded by the Toltecs. Recent attention has been focused on La Quemada as investigations by Charles Trombold, Ben Nelson, and Mari-Areti Hers have revealed new information that have altered earlier misconceptions as to chronology and interaction between central Mexico and this northern frontier. Not all the reports are completed and what follows is culled from preliminary interpretations and is still tentative.

Settlements in the Malpaso Valley in southern Zacatecas represent a northern expansion of Mesoamerican culture during years of favorable climatic conditions. La Quemada was one of several isolated sedentary polities surrounded by nomadic peoples that occupied this northern frontier.

The huge site of La Quemada is perched on the top of a cliff backed by a massive defensive wall. A broad causeway leads up from the valley floor to one group of structures. Other roads radiate to smaller settlements in the surrounding valley and to a small pyramid on a hill to the east. Since little is known of its history, it has been very difficult to place La Quemada chronologically and for many years it was considered to be Postclassic.

It is possible that La Quemada was one of the largest and most important sites in north-central Mexico during the Classic Period. Trombold (1990) calculates the fall of this site, or at least the end of construction, to have taken place between A.D. 835 and 850. The place was probably abandoned after the fall of Teotihuacan and before the rise of Tula. Therefore, instead of receiving influences from, it more likely contributed to the growth of Tula. No Toltec material has been recovered from the excavations: no metal, *molcajetes*, Plumbate, or mold-made figurines (Nelson, 1990). Even so, there may have been some Postclassic residents that occupied the site according to Kelley (1990b) and Weigand (1982).

The remains themselves are of more than usual interest. The ruins cover most of an elongated hill: a great stone wall and ramparts encircle the hilltop. Interior structures were found in the fortifications (staircase, residential quarters, and middens), indicating a long history of construction and the fortifications may have been a late addition.

Lower on the hillside are courts surrounded by walls or pyramids; others contain small pyramids and altars. There are colonnaded courts, great stairways, and a subterranean passage, perhaps roofed by a corbeled arch. In the lower part of the citadel a wide walk leads to the Hall of Columns that is a rectangular open area paved with red plaster and studded with 11 round stone pillars. These are not unique, as there are others in the core area as well as in hinterland sites. Both square and round columns are found. This is a standard architectural feature of the region. The Hall of Columns was once the scene of a brutal massacre, leaving hundreds of skeletons without feet or skulls. A layer 10–20 m deep of charred human bones was found along three sides of the interior walls, extending out for 3 m. The bones lay directly on the floor, covered by debris when the building burned (Kelley, 1978). The large colonnades and much of the construction are built from small flat slabs of stone and adobe brick. A large I-shaped ball court lies between the Hall of Columns and a steep-sided votive pyramid (Figure 6.8). These structures are connected by raised causeways formed by parallel masonry walls that have been filled with rubble and smoothed to make the roadbed. These are very similar to the roads of Xochicalco and the *sacbeob* of Yucatán.

Much of the public area has been cleaned and preserved but not excavated, so there will be much yet to learn. The recent excavations by Ben Nelson (n.d.) have centered on terracing on the western flank of the citadel. He has found habitation rooms and both public and ritual spaces. These were strictly residential terraces, for the stairways, platforms, landings, and middens would not have been suitable for agriculture. One terrace connects a staircase and causeway to the central ceremonial precinct.

The largest terrace, No. 18, with level space of 40 × 70 m, supported adobe

FIGURE 6.8   Votive pyramid at La Quemada, Zacatecas. (Courtesy of the Instituto Nacional de Antropología e Historia, Mexico.)

structures on platforms around a large sunken patio. This terrace also had a small open-ended ball court with masonry walls that had been replastered several times. At the end of one wall was a headless stone statuette of a ball-player 40 cm in height.

Nelson sees La Quemada as a product of local growth, not a colony or built in haste as a commercial outpost. Its long history shows gradual and slow construction. Population is difficult to estimate with the material at hand, but it must have been substantial to judge from the 48,000 m² of terracing (excluding public architecture) revealed by the mapping. If this area was indeed occupied by residents, 4000–8000 population is possible. This is far larger than formerly anticipated.

La Quemada was in a prime location for north–south trade. Turquoise from the Cerrillos mine in New Mexico has been found in the Malpaso Valley (Weigand et al., 1977; Weigand, 1982), so rare resources did find their way through without needing a state-controlled infrastructure. Turquoise began to be used heavily after A.D. 700 (Weigand and Harbottle, 1987) although it did not replace malachite until the epiclassic years.

There may have been two distinct periods of development at La Quemada. The first corresponds to Alta Vista's early Canutillo phase that Kelley envisions as a derivative of the Lerma-Santiago River corridor, and a second one between the years A.D. 600 and 800. There is a C-14 date of A.D. 930 ± 120 from a sample taken from a hearth above a collapsed roof. Presumably this dates a later group of people that may have lived among the ruins from A.D. 810 to 1050. La Quemada is another site that shows evidence of a fire, date unknown. We expect that some of the smaller sites will eventually help reconstruct the history of this Malpaso Valley.

Alta Vista Approximately 175 m northwest of La Quemada, west of the Río Colorado and the town of Chalchihuites lies the site of Alta Vista, still in the state of Zacatecas. The people of Alta Vista were remarkable and sophisticated despite all their unappealing sacrificial customs. Archaeologist J. Charles Kelley and his wife, Ellen, have worked for many field seasons at Alta Vista in order to understand and make sense out of a complex jumble of remains. The simplified account that follows is based on Kelley (1990a), a summary of investigations at Alta Vista dating back to 1956.

Two environmental features have dominated the cultural development of Alta Vista. First, it is located close to, or actually on, the Tropic of Cancer, a fact that may well have dictated its founding by Teotihuacan (Aveni et al., 1982). Second, the area was the scene of tremendous mining operations exploiting the great variety of mineral deposits. We think the Teotihuacanos were lured to this northern frontier by its deposits of malachite, jadeite, green stones, hematite, weathered chert, and flint. Extraction of these exotic materials began in Late Preclassic years, but the operation was greatly expanded after A.D. 400.

Attention in recent years has focused on the surprising extent of these mining enterprises. Deep pits and tunnels several kilometers long have debris taluses associated with mining operations. The defensible hilltop or mountain sites protected the commercial enterprise as well as the frontier, for there is evidence of perpetual conflict with the nomadic Chichimecs. Not only was this region exploited, but expeditionary trips were made as far north as Cerrillos, north-central New Mexico, for only the North American Southwest possessed large deposits. Thus trade routes were opened between these areas, which stimulated continual social and cultural contacts. Turquoise sources can be identified by neutron-activation analysis, and Garman Harbottle and Phil Weigand have analyzed over 2000 pieces from 28 archaeological sites in Mesoamerica and the Southwest. Over two dozen Mesoamerican artifacts have been traced to specific mines more than 1000 miles away in New Mexico, Arizona, and Nevada (Harbottle and Weigand, 1992).

The first area to work turquoise extensively was Alta Vista. Here it was worked into artifacts for ritual use from raw nodules at a huge workshop (Weigand and Harbottle, 1987). A second source of turquoise, one within Mexico, was the Concepción del Oro region on the Coahuila-Zacatecas border. These were small natural outcrops and exploitation was done by expeditionary groups, not colonizers. Teotihuacan is believed to have had complete control of the Alta Vista mines and the minerals were carried south to the city for processing. It must have been an oppressive colonial enterprise, making virtual slaves of the local inhabitants.

The selection of the site for Alta Vista had been carefully planned. It lies directly west of a mountain peak called Picacho Pelón, over which the sun rises on the equinoxes. In addition, the site is equidistant from other mountains to the north and south. The summer solstice rising over Pelón at this time can be viewed from the southern mountain, an event noted on a petroglyph with a cross and concentric circle, the same symbol found at Teotihuacan and at Uaxactún. It follows that from the northern mountain, one can watch the sun rise over Pelón on the winter solstice. In the heart of the central ceremonial core, a colonnaded gallery leads east to a stone column placed between two slits in a stone masonry wall. Called the Labyrinth, this was actually an observatory. The column casts no shadow at noon on the summer solstices, demonstrating its position on the Tropic of Cancer. No doubt other astronomical sightings could have been taken before the deterioration of the building.

The center of the ruins was originally a large rectangular court surrounded by raised stone walled walkways with stairs leading down on all sides. Toward one side was a temple with thick walls of cobblestone and adobe mortar with a roof supported by 28 round columns. In front of the temple was a kind of roofed porch called a Hall of Columns. Eventually alterations were made, but the building was probably constructed as a shrine to Tezcatlipoca (Lord of the North, the four directions, and the night skies). It seems likely that this shrine was built by Teotihuacanos or people from one of their satellites. From A.D. 700 to 750, after the fall of Teotihuacan, many changes took place; new pottery types were produced and the mining industry was revitalized. Apparently the exotic goods that had once been exported now became available to the local populace.

A new human sacrificial cult, complete with *tzompantlis*, cannibalism, and representations of warriors with shields and weapons appears. The peak of development was reached from A.D. 800 to 850 when the central temple was remodeled into a pyramid as part of a 3-temple complex. Courts, columns, porches, walkways, and walls proliferated. Some covered walkways had once supported hanging femurs and pierced skulls. One of these areas, (Structure 4) also known as the Temple of the Skulls, contained a 20-cm layer of human skeletal material on the floor where it had fallen from racks above. Trophy-head displays and long-bone suspension was not uncommon at Alta Vista (Kelley, 1978).

In the final years, some spaces were allowed to deteriorate and refuse was dumped in areas previously neatly maintained. As to pottery, champleve, pseudocloisonné, and negative painted vessels were no longer produced. By A.D. 900 parts of the site were burned and some people had emigrated.

The population dropped sharply but some villagers may have remained. Of the emigrants, warriors may have been the first to leave, heading south with some joining the Caxcanes and others forming part of the Tolteca-Chichimeca intrusion we will find at Tula (Hers, 1989). This exodus did not cause major problems in the north, however, for others after leaving Alta Vista took up residence nearby at the Schroeder site in the Guadiana Valley in Durango.

At Schroeder, a number of hamlets grew up, rather than having a typical central ceremonial center. There is a small oddly shaped pyramid and a small open-ended ball court. Construction was centered around small courts, stone walkways, and walled house platforms built of slab stone masonry (Kelley, 1990b). Thus the Chalchihuites culture was carried on by other centers that continued to prosper. The area maintained its contact with the American Southwest and Cerrillos turquoise continued to flow south.

Cerro de Huistle   There were manifestations of the Chalchihuites culture all along the northern rivers that flow south into the Río Grande de Santiago (Hers, 1989). Of these I will mention only the Cerro de Huistle that lies almost due south of Chalchihuites in a desolate area of barrancas and mountains, about 5 km west of Huejuquilla el Alto in the very northern tip of Jalisco.

The site of Huistle on the south part of the mountain has an 18-m plaza surrounded by structures. On the staircase of the small temple on the east side was a tumbled down sculptured stone thought to be proto-*chacmool*. This is a crude human figure that lies on its back looking up to the heavens. The flexed limbs are simply indicated by incisions and the horizontal flat belly would have served to receive offerings (?). The features are formed of punched holes. This sculpture is believed to date between A.D. 550 and 900 based on ceramics and eight C-14 dates, making this the earliest and only *chacmool* known of Classic date. Nearby were two human skulls with drilled holes in the vertex permitting suspension, evidence of a *tzompantli*. From the location of the proto-*chacmool*, Hers believes that originally it had been placed at the top of the stairs at the entrance to the temple or shrine. Its association with a *tzompantli* indicates a close relationship to human sacrifice and bellicose ritual. This formed part of the Tolteca-Chichimeca contribution to Tula (Hers, 1989).

Querétaro   In addition to the mining operation in the far north, exploitation of cinnabar deposits in northern Querétaro in the A.D. 600s was also undertaken by the

Teotihuacanos. These mines had been known and exploited long before by the Gulf Olmec, but the most intensive mining operations were carried out toward the end of the middle Classic period. Judging from pottery and stone yokes recovered at the site, both Teotihuacanos and central Veracruz groups were present. We do not know how the mines were controlled, but the objective was to extract cinnabar, one of the special commodities prized for decorating fine pottery and a substance deemed necessary for ritual. It was also the source of red for painting pyramids and elite residences.

From Langenscheidt and Tang Lay's reconstruction of the mining operation (1982), this would have been a tough way to earn a living. The rock face of the mountain was attacked with hammers of diorite or andesite. Attrition eventually created great cavities, actual pits, rooms, and galleries. Where possible, hard wooden wedges were driven into cracks to break off fractured pieces of rock. The debris was allowed to accumulate under foot; this raised the level of the floor and permitted the miners to get at the roof. Remains of baskets and cordage indicate how the stone was removed to be subsequently pulverized and subjected to a flotation process.

The Querétaro mines have been exploited periodically since 300 B.C. (?) and, although deposits are not yet exhausted, the destruction of a round temple, terraces, and walls near the face of a mountain are rather thorough. It is possible, although undocumented, that native mercury was also mined (Langenscheidt and Tang Lay, 1982).

The West

Teotihuacan's primary interest in the north and west was the exploitation of minerals and fine stone resources. The exotic Teotihuacan exports of Thin Orange and beautifully crafted cylindrical tripod vessels are found sporadically in the west but the only areas with a strong Teotihuacan influence were Michoacán and the Balsas region of Guerrero.

Near Cuitzeo at Tres Cerritos, and at Tingambato midway between Uruapan and Pátzcuaro, and farther west near Jiquilpan at the site of El Otero, are Teotihuacan-like centers with public architecture (pyramids and ball courts, Figure 6.9,) with talud-tablero construction placed around plazas (Figure 6.10). Siller (1984) has pointed out however that although the talud-tablero appearance resembles that of Teotihuacan, the construction differs, being reproduced in the west as a decoration by local workers. Stone masks, conch shell trumpets, frescoed vessels, and offerings of turquoise, rock crystal, and pyrite mirrors are all familiar Teotihuacan artifacts. All three centers, however, buried their dead non-Teotihuacan fashion in large tombs containing 30–40 individuals. The ceramics, regardless of style, were all of local manufacture (Piña Chan, personal communication; Pollard, 1991). Thus it seems that the talud-tablero architecture and ceramics were inspired from, or were imitations of those of Teotihuacan, and do not necessarily imply a direct relationship.

Passing into Jalisco's Atemajac Valley where the modern city of Guadalajara lies today, the inhabitants of the sites of Ixtepete and El Grillo constructed talud-tablero architecture. Another such site, Coyutla, is similar to Ixtepete only on a monumental scale. This site was well fortified by cliffs and terraces, serving as a natural gateway

FIGURE 6.9   Talud-tablero style construction at Tingambato, Michoacán. Narrow end-zone of a ball court. (Courtesy of Roman Piña Chan.)

from the Lerma River to the Jalisco highland lake area. Only 10 km west of the Atemajac Valley we find an entirely different scene: the extraordinary independent societies of the Teuchitlán region.

The explorations of Phil Weigand since the 1970s have yielded a unique architectural complex of major significance that occupied the highland lake districts of Jalisco and Nayarit. The area to be discussed is the fertile Teuchitlán Valley, an area of great ecological diversity located near deep canyons and high mountains, with rich soils and a nutrient-rich lake basin. Not overlooked by the early people were the rich resources of copper, silver, gold, malachite, pyrite, hematite, and fine quality quartz and obsidian.

The earlier Preclassic shaft tombs had by now been replaced by a monumental circular architecture of a form without precedent in Mesoamerica: hundreds of sites of which the Teuchitlán-El Refugio zone will serve as a good example (Weigand, 1990).

This zone is one of six great settlements loosely ringing the base of the Volcán de Tequila. Most of the building activity here is confined to a nucleated core area of 32,000 ha with smaller zones of 3000–5000 ha, each in turn having cores of 300–500 ha. Population for the zone is estimated at 20,000–30,000 individuals. This was a

FIGURE 6.10   Large platform supporting a series of rooms. Talud-tablero construction. Tingambato, Michoacán. (Courtesy of Roman Piña Chan.)

major development of enormous proportions. Each habitation zone is dominated by a monumental multiple circle complex accompanied by lesser circles. The pattern was completed with at least one great ball court and residential compounds of rectangular patios and platforms (Weigand, 1985a, 1990).

In the typical pattern, a concentric circular construction was placed atop a huge circular terraced pyramid. On the flat top was a semisubterranean room, surrounded by a circular elevated patio, in turn enclosed by a circular banquette. Within this enclosure might be as many as 8–16 terraced pyramids with stairways leading into the patio. Underneath the patio are "reenterable family crypts" with shafts and one or more side chambers to contain the dead and offerings (Figure 6.11).

What led to this curious arrangement is not known. We are told that the proportions and symmetry follow set rules and the final result is a scene of grace and elegance. Architecture such as this is indicative of careful planning, and represents considerable social investment in resources and ideology. This was the prevailing architecture throughout the highland lake districts of Jalisco and Nayarit (see Map 6.4).

Agriculture intensified in response to the resulting population boom and good land was plentiful. *Chinampas* were developed along the lake shore; terraces increased and check dams were constructed.

A local obsidian industry was a sophisticated specialization carried out in four

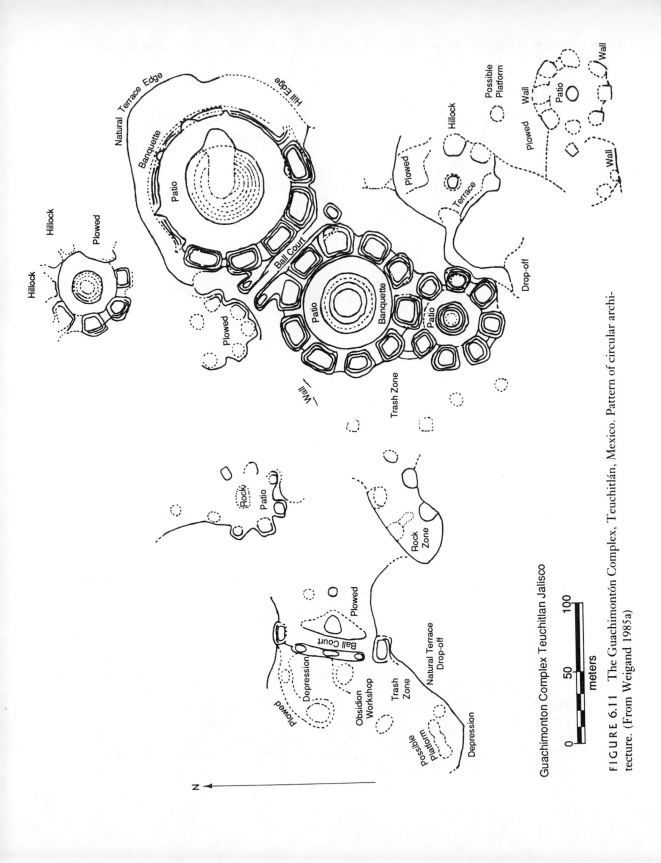

FIGURE 6.11 The Guachimontón Complex, Teuchitlán, Mexico. Pattern of circular architecture. (From Weigand 1985a)

Guachimonton Complex Teuchitlan Jalisco

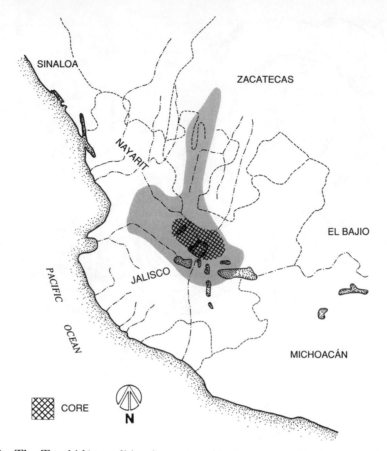

MAP 6.4 The Teuchitlán tradition in western Mexico, geographical extent. (Courtesy of Phil C. Weigand.)

different locations. The raw material was first extracted and transported to a workshop. There cores were produced and moved to another site where prismatic blades were struck. A final stop took care of producing and retouching a wide range of other artifacts. This complex arrangement required efficient management and control.

The differences in architecture and cultural remains between the Teuchitlán and Atemajac valleys are striking. They are separated by a distance of only 10 km with no natural barriers or obstructions forming a frontier. No intermediate or transitional architectural styles are to be found in the marginal areas although derivatives lived on in Bolaños Valley sites to the north. The rectangular and square forms and grid patterns of central Mexico are a far cry from a configuration of concentric circles. No jade is found at Teuchitlán sites. The small quantity of Thin Orange pottery, regardless of its prestigious value elsewhere, seems to have been of little consequence in this west Mexican region. There are few imports of any kind.

Thus these valley folk coexisted with their fundamental cultural differences side by side until around A.D. 700 when the Teuchitlán tradition begins to weaken. Teotihuacan had withdrawn from distant affairs and in the Teuchitlán sites less care was taken in forming the circles and maintaining the strict patterning of superstructures. Secular architecture became more popular and less of an investment. Residential zones began to disperse, breaking up the core.

A logical question is posed by Weigand (1985a). This leads to other questions. If the new order under Teuchitlán was so prosperous, why should it decline instead of expand to take over neighboring activities? There must have been internal social or political problems as yet not understood, but it can hardly be a coincidence that the early Postclassic years see the simultaneous collapse of both the Atemajac-Teuchitlán valleys. After A.D. 900 the circular architectural tradition that affected much of the west in the Classic Period was abandoned.

Before leaving this unusual area, I should mention the fascinating possibility of a Classic Period codex-style writing on *pseudocloisonné* vessels that has been reported by Phil Weigand (1992). Human figures occur on panels; one appears to represent Ehécatl; in another case, an elite person with a name glyph wears a ball game yoke around the waist. Over 2000 vessels of this type are known to exist in private collections, and museums are currently being studied.

A Salt Industry   About the time Teuchitlán began to decline, a remarkable salt-producing enterprise was growing up south of Guadalajara in the Atoyac Basin, flourishing from A.D. 700 to 1300 (Neal and Weigand, n.d.).

Known as Techaluta near Atoyac, an area of 2,000 ha is covered with a great concentration of pyramids, courts, and platforms of all sizes that served as production and processing centers for salt. This industry in turn created a major ceramic center that turned out a variety of wares for boiling, evaporating, and transporting the salt. For evaporite pans, the clay was pressed directly into a hole in the earth and only smoothed and polished on the interior surface. Luxury pottery was also manufactured as the workers resided on the lakeside platforms year-round. Salt production was a full-time operation estimated at attaining a yearly yield of 1460 tons, or 1.5 tons of salt per day! The salt wares are so distinctive that future studies should show their distribution and thus the extent of the network.

Behind the lakeside platforms and evaporite utility areas are complexes of pyramids, courts, and more conventional construction. Residents in this area must have had to support the salt workers by cultivating the agricultural land beyond. This is a particularly well-documented enterprise to be added to our growing inventory of salt-producing stations in Mesoamerica (see page 272).

West Coast

During this same period of time extraordinary changes took place in Nayarit at the site of Amapa near the mouth of the Río Grande de Santiago. It will be recalled that considerable Preclassic remains were found here (Gavilán and Amapa phases).

Following a hiatus (A.D. 400–600), Amapa suddenly looks very much like central Mexico with mounds grouped around plazas oriented to the cardinal directions and some cut stone used in stairways and as trim on buildings. This layout is typically Mesoamerican and proved to be of lasting effect as it continued until the Conquest. Pottery became very elaborate with polychrome and engraved decorations. Special cemeteries were initiated in which the dead were placed in a seated position surrounded by many grave goods and metal artifacts (Meighan, 1976). The appearance of metal here is one of the earliest on record, so Amapa brings us to the introduction of metallurgy, meriting a momentary digression.

Metallurgy   The fact that metallurgy was brought to Mesoamerica from South America always stirs the imagination with thoughts of slashing through jungles with machetes, or waiting for the wind to blow your craft into shore. Probably both scenarios are likely because we think a maritime route was followed from South and Central America into west Mexico, and an overland route through Central America into the Maya region. We note (see page 271) the finding of a gold pendant in Belize around A.D. 550, that was undoubtedly an import from lower Central America. In west Mexico, the establishment of the technology appears between the years A.D. 800 and 1200 (Meighan, 1976; Hosler, 1990). New elements were introduced after this period in a second phase of development. One of the most interesting aspects of the introduction of metallurgy is that although the technique was acquired from abroad, west Mexicans transformed and restructured the technology to accommodate local tastes and needs (Hosler, 1988).

In the early period there are striking similarities with the same inventory of artifacts in both west Mexico and southern Ecuador: bells, needles, open rings, tweezers, axes, awls, and fishhooks (Figure 6.12). In the case of open rings, not only is the technology the same, but they are found in both areas under identical circumstances—in private graves placed near the head. A ring of this type might be used to hold back the hair or as a nosering or earring. Bells, by far the most common artifact produced, were made with a ring for suspension and usually contained a loose clapper. Metallurgists using the lost-wax casting had probably been in touch with the Colombians or lower Central Americans who were highly skilled in this technique (see page 461).

After A.D. 1200, alloys became popular such as copper–tin, copper–arsenic, and copper–silver. These were fashioned into new designs, thinner blades, sheet ornaments, and lost-wax cast ornaments. Bells remained important for a special sound might enhance your status. A man with "good sounds" was respected and had admirable qualities. Since resonance was important, bells were the most popular artifact. Color too was of special interest, and craftspersons learned that by adding arsenic to copper a silver metal was produced, and tin mixed with copper created a very desirable golden cast. The association of gold and silver colors with the sun and moon deities in South and Central America became widespread in the western hemisphere. Both sound and color denoted status and power. Other combinations such as tumbaga (alloy of silver, copper, and gold) (Bray, 1978) were tried, but are less frequent.

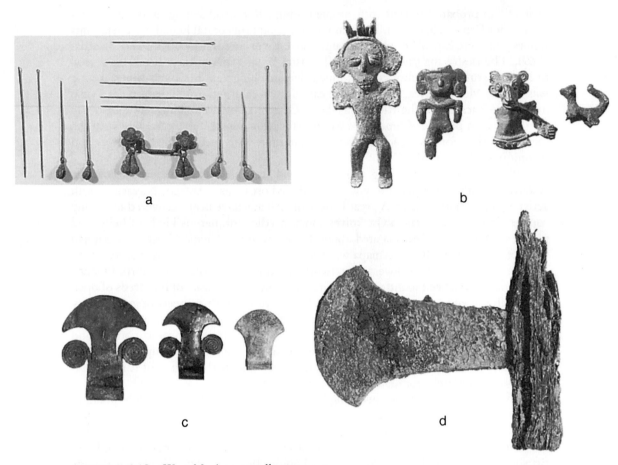

FIGURE 6.12 West Mexican metallurgy.
a. Pendant, needles, and pins of copper from graves at Tzintzuntzan, Michoacán. Maximum length needle: 7 cm; maximum width pendant: 5.5 cm.
b. Copper figurines, Michoacán. Tarascan culture. Height largest figurine: 5.5 cm.
c. Copper tweezers, Michoacán. Tarascan culture. Height largest: 7 cm.
d. Copper axe hafted to wooden handle from Tzintzuntzan grave, Michoacán. Length: 11 cm.
(All photographs courtesy of the Museo National de Antropología, Mexico.)

Most objects were produced for the elite with little attention given to the advantages of a metal tool. Perhaps as Hosler (1988) points out, by the time metallurgy reached west Mexico, stone, wood, ceramics, and shell were used so efficiently that little effort was made to develop a substitute.

Evidence of intercontinental exchange of ceramic styles, forms, and design motifs has been frequently mentioned in the literature (Green and Lowe, 1967; Kelly, 1980; Meighan, 1969; Paulsen, 1977; Edwards, 1969; West, 1961; Hosler, 1988). Initial contact had probably started with simple trading. Rafts and sailing canoes are documented for Ecuador and Peru. The Manteño merchants of coastal Ecuador were famous sailors and were capable of making long, nonstop voyages on the open sea (Edwards, 1969). The desire for *spondylus* shell off coastal Sinaloa might have been one reason to head north. This shell was in as much demand for ritual in South America as it was within Mesoamerica. In 1526 rafts carrying 20 men reportedly stayed for 5 or 6 months at Zacatula in the Río Balsas delta, Guerrero, before making the return trip south. In such periods of time there would have been considerable mingling with the locals and time for discussion and experimentation with metallurgic properties and techniques (West, 1961).

By A.D. 900 metalworking was understood in west Mexico where the natural resources of silver, copper, tin, gold, and alloyed ores exist. Amapa, Nayarit was an active metalworking center. A great variety of artifacts have been recovered including copper rings, beads, axes, awls, knives, pins, needles, numerous kinds of bells, and plaques (Meighan, 1976). Located about 50 km from the Pacific Coast on the north bank of the Santiago River, Amapa was conveniently accessible to maritime travelers.

Another west (or southwest) metalworking center was coastal Guerrero. Quantities of metal have been found near Zihuatenejo. The finds consist of hundreds of open rings, often hooked together in jumbles, along with bells, thin sheets of gold, a gray metal resembling silver, and pieces of slag. Ellen and Charles Brush excavated nearby at the Barnard site and recovered metal associated with polychrome pottery and large quantities of *malacates*. They believe the site to have been occupied just after A.D. 900 (C. F. Brush, n.d.). Analysis of the metal shows that much of it is bronze, probably deliberately compounded of copper and tin alloy.

After the concept of metalworking became understood, it became widespread in Mesoamerica shortly thereafter.

Guerrero   Further to the east along the coast of Guerrero near Acapulco, C. F. Brush (1969), E. S. Brush (1968), and Ekholm (1948) reported Teotihuacan-type pottery and mold-made figurines. This contact seems to have been short lived, however, and was replaced by remains with more Mayoid flavor. The latter was not limited to the coast, for a double-corbeled Maya vault roofed a tomb at Oztotitlan in the northern Río Balsas. Late Mayoid stone sculptures are also reported in the area (Reyna Robles and Rodríguez, B., 1990). Farther west in the middle Balsas Valley both central Mexican and Maya influences are found in the region of Huetamo, Michoacán. A variation of the talud-tablero architecture, resembling that of Xochicalco with the flaring cornice, along with sculptured Mayoid stelae are reported. Guerrero and the eastern Tierra Caliente of Michoacán are known only from spotty data such as these, but what there is indicates that the Río Balsas drainage, although not densely populated, was not isolated from other Classic peoples to the east.

Many objects of Teotihuacan influence (?) are known to come from the upper Balsas River basin near Mezcala, again exposed by looters rather than scientific explorations. Because of their style, these Mezcala stone artifacts have been tentatively placed in an early Classic context, but some may prove to be earlier. Stone vessels, masks, human and animal figures, tools such as axes, chisels, and punches, and curious models of columned temples in a severe and rectilinear style are typical (see Figure 8.10a,b).

More Teotihuacan-style masks come from Guerrero and Puebla than from Teotihuacan itself, and the Guerrero examples are too numerous to be explained by trade. Guerrero was a source of minerals and particularly marine shell that was valued for making jewelry and used in ritual. Preferred stones were serpentine, jadeite, andesite, white nephrite, quartz, chalcedony, amethyst, garnet, alabaster, soapstone, and diorite. Having these natural resources at hand, Guerrero spawned many lapidary artists.

The intrusive features in Guerrero have attracted more attention over the years than the local development as they are quickly isolated. The local attributes of Guerrero far outweigh the importance of outside influences. On the Preclassic level this idea has long been supported. Paul Schmidt (1990) who has worked in Guerrero since 1975 questions the validity of culturally linking Guerrero to west Mexico.

When investigations of a few sites such as La Organera, for example, are better known, there may be some surprises. La Organera is a site of approximately 10 ha located 3 km southeast of the town of Xochipala. The ruins consist of a large civic-religious center, only partly cleared. Six terraces form a north–south axis with the tallest features at the north. There are patios or courts, accompanied by pyramidal structures, platforms, and rectangular rooms with connecting stairways and passages. Reyna Robles and Rodríquez Betancourt (1990) report the presence of square and possibly round columns.

Toward the south are two courts enclosed by structures at least 4 m in height. A low passageway (so low one must crawl!) on the west side of one court is roofed by a corbeled arch, Maya style. Another such "false" arch roofed a closed tomb that contained remains of three individuals (two females and one male). Floors, stairs, and walls were once stuccoed but remains are in poor condition as the zone has been badly looted over the years. Based on his ceramic studies, Schmidt (1990) estimates La Organera to be of late Classic date, and probably much more extensive than has been reported to date.

Final Years at Teotihuacan

The decline started after A.D. 500 and commercial ties were first severed with northwestern Mexico and the Guatemalan highlands. Gradually Teotihuacan withdrew into central Mexico and after a century, the only remaining relationship outside the valley was with El Tajín in Veracruz. The Teotihuacan Corridor had been closed by eastern competitors. The great capital had wielded unprecedented power for 500 years and perhaps her allies became resentful. It is also possible that the authorities had overextended the commercial networks and there may have been mismanagement at home. Some or all of these reasons are possibilities (Diehl, 1989).

Nonetheless, for many years the city itself maintained its usual momentum and to outward appearances was unaffected by the retrenchment abroad. During Metepec (A.D. 650–750) no new construction was added, but the city looked very prosperous.

Prominent in these days were larger, mold-made figurines representing deities or elites, often seated on thrones with attire and insignia included in the mold. Important ceramic features were ornate incense burners, annular-based bowls imitating Thin Orange forms, pottery stamps, and spindle-whorls. Hundreds of clay Metepec figurines depict warriors. Metepec murals are more secular in nature and the beginning of a dynastic pride is apparent (Pasztory, n.d.a). This is explicit in the Techinantitla murals in which a wealth of glyphs and insignia are displayed.

The exact date of the fire is not known but the results were devastating (R. Millon, 1988a). An estimated date is A.D. 750. The fire was deliberately set and well planned to systematically destroy the religious and political center of the city. The monumental architecture on the Street of the Dead was savagely burned and smashed as were temples in the rest of the city. This was not easily done. For example, enormous stones from the balustrade of the great staircase leading to the Temple of the Moon were wrenched out of place and hurled hundreds of yards. Sculptures were shattered. In the Ciudadela, fragments of a carved human figure 60 cm in height had been smashed to bits on top of the temple and then pitched off over the edge in all directions. Looting, smashed skeletons, bodies dismembered or cut to pieces, broken pottery, and the destruction of deity effigies reflect an unleashed fury. More than 2 km of architecture was thus torn down, burned, and smashed in a seemingly excessive devastation so complete as to preclude any idea of reconstruction or restoration. It must have taken days or weeks to accomplish, needing a sizable task force to destroy every vestige of ritual and political power. Events leading up to it may have been gradual, but the actual event was sudden and total.

Who was responsible? Foreigners are not blamed, nor was there a coup d'etat or evidence of warfare. The "who" is still unanswered but speculation leans to the local residents who may have become tired of an antiquated static system of regulated economy, perhaps mismanaged and unwilling or unable to change.

The Coyotlatelco Period

The city was not abandoned but the main center was deserted. Even with only one-fifth of its former population, Teotihuacan remained the largest urban center in the Basin of Mexico for the next 100 years.

This Epi-Classic period (A.D. 750–950) is known as Coyotlatelco, named for a distinctive pottery style of red motifs on a buff or yellowish background. This ware is characteristic of settlements from the Toluca Valley to the Puebla-Tlaxcala region and although its origin is still unknown, likely sources are the regions of Puebla or the Bajío (see page 388). Among other crafts, Teotihuacan seems to have been a large center of Coyotlatelco production.

The Teotihuacan Valley had the largest population of any center in the Basin of Mexico at this time, estimated at 75,000 to 80,000 people (Sanders *et al.*, 1979), with half of them living at Teotihuacan itself. These settled to the east, south, and west of the city, but not in its immediate surroundings. Whether these Coyotlatelco people were descendants of the Teotihuacanos or outsiders, it seems that no one wanted to reoccupy or attempt to rebuild the old capital. This may signify a conscious rupture and desire to eradicate any prolongation of Teotihuacan tradition or association.

The whole power structure in the Basin of Mexico was now changed. There was no longer a centralized authority but a number of settlements grew up in the more sparsely occupied parts of the Basin. These were Zumpango, Cerro Portesuelo, Cerro de la Estrella, Xico, and Azcapotzalco. Aside from the Teotihuacan Valley, the most densely settled area was the central part where the lake was exploited and salt was produced. The lake and forests were also exploited in the south by the residents of small hamlets, while in the north activity centered on the extraction of limestone at a single nucleated village (Sanders *et al.*, 1979; Diehl, 1989).

These are rather undistinguished and colorless years after the glory days of Teotihuacan. There is no visible elite society. Teotihuacan did not perpetuate its ideology and we find no signs of the Great Goddess, the Storm God, or Feathered Serpent. There is no monumental architecture or a definable art style. These central Mexicans had turned over a new leaf.

PUEBLA-TLAXCALA

The Puebla-Tlaxcala region constitutes a key geographical link between highland and eastern lowland cultures. Development in this area was several hundred years ahead of the Basin of Mexico and in its Tezoquipan phase (300 B.C.–A.D. 100) experienced a florescence represented by more than 25 planned civic-ceremonial centers with the earliest known talud-tablero construction in central Mexico (García Cook, 1981).

Teotihuacan's trade routes had been well established in Preclassic days, and a major Classic thoroughfare from Teotihuacan eastward has been plotted by García Cook and Merino (1977) called the "Teotihuacan Corridor." Calpulalpan, Tlaxcala, a gateway point located near the beginning of this route leading to the southern lowlands, was probably a major distribution center for urban products. It seems likely that trade networks and the market system in Teotihuacan proper and the Basin of Mexico functioned separately from the Tepeapulco obsidian industry mentioned above, which was a special enterprise.

The Teotihuacan Corridor carried the major traffic east and south. From Teotihuacan one would start out from the East Avenue and follow the natural drainage system and ridge tops through a pass to the east to reach Calpulalpan. From there the "corridor" continued southeast to Huamantla where it split, one branch turning east to Veracruz, the other going south, probably via Tehuacán (R. Millon, 1988a). The gateways and passes were ideally located to monitor travelers and regulate trade. They probably functioned as major control points for both raw materials moving in and finished products moving out of the city. Another route led east to Tepeapulco and

Tulancingo that was the most direct route to El Tajín. In the other direction, traders and travelers would make the slow ascent to the highlands from the hot lowlands via this Teotihuacan Corridor and enter the big city close to the Great Compound, possibly the main market (see Map 6.1).

It is interesting that although Teotihuacan dominated the entire Basin of Mexico, its influence in Tlaxcala was concentrated in the northern part of the state. The well-known site of Cholula to the south has a paucity of Teotihuacan artifacts and cultural remains at this time.

Cholula in the state of Puebla has been well known and visited by thousands since the Spaniards first publicized it in the sixteenth century, yet it is only through work by the German Foundation of Scientific Investigations and through renewed interest and field work by INAH that a general perspective of the highland areas of Puebla and Tlaxcala is emerging.

The great pyramid at Cholula was begun in the Preclassic Period and the site was remodeled and expanded many times in succeeding years. Archaeological sequences in general parallel those of the Basin of Mexico. Some of the structures are built in the talud-tablero style. An example of this can be seen south of the pyramid where an elegant residential palace is decorated with 50 m of murals of beautiful polychromed frescoes dubbed "the Drunkards." Life-sized figures are shown serving one another and drinking pulque. All the figures have different faces, a rare example of realism. More than a dozen of the illustrated vessels can be duplicated in the archaeological collections.

Contact with Teotihuacan is evident in early Classic ceramics at Cholula, but later the Gulf Coast cultures are more strongly represented. The Classic Period looks rather impoverished. There are no frescoed vessels, no *candeleros*, and few Tlaloc effigy vessels. A smudged variety of Thin Orange occurs. In the years A.D. 100–650, no new hydraulic constructions were built nor was more land cultivated. In fact, a kind of cultural stagnation ensued and even religion seems less important. Smaller, more dispersed rural settlements and fewer sites with formal architecture are found. Of interest is the appearance of fortified sites such as Tetepetla and settlements located in defensible positions. A sharp decline in the general quality of material culture can be seen in pottery and in the absence of, or poorly made, figurines. Outside of the Teotihuacan Corridor, the extreme northwest region, there is little or no indication of contact with Teotihuacan.

Around A.D. 600 Cholula "fell" (García Cook, 1981) and does not resume importance until the end of the ninth century. Flooding also occurred in the area but the damage is not known (Dumond and Muller, 1972). Perhaps people moved over to Cerro Zapotecas where a considerable population is noted about this time. (Was this move due to the arrival of the Olmeca-Xicalanca at Cholula?)

Cerro Zapotecas (Mountjoy and Peterson, 1973) only 3.2 km west of Cholula, is an extinct volcanic crater rising 240 m from the floor of the valley. Most remains date from Middle to Late Classic periods. Considerable building includes two temple/pyramids, possible residential structures on terraces, and a ball court. Stone-lined ditches and some kind of waterworks were found in association with the upper residential terraces. The presence of Plumbate and Fine Orange pottery points to a later occupation, but in general Late Classic-Early Postclassic remains are rare.

This period is one of conflict, struggles for supremacy, and general instability, and at some point the Teotihuacan Corridor was closed. Cholula was of minor importance and we know little about its occupation during these years. Late in the ninth century, it was reoccupied by Tolteca Chichimeca and Mixtecos to again become a prominent center.

There is considerable confusion about the arrival of the Olmeca-Xicalanca people, but there is general agreement that they came from the Gulf Coast. Most scholars now believe they came in the seventh century and were driven out in the ninth (Davies, 1977; García Cook, 1981; Fox, 1987). Presumably they made Cacaxtla their capital, maintaining a hegemony in the Puebla Valley and central Tlaxcala until they were forced out.

Cacaxtla

Cacaxtla is famous for its spectacular mural paintings, but there is more. It consists of a huge fortress built up over many years of construction probably dating back to Preclassic times. Its great period was roughly from A.D. 650 to 900. The hill on which it was built actually forms part of the larger archaeological complex of the ruins of Xochitécatl.

Cacaxtla is mentioned in some early sources as the capital of the Olmeca-Xicalanca, an intrusive group from the southern Veracruz-Tabasco area of the Gulf Coast. These people are believed to have settled first at Cholula and soon thereafter took over Cacaxtla and remained until their expulsion in the ninth century. According to carbon dating the battle murals were painted between A.D. 655 and 835 (Baird, 1989).

The ruins are tucked behind the site of Xochitécatl, not far from Texmelucan, Tlaxcala. The local springs, serving the needs of the modern community, may well have been an important factor in choosing this site for ancient settlement. The ruins occupy the hilltop of a promontory less imposing than Xochitécatl, but command an impressive view nonetheless, sweeping over the Tlaxcala Valley to the great volcanoes of Ixtaccíhuatl and Popocatépetl. The entire summit is covered by a ceremonial area of shrines, rooms, patios, staircases, passageways, altars, and a palace structure.

Attention was drawn to Cacaxtla when the first murals were discovered in October 1975 by looters who tunneled into Building A and suddenly found themselves looking up at some of the most remarkable paintings in Mesoamerica. Fortunately, they were so overwhelmed that they reported their finds to the local priest, who immediately notified INAH. Controlled excavations followed, revealing truly spectacular murals and an amazing building complex embracing the entire hill.

From a large parking area, the visitor now enters the archaeological zone from the east side and passes a museum, bookstore, and restaurant. Despite the gigantic roof erected to protect the paintings (Figure 6.13), the views over the surrounding valleys are magnificent. Cacaxtla does not present the ordinary layout of a planned ceremonial center. Archaeologists have identified five phases of construction with numerous

FIGURE 6.13   Cacaxtla, Tlaxcala, the site. (Photographed by the author.)

renovations and alterations. A distinctive feature are the elongated constructions entered through a series of doorways between rectangular pillars. These were not rooms but long galleries surrounding patios connected by passageways and short staircases leading from one level to the next. Although not originally designed as a fortress, these staircases provided an important defensive mechanism, as access to the summit could have been easily controlled.

Offerings   Between 1975 and 1989, excavations uncovered great concentrations of bones, totalling 208 of which 199 belonged to young children. Although preservation was poor, some were identified as unborn infants. The majority were found on the floor of patios and doorways, and had been sacrificed by cremation, mutilation, dismemberment, or by crushing the skull. The remains lay in complete disarray as if they had been scattered. With them were points or scrapers of flint or obsidian, bone needles, earspools, animal figurines, lipplugs, and *malacates* of clay, shell beads, stone, or clay pendants, randomly distributed. In one passageway 10 individual skeletons of children were each accompanied by a dog.

Reviewing the early source material, both Durán (1967) and Sahagun (1946) mention the sacrifice of children upon two occasions: (1) during annual Tlaloc festivities held to produce rain; and (2) upon completing a temple or building in order to give it strength and protection. Children were usually sacrificed at night as the ritual was probably unappealing. Sahagún mentions Xochitécatl. These references could well apply to Cacaxtla.

Murals.   The battle murals of Building B are seen immediately as one reaches the great patio. They decorate either side of a small stairway that leads up to a long chamber with seven entrances. Colors are vivid: bright blue, brick red, white, and black. These represent the aftermath of ritual battle between Mexicans of the Gulf Coast region ("Mayanized Mexicans" of mixed Teotihuacan and Maya ancestry) (McVicker, 1985) and a Maya group. The scene of the battle might be southern Veracruz or Campeche or even the Usumacinta or Pasión River (Baird, 1989) (Figure 6.14).

The paintings are beautifully executed, but illustrate a very bloody, gory performance. Torture predominates as blood pours from open wounds. Drawing blood was the main objective of this ritual battle garnering public support for the king as one way of reinforcing his legitimacy.

The victorious Gulf Coast Mexicans wear Teotihuacan-related warrior outfits and went into battle elegantly attired. The Maya (bird-people, so-called for a great bird helmet and beak), wear many personal ornaments but no clothes. Some bodies were painted blue, a color often associated with ritual sacrifice and offerings (Baird, 1989). They are easily identified as Maya by the deformed head and facial features.

Execution is fluid and surprisingly realistic. Many figures overlap. One figure stands against a border of half-stars. This motif, a 5-pointed star or 1/2 star was associated with war and sacrifice at Teotihuacan. It has a particular significance as a Venus symbol and was closely associated with warfare and sacrifice among the southern lowland Maya (Schele and Miller, 1986).

It is seen again in Building A, reached by a short stairway on the right. Here there are four large figures on each side of a doorway and the door jambs. They are

FIGURE 6.14 Cacaxtla battle mural. (Courtesy of Elizabeth Boone and Dumbarton Oaks, Washington, D.C.)

all elaborately dressed. One dances with his heel raised; another is pouring water from a vessel. All are accompanied by glyphs and many signs indicate ties to various Classic lowland Maya sites (Baird, 1989).

In Building A and B murals, there are 19 glyphic signs that, aside from being a form of writing, are also part of the pictorial representation. They are usually found floating in the area around the head, but at times are included in the warrior's dress. The wonderful owl on the east mural of Building B is a common war symbol but here it also names the figure. Two other glyphs on Building A name people as Winged Eye and Three Deer. The Reptile Eye (RE glyph), familiar from Teotihuacan pottery, appears three times in Building A murals. The trapeze-and-ray glyph is also present, possibly relating to Oaxaca urns or Maya stelae where it is found with more frequency than at Teotihuacan. Of the 12 complete standing warriors, 9 are named.

The murals are painted in an eclectic combination of Maya, Teotihuacan, Xochicalco, Oaxaca, and Gulf Coast styles. But it is Maya that predominates, seen in the overlapping and posing of the figures and elements of attire such as the Tlaloc mask with trapeze-and-ray headdress, tied rope collars, and a 3-knot insignia (Maya reference to sacrifice) (Nagao, 1989). Nagao sees specific parallels with Oaxacan glyphs. Most of the portable objects at Cacaxtla are attributed to Veracruz and Oaxaca. In essence there is little that can be traced directly to Teotihuacan.

By the Classic Period the basic features of writing were shared by these regions and were presumably understood at least by the elite members of society. In the case of Cacaxtla, common signs were deliberately used and were designed to be "read" by the local inhabitants (Berlo, 1989).

The Venus Temple It was not until 1986 that the Venus Temple was found (Baus, 1990). A pair of dancing figures, male and female, are painted on either side of a doorway on two rectangular pillars of a temple in the southwest corner of the ceremonial center. In vivid hues of black, blue, white, and ocher on a brick red background, the simple uncluttered dancers are in striking contrast to most other Mesoamerican murals. In style and color, however, they resemble Building A murals, as these figures are also bordered by wavy water containing aquatic creatures.

On both pillars there are two half-stars with a central eye outlined by a blue ring. Bodies of the figures are painted blue and wear a short jaguar skirt over which hangs a large 5-lobed Venus symbol. Unfortunately, head and arms of the woman and part of the torso are missing. Only one long drooping breast denotes her sex (Figure 6.15).

The representation of the man is almost complete. In his upright hand (or jaguar paw?) he holds another half-star. His most distinctive feature is the yellow scorpion tail that he wears as his own (Figure 6.16). Scorpions are frequently represented in Postclassic códices and their tails are also worn by Maya deities.

The Red Temple Thought to be built at the same time as the Venus Temple, the Red Temple was another gallery-type construction with multiple doorways. The building had been renovated to create a staircase leading up to the next level. In the

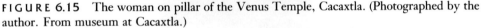

FIGURE 6.15 The woman on pillar of the Venus Temple, Cacaxtla. (Photographed by the author. From museum at Cacaxtla.)

course of this ancient renovation, some murals were partially covered up and others obliterated, the only example of this type of destruction at Cacaxtla.

The murals of the Red Temple to be seen today are found on the east and west walls leading to the staircase mentioned, and are framed by long feathered serpents above a border of water. A graceful tall tree (cacao?) springs forth bearing flowers and fruits, while a bird of gorgeous plumage perches near the top. Continuing up the staircase is a scaly amphibian mounting the stairs, as water drips on his back. At the second step a corn plant bears human faces. This seems to be a panorama of the watery Underworld and its creatures who climb up into the *axis mundi* of the terrestial habitat.

This east wall is the larger of the two and shows an old man (named by his glyphs as "4 *tlacuache*" or "dog") wearing a blue mask and a jaguar head. He has been dubbed the "merchant" because of the staff he carries in his right hand and a huge basket at his back, containing tropical products to sell (?)

The west wall presents a similar scene with double borders of water and serpent, but without a human figure. The maize plants are duplicated but with long tassels on ears of maize. A spotted amphibian mounts the first step with parts of his back covered with armadillo scales. Again water is dripping from above. A jaguar heads for the

FIGURE 6.16   The man with scorpion tail on pillar of the Venus Temple, Cacaxtla. (Photographed by the author. From museum at Cacaxtla.)

surface in a rain shower, while north of him in a corn field is another jaguar bearing a tortoise shell on his back.

The Cacaxtla murals are very much a local product but the prevailing outside influence is from the Maya region. The tall sloping talud-tablero architecture is like Cholula or Xochicalco. The framing of murals with an aquatic border represents Xibalbá, the watery Underworld where water moves, undulates, and is divided in segments embracing crabs, fish, mollusks, snakes, herons, various amphibians, and aquatic plants. Most similarities with Teotihuacan are symbolic or iconographic ones that are also shared with the Maya area. Closest ties to Teotihuacan may be the RE glyph and the half-star motif. So marked is the paucity of Teotihuacan influence, taking into account the proximity and its powerful domination of highland Mexico for several hundred years, one cannot help but wonder if the Cacaxtla murals do not represent a conscious rejection of the great center (Nagao, 1989).

I hardly need add that the Cacaxtla murals are a discovery of tremendous importance giving us a graphic example of elements of ideology, glyphic signs, and astronomy shared among elite Mesoamericans over great distances. This is an excellent example of the importance of blood sacrifice as the aim of warfare and its meaning for the institution of kingship (Schele and Miller, 1986). The Cacaxtla battle murals present the standard pattern of Maya warfare prior to the mid-eighth century, illustrated in highland central Mexico.

XOCHICALCO

Forty km west of the modern town of Cuernavaca is a major fortified site called Xochicalco, "Place of the House of Flowers." Xochicalco had been settled briefly and abandoned in the Late Preclassic Period and it had not shared in the Amatzinac trade of earlier days centered at Chalcatzingo. This region had had a symbiotic relationship with the Basin of Mexico early in the Classic Period. Some Teotihuacan ceramics are found but become less abundant by A.D. 600, and Xochicalco was never a part of its domain. A glance at the map will help keep in mind the locations of eastern and western sites in Morelos, for they have very different histories of development.

Xochicalco, in contrast to the eastern valleys, is located on a steep hillside, with water supplied by springs, lakes, and rivers. It fortified itself with impressive construction of walls, ramparts, ditches, and dry moats. The latter are cut directly into the bedrock, in some places up to 3 m in depth (Hirth, 1988). The defenses were not continuous around the hill but when combined with platforms and terraces at the base of the hill, made an effective barrier. The city above was planned with concentric terraces that were built up with steep façades on the outside edge, sometimes with free-standing walls. The site was divided into compartments with access restricted by paved ramps, some enclosed by walls. In addition, six outlying civic-ceremonial precincts about 1 km from Xochicalco were fortified. Four of these had few if any residences and must have been designed purely as protective outposts. The story of Xochicalco is one of warfare, sacrifice, and conquest.

This was a key highland site for the Epi-Classic period (A.D. 700–900). Its importance lies in its geographical and chronological focus, both important for the reconstruction of this rather unsettled period. Moreover, the carved stone monuments here provide the largest corpus of inscriptions for this period in central Mexico.

The main group of public buildings completely modified this fortified hill. The most imposing structure is the Feathered-Serpent Pyramid (Figure 6.17) supporting remains of a second story and covered with a wonderful corpus of carved human figures, hieroglyphs, and feathered serpents. The profile is basically talud-tablero construction but in different proportions from those at Teotihuacan. Here the talud is tall and the tablero short, and both elaborately carved. The latter contains no niches or recessed panels but is surmounted by a flaring cornice, typical of El Tajín. The talud is faced with slabs of andesite carved in reliefs depicting feathered serpents with undulating bodies that wind between Maya-like figures that some consider Chontal (Fox, 1987; Figure 6.18). The accompanying glyphs are related to calendrical adjustments and fire ceremonies. The tablero and the fragmented second story talud are

FIGURE 6.17   Main pyramid at Xochicalco, Morelos. Feathered serpents carved in low relief adorn the talud. (Courtesy of the Instituto Nacional de Antropología e Historia, Mexico.)

FIGURE 6.18   Detail of sculptured relief of Xochicalco pyramid. (Courtesy of the Instituto Nacional de Antropología e Historia, Mexico.)

carved with reliefs of warriors. These are elite figures that wear a trapeze-and-ray headdress and carry a strap bag. The iconography identifies them as warriors with militaristic emblems derived from Teotihuacan that are also found on public monuments in the Maya region (Schele and Miller, 1986; Berlo, 1989). Several toponyms have been identified and are believed to denote conquest and subsequent tributary status of the towns represented. This information is conveyed by a glyph of an open jaw about to snap up a 4-part circle linked to a seated figure.

Many similarities in style are found with Cacaxtla and Teotenango, the fortified hilltop in the Valley of Toluca to the west (see page 452). These three contemporary sites shared the same basic Mesoamerican-type writing with calendrical information, both numerical systems (combining bars and dots, and dots only), and use of the reptile eye, bone, and blood glyphs. Oaxaca is seen as the major inspiration for glyphic signs at Xochicalco. Here there was no more attempt to preserve Teotihuacan traditions than at Cacaxtla, but in adopting nonlocal traits, Xochicalco was more subtle in their assimilation than the artists at Cacaxtla. As it turned out, Xochicalco with its own sophisticated eclectic art style survived to be a focus for later cultures, whereas Cacaxtla was forgotten once it was abandoned (Nagao, 1989).

A small building complex called Structure A, located about 30 m south of the main pyramid, houses the Temple of the Stelae, named for three finely carved stone stelae recovered in the debris of the sanctuary (Figure 6.19). These magnificent monuments dated at about A.D. 600–700 had been intentionally defaced and broken, and were assembled again only after archaeologists broke through a stucco floor to recover the remaining fragments. Associated with the stelae were Teotihuacan figurines, eccentric obsidians, and shell, jade, and turquoise beads, as well as late Classic pottery of Teotihuacan, Tula, the Mixteca, and Fine Orange (Sáenz, 1961).

Each of the stelae is carved on all four sides with 16 glyphs that together constitute a set. Each stela has a human form with some kind of face on the front, and feet on all the other sides. The reliefs have been interpreted by Pasztory (1976b) as depicting three deities (Tlaloc, the Sun God, and his wife, a fertility and moon goddess) and deal with major events in the agricultural cycle. On these stelae they offer a prayer or appeal for bountiful crops. Alternatively, Berlo (1989) suggests that these stelae may deal with rulers, reigns and conquests, and believes two regional towns are named.

Extensive terraces were so densely occupied by dwellings that they are difficult to study in terms of household units. Other residences were scattered between major terraces in low platforms. These often hold 3 structures each and the platforms were clustered at distances between 10 and 20 m apart. Residences might be built on several levels connected by ramps or stairways. No large multi-family apartmentlike structures have been found such as those that characterize Teotihuacan. Xochicalco housing resembles more the arrangements we will see at Tula.

Paved causeways linked groups of structures within the site. One leads down the hill to a ball court (Figure 6.20) that originally had rings and is almost identical to one at Tula. The style is that of many Classic courts. Other roads extend out linking

FIGURE 6.19   Three stelae at Xochicalco constituting a set. Found in debris of sanctuary of Structure A. Height: 178 cm. (Courtesy of the Instituto Nacional de Antropología e Historia, Mexico.)

Xochicalco with smaller sites possibly forming a network like that of La Quemada, and Cobá in Yucatán.

When Teotihuacan began its withdrawal, its ceramics became less abundant at Xochicalco and fewer imitations were made (Hirth and Angulo, 1981). The common Metepec trade wares including Fine Orange are scarce. Very prominent is a distinctive granular ware shared with Xochipala, Guerrero, that constitutes the greatest percentage of imported pottery throughout the various periods. Coyotlatelco (red-on-buff or yellow) spread through the Toluca Valley and even to eastern Morelos and Puebla, but not to Xochicalco. This site had already asserted an independence and dealt instead with Guerrero, Oaxaca, Veracruz, and the Maya region. This dramatic shift away from the Basin of Mexico is also reflected in the procurement of obsidian, dropping Pachuca and Otumba and importing instead from Zinapécuaro in Michoacán.

FIGURE 6.20   Xochicalco ball court with stone rings in lateral walls. (Courtesy of the Instituto Nacional de Antropología e Historia, Mexico.)

In this period of conflict and regional militarism, Xochicalco was one of the primary centers to expand by conquest into a regional tribute-supported polity. Its domain is thought to have extended into the Ajusco Mountains on the southern fringe of the Valley of Mexico, southwest into the Mixteca Baja, and into the Balsas depression (Hirth, 1989). This tribute-based state may have been supported by its warrior sodalities, in which ranking was important and upward mobility possible. Perhaps the symbolism for human sacrifice and the religious desire to nourish the gods so pervasive a few centuries later was already being anticipated in the tenth century.

We know Xochicalco ceased to be of any significance after A.D. 900. Therefore, it did not replace Teotihuacan as a major center of the Postclassic Period, for by then it too was weak; nor could it have offered Tula much competition. By A.D. 950 Xochicalco may have been replaced by one of its own tributary centers, Miacatlán (Davies, 1977; Berlo, 1989).

THE ÑUÍÑE

The Ñuíñe, meaning "hot lands" as defined by Paddock (1966), refers to an area and a style. The area is the Mixteca Baja that embraces northwestern Oaxaca, southern Puebla, and northeastern Guerrero (see Map 6.3). Although its general features have been known for years, there has been little scientific work done in the area and it is known largely from private collections and surface material.

The presence of Thin Orange pottery is one of its outstanding characteristics. It is also the region of small heads about the size of grapefruit, known as *cabezitas colosales*. Moser (1977) believes they may represent shrunken or decapitated heads, perhaps of revered leaders, warriors, or ball-players. With few exceptions they had no bodies or necks. Large orange paste effigy urns and a rather strange spouted olla with turned down rim are other unusual products.

The Ñuíñe is best known for its handsome stone carving style and a glyphic "writing" system most similar to that of Monte Albán and the Mixteca Alta. Glyphic signs denote dates and place names in a distinctive style. Those in a rectangular cartouche contain a day-sign with numerical coefficient below. A circular cartouche may have a day- or month-sign with additional affixes. Glyphs associated with toponyms are probably names or record conquests (Moser, 1983). Ñuíñe-style glyphs are present on Building A at Cacaxtla (Berlo, 1989). Nagao feels they are more stylized and abstract than the representational type glyphs of Cacaxtla (Nagao, 1989).

The Ñuíñe emerges as a kind of regional development that peaked around A.D. 400–700. It is seen as a fused eclectic style of Teotihuacan, Monte Albán, and Maya with a long relationship with Monte Albán (Moser, 1983). Later counterparts can be found with Xochicalco, Puebla, and Tula.

The map shows this region to lie on a kind of low altitude path between the Gulf lowlands, Xochicalco, and Guerrero. When Teotihuacan declined, the Ñuíñe was one of the regional centers that prospered. Perhaps it was a desirable area where some Teotihuacanos resettled (Paddock, 1978).

OAXACA

Monte Albán

We have seen that the Zapotecs established residence in the Oaxaca Barrio at Teotihuacan, and now we will see that some Teotihuacanos visited the great Zapotec capital at Monte Albán. This center always remained staunchly Zapotec and in many ways is unique as a major center of Mesoamerica. We will resume the history of this hilltop center in its Period III (IIIa and IIIb) and IV that fall in the Classic years of A.D. 300–1000.

Monte Albán IIIa   From A.D. 300 to 500 (Monte Albán IIIa) a renewed growth in population took place, particularly in the southern valley, while the area around the capital was still sparsely inhabited. Administrative centers were established away from Monte Albán such as Zaachila in the south, but these did not erode power at the capital. Nine pottery workshops operated from these centers producing a more standardized vessel, requiring less labor and resulting in less competition between the centers. In Period IIIa many farmers began to plant two crops instead of one and relied on other specialized farmers for utilitarian items (Feinman *et al.*, 1984). This promoted a market system that brought farmers into a centralized location for other goods. This would have increased interaction among the valley communities and encouraged their consolidation. It is possible that the market was located near the base of the north slope of Monte Albán (Blanton and Kowalewski, 1981). Specialization increased and both rural and urban areas were well served.

Monte Albán IIIb   Construction continued at Monte Albán where the heart of the city, the Main Plaza, was designed for public ceremonies. By now Building L was very visible at the southwestern corner of the Main Plaza with the galleries of prisoners and sacrificed victims on display, and Building J was located so that people could walk all around it to be reminded of the state's conquests. Conquests began to decrease, however, and tribute was lessened accordingly.

In Period IIIb the capital was built up on a massive scale. It extended over 6.5 km with a maximum population around 24,000 (Blanton and Kowalewski, 1981). The South Platform fronting on the Main Plaza was a gigantic pyramid 15 m high, measuring more than 100 m at the base along one side. At each of the four corners stood a stela carved in relief showing two figures and hieroglyphs. The message on all four stelae is the same. The scenes show a Teotihuacan ambassador (known by his tasseled headdress), leaving his Tepantitla-like home at Teotihuacan and traveling to Oaxaca, where upon arrival he is greeted by a Zapotec official. At the foot of the stela at each corner was a stone box containing special offerings of sea shells, jade, and Period III pottery. No dates are given, but very likely the recorded scene took place upon the dedication of the South Platform. All the figures are decked out in fine ceremonial attire. The Teotihuacanos carry their incense pouches of copal as they do in their own painted murals.

On another occasion a Teotihuacan emissary named Eight Turquoise came to Monte Albán wearing a tasseled headdress to confer with Three Turquoise, a Monte Albán lord. This peaceful meeting is recorded on a *tecalli* plaque known as the Lápida de Bazán, found in 1931 in the debris of Mound X.

The Teotihuacanos on these monuments are not armed or escorted by armed men (R. Millon, 1981). What kind of "special relationship" existed between these two great centers? Possibly the Teotihuacanos wanted to learn from the Zapotecs new devices for measuring the sun accurately and perhaps combine this knowledge with the 260-day ritual calendar (Coggins, 1983). Oaxaca was a leader in this field, having gotten off to an early start after carving early calendrical signs at San José Mogote. Writing is not easily interpreted in Oaxaca because it is difficult to figure out the order and composition of the glyphs. Lists of names, numbers, and verbal functions have been deciphered but these alone do not produce a meaningful text. The scenes with people noted above and new themes are a radical change from the early slab reliefs of Building J (Clancy, 1983).

A curious structure, Building III, atop the large southern platform, has recently been reported by Marcus Winter (1990). It is associated with a patio and shrine, but its single staircase is located on the east side rather than facing north to the Great Plaza. A reused stone at the foot of the balustrade depicts a seated figure in profile under some glyphs that may give his name, and others in front with some kind of additional information. The construction resembling that of Lambityeco, along with other details, have led to an estimated date of A.D. 730.

The North Platform also built at this time was reached by wide stairs, leading to a colonnaded hall overlooking a huge sunken patio enclosed by high pyramidal platforms. As a public building, this was stunningly impressive. The rest of the Main plaza was bordered by 14 buildings, perhaps each representing one of the 14 Oaxaca barrios. There is no archaeological documentation for this assumption but the existence of 14 buildings and 14 known Oaxaca barrios seems more than random coincidence and might represent lineages (Blanton, 1978). A building complex known as System IV (Figure 6.21) is one of six structures that line the west side of the plaza. It was designed for privacy with its courtyard enclosed by walls. The main ball court occupied a prominent location at the northeast corner, and the game was played without rings. Niches were placed in opposite diagonal corners perhaps involved in scoring. The ball court rather effectively limited access to the plaza. The latter was no more accessible to the general public than other areas of the city that were enclosed by steep walls and passageways.

To find one's way into a fine residential palace, probably that of the ruler, required all one's wits. From the sunken patio of the northern public building, one climbed a short staircase and passed through a gate into a narrow hallway, up another stairway, through a room with two columns, a door to a hall, eventually reaching the central patio. This sense of seclusion was typical of elite residences. Access was restricted and probably controlled. Happily, in this case the owner had a small private entryway via a discreet gate.

The desire for privacy is reflected throughout construction on the hilltop and is one of Monte Albán's most distinctive features. Barrio Siete Venado, built at the end of Period IIIb, surrounded itself with double walls. Even the two main roads from the north led to points in the residential areas on east and west sides of the mountain, but not within easy access of the Main Plaza (Blanton and Kowalewski, 1981). The modern tourist road that leads to the parking lot has been built over an ancient wall. When the hilltop itself was so built up that it could accommodate no more, additional settlements were made on the slopes and tops of other nearby hills.

In regard to construction, façades form a series of rectangular tableros in two planes that alternate with recessed spaces. Also, rather than standing out as separate additions, many staircases are set into the structures.

The typical gray ceremonial ware of Monte Albán persists. Some of the earlier types survived, including spout handles, spider-foot vessels, perforated incense burn-

FIGURE 6.21   Oaxaca, system IV building complex. (Photographed by the author.)

ers, and bird-shaped bowls. New forms in Teotihuacan taste were added, such as *floreros* (see Figure 6.27f) and *candeleros* (6.27d), stucco coating, cylindrical tripods, so-called Tlaloc jars (6.27e), ring bases, and some Thin Orange ware and resist painting. Common in Monte Albán are gray-ware vessels in the form of a jaguar foot, a spouted tripod, and a bowl with interior cup. (See Figure 6.27 j, k, and l). Distinctive local developments are a serpentine motif and the urn, in particular the funerary urn, a Zapotec specialty (Figure 6.22). Made of gray, unpolished clay, it is composed of an elaborate deity usually, but not always, seated cross-legged against a cylindrical receptacle.

Mural paintings are largely confined to tombs where mineral colors were applied *al fresco* to a white base color. People and animals are shown in profile without shading. The best preserved of all painted tombs is Tomb 104, where on an urn a god wearing Cocijo (Zapotec rain diety) as a headdress gazes down from his niche over the entrance. The people in the murals resemble toothless old men with protruding chins. They are reminiscent of the figures in Teotihuacan's Tepantitla. A scene in Tomb 105 shows nine paired dieties in a procession.

The murals and urns have been the main source of information on deities and religion. Cocijo was the equivalent of the rain god (Figure 6.22a) Tlaloc. Other well known gods were a bat god associated with fertility and maize (see Figure 4.13), the serpent associated with Quetzalcoatl, especially in his role as the wind deity, and even a flayed deity that is later known as Xipe (see Figure 8.20). Nearly all the art and architecture now visible date from Period IIIb.

Obsidian workshops were located northeast of the Main Plaza situated near elite dwellings, along with several crafts from marine shells and special minerals. All obsidian from the Oaxaca Valley was produced at Monte Albán. This is an example of an industry with production and distribution tightly controlled. It must have been considered an exotic item (Santley, 1983). Not surprisingly the greatest amount of green obsidian belongs to the years of contact with Teotihuacan.

An unusual specialization is seen in the medical profession. Monte Albán provides the best evidence of skull trepanation in Mesoamerica. Ten adult skulls, six of which were female, all dating to Period IIIb, showed drilling, scraping, and cutting of the bone. Since none were buried in tombs, presumably these were people of low social rank. One individual endured five operations before he expired, and most had undergone two. Apparently only two lived long after surgery (Wilkinson and Winter, 1975).

The settlements in the southern valley had not proved successful and the piedmont region lost most of its residents. Many people moved closer to Monte Albán to the mountainous area north and west of the capital where wood and other products were available. The state was still highly centralized; pottery was standardized with a gray ware of lower quality.

There is no evidence that Teotihuacan ever attempted colonization or exploitation of Monte Albán. The relationship appears to have been peaceful and one of respect. When Teotihuacan lost its great power and prestige abroad, any threat Oaxaca may have felt was removed. Although a few more walls were erected at the Zapotec capital, the Main Plaza was abandoned and the population gradually declined. There was no

a   b   c

FIGURE 6.22   Monte Albán urns.
a. Gray-ware funerary urn representing the god Cocijo, wearing a mouth mask with forked serpent tongue. Monte Albán IIIa. Height: 48 cm. (Courtesy of the Museum of the American Indian, Heye Foundation, N.Y. [23/5554].)
b. Funerary urn representing goddess "13 Serpent," Monte Albán III. Height: 50 cm. (Courtesy of the Museo Nacional de Antropología, Mexico.)
c. Jaguar figure (urn?) with Zapotec-style claws and mouth. Oaxaca, exact provenance unknown. Height: 38 cm. (Courtesy of the Museo Nacional de Antropología, Mexico.)

wholesale destruction but by Period IV only 4000 people are estimated to have resided on the hilltop.

Monte Albán IV   By A.D. 900 the Oaxaca Valley was no longer under a centralized authority but was inhabited by a number of autonomous political settlements. Monte Albán itself may have been reduced to being one of the resulting small petty states (Blanton and Kowalewski, 1981). Marcus (1989) suggests that the 14 wards (lineages?), each of which had maintained a building on the Main Plaza, may have moved out to an administration center of its own at Cuilapan, Zaachila, Macuilxóchitl, Matatlán, or Lambityeco.

Lambityeco, located in the Tlacolula branch of the Oaxaca Valley about 30 km southeast of Monte Albán, is often considered representative of this period. About 70 mounds have been reported from this site (Paddock, 1983a) with remains indicating local salt production. It also exhibits close similarities to Monte Albán IIIa–IV in urns, painted murals, residential layouts, and certain tomb patterns (Winter, 1989). In fact, Marcus Winter argues that development at Lambityeco overlapped with

Monte Albán and was confined to the years from A.D. 550–800, leaving an unexplained gap in our Oaxaca record thereafter.

Another center was Jalieza with 16,000 inhabitants, one of the largest in the valley. It could not be considered a capital or even an administrative center, as it had no central plaza or public buildings. It consisted of isolated elite residences scattered along a ridge.

Period IV is admittedly a weakly defined period in Oaxaca but one in which such centers as Yagul, Mitla, and others in the Tlacolula region were already developing the new configurations that are so apparent after A.D. 1000.

Comments

The general character and history of Monte Albán is very different from other centers examined up until now. Monte Albán had had a vibrant, exciting history from 500 B.C.–A.D. 750, from its early precocious founding to problems in the eighth century. Did the withdrawal of Teotihuacan have much effect on Oaxaca? It seems that Monte Albán began a decline of its own about the same time (R. Millon, 1981, 1988a). It is also possible that contacts between the two centers were not as close as has been implied. Actual imports are few. From 2000 residential terraces, not one import from Teotihuacan could be identified (Blanton, 1978). Aside from some mural features, most of the "influence" is seen in portable goods that could have come in indirectly from Xochicalco or the Ñuíñe.

A major contributing factor to the decline of this polity surely stemmed from the cost of maintaining a powerful, centralized government. When people decided to stop supporting the expensive capital and operate out of local autonomous centers, it was a fundamental change. Their future concern was now to be the relationship with their aggressive neighbors to the north and west, the Mixtecs.

EL TAJÍN AND THE BALL GAME

Sites in the Veracruz area are less extensively excavated than those of the highlands, so it is likely that the importance of this region has been greatly underestimated. At one time a very important development was centered at El Tajín, Veracruz, 8 km southwest of the town of Papantla in the humid, heavy, tropical rain forest where the present-day Totonac Indians make their home.

In the Early Classic, El Tajín was a small settlement closely allied to Teotihuacan. The visible ruins belong to the ninth to eleventh centuries. They are deceptively small, as the exposed buildings are tightly clustered, but untouched mounds extend for 5 km into the lush, tropical growth that covers the surrounding small hills. Although Krotser has estimated a population at 3000–5000, a large sustaining area could perhaps triple this figure (Krotser and Krotser, 1973).

The heart of the ceremonial center was the Pyramid of the Niches and associated large stone structures and ball courts that occupy a flat area open to the south. Long ridges limit the east and west sides while to the north rise a series of hills with a central ridge. The latter has been terraced to support fine residential structures called Tajín Chico. The core area is composed of more than 200 mounds, consisting of temples, courts, elite residences, and no fewer than 12 ball courts, for this is the region where we think the game began.

In 1984 the Universidad Veracruzana together with INAH authorized the Projecto Tajín to continue exploration and to restore the Pyramid of the Niches. This is the most important and commanding structure, built in 6 tiers over a similar earlier one. It is outstanding for its variation of the talud-tablero form incorporating 365 niches into its façade, surmounted by a flaring cornice (Figure 6.23). It has always been tempting to imagine that each niche held a figure, but this has no scientific basis.

Nearby are 2 of the 12 ball courts. The vertical walls of one are elaborately carved with narrative bas-reliefs in the interlaced scroll-and-volute pattern for which Tajín is famous (Figure 6.24). In a scene rarely portrayed, a ball player is about to be sacrificed by the flint knife held over him. A small court in a plaza to the north is built with sloping benches, unlike the usual vertical-walled courts.

Beyond El Tajín's ball courts and the Pyramid of the Niches, at a slightly higher level to the north, are a series of palacelike structures called Tajín Chico, with roof combs and corbeled vaulted rooms and colonnaded doorways. A retaining wall acted as a barrier separating this area from the lower one with the pyramid. This may have served to limit access or control circulation. Another such wall was raised between Tajín Chico and the area to the west.

This area occupies the highest part of the site, presumed to be the home of 13 Rabbit, one of Tajín's rulers (Wilkerson, 1984). He is well represented on reliefs in

FIGURE 6.23   Pyramid of the Niches, El Tajín, Veracruz. (Courtesy of the Instituto Nacional de Antropología e Historia, Mexico.)

FIGURE 6.24   Relief carving of south ball court showing sacrificial scene. El Tajín, Veracruz. Length of this panel: 1.98 m. (Courtesy of the Instituto Nacional de Antropología e Historia, Mexico.)

the Building of the Columns where most of the glyphs are found. Reliefs reveal a predilection for toads, jaguars, and serpents, as well as people. Bar-and-dot numerals with day-glyphs are evidence of the Tonalpohualli (260-day) and Xíhuitl (365-day) cycles. Among the historical figures in processional scenes of conquest and ritual sacrifice, 13 Rabbit is the most common. Names float above the figure as at Cacaxtla (Berlo, 1989).

A rather special feature at El Tajín is the massive masonry, constructed of a concrete mixture of sand, seashells, and wood, poured in sections using wooden molds. The architecture includes niches, mosaic decorations found mostly on residential structures, friezes of frets, a flaring cornice, flat roofs, and corbeled arches. Some buildings were stuccoed and brightly painted in red or blue (Brueggemann and Ortega, 1989). The rainy season in this area brings torrential downpours. Consequently, a number of complex drains, subterranean canals, and storage tanks were devised to take care of the run-off or divert the water to storage tanks.

We know that El Tajín became very influential in the Classic Period and that contact with Teotihuacan was close. The precise nature of this relationship is not known, but at the time of Teotihuacan's retrenchment, El Tajín was a powerful and militaristic society (Zeitlin, 1982). It was at this time that it reached its maximum size and became one of the major centers of the epiclassic period.

Artifacts and architecture of El Tajín style have been found at Zaragoza and Oyameles, the obsidian deposits in central Veracruz that supplied El Tajín as well as Matacapan with gray-black obsidian. This presence of El Tajín in the Zaragoza region suggests a close relationship, if not conquest or colonization. Santley believes that when Teotihuacan declined in inportance, El Tajín took over control of its obsidian distribution system on the south Gulf Coast, but established no enclaves of its own. Perhaps El Tajín was not able to muster the power and prestige of Teotihuacan and could not have outfitted large caravans of porters for overland trading expeditions. Its solution may have been to operate with canoes. These could move large loads efficiently and carry the same Zaragoza obsidian to the markets of the southern Gulf Coast communities (Santley, 1989).

The Ball Game

It is logical that the ball game would have originated in the Gulf coastal lowlands, the land of the "rubber people." If El Tajín was not one of the earliest founders, it became a rapid adherent and promoter. Having 12 ball courts of its own, it seems fitting to discuss the game here, for we will refer to the game often in the pages ahead.

Many peoples from the American Southwest to South America played a ball game. In Mesoamerica this was of great signifiance not only as a sport but also for its religious and ritual aspects. There are good descriptions of the game from early accounts by Durán (1971) and Sahagún (1946) but also a comprehensive study by Stern (1948), and for the Maya, Jones (1985) and Schele and Miller (1986). We know that the Aztecs played the game in an I-shaped enclosed court with rings in the center of side walls. This was a rough game, played by two opposing teams, each numbering from 2 to 11 men, using a heavy, solid, rubber ball that measured approximately 6–8 inches in diameter. According to the rules, the ball had to be kept in motion by using only the hips, knees, and elbows, but no hands or feet. We are told that spectators arrived decked out in jewels and fine clothes to watch and encourage their team. If perchance the ball passed through the stone ring, a difficult and not too common feat, the game was immediately terminated and to the winners belonged the spoils: any belongings of the spectators. Consequently, upon seeing the ball pass through the ring, the public fled with the winning team in hot pursuit. There were easier ways of scoring involving markers and end-zones.

The form of most Mesoamerican courts was I-shaped but the lateral sides vary from being low and sloping, as at Copán (see Figure 6.39), to tall and vertical, as at Chichén Itzá (Figure 6.86). Within this general framework there were many variations. At Teotihuacan, for example, the game was not played in a formal court, but in open space with end-markers. In the Tepantitla murals, some figures play ball using bats, but another scene shows the typical hip-ball game in progress. In west Mexico, the court at Amapa, Nayarit, has a central marker topped with a cup. This is unique, for most center markers take the form of round flat disks, or stone tenoned heads, animal or human.

A painted line divided the alley between the rings, and among the Maya three flat, stone markers were often set on a central longitudinal line. These lines and markers clearly designated zones where the ball could bounce but not die. The end-zones were areas where it could not even hit the floor. Rings and closed end-zones are rare before A.D. 1100, so some of the variations in courts reflect temporal changes in rules and architecture.

In Mesoamerica, the ball game dates back to the Preclassic Period, for there are numerous ball-players represented in the clay figurines of San Lorenzo, Tlatilco, Tlapacoya, Cuicuilco, and Xochipala. They are often represented with one padded knee, a wrapped hand or forearm, and wearing protective belts. They are frequently shown down on one knee attempting to return the ball (Figure 6.25a).

The earliest court on record may be two parallel mounds at San Lorenzo (Coe and Diehl, 1980a). By the Late Preclassic a number of courts have been reported from Oaxaca, Chiapas, highland Guatemala, and Belize. Pasztory (1972) places the peak of this game from A.D. 450 to 700, a period of great mercantilism throughout Mesoamerica. At this time outstanding centers were El Tajín, Cotzumalhuapa, and Chichén Itzá.

Associated with the Classic ball game were objects we know as yokes, *hachas* (thin stone heads), and *palmas* (palmate stones). The U-shaped stones called yokes, often elaborately carved on the outer surfaces and weighing from 40 to 60 pounds, were imitations of the protective belts worn by ball players. The *palmas* are about 15–18 cm in height, usually fan-shaped, and notched at the top, and have a concave surface at the base as if meant to be supported by a curved edge. The back is smooth and left plain. The front may be decorated with motifs of birds, animals, or human figures. Pictorial representations suggest that the *palmas* were held or tied somehow on the yokes that were designed to be viewed from the front. We do not know how the *hachas* were used, but they formed part of the game paraphernalia. *Hachas* often have a deep cut or notch at the back, or an undecorated projecting tenon. Like *palmas* and yokes, they are beautifully carved. Artistically these are some of Mesoamerica's finest stone sculptures.

The game was played as a sport, a wager, and a ritual. The game sometimes reenacted a myth in which the Sun God descends to the Underworld and is reborn as the Maize God, representing fertility. A ritual game might be played to hasten the rains and ensure fine crops. A plant usually figures in the sculptured narrative panels, whether maize, cacao, or maguey. The Sun God is often shown with his twin partner, the planet Venus.

Among the Maya the game was also related to fertility, the sun, warfare, and sacrifice by decapitation. A high-ranking captive might be forced to play a game in which he might lose his head. Courts were often built against staircases. In some well-documented instances, the loser in the game was taken to the top, bound up to form a ball, and rolled down the stairs to his death (Schele and Miller, 1986). Kowalski and

FIGURE 6.25   Ball game artifacts.
a. Hollow figurine representing ball-player wearing yoke about the waist, and knee and arm guards. Santa Cruz, Quiché, Guatemala. Length: 37 cm. (Courtesy of the Museum of the American Indian, Heye Foundation, N.Y. [12/3347].)
b. *Palma* or palmate stone, Veracruz. Height: 20 cm. (Courtesy of the Museum of the American Indian, Heye Foundation, N.Y. [16/3473].)
c. *Hacha* or thin stone head with projecting tenon. Height: 29 cm. (Courtesy of the Museum of the American Indian, Heye Foundation, N.Y. [16/3474].)
d. Stone yoke with carved decoration of the Tajín-style volute. El Tajín, Veracruz. Length: 44.2 cm. (Courtesy of the Metropolitan Museum of Art. The Michael C. Rockefeller Memorial Collection. Bequest of Nelson A. Rockefeller, 1979. [1970.206.423].)

Fash (1991) give a vivid description of the game and the court iconography at Copán, Honduras, where the ball court was the arena for a cosmic conflict, and acts as a portal to the Underworld. The Copán lords reenacted the Hero Twins' myth in which they manage to defeat the lords of Xibalbá by trickery in a ball game. In this case, one of the beautiful markers of the Copán ball court illustrates the ruler himself playing the part of a Twin. Once again the Twins ensured the rebirth of the sun, "promoting the growth of the maize, and manifesting their sacred role as mediators between the world of the gods and that of men."

CENTRAL AND SOUTHERN VERACRUZ

The ruins of El Tajín are not unique. There are others with niches, profiles with flaring cornices, and step-fret designs. With slight variations, the complex extended into the Sierra de Puebla, a good example being Cuetzlán, Puebla on the very edge of the altiplano. This site has a pyramid with niches like El Tajín with step-frets up the balustrades, a ball court with vertical low walls, yokes, and *palmas*.

Not far from the port city of Veracruz the potters of Remojadas busied themselves producing masses of hollow figurines turned out by molds. Mostly of Late Classic date, they are quite distinctive. Their jolly, laughing faces often expose filed teeth through great smiles (Figure 6.26). Men and women as well as infants are represented, along with ball-players and warriors. Black asphalt paint from natural outcroppings in the area was used to highlight the features and ornamentation (Figure 6.26c). The happy figures may depict a forced gaiety as the result of drinking hallucinogens in preparation for being sacrificed. To have met this fate looking gloomy would have been considered an evil omen (Heyden, 1970).

This is also a region where small wheeled figures (10 cm long × 8 cm high) may have originated. These were probably not toys but were used in some ceremonial context as a few have come from dedicatory caches (Diehl and Mandeville, 1987). They may be of Late Classic date in Veracruz but elsewhere are Early Postclassic. A large number of fragments were recovered at Tula (see page 405). Without a suitable domesticated animal to pull a load, and given the broken terrain in much of Mesoamerica, merchandise was moved not by wheels, but by tumpline and canoe. An explanation for the lack of wheels in Yucatán is more difficult to understand (see page 362).

In southern Veracruz, Cerro de las Mesas, whose roots go back to 600 B.C., is also an important center of Classic times. Although its several dozen mounds have been known for a long time, little scientific work has been done at the site. Among the stone monuments, carved stelae with bar-and-dot numerals bear Long Count dates of A.D. 468 and 533. Some glyphs look derived from Oaxaca, whereas many stone carvings resemble Cotzumalhuapa and Izapa. Cerro de las Mesas seems to mark the northern limits of the Long Count dating system.

A famous Classic period cache reported many years ago by Drucker (1943b) included jade hierlooms, many carved pieces of jade, serpentine, and other stones, altogether over 800 selected pieces of elite pottery. Cylindrical tripod vessels, *candeleros*, mold-made figurines, and large, clay sculptures of familiar deities are relics of Teotihuacan.

Matacapan Continuing south is the site of Matacapan, located between Lake Catemaco and the slopes of the San Martin Tuxtla volcano, 5 km east of the modern town of San Andrés Tuxtlas. Matacapan had been inhabited earlier by Preclassic

FIGURE 6.26 Classic Gulf Coast figurines and mirror.
a. Hematite mirror back with perforations for suspension. El Tajín, Veracruz. Diameter: 8 cm. (Courtesy of the Museum of the American Indian, Heye Foundation, N. Y. [22/6252].)
b. Wheeled pottery cart in form of a crocodile. Veracruz, Mexico. Length: 25 cm. (Courtesy of the Museum of the American Indian, Heye Foundation, N.Y. [22/5562].)
c. Remojadas standing figure decorated with asphalt paint. Central Veracruz. Height: 31.8 cm. (Courtesy of The Metropolitan Museum of Art. The Michael C. Rockefeller Memorial Collection. Bequest of Nelson A. Rockefeller, 1979 [1979.206.578].)
d. Hollow "laughing face" figure, central Veracruz Remojadas culture. Height: 36 cm. (Courtesy of the Museum of the American Indian, Heye Foundaton, N.Y. [23/3925].)
e. Solid clay figurine with asphalt on the legs. Pánuco, Veracruz. Height: 19 cm. (Courtesy of the Museum of the American Indian, Heye Foundation, N.Y. [23/8529].)

villages, but a volcanic eruption had left it uninhabited until the middle Classic years. The Teotihuacanos selected this fertile plain as a pleasant base to establish an enclave for their busy trade network. This was an astute choice, for the strategic location gave them easy access up and down the coast as well as to the great rivers leading inland. It also offered a local source of kaolin for producing fine paste pottery. This not only makes an elegant and attractive ware, but requires minimal grinding and little sieving. Black volcanic ash could be procured from the Catemaco River for tempering coarseware jars. Salt, cinnabar, and igneous rock were also available. Most of the foreign pottery found at Teotihuacan had come from this area (Rattray, 1989). Ceramic production was a major industry and highly specialized. Some household areas manufactured pottery for local consumption. Another group specialized in elite wares and still others combined to produce in quantity. The wares include imitations of typical Teotihuacan products. The figurines are nearly twice the size of those made in Teotihuacan.

The main center of Matacapan consists of 62 mounds, arranged in little plaza groups around a large central plaza. There is one very large mound of 2 tiers of talud-tablero architecture, and there may well be other buildings in this style. Around this central core is a dense urban area of 4.5 km. The total living area covers about 20 km. The entire area of Matacapan yields Teotihuacan remains both ritual and domestic. There is one Teotihuacan-type residential compound (Mound 61) with apartments, patios, and corridors with burials placed under the floors. The general feeling is that of an enclave of Teotihuacan immigrants and their descendents who lived here around A.D. 400–500.

Of the obsidian, 90% came from central Veracruz at Zaragoza and Oyameles, a very small amount from Pachuca, and none from Otumba or Guatemala.

When Teotihuacan declined, Matacapan immediately followed and soon lost its role as a commercial center. It was probably replaced by El Tajín (Santley, 1989).

From Matacapan on the Gulf side, if one crosses the Isthmus to the Pacific side, by following the well-traveled Soconusco route along the Chiapas coast to Guatemala, Balberta is our next stop. It lies on the coastal plain almost due south of El Baúl.

Balberta   At a time when many highland and southern coastal sites as well as Chiapa de Corzo and Izapa were either abandoned or experienced a disruption, Balberta, 90 km southwest of Kaminaljuyú (see Map 6.5), underwent a transformation from an earlier chiefdom-type settlement toward a statelike organization. A new layout placed structures in rows around a central pyramid in a huge plaza. The populace moved in closer, giving up a more dispersed living arrangement. The 20-ha center of town was enclosed by a wall-and-ditch combination, another example of fortifications. The cessation of figurine manufacture is usually taken as a sign of a state religion replacing household ritual, and in this case, when the figurines went, so did pot-bellied sculptures and Usulután ceramics.

These dramatic changes are seen as local developments. Foreign goods consist mainly of green obsidian tools of Teotihuacan manufacture. A vigorous trade was no doubt a main factor in the growth of Balberta's thriving economy of cotton and possibly cacao production, but competition for commercial markets may have led to the fortification of the center and nucleation of population. This area, only now being investigated, holds considerable promise for the study of interrelationships with Mexico as well as the emergence of Maya civilization (Bove, 1991).

EL SALVADOR

The ash-fall from the devastating eruption of Mount Ilopango in A.D. 250 abruptly terminated the previous period of great florescence and buried all the fertile valleys and basins of western El Salvador. In such situations people usually seek out relatives in safe areas and/or where environmental conditions are familiar and offer similar economic possibilities (Demarest, 1988). Most of the people probably went no farther than the western highlands of El Salvador and Guatemala. An example of a more distant migration may be a case of small family units moving to Copán, Honduras, to be gradually followed by others in the fourth to seventh centuries. The circumstances would have met the goals of the migration to the benefit of all parties (see page 283).

The Ilopango eruption rather effectively cut off Quelepa and eastern El Salvador from the west. Consequently this region renewed a relationship with lower Central America and became part of Mesoamerica's frontier (Lange and Stone, 1984; Sheets, 1984). Following A.D. 650, however, Quelepa once more became "Mexicanized." Architectural features include an I-shaped ball court and buildings grouped around plazas, an arrangement not limited to Mesoamerica, but a departure from the usual southeastern linear alignment. Imported goods include ball-game paraphernalia (yokes, *palmas*, and *hachas*), wheeled figurines, and fine paste ceramics. In these years Quelepa's relationships were particularly strong with Veracruz and the Gulf Coast cultures (Andrews V, 1977).

Although the political organization of Chalchuapa society had been shattered, most of the people survived as testified by the continuity of ceramics in western El Salvador thereafter. Eventually Tazumal was once more enlarged and a close commercial relationship with Copán and the southeast periphery contributed to a resurgency of power and prestige of the elite.

The Zapotitán Basin was also reoccupied, most likely from the west and a new center was established at Campana-San Andrés. Other noteworthy settlements were made in the Cerrón Grande basin to the north. In the Early Classic, the Chortí Maya moved south out of the Petén through the area of Copán and Quiriguá, and some people came to the Zapotitán Valley. This region was still affected by the vulcanism of A.D. 250. Nonetheless, before the soil had fully recovered, farmers settled at the site of Cerén by A.D. 550. A farmhouse and outhouse were still well preserved by another volcanic eruption in A.D. 600 only 1.5 km away. A wattle-and-daub house was found with beans still in pots in the kitchen, remains of a codex (beyond hope of restoration), and weaving and pottery-making areas could be identified. The fields at Cerén were not irrigated, but many had been planted in ridges to retain rainfall (Sheets, 1982).

A primary factor in the recovery of western El Salvador was the prevailing interaction with the southeastern periphery where centers participated in an economic network that shared lithic technology and obsidian from Ixtepeque.

A polychrome pottery known as Copador was brought on the market and enjoyed a phenomenal success. Produced in Copán commercially as a non-elite item, it was widely distributed in the southeast. By carrying Mayoid symbols and motifs it was accompanied by a prestigious aura of Maya culture. The possession of a Copador vessel bore a significance far beyond its economic or aesthetic value (see page 283; Demarest, 1988).

GUATEMALA VALLEY

Returning now to the Valley of Guatemala, many earlier centers had continued without interruption, and some architectural styles and techniques were still in use in A.D. 300. Ceremonial offerings were thrown into the waters at Lake Amatitlán, presumably to ask favors of or placate the gods. Positive results were forthcoming to judge from the tremendous increase in the practice. Lake Amatitlán remained a center for groups throughout the long history of the region. Its location at the southern entrance to the valley lay directly on the path of many travelers. The lake region was utilized for resources such as fish, waterfowl, and salt, but it was also an area rich in vital raw materials such as columnar and vesicular basalt, and thin slabs of rock (lajas) used for lining stone drains. These lajas occurred as natural outcrops. Wild amate trees supported a growing industry of cloth and paper-making to judge from the numbers of stone bark-beaters.

Although the several phases following Miraflores are undistinguished, by A.D. 400 the outlines of the great Esperanza phase had been formulated. In 1968–1969 a team from Pennsylvania State University explored additional mounds in the valley that had been reported years earlier by the Carnegie group (Kidder *et al.*, 1946). The massive ceremonial complexes were reappraised and extensive pits and trenches dug in residential zones and in the surrounding sustaining areas. The reader is referred to articles by Brown (1977a,b), Cheek (1977a,b), Michels (1977, 1979), and Sanders and Murdy (1982).

Kaminaljuyú was still the predominant site in the valley but another complex center was located to the south, Frutal (Amatitlán), and a smaller settlement of Sólanos in between.

At this time Kaminaljuyú consisted of two major areas of mounds known as the Palangana and the Acropolis. Originally estimated to have occupied a 7.5 km², the area known today as the Kaminaljuyú Park set aside by the Guatemalan Government probably occupies only 3% of the ancient site, the rest having fallen prey to weather, looting, and the bulldozer when the modern capital expanded to the north.

Population estimates were worked out by obsidian dating since sherds were too eroded to use. A standard house lot was assumed to be inhabited by 7 people, and each lot was estimated at 2500 m². With the aid of aerial photography and this means of calculation, the population of Kaminaljuyú polity was found to have peaked around A.D. 650 at 22,712 for the central core, with a sustaining area population of 16,244. By A.D. 900, the population had dropped almost 75%. Building activity is estimated to have taken place over a period of perhaps 100 years. Architecture shows a combination of local style and techniques using puddled mud and talud-tablero combinations. Almost all of the buildings are placed on new ground instead of being superimposed on old buildings. Some are faced with neatly cut volcanic-pumice blocks covered with clay and plastered.

Tombs were still constructed according to the old practice of building rectangular burial chambers roofed with logs. On the floor of the burial chamber the honored dead were laid in an extended position accompanied by retainers (men, women, and children) and given lavish offerings of pottery, jade, obsidian, and pyrite mirrors. Eventually the dead were seated cross-legged, Maya style, and instead of placing the tomb in a prominent position in the mound as the Miraflores people had done, the Esperanza builders now located the graves in front of the structure or in the subsoil beneath. These tombs are plain rectangular pits, very different from the elaborately constructed tombs of their predecessors and belonged to the highest ranking and most powerful members of society. The rich contents include objects from many regions, including some of Teotihuacan style (Figure 6.27): the familiar lidded slab-leg cylindrical pot, Tlaloc vases, *candeleros*, *floreros*, and Thin Orange ware. These fine goods were reserved for tombs and ritual contexts and did not appear in residences, even those of the elite.

Kaminaljuyú had real competition from the other large polity 13.5 km to the south known as Frutal or Amatitlán. Spread out on the flat valley floor, San Antonio Frutal was as large as, if indeed not larger than, Kaminaljuyú and was composed of an acropolis and 30 principal mounds with approximately 200 others scattered about. Frutal traded exclusively with Maya contacts on the Pacific coast, Copán and Guaytán to the southeast, and Nebaj, Zaculeu, and Chamá to the north.

Between the two large polities lay Sólanos, occupying a tongue of land between two deep barrancas. It is estimated to have had 15 mounds grouped around 3 plazas and an acropolis. Fine, exotic goods are present from virtually every direction. These were prosperous days for farmers, too, as the older methods of swidden farming (see page 241), were improved by the introduction of short fallowing cycles. The stone hoe blade was widely adopted, making the work easier. Terraces were constructed and farming could be extended to marginal soils.

Despite the influx of foreign goods, building styles and techniques remained essentially Maya. The most spectacular tombs, those of Mounds A and B, were erected by A.D. 450–550. Thereafter some crucial changes took place. Sanders (1977) believes the aristocratic old center was replaced by a state-type political system, and Mounds A and B were abandoned. Although the massive Acropolis in talud-tablero style was built after this, tombs are few in number and their contents are shabby compared to those of earlier ones. Quality visibly declined. Simple stelae were carved but no longer were the old 3-pronged incense burners produced that had served the masses well for so long. Gone, also, are figurines, frog-effigy altars, and the old Izapa-style carved stelae.

Why the sudden changes, and how can we account for the presence and distribution of foreign goods? Was this merely a trading relationship? Were Teotihuacanos actually present? Could they have conquered Kaminaljuyú? We know the Teotihuacanos were knowledgeable in the art of warfare. We have only to recall their murals, and remember the sacrificed warriors at the old Temple of Quetzalcoatl (C. Millon, 1973; Cabrera Castro *et al.*, 1991). Yet the Guatemala Valley has produced no weaponry, defense systems, or evidence of warfare. To outward appearances, at least, life was peaceful.

According to Brown (1977a) the valley may have been a major commercial center where merchants gathered from central Mexico and the various Maya regions. Perhaps the whole system grew out of exchanging cacao and obsidian between the two chiefdoms (Michels, 1979). Sanders (1977a) suggests trade may have been organized along the lines of the Aztec's *pochteca* (see page 471), and operated like a port of trade.

Without a doubt, interregional exchange networks between the lowland Maya to the north and the Pacific slopes to the south worked to everyone's advantage. From the lowland Maya cities came lime, indispensable for building, and other products such as pelts, feathers, and eccentric flints. Basal-flanged Tzakol vessels (see Figure

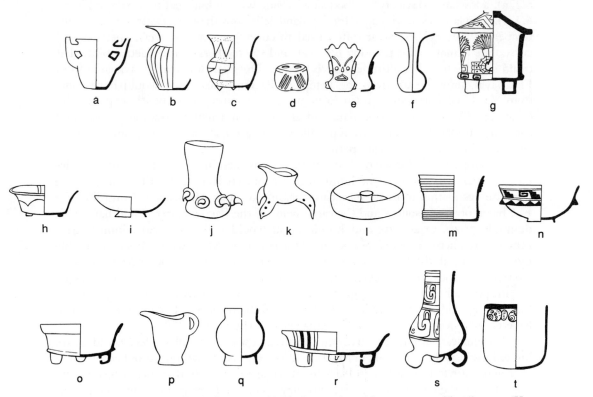

FIGURE 6.27   Classic Period pottery. (a) Black-ware jar with two spouts, Teotihuacan (Xolalpan); (b) black incised jar, Teotihuacan (Xolalpan); (c) polychrome vessel with three tiny solid supports, Teotihuacan (Xolalpan); (d) *candelero* (incense burner); (e) so-called "Tlaloc" vase, Teotihuacan (Tlamimilolpa); (f) *florero* form, Teotihuacan (Xolalpan); (g) painted cylindrical tripod with lid, Teotihuacan (Xolalpan); (h) incised brown tripod bowl, Teotihuacan (Xolalpan); (i) Thin Orange bowl, annular ring base, Teotihuacan (Tlamimilolpa); (j) gray-ware vessel in the form of a jaguar foot, Monte Albán IIIa; (k) gray-ware spouted tripod cup, Monte Albán IIIa; (l) bowl with interior cup, incense burner (?), Monte Albán IIIa; (m) cylindrical vessel with moldings, Cerro de las Mesas, II; (n) polychrome basal-flanged bowl, Early Classic, Copán; (o) negative-painted black tripod bowl, basal molding, hollow cylindrical feet with a square vent on the inner side, Early Classic, Nebaj, Guatemala; (p) brown-ware Tzakol pitcher, Kaminaljuyú; (q) vessel with ring stand, Uxmal; (r) polychrome Tepeu tripod, Uaxactún; (s) Fine Orange Tepeu tripod, Chichén Itzá; (t) polychrome Tepeu vessel banded by glyphs, Zaculeu. (From the following sources: a, b, c, g, Piña Chan, 1960; d, e, f, h, i, Sejourné, 1966; j, l, Caso and Bernal, 1952; k, Caso and Bernal, 1965; r, s, Smith and Gifford, 1965; t, Rands and Smith, 1965; all copywright © 1965 by the University of Texas Press; m, reproduced by permission of the Smithsonian Institution from *Smithsonian Institution Bureau of American Ethnology Bulletin 141* (*Ceramic Stratigraphy at Cerro de las Mesos, Veracruz, Mexico*), by Philip Drucker; Fig. 12r, Washington, D.C.: Government Printing Office, 1943; n, Longyear, 1952; o, Smith and Kidder, 1951; p, Kidder *et al.*, 1946; q, Ruz Lhuillier, 1963).

6.27n), a lowland Maya style, stood side by side with cylindrical tripods (see Figure 6.27g). Lowlanders were eager for highland jade, obsidian, volcanic ash (used for tempering pottery), cinnabar (often used to cover jades and graves), specular and crystalline hematite (for painting pottery), and the feathers of the quetzal bird, that could only be found at altitudes above 1500 m. Obsidian was readily available from El Chayal, only 25 km from the Petén or Pacific Coast. Jade would have come from Manzanal near San Agustín Acasaguastlán, a source conveniently exploited by Guaytán. The Pacific coastal plain had always been a natural trading partner and continued to bring up agricultural products such as cacao and cotton from the lower altitudes along with utilitarian pottery.

The apparent influence of Teotihuacan that is seen in architecture and ceramics has given rise to the view of Kaminaljuyú as an enclave of Teotihuacan and the ultimate destination of many merchants passing through Matacapan. Control of the El Chayal obsidian source and the cacao fields of the Pacific Coast would have been desirable prizes to acquire and Kaminaljuyú would make an ideal administrative center. From here the door was open to all the rest of the Maya world. It was a credible hypothesis as talud-tablero style architecture began to appear in other Maya sites, as well as cylindrical tripod vessels, representations of the Mexican rain deity, Tlaloc, and the possibility that a Teotihuacano might have married into Tikal's ruling dynasty. Supporting evidence thus accumulated for a number of years, but more recent finds have raised questions that challenge this premise (Demarest, 1988).

Teotihuacan "influence" in ceramic forms and wares as well as green obsidian are limited exclusively to burials in Mounds A and B at Kaminaljuyú. No Teotihuacan-type goods are found in domestic debris. It seems more likely that these objects were imported by the elite for ritual or as prestige objects bolstering and reinforcing their social status, for the distribution indicates a tight control.

Actual imports have proven to be few in number, most being produced locally as imitations, emulating Teotihuacan style (Ball, 1983). It is also possible that some imports were brought in from the Gulf Coast and do not represent direct contact with Teotihuacan. The talud-tablero that looks much like that at Teotihuacan, was built with a different technique. In addition, this style architecture recently discovered in the Mundo Perdido Complex at Tikal seems to predate that at Teotihuacan (Laporte, 1987a; Laporte and Fialko, 1990). In other words, what we have could well be the result of an exchange arrangement between elites at Kaminaljuyú and Teotihuacan or possibly with Veracruz, without necessitating actual occupation or contact. There is no evidence of a military takeover or physical occupation of the Guatemala Valley by foreigners. We will see this same question arising again and again in the Maya lowlands. There is no doubt that Teotihuacan played a powerful and influential role in Mesoamerica at this time. It is only the nature of the contact that is being questioned.

Kaminaljuyú dealt with many areas and no doubt competition was intense. She may well have controlled the production and/or distribution of El Chayal obsidian that would have been a tremendous commercial asset. But the prosperity lasted only until A.D. 550. Thereafter some changes in the valley could reflect events taking place in central Mexico that resulted in the withdrawal of Teotihuacan from participation in foreign affairs.

A gradual breakdown of the Guatemala Valley cultures culminated around A.D. 800, by which time population had expanded until no more arable land could be found. Friction and competition could have led to a marked deterioration of the former way of life that is expressed in the following phases called Amatle (A.D. 650–800) and Pamplona (A.D. 800–1000). For a while, ceremonial centers continued to be constructed in tightly knit, compact groups in open country such as valley floors, where stone and talpetate (see Glossary, Tepetak) masonry platforms were built. But around A.D. 800 the valley sites were abandoned for more favored defensive positions along hilltops.

Pottery is degenerate when compared with the finer quality and taste of Esperanza wares. Even so, new types appear such as Fine Orange and a distinctive ware called San Juan Plumbate (see Glossary, Neff and Bishop, 1988). The latter, produced in western coastal Guatemala, is a fine-textured ware with a high percentage of iron compounds that, upon firing, acquires a hard, metallic, lustrous finish. A later Plumbate called Tohil, is similar but differs in paste, shape, and decoration. San Juan Plumbate was made into tall, cylindrical vessels that contrast sharply with later effigy forms.

In our next encounter with Guatemala Valley people, we will find them living on hilltops, concerned with defense about the year A.D. 1000. In highland Chiapas to the west, settlements were already located on heights or on ridges bordered by easily defended ravines or cliffs (Adams, 1961).

THE LOWLAND MAYA: A.D. 300–1200

These years in the lowland Maya area are usually divided into an Early Classic Period, A.D. 300–600 (Tzakol) and Late Period, A.D. 600–900 (Tepeu). Tzakol and Tepeu are terms for the corresponding ceramic phases. The following years, A.D. 900–1200, are often called the Early Postclassic. A division into early and late periods is warranted in some areas by ceramic and art styles and major changes in the fields of writing, architecture, and sociopolitical development.

It is now possible and advantageous to see this entire time span of Maya civilization as a continuum with regional centers taking turns of prominence. Instead of a catastrophic "collapse" in the south in the ninth century, we will view it instead as a change with a transfer of focus to the north. In northern Yucatán, Maya civilization readjusted to a new order while continuing many lowland traditions until major changes occurred upon the fall of Chichén Itzá in the thirteenth century. This contributes to a long chapter, but presents an uninterrupted sequence.

General Maya Concepts

A short explanation of several Maya concepts or beliefs will furnish a better understanding of the behavior or these people and the architectural organization of various sites. These involve (1) cycles of time, (2) a template for site planning, (3) Maya cosmology, and (4) the Myth of the Hero Twins.

Cycles of Time   The Books of Chilam Balam contain compilations of ancient Maya prophesies that are filled with the Maya's great preoccupation with warfare, death, and the Hereafter. Closely associated with this is their fatalistic belief in cycles of time. The passage of every period of 13 katuns or 256 years (13 × 20 years) was carefully recorded and celebrated. Katuns were named and the Maya believed that past events would recur with the reappearance of the same katun. Thus the future was predictable, inevitable, and usually unlucky. One had to try to get around impending misfortune or accept the fate ordained by higher forces.

Dennis Puleston (1979) pointed out that this preoccupation of the Maya with the 13-katun period (Short Count), along with a fatalistic attitude, could be a contributing cause of the ninth century "collapse." More recently, Arlen Chase (1991) compared events in these years with three katun ending dates with disarming but convincing results. They signaled such events as decline, instability, and warfare. These cycles of time are not all-explanatory but point up a fatalistic belief among the Maya that for them constituted a powerful force as certain dates approached. It is something to bear in mind in the pages ahead.

A Template for Site Layout or Planning   There were certain principles based on the cardinal directions that dictated the positioning of structures in a site. A template was established by late Preclassic times that was followed through the late Classic Period. These principles as outlined by Wendy Ashmore (1991) include

1. Emphasis on a north–south axis in site organization.
2. Formal and functional dualism between north and south.
3. East and west elements form a triangle with the north. The southern position is often suppressed or implied.
4. A ball court is sometimes placed as a transitional element between north and south.
5. Causeways are often used to link these elements, stressing a symbolic unity of the whole scheme. We will see examples of this pattern at Tikal and Copán.

Maya Cosmos   Related to the template above is the Maya view of their cosmos. The Mexicans visualized the world divided into quarters as we have seen at Teotihuacan, and their cosmos was horizontal. The Maya also recognized four quarters, plus a central fifth position and emphasized east and west as the path of the sun. The king was identified with the sun during the day as he ruled; upon death he traveled to the Underworld with the setting sun and eventually the World Tree in the center of the universe would provide his access to the heavens above, where he would join his ancestors and could communicate from there with his descendants on earth below.

North was the sphere of celestial supernaturals and the south was the Underworld. A ball court often located in between the north–south structures acted as intermediary and as one gateway to the Underworld. The Maya universe was not flat, for both the heavens that housed the ancestors and the Underworld were multi-layered. The latter was the setting for tests and trials, scene of the adventures of the mythical Hero Twins. The movements of the Sun, Venus, and other deified entities took place between these layers and certain other elements functioned as connecting devices, such as mountains (or pyramids), caves, and the Four Bacabs that held up the corners of the sky. The Twin Pyramid Complex of Tikal furnishes a good examples of this scheme.

By the time we touch on patterns at various lowland sites, the reader will see how the Maya adapted their city layouts to the natural features of the landscape. Certain aspects of this pattern are found elsewhere in Mesoamerica. It provided a theater for public affairs, official activities, and commemorative events as well as demonstrating power and prestige of the ruling authorities. Upon entering another polity a traveler would recognize the pattern and immediately orient himself.

Myth of the Hero Twins   The Maya elite established their right to rule by dynastic ties to ancestors and through adherence to shamanistic ritual. They based their beliefs in the mythology of the Hero Twins found in the Popul Vuh. Royalty claimed descent from these twins, and in this way acquired supernatural power.

In essence the myth relates how the Hero Twins (Hunahpu and Xbalanque) were summoned to the Underworld (Xibalbá) to take part in a series of trials. Their father and uncle had been defeated by the Lords of Xibalbá and consequently sacrificed. Hunahpu and Xbalanque played ball against the Lords day after day, and finally outwitted them and won. They then took their place in the heavens to become the Sun and Moon (or Venus). The ball game became a way for the living to reenact the myth of the Hero Twins providing the defeat of the forces of death and achieving rebirth, giving hope to others for eventual resurrection.

Population and Settlements

The Petén region was already well populated long before 300 B.C., probably by people following the rivers to the interior (see Map 6.5). Rivers are rare in this region, and the most reliable sources of water were water holes called *aguadas*. These were favored habitation areas as were natural elevations, the edges of lakes, and near *bajos*, low depressions that became swampy in the rainy seasons. The rains here fall mostly between June and December, contributing an average of 135 cm annually.

Tikal is located in hilly tropical terrain, which was obviously unsuited for a grid plan of settlement. The location was apparently chosen for its large natural supply of flint, valued for tools, along with a natural elevation of land that was to form the center of the city.

A concentration of ruins form a compact core and the density falls off as one retreats from the center. In the outer area structures are distributed around plazas, and these groupings in turn are scattered at random.

The basic housing pattern was that laid down in earlier times in which low platforms supporting houses were grouped around patios. The simplest house was made of pole and thatch of which nothing remains. Better housing used stone in construction. The presence of utilitarian artifacts denotes living quarters as opposed to workshops or rooms designated for ceremony or ritual. Living quarters, kitchens, storage facilities, and sometimes workrooms were identified.

From a single house presumably of a nuclear family, it was but one step to larger, residential arrangements of patio-type groupings that would have included extended families or lineages. It was not unusual to find that one building facing the main plaza of several such groups had no domestic function. This probably functioned as a shrine. A cluster of these patio groups might include several extended families, and larger and more complex settlements were simply aggregates of the same features. The civic-ceremonial center itself can be seen as the final elaboration of these arrangements occupying a larger area, with greater structures and taller buildings using dressed stone masonry. Now the shrine had been replaced by a temple/pyramid.

The elite lived in more elegant and substantial structures that were merely larger, all-masonry versions of the smaller, perishable home.

Long, vaulted structures called palaces are often thought to have housed the ruler and his family. These were groups of long, multi-chambered galleries grouped around plazas, furnished with benches, skins, mats, and textiles that made them more comfortable and attractive. Benches and thrones were a particular feature of these structures. These structures also served a number of other purposes such as administrative offices, receiving dignitaries, displaying captives, or performing rituals. Actual living quarters sometimes adjoined these buildings or were located nearby. Multi-purpose residential quarters were centrally located near funerary pyramids and ball courts.

Estimating population of Maya settlements is a complex task (Culbert and Rice, 1990). Some of the difficulties involved in using a housemound count can be appreciated when one realizes that the Maya often had the disconcerting habit of moving out of their houses after burying the dead therein, usually under the floor. Cemeteries are nonexistent. Other than for a death in the family, housemounds might be abandoned for a number of reasons such as the exhaustion of the soil, epidemics, fear of an enemy, or even to avoid some undesirable social situation. A physical move would involve only a small expenditure of time and labor, for the Maya did not accumulate household goods on the scale that we do. Adding to confusion, houses were sometimes rebuilt at a later time on the same mound. Any meaningful population estimate would have to be based on the number of houses inhabited simultaneously. The fact that the great majority of burials in the structural platforms of Tikal remained undisturbed is viewed as proof of continuous occupation.

Willey cites figures of 72,000 in 120 km at Tikal, calculated at 800 persons per km^2, 500 persons per km^2 around Becán, Río Bec, and Xpuhil, and 2000 persons per km^2 at Dzibilchaltún in north Yucatán at its zenith. The overall population of the Maya lowlands must have been in the millions (Willey, 1980).

The following data for the central Maya lowlands, excluding the Río Bec region, is from Turner II (1990). After 300 B.C. the population grew slowly for 600 years and reached a little over 1 million about A.D. 300. Then it stabilized for about 300 years and after A.D. 600 experienced a great population explosion for 200 years until A.D. 800. At that all-time peak the population is calculated at 2.6 to 3.4 million. A sharp decline set in thereafter. At European contact there were less than 75,000 people living in the central Maya lowlands.

Food Production

The basic economy of Tikal was probably based on slash-and-burn agriculture of maize, squash, and beans, but not exclusively as once thought, nor as primitively accomplished. A swidden farmer does not have an easy life. First, the land must be laboriously cleared, and the subsequent burning off may take several days. Planting is done at the beginning of the rainy season by dropping one seed at a time in a hole made by a sharp stick and covered over. After working a field for about 3 years, the land must be fallow for at least 4, and possibly 8, years to replenish the minerals, after which the cycle is repeated. This usually results in a shifting population, although the evidence from Tikal shows that some house platforms were in continuous use from 500 B.C. on, so a slash-and-burn economic base does not always require nomadic farming. Numerous studies comparing yields of this type of agriculture have shown a crop surplus is possible (Carneiro, 1960; Cowgill, 1962; Dumond, 1974; Turner II, 1974).

In addition, the combination of maize, squash, and beans makes optimum use of the natural resources: the vines of the squash protect the soil from erosion, the corn grows tall, breaking the force of the rain, and beans grow up the corn stalks, increasing the foliage.

It has recently been shown that the Classic Maya prepared maize in the form of a tamale instead of a tortilla as among the central Mexicans. The clay griddle (*comal*) for baking is conspicuously absent among the Maya until very late Postclassic times. The numerous examples from Classic Maya inscriptions and murals leave little doubt that the tamale was the primary maize food, frequently used in ritual and associated with Ah Mun, the corn god (Taube, 1989; Figure 8.1).

Another source of dependable food was the breadnut or *ramon* tree (*Brosimum alicastrum*), that yields a fruit of high nutritional value and grows throughout the Petén. By a series of experiments, Puleston discovered that these nuts could be stored in underground chambers called *chultuns* for up to 18 months, whereas maize rotted within 2 weeks. Once planted, the breadnut tree will last for nearly 100 years, requires no tending, and is not so dependent on rainfall. It would have added a substantial vegetable protein to the Maya diet. Ramon trees probably formed part of kitchen gardens grown close to the house that, together with other plants easily tended in household rubbish, were capable of high productivity. The widespread use of the ramon tree for food has not be proved, but it seems to have served the inhabitants of Tikal well during the seventh to ninth centuries (Puleston, 1971).

Marine resources provided additional food and the sea was heavily exploited all around the Yucatán coast. Fish may have been trapped and bred in canals between raised fields along the levees, an idea advanced by Thompson (1974) when studying the Río Candelaria Basin. Fish could also have been dried and traded inland. Apparently freshwater snails, *Pomacea* and *Pachychilus*, provided a supplementary source of protein

(Moholy-Nagy, 1978; Nations, 1979). *Pachychilus*, once thought to have been consumed in great quantities, was not eaten, but its shell was burned and added as powder to boiling water in the preparation of maize, thus providing a wonderful source of alkali. Although the Petén is rich in limestone, this source is not pure enough to use in cooking. Our present knowledge of the archaeological distribution of *Pachychilus* shells includes Piedras Negras, Tikal, Uaxactún, and some Belize sites.

The above does not mean that a tropical forest or jungle is resource rich and provides a limitless environment. It does have the potentials outlined above but is a fragile environment, easily upset by overexploitation in concentrated areas. A balanced subsistence can be maintained by shifting cultivation, multi-cropping programs, terracing, and planting household gardens. To encroach on nature's biodiversity of habitats is to court disaster as may well have taken place in the Petexbatún.

Distribution of sites suggests utilization of ridged fields and *bajos* for a *chinampa*-type agriculture in certain areas. In this system soil or muck is piled up in an area of swampy or seasonally wet lands, creating ditches or canals between ridges or plots of higher ground. The result is an extremely fertile area for agriculture. These were first identified as ridged fields along the Río Candelaria in Campeche and have also been found along the Río Hondo in northern Belize where they have been dated to 1100 B.C. (Puleston, 1977). The raised-field patterns of Quintana Roo indicated that *bajos* there had been cultivated. It seems likely that sites in the Petén region may have been settled according to the availability of *bajos* where this type of agriculture would have contributed substantially to the food supply (Harrison, 1990; Harrison and Turner II, 1974). The *bajos* at El Mirador, however, seem to have been an exception and apparently were not suitable for agriculture.

Another special situation is that of northern Belize where settlements were strung out along the rivers. Here both cacao and cotton could have grown on the ridged fields where soil was renewed from the canals or swampy depressions between the ridges. Cacao needs high rainfall and humidity and these conditions were excellently met in both northern and southern Belize. The area around Lubaantún was a large cacao-producing center in the eighth and ninth centuries as it is today (Hammond, 1988). Cacao is pollinated by midges, which Dahlin says would breed in the swamps; their larvae also provided good food for fish that could have been exploited by traps as well (Dahlin, 1979).

Although hunting does not seem to have been a major food-producing activity, a number of different animals were presumably eaten at Cuello, Belize: white-tailed deer, musk-turtle, armadillo, pond turtle, and brocket deer were the most abundant, but dogs, rabbits, and peccaries were also found.

Evidence of rather sophisticated food-producing techniques have been forthcoming from other regions in late years. Hundreds of thousands of stone-walled terraces line the hillsides around Río Bec in central Yucatán. These may not all be agricultural, as terraces also make good living sites, but the vast majority were designed to intensify food production (Turner II, 1979). Not only did they serve to impede erosion with carefully planned drainage techniques, but short-crop fallowing would have been facilitated. Pot irrigation could have improved the yield in dry seasons. It is not known exactly how old these earthworks are, but some were in use between A.D. 400 and 900.

In this same region Eaton (1975) identified what he calls farmsteads. A farmstead accommodating 8–10 people would consist of a house or group of houses with walled enclosures or courtyards set aside for storage, or workrooms containing tools, utilitarian pots, and debris. These houses would be adjacent to agricultural land. The farmsteads, in contrast to ridged fields and agricultural terraces, have been dated to the eighth to tenth centuries in this area. They seem to have been rather privileged landholdings, some houses having benches or sleeping platforms, and floors were plastered as skillfully as in the temples.

One more subject is root-crop agriculture. Its evidence is very difficult to find but we believe that some farmers cultivated manioc. For a people inhabiting a dense rain forest, root crops offer greater subsistence potential than maize (Bronson, 1966), and could be grown belowground in the same field as maize and beans. Manioc cultivation could have spread north from the South American lowlands in the second millenium B.C. (Lathrap, 1973) and has been found at Cuello (Hammond and Miksicek, 1981).

All told, a variety of food was available to a people who maintained the complexity and diverse nature of the tropical forest and were able to adapt to its dry periods and yearly fluctuations in rainfall. By developing special farming techniques of ridge-filled agriculture in some areas, *chinampa*-type cultivation in the *bajos*, terracing, trapping fish, storing breadnuts, and controlling and storing water, the Maya were energetic, resourceful, and imaginative native farmers.

Commercial Enterprises

During earlier years exchange was not so much a large commercial enterprise as a private affair between trading partners. As we have noted, the goods that moved around were largely exotic, special items for a select few, who acquired prestige and status through their possession and display.

By A.D. 300, as stratified societies became more complex, so did economic activity. By now trade was well organized, controlled, and managed. There may have been large-scale expeditions dealing not only with luxury items but also with provisions and basic commodities moving through the system for further processing and redistribution. Long-distance exchange networks increased interaction between major polities.

Of traded commodities, obsidian is of great value to the archaeologist because it is durable and because its origin can be traced. Ancient Mesoamericans valued it for the fine prismatic blades that could be struck from its cores. Some finished blades at Tikal had probably been produced by specialists at Kaminaljuyú (Clark *et al.*, 1989), but more often cores were imported for local tool production and redistribution. Certainly it would have been less risky and more practical to carry a bag of cores than the delicate finished blades.

Although El Chayal exported to the Petén, central Yucatán, and Belize, merchants with Ixtepeque obsidian shared the same markets. It was not at all unusual for a center to import from several sources (Jack *et al.*, 1972). Seibal for example, imported from both El Chayal and San Martin Jilotepeque, and even yielded a specimen from Zaragoza, Puebla, 800 km to the northwest (Graham *et al.*, 1972).

The presence of green obsidian in such diverse Maya sites as Tikal, Uaxactún, Altun Há, Becán, Dzibilchaltún, Palenque, Yaxhá, and Kaminaljuyú are often cited as evidence of contact with Teotihuacan in central Mexico. Although Cerro de las Navajas at Pachuca near Teotihuacan is the only known source of green obsidian, this could have passed through many intermediaries before reaching Maya settlements. It is easily carried, but is difficult to date outside of a controlled context and may well have been only sporadically distributed to the elite (Demarest and Foias, n.d.). More-over, Cerro de las Navajas obsidian never constitutes more than a minor presence at these Maya sites (Moholy-Nagy and Nelson, 1990). Green obsidian does not necessarily indicate direct contact with Teotihuacan.

Another marketable commodity was volcanic ash used for tempering pottery. Chalchuapa in El Salvador had a long-standing relationship with the eastern lowlands and provided ash for pottery at San José, Barton Ramie, and Benque Viejo. From the east coast, merchants bearing ash could easily travel the earlier river routes inland to the Petén where ash-tempered pottery became abundant as it did in northern Yucatán after A.D. 600. Several networks must have been in operation (and competition) as different sources were used. A sea route would have certainly facilitated the movement of the large quantities of ash that were apparently transported.

Ash and obsidian were not the only highland commodities in demand. Jade from Manzanal on the Motagua River was the most highly prized article of all times. The mark of the truly elite was to be buried with a jade bead in the mouth, jade ear ornaments, rings, and a figurine or two, or as many as the family could afford. The term jade is used here loosely to apply to a number of green stones. The Olmec had preferred a dark blue-green jade. There was also a fine translucent emerald green color especially prized by the Maya, but many varieties exist and all were considered gems, enhanced no doubt by their scarcity. Most jade was made into jewelry, plaques, beads, pendants, earspools, mosaics, even dental inlays, but one famous 9-pound lump was turned into a head of the Sun God at Altún Há (Pendergast, 1969).

Products mentioned so far have been highland exports to the lowlands. What lowland products would have made the return trip? Salt, a universal necessity, was a major item, obtainable only from salt lakes, streams, wells, or the sea. Since salt was the heaviest and bulkiest of long-distance traded items, the southern highlands obtained most of their salt from salt springs via highly localized trade networks. The finest salt was that from the coastal lagoons of northern Yucatán (Andrews, 1983). The Petén imported thousands of tons of Yucatán salt annually using large fleets of canoes.

Cacao (Figure 6.28) was a highly commercial crop in great demand as it was used for ritual, as currency, and as a beverage prized by the nobility. It was a major commodity on the tribute rolls in the Postclassic Period (Millon, 1955). It is believed to be of South American origin but little is known of its history and domestication in Mesoamerica. Its culivation here goes back to early Preclassic time at Cuello, Belize,

FIGURE 6.28   Cacao growing in the Río Grijalva delta region of Tabasco. (Photographed by the author.)

and in Soconusco (the Pacific piedmont area of coastal Chiapas-Guatemala) (see references in Sharer and Grove, 1989). There is ample evidence for cacao in the Classic Period, in códices, inscriptions and ceramics, even to recovering its remains in pottery vessels at Río Azul (Stuart, 1988).

The greatest areas of cacao production were Belize, the Motagua River valley, and Soconusco. Since cacao requires deep soil and year-round humidity, Yucatán has never figured as a potential area of cultivation, despite its production mentioned by the sixteenth century chroniclers. Today cacao (*Theobroma cacao L*) has been found growing naturally in *cenotes* and sinkholes near the modern city of Valladolid (Gómez-Pompa *et al.*, 1990). Northern Yucatán may not have been an exporter but cacao could have been cultivated in the Late Postclassic for the local elite.

Of cotton there is no doubt. Cotton clothing is well represented in murals, in paintings, and on ceramic figurines from the time of their appearance. The finding of spindle whorls is usually taken as a good indication of cotton cultivation, but we know that cotton was cultivated and woven into cloth long before their appearance. Textiles of cotton yarns were recovered in the Tehuacán Valley, probably produced on the back-strap loom we find in use today. Evidence of cotton occurs as early as 200 B.C. continuing until the Conquest (Johnson, 1967). Remains of cotton have been recovered in core samples along the Río Hondo raised fields in Belize (Hammond, 1988). Both northern Belize and El Salvador had appropriate conditions for raising both cotton and cacao. Merchants would have found eager customers among inhabitants of the highlands and the Petén.

From the tropical forest itself came such marvelous items as jaguar skins, feathers from the toucan, parrot, macaw, and hummingbirds. Quetzal feathers of a gorgeous, emerald green iridescent color went the only way, from highland to lowland, for these birds live only in the cloud forest of the southern highlands, between 1200 and 2700 m elevation (Dillon, 1975). Other lowland products were flint and polychrome pottery, both heavy items that would have traveled easier by canoe than by tumpline.

Movement of all these products involved planning, administration, and a considerable team of traders. Several well-established routes had been used for hundreds of years. From highland Guatemala there were several ways to reach the lowlands: from Alta Verapaz via Sakajut and El Portón down the Chixoy and Pasión Rivers to the Petén (Map 6.5). From there one could continue down the Usumacinta River system to the Gulf of Mexico and travel either west to Tabasco, or north around the Yucatán Peninsula. Another route led down the Motagua River valley to the Gulf of Honduras from where goods could be redistributed along the east coast riverine sites.

Adams (1978) calculates a canoe trip could be made from northern Belize to El Cayo, 250 m into the Petén, in about 8.5 days, traveling 10 hours a day at 3 km per hour. From there it is another half-day to Naranjo and three more to Tikal. Simultaneously, porters (*tamemes*) probably made the trip overland even as they do today along the flanks of the Maya Mountains. Foot travel is not hampered by the obstacles we encounter with wheels, and coping with changes in altitude, ravines, and rivers would have been easier on foot. An overland route, of course, could have been used all the way to Yucatán via Becán and northeastern Petén with possible stopovers for the merchants to transact a little tropical forest business along the way.

The frequent references to communication and interregional relationships might give the false impression that travel was for everyone. This is not so. There were several restraints on travel. First, one would have to be able to leave his crops or professional duties at home; second, the expense of guards, porters, and servants limited travel to rulers, nobles, priests, and merchants; and third, travel was seen as a dangerous undertaking. Routes were associated with serpents and used by animals and robbers (Kubler, 1985). Royal visits between the Usumacinta sites are notable. The distances were not great and there were many in attendance. Long distances would have been covered primarily by merchants.

Sociopolitical Organization

We do not know exactly how or when kingship first appeared among the lowland Maya but by A.D. 1 a supreme ruler we call a "king" was already the authority at Cerros, Lamanai, El Mirador, Uaxactún, and Tikal. By A.D. 300 this system was deeply rooted in Maya society and had spread across the land.

A king was not only the supreme political authority and power but was seen as

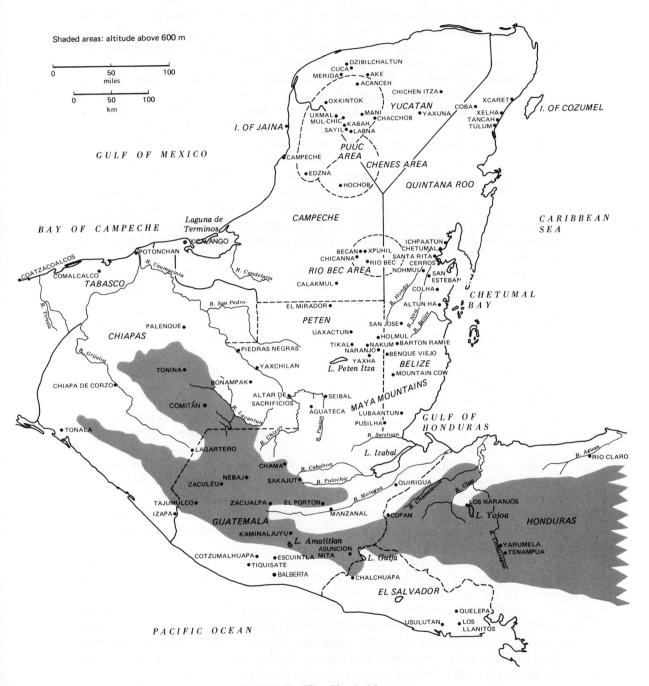

Shaded areas: altitude above 600 m

MAP 6.5 The Classic Maya.

divine. He was the human representation of the supernatural. Through his actions, gods and humans and the natural world were nourished and controlled for he had the power to act as intermediary between humans, deified ancestors, and supernaturals. There was no higher authority (Schele and Miller, 1986).

In the tightly stratified Maya society, the ruler and nobility were ranked at the top. The royal family might include 100 people (?) for the king was permitted to have more than one wife. The king's duties included bringing the gods into humans' presence through a rite performed at certain period endings. He was to maintain contact with the gods and maintain his power by offering sacrifices and bloodletting. Much time was spent in reinforcing his power and authority through public display of his ancestral background, his attention to the ritual and his prowess in war. His image was important not only in his immediate kingdom but in all the nearby regions. The king surely relied on religious personnel for interpretations of the calendar, cycles of the cosmos, and predictions, but we do not see craftspersons or theologians in murals or inscriptions. Only ancestors, deities, and supernaturals shared billing with royalty.

Also of high rank were the nobility with many titles of royalty. There was an administrative class and those who carried out the orders, a kind of executive bureaucracy. *Cahals*, a term used among the Usumacinta cities, were a kind of regional governor or military captain who were directly responsible to the king. The position might be inherited or bestowed on a deserving individual.

A number of talented individuals were also privileged: court entertainers, musicians (always male), probably fine sculptors, painters, and artisans of all kinds. The role of scribe was very special and they were viewed as almost geniuses.

Further down the scale would be architects, plasterers, stone masons, potters, laborers. The lowest strata of all consisted of the peasants who offered nothing more than their manual labor in the fields, but which made the whole system possible.

Maya society was patrilineal and patrilocal, that is, upon marriage, the wife went to live with her husband's family. The oldest son inherited (primogeniture), and seniority of generation was recognized. The settlement pattern of patio-grouping might well represent housing of extended family or lineages (Willey, 1980). This could result from a craft specialization in which the sons are apprenticed to their father and grow up in the trade. Even the lineages could become endogamous and ranking of craft specialties develop (Haviland, 1985).

There were some prominent women in Maya history who are represented on major monuments and in paintings. A few became rulers. They are the exceptions, however, for men predominate in the Maya world.

Mobility in this society was probably not flexible, perhaps confined to permanent urban residents of the elite. Wealth would have been difficult to accumulate outside of the upper ranks. Perhaps warfare eventually became an activity in which one could gain prestige and improve one's social status. A talented sculptor who could portray in bas-relief a ruler with his elegant trappings surely merited royal blessings.

If one had an aristocratic background, observed the rules of ritual, had some talent or profession, and could avoid capture, one could live well in Maya society.

For the lowland Maya, there is no equivalent of Teotihuacan, in the sense of one huge urban center that dominated the entire region. Instead, the Maya lived in hundreds of scattered settlements ranging from villages of 2000–3000 population to centers of more than 50,000. These had all long since outgrown their simpler egalitarian existence and were now sophisticated, wealthy, stratified societies, interrelated, competitive, warring, kingdoms or city-states. The most successful example of a conquest state is found in the Petexbatún (Map 6.8) in the seventh to eighth centuries, led by the rulers of Dos Pilas.

Of primary interest are the recent excavations in this region, revealing evidence of intensive and devastating warfare (Demarest, n.d.). Until the mid-seventh century, warfare was conducted along set rules and captives were taken to be sacrificed at home, reaping public acclaim and prestige. Dwellings, temples, or fields were not destroyed nor was territory annexed. Raids and skirmishes followed a pattern that was honored by all participants. There was no need for fortifications and settlements could be made in open areas with easy access.

About A.D. 670 a shift in this pattern took place in the Petexbatún as Dos Pilas began to expand its domain down the Pasión River incorporating other settlements. A century of intense fighting followed when endemic warfare swept over all the petty kingdoms with devastating environmental consequences. Massive fortifications were erected. By A.D. 850 the Petexbatún was almost depopulated and many other lowland sites had erected their last inscriptions. This regional war has important implications for the "collapse" of the lowland Maya.

I have selected several major sites to examine in detail: Tikal, Dos Pilas, Copán, and Palenque. These will provide geographic diversity representing the northeastern Petén, the Petexbatún, southeastern Mesoamerica of western Honduras, and the northern edge of the Maya world in Chiapas, Mexico. Pertinent, also, is the fact that each has been the object of intense excavations in recent years, some work currently taking place. The dynastic history of each is partially known, and their monuments provide examples of some of the most beautiful and distinctive examples of Maya art. In using these sites as a focus, we will learn something about their neighbors with whom they fought, formed alliances, married, and traded. This will take us to the year A.D. 889, a date at Seibal that is one of the last recorded in the lowlands. The history of this site will lead us to central and northern Yucatán.

TIKAL

Neither the highland or lowland Maya region was ever unified politically but in the mid-sixth century Tikal was the most prominent and powerful center. Due to its position on crossroads of communication from highlands to lowlands and between rivers flowing west and east, it could control the movement of goods and handle their distribution. Tikal had an important resource of its own: local chert or flint used for tools.

El Mirador, the enormous center to the north, had slipped into decline by now

Tikal

and although Calakmul may have profited by this retrenchment, it is not yet a major polity. It is Tikal that became the primary focus of religious and royal activity. In A.D. 292 on Stela 29, Tikal displayed its own emblem glyph as a "tied pouch," a prestigious sign of power. From then until A.D. 534 Tikal was to have no real political competition.

The dynastic history of Tikal in the fourth century rightfully begins with Jaguar Paw III, already mentioned in Chapter 4. We believe he died in A.D. 378 and was appropriately entombed in the Mundo Perdido and immortalized on Stela 29 (see page 129). The next ruler to follow is Curl Nose. This figure is thought by some to be an outsider, perhaps from Kaminaljuyú. Coggins (1979b) has built a strong case for some type of Teotihuacan takeover of Tikal by Curl Nose, perhaps through intermarriage. Schele and Freidel (1990) do not see actual conquest or dominance by foreigners. Rather they explain the evidence as representing a Teotihuacan ritual complex that the Maya embraced, finding it compatible with the religion already in place. These scholars further believe they have a firm dynastic sequence of local rulers dating back to Jaguar Paw I. They suggest that if any Teotihuacanos were present in the city, they may have formed part of a trade network. Whatever his background, origin, or mission, Curl Nose creates some kind of disjunction in the dynastic sequence at Tikal and a number of new features appear during his reign.

Group 6C-XVI

About 350 m south of Mundo Perdido, a Late Classic architectural complex of residential platforms (6C-XVI) has been found overlying abundant material of the Early Classic. The latter consists of pyramidal platforms, rooms, porticos, patios, and buildings grouped around small plazas. Laporte and Fialko (1990) believe this complex represents a second lineage or dynasty that prevailed after the reign of Jaguar Paw III. They call this the "Ma cuch" dynastic lineage and believe it was closely associated with the ball game, architecture of talud-tablero style, and certain iconographic elements (Figure 6.29).

Stylistic elements of this architecture appear prior to A.D. 1 in the Mundo Perdido Complex and thereafter are manifested on numerous buildings at Tikal (Laporte, 1987b; Laporte and Fialko, 1990). Laporte believes it may be derived from sites intermediate between Tikal and the Basin of Mexico (see discussion in Demarest, n.d.).

An outstanding discovery of a beautiful ball-court marker was found in this compound by the Proyecto Nacional Tikal in 1982–1984. The marker was not designed to be used on a ball court but was erected as a public monument for display in A.D. 378, after Tikal's victory over Uaxactún (see below). Similar markers are known from a few other sites (see page 118). This one was originally set on a talud-tablero style altar in the north patio of Group 6V-XVI. Around A.D. 425 the whole plaza was covered over, the marker taken down, and included as part of a ritual

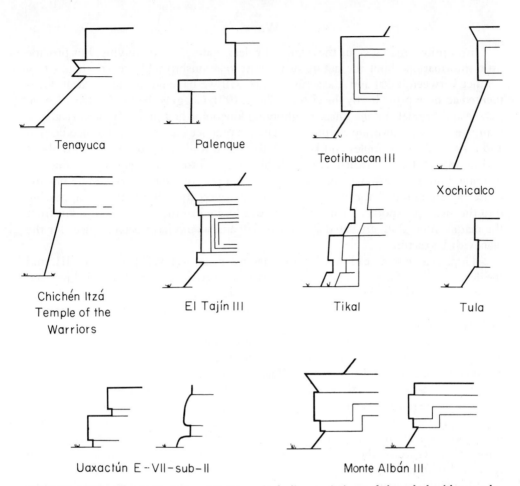

FIGURE 6.29 Classic Period architecture, including variations of the talud-tablero style. (Adapted from Marquina, 1951).

offering. It is 1 m in height, and elaborately carved with the names of Curl Nose and Smoking Frog and an inscribed text of 36 hieroglyphs and dates. The iconographic theme is clearly one of sacrifice, death, and war.

A ball game is shown in progress in nearby murals. A staircase forms part of the scene, a fact that may be significant in relation to the game, as is the fact that Group 6C-XVI lies directly south of the Tikal epicenter, implying a connection to death and the Underworld. The lineage that occupied this complex may have been specifically dedicated to the ball game, its preparation, and ritual (Laporte and Vega de Zea, 1988; Laporte and Fialko, 1990).

War

Inscriptions may give us the names of rulers, dates, and toponyms, but provide little information about the nature of intersite relationships. However, thanks to a conflict between Tikal and Uaxactún in A.D. 378 we have an unusually well documented account provided by the victors (Chase, 1991; Coggins, 1979b; Culbert, 1991a; Schele and Freidel, 1990). These neighboring kingdoms had probably been rivals for many years, each capturing victims to sacrifice, a practice accompanied by bloodletting and a ritual duty of nobles and kings. A defensive wall and moat was found about 4 km north of Tikal's Great Plaza, probably designed to guard against such raids or warring groups (Puleston and Callendar, 1967). This great moat, bridged by narrow causeways, continued almost 9.5 km in an east–west direction before disappearing into the swamp. Another such earthwork was located to the south about 8 km from the main center. Both are dated about A.D. 350 and would have been in place for the war with Uaxactún.

Things came to a head in A.D. 378 when the ruler of Tikal, Jaguar Paw III, and the leader of his forces, Smoking Frog, won a decisive victory "demolishing and throwing down the buildings of Uaxactún" (Schele and Friedel, 1990: 148). Whereas formerly Tikal had been satisfied with raids to capture victims, this time it apparently took over Uaxactún.

The name of Uaxactún's ruler is not known, but he ceased to figure in history after being hauled off to Tikal for certain sacrifice. The victors had their portraits carved on stelae at both Uaxactún and Tikal to celebrate and record this event for all posterity. Tikal now was to dominate the central Petén for nearly 200 years.

The battle must have been the final major event in the life of Jaguar Paw III who died shortly thereafter. We know little about him personally but believe that he is the figure on Stela 39 dressed as a warrior and standing over a captive. We have little information regarding the enigmatic figure of Smoking Frog. He seems to have been rewarded with rulership of Uaxactún but is never named as king of Tikal.

On the monuments erected after the battle we see Teotihuacan symbols blending with Maya art to form a new war-sacrifice imagery. For example, on Stela 5 at Uaxactún, Smoking Frog looks out over his domain dressed in a Tlaloc-Venus costume that was becoming the standard uniform of a conquering warrior. The entire regalia contains war-sacrifice symbols prevalent in Teotihuacan iconography.

The Maya associated these new symbols with the movements of the planet Venus and perhaps Jupiter and Saturn. There is convincing evidence that following the battle with Uaxactún in A.D. 378, the Maya programed their wars according to the heliacal risings of the morning and evening stars and the stationary points of Jupiter and Saturn (Schele and Freidel, 1990:444–445). In other words, from this time on, ritual events were coordinated with astronomy. The Maya had recorded historic dates of importance in the life of a ruler earlier, and at Uaxactún periodic celebrations were already recorded at the end of 20-year periods, the katun. Now these became of primary importance and the focus shifted to celebrating calendric events (Coggins, 1983).

When Curl Nose took over as tenth ruler of Tikal in A.D. 379 following the death of Jaguar Paw III, he is depicted on Stela 4 dressed in Teotihuacan imagery, and instead of a Long Count date the stela records a Calendar Round date more in keeping with Mexican traditions. When he was laid to rest in Burial 10, about A.D. 426, his grave was placed in front of the North Acropolis with his inaugural monument Stela 4 set in front of the tomb. This was a prestigious innovation that was to continue through the seventh century. His elegant grave goods emphasized his elite status with many foreign-style ceramics.

His son and successor, Stormy Sky (eleventh ruler) was one of Tikal's most celebrated and influential rulers and was inaugurated in A.D. 436. His reign saw the expansion of Maya culture over a wide area to the east. This was the time when Copán and Quiriguá began to erect monuments, and they reflect a style similar to the stelae of Stormy Sky. At Río Azul actual conquest may be indicated with a royal grandson of Stormy Sky installed as Ruler X, perhaps representing an expansion of Tikal's commercial interests in this direction (Adams, 1990).

Stela 31 is Stormy Sky's most famous monument and one of the most informative in Tikal history (Figure 6.30). On the back in a long inscription Stormy Sky identifies his parents, commemorates his accession in A.D. 436, and records some calendrical information. On the front, his father Curl Nose floats overhead in the sky as his ancestor and appears again on either side of the central figure of Stormy Sky himself. Stormy Sky is dressed like his Jaguar Paw ancestor on Stela 29 while with one arm he reaches up to his father in the sky.

Upon his death he was given a sumptuous burial (Burial 48) in a painted tomb tunneled into bedrock in the North Acropolis. He was buried in a seated position but his skull and extremities were never found. Befitting his high rank, not only were two teenagers sacrificed, but the walls of his tomb were stuccoed and painted with the Long Count date of his death, A.D. 457. Among his rich offerings were elegant pots, a fine Teotihuacan-type cylindrical tripod covered with painted stucco, and an alabaster bowl stuccoed in apple green and decorated with a band of incised glyphs. There are hundreds of beautiful jade beads, two pairs of jade earspool flares, marine products, green obsidian, and abundant food.

The Hiatus

Just as Tikal seemed headed for great prosperity, we are suddenly faced with a gap in the written record. Changes in stela carving style and the rapid succession of seven rulers suggest some turbulent years. Rulers named Kan Boar and Jaguar Paw Skull (Ruler 14) succeeded Stormy Sky and from then until the accession of Double Bird (21st ruler) in A.D. 537 we have scant knowledge. This gap is known as the hiatus, a period around the years A.D. 534–593 when few inscriptions were recorded in the Petén and activities slumped at some sites. At Tikal inscribed monuments ceased from A.D. 527 to around A.D. 570 (?), followed by a second gap until A.D. 692.

During the first half of the sixth century Tikal must have had political troubles,

FIGURE 6.30   Drawing of front and lateral faces of Stela 31, Tikal, Guatemala. The main figure is Stormy Sky, elaborately dressed, and accompanied by Curl Nose, his father, outfitted as a warrior on both sides of the stela, bearing the tasseled headdress and Storm God insignia of Teotihuacan. (Courtesy of the University Museum, Philadelphia, University of Pennsylvania.)

but despite them the ritual center of the city was renovated over a period of 70 years. By now the early causeways were well-used thoroughfares and the Maler Causeway was begun leading north from the East Plaza. The North Acropolis was once again redone, creating buildings that were to remain for the life of the city. Structure 5D-33-2 covered the old tomb of Stormy Sky and revived the fourth century tradition of decorating façades with large stucco masks. This was one of the most impressive and beautiful buildings of Tikal.

Early in the sixth century, twin pyramids set off by new floors were erected in the East Plaza, probably to celebrate tun- and katun-ending ceremonies. This was the beginning of the East Plaza's transformation into a special area for public functions, an arrangement to last for a hundred years (Jones, 1989).

This general period of unrest, political upheaval, and instability is unevenly manifested in the southern Maya lowlands, with some sites such as Uaxactún, El Perú, and Naranjo periodically breaking the silence. However, it was during this hiatus that the custom of inscribing stelae and altars spread widely to such distant sites as Toniná and Palenque in Chiapas, Pusilhá in Belize, and Cobá in northern Yucatán where Long Count inscriptions were now begun. Closer to Tikal, Yaxhá recorded dates whereas Río Azul did not. The area least affected was the southeast where activity at Copán and Quiriguá continued unabated with hardly a pause and where there may have been an influx of settlers in these very years. Caracol in Belize enjoyed some of its finest years.

Who were these Caracoleros? Their own inscriptions provide us with one view of what happened, portraying them as the terror of the sixth century Petén. If they were not directly responsible for the devastation at Tikal, they were at least full participants.

Caracol

Caracol in the southern Cayo District of Belize can hold its own in the Maya realm of art, hieroglyphic texts, and monuments. At 1600 ft. elevation it is one of the highest sites in the southern lowlands and is perched on a plateau on the western side of the Maya Mountains, where a deep canyon falls away to the northwest and hilly terrain rises to the southeast. Here the Maya initiated a vigorous building program around A.D. 500 using both skilled and unskilled labor. Seven long causeways lead out from a densely occupied core area of two major building complexes. The population after A.D. 600 may have occupied an area of 314 km (Chase, 1991). Water was apparently of great concern considering the abundant reservoirs and a pronounced dry season. The nearest bodies of water were nearly 10 km distant. There are a great number of terraces, tombs, monuments, and inscriptions that proudly reveal a dynastic sequence of rulers.

Caracol is renowned for winning a long war with Tikal, but also for the fact that it was continuously occupied from at least 300 B.C. until A.D. 1150 (Chase and Chase, 1987; Chase, 1991). In other words, there is no Maya hiatus here in the sixth century, nor a "collapse" in the ninth.

So Caracol flourished during the hiatus in the Petén, but not until the ball court was excavated in 1986 did the story come out. In the center of the Caracol playing field, a round monument (Altar 21) was found to have an inscribed text relating how after several attempts, an aggressive king of Caracol, Lord Water, finally defeated Tikal on May 1, 562. Details are not known, but it could not have been swift or easy. This was a stunning blow for the powerful polity of Tikal. Furthermore, Tikal's ruler, Double Bird, lost his life in one of the battles. Now we can better understand the ensuing silence from Tikal: its monuments were being uprooted, deliberately broken, and defaced around A.D. 557–682. The gorgeous Stela 31 was wrenched from its prestigious setting in front of Temple 5D-33-2 and, along with others, was dumped as trash in the Great Plaza (Schele and Freidel, 1990).

Caracol waged war brutally, relentlessly, and successfully in the entire Petén region for over 100 years, programmed according to the movement of Venus. For 46 years Lord Water reigned and then one of his sons, Lord Kan II, continued the aggression. With Tikal subdued, ten years later the great site of Naranjo also fell. Thereafter in A.D. 642, the exhausted residents of this site were forced to dedicate their hieroglyphic stairway to Caracol as a daily reminder of their submission.

A stairway such as this might sometimes commemorate victories, but in this case it became a daily humiliation for the surviving elite. No new monuments were inscribed for another 40 years.

The Petén wars in the seventh century are familiar tales of intrigue and realignments of friends and foes, dominated by bloody wars and Venus rituals. Tikal, Naranjo, Dos Pilas, Caracol, Yaxhá, and Calakmul were all participants.

These were disturbed years in the lowlands as Caracol was not the only aggressor. Dos Pilas figures largely in Maya history at this time as the best example of an expansionist polity. An astute political move of Dos Pilas was to send off a sister to marry into Naranjo's downtrodden royal family, producing an heir (Smoking Squirrel) after 5 years. As a young warrior, taking cues from his Dos Pilas mother, and carefully timing his battles and war-related activities to the position of Venus, he eventually managed to restore Naranjo to its former independence and power in A.D. 713. Next, Smoking Squirrel ordered the disgraceful stones of the hieroglyphic stairway dismantled and rearranged in an illegible jumble in an attempt to eradicate the memory of defeat.

The beauty and delicacy of Maya art and inscriptions tend to mask the cruelty of these people. For example, high-ranking captives taken in battle were not merely tortured and sacrificed but death might be prolonged for several years, during which time they were brought out periodically to participate in gruesome rituals and be publicly humiliated. Smoking Squirrel's mother stands over a captured lord on Stela 24. She remained prominent in Naranjo's history, appearing on monuments of her own. She is but one of a number of outstanding women in Maya history. Some rated splendid tombs as at Tikal and Caracol; others at Yaxchilán and Palenque attained rulership.

Tikal Regains Momentum: The Finest Years

Animal Skull   Meanwhile Tikal had started to regain her vitality. About 25 years after Double Bird was killed in the war with Caracol, a ruler named Animal Skull acceded as Tikal's 22nd ruler and reigned about 20 years. He seems to have been an outsider, for his father did not bear Tikal's emblem glyph. He might have been placed in power by Caracol. Whatever his background, he was respected and revered for he was given a burial (Burial No. 195 ?) in royal ground in front of the North Acropolis (Figure 6.31). He is remembered today as the distinguished ruler whose grave goods included a ball-game yoke and remains of a rubber ball (Jones, 1985).

Records in the early seventh century are few in number but the Tikaleros were

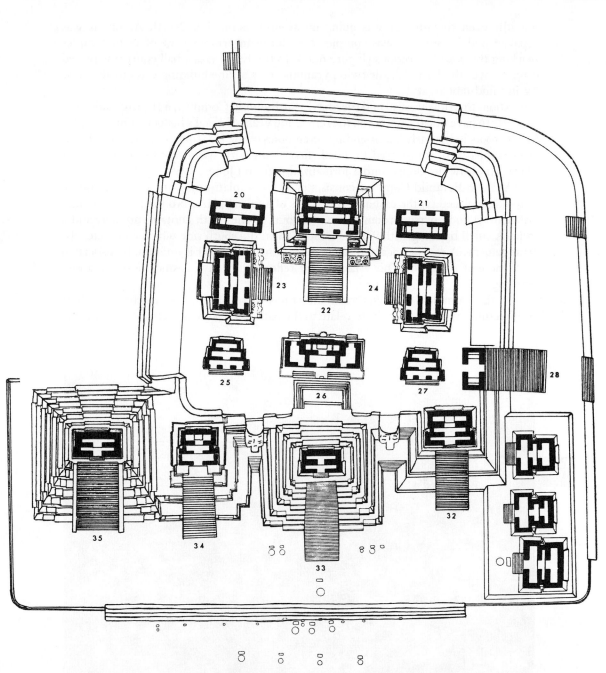

FIGURE 6.31 Plan of the North Acropolis, Tikal, in A.D. 800. (From W. R. Coe, 1988. Courtesy of the University Museum, Philadelphia, University of Pennsylvania.)

not idle even though war was going on around them. The North Acropolis was repaved and its summit was completed to form an arrangement of eight temples marking the world directions (Figure 6.32). In the East Plaza a ball court was placed directly over the Early Classic twin pyramids and a shrine building was erected close by in talud-tablero style.

About this time we also find the first Twin-Pyramid Complex, a group of buildings that was to have a lasting effect on the remaining years of Tikal's history. This complex had its roots in the early katun-ending ceremonies of the E-Group at Uaxactún. These celebrations were transferred to Tikal, first at the early twin pyramids in the East Plaza, and now developed into a formalized pattern (Jones, 1989, 1991).

A Twin-Pyramid Complex consists of two low platforms with stairways on all four sides, placed on the east and west sides of a raised plaza. No temples were built on them. A long narrow room across the court to the north contains an altar and a stela. A small building with 9 doors is situated on the south side which completes the arrangement. A row of uncarved stelae each with a plain altar is unfailingly associated with the east pyramid. This arrangement reflects the Maya cosmos outlined above (see page 238).

In this complex, east and west directions were of primary importance. The architectural design is thought to relate to the path of the sun as it crosses the sky and

FIGURE 6.32   View of the North Acropolis from Temple I. Note that Temple 33 is no longer standing. (Photographed by Lorraine Matys.)

descends to enter the Underworld. This can be symbolically compared to the life and death of the ruler before he joined his ancestors in the sky. The north represents the zenith of the celestial world, the heavens, while the 9-door building to the south stands for the Underworld with its 9 Lords of the Night. This building complex was the setting for public celebrations of katun-ending rituals that had been introduced many years before and were revived at this time to become Tikal's principal public cult. By the next century, a new Twin-Pyramid Complex would be erected at the end of each katun (20-year period) (Jones, 1991).

Shield Skull   Tikal's next ruler named Shield Skull was an industrious builder, perhaps a son of Animal Skull (?). When he died he was placed in the pyramidal base of Temple 5D-33-2 (Burial 23). Who was he? He is most renowned for fathering Ah Cacau (Ruler A or Double Comb) who was to become one of Tikal's most illustrious rulers. There are reasons to believe that Shield Skull was either from Carcacol or the general area, as eastern influence is abundant (Chase, 1991).

Ah Cacau   Eastern influence continued with his successors who not only introduced new features but integrated them with old Tikal traditions. Before his death, Ah Cacau declared himself the "260-tun reincarnation of the spirit of Stormy Sky" (Jones and Satterthwaite, 1982). Thus the beautiful Stela 31 of Stormy Sky was retrieved from the rubbish and buried with great ostentation in Structure 5D-33-2 containing his tomb and the grave of Shield Skull, his father. In the center a new temple (Structure 5D-33-1) was superimposed.

Another masterpiece, Stela 26 or the Red Stela (Shook, 1958), was also rescued (Figure 6.33). An elaborate figure of Jaguar-Paw-Skull (a hiatus ruler) had been carved on the front, with double rows of fine glyphs down the sides, and the entire stone painted red. The monument had been deliberately smashed and broken into pieces. These were now reburied in the bench of Temple 5D-34-1, along with a great variety of marine shell material, fragments of jade and obsidian, a mosaic plaque of jade, and crystalline hematite mounted on mother-of-pearl. Eccentric obsidians and small incised obsidians in this offering represent some of the finest and rarest objects recovered at Tikal.

With the completion of Temple 33-1 over Burial 23, the Great Plaza was now surrounded by huge structures. Access to the North Acropolis with its ancestral tombs was henceforth restricted by these buildings placed across the south face.

While Temple 5D-33-1 was being raised, Ah Cacau not only built a Twin-Pyramid Complex, and raised his own Stela 30 paired with a round altar in Caracol style, but he attacked Calakmul and brought its defeated king, Jaguar Paw-Jaguar and captives back to be sacrificed, probably for the completion of his new temple (Schele and Freidel, 1990).

The seventh century saw the building of other Twin-Pyramid Complexes. The Tozzer Causeway on the west was built and rebuilt, and the East Plaza marketplace was begun.

Culbert (1991a) refers to the years between A.D. 672 and 771 as "a golden century

FIGURE 6.33   Detail of hieroglyphs from Stela 26, the Red Stela. (Courtesy of the University Museum, Philadelphia, University of Pennsylvania.)

for the Maya elite." Ah-Cacau at Tikal had a brother (?) at Dos Pilas, and an influential niece married to Smoking Squirrel of Naranjo. Palenque was ruled by Pacal and his son Chan Bahlum, while Shield Jaguar was king of Yaxchilán. Smoke Jaguar was one of Copán's "greats" and his son, XVIII-Jog, accedes and meets his death during these years. Not only were these figures contemporaries but in most instances we have evidence that they were acquainted. Royal exchange visits were important politically. It was important to maintain prestige, to see and be seen.

A physical giant for his day at 5 ft. 5 in., Ah Cacau ruled Tikal for 60 years. He died in A.D. 722 soon after dedicating a second Twin-Pyramid Complex, and was royally entombed in Burial 116 on the south side of the Great Plaza. He was laid to rest with the finest offerings available: 180 pieces of worked jade, pearls, alabaster, and shells. Quite remarkable is a pile of 90 bone slivers, located in one corner of the dais on which he had been extended. Thirty-seven of these bones were delicately carved depicting deities in naturalistic scenes such as canoeing. Some have hieroglyphic texts.

Above his tomb, Temple I (Structure 5D-1) was raised to imposing heights (Figure 6.34). Its nine sloping terraces were perhaps designed to correspond to the nine layers

FIGURE 6.34   Temple I, Tikal, Guatemala. (Photographed by Lorraine Matys.)

of the Underworld, an arrangement that would facilitate the king's ascension to the heavens above. Temple I has three rooms, recessed one above the other, each vault supported by the exceedingly hard wood of the sapodilla tree, preserving some magnificent carved lintels.

Directly across the Great Plaza rises Temple II (Structure 5D-2), completed before Temple I during Ah Cacau's lifetime. Although it contains no tomb, a hieroglyphic text on the doorway lintel informs us that this temple was dedicated to a woman, probably a wife of Ah Cacau.

Four more temple/pyramids (III–VI) followed the 9-tiered style of I and II, and probably house later kings that still await discovery. Temple IV, dated about A.D. 741, and believed to contain the tomb of Yax-Kin (27th ruler), is the tallest of all (212 feet from the plaza floor) and built where the Maudslay and Tozzer Causeways meet. Temple VI, dated about A.D. 788 (Tikal's Temple of the Inscriptions), may be dedicated to a lesser royal figure and instead of carved lintels, was decorated with a stucco roof comb with a long text. These structures were carefully placed in accordance with the basic cosmological design (Figure 6.35 and 6.36).

The temple/pyramids were giant funerary structures built for a specific individual, and designed only for ancestor worship, not for public ritual or celebrations. Temple

FIGURE 6.35   Temple II, Tikal, Guatemala. In the distance Temples III and IV can be seen. (Photographed by Lorraine Matys.)

I and II of Ruler Ah Cacau and his wife faced each other across the Great Plaza to the right and left of the North Acropolis. Nothing would thereafter restrict the view of Temple I.

Yax-Kin   The tomb of their son, Yax-Kin (Ruler B), was placed at some distance but in sight of his parents with a magnificent panoramic view. The temples are posthumous, so although planned by one ruler, they were built or completed by his heirs (Miller, 1985a).

Yax-Kin ruled for nearly 20 years (A.D. 734–766) after his father died and it fell to him to complete much of the work already begun. Between Ah Cacau and Yax-Kin, they restored Tikal to her former prestige and effected a true renaissance in monumental architecture and inscriptions. The iconography of this period suggests that they were also great warriors as their monuments abound with carvings of captives under foot and sacrificial scenes, yet historically only two major conflicts are recorded: the capture and sacrifice of Jaguar-Paw-Jaguar of Calakmul by Ah Cacau in A.D. 695, and a defeat of Yaxhá by Yax-Kin.

Chitam   The 29th and last ruler of Tikal's long dynastic history was Chitam (Ruler C). He is credited with erecting two huge Twin-Pyramid complexes, both east of the Maler Causeway, Although the last dated stela we have records the year A.D. 869, and Tikal was already in decline, still later in A.D. 889 Tikal managed to send a representative to attend the katun celebrations at Seibal (see page 359).

Comments

The central core of Tikal covered 16 km and included over 3000 structures. The city consisted of an East, West, and Great Plaza and the huge complexes of the North and Central Acropolis. Temples I and II are located on the Great Plaza. These giant temple/pyramids together with lower buildings, courts, and plazas make up the central ceremonial cluster.

Recalling the basic Maya template of site planning, we can appreciate that the placement of structures at Tikal meets the prescribed pattern. The North Acropolis was the focus of ancestral tombs and the early rulers that had reached the heavens above (north). East and West positions were occupied by Temple I and Temple II. A ball court in the East Plaza functioned as a gateway to the Underworld located between the North and Central Acropolis to the south that was the domain of Underworld supernaturals. This plan can be expanded on a larger scale with Temple IV and Temple VI representing west and east and the north position filled with Twin-Pyramid Complex 3D-2 (Figure 6.36). The south was either left open or understood to lie below—the Underworld. The three causeways united the whole plan and completed the cosmology.

Other features of Tikal, perhaps less prominent, constituted important aspects of the city. The first of these is the ball courts, of which there were five. The smallest and oldest court with low, sloping benches, much like one we will see at Copán, is located in the southeast corner of the Great Plaza. A second is found in the center of the East Plaza, and a triple court (3 playing alleys), unique among Mesoamerican courts, is situated southeast of the Great Plaza across the ravine. Nearby is Tikal's sweat house consisting of a single room with a low doorway from which a channel leads to a firepit at the rear. Sweat baths, or *temescals*, probably had a ritual significance, and were associated with the ball game. They are found in both highland and lowland regions. The presence of the triple ball court and sweat bath highlights the importance of the East Court area as a center of concentrated public activity. The quadrangular buildings that were constructed nearby have led archaeologists to identify this as the ancient marketplace (Jones, 1989). On a separate causeway directly west of Temple V is the Mundo Perdido Complex, and well beyond it, the Group 6C-XVI.

Realm

It is difficult to determine the territorial limits of any of these Classic polities for we find no record of boundaries. However, it is usually assumed that any center exhibiting its own emblem glyph was independent. If a smaller center displayed a

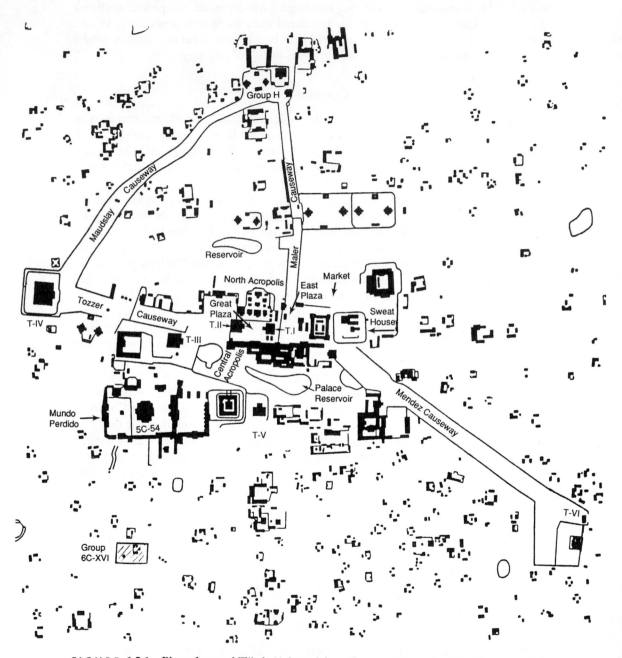

FIGURE 6.36   Plan of central Tikal. (Adapted from Carr and Hazard, 1961. Courtesy of the University Museum, Philadelphia, University of Pennsylvania.)

glyph of a larger polity, it is reasonable that it was subservient to it. (This may sound logical but there are conflicting situations and relationships are not very explicit). Tikal, however, was the largest and most powerful polity of the lowland area in Early Classic years, that is, before A.D. 600. As to the area under its political control, there is general agreement to include a region from Lake Petén Itzá to Naranjo on the east, through Uaxactún and around to El Perú (?) on the west. This would embrace an area of 2500 km with an estimated population of approximately 360,000 (Culbert, 1988a) (see also discussion of populations in Culbert *et al.*, 1990). The realm may well have extended north to Xultun and possibly Río Azul (Culbert, 1991a; Adams, 1990). Although Calakmul was defeated by Tikal in A.D. 695, there is no suggestion of its incorporation into Tikal's domain. From this it seems that Tikal's interests and expansion were directed to the northeast. The aggressive Petexbatún to the southwest may have curbed her moves in that direction.

One can see continuity at Tikal throughout these years, even through the turbulent seventh century, while undergoing changes during the hiatus. Thereafter Tikal lost her earlier political dominance of the Petén as regional city-states proliferated and many more emblem glyphs appeared. The dynastic sequence is interrupted by intrusions from the east under Animal Skull, an outsider. Under Ah Cacau many earlier traditions were revived and a new prosperity was realized. His successor continued the massive building program with the completion of the great funerary temples and the stone-roofed marketplace. But after A.D. 810 building ceased and the population rapidly declined.

Thereafter some small residential platforms went up in the East Plaza and the ball court continued in use. People were still around to inscribe the last date at A.D. 869 but leadership was badly lacking. Just when all activity ceased at Tikal we do not know, but Uaxactún and Yaxhá hung on a few years longer and the Tikal emblem glyph made a late ninth century appearance at Seibal, Jimbal, and Ixlú. This period of decline will be seen with greater perspective after taking up other southern lowland sites.

I would like to add a few words here about Yaxhá, Río Azul, and Calakmul before crossing into Belize.

Yaxhá

Located on a bluff on the north side of a chain of lakes southeast of Tikal, Yaxhá has a long history known mostly from the work of Nicholas Hellmuth in the early 1970s (Hellmuth, 1972).

Classic Period temple/pyramids, palaces, patios, and *sacbeob* have not attracted as much attention as Stela 11, depicting a typical Teotihuacan-style warrior. Other Mexican features of the site include a nonvaulted building with 6 round columns and 7 doorways, and formal streets laid out in north–south, east–west directions intersecting at right angles. There is also a Twin-Pyramid Complex and a fragmented round altar with floating sky gods, a Late Classic feature of this area (Hellmuth, 1986;

Chase, 1985a). About half of Yaxhá's 40 stelae are carved but the site has suffered from looting and part of what is known is derived from notations at other sites.

Although Yaxhá is little known today, it was prominent in the Late Classic Period. Along with neighboring Ucanal, Yaxhá was positioned in a precarious border region between Caracol and Tikal. It was conquered by Naranjo in A.D. 712 and by Tikal in A.D. 743, during the Petén wars. Some ceremonial event was also celebrated at Yaxhá in which Calakmul and Dos Pilas participated (Schele and Freidel, 1990).

Río Azul

Río Azul, located in the very northeastern corner of the Petén, became an active urban center in the Early Classic Period, suffered a hiatus, and was reoccupied thereafter but with little new construction. Rather curiously, the great amount of construction in the Early Classic would seem to exceed the needs and ability of the 3500 residents. Nonetheless, this is seen as the great period at Río Azul. The ruins are situated on a defensible, leveled ridge in a bend of the Azul River and were first reported in 1962. News of heavy looting of temples and painted tombs in 1981 brought out the archaeologists and Richard E. W. Adams led the Río Azul Project from 1983 to 1987 (Adams, 1986, 1990).

The total site of 7–8 km is composed of temples with their associated palaces linked by causeways and paved patios. Other palace groups lie outside the .5-km core center along with small groups of housemounds. Temples are embellished with modeled stucco reliefs and glyphic texts.

Adams believes Río Azul was conquered by Tikal around A.D. 390, perhaps with help from Teotihuacan, for the purpose of establishing a kind of commercial frontier outpost. Three round altars document the execution of a number of elite personages and date to the time of this presumed takeover. Río Azul lies less than 100 km from Tikal and is very conveniently located on the way to Río Hondo and centers in northern Belize. The general area is thought to have produced cacao, reason enough for a possible incursion. Most scholars feel that Tikal's domain did not extend this far, but agree it is possible (Culbert, 1991a).

Río Azul had its own emblem glyph but in Tomb 1 dated at A.D. 460, Ruler X recorded parentage statements with names of Stormy Sky, his wife Bird Claw, and grandfather Curl Nose. This would imply that he was a son of Tikal's Stormy Sky. A painted Storm God mask and numerous Chacs (rain gods) decorating painted tombs of the fifth century might also be the insignia of a Río Azul dynasty. If so, it did not survive the hiatus.

Between A.D. 390 and 530 a series of large temples were raised over the altars and painted tombs. A number of the latter have been found. Tomb 19 dated A.D. 450–500 was rich and unlooted. The deceased was a middle-aged non-Maya warrior, wearing a jade necklace of carved heads and skulls. He had been wrapped in brocaded cloth and laid out on a wooden litter with a mattress of ceiba tree cotton (kapok). More than a dozen pottery vessels accompanied him. Six of them are of Teotihuacan style.

Another has a screw-on lid, locked in place with lugs. Tests and interior scrapings analyzed by the Hershey Food Coporation Technical Center proved to be cacao, further confirmed by David Stuart when he deciphered the hieroglyphs on the lid (Stuart, 1988). Four other vessels also proved to be used for drinking chocolate.

A corbel-vaulted tomb (No. 12) with the Río Azul emblem glyph dated at A.D. 450 had been looted, but the painted walls could be "read" by John Carlson. The tomb faced west with a text of six glyphs noting that "He [name glyph], has been raised up into the sky." Lords of the Four Quarters of the sky decorated the walls while the four corners of the tomb marked the solstice directions. This was not a grave of a king, simply an elite, but Maya cosmology was understood and the precepts observed.

A cremated burial and abundant cylindrical tripod vessels made locally and at Teotihuacan strongly suggest foreign influence. The vessels do not necessarily indicate direct contact, but cremation was not practiced among the Maya. A small altar built in talud-tablero style is much like one in Group 6C-XVI at Tikal.

Río Azul certainly had all the turmoil found in a frontier outpost. After willful burning and destruction of buildings and desecration of some early burials, the site was apparently abandoned in the sixth century (A.D. 530–600) during the hiatus years at Tikal.

In the Late Classic, population increased and there was some attempt at renovations. A late stela was erected in A.D. 774 showing a captured victim under foot, but there was little new construction. In A.D. 830 Río Azul was overrun by northern Maya from the Chenes/Puuc area. The closing chapter is marked by Stela 4 (A.D. 830–880) on which a figure is dressed in the style of Chichén Itzá, Yucatán, wearing sandals and a serpent skirt, carrying spears and a round back-shield. This was a new warrior from the north.

Calakmul

We pause a moment for a glimpse of Calakmul, an unusual site in many ways. It played a prominent role in the Petén wars of the seventh century. Being tucked away in southern Campeche, not easily accessible even today, it has escaped pillage by looters and 113 of more than 140 stela are inscribed.

The site is huge. Of nearly 1000 structures, 92 are pyramids or other public buildings; approximately 300 contain corbeled vaults. Some of the quadrangular arrangements are said to compare in size with the great Nunnery (Las Monjas) at Uxmal in Yucatán, which has awed visitors for many years. The bases of Structures 1 and 2 at Calakmul equal Edzná's entire acropolis and Structure 2 compares favorably with the base of El Tigre Pyramid at El Mirador.

The great wall raised toward the end of the Preclassic has already been mentioned (see page 134). It has many entrances, one leading to a possible marketplace. It was probably a defensive structure but could also have served to mark off the center of the city with its short *sacbeob*. The center of town (1.75 km) was compact and housed the wealthy in fine residences placed close to public buildings. Other dwellings were located in the countryside and even within *bajos* on elevations where groups of houses resembled small islands (Folan, Jr.,1990).

Inscriptions span the years A.D. 514–830. The glorious years of Calakmul were A.D. 600–850. Although the first stela was raised in A.D. 514, 109 years elapsed before the next. Was there a haitus? perhaps, but the missing stelae could have been destroyed by rulers or are yet to be discovered. At Calakmul the stelae stand where they were erected, each in front of an associated building. Sadly, the inferior quality of the limestone has led to considerable deterioration. However, Joyce Marcus arrived in time to study them and has identified ten possible rulers. Women often appear with their husbands and five royal couples are portrayed (Marcus, 1987).

Calakmul was a regional capital believed to have coexisted with El Mirador at an early time, and eventually inherited its power upon its demise (Marcus, 1976; Schele and Freidel, 1990). Its Late Classic domain included the neighboring centers of Balakbal, Naachtún, Uxul, Oxpemul, La Muñeca, and Altamira (see Map 6.6). Jaguar Paw-Jaguar was its most renowned king, acceding to power in A.D. 686. In the seventh Century, Calakmul allied itself with Caracol in its warring throughout the Petén. Friends, enemies, politicians, and marriages have been sorted out by comparing site inscriptions as to which dignitaries attended what accession ceremonies, katun-ending celebrations, and building dedications. For example, at Jaguar Paw-Jaguar's accession, the ruler of Dos Pilas and El Perú were in attendance. The occasion was recorded at all three sites.

After Ah Cacau of Tikal captured Jaguar Paw-Jaguar in A.D. 695 and sacrificed him (see page 259), Calakmul continued to erect monuments, and our last news is from Seibal, where a Calakmul noble traveled to witness a katun-ending ceremony in the late ninth century.

BELIZE

We have already seen the early evidence of kingship at Cerros and noted the abundance of settlements in Belize during the Preclassic Period. Most of these were easily reached by water and throughout its history Belize reaped advantages from its strategic location on the Caribbean Sea. This enabled it to both receive and distribute goods along the major river systems leading to the heart of the Petén and Campeche as well as to have contacts with highland Guatemala via the Motagua River. These routes formed natural corridors for the transmission of goods and ideas. (McKillop and Jackson, 1989).

In the Classic Period, Caracol was the only military power in Belize to go on a rampage. Pyramids, temples, and tombs proliferate at the largest sites, but many settlements are more modest and vary in outlay. Inscriptions are not always present. Belize was densely populated and maintained an important role commercially. In the early periods exchange of goods was predominantly between coastal and inland sites with little seagoing activity. After A.D. 600, however, the population increased dramatically along with trade and great changes were brought about in Belize. Agricultural techniques had led to the appearance of raised fields where beans, maize, squash, root crops, cacao, and cotton were grown. Thus the inhabitants were full participants in lowland Maya culture and many settlements were able to adapt to the changes that took place at the end of the Classic Period and move along with the new trends of the Postclassic era. The following sites are but a few of the most outstanding (see Map 6.6).

Ambergris Cay

Several interesting sites have been reported from Ambergris Cay off the coast of northern Belize. This island is 40 km long by only 1.5–3 km wide with few surfaces over 3 m elevation. Sea travel is treacherous, with vessels having to maneuver through narrow openings in the reef. In A.D. 650 a canal 3–4 m wide was cut through the

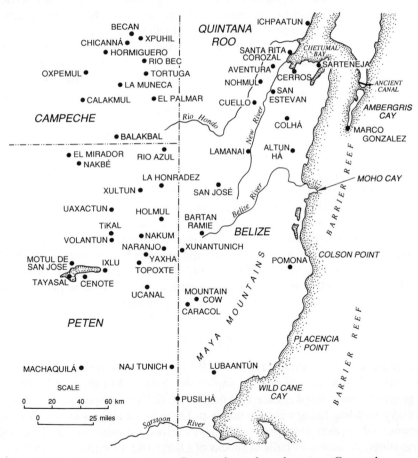

MAP 6.6 Belize, eastern Guatemala, and southwestern Campeche.

narrowest point of the peninsula to permit easier passage to calm water. Understandably, settlements were made on the leeward side: San Juan and Chac Balam, and at
the very southern tip, Marco González (Guderjan *et al.*, 1989).

These functioned as trans-shipment points probably funneling goods back and
forth to the mainland. San Juan was active all during the Classic Period. Six platform-
mounds are mapped, and around A.D. 900 a round, 2-tiered structure was erected
similar to Nohmul's Structure 9. These sites were all influenced by Chichén Itzá.
Obsidian was mostly from El Chayal but Mexican sources constituted 18%.

Marco González, a small site, functioned in a similar way. It became even more
active in the twelfth and thirteenth centuries when it carried on an active relationship
with Lamanai (see page 433) (Pendergast, 1990).

Santa Rita Corozal

After Cerros faded away, Santa Ritz Corozal replaced it as the leading settlement
in the community. It began to construct monumental architecture with stucco mask
façades, and by A.D. 450, a prominent person (a ruler ?) was buried in Structure 1
with all the furnishings befitting his high rank. Many of these items were associated
with bloodletting and the sea (Chase and Chase, 1989). After A.D. 600 social differences
became less apparent and pronounced regionalism spread. The Petén does not seem
to have maintained its former importance for this area. But Santa Rita Corozal is a
site to keep in mind, for its prime years are yet to come in the Postclassic era.

Nohmul

This is a large site on the Río Hondo, and a good example of the mixed economy
mentioned above. Hammond (1975) suggests that the raised fields, which could be
renewed annually by silt from the canals, were constructed in response to the demands
of a growing population. As a result, the community was placed under firmer control.
The massive building projects required a large labor force and at the same time
commercial activities expanded. The three large mounds begun in the Late Preclassic
were in continual use and Nohmul thrived until the terminal Classic. A rather special
relationship with Chichén Itzá in the ninth century brought in new people from the
north along with innovations in architecture (see page 429).

Colhá

Located also in the northern region, Colhá lies on a broken ridge among swamps
not far from the coast. It is a rather complex site, founded in the middle Preclassic,
but is generally considered a Late Classic site. Colhá was a specialized craft town,
nearly every building being a chert workshop. Debitage of chips and nodules identify
the commercial aspects that produced quantities of various tools and prestigious
eccentric flints. A *sacbé* was built of blocks of chert, and a number of chert nodules
(1 m in height) connected structures in the southern part of the site. The ceremonial

center was small, consisting of a single pyramid, a miniature ball court, and several large enclosed courts. This was a settlement of dense occupation, with more interest in commerce than ideology and ritual. A busy export business was probably conducted via the sea.

Altun Há

North of Belize City on the central coastal plain is a smallish ceremonial center surrounded by dispersed settlements. Of its two plazas, one is bordered by pyramids, the other has one large pyramid with multi-chambered buildings on the other three sides. In a zone west of the center of town, one structure (C-13) seems to have fulfilled the ritual needs of the community from the earliest time in the Preclassic until the abandonment of the site in the ninth century. Although there was some reoccupation in the Postclassic, the years of Classic elite life were never resumed (Pendergast, 1979-1982).

This is a modest isolated site, but Altun Há is renowned for its great jadeite carving of the Sun God in the Preclassic and in the Classic Period for its rich tombs, jade, and a famous cache of eccentric obsidians (Pendergast, 1969). Buried in the upper level of the tallest ceremonial structure (B-4) near the main ceremonial precinct, a great cache contained shells, pottery, jadeite beads, and 245 eccentric obsidians along with 13 green, stemmed, obsidian blades. Not only is the workmanship fine, the quantity staggering, but the green obsidian could only have come from the Cerro de las Navajas mines in central highland Mexico. Stelae were never erected here. Early Classic trade brought great wealth and prosperity to this center so conveniently located for intersite communication. Altun Há has also yielded the oldest metal import into the Maya area, which is a small tumbaga claw of Late Classic date A.D. 550 from the region of Panama (Bray, 1989). Apparently there was no shortage of land or tight residential control. People could live wherever they chose. When abandonment took place at the end of the Classic Period, every accessible tomb was looted.

Lamanai

The nearby site of Lamanai, 40 km west of Altun Há at the head of the New River, had been very active in the Preclassic Period, and its occupation and prosperity continued uninterrupted until A.D. 1675. Excavations were carried out at the site from 1974 through 1982 by David Pendergast (1986, 1990), who points out the sharp contrast between Lamanai and Altun Há. At Lamanai, ceremonialism was strongly developed, providing evidence of a ruling authority with tight control over the populace. An early center was developed in the northern sector, but after A.D. 850 when many other Maya centers were failing, Lamanai residents moved to new locations and devoted their energies to the construction of a new focus to the south.

A large temple was built and a single ball court, where a spectacular offering had been placed under its giant central marker. A lidded bowl contained 100 g of crystalline hematite, 19 g of cinnabar in a miniature vessel, and other objects of jade, shell, and pearl, all atop a pool of 131.9 g (9.7 cm) of mercury (Pendergast, 1982). Previously mercury had been found at Copán, Quiriguá, and at Kaminaljuyú and Lake Amatitlán, but not in such quantity. This large deposit at Lamanai had probably been collected for ritual use.

The relocation of the center at Lamanai did not result in a disruption or upheaval. On the contrary, these people were planning ahead with confidence in the future. Trade apparently continued unabated.

A great frenzy of housing construction took place in the ninth, tenth, and eleventh centuries. Three structures were sometimes placed around two contiguous courtyards. The façade of one was decorated in stucco like a contemporary building at Seibal. One platform supported three structures. An enclosed courtyard with a single platform and colonnaded halls was a plan that became typical of terminal Classic and Postclassic arrangements in northern Yucatán.

Eventually courtyards were filled in to create a huge platform with residential structures at both ends—a tremendous undertaking requiring direction, authoritative control, and massive manpower. Ceramics gradually adopted new styles as well. Unfortunately for us, by the end of the Classic, the norm here for burial custom was to smash vessels prior to interment. Lamanai adjusted independently to new trends of the Postclassic while maintaining some of its former ties to ritual and architectural design. No radical changes are noted and a stable existence continued throughout the Postclassic years.

Barton Ramie

Lying due east of Tikal and Holmul in the upper Belize River valley is one of the best-known sites in the area with early beginnings of ordinary housemounds built on alluvial clay terraces. Eventually more than 200 structures were placed at random. The site has a long history of occupation reaching back to 750 B.C. and continuing beyond A.D. 1000 (Hammond and Ashmore, 1981). The general ceramic sequence followed conventional patterns and included the Floral Park manifestation. Not far to the southeast is Pomona, the site of the famous Preclassic jadeite flare. To the southwest is Xunantunich (Benque Viejo) noted for a building complex with an exceptionally tall building 40 m in height that was decorated with elaborate stucco and stone mosaics (Morley et al., 1983).

Coastal Belize Salt Production

Salt production must have been a lively enterprise along the coast of Belize during late and terminal Classic years (MacKinnon and Kepec, 1989; Valdez and Mock, 1991). The great quantity of faunal and marine life remains, together with ceramic artifacts for salt-making, point to the use of salt in the preservation of meat and fish for transport to inland centers. This salt was inferior to that of northern Yucatán but may have satisfied demand in many localities of the southern lowlands. A number of sites have been reported from the Northern River Lagoon to Point Placencia on the south coast.

Lubaantún

This site flourished in the Late Classic from A.D. 700 to 850. The ceramic assemblages attest to an exchange network that brought in Fine Orange from the Pasión Valley although most pottery proved to be made from local clay. Its figurines have been found at neighboring Pusilhá. Obsidian was imported from El Chayal. There is a single acropolis center, a great plaza and two ball courts using the local green sandstone for construction. No stelae were erected nor were buildings vaulted. Elite residences were concentrated in one area west of the center with their own shrines. This would have been a suitable area for cacao production (Hammond, 1988). This is an unusual site and is best understood along with other southern Belize sites, such as Pusilhá.

Pusilhá

Thirty-two km southwest of Lubaantún along the foothills is Pusilhá, an interesting site divided by the Moho River, but connected by a stone-braced bridge. One side of the river was dedicated to agriculture with terraces while the other was the ritual center with a plaza and 20 stelae, one of which bears the emblem glyph of Quiriguá, notable for being the only one outside of its main site. About the time Lubaantún was founded (soon after A.D. 700), Pusilhá inscribed its last dated monument (A.D. 731). However, it continued to make fine pottery for another 100 years (Hammond, 1988). This lets us know that the cessation of dated monuments is not necessarily indicative of immediate abandonment or collapse.

Pusilhá and Lubaantún are two major sites in a regional area of southern Belize geographically limited by the Maya Mountains (north and west), the Caribbean (east), and two major rivers making a swampy southern border. Leventhal (1990) calls attention to the internal cohesion of Maya sites in this area during the late Classic. There are distinctive features of each noted above, but shared similarities can be found in three features: (1) ball courts enclosed by free-standing walls; (2) "façade-natural construction," that is, the stone façade is placed over the natural terrain to form terraces and pyramids; and (3) the reuse of tombs. In one example at a site called Nim Li Punit, five individuals had used the same tomb sequentially. This is not a unique situation, but seems to be particularly characteristic of this area. Greater use of such regional studies may prove to be more beneficial than approaching the Maya in terms of the general overarching view, the "big picture."

COPÁN

We emerge now from the tropical forest and Belize and proceed to the southern highland city of Copán, nestled in a beautiful little valley of western Honduras. Here in Preclassic days early settlers had lived and farmed the rich bottomland that was bisected by the Copán River and circumscribed by forested hills. The heart of the valley is the Copán pocket, 9.25 square miles, containing 2500 mounds with probably 1000 more up and down the valley.

Copán

It is becoming increasingly common for a series of scholars and institutions to participate in major excavations, and so it has been at Copán. Among organizations, the Carnegie Institution of Washington, the Peabody Museum of Harvard University, the National Geographic Society, Dumbarton Oaks of Washington, the University of Texas, and the University Museum, University of Pennsylvania have all been enthusiastic supporters.

In 1976 the Honduran Government with the Instituto Hondureño de Antropología e Historia, initiated a major project at Copán that has focused on both the Main Group of structures as well as others in the surrounding countryside under the overall direction of William Fash. Partial results of these current investigations can be found in the writings of a large number of individuals, specialists and graduate students. In compiling the history of Copán and Quiriguá, I owe much to the following scholars: Ashmore, 1986, 1991; Baudez, 1986, 1991; Demarest, 1988; Fash, 1986, 1988, 1991a,b; Fash and Sharer, 1990; Fash and Stuart, 1991; Jones and Sharer, 1986; Leventhal *et al.*, 1987; Riese, 1986; Schele and Freidel, 1990; Schele and Miller, 1986; Stuart, 1992; Miller, 1988a; and Webster, 1988, 1990. Already these scholars have been able to tell us much about settlement patterns, housing, monuments, structures, and history of hieroglyphic inscriptions. The dynastic sequence of Copán rulers now seems well defined, permitting rulers to be referred to by number such as Ruler 8 or Ruler 13 for example. The reader should bear in mind that the commonly used nicknames such as Smoke Jaguar or 18 Rabbit may not be accurate transliterations. An exception is Ruler 1, whose name reads K'inich Yax K'uk' Mo' (Stuart, 1992).

The Site   The Main Group of ruins includes an Acropolis, a massive conglomerate of courts, platforms, temples and ball courts. From the Great Plaza (Figure 6.37) the city was divided into quarters marking the cardinal directions. A sight line ran from a mountain in the north to Temple 11 in the south; east and west were formed by two causeways leading out from the plaza. This division into quadrants is known elsewhere and was not only an important cosmological design, but created a frame for ritual activity (Baudez, 1990). From the top of the Acropolis one commands an imposing view of the main courts and their surrounding buildings and stepped terraces as well as an impressive view of the Copán River 100 feet below. The Copán River once flowed by the ruins eroding the east face of the Acropolis, exposing a vertical "stratigraphic" cut 37 m in height. Fortunately the course of the river has been rechanneled to prevent further destruction. The exposed cross-section (the *corte*), has allowed access by tunneling to earlier structures revealing an architectural sequence of the Acropolis without destroying later superimposed constructions (Sharer *et al.*, 1992).

Most of the spectacular remains to be seen today date from the eighth century, the apogee of the Late Classic period. A large group of structures on the southern edge of the Acropolis is now believed to be the residence of the royal family around A.D. 800 to 900 (Andrews V., and Fash, 1992). Aside from the site core of the Main Group with the Acropolis, settlements are found all along the northern foothills with mounds occupying natural terraces or small hillocks. There are also small clusters of

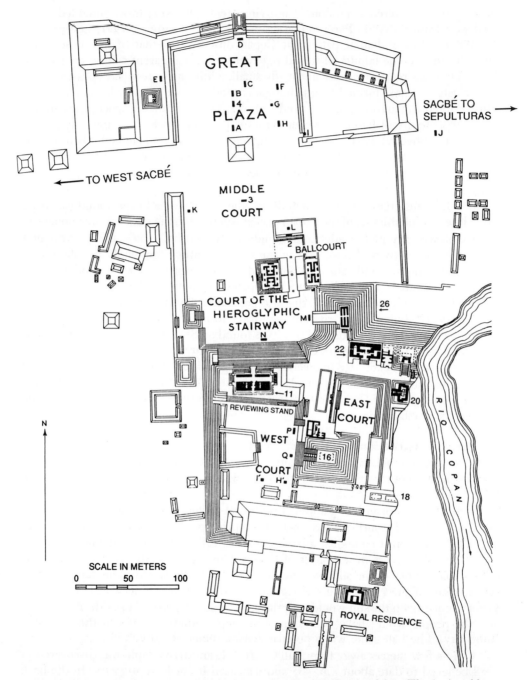

GREAT

PLAZA

SACBÉ TO
SEPULTURAS

TO WEST SACBÉ

MIDDLE
COURT

BALLCOURT

COURT OF THE
HIEROGLYPHIC
STAIRWAY

REVIEWING STAND

EAST
COURT

WEST
COURT

RIO COPÁN

ROYAL RESIDENCE

N

SCALE IN METERS
0   50   100

FIGURE 6.37 Copán: ceremonial precinct and acropolis. (*Reprinted from The Ancient Maya, Fourth Edition*, by Sylvanus Griswold Morley and George W. Brainerd; revised by Robert J. Sharer with the permission of the publishers, Stanford University Press. © 1946, 1947, 1956, & 1983, by the Board of Trustees of the Leland Stanford Junior University. Additions from Baudez, 1990 and Fash, 1991.)

housing units scattered at random in outlying areas. One *sacbé* (now gone) led west-northwest from the Main Plaza to one residential area (Ashmore, 1991; Leventhal *et al.*, 1987). The residential pattern at Copán differs from that of Tikal (see page 239–240) in that the family all stayed together with no apparent ceiling on growth. Although house platforms were unusually small, additions were always possible until tight clusters almost formed "a quadrangle around a plaza" (Leventhal *et al.*, 1987). This resulted in narrow walkways and utilization of all available space, indicating a different structure of family organization. One patio-group was occupied by several generations (Sheehy, 1991). The largest aggregation of mounds outside the center is only a short distance down the eastern *sacbe* from the Main Group and is called Las Sepulturas (the Tombs), a modern misnomer, for this was an area of elite residential compounds.

It is here that remains of an early Preclassic cemetery had been found (see page 70). The early inhabitants of the Copán pocket belonged to the same ethnic population as that of western El Salvador and Honduras (Leventhal *et al.*, 1987). Although population and activity dropped off in the second century, gradually people moved back into the bottomlands and also occupied a promentory where the modern town of Copán is located. The earliest date at Copán corresponds to October 14, 321 B.C., recorded on a monument (Altar I') that was erected 1000 years later in the West Court (Stuart, 1991). This curious citation may refer to a mythological event in Copán's ancient past. Another early date, A.D. 159, is found on Stela 1 along with the representation of a ruler (?) and Copán's emblem glyph of a bat. In this Early Classic period, living sites were concentrated in several competing polities: (1) in the area which would become the Main Group at Copán; (2) in the location of the modern village of Copán; (3) a hilltop site called Cerro de las Mesas; and (4) in three other settlements on the low terrace north of the river.

Early Construction and Rulers   While the residents of the Copán village area began carving hieroglyphic monuments, the Great Plaza of the Main Group began with a stuccoed courtyard, a large unstuccoed plaza, a temple and a ball court. (Figure 6.39).

The Mesoamerican ball game had profound religious associations, and Copán's earliest court (Ball Court A-I) was one of the principle features of the Main Group. From its inception it embodied a basic cosmological symbolism. The alley markers show the ball-players in a contest of dark versus light, death versus life and the predictable victory of the sun over the Lords of the Underworld. This represents an reenactment of the Hero Twins' defeat of the Lords of the Underworld. With their victory, once again the sun would rise, the crops would ripen and provide abundance, and the people would have witnessed their king mediating between the gods and humanity. The ball game was a popular artistic theme (Figure 6.38).

Only a few meters away from Ball Court A-I, an early temple was discovered in 1988 believed to date about A.D. 435 and was used for at least 30 years. In the back chamber of this early Classic temple (dubbed "Papagayo"), Stela 63 lay broken in three pieces. Its inscriptions refer to a former ruler, K'inich Yax'-K'uk'M'o, believed

FIGURE 6.38 Ball game scene on polychrome Maya vase. (Courtesy of the Dallas Art Museum. Photographed by Justin Kerr.)

FIGURE 6.39 Ball court (A-III) at Copán. (Photographed by the author.)

to have been in power from A.D. 426–435 (?). He is mentioned on other monuments as the founder of Copán's ruling lineage and he appears with his successors on Altar Q (see page 278). He may also be the figure on Stela 36 (a stela reused in Structure 10L-4), contemporaneous with Stela 63 (Fash and Stuart, 1991). Ruler 4, Cu-Ix, refloored the Papagayo and added a hieroglyphic step (Fash and Sharer, 1991).

There is evidence however of even earlier rulers, associated with monuments or structures and platforms with gigantic stucco sculptures. The east side of one of these buildings has a large crocodilian creature floating above a water lily and a tun (stone) glyph, a familiar representation of the Mesoamerican belief that the earth was represented as the back of a giant crocodile that floated on a pond (Fash, 1988). These are the first signs of art, iconography, and hieroglyphic inscriptions that belong to the elite Maya culture of the Petén. An early colonization of both Copán and Quiriguá has often been suggested. Stela 36 is carved in the low-relief style of the southern lowlands lending credence to an early Petén intrusion.

There is, however, no evidence of elite trade with the Petén (see discussion in Baudez, 1986; Fash and Stuart, 1991). Iconographic and ceramic features tie Copán more closely to the Guatemalan highlands. The elite Maya features of the Petén were gradually absorbed into the non-elite composition of the local population at Copán, and eventually produced the special blend of the Copán polity in its prime.

While the Main Group was becoming the center of ceremonial activities, over in the Sepulturas area, a prominent individual died around A.D. 450 and was buried with fine pottery, jade jewelry, and a curious assortment of objects: divining stones, turtle shells and rattles, a codex (now deteriorated), and animal teeth and bones. These are just the types of tools a shaman might have had in his bag of tricks. Among the pottery vessels were lidded cylindrical tripod jars typical of Classic Teotihuacan. Other graves of the same period were devoid of offerings, but the Sepulturas shaman and evidence of named rulers (kings), indicate that already in the fifth century, inhabitants of the Copán Valley were living in a stratified society.

There may have been several early local lineages competing for power in the Copán Valley, but K'inich Yax K'uk'Mo' seems to have initiated the lineage that was to provide Copán's kings for 400 years (Fash, 1991).

Several fine burials of unidentified individuals have been found in and around Structure 10L-26. One male skeleton seated in a stone cist was given grave goods of Thin Orange ware imported from Central Mexico, a beautiful carved bowl of Kaminaljuyú style, shell ornaments, a slate-backed pyrite mirror, and polished jade pieces. Two other elite graves lay immediately east of the Papagayo Structure.

Tunneling in from the eroded east side of the Acropolis into Structure 16, the team from the University of Pennsylvania directed by R. J. Sharer, discovered a masonry chamber 12-feet long plastered in red and roofed by stone beams. A well-preserved skeleton lay on a stone slab and was covered with jade beads, carved shell, and surrounded by abundant ceramics. Inscriptions may identify the deceased as Waterlily Jaguar (Ruler 7) who reigned for forty years. He is depicted on Alter Q and Stela E and may be the early Copán ruler mentioned on a Stela 16 at Caracol in Belize (?). If not the tomb of Waterlily Jaguar, it may belong to one of his three immediate successors of the sixth century: one of two younger brothers or a son, Moon Jaguar (Ruler 10).

Possibly dating to the reign of Ruler 11, Butz' Chan, is a small elegant temple known as Rosalila, discovered beneath three later buildings inside the massive Structure 10L-16 that faces the West Court. A coating of rough plaster had preserved it well; even the roof-comb was still in place. The façade was decorated with stucco sculptures of two large birds with the old god Itzamná emerging from their mouths. The upper story bears sacrificial iconography. The finest treasure in a caché containing knives, beads, spiny oyster shells, and shark vertebrae was nine eccentric flints (sculptures of chert), still wrapped in fragments of colored cloth. Such objects mounted on a staff may have been carried in ceremonies as symbols of supernatural power (Agurcia, F., and Fash, 1991).

During this same reign the earlier Papagayo Structure was burned and ritually "killed" between A.D. 575 and 650, and a curious larger construction called Corcha was superimposed. Its presence and architecture are unaccounted for as it is a long, colonnaded, open, public building with no antecedents at Copán, nor was its style repeated thereafter.

Smoke-Jaguar Beginning with the twelfth ruler, Lord Smoke-Jaguar (also called Smoke-Imix God K) in A.D. 628, dynastic history is more complete, ending with the last inscribed date in A.D. 832. Lord Smoke-Jaguar was one of Copán's "greats." At home he erected more stelae and altars then any of his predecessors. One of the most important stelae he erected was of Stela I, set up in a niche on the east side of the Great Plaza. It refers to an ancient date of A.D. 159 (8.6.0.0.0) which, although the valley had even earlier inhabitants, may refer to the founding of Copán as a polity (Schele, 1987). In A.D. 652 an important calendar period-ending, Smoke-Jaguar set up six stelae at different high points around the Copán Valley, presumably to mark off the limits of his kingdom. Or they may have been placed for astronomical sightings, to facilitate communication with defense in mind, or to reinforce a connection between his ancestors and the surrounding sacred mountains. Whatever the reason, it was a unique occurrence and unusual role for stelae.

The very next year, A.D. 653, an inscription on Altar L at neighboring Quiriguá, tells us that this center fell to Copán. Although unrecorded at Copán itself, it was not forgotten by Quiriguá. Copán's expansion down the Motagua Valley was surely well planned with an eye on the jade and obsidian trade operating down the river from highland Guatemala. Copán holdings were also expanded to the northeast outside the Copán pocket to include Río Amarillo, La Florida, and Los Higos. The latter has an eighth century inscribed Maya stela (Riese, 1988). (See also Vlcek and Fash, 1986).

On Smoke-Jaguar's stelae he appears in full warrior regalia complete with Tlaloc year-sign, sacrifice symbols, sometimes wearing a turban-type headdress with an iconography close to that of Cotzumalhuapa and the Pacific slopes of Guatemala (Baudez, 1986). According to Schele and Freidel (1990) Smoke-Jaguar died in A.D. 695 at around 80 years of age. In her study of Copán's Acropolis, Mary Miller (1988a) tells us that Building 16 in the West Court is one of the oldest visible structures. This is a 9-tiered pyramid such as those built as mortuary temples at Palenque and Tikal.

Miller believes Structure 16 at Copán may contain the tomb of Smoke-Jaguar although as yet no royal tombs have been found. Having given to Copán a long period of stability, Smoke-Jaguar left to his son XVIII-Jog (18 Rabbit) a prosperous kingdom, perhaps the largest of its time.

In Maya society, the eldest son inherited. Younger ones were often trained as scribes, a worthy occupation. We think one such son of Smoke-Jaguar was the elite individual that was placed in a vaulted tomb inside Structure 10L-26. This person, accompanied by a sacrificed youth, had been given the finest of Maya jewels: jade ear ornaments and a necklace with jade carvings of a noble and an owl. The decoration of the pottery and a paint pot identified the deceased as a scribe.

XVIII-Jog   It would have been this scribe's elder brother, XVIII-Jog, who succeeded Smoke-Jaguar in A.D. 695 to rule for 50 years. He was not the empire builder with the political acumen of his father, for his interests lay elsewhere. Having inherited wealth, prestige, and a prosperous kingdom, he devoted his energies to making the royal city of Copán worthy of the power and stature it had acquired. The entire center of the city was transformed as he guided artisans, architects, sculptors, and scribes into executing some of the Maya's finest examples of monumental art.

An earlier temple (Temple 22), the most important of the East Court, was now remodeled to have a perpendicular façade exquisitely decorated in the Yucatán style of Chenes, Río Bec, and Puuc. This was decorated with deeply carved stone sculptures. Great Witz Monsters made of mosaic pieces were placed at the four corners. Access to the sacred precinct was gained by passing through a huge Celestial Monster mouth like the Chenes's façades in Campeche (Figures 6.40 and 6.41). The heavens were held up at the corners by four pauahtuns (bacabs) seated on the skull of the Underworld and supported a giant bicephalic monster whose "body arches over the doorway" with Sun and Venus symbols (Miller, 1988a).

The ball court was remodeled to become the most beautiful at Copán, altering the markers to emphasize the king's role incarnating the ancestral Hero Twins. The bench and façade sculptures now included pertinent symbolism of the ball game with macaws (sun and light), the Underworld (bones and kan crosses associated with *akbal*, or night), and maize plants with cobs and kernels (abundance and fertility).

XVIII-Jog also set up a "forest" of his own stelae (tree-stones) in the Great Plaza (Figure 6.42). Of his monuments, none is more puzzling than Stela A (A.D. 731), for it records the emblem glyphs of Tikal, Palenque, Calakmul (or El Peru ?), and Copán, each associated with a glyph of the four cardinal directions. Did this refer to a political alliance? a meeting or celebration? What role did Copán have among these leading Maya polities of the eighth century? We can only speculate, for XVIII-Jog had only a few more years to live. We have, however, fine examples of his artistic taste shown in the execution of the royal figures on his stelae (Figure 6.43). The iconography here is markedly different from that of earlier ones. The war-sacrifice-death complex is associated with the Sun God rather than with the jaguar that is no longer found in the headdress or belt. Instead, new images feature the Maize God, Cauac Monster, the Crocodile, and God K with special emphasis on earth and rain fertility. Most of these changes took place under XVIII-Jog (Baudez, 1986).

FIGURE 6.40   Entrance to sanctuary of Temple 22, Copán. (Photographed by Justin Kerr, 1987).

FIGURE 6.41   Detail of the entrance to Temple 22, Copán. One of the skulls of the Underworld. (Photographed by the author.)

FIGURE 6.42   The Great Plaza of Copán. (Photographed by the author.)

FIGURE 6.43   Stela depicting Ruler XVIII-Jog. (Photographed by the author.)

He seems to have taken great interest also in the old trade route to the Petén lowlands via highland Guatemala, perhaps even controlling the quetzal feather trade (Coggins, 1988a). At least we find Copador-related wares in Piedras Negras and a shared iconography with Usumacinta sites. There may have been some kind of special relationship with Chamá, Alta Verapaz, since they both portray a sign of a leaf-nosed bat with spread wings. Bats form part of Copán's emblem glyph and as we will see, they adorn a later building at Copán (see page 288).

At this point, kingship began to undergo certain modifications, becoming less rigid and more tolerant of other ideas. XVIII-Jog began to sanction the use of royal perogatives by the noble lineages in Las Sepulturas households and these patriarchs started erecting inscribed monuments formerly permitted only to kings. Although not apparent in his own inscriptions or monuments, XVIII-Jog seems to have relaxed his public stance to accommodate some non-Maya beliefs.

Another element was the growing multi-ethnic nature of society. Population increased so dramatically that it could not have been a purely local expansion. Artifacts reflect a non-elite intrusion from the southern periphery that already had an early ceramic base in the region. Demarest (1988) suggests this population increase may have been caused by a gradual build-up of household settlers coming in from the Chalchuapa regions, perhaps seeking work as potters and stone artisans during the lean years in western El Salvador when people were still recovering from the effects of vulcanism. Families may have begun coming in as early as the seventh century, which would account for the otherwise puzzling presence of a red-painted Usulután style in the Copán Valley. In the Late Classic these settlers may have constituted an important addition to the labor force. Demarest visualizes no mass movement of people, but a population that grew gradually from a few families who were followed by their relatives. The immigrants would no doubt have been grateful to Copán's ruler for their reception and opportunity to reestablish themselves. Likewise, the ruler would have been pleased to expand his constituency with loyal supporters. They were loyal, yes, but the newcomers may not have viewed the ruler as a divine king with the same reverence of those raised in the old tradition.

As population increased pressure mounted in the valley as arable land was becoming more scarce. Craftspersons were busily trying to satisfy the demands for household goods and commodities. Ixtepeque obsidian was imported, *metates* were produced from the local rhyolite, and after A.D. 737 an elegant polychrome pottery known as Copador was turned out in Copán in large quantities (Leventhal, 1986). This combined ceramic features of El Salvador with Maya styles of the western highlands and was widely traded in the southern region. Copador combined a deep purple-red, black, and usually an orange color on a cream or orange-tinted background. Motifs might be in the form of glyphs, human, bird, or geometric designs. In the late Classic, every household in western El Salvador had a few examples of Copador. It was a non-elite item, decorated with rather imprecise Maya imagery, lacking any dynastic significance. Glyphs were purely decorative, at times placed backward and were meaningless (Demarest, 1988; Coggins, 1988a). Distribution of Copador skirts Quiriguá but is abundant in a radius of 50–75 km around Copán.

Following A.D. 725 Quiriguá was ruled by its greatest king, Cauac Sky (Two-Legged-Sky). It is possible that there was some kinship tie with Copán but this is unclear. Remember that Smoke-Jaguar had brought Quiriguá into the Copán domain back in A.D. 653. Now after 14 years in power, Cauac Sky had learned rulership, and had adopted so many concepts of royalty from Copán that he incorporated Copán's emblem glyph into his own name clause. Details are not known but somehow conflict broke out in A.D. 738. Cauac Sky captured XVIII-Jog and promptly beheaded him in Quiriguá, where the event was well documented and publicized.

Apparently no cultural slump ensued at Copán as we saw after conflicts in the Petén. Quiriguá made no attempt to occupy or wreak destruction on Copán, and the latter reacted by downplaying this loss and moved to renew faith in its ancestral history and exalt their kings.

Smoke-Monkey   Lord Smoke-Monkey immediately took over the empty throne at Copán to rule for only ten years but in some of his constructions we can see a harbinger of the future. Instead of erecting traditional monuments, scribes and carvers turned away from stelae-carving to design and produce the great Hieroglyphic Stairway that would be completed by his son (Figure 6.44). This was a feat that Riese (1986) considers equal to producing 30 stelae! It was designed to revitalize and restore the power and prestige of Copán.

A second construction was the "Council House" (Structure 10L-22a), erected late in his reign bearing a date of A.D. 746. This edifice is a rather dramatic sign of the increasing decentralization of political authority in the eighth century. Each of eight human figures sit cross-legged in a niche over a large hieroglyph believed to name his

FIGURE 6.44   The hieroglyphic stairway at Copán. (Photographed by the author.)

home town. These figures are placed at the corners and sides of the building and may well be portraits of officials representing various local lineages. Large mat designs and *ahau* glyphs together with dance platforms and small artifacts support the function of this structure as a governing house (Fash and Stuart, 1991; Fash and Sharer, 1991).

Smoke-Shell   It was the following ruler, Smoke-Shell, who embarked on a renaissance program that finished the magnificent stairway. Probably well aware of the ancient temples underlying Temple 26, he chose to place this staircase on the west face of the Temple of the Hieroglyphic Stairway (Structure 10L-26). This tremendous undertaking documents the whole dynastic history of Copán (including the decapitation of XVIII-Jog) up to the year of the stairway's dedication in A.D. 755. The text emphasizes the role of the ancestral kings as warriors. The stairway measures about 85 ft. high by 50 ft. wide. The 1 1/2 ft. riser of each of the 72 steps is intricately carved with hieroglyphs, 2500 in all, constituting the longest Maya text in existence. Spaced at intervals up the steep flight of steps are life-size stone images of the last five successors of the dynasty, each almost 6 ft in height and dressed in the old Tlaloc imagery with the year-sign attire of conquest war, each bearing a shield and lance. Unfortunately in the late 1800s many of the steps fell off, leaving only 30 risers in place and a heap of carved stones at the bottom. What promises to be a rewarding, if painstaking, task is that of redrawing each stone from scale photographs of glyph blocks by Barbara Fash. This may enable the epigraphers to "read" the historic text that, together with the inscriptions from Temple 10L-26, convey 200 years of dynastic history. In general, we know that Cauac Sky is not mentioned, the reign of Lord Smoke-Jaguar is emphasized, and the name of XVIII-Jog appears on both the stairway and in the temple. The overall theme is one of renewing ancestor worship and displaying pride in war and sacrifice. Under a large altar at the foot of the stairs was an offering of jade, sting-ray spines, and flint, reflecting all the war imagery depicted above. Finally an annex (Structure 10L-230) was placed on the south side of Temple 10L-26 furthering the war-sacrifice theme with motifs of long bones and skulls. A flint knife was actually found on the floor. Names and dates are all Copanec.

This final remodeling of Structure 10L-26 and associated buildings illustrates a marked contrast with earlier versions. Perhaps Smoke Shell himself was a war captain, furthering the theme of war iconography on Structure 26. The loss of XVIII-Jog was deeply felt and more disruptive than was immediately apparent. Portraits of rulers, hieroglyphic texts and martial themes from this time on show a radical change from the earlier plaster sculptures of birds and supernaturals in cosmological scenes (Fash *et al.*, 1992).

Lord Smoke-Shell is remembered for one other dramatic feat. Nine years before acceding to the throne in A.D. 749, he sent off for a royal wife all the way to Palenque, at the other end of the Maya world. Political marriages were common among the Maya elite in such centers as Naranjo, Tikal, Uaxactún, and Dos Pilas. The distance involved here is exceptional, but perhaps not extraordinary to the Maya when we recall the trade network that functioned under XVIII-Jog with the Petén and Usumacinta region and continued after his death. Perhaps Palenque was so admired that nothing else would equal the prestige to be gained from a royal alliance with its dynasty. Whatever the reason, a royal Palenque woman made the trip across the jungle to wed Smoke-Shell at Copán. From Palenque she may have introduced a new feature of ritual use—a special *incensario* (Riese, 1988). This is a stone cylinder with a lid, often decorated with deity heads, monsters, and sometimes short inscriptions. Over a hundred of these have been found at Copán, otherwise known only from Palenque and the Tabasco region. Exceptions include Yaxchilán and Salinas de los Nueve Cerros (Dillon, 1987). The latter is a Classic site transitional from the Maya lowlands to the highlands in Alta Verapaz, Guatemala on the south bank of the Río Chixoy. This was a salt source very important to this area. If Yaxchilán and Salinas de los Nueve Cerros are construed as royal stopovers, we can plot the bride's journey up the Usumacinta to Yaxchilán, on to the Río Chixoy, followed by a rough climb to the highlands, and from there east to her ultimate destination of Copán. The son born of this union was the last major ruler in Copán's history: Yax-Pac (also known as Rising Sun, or Madrugada). Although Smoke Shell is often assumed to be the father of Yax-Pac, he is never named. Stuart (1992) believes the father was an unknown individual as yet unidentified.

Yax-Pac   The reign of Yax-Pac (A.D. 763–820) had some moments of glory and great satisfaction, but he must have felt sad toward the end of his reign to see the divinity of the dynasty slipping away. Many problems were coming home to roost. Studies on the osteological remains hint of malnutrition and disease. As the valley farmers felt pressed for space, more trees were felled in the uplands, and more land was cleared first in the valley, then the foothills, and finally on the mountain slopes, exposing the surface to the forces of erosion. Shorter fallowing seasons and a decrease in the food supply were other unfortunate results.

A calendar of Yax-Pac's activites is exhausting to read as this energetic man struggled to keep his family's traditions alive: dedication after dedication, period-ending celebrations, inaugurations, public command appearances, and ritual (see list in Schele and Freidel, 1990:31). There were notable accomplishments among them with stylistic qualities of Palenque (Miller, 1988a).

His greatest achievement was Temple 11, a gigantic structure facing north over the Hieroglyphic Court to the Great Plaza in line with a saddle in the mountains in the distance. In fact, a line from the center doorway and stairs is exactly true north (Miller, 1988a). One could enter Temple 11 from all four sides to read texts about the political prowess of Yax-Pac and the dedication of this temple. The entrance to the 2-story temple was formed by the open mouth of the Witz Monster. On the north side a bench shows a procession of ancestors honoring the accession of Yax-Pac. The south face overlooking the West Court took the form of an imitation ball court with a sacrificial platform from which victims could be rolled down the stairs. This so-called Reviewing Stand is decorated with three huge conchs and a central deity figure who presided over the ritual sacrifices (Figure 6.45). The entire West Court formed the setting of an elaborate theatrical ball court, full of symbolic reminders of the Underworld of Xibalbá (Schele and Freidel, 1990). The construction of this edifice is

FIGURE 6.45   The executioner god presiding over the sacrifice of victims, rolled down the stairway like a ball. Reviewing Stand, Temple 11, West Court, Copán. Photographed by the author.)

not the finest and the sculpturing is not Copán's best, but it is a massive tribute to the supreme effort of Yax-Pac to honor his ancestors and the tradition of royalty.

On the east side of the West Court is Structure 16 overlooking the imitation ball court. Resting in its original position at the foot of the staircase is a great block of greenish andesite known as Altar Q. It is carved on all four sides with portraits of 16 Copan kings, each one royally dressed, sitting cross-legged on his name glyph. The stone was commissioned by Yax-Pac and dedicated 3 years after Temple 11 (Figure 6.46). On this stone he is shown as the central figure receiving his badge of authority in A.D. 763 from Yax-Kuk-Mo', credited with having founded the Copanec dynasty in the fourth century. In 1991 the discovery of a small temple (Rosalila) was reported buried beneath three others inside Structure 16. This structure, recovered in exceptionally fine condition, has already been noted (page 279). For some reason the Maya carefully buried it intact instead of following their usual practice of demolition before beginning a superstructure. Under Yax Pac, Structure 16 was enlarged to massive proportions and by placing Alter Q at the base of the staircase, he reasserted his supernatural powers derived from his 15 ancestors. A most unusual tribute to them was to inter closeby the bones of 15 jaguars (one per ancestor), in a carefully constructed underground crypt. The jaguar, protector and symbol of royalty, was seen as a link between the living and the dead (Fash, 1991). The significance of this cache would have been understood and appreciated by an admiring Copanec public.

Access to the East Court is restricted by the massive pyramidal Structure 16 forcing one through a narrow passageway to the south. The East court with its private Temple 22 was almost a mirror image of the West Court, another setting for a ball

FIGURE 6.46   Altar Q, commissioned by Yax-Pac, and dedicated in A.D. 775, sixteen successors of the Copán dynasty. (Reproduced by courtesy of the Trustees of the British Museum.)

game sacrifice. On the west side a staircase framed by rampant jaguars with a central Venus symbol at the top, was likely used to display captives before they were bundled up and rolled down the stairs in sacrifice after a ritual ball game. Thus in both East and West Courts a sacrificial deity presided over a sacrificial ball court next to a major building of rulership where bloodletting of the nobility took place.

Another Yax-Pac edifice was a circular towerlike substructure of Temple 20 in the East Court of the Acropolis of which little remains. The sculptured remnants show that once the façade was decorated with bat motifs. Turning to the Popol Vuh, Barbara and William Fash read how one of the Underworld trials of the Hero Twins was to be locked up in a "House of Bats." Since Temple 20 could be locked only from the outside, an "unlucky" individual could have been incarcerated here (Fash and Fash, 1989).

Other signs of change are evident in the Sepulturas area giving us a good idea of suburban living in this 8th century. The largest compound, 9N-8 was composed of 40-50 buildings around 11 courtyards. The compound could have housed as many as 250 people and it included temples, shrines, kitchens, storage rooms and workshops, structures for young men and even a dressing room for ball players. Residential quarters were identified as those having benches used for sleeping but probably used as seats for receiving officials and other purposes as well. Refuse dumps, always a fertile source of information for archaeologists, yielded clues as to local crafts and traded goods.

The largest of these structures (9N-82) was the House of the Bacabs (Webster, 1990), home of the powerful patriarch of the local lineage who, along with his ancestors, paid homage to God N as patron of Maya scribes. We have noted the prestigious position of scribes in Maya society. They were viewed with great respect and regarded as almost geniuses. The discovery of this elegant House of the Bacabs or scribes reveals how far the king, Yax-Pac, had gone to ensure loyalty and support from high-ranking individuals.

This house must have been elegant in its prime. Eight fully 3-dimensional relief sculptures of scribes, life-sized, were tenoned to the upper façade. With human face and simian features, each holds a paint pot (half shell) in one hand and pen in the other (Figure 6.47). On the north façade the central scribe wears a distinctive long pectoral, possibly some kind of lineage insignia for the astronomer. This might well indicate ancestor worship in the ritual-compounds (Fash, 1991). On either side of the lower façade are other scribes, each holding similar tools. Inside the house, a bench help up by four *bacabs* (as in Temples 22, 26, and 11) was inscribed with a dedication date of A.D. 781. Yax-Pac's presence at the ceremony is clearly depicted, a radical departure from all precedents.

Once the Yax-Pac began traveling to lineage households and participating in such celebrations and rituals, he was in fact undermining his own power. The Acropolis

FIGURE 6.47   Scribe (God N) from Structure 9N-82, Sepulturas, Copán. In one hand he holds a writing tool and in the other a shell fragment to serve as his ink or paint pot. (Photographed by Justin Kerr [No. 2870].)

had always been the precinct of royalty. This was the sacred hearth that drew the populace to it for its vicarious participation. The humanizing of royalty somehow diminished the institution of kingship.

Yax-Pac then celebrated his first katun anniversary. For this he dedicated two altars (T and U) in the settlement underlying the present village of Copán. Altars were not a new sculptural form but had usually been paired with stelae and rarely did they combine inscriptions with figures. The altars that Yax-Pac now erected were large boulder altars unaccompanied by stelae, which combined zoomorphic figures with glyphic texts. These were likely inspired by Quiriguá where sculptors excelled in this style monument and elaborated it to produce gigantic examples. On one of his altars, Yax-Pac publicly introduced his half brother (?) (Yahau-Chan-Ah-Bac), who had come to Copán from Palenque with their mother. Now he was being honored by appearing prominently on Altar T with the king (Schele and Freidel, 1990). A full brother is also brought to light in inscriptions and images of all three brothers are found on a carved throne in the back chamber of the Council House built by his grandfather. Clearly Yax-Pac was trying to magnify or simply maintain his power and incorporate elite leadership in the decision-making process (Fash and Sharer, 1991). This idea was even less successful than his gestures toward the nonroyal patriarchs of the lineage households. Divinity could not be shared successfully. A final gesture in A.D. 800 was made by setting Altar G-1 in the very center of the Great Plaza, the most sacred precinct of the kingdom. On this great stone, a double-headed image of the Cosmic Monster, Yax-Pac affirmed his political duality with his half brother. The divine sanctity of the lineage was broken.

The kingdom was slipping downhill. A year later, A.D. 801, Yax-Pac dedicated his own mortuary Temple 18. Tucked away in the far northeast corner of Copán, a rather modest building contained his elaborate vaulted tomb. When found, it held only the fragments of bone, jade, and alabaster that looters had left behind. The building was not a cosmic sanction of the divinity of Yax-Pac and his royal ancestors. Instead it was a war monument, showing Yax-Pac and probably his brother headed for battle with shields and weapons. The kingdom was now preoccupied with local political problems and security of the realm. It was a sad end for this vigorous ruler.

A complex of buildings south of the Acropolis housing royalty centered around Structure 10L-32 plaza. After A.D. 800 when the power of the nobility was broken, access to the complex became more restricted. Soon construction ceased, monuments were no longer carved and debris began to accumulate. By the end of the century this group of structures was burned and willfully destroyed, perhaps by outsiders or a disillusioned local population (Andrew V. and Fash, 1992).

A final king, U-Cit-Tok was inaugurated in A.D. 822, but the great days of royal pomp and glory were over. Copán did not undergo a sudden "collapse" or catastrophe, but the political authority was decentralized and the population gradually declined. The Copán pocket had probably been overexploited causing deforestation but there was enough arable land to sustain a dwindling population until A.D. 1100–1200.

Additional Comments

Before leaving Copán, there are several points that should be emphasized. Already, Quiriguá has been mentioned with some frequency because the history of the two sites are intertwined. Even so, their orientations are different in many ways. They had independent trading patterns. Their relationship must have had ups and downs, exhibiting at various times jealousy, friendship, competition, rivalry, and warfare. Each conquered the other at some point. They shared elite customs, and may even have had royal kinship ties. Quiriguá's interesting history will be examined shortly.

The reader may have wondered about a hiatus. Copán did not respond to, or was not affected by, the hiatus that was noted in the Petén heartland. The hiatus is no longer perceived as the general phenonemon it once was. Copán maintained a long-standing relationship with the western highlands that continued uninterrupted. If there was a lessening of activity at Copán, it could have been during twenty years following the capture of XVIII-Jog in A.D. 738 when no inscriptions were added to the Great Plaza, but these years may only reflect a shift to initiate work on the great stairway.

Copán's iconography shows non-Petén influence and is freer and more creative in style than seen in the stiff sculptural forms of Quiriguá and Tikal (Jones and Sharer, 1986). The special beauty of Copán may result from adapting intrusive features to produce its own creation. The early similarities with the Petén such as site layout and stucco monster masks on façades, that is, the institution of kingship, could have been derived from Belize.

Copán's underlying culture was that of the southern periphery, maintained in the non-elite aspects of daily life such as *manos* and *metates*, and particular ceramics that evolved out of the Uapala Ceramic Sphere, and from Honduran traditions.

The elite Maya overlay consisted of monumental art, calendrics, hieroglyphics, exotic goods, and the major layout of settlement patterns (Leventhal *et al.*, 1987). The cosmic plan at Copán is similar to that of Tikal with a ball court centrally located; east and west residential groups placed at the end of causeways; north marked by two residential compounds and south being the watery Underworld of the West Court, or beyond the Copán River, a small complex with frog sculptures. The two northern elite compounds may themselves represent a miniature north–south axis, the northern one oriented toward ritual activity, the southern more private, enclosed, and oriented toward worldy affairs (Ashmore, 1991).

Copán's outside trading relationships were strong with its old Preclassic connections, predominantly with areas of the Ulua-Comayagua drainage basin, Chalchuapa, and the southern Guatemalan highlands. These golden days were short-lived, for after A.D. 735 Copán was "no longer the controlling power of the Maya southeastern frontier region" (Leventhal, 1986). Thereafter, Copán produced its own Copador polychrome and carried on a brisk trade without needing or seeking either support from or contacts with its Maya neighbors. The final years until A.D. 1200 were spent quietly as families gradually moved away.

QUIRIGUÁ

Quiriguá

Archaeologically, Quiriguá in today's banana land of Guatemala has been over-shadowed by its larger neighbor Copán, but Quiriguá had a life of its own. It was located on the economic crossroads of the southeastern Maya region. At that time a bend of the Motagua River flowed close to the site, providing the primary route for travelers and commerce going and coming from highland Guatemala to the Caribbean coast. Quiriguá was also on a natural overland route connecting the Petén to the north with Central America to the southeast. Surrounded by a fertile alluvial flood plain, these Maya could have grown a variety of agricultural products for easy export. This was a site endowed with advantages.

Quiriguá has been renowned since J. L. Stephens mentioned visiting its elaborate monuments in his early travels around 1841. Since then, many have retraced his footsteps, but little was known about the ruins other than that, like Copán, the period of Quiriguá's greatest florescence was reached in the Late Classic Period.

At the end of 1971, the University Museum of the University of Pennsylvania, together with the Guatemalan Government, initiated a program designed to investigate Quiriguá and learn something of its history and the role it played among other lowland Maya sites. Directed by William R. Coe and Robert J. Sharer and assisted by Wendy Ashmore, excavations have been carried out since then in the 95-km zone around the site-core, with reconnaissance and surveys made in the surrounding areas.

Quiriguá is both blessed and plagued by plentiful water. The Motagua River affords easy access to other regions, but it has also caused severe flooding. As a result, alluvial sediments have effectively buried many of the early settlements and it was not until a decade ago that the origins and background of Quiriguá could be reconstructed. In the late 1970s, the Del Monte Corporation, while excavating drainage ditches for a new banana plantation, happened to uncover remains of early constructions and monuments. Alerting the archaeologists, and with the cooperation and assistance of the Corporation, it was possible to gather valuable information heretofore inaccessible. The following sketch of events is based on writings by Ashmore (1984, 1986), Jones and Sharer (1986), Kelley (1962), and Sharer (1978a, 1990).

Prior to A.D. 400 there are few signs of settlements along the river, but by the fifth century a lookout station had been placed on a ridgetop in a peripheral area, and a small masonry compound (Group 3C-7) was established on the wide flood plain. The earliest known date at Quiriguá (A.D. 478) was inscribed on Monument 21, a stela at the lookout station. Meanwhile, in the course of excavating for a new drainage canal, another stela, Monument 26, was fortuitously recovered. It had been broken in antiquity, but probably once rested on a low platform cut by the dragline near Group 3C-7. Upon investigating further, a rather elaborate cache was found in a platform structure. This contained Early Classic vessels with burned jadeite artifacts, mirrors, and cinnabar.

Monument 26 provides evidence of an established ruling dynasty at Quiriguá. It depicts a Maya ruler, records a Long Count data of A.D. 493, and refers to two earlier anonymous rulers. These two stelae (Monuments 21 and 26) date from the late fifth century. Made of bluish schist, they are similar in size and shape, and the carved frontal figure in both cases continues the carving around the side. This distinctive wraparound style was shared with Copán and came close to being a free-standing sculpture. It has been suggested (Schele and Freidel, 1990) that the inscription refers to Rulers 3 and 4 of Copán. This might mean that this large neighbor controlled Quiriguá from a very early time (Fash and Sharer, 1991). Iconographic elements of the two Quiriguá stelae closely resemble Stela 2 at Tikal and Uaxactún's Stela 20, both of comparable date.

The flood plain area would have had two good entry points from outlying sites. Two of these are well separated, and when combined with the ridgetop lookout station where Monument 21 was located, they might have formed some kind of communication network for the valley. In one of these sites (Location 011) overlooking the Quiriguá River, structures formed a triadic arrangement that is a familiar pattern in the northeastern Petén and thought to be derived from Late Preclassic layouts at Tikal, Uaxactún, and Cerros. This was a cosmological arrangement consisting of structures on the west, east, and north sides of an elongated patio with the northern one predominating (the southern point may be omitted.)

Ashmore (1986) sees this layout as an elite element that was exported from key centers in much the same way the Maya exported inscriptions, sculpture, or an architectural style. Local inhabitants might not have been aware of the political link involved, but dignitaries or emissaries would have recognized it, felt comfortable, and been impressed.

The combined evidence of ceramics, inscriptions, and construction provides good reason to postulate a founding of Quiriguá by some Petén group, possibly from Tikal itself. The commercial advantages of its geographic location would surely have attracted the attention of any expanding trade network. Quiriguá could have monitored (or controlled?) the riverine traffic and was in a position to forestall any obsidian monopoly envisioned by inhabitants of Kaminaljuyú. Jade, although in lesser quantities than obsidian, would also have passed by Quiriguá en route to the eastern lowlands.

Sometime around A.D. 500–650? the little Classic center on the flood plain was severely flooded and some kind of cultural decline ensued, reflected in the lessening of activity and an absence of polychrome pottery. These were unsettled years at Quiriguá, for in addition to the flood and perhaps an economic slump, Quiriguá was possibly taken over by Copán's Lord Smoke-Jaguar in his territorial expansion down the Motagua Valley. On Altar L at Quiriguá Lord Smoke-Jaguar's name appears with the 9.11.0.0.0 period-ending date of A.D. 652. How long this state of affairs lasted is not known, but Schele and Freidel (1990) believe it continued into the reign of XVIII-Jog who acceded in Copán in A.D. 695. About this time (A.D. 700), the main center at Quiriguá was transferred to a permanent location that became the Acropolis. This seems to have happened following the flood, and architects replaced the use of old earthen and cobble construction with rhyolite masonry.

The Acropolis started off as an elite residential complex. A distinguished person (ruler?) with notched incisors and front teeth inlaid with jade was found in a stone-lined crypt under a shrine. This was a dedicatory burial, a practice we have noted at Tikal. Quiriguá was approaching its period of greatest florescence (A.D. 740–810).

The Acropolis was eventually enlarged three more times and construction soon switched to using sandstone. Settlements increased and extended farther out into peripheral areas, some of which can be regarded as elite residential administrative satellites. Although some of the peripheral residences were located downstream on higher terracing, most settlements were spread along the river on the first terraces.

Of the five Late Classic rulers at Quiriguá, it is Cauac Sky (Two-Legged-Sky) that is the most distinguished, and to whom Quiriguá owes its greatest debt (Figure 6.48). He ascended the throne in A.D. 724 and commissioned most of the known structures in the core area and over a third of the 30 monuments known. As king, he lived regally in elaborate quarters in the southwest corner of the Acropolis that had replaced the earlier residential compound. It was Cauac Sky who led his people during the A.D. 738 conflict with Copán, emerging victorious and taking XVIII-Jog home to be beheaded.

The details of their encounter are a mystery, but the defeat of the major power

FIGURE 6.48   Detail of Stela C, portraying ruler Cauac Sky, A.D. 775, Quiriguá, Guatemala. (Photographed by the author.)

in the southeast by a small upstart down the river has the makings of real drama. As the greatest event in Quiriguá's history, it was not to be forgotten and the date A.D. 738 was recorded five times. No Quiriguá ruler is mentioned at Copán, although the date A.D. 738 appears on its Hieroglyphic Stairway, step 41. This date may mark Quiriguá's real independence from Copán.

Cauac Sky did not attempt to occupy or deface Copán, but concentrated on increasing the fortunes and magnifying the appearance of Quiriguá by undertaking a massive building program with larger and taller stelae and greater zoomorphic altars.

A huge plaza to the north was enclosed on three sides by an enlarged Acropolis. Here Cauac Sky placed his great monuments. The west side of the plaza was entirely rebuilt, burying an earlier ball court. Now a new ball court went up with a plaza connected by a wide staircase to the Acropolis. Over the west platform of the plaza, overlooking the Motagua River, a huge wall was raised and embellished with three great masks of Kinich Ahau (Sun God), easily identified by his crossed eyes and notched front teeth. In this general layout, together with the carving of bench panels and frieze inscriptions. Quiriguá began to take on an outward appearance of Copán. At Copán, Stela J with its mat-pattern symbolizing royal power had been erected in A.D. 695 at the east entrance to the Main Group at the beginning of the causeway. Admiring this prestigious feature, Quiriguá decided it, also, should have a comparable monument in a prominent location. As the Motagua River passed close to the Acropolis, a basin of water provided good docking space where canoe traffic could pull up to the center of town. Stela H, Quiriguá's only mat-pattern stela, was set precisely at the entry to the city from the canoe port.

Quiriguá's Acropolis eventually contained a fine residential complex, providing the occupants with such amenities as benches, curtain holders, and windows. There were also areas for services, storage, and less elegant living quarters nearby. The Great Plaza, as at Copán, was the focal point for displaying stelae and other great monuments. It would have served as a fine public gathering place, and the monuments face the open side of the court for all to appreciate.

Quiriguá is rightly renowned for its gigantic sandstone stelae, the largest of which, Monument 5, bears the portrait of Cauac Sky and records the date of his victory in the conflict with Copán. This stela is 35 ft. in height, 5 ft. wide, and weighs an estimated 65 tons! In general, the figural style of Quiriguá, like that of Tikal, is stiff and formal in contrast to Copán where the rulers seem less rigid and more relaxed. Eventually, the stelae format was abandoned and huge boulders were carved and subsequently called zoomorphs. These were strange stones carved with earth monsters and sky deities, with humans often intertwined with serpents or shown emerging from their jaws (Figure 6.49).

The successors of Cauac Sky fell far short of his accomplishments but these were prosperous years. Sky Xul (A.D. 784–795), probably Cauac Sky's son, ruled 11 years. Imix-Dog reigned only a few years after that to be followed by Scroll-Sky, who occupied the throne for only a short time in A.D. 800. His record is rather vague, but Jade Sky ascending the throne in A.D. 800 renewed the building program, using some marble in construction. The hieroglyphic frieze on Structure 1B-1 mentions the

FIGURE 6.49   Late Classic zoomorph sculpture, Quiriguá, Guatemala. (Photographed by the author.)

presence of Yax-Pac of Copán at a special ritual event in A.D. 810. The two leaders either overcame their differences by this time or Yax-Pac was seeking refuge due to problems at home in Copán (?). Twenty years later, the largest structure ever erected at the site was completed (Structure 1B-5). This may have been Jade Sky's living quarters. Thus the good times lasted throughout the remaining years of Quiriguá's Classic Period.

We know little more until around A.D. 1100 when some inhabitants left behind Plumbate pottery, some copper objects, and even a *chacmool* (Richardson, 1940), which has spent the last fifty years in the Museum of the American Indian in New York. These late residents of the region were also merchants, but, as we will see, their markets lay with the seagoing traders of the east coast of Yucatán.

Among lowland Classic centers, Quiriguá is a particularly fascinating site and nonconformist in some ways. It has the elite characteristics of a southern lowland Maya center with the exception of great temples and causeways. Its giant stelae and great carved zoomorphs are impressive. Quiriguá astounded the public with news of its victory over Copán, the defeat of a major Maya polity. This was a defeat, but not necessarily a conquest, for Cauac Sky did not choose to smash, plunder, or occupy Copán. This was the traditional style of Maya warfare. Victory for Cauac Sky was complete with the sacrifice of Ruler XVIII-Jog and the public recording of the event in his own plaza. Thereafter he concentrated on enlarging the Acropolis on a grand scale. This reflects an increasing wealth and power base, probably the result of expanding his commercial ties.

In the peripheral areas and the lower Motagua Valley, multi-room structures, vaulted masonry, and ball courts have been found, although cut stone masonry, plastering, and sculptures are rare; stelae were left plain. Much of this expansion was done in the reign of Cauac Sky.

Quiriguá has no towering temple/pyramids, no causeways, few caches, or elaborate tombs, very little jade to date (curious in view of its role as a distribution center), an absence of Copador pottery, and no prominent women. For whatever reason, it did not engage in political marriages or alliances. Its emblem glyph was kept at home with one exception: Pusilhá. It made its way by controlling and redistributing Ixtepeque obsidian and jade in the movement of commodities up and down the Motagua River (Figure 6.50) and it may have produced and exported some cacao and cotton along with other crops (Ashmore, 1984; Sharer, 1990).

Whether from drainage ditches or peripheral areas, there will surely be more to learn, but Late Classic remains so far lead one to conclude that Quiriguá's inhabitants were thoroughly Maya with an independence streak, while enjoying a rather exciting life on the busy crossroads of the southeast.

THE SOUTHEAST PERIPHERY

The area of eastern Guatemala, western Honduras, and eastern El Salvador has received much attention from investigators in the last ten years (Urban and Schortman, 1988). Consequently, we now have a much better idea of the extent of Maya culture and of the basic features of the local indigenous development in these areas. Again, familiarity with a map is necessary because rivers and their drainage basins influenced the choice of living sites, determined the agricultural potential, and were cultural corridors of communication (Map 6.7).

The major centers of Copán and Quiriguá are considered to lie on the southeast frontier of Classic Maya civilization. The Lower Motagua region is a simpler version of the manifestation at Quiriguá without many of its elite features. The region of Naco, the Sula Plain, and the Yojoa, Ulua-Comayagua drainage basins constitute the Southeast peripheral area of Mesoamerica.

We noted the presence of Olmec-related influence from the Gulf Coast lowlands in the Sula Plain, Aguan Valley, and at Copán in the Preclassic Period. It is during the Late Classic Period that this large area had strongest ties to the Maya, but such elements as hieroglyphic writing, vaulted architecture, and carved stelae never spread beyond Copán and Quiriguá.

The best information we have for the Early Classic Period comes from the area of central Honduras, the Ulua-Comayagua drainage basin. In the years from A.D. 300 to 500, Yarumela and Los Naranjos were prominent nucleated settlements with large-scale public architecture and ceremonial centers with formalized ritual. The greatest platform ever raised in central Honduras was built at Yarumela on the Comayagua

FIGURE 6.50   Miscellaneous Classic Maya artifacts.
a. Late Classic incised obsidian flakes and blades, often found in caches. Tikal, Guatemala. Scale is in cm. (Courtesy of the University Museum, University of Pennsylvania.)
b. Carved jadeite figure. Copán, Honduras. Height: 20 cm. (Courtesy of the Museum of the American Indian, Heye Foundation, N.Y. [10/9827].)
c. "Eccentric" flint of ritual use of great value and widely traded. Río Hondo, Orange Walk, Belize. Length: 36 cm. (Courtesy of the Museum of the American Indian, Heye Foundation, N.Y. [13/5547].)
d. Human effigy "mushroom stone." Momostenango, Guatemala. Height: 33 cm. (Courtesy of the Museum of the American Indian, Heye Foundation, N.Y. [9/8304].)
e. Carved wooded figure of a dignitary or priest, Tabasco. Height: 36 cm. (The Metropolitan Museum of Art. The Michael C. Rockefeller Memorial Collection. Bequest of Nelson A. Rockefeller, 1979 [1079.206.728].)
f. Marble vase carved in the volute-style of El Tajín. Ulua River Valley, Honduras. Height: 13 cm. (Courtesy of the Museum of the American Indian, Heye Foundation, N.Y. [4/3956].)

MAP 6.7 The southern periphery.

River. This site was arranged in a linear settlement pattern that probably represents an indigenous development. Not far north is Los Naranjos, well known for its formidable defensive moat. Smaller nucleated settlements were located all along the river systems, usually in linear arrangements. Plaza groups are less common but more closely resemble lowland Maya patterns.

The predominating sculptural form was a pedestal-base stone shaft that in the Ulua-Comayagua region might have human figures. To the west the relief carvings are more complex, with a strong resemblance not to lowland Maya stelae, but to the kind of sculpture popular among the late Preclassic peoples of highland Guatemala and El Salvador. Obsidian was largely from La Esperanza, a source in southern Honduras, but a few examples were from Guiñope in southeastern Honduras, El Chayal, and even Cerro de las Navajas in highland Mexico.

A spectacular find at Salitron Viejo, east of Los Naranjos, yielded over 2400 jade and marble artifacts. Among these a carved jade pendant of a hunchback or dwarf can be matched by specimens at Copán, Kaminaljuyú, and Chichén Itzá. Other jade crescents (Teotihuacan-style nose ornaments) were carved to represent a Tlaloc and found in association with green obsidian. Talud-tablero architecture is reported from this site. This could have resulted from contact with Copán that was in turn in close contact with Kaminaljuyú (see page 291). Apparently jade and jadeite artifacts were widely traded throughout eastern Mesoamerica around A.D. 400–500.

Southeast of Yarumela is the impressive fortified hilltop settlement of Tenampua. Rising 240 m above the valley floor, it is perched on a plateau to which walls were added. Over 300 mounds were aligned here in roughly north–south orientation. Stairways mounted the west side of the larger mounds that presumably supported temples. Noteworthy is an open-ended ball court surprisingly well preserved, and considered a Late Classic feature. Unfortunately this scenic site has suffered from its popularity among weekend pot-hunters during the 1950s and 1960s. No wonder, for Tenampua yields beautiful Ulua Polychrome vessels (Agurcia F., 1986).

Major changes occurred around A.D. 500. Large centers like Los Naranjos, Yarumela, and Tenampua were replaced by smaller independent competing communities. This coincided with a increase in population and now people chose to live in smallish village polities, each with its own ceremonial precinct. A new religious theme featured agricultural deities and fertility. No longer were human figures represented in sculptural art. Crude or well-dressed shafts of stone might be plain, carved, or stucco painted. Motifs were a stylized serpent associated with water, or a curious simple figure with some vague similarity to a Tlaloc. Burial customs were also affected by this new order. With a diminished religious leader or central authority, ceremonial centers were reduced to platforms, no more than 3–4 m in height. No longer were elite individuals given burials with fine offerings in a large ceremonial precinct. Graves were found in domestic areas with goods of far less quality than before. Yet caches in nonmortuary contexts such as had begun at Salitron Viejo were continued throughout the Classic Period at Travesía, Cerro Palenque, and Gualjoquito. Deities were more abstract and less personalized in direct contrast to Maya patterns. Hirth (1988) believes these changes evolved locally and were not due to any outside intrusion.

Gualjoquito

A good sequence of development is that seen at Gualjoquito northwest of Los Naranjos and 10 km north of Santa Barbara, the Honduran department capital (Ashmore *et al.*, 1987). This is an example of a small regional development of 8 ha of alluvial terrace, that reached its apogee after the large centers of Los Naranjos and Yarumela declined. Located in relatively level terrain near the confluence of the Ulua and Jicatuyo rivers, it was situated on a busy communication route. The Ulua River formed a north–south corridor: its tributary, the Jicatuyo River, leads westward, and to the east, Lake Yojoa could be easily reached via an overland pass.

The site was occupied from Preclassic (400 B.C.) to the Late Postclassic (A.D. 1200) with fortunes closely paralleling those at Copán, approximately 125 km to the west. Gualjoquito reached its zenith in the Late Classic from A.D. 600 to 950. With stone a scarce resource, construction was largely earthen faced with cobbles, but building techniques and layouts of prominent buildings follow the general Maya pattern.

The most imposing structures were Structure 12, a building with its platform, and Group 1, a plastered court with buildings on the north and west sides. Both of these were initiated in the Early Classic and remained the principal features throughout the Classic occupation. There are more ties to Copán than with any other outside source, and ultimately when Copán declined, Gualjoquito followed shortly thereafter. Ashmore (1987) can also see similarities with the Early Classic group at Los Naranjos, but favors a derivation from Copán because of the use of cut stone blocks and the elaborate multi-layered plaster floor. However, at Gualjoquito there are no carvings or hieroglyphs.

The overall site plan reflects the Maya cosmogram with residences located to the south and public and/or ceremonial features to the north. A ball court was not part of the original plan, but when it was added at at later time, it was placed according to the traditional Maya design. This was an elite center with trade a factor; its growth was seen in imports of Ixtepeque obsidian, abundant Copador pottery, and, from the Pacific, *Spondylus* valves.

Fourteen km to the south on the Ulua River, Tencoa is a contemporary valley site. It was better situated for agriculture than Gualjoquito and could sustain a larger population but was less well positioned for external communication. Layout of the structures in the 31 sites recorded reflect less formal planning with locations determined by elevation, access to water, availability of building stones, and well-drained soil. This non-elite region peaked in the Late Classic and may have been politically subordinate to Gualjoquito. There is no mention of Copán or external influences. The differences apparent in these two regions illustrate the fallacy of judging a local society by examining a single site.

Gualjoquito exhibits some specific ties to Copán in layout and architecture but in most of west-central Honduras, the ceramics provide the most obvious clues to outside relationships. Hirth (1988) identifies four major Classic types, each of a different origin.

a   b   c

d

FIGURE 6.52   Fine Classic Maya pottery.

a. Polychrome pictorial vase from Nebaj, Gautemala, in which a lord receives tribute and the payment is being recorded. Late Classic.

b. Cylindrical tripod vessel with incised panel decoration. Lid has a modeled parrot at the apex. Kaminaljuyú, Esperanza phase. Height: 35 cm. (Courtesy of the Museum of the American Indian, Heye Foundation, N.Y. [16/6235].)

c. Black incised bowl with basal flange, jaguar lid. Holmul, Guatemala. Early Classic Maya. Height: 24 cm. (Courtesy of the Peabody Museum of Archaeology and Ethnology, Harvard University. Copyright by the President and Fellows of Harvard College.)

d. Roll-out photograph of the Nebaj pot above. (Both are reproduced by courtesy of the Trustees of the British Museum, London.)

THE USUMACINTA SITES

Altar de Sacrificios

Due west of Dos Pilas is Altar de Sacrificios (Willey, 1973, 1977a,b; Willey and Smith, 1969), strategically located on the Pasión River where it is joined by the Chixoy River, providing a trade route to Alta Verapaz in the Guatemalan highlands. Below this juncture the river is known as the Usumacinta, a main thoroughfare of communication from the western regions of Tabasco to the Petén. By making a rather complicated portage across the Petexbatún region to the Sarstoon River, canoes could reach the Bay of Honduras on the east coast of Yucatán. Altar de Sacrificios occupied a prime location for commercial and intersite relationships.

A leading ceremonial center, Altar de Sacrificios reached its zenith in Late Classic times. The first Long Count date of A.D. 455 is carved on a red sandstone stela. Although the preferred building material was limestone, sandstone was available only 9 km upstream. Obsidian, quartzites, jadeites, and other igneous rocks all had to be imported from the Guatemalan highlands. Communication with outlying areas was so well pronounced that these products could be easily obtained and are found in the richly stocked graves. There is a pronounced differentiation between ordinary and ritual or luxury wares. The Floral Park manifestation also reached the Pasión River. Only the strategic location of Altar de Sacrificios can explain its growth out of the Early Preclassic Xe complex to the Early Classic and the wonderful 200 years of prosperity following the hiatus of A.D. 534–593.

Here in the southwestern Petén, the Maya erected a pyramid of 9 or 10 terraces with almost vertical walls. An elaborate staircase led up to the summit, once crowned by a perishable temple. Stelae and altars were placed on the stairways of platforms and buildings rather than in the courts and plazas as we have seen elsewhere. But consistent with prevailing trends, the buildings were arranged around courts and plazas and a ball court resembles that of Copán.

Among the remains from burials, one beautiful polychrome vessel with figure painting is particularly noteworthy. Known as the "Altar Vase" it was found in a double burial of women during the Peabody Museum excavations of 1959–1963. The scene is thought to represent the elaborate funeral in A.D. 754 of a prominent woman in her forties. A dancing figure in jaguar trousers is none other than Lord Bird Jaguar of Yaxchilán (see page 315), the site where this cylindrical vessel may well have been made. Another figure is thought to be the brother of Ruler Yax-Kin of Tikal (see discussion in Hammond, 1988). Emblem glyphs of both Tikal and Yaxchilán appear on the pot. The younger woman is cutting her neck with a knife, thus ending her earthly existence to accompany the deceased. Adams (1977b) has suggested that notables possibly related through marriage gathered for this funeral, giving an idea of the political significance of elite kinship ties.

Linda Schele (1988) agrees with the identification of the figures but suggests that the scene might instead represent a dance of the dead lords in Xibalbá, a rite of passage in an afterlife myth of the Popol Vuh corresponding to a similar scene on a carved tablet in Temple XIV at Palenque.

Toward the end of the great Classic Period, one sees in Altar de Sacrificios art faces and motifs that reflect a new strain. This outside influence is apparent in the pottery and figurines of the local Ximba Phase. Fine Orange, particularly the variety known as Y or Altar type, and Fine Gray wares predominate. Fine Orange paste was also used in producing figurines with non-Maya features.

The last dated monument at Altar de Sacrificios was erected in A.D. 849. This does not mean that the center was immediately abandoned, but it does mark both the influx of outside ceramic styles and general impoverishment.

If location controlled the growth and prosperity of Altar de Sacrificios, so, also, does it help explain its ultimate collapse, for eventually it was outside pressures and intrusions of foreigners who pushed up the rivers that may have hastened the end of this site.

J. Eric Thompson (1970), basing his observation on the study of linguistics and historical source material along with archaeological data, believed that the Chontal Maya people, whom he identified as Putún, were responsible for the outside influences noticed first at Altar de Sacrificios about A.D. 771–790, and later in A.D. 830 at Seibal. The Putún Maya lived in the large delta lands of the Grijalva and Usumacinta Rivers in southern Campeche and Tabasco, an area culturally marginal to the great Maya centers.

These people are known to have been aggressive traders and merchant seamen who eventually controlled the sea routes around the peninsula of Yucatán to the Bay of Honduras on the east, probably seeking salt, slaves, or honey. Groups undoubtedly traveled by both land and sea to penetrate the Maya region at various times. The Putún exemplify the mercantilism that increased at this time. Their center of operations was Chakanputún, in Tabasco. Possessing Mexican neighbors, intermarriages undoubtedly took place, resulting in the adoption of some Mexican tastes and habits.

In Late Classic years, these Putún made incursions by canoe up the Usumacinta River, bringing in the blend of Maya and Mexican elements that appears at this time along interior river sites. These merchants will be referred to often in the pages ahead.

Bonampak

Farther along the Usumacinta drainage, western centers of Maya civilization were also constructing temple/pyramids, erecting stelae, and recording dates and events in hieroglyphic carvings. Bonampak in Chiapas, a contemporary of Yaxchilán and Palenque, is a site renowned for its unique mural paintings of the ancient Maya, that provide us with infinite detail of dress, processional scenes, musicians, sacrifices, sacred rites, and warfare. Bonampak lies deep in the jungle home of the modern Lacandón Indians, who bear great physical resemblance to their Maya ancestors.

The ruins of Bonampak lie on the banks of the Lacanjá River and are so completely covered with dense vegetation that one is close upon them before they are seen (Figure 6.53). Moreover, the site has been only partially excavated. Natural elevations have

FIGURE 6.53   Entrance to the ruins of Bonampak, Chiapas. (Photographed by the author.)

been modified by raising platforms, retaining walls, stairs, and terraces to support temples and residences at varying levels. Five great buttresses to the northeast of this acropolis might have functioned as parapets. No palace structure has been reported to date.

The temple with the murals, Temple I, lies just to the right of the large rectangular plaza. It contains three rooms, each with a stone lintel carved in relief, and fresco paintings that covered the entire wall from floor to ceiling. The walls were first prepared with a lime coating 3–5 cm thick, and while they were still damp, the paintings were executed in orange, yellow, green, dark red, and turquoise blue. From the date of their discovery in 1946, efforts have been made to preserve the vivid colors. Inevitably the exposure to light and humidity have taken a toll, but not before accurate copies were made (Miller, 1986, 1988b).

Murals of the three rooms are now known to relate events surrounding an heir-designation rite, a 2-year process lasting from December 14, 790 to August 6, 792. A Bonampak king, Chaan-Muan, staged the event that opens in Room 1, where high-ranking nobles display the child-heir from the edge of a pyramid. In Mural 14 important individuals are the only spectators, but undoubtedly the entire community came out to witness the event.

A group of 12 musicians enliven the scene. Although we have other representations of musicians, this is the most comprehensive band known (Miller, 1988b). The composition shows the same order of instruments as depicted in ceramic scenes. From this we surmise that a late Classic band would lead off with rattle-shakers, followed by drummers, turtle-shell beaters striking with deer antlers, and probably flutes and whistles. The drum was mounted on a litter when carried due to its weight (Figure 6.54). A few masked participants have not been identified.

FIGURE 6.54   Wall painting showing part of the Bonampak band. (Courtesy of the Instituto Nacional de Antropología e Historia, Mexico.)

After the presentation of the heir, next in order was to take captives to be sacrificed. This is portrayed in Room 2. A great battle is shown taking place during the inferior conjunction of Venus, with stars being "thrown out into the heavens" while on the earth below King Chaan-Muan, aided by his Yaxchilán allies, seizes a number of victims (Schele and Miller, 1986).

The final scene culminates in displaying, torturing, and sacrificing 9 captives, graphically illustrating mutilation with blood flowing freely from wounds, while captives in anguish and pain await their inevitable heart sacrifice. A decapitated head rests on the staircase while the king surveys the scene in his jaguar robe (Figure 6.55). For the victorious celebration, the band once more appears and Chaan-Muan, the father of the heir, mutilates his own tongue in a sacrificial rite. This entire procedure is really to honor and promote the king, not the child. It is he who organizes, celebrates, goes to war, and benefits (Schele and Freidel, 1990).

The murals provide us with invaluable, seldom-preserved ethnographic data. Dancers are shown with heels raised. We see elaborate masks, parasols, fancy head-dresses, and decorative wearing apparel. Figures seem to portray actual individuals, not just the Maya ideal of beauty. Perspective is achieved by placing horizontal registers above another and nowhere else do so many figures appear together, some with a short glyphic text near the head.

Bonampak and Yaxchilán were closely knit neighbors, related by marriage. The

FIGURE 6.55 Continuation of the celebration begun in Figure 6.54 (the presentation of a new heir). In this case captives have been sacrificed while the king in his jaguar robe observes. (Courtesy of the Peabody Museum of Archaeology and Ethnology, Harvard University. Copyright by the President and Fellows of Harvard College.)

only setback in Bonampak's fortunes was the short span of time it spent as subordinate of Toniná, the bellicose highland center in Chiapas (Schele and Freidel, 1990). By the end of the seventh century, Bonampak disappears from our record about the same time as the larger Usumacinta centers.

Yaxchilán

Yaxchilán

Yaxchilán in the modern Mexican state of Chiapas is one of the oldest names in the lowlands, a site that so impressed Alfred Maudslay that in 1882 he shipped some of its beautifully carved monuments to England, where they may be seen today in the

British Museum. Its location is dramatic, set on a bluff high above a large loop in the Usumacinta River about 80 km downstream from Altar de Sacrificios.

Like Dos Pilas, Yaxchilán may have been founded from Tikal (Coggins, 1979a), but its urban development began in the Early Classic Period on a flat terrace overlooking the river and green panorama of the jungle. To create more space, steep depressions were filled in on the east and west sides and eventually the great citadel-like hill was terraced and dotted with structures and staircases.

Architecturally Yaxchilán shares the mansard-type roof and perforated roof combs with the more westerly Palenque. Many other features recall Petén construction with very thick walls. At least two ball courts have been identified. Palace-type buildings rather than the temple/pyramid prevail. The 3 to 5 doorways of these elongated stone buildings afforded communication with deities in the cosmos (Figure 6.56). As elsewhere, the earth represented the central world axis that connected the heavens above with the sacred Underworld beneath and the king was the personifying link between the three realms. Rather than orienting structures to the cardinal directions, the important points of reference were the solstitial rise and set points for the sun (Tate, 1985).

The dynastic history of Yaxchilán is almost complete for the years between A.D. 600 and 830, owing to more than 125 inscriptions carved on lintels and stelae. These scenes portraying people performing ritual and recording historic events are much more informative than the formal single- or double-figure stelae of Tikal, Copán, and Quiriguá. For example, lintels and panels on door jambs were carved in a sequence that usually relate an entire celebration.

The lives of two rulers, father and son, will serve to illustrate the tribulations of these kings on the Usumacinta. At Yaxchilán one dynasty ruled throughout its re-

FIGURE 6.56   Building 19 at Yaxchilán, Chiapas. (Photographed by the author.)

corded history. Lord Shield Jaguar, born in A.D. 647, lived to be more than 90 years of age. His principal wife was his cousin, Lady Xoc, who was prominent, powerful, and influential, appearing in many carvings, but never as ruler. Shield Jaguar erected numerous stelae in plazas, in front of buildings, and commissioned many constructions (Figures 6.57 and 6.60). One of his great artistic achievements was Temple 23 placed in the center of the first terrace, dominating the plaza (Figure 6.58) as a tribute to Lady Xoc. When the king was in his 60s he took another wife, this time from Calakmul; although of noble birth, she was an outsider, a "foreigner."

The child of this marriage, Bird-Jaguar, was his father's chosen heir, but his claim to the throne could be challenged by other sons and grandsons of Shield Jaguar who could claim a pure ancestry without any alien imput. Many monuments were carved to assert Bird-Jaguar's right to rule by showing him participating with his father and grandparents at important celebrations. On Lintel 15 (Figure 6.59), one of Bird Jaguar's wives is depicted with the Vision Serpent during an important bloodletting event. Upon Shield Jaguar's death, it took 10 years for Bird-Jaguar to gain the throne. In his campaign to accede, he first staged a ball game on the steps of his great Temple 33 that was to become his accession monument (Figure 6.60). For this occasion he

FIGURE 6.57   Bloodletting on Lintel 14, Temple 20, Yaxchilán. Depicted about A.D. 741 at the end of Shield Jaguar's life. (Photographed by Lorraine Matys.)

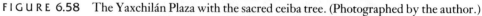

FIGURE 6.58   The Yaxchilán Plaza with the sacred ceiba tree. (Photographed by the author.)

bounced a captive tied up as a ball down the steps as a sacrifice. Two years later he celebrated his first big period-ending and one inscription reads "in the land of Bird-Jaguar" (very presumptuous, for it was not yet "his" land). Finally he had to capture a prestigious victim worthy of being sacrificed for his accession ceremonies, and not least of all, he had to father an heir of his own. We are not told what other contenders there were, nor is the opposition portrayed. But according to Bird-Jaguar's monuments, he managed it all, and acceded as king in A.D. 751. Of his 4 wives, two are from Motul de San José. Politician to the core, Bird-Jaguar immediately set forth on a campaign to secure the succession for *his* son, and so the pattern continued.

The proven path had always been to publicize the exalted status of ancestors, but Bird-Jaguar went a step further by appearing with high officials on monuments. At times he is shown with his son and a *cahal* (provincial governor)—good exposure for the son. Similar tactics tested by Yax-Pac at Copán were unsuccessful, but the strategy

FIGURE 6.59   Lintel 15, Temple 21. In this scene, one of Bird Jaguar's wives from Motul de San José, has let blood. The Vision Serpent appears above, and the ancestor she wanted to contact emerges from its mouth. A.D. 770. Height: 87.6 cm. (Reproduced by the courtesy of the Trustees of the British Museum, London.)

worked at Yaxchilán and was followed up and down the Usumacinta kingdoms after the example set by Bird-Jaguar.

This, in brief, is the rendering of inscribed events from the viewpoint of Bird-Jaguar. How slanted the view is we do not know, but similar patterns are found at contemporary sites of Palenque, Piedras Negras, and Bonampak.

Large kingdoms did not develop in this region, only small polities controlling perhaps 25 km. Marriage alliances and visits among royalty were frequent. Marriages are recorded between Yaxchilán and Calakmul, Motul de San José, and Bonampak. Royal visits are depicted between Yaxchilán, Piedras Negras, and Altar de Sacrificios. Although battle attire and capture scenes are frequently represented, little evidence of actual warfare is shown. Yaxchilán apparently defeated Lacanhá in A.D. 564, but lost some later military encounter with Dos Pilas. A major personal victory of Bird-Jaguar was the capture of an individual called Jeweled Skull in A.D. 755. Although these figures are artfully portrayed on Lintel 8, we do not know where Jeweled Skull came from or the significance of his capture.

The history of the Jaguar Dynasty is unusually well documented, probably in an effort to overcome its political anxieties. Out of their problems, they left us some of the finest carved Maya monuments on record. Workshops of artists and scribes were well organized, some trained in how to depict the proportions, compositions, and

FIGURE 6.60   The great Temple 33, commissioned by Bird-Jaguar. (Photographed by Lorraine Matys.)

gestures of figures; others specialized in hair styles and textile designs, while the scribes worked out the hieroglyphs (Tate, 1989). This was a collaborative workshop effort that trained later groups at Yaxchilán, resulting in the corpus of outstanding monuments we have today.

Yaxchilán, also, was affected by the intrusion of foreigners in the eighth century. At least some Yucatecan-style inscriptions are evident, and influence from the Campeche region is seen in a particular method of recording dates, examples being the Calendar Round dates recorded on Stelaes 18 and 20 (Graham 1973). Yaxchilán provides a hint of the unrest and change soon to come, for prominent themes in late art are group compositions of strife and conflict (Proskouriakoff, 1960, 1961; Thompson, 1970). The last date found at Yaxchilán is A.D. 808.

Piedras Negras

Piedras Negras

About 50 km downstream from Yaxchilán, Piedras Negras is situated in another big loop of the Usumacinta River, this one on the east, today's Guatemalan side. The terrain is very steep and the ruins of Piedras Negras rise from a high hill. Leaving the river one enters the shade of the deep jungle and climbs up past a huge ceiba tree to the sound of birds and monkeys in the upper canopy of the forest (Figure 6.61). Unfortunately, the jungle has reclaimed the ancient city and only with map in hand and imagination can one locate a particular structure. Some deterioration can be

FIGURE 6.61   The Usumacinta River below Yaxchilán. (Photographed by Jack Lissack.)

attributed to ancient construction using wooden beams and thatch instead of stone masonry vaults. Here, as in most Usumacinta sites, height was achieved by leveling and terracing natural elevations. (Figure 6.62).

The ruins consist of tightly grouped courts, structures with wide stairways, two ball courts, and eight sweat houses with dressing rooms and lounging quarters (Coe,

FIGURE 6.62   *Temescal* at Piedras Negras. (Courtesy of Jack Lissack.)

1959). Architects at Piedras Negras were slow to take up the corbeled arch, but eventually ceilings were vaulted in pure Maya style. Other Petén influence can be seen in stucco masks that flank the staircases, although colonnaded doorways are more like those in Palenque. Buildings let in much more light and air than earlier Petén construction permitted (Kubler, 1984).

A specialized palace-type structure at Piedras-Negras was a building designed primarily for administrative purposes that also served as a royal residence. The Acropolis at Piedras Negras has 13 long structures arranged around 6 courts at various levels. From below, a visitor would ascend a wide staircase and pass through a long double-chambered building or gallery to emerge at another court. The view at this point would have been stunning, for a person would look up to see a massive structure with an elaborately adorned stucco façade. To enter this building, one crossed the huge court and ascended another monumental staircase that led to a spacious room that served as an audience chamber, the principal public room of the palace. Sometimes this room might be provided with a bench used by the ruler as a throne. In Building J-6 at Piedras Negras a carved hieroglyphic throne in a vaulted niche was centered in line with the doorway. Here the king would receive his visitors. Royal visits were common and are the subject of many carved panels.

Beyond this huge complex a West Acropolis rises precipitously to a series of terraced galleries on staggered levels. Many structures are reached with difficulty because of intentionally restricted access. Structure O-13 is a 9-level funerary monument, possibly containing tombs of eighth century rulers.

The stelae at Piedras Negras were superbly carved, exhibiting great detail in styles of clothing and unusual care in the execution of the hieroglyphs. Both wall panels and stelae are examples of some of the finest of Maya stone carving and it was groups of stelae at this site that consistently recorded hotun-endings (1800-day periods) that led Proskouriakoff (1960) to her remarkable study of the personal histories of important leaders (see page 153).

About 40 stelae have been found at Piedras Negras that often depict a ruler sitting cross-legged in a niche above a scaffold after having performed ritual sacrifices. The martial motifs of the seventh century often include a bound captive or prisoner beneath the feet of a warrior. Such monuments are common with the ruler standing erect with one or more captives kneeling at his side and being smaller in size. The Tlaloc war costume of the Late Classic is again seen here. Piedras Negras art is rich in iconographic detail exhibiting many traits not only from the Petén and Palenque, but also from the more distant regions of Cotzumalhuapa, Xochicalco, and Teotihuacan (Parsons, 1969).

Trade brought in shells from both coasts, obsidian, and jade. Caches rich in such objects and eccentric flints are found either associated with altars or with structures. Some are contained in a special lidded cache vessel. Although rulers are heavily garbed in all the trappings of a warrior, and stone panels frequently portray martial scenes, few weapons are found and Piedras Negras does not appear to have been an aggressive or imperialistic polity. The only mention of some military action was that associated with Tikal (Culbert, 1988a). There are signs of violence and willful destruction of monuments, but no sign of conquest or later occupation. The last date recorded is A.D. 810.

Palenque

Palenque

We come now to Palenque, a great Classic Maya center of the west, yet very different from anything we have seen so far. Carved inscriptions and Long Count dates abound, but only two stelae are known. There is no acropolis, no great plazas with paired stelae and altars, no *sacbeob*, no great caches of eccentric flints or obsidian. The polychrome wares typical of the Petén were short lived, and although misleading at first glance, there appears to be no city planning. Despite these differences, Palenque belonged to the Maya world and became one of its leading centers or capitals of the eighth century.

Palenque has long been famous for the beauty of its sculpture in stucco and marvelous carved panel reliefs as well as for the harmony and charm of its crested temples with mansard roofs. Archaeologists are intrigued by the vaulted aqueduct to channel waters of the Otolum River beneath the ruins, a vaulted bridge over the river, trefoiled vaults reducing the massiveness of walls, a 4-story tower, IK or T-shaped "windows," and a completely new concept in temple building.

The combined result is a lighter, airier temple than the dark massive-walled structures of Tikal. Palenque does share with Tikal and Dos Pilas the custom of placing tombs within pyramids, thus the Temple of the Inscriptions was the scene of one of the most spectacular funerary rites in Mesoamerica. In addition, it is here that true portraiture was developed, not just the idealized Maya figure, but naturalistic models of distinct personalities, even to the point of portraying their physical defects.

It is little wonder that Palenque has been a favorite of many visitors since early days of visits and drawings by John Lloyd Stephens and Frederick Catherwood in the nineteenth century. Nestled in the foothills of the great Chiapas Mountains that are covered with forests of mahogany, cedar and the sapodilla tree, the temples of Palenque command a magnificent view far out over the low coastal plain that extends to the Gulf of Mexico some 128 km away. Although a few Chicanel sherds have been recovered, and a small ball court and tomb with rather undistinguished pottery date from the Early Classic Period, Palenque was in most respects just one more modest or rural settlement until the seventh century. The extraordinary florescence of the site is confined to a mere 150-year span of time and can be attributed to the energy and inspiration of some remarkable personalities. The ruins we see today can be best understood by attempting a historical reconstruction (Griffin, 1976; Mathews and Schele, 1974; Robertson, 1983; Robertson *et al.*, 1976; Schele, 1976; Schele and Freidel, 1990).

Pacal Palenque's most remarkable ruler, Lord Pacal (Shield) was born in A.D. 603, ascended to power at the age of 12 1/2 years, enjoyed 68 years on the throne, and merited all the pomp and ceremony accorded him upon his death in A.D. 683. He boasted of mythological ancestry, establishing himself as semidivine, a power he inherited from his mother whose husband was a figure of no importance.

The shift to emphasize his mother in a good Maya patrilineal society required a bit of manipulation and interpretation of ancestral history. The upshot was that Lady Zac-Kuk, his mother, was found to be divine, in fact a kind of Mother Goddess, equated with the First Mother of Creation. It would then follow that her son would inherit this divinity, establishing his right to rule. The two most important kings were Lord Pacal and his elder son Lord Chan-Bahlum (Snake-Jaguar). Between the two of them they compiled and publicized four king lists, producing the most detailed dynastic history we have of Classic times, running from A.D. 431 to 799 (Schele and Freidel, 1990).

Having settled the matter of divinity, Pacal had another problem involving heredity: a physical abnormality needed sanctification. In the preceding generation, an uncle was decapitated, an event graphically recorded on a stucco relief. This uncle had a badly deformed clubfoot that was now displayed as a divine attribute. Lord Pacal may have been born with a clubfoot also, but this is hard to determine from the stone sculptures. The matter will be settled one day when his skeleton in the sarcophagus is studied. He may have flaunted his foot as proof of his divinity and his relationship to his divine but decapitated uncle. The clubfoot becomes significant as it was eventually conceptualized and transformed into a serpent. The serpent-footed deity, God K, rapidly became prominent as a symbol of divine rulership. After A.D. 912 we find God K, the manikin-scepter deity with a serpent foot and a flare in his forehead, as a common symbol of kingship throughout the Maya realm.

As is frequent among divine royalty, intermarriages prevail, for the divine must choose for marriage one of their own rank. Thus it is possible that Pacal married Lady Zac-Kuk, his mother, in name only or perhaps in actual fact. She died when he was 27 years old. He also married his sister, Lady Ahpo-Hel. The genes for physical deformities were thus closely retained and best explain the abnormalities in the Palenque ruling family. Lady Zac-Kuk was also abnormal, depicted with a massive head and jaw, the victim of acromegaly (Robertson et al., 1976).

Lord Pacal fathered two sons who succeeded him: Lord Chan-Bahlum and Lord Kan-Xul (Lord Hok), the first of whom had 6 toes on each foot and 6 fingers on his left hand, an example of polydactyly and illustrated on the piers of the Temple of the Inscriptions. Chan-Bahlum's tomb under the Temple of the Cross is still unexcavated and perhaps one day his 6 toes and 6 fingers will come to light. To have a deformity of this nature became an indication of royal blood.

Finally at age 44, Pacal, now free of both parents, began to build. His first project in A.D. 647 was erecting the Temple Olvidado (the Forgotten Temple) 1/2 km south of the Palace, near a residential zone and one of the water sources. It was built facing north along a steep escarpment, reached by a series of stairs up four platforms. This was a truly innovative structure and was thereafter reflected in the architecture of Palenque. The temple had two inner galleries with trefoil vaults, walls were much thinner than in previous constructions, and the three doorways were wide and spacious. The roof comb was unusually elaborate, composed of six large glyph blocks with pairs of holes suggesting owl eyes (Temple of the Owls ?).

Aside from the architecture itself, the four piers on the north façade are perhaps the most interesting features. The inscriptions are enclosed in circular cartouches, each containing six glyphs that identify Kan-Bahlum Mo' as Pacal's father and Lady Zac-Kuk as his mother. His mother is named and portrayed elsewhere at Palenque, but his father is mentioned only here and on his sarcophagus stone (Mathews and Robertson, 1985).

Next, Pacal initiated more ambitious programs, constructing the Temple of the Count, subterranean galleries beneath corbeled passages of the Palace and a number of its houses, making the Palace unique among Maya structures. The entire complex is situated on an artificial platform some 90 m long by 73 m wide. Its pillars and walls were lavishly decorated and covered with stucco reliefs of masks and figures. Traces of the hieroglyphs and scenes that once adorned the wall reliefs celebrate his ancestry and may still be seen.

He also laid out the plaza south of the Palace and commissioned his huge mortuary temple/pyramid (Figure 6.63). A crypt was dug 1.5 m below the plaza floor at the foot of the large sacred mountain into which was placed an empty stone coffin. This was protected by a wall and filled with sand as the great pyramid was carefully raised above it. By the time he died in A.D. 683 his final resting place had been prepared and his funeral must have been the most sumptuous Palenque ever witnessed.

He was carefully laid out in the crypt in a great stone sarcophagus with a jade piece in his mouth, and one in each hand; he wore a jade ring on every finger, bracelets, a diadem of jade disks, jade and mother-of-pearl earspools, and his favorite tubular jade bead necklace. On his forehead was placed that symbol of kingship, the three-pointed headband, and finally his face was covered with a mosaic mask with eyes of shell and obsidian (Figure 6.63a). Beside him lay 2 jade figures. Everything including the corpse had been coated with red cinnabar to emphasize his eternal life after death. A lid was carefully fitted over the U-shaped box, and removable stoppers were dropped into holes for lifting the stone into place for the last time. Over this lid, another gigantic one, 4 m long and exquisitely carved, was slowly lowered into place (Figure 6.63.) This beautiful sarcophagus cover shows Pacal as a clubfooted young man, wearing the headdress of God K, falling into the jaws of the Underworld along with the dying sun. According to M. Coe (1988), Pacal identifies himself both with God K and Tezcatlipoca, for in his headdress is the tube of the Smoking Mirror God, patron of royal descent. Above his figure the World Tree spreads its limbs to welcome his soul after he ascends from Xibalbá.

No fewer than 14 dates are inscribed on the lid, including his birth and death dates, as well as names, dates, and pictorial representations of his ancestors. The walls of the crypt were entirely covered with stucco reliefs, perhaps of the Nine Lords of the Night or ancestors. Two stucco heads and simple vessels containing food were left on the floor. The final sealing of the crypt was accomplished by fitting a triangular slab into one of the vaults, whereupon five or six youths were promptly sacrificed and left to accompany (or guard?) the privileged deceased. A solid masonry wall in turn sealed in this macabre scene, after which attention turned to concealing the crypt.

In anticipation of these funeral rites, the pyramid had been built along with the interior staircase with its neatly vaulted roof. The stairs turned at a landing and, keeping pace with the exterior construction, finally reached the summit.

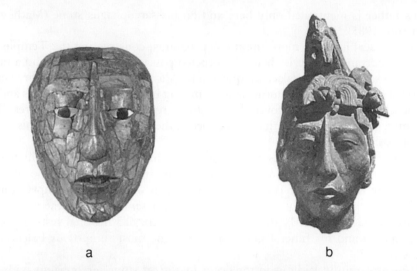

a   b

c

FIGURE 6.63   Pacal's Tomb: Temple of the Inscriptions, Palenque, Chiapas.
a. Jade mosaic mask with eyes of inlaid shell and obsidian. Found as death mask of Pacal in sarcophagus in the funerary crypt. Height: 24 cm. (Courtesy of the Museo Nacional de Antropologia, Mexico.)
b. Beautifully modeled life-size stucco head believed to represent Pacal. Found on the floor of the funerary crypt. Height: 31 cm. (Courtesy of the Museo Nacional de Antropología, Mexico.)
c. Temple of the Inscriptions, Palenque, Chiapas. (Courtesy of the Instituto Nacional de Antropología e Historia, Mexico.)
d. Funerary crypt underlying the Temple of the Inscriptions. The carved stone, lid of the sarcophagus, shows Pacal falling into the open jaws of the Underworld. (Courtesy of the Instituto Nacional de Antropología e Historia, Mexico.)

d

Chan-Bahlum Chan-Bahlum, Pacal's elder son, succeeded his famous father in A.D. 684 and ruled for 18 fruitful years. Now he completed his father's funerary temple, the Temple of the Inscriptions, using the same skilled architects and sculptors that had worked for Pacal. The temple was modeled on that of the Temple Olvidado with mansard roof and central roof comb. The finishing touches afforded him a fine opportunity to show that he, also, was the direct recipient of divine power. For maximum effect he decorated the outer piers of the temple, visible from the court below. Here in brilliant painted stucco relief he illustrated himself as a child with his deformities, receiving from Pacal the sanction of his new status as a "divine human." This presentation ceremony corresponds to the heir-designation scene of the Bonampak murals.

The great stone panels at the back immortalize the Long Count date of A.D. 683. Easily overlooked among the neatly cut and fitted stones that form the paving of the floor is one with a double row of stone stoppers, the only clue to the interior staircase leading to Pacal's crypt. When the Mexican archaeologist Alberto Ruz lifted this stone in 1949, the vaulted stairway was found choked with rubble. Four field seasons later, on June 15, 1952, the crypt and its secrets were revealed (Ruz Lhuillier, 1960).

One of its secrets was the so-called psychoduct, a small tube that passed out of the foot of the sarcophagus and led to a hollow pipe at the bottom of the staircase to lead up to the Temple above. This permitted Pacal's soul to communicate with his descendants via the Vision Serpent. This is not the only temple/pyramid with a psychoduct at Palenque, but it is certainly the most elaborate. Puzzling is why the vaulted staircase was built with removable entry lid and stoppers if Pacal was to be sealed in for all eternity. Debris that filled it dates from the building's construction (Griffin, 1976), so access was blocked as of the time of the interment.

Pacal would surely have been gratified to witness his continued impact on Palenque. Inspired by his father and anxious to immortalize the legitimacy of his birthright, Chan-Bahlum next erected the Group of the Cross temples (Temple of the Cross, the Foliated Cross, and the Sun) (Figure 6.64e) that served to heap glory upon and reinforce the divinity of this dynasty.

These temples are arranged at different levels around a plaza on the east side of the site. Each is placed on a pyramidal base with frontal staircase leading to a stone temple in the new architectural style. Passing through the doorways, a broad inner chamber leads to the "sanctuary," actually a small inner temple with its own roof set in the back chamber and representing the Underworld. Here the deceased king would be confronted with trials as were the Hero Twins, and upon victory, he would rise again to bring prosperity to his people. On the back wall of this little inner temple is a magnificent bas-relief stucco panel. The panels on all three temples of this Cross Group feature two central personages: a tall Chan-Bahlum and a short Pacal, accompanied by long hieroglyphic texts that record historical information about Chan-Bahlum's ancestors in support of his divinity.

To accomplish this, a mythological founder of the Palenque dynasty born in 993 B.C. is connected to the First Mother and First Father and to their three children, the gods of the Palenque Triad. These three gods formed part of the earliest kingship symbolism at Cerros, but they became intimately associated with kingship at Palenque when Chan-Bahlum connected their detailed history with the Palenque dynasty (Schele and Freidel, 1990). The three temples together form an integrated architectural group. Their inscriptions form a set, closely related through their sculptural reliefs. In essence the Palenque Triad verifies and supports the accession of Chan-Bahlum in A.D. 684.

There is a marvelous head of Lord Chan-Bahlum from Temple XIV that portrays him realistically with a very large nose, thick, pendulous lower lip, and even anxiety in his facial expression (Griffin, 1976). Portraiture was probably ordered by Chan-Bahlum, for prior to his reign we find the standard archetype Maya sculpture exemplified by the stucco head of Pacal found in the crypt (see Figure 6.63b). Not only was sculpture standardized but also mural painting. At Palenque, as well as at Seibal and at Teotihuacan, patterns of stencils were sometimes used (Robertson, 1975, 1977).

Kan-Xul   Lord Chan-Bahlum was succeeded by his younger brother, Lord Kan-Xul. This new king was now 38 years of age and reigned for the following 23 years. As each ruler looked for some way to leave a lasting mark, it fell to Kan-Xul to remodel the Palace and extend it to its massive proportions, adding more rooms, galleries, and

FIGURE 6.64 Views and details of Palenque. (All photographed by the author.)

a. The Palace with tower, on the huge artificial terrace.

b. The Palace West Court, with crude bas-relief slabs.

c. Fine Palenque stucco sculpture from the Palace complex.

d. An IK window in the Palace.

e. The Cross Group: (left, Temple of the Cross; center back, Temple of the Foliated Cross; lower right, Temple of the Sun; unexcavated mound in center foreground, Temple IV).

f. West view from Palace.

c

d

FIGURE 6.64—Continued

e

f

FIGURE 6.64—Continued

courtyards. Somewhat out of character are rather grotesque figures of captives carved on slabs on the sides of a Palace patio (Figure 6.64b). The workmanship is generally poor and inconsistent, striking a curious discordant note in an otherwise harmonious setting.

Every visitor to the Palace can be found on tiptoes peering through the IK or T-shaped "windows." These openings are ubiquitous in, but not limited to, the Palace complex. IK, a day-sign (see page 146) means both "wind" and "breath," considered a metaphor for "life." It has been difficult to interpret the function of the openings since they are not all at eye level as a functional window would be. Some are placed upside down, some are paired. In the Cross Group for example, IK "windows" are too high for sighting but might have served to let both light in and smoke from incense or ritual fires out. For us these 85 "windows" add grace, charm, and light to an otherwise dark room, but we do not know what meaning or function they may have had for the Maya (Peterson, 1985).

Kan-Xul is also seen as the builder of Temple XIV, located in such a way as to obstruct access to the Cross Group, that for many years seemed to be out of place in Palenque's architectural scheme. After a close analysis of the inscriptions, Linda Schele (1988) explains the positioning of this structure as a deliberate obstruction constructed after the death of Chan-Bahlum by his brother, that acts as a cork to bottle up the special three Cross Group temples. Temple 33 in the North Acropolis at Tikal performs a somewhat similar function. In both cases, ceremonial space used by earlier rulers is blocked or protected.

We do not know where or how Kan-Xul made his error, but somehow he found himself captive and was hauled off to Toniná in western Chiapas, a supreme humiliation for the second son of Pacal. Toniná was well known in the Late Classic Period for its bellicose nature and military prowess. The capture and decapitation of Kan-Xul was its greatest moment of glory. The event is depicted on a panel of skeletal figures on the side of a Toniná building where David Freidel (Robertson, 1991) read the text naming Kan-Xul as the victim. His untimely demise created some confusion at Palenque but not enough to derail the traditional dynasty.

The following ruler was Chaacal, not a son of Kan-Xul or Chan-Bahlum, but perhaps one of their nephews (?). He was followed by a *cahal*, Chac Zutz, a war captain who had been an important figure during the reign of Chaacal. We know little of the last ruler, Kuk, other than that he reigned about 20 years, until around A.D. 784, for Palenque is one of the first cities to "collapse", inscribing its last date in A.D. 799.

Comments

The curious Palenque tower with interior staircase was built by one of the last rulers, possibly Kan-Xul. This square 4-story building was supported not by corbeled arches but by horizontal beams of wood. A Venus glyph on a landing suggests that it might have been used as an astronomical observatory, but there are other possibilities as well. The tower offers a superb view of the immense coastal plain but seems to have been primarily a cosmic-magical symbol unifying the entire site. It may have been placed so as to observe the winter solstice sun entering the Underworld via the tomb of Lord Pacal (Schele, 1976; Carlson, 1976). The sound of a conch shell trumpet carries so well when sounded from the tower that it makes one wonder if signaling was another function.

From very humble beginnings, Palenque became the most important center in the west, a sacred city, leader, and capital, only to decline by A.D. 799. Through the years Palenque has managed to retain more of its ancient character than many other sites, for even today one feels an ageless unity between the Underworld, the heavens, and the temples that serve to join the different realms.

Only casual mention has been made of Palenque's relations to other sites. In contrast to Tikal whose rulers were involved with intersite marriage and alliances as well as long-distance trade, Palenque retained a regional character. Even in the Early Classic, Palenque had few ceramic ties to the Petén heartland, with none of the polychromes or orange-slipped wares. There is little that looks like Tzakol until the middle Classic years when Petén wares were both imported and imitated, and contacts with nearby Piedras Negras were strong. By A.D. 600–700, styles were localized and thereafter Fine Paste wares increased. In Palenque's final days, Fine Gray wares and a Fine Orange of Balancan type (z) heralded the presence of a non-Classic tradition. Most of the products were made in specialized communities for the local market (Rands, 1977).

Architecturally Palenque's influence extended to northeastern Yucatán where temples are also built with double galleries (see page 336). An area closely related to Palenque is the alluvial plain of Tabasco, where the large site of Comalcalco shows similarities in art and architecture (Figure 6.65). Here are systems of courts and plazas and a huge artificial platform that supported a number of buildings constructed of kiln-fired bricks. Situated in the homeland of the Putún or Chontal Maya, these people mingled with their Mexican neighbors. In effect, some of the stucco reliefs reflect both Maya and non-Maya features. This marks the western edge of the Maya world.

Toniná

The site of Toniná, Chiapas, excavated by the French Archaeological Mission in Mexico in the 1970s, is well known for two feats: it captured and sacrificed a Palenque king, and also recorded the last-known Long Count Maya date on a stela. Toniná is

FIGURE 6.65   Ruins of Comalcalco, Tabasco. (Courtesy of Jack Lissack.)

only 50 km south of Palenque, but at nearly 3000 ft. elevation it is transitional to the western highlands. (See Map 6.5.)

The ruins are located near the modern town of Ososingo where the Maya modified a hillside into a series of terraces that overlook a large plaza. The latter is bordered by a ball court to the east, a massive pyramidal structure to the south, and a series of north–south buildings aligned along the west side, all dominated by the northern terraces. The major concentrations of housemounds lie across an arroyo (Mathews, 1983).

Of the 250 scattered monuments (altars, stelae, disks, panels), less than half are inscribed and few are found *in situ*. The stelae are small, under 2 m in height, and are carved in the round, a distinctive feature of Toniná.

Dates are largely confined to the Late Classic when Toniná seems to have warred against both Bonampak and Palenque. A large panel shows a figure holding a decapitated head, named in hieroglyphs as Lord Kan-Xul of Palenque, the greatest coup of Toniná (Robertson, 1991).

The last-known Long Count date of the southern lowlands was recorded here on Monument 101 in A.D. 909 (Schele and Freidel, 1990).

Lagartero

Lagartero is an island and peninsular settlement in the swamps of Chiapas near the border of Guatemala. Its watery environment is due to being located on small tributaries of the great Río Grijalva.

Temple/pyramids, palaces, and other buildings were grouped around plazas and patios, but it is the large refuse dump that has attracted attention. At first, unusual clay figurines were reported by Susanna Ekholm of the New World Archaeological Foundation, but further excavation uncovered an enormous pit 24 m × 12 m × 2 m deep filled with all manner of refuse deposited at one time. It contained abundant ceramics, as Lagartero was a center of production, but the pit also included ornaments, tools of all kinds, objects of bone, stone, and shell, and undoubtedly perishables.

This great refuse deposit is thought to represent a ceremony described by Landa (Tozzer, 1941) as taking place at year-end during the Uayeb (see page 145), but it might also mark the end of a 52-year cycle.

Sixty percent of the broken clay figurines are women, elegantly attired and surely of elite status with an important role in this society. Men are less numerous in figurines but dominate the figures on polychrome pottery of Late Classic style. The estimated date of the dump is A.D. 800–900 (Ekholm, 1990).

Cotzumalhuapa

Cotzumalhuapa refers to an area of Guatemala with an enigmatic art style that seems to defy a clear placement or role in Mesoamerican archaeology. Bilbao is one of the main centers in this region, located a short distance northeast of the town of

Santa Lucía. Cotzumalhuapa lies on the sloping piedmont in a natural rain forest 50 km from the Pacific Ocean.

The ceremonial center is made up of four main groups that include 17 pyramids, plazas, and courts faced with stone rubble or adobe plaster along with some finely dressed stone-block stairways. Hundreds of cylindrical tripods have been turned up by bulldozers preparing the land for cultivation of sugar and cotton (Hellmuth, 1978). Mold-impressed designs, as well as carved decorations record scenes of ball-players and decapitation. Motifs are similar to those of Teotihuacan, Monte Albán, Xochicalco, and the Gulf Coast.

In general, there are two main themes: a preoccupation or obsession with death, and the ball game. The characteristic stone-carved narrative scenes center around the ball-game cult. Decapitation is graphically illustrated; skulls and skeletal figures are common, executed in a stiff unsympathetic style with "no aesthetic merit" (Parsons, 1969; M. D. Coe, 1988). Providing some relief to the austerity of a scene is the frequent use of leaves, branches, and pods of the cacao plant, for this was one of the richest cacao-producing regions in Mesoamerica.

Cotzumalhuapa most likely represents a Mexican intrusion from the Gulf Coast region, perhaps from El Tajín itself, based on close parallels related to the ball-game cult. In addition, religion reveals Mexican deities with representations of Tlaloc, Xipe Totec, Huehuéteotl, and Quetzalcoatl. Carved hieroglyphs enclosed in cartouches have Mexican day-names and numbers that use dots or circles instead of a bar for number 5, Maya style. These were people who spoke a Náhua language known to have been in the area (M. D. Coe, 1988; Morley *et al.*, 1983). At present, the best estimate is for a date around A.D. 900 or shortly thereafter, possibly associated with Pipil migrations.

THE "COLLAPSE" IN THE SOUTHERN LOWLANDS

It may come as a disappointment to some to learn that the Maya civilization did not collapse overnight with people and cities suddenly disappearing to who knows where or why. For years this great mystery of the Maya has been a challenging enigma. But Maya civilization did not collapse and vanish into nothingness. Rather, it underwent sociopolitical and economic changes that led to a shift of power and focus to other Maya regions of the Yucatán Peninsula. Classic Maya features of architecture, hieroglyphic writing, religion, and ceramics survived and underwent modifications as new contacts, environmental conditions, basic goals, and lifestyles brought about adaptations and innovations.

Unfortunately, the inscriptions do not tell us about economic affairs or social problems, so we must rely on the study of cessation of dates, construction, deterioration in quality of remains, signs of malnutrition, warfare, and outright abandonment of sites to interpret the decline of these southern centers. A special conference (Culbert, 1973) was once held to deal exclusively with the "collapse," and the literature is replete with ideas concerning this continuing problem. I am grateful to the following authors for their scholarly views that are subjected here to my interpretation. See Ball and Taschek (1989), Chase (1991), Cowgill (1979), Culbert (1973, 1988a,b), Demarest (n.d.a,b), Diehl and Berlo (1989), Freidel (1985, 1986), Kowalski (1989), Puleston (1979), Robles and Andrews (1986), Sabloff and Andrews V (1986), Sabloff (1990), Sanders (1973), Sharer, (1983), Thompson (1970), Willey (1974), and Willey and Shimkin (1973).

The Maya power structure was always unstable. These pages are filled with the rise and fall of kingdoms and rulers struggling to increase their prestige, status, and economic advantage. Political unity that would have maintained some prolonged peace from time to time was never achieved. The Maya realm never expanded beyond the territory it occupied in the mid-eighth century. Thereafter buildings continued to be built and inscriptions inscribed, but all within cities or kingdoms already established.

During the second half of the eighth century, commercial relations with highland Mexico broke down, interregional relationships were strained, warfare increased, and births could not keep pace with the death rate. The ninth century is a scene of disjunction and decline in many aspects, but the seeds of destruction were inherent in the system. The changes that ensued were not brought about by a single cause, but one asks why they occurred at all, why this great civilization was not able to perpetuate itself. It had seemingly learned how to cope with its fragile and diverse environment, feed itself, communicate, engage in warfare according to a system with well-established rules of containment, manipulate the supernatural, and support its royal dynasties as well as an extravagant elite. Some early day-to-day pressures had been alleviated, because food could be stored, dried fish kept well, and the steady stream of merchants kept hard-to-get commodities in stock. Local crops were doing nicely with terracing and the flow of water under control. Obsidian was always available from a variety of highland sources. Many households now had a few quality imports such as a fine *metate* of highland limestone, and perhaps a few jade beads, although these were a luxury.

Nonetheless, warning signs were there. Warfare was a constant threat, a frequent reality, and times had changed. There were lessons to be learned from the devastation wrought by the Petexbatún wars. Repercussions from Teotihuacan's withdrawal were widely felt and created a serious void in the economic networks. After the Petén wars of the seventh century, Tikal had found she must share power with peripheral centers such as Copán, Palenque, Piedras Negras, and Cobá. The energetic and astute Putún were trying to fill the gap. Bolder merchants were taking to the sea, and instead of crossing the peninsula by river and portage, more and more frequently they went around Yucatán to their east coast counterparts in Cozumel and Belize. Heavy objects could be more easily transported by sea than by a river-portage combination through the jungle. For the cities of Petén, an all-sea route removed them from competition and participation.

A serious gulf between classes due to exploitation and inequalities has often been cited as another possible factor contributing to the weakening of the system. Perhaps the elite had expanded to the point where their maintenance demanded an excessive amount of labor to be diverted from the pool of farmers. Were there too few to support so many, or was food production being mismanaged? Was the carrying capacity of the land at its limit? The agricultural system relied on a careful program of diversifying, spacing, and fallowing of crops. If erosion and overexploitation set in, there was little hope of recovery.

We know that the Maya, like most Mesoamericans, were obsessed with the concept of time and recurring cycles, and a fatalistic attitude is very demoralizing. This, combined with setbacks in warfare and the economy, would certainly have been a contributing factor. Warfare seemed inevitable.

The example of rampant warfare in the Petexbatún illustrates how within a century a small state could be obliterated. The warring alone did not wipe out the population, but was responsible for ruining its subsistence potential. No other dramatic examples of warfare have been documented to match the demise of Dos Pilas, but fortifications are known from a long list of sites. It is unlikely that the Petexbatún is unique.

When southern and northern lowland Maya temples are compared, (Figure 6.66), one can see a change from the characteristic early thick walls and narrow dark rooms of Tikal, to the lighter, structures with wider doorways at Chichén Itzá. This transition is apparent at Palenque. An inner sanctuary and the corbeled arch were features maintained by the northern architects.

The changes that occurred in Maya society after these eighth century failures are reflected in the epigraphy. The depictions of ritual, mythology, and elite activities that prevailed in southern Classic Maya art are noticeably absent. With the old beliefs went the behavior associated with prescribed duties and celebrations. In the continuation of Maya civilization, we will see traces, reminders, and echoes of kingship, but they are now submerged in a new order that is more mundane, with some sharing of authority. Worldy pursuits like the accumulation of wealth were now within the grasp of the ambitious. Social mobility was possible.

In essence then, what "collapsed" was the institution of kingship with its built-in support systems, not the Maya civilization.

In continuing the story of the Classic Maya we will move to central Yucatán and southeastern Campeche before proceeding north to discover how these changes were reflected in a new blend of Maya civilization.

SOUTHERN CAMPECHE AND CENTRAL YUCATÁN

The still poorly known area of southern Campeche and central Yucatán was naturally affected by the major developments taking place in the south and north. The Maya of this region were sophisticated farmers. Some produced extraordinary buildings and fortifications, and remains of their settlements are providing information linking all corners of Mesoamerica.

This vast area did not produce the same type of cities as those of the south, nor

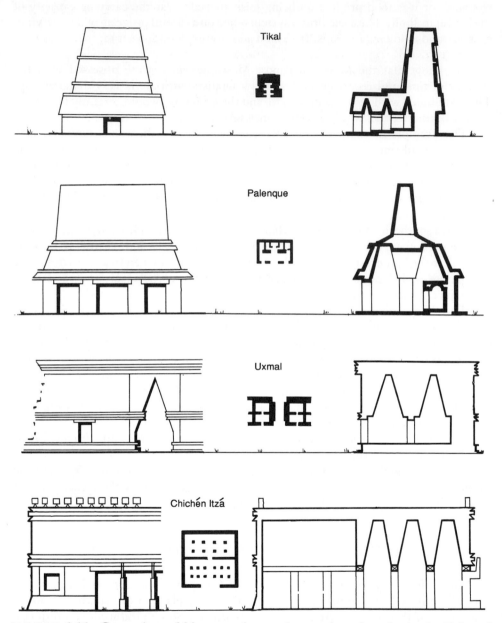

FIGURE 6.66 Comparison of Maya temples, northern and southern lowlands. (Adapted from Marquina, 1951).

did they ever create vast territorial empires. They did, however, excel as builders, farmers, and possibly as warriors. Only the most outstanding sites will be briefly mentioned. Let us return to a group of regional centers of southeastern Campeche, just north of the Petén (see Map 6.6.)

Settlements here are rather compact with groups of structures arranged around courtyards, much in the style of the Petén. In general, there are no *sacbeob* or hillside staircases, and much of the area was swampy. Calakmul, already noted (see page 267) for its large size and proliferation of stelae, is one of the fortified centers of this region. Oxpemul and El Palmar are others. Oxpemul, north of Calakmul, is the last site in this area with Petén-style architecture. A hill was leveled and a stone terrace was built to create the fortress. If the terrace had been combined with palisades or some other perishable feature, as was done with ditches at Tikal and Becán, this would have made an effective citadel. East of Calakmul, El Palmar, built around two lakes, could have been easily fortified, but no formal structures are visible. We have little evidence that there was an organized defense system, but there must have been good reason to muster the manpower devoted to these constructions.

Río Bec Region

The Río Bec region is located in southeastern Campeche and southwestern Quintana Roo (see Map 6.5.) This is an area ecologically transitional between the Petén rain forest on the south and the dry scrub plains of Yucatán to the north. Ridges of hills are covered with dry forests of breadnut and *sapote* trees; water runs down the gullies to be caught in low-lying areas. The Maya settled here where rainwater could be accumulated in reservoirs. A new style of architecture is shared by a cluster of sites, the most important being Río Bec, Chicanná, Becán, la Hormiguera, and Xpuhil (Figure 6.67). In general, layouts are less dense and more scattered than in the Petén. Many of the 38 known centers have not yet been surveyed or investigated (Adams, 1981). Río Bec architecture combines features of chambered palaces with pyramidal platforms. Heavy use of stucco and fine uncut masonry, vertical façades, and elaborate ostentatious decorations are characteristic. Roof combs are sometimes replaced by towers, and masks of a long-nosed god often decorate corners and façades. Two-story structures are known in which the second story is recessed to rest on solid fill.

Chicanná

Chicanná is located 3 km southwest of Becán. It is small, but it is a jewel of the Río Bec region. This was an elite center of five groups of mounds and buildings. Structure I has end towers simulating pyramids after the style of Tikal. The façade is completely adorned with mosaic masks, and in passing through the doorway, one is entering the open mouth of a serpent. Appropriately named, Chicanná means "serpent-mouth-house" (Eaton, 1974).

a

FIGURE 6.67   Architecture of central Yucatán.
a. Building XX, Chicanná, Campeche. (Courtesy of Román Piña Chan.)
b. Building, II, Chicanná, Campeche. (Courtesy of Román Piña Chan.)
c. Building I, Xpuhil, Campeche. (Courtesy of Román Piña Chan.)
d. Example of Río Bec architectural style. Reconstruction of a building at Xpuhil, Campeche. (Drawing by Tatiana Proskouriakoff, 1946. Courtesy of the Peabody Museum of Archaeology and Ethnology, Harvard University. Copyright by the President and Fellows of Harvard College.)
e. Building 1, East Group of Becán, Campeche. (Courtesy of Román Piña Chan.)
f. Example of Chenes-style architecture. Model of temple at Hochob, Yucatán. Museo Nacional de Antropología, Mexico. (Courtesy of Victoria Bach.)
g. Building of Five Storys, Edzná, Campeche. (Courtesy of Román Piña Chan.)

b

c

d

e

FIGURE 6.67—Continued

f

FIGURE 6.67—Continued

g

FIGURE 6.67—Continued

Xpuhil

At Xuphil (Figure 6.67) ornamental tower/pyramids have front and back stairways with treads too narrow to use. Ostentatious façades of veneer masonry are heavily decorated with bas-reliefs, the final details being carved into thick stucco and brightly painted.

The small sites of Pechal and Peor es Nada are special for having the only examples of amphitheaters in the Maya lowlands, with a seating capacity estimated at 8000 (Adams, 1981).

Becán

Becán, just north of Xpuhil and Chicanná, differs by being the only fortified site in the group. Around A.D. 100–250 it built a remarkable ditch or dry moat that, combined with a palisade, could have been extremely effective. Much of the history of this site has been reconstructed by Ball (1977a,b) who has demonstrated a close relationship with the Petén based on his ceramic studies. A major conflict took place around A.D. 450–630, a time of turmoil in the south, which resulted in the breaching of Becán's great fortifications. An abundance of skeletal material was found scattered about and buildings were wrecked and demolished.

An extraordinary cache of Teotihuacan-style figurines was contained in a typical Maya vessel. Known as Cache 69-2, it had been placed at the time of a public ceremony representing an overturn of political power about A.D. 550–560 (Ball, 1983).

The carved cylindrical tripod vase that contained the figures was made in the Guatemalan highlands and was probably imported earlier for an elite burial at Becán that was subsequently violated and pillaged and reused at this time. When discovered in the rubble of an elite residence, this vessel held a large, hollow 2-part Teotihuacan-style figure that in turn contained 10 small, solid figurines representing Teotihuacan deities and warriors along with jade ornaments. The pervading theme of the figurines, representing owl and jaguar military orders of Teotihuacan, is warfare. This was not the usual dedicatory cache, but a victory offering. It is an unprecedented find that suggests actual military presence of Teotihuacanos from central Mexico, along with ethnic groups of lesser rank (Ball, 1983). Just who these parties were we do not know, but it is a fortuitious discovery, happily found under controlled archaeological conditions.

By the eighth century, pottery styles had deteriorated; the ditch at Becán was filled in, and with the appearance of slate ware imitations, we find that attention had turned to northern Yucatán.

Chenes Region

Farther north still is an area called Chenes where the architecture is essentially the same as that at Río Bec. Hochob is the largest of this group and is a good of Chenes style. (Figure 6.67f). At this site a long platform supported three buildings. The doorway to the palace-type structure forms the mouth of a monster, and the entire vertical façade is elaborately decorated in deep relief. This same architecture is known from Dzibilnocác, El Tabasqueño, and Chichén Itzá. Years ago Kubler (1984) pointed out early antecendents for this remarkable architecture in the elaborate façade of Temple 22 at Copán, and also at Holmul.

Edzná

Although not considered a Chenes site, Edzná is not far west of Hochob. Its greatest days were earlier in the Late Preclassic when the great waterworks were constructed, but there are interesting features of Classic date as well. A great 5-story temple/pyramid (Structure V8-19, Figure 6.67g) was built in two or three distinct sectors, one of which was for civic-ceremonial purposes, the others residential. The 19 known stelae all bear Calendar Round dates (G. Andrews, 1984). Thompson (1970) observed that these had an aberrant method of recording dates similar to that of Yaxchilán. He also felt that the features of the people on the monuments did not look Mayan and suggested that these were Putún folk coming south from Yucatán that stopped on their way to Yaxchilán and Altar de Sacrificios (see page 318). An Early

Classic stairway is flanked by two well-preserved stucco masks, but the ball court finished in Puuc style veneer would lend support to the presence of Thompson's Putún. (See Mexicon, 1987).

NORTHERN YUCATÁN

The northern lowlands replaced the southern traditions of carving hieroglyphic texts with an architectural style that communicated by means of bas-reliefs on walls, columns, lintels, and through elaborate painted scenes.

A long-standing debate has centered around chronology in an effort to coordinate the archaeological sequence in northern Yucatán with other areas of Mesoamerica. Involved is the problem of dating and correlation of the archaeological remains with carbon 14 dates and the Maya calendar; the relationship between northern and central Yucatán to the so-called "collapse" of the southern centers; and the relationship between Chichén Itzá in northern Yucatán and Tula, Hidalgo, in central highland Mexico. It is a basic concern since the chronology of all areas in Mesoamerica is ultimately cross-tied to the Maya Long Count system.

The correlation problem has centered around choosing between several possible dating systems. The archaeological data and most of the scientific processes strongly continue to support the Maya Long Count date of the 11.16.0.0.0 correlation with the Christian calendar year 1539. Nonetheless, a correlation of 11.3.0.0.0 or even 11.5.0.0.0 would still fit the northern Yucatán archaeological sequence for the terminal Classic-Postclassic Period (see discussion in Ball and Taschek, 1989; 191, note 6). While the debate is still unsettled, I continue with the 11.16.0.0.0 correlation.

The view has long been held that Puuc architecture belongs to a Late and terminal Classic Period, that is, A.D. 800/900–1000. So-called "Toltec" influence was then dated to the following early Postclassic. These were seen as consecutive periods of development. It was a neat arrangement but has not worked out as more information becames available.

A number of Toltec themes and motifs in Puuc sites were pointed out long ago by Proskouriakoff (1950). Carvings in a Toltec structure at Chichén Itzá were Classic Maya. The carbon dates from the Balankanché Cave proved beyond doubt that an offering of Toltec censers had been sealed in by A.D. 900. It became clear that different architectural and ceramic styles and motifs reached northern Yucatán from western Mesoamerica over a number of years via some kind of trade, direct or indirect, or movement of people. These would have been Mexicans but not Tula Toltecs.

The relationship between Chichén Itzá and Tula, Hidalgo, is still subject to various interpretations. The history of the debate has been summarized elsewhere (Cohodas, 1989), so I will try to present some of the current ideas about these confused years based on Willey (1986a); Andrews and Sabloff (1986), Schele and Freidel (1990), and Sabloff (1990).

I have extended the Late Classic Maya Period in this text to the year A.D. 1200 in order to accomodate the Itzá occupation of northern Yucatán. This will take us to the demise of Chichén Itzá and the rise of Mayapán. The departure of the Itzá from northern Yucatán marks the beginning of a whole new phase of Maya history.

I will consider three distinct regions: first the Puuc area of northwest Yucatán with a number of prominent sites, the most important being Uxmal; second, Cobá, a Classic center that reached its prime between A.D. 900 and 1100 and retained its old traditions and independence; and third, Chichén Itzá, the cosmopolitan capital of a large territory eventually extending from Campeche to the Caribbean coast. Although these three regions have well-defined differences, they partially overlap temporally and share some cultural content.

Puuc

The word Puuc refers to a series of hills in northwestern Yucatán where a number of rather well-preserved remains have been found. This region has very fertile soil, but little water. Nonetheless, this is the most densely populated area of Yucatán. The ruins are all located close to *chultuns*, water-storing devices. These were either cut into the limestone or dug into plazas, lined with stone, and plastered. (The *chultun* of northern Yucatan therefore had a different function from the food-storage pits of Tikal by the same name.)

Archaeologically Puuc refers to a new cultural tradition, a development spawned by northern Campeche together with indigenous cultures of western Yucatán. It also absorbed architectural features from the Chenes and Río Bec areas and gradually assimilated intrusive foreign elements. By A.D. 800 Puuc was the dominant architectural style in western Yucatán and as population increased, it spread to other sites such as Dzibilchaltún, Oxkintok, Ake, and Yaxuná.

The beginnings of Puuc architecture (proto-Puuc) can be found at Edzná from A.D. 633 to 810 when part of its 5-story pyramid may have been built. Early Puuc is dated at A.D. 700–800 and the late or Classic Puuc from A.D. 800 to 900/950 (Kowalski, 1987). This latter period embraces the visible Puuc structures seen today which are believed to be partly contemporaneous with some of the Mexican buildings at Chichén Itzá.

In Puuc style of construction, small mosaic stones are tenoned into a rubble concrete core. Prior to construction, quantities of presculptured stone elements were assembled and then combined as needed into masks and geometric designs producing repetitious motifs. This is in contrast to older block masonry construction where big slabs of stone faced with mortar carry the load. In addition, a storied effect is created in Puuc buildings by setting back rows of chambers in a staggered formation.

Although Puuc sites do not seem to conform to any particular plan, they paid special attention to the twice yearly zenith passage of the sun. Orientation of buildings are skewed to the sunset, anticipating the zenith passage by 20 days, one uinal (Aveni and Hartung, 1986).

Uxmal   The largest of all the Puuc sites and a very beautiful one is Uxmal, a well-known center about 78 km south of Mérida (Andrews IV, 1965; Morley *et al.*,

1983; Kowalski, 1985a,b, 1987). The greatest structures are grouped in rather close proximity: the effect is stunning. Despite being known for a long time, there is still little information regarding population of the site or settlement patterns.

The Nunnery or Las Monjas, is a huge quadrangle of four separate buildings that surround a great court, accessed either at the corners or via the main entrance formed by a corbeled arch on the south side. The long buildings contain numerous chambers, each with its own doorway. Façades are intricately decorated by small cut stones set in masonry (Figure 6.68). Motifs in the friezes are huts among latticed panels, rain-god masks, small columns, and serpent heads. The decoration of the north building includes Tlaloc with the year-sign headdress, bound captives, and exposed genitals. Uxmal is unusual in having a number of phallic sculptures. To the south of the main center, the Temple of the Phallus is named for its façade decorated with this motif (Morley et al., 1983).

The Pyramid of the Magician (El Adivino), rises sharply just east of the Nunnery Quadrangle (Figure 6.69). It has a roughly elliptical base and was remodeled five times, containing styles ranging over four centuries. The earliest structure (A.D. 569) is decorated with Teotihuacan features such as those seen in the southern lowlands. Most Mexican elements occur during the ninth century, for example, the feathered serpents on the west façade of the Nunnery and in the ball court, and skull and bone motifs in the Cemetery Group.

The Uxmal ball court has high vertical playing walls and tenoned stone rings

FIGURE 6.68   Las Monjas (the Nunnery) at Uxmal, Yucatán. Puuc style architecture of stone mosaic façades. (Courtesy of the Instituto Nacional de Antropología e Historia, Mexico.)

FIGURE 6.69 El Adivino (the House of the Magician) pyramid at Uxmal, Yucatán. (Photographed by the author.)

typical of seventh century Yucatán ball courts. The ring is inscribed with a date of A.D. 649. Ball-players in 3-dimensional stone sculpture were found in a pile of fragments in the Nunnery Quadrangle dated about A.D. 653.

Impressive for its tremendous size, the House of the Governor is the culmination of Puuc architecture. It consists of a massive central building with a tripartite façade and contains a series of spacious interior chambers. The façade is decorated in Puuc style with long-snouted mask panels, stepped frets, and lattice or mat-motifs (symbols of royal power), an outgrowth of Classic Maya tradition with antecedents found at Uaxactún, Tikal, and Altun Há. The entire structure rests on a stepped platform some 122 m long by 27 m wide, set on a natural elevation. This may be the last structure erected at Uxmal and is a tribute to its fine workmanship. The masonry is expertly finished. Stones of the vaults are cut, pecked, and ground smooth. The mosaic façade is sharp in detail (Figure 6.70) (Kowalski, 1987).

Little Puuc architecture was built following A.D. 900. The last monument was probably Stela 14, dated at A.D. 907. Kowalski dates the House of the Governor at A.D. 900–915. This brings us to a personality named Lord Chac, Uxmal's most famous ruler. He commissioned this remarkable building to serve both as his residence and as the seat of power and administrative center. The broad central stairway leads to large chambers suitable for holding formal audiences.

Lord Chac headed one of the powerful dynasties in northern Yucatán and is mentioned in texts at both Kabah and Chichén Itzá. He is named on a small cylindrical altar south of the House of the Governor along with his father, Chac Uinal Kan, and

FIGURE 6.70   Detail of fine Puuc workmanship on the façade of the Governor's Palace, Uxmal. (Courtesy of the Instituto Nacional de Antropología e Historia, Mexico.)

his mother, Lady Bone. Lord Chac is probably the richly attired figure depicted on Stela 7, standing on a bicephalic jaguar throne. A throne like this is still in place today in front of the central doorway of the House of the Governor. Such jaguar thrones or seats are known from Copán and Piedras Negras, but the closest parallel to the one at Uxmal is the bicephalic throne represented on the Oval Tablet in House E at Palenque.

The House of the Governor shares with Piedras Negras the specialized palace features of serving both as a royal residence and as an audience chamber; the same broad stairway; large central chambers; an axially placed throne; and the sculpture of a seated figure of royalty (Lord Chac?). In this case the figure is placed over the central doorway instead of using the stela format common in the south.

Aside from these functions, the House of the Governor served as some kind of astronomical observatory associated with a Venus cult whose symbols also appear on the House of the Magician and in the Nunnery Quadrangle. At Uxmal most buildings are oriented 9° off cardinal directions clockwise, but the House of the Governor is oriented 20° clockwise. This deviation places it in line with a particular mound on the horizon corresponding to the azimuth of Venus as it rose over the Yucatán plain (Kowalski, 1987).

Uxmal was abandoned toward the end of the tenth century for reasons as yet unknown, but was used later on as a shrine of the Xiu after the fall of Mayapán (see page 431).

Kabah   Kabah was once approached through an arch connecting this site with Uxmal 18 km away (Figure 6.71). One arrives today on a road beside the arch to see one of the most lavishly decorated Puuc buildings in existence. Known as the Codz Poop or Palace of the Masks, its façade is completely covered with stone mosaic masks with long hooked noses and door jambs carved with figures engaged in taking captives with *atlatls* and spears (Figure 6.72). Ten doorways lead to pairs of inner chambers one behind the other. Set on a huge artificial platform, the Codz Poop is the most elaborate and imposing structure at Kabah.

Sayil   Five km south of Kabah is Sayil. A Puuc site known for its impressive 3-tiered Great Palace structure, it has only recently been investigated (Sabloff, 1990). Until these excavations, directed by Jeremy Sabloff and Gair Tourtellot, our knowledge of Sayil was limited to an early survey map done by Ed Shook and Harry Pollock for the Carnegie institution of Washington, and descriptions of the impressive Great Palace that dominates the site. Now, after five field seasons (1983–1988), we know that Sayil was occupied for a relatively short span of time. It was a city with an urban population of 10,000 with approximately 7000 more living in the suburbs. The platforms that once supported perishable dwellings were so well preserved that floor plans could be accurately mapped. Inhabitants surrounded their platforms with garden plots, and *chultuns* provided them with potable water. However, by A.D. 900 the carrying capacity of the land had been reached, which probably hastened the sudden

FIGURE 6.71   The arch over the *sacbé* at Kabah, Yucatán. (Courtesy of the Instituto Nacional de Antropología e Historia, Mexico.)

FIGURE 6.72   The Codz Poop structure at Kabah, Yucatán. Puuc style architecture with a façade solidly decorated with mosaic masks. (Courtesy of the Instituto Nacional de Antropología, Mexico.)

demise of the city. The work at Sayil is a good example of the type of intensive excavation that is needed to understand these ancient sites.

Labná   A 2-story palace similar to that of Sayil was built at the neighboring site of Labná, only 18 km to the southeast. From this structure a short *sacbé* leads to a small palace group reached by passing under Labná's most famous monument, an elegant stone mosaic arch, considered to be one of the finest examples of Puuc architecture. Beyond, a small group of buildings contain an edifice known as the Mirador. Although now collapsed, its frontal roof comb was once decorated with a stucco relief over the door showing two ball-players in action.

Dzibilchaltún   Moving north of Uxmal, activity at Komchén on the northwestern plain ceased at the close of the Late Preclassic and the Dzibilchaltún area was almost unoccupied during the Early Classic. During the Late Classic (A.D. 700–1000), Dzibilchaltún achieved a population of 50,000 and the city expanded to its maximum size (Kurjack, 1974). This is one of the few sites where extensive and systematic investigations have been carried out in northern Yucatán (Andrews IV and Andrews V, 1980).

The presence of outsiders around A.D. 600 led to the erection of a platform in talud-tablero style in one of the outlying areas to the west. This may have been the work of Mexicanized merchants involved with the coastal salt beds a short distance away. It was of short duration, at which time the center of Dzibilchaltún was almost deserted. A century later it suddenly embarked on a massive building program that raised huge temple/pyramids, small platforms, and multi-room vaulted structures. These were concentrated around the Xlacah Cenote, the fresh water supply, located in a corner of the main plaza. Another was outside the center (Figure 6.73). Low platforms supported stone-walled, thatch-roofed houses. Most of these had a single doorway in the center front and activity would have taken place outside on the platform. Some of these platforms were higher than others, height perhaps being a sign of status. Residential property walls and grouping of structures provided considerable privacy (Kurjack and Garza, 1981).

The most interesting building is the Temple of the Seven Dolls (Figure 6.74). The original structure built in A.D. 700 was square-shaped with stairs on all sides. The interior consisted of a corridor surrounding a vaulted room with a raised roof that formed a low tower. Elaborate stucco masks once decorated the exterior upper façades, and windows were placed beside two of the entryways. Eventually the entire structure was covered by a large pyramid still maintaining the radial plan. In the Late Postclassic, the original building was uncovered and after adding an altar, it was used as a shrine. The name of Seven Dolls is derived from the finding of seven clay figurines on the floor in front of the altar (Morley *et al.*, 1983).

The ground plan and masonry of the Seven Dolls is similar to the Palace at Palenque. Andrews V (1981) sees many features shared both with Palenque and other Classic sites in the southern Maya lowlands. Even some of the pottery at Dzibilchaltún may have been derived from western prototypes.

Dzibilchaltún was the most powerful of a number of independent polities in northern Yucatán in the seventh and eighth centuries. Izamal and Tihoo (the site of

FIGURE 6.73   The Xlopah Cenote at Dzibilchaltún. (Courtesy of the Instituto Nacional de Antropología e Historia, Mexico.)

FIGURE 6.74   The Temple of the Seven Dolls, Dzibilchaltún, Yucatán. (Courtesy of the Instituto Nacional de Antropología e Historia, Mexico).

Mérida) were other large inland centers and a number of these were connected by causeways. Puuc architecture did not arrive here until about A.D. 830. Then the earlier block-masonry walls and slab-vaults were replaced by vaulted buildings of concrete walls. Cut veneer mosaic stones replaced modeled stucco facades. The city now reflected the wealth acquired by the enterprising merchants, but as we approach the end of the Late Classic Period, deterioration becomes evident in construction and artifacts.

We do not know exactly what role Tihoo played in the downfall of Dzibilchaltún, but we do know that it benefited, outstripping her neighbor in size and prosperity and no doubt assuming control over the salt beds as well. Tihoo was fortified along with many other sites at this time such as Izamal and Chunchucmil, but apparently not Dzibilchaltún.

The foreign intrusions at Chichén Itzá effectively eclipsed Dzibilchaltún around A.D. 1000 and its early prominence in the mercantile world passed to Chichén and to coastal communities such as Cozumel. As often happened, Dzibilchaltún settled down to become a terminus of pilgrimages.

THE PUTÚN (CHONTAL-MAYA) AND THE ITZÁ

I have already referred briefly to Putún merchants, Itzá, and Mexicans. Before going further, it would be well to leave the ruins for a while to look at the background of these diverse groups that have a prominent role in the remaining Maya history. The following is a partial reconstruction of Maya history from the eighth to the twelfth centuries, based largely on Andrews and Robles (1985) Carmack (1981), Chase (1985a), Rice and Rice (1984), Robles and Andrews (1986), Ball and Taschek (1989), Fox (1987), Sabloff (1990), Kowalski (1989), Sharer (1983). These authors have worked with the ethnohistorical data of the Books of the Chilam Balam and with the archaeological remains including epigraphic material. The complex picture that follows should be considered as highly speculative because of the fragmentary archaeological record and the nature of the literary sources. However, we have come a long way in the last few years from the time the Itzá were seen as aimless wanderers constantly coming and going in many directions. The many directions are still there, but the Itzá are emerging as smart, purposeful, ambitious, aggressive entrepreneurs. Our tale opens in the Late Classic years of the Chontalapa. (Map 6.2).

The Chontalapa

A great movement of peoples in Mesoamerica in the eighth and ninth centuries had a profound effect on the Maya. The lowland area of the Gulf of Mexico known as the Chontalapa (coastal Tabasco and southwestern Campeche) became a kind of staging area for ensuing migrations (Fox, 1987). In the northern part, Mexican influence was strong, but rounding the Gulf of Mexico toward Yucatán, Maya features predominated. In between, central Tabasco was a hodgepodge of Mesoamerican languages (Zoque, Náhuatl, Mayan) and cultural currents.

The importance of the Chontalapa can hardly be overemphasized. It was a frontier region where the very edge of the Maya world came in contact with the local Chontal population. This was the homeland of peoples we call the Itzá, Xiu, Quiché, and Cakchiquel, the best known of various lineage groups who moved out from this area to highland Chiapas and Guatemala, to Yucatán, Belize, and eventually to the far eastern edge of Mesoamerica around Nito and Naco, Honduras.

West Population in the Chontalapa greatly increased in the Late Classic when the Olmeca/Xicalanca were expelled from the region of Cholula in highland central Mexico. Timing is debatable. These people are also referred to as the "historic Olmec" or Mixteca/Popoloca, who had ancient ties to southern Veracruz and Tabasco (Davies, 1977; Fox, 1987). Some Maya were already known to these Olmeca in view of their contacts at Cacaxtla, so by moving down to the Gulf Coast they were hardly entering an alien society. Both groups already shared the ancient concept of the feathered serpent and as intermarriage took place, Mexican cultural patterns were easily incorporated into the local social fabric.

The region settled by the Olmeca was Acalán, an area lying inland between the Candelaria and San Pedro rivers in southwestern Campeche (see Map 8.1). This offered fine farmland and a strategic location on a navigable river system that provided an excellent base for departing groups of émigrés.

Coastal Yucatán was easily accessible by canoe and other parts of the Maya world could be reached by canoeing up the major rivers and making portages between tributaries. Fox (1987) deals at some length with migrations that either expanded outward from a center, or what he calls "leap-frog migrations" of small groups who broke away to take up land at great distances where they found economic and environmental conditions compatible with those they left behind.

The very Late Classic diaspora took place from this Gulf Coast region, including the adventurous Chontal-Maya incursions to northern Yucatán and various sites along the Usumacinta River drainage. Thompson (1970) called these people the Putún and emphasized their mercantile interests. Trade no doubt played a role, although Fox feels that trade cannot account for all the movements of people that took place at this time. Not all Chontal migrants were merchant minded. Some communities of less social stature moved out of Acalán into remote mountain regions of the Chiapas highlands. They used the same riverine routes inland to the Pasión region and from there the Río Chixoy led the way to the Chiapas mountains.

After Teotihuacan withdrew from the commercial world in the eighth century, the Chontal-Maya (Putún/Itzá) were no longer content to be in the middle between the Mexicans and the Mayans. They moved immediately to assume a more aggressive posture and transform what had been a passive role as intermediaries into a whole new system of relationships with the political and economic environment. Toward the late eighth century, they began to seize land and establish their own outposts and distributive centers, and organize the takeovers of commodity resource zones. In this they were highly successful. From the Chontalapa some based themselves at Palenque between the seventh and ninth centuries. Others pushed up the Usumacinta river to Yaxchilán and still others continued on to the Pasión sites of Altar de Sacrificios and Seibal.

These incursions brought fine paste wares and Mexican iconography to the Usumacinta sites in the eighth century, affecting much of the southern lowlands. One western Itzá intrusion (perhaps originating in the north; see Edzná, page 343) around A.D. 771 brought new ideas that led to a de-emphasis on the stela cult. At Palenque, Piedras Negras, and Yaxchilán we find few stelae but abundant carvings and texts on lintels and tablets and also wall paintings. Proskouriakoff (1950) noted ties between Piedras Negras and the island of Jaina, and thought Yaxchilán might have been under the control of foreigners. A Yucatec style of dating appeared early in this western region. The cessation of stela erections spread to a number of sites, including Tikal, Uaxactún, and Seibal around A.D. 800.

Thus a kind of "stelae hiatus" is seen, after which their carving was resumed. No Cycle 10 monuments (i.e., Baktun 10) were erected at Usumacinta sites. The same influences reached the Motagua River drainage at Copán and Quiriguá. Some of this outside influence in the ninth century is derived from western Yucatán, not Chichén Itzá.

North   The Itzá appear in our history as the Putún or Chontal Maya around the year A.D. 751 when we first see their intrusions in the western river regions. In the north the Itzá came as merchant-intruders with well-defined goals of conquest, and after taking Chichén Itzá they became the dominant rulers of this capital, controlling the largest Maya territory in history. The Late Classic years in northern Yucatán form a single continuous development through the terminal Classic and Early Postclassic Periods lasting until A.D. 1200. In this I follow several authors who stress this unity (Andrews V and Sabloff, 1986; Schele and Freidel, 1990; Sabloff, 1990). In the light of our present knowledge the fall of the Itzá (ca. A.D. 1200) initiates another regime and chapter in Maya history.

From the Chontalapa the Itzá are thought to have first established settlements along the west coast of Yucatán (at Champotón?) and possibly farther north at Chunchucmil located near rich salt beds. According to the Books of the Chilam Balam these early Itzá moved inland from the east coast. Folan, Jr. *et al.* (1983) tell us that in the ninth century some Chontal-speaking Maya (the Itzá) arrived on the east coast, stopped at Cobá, and continued on to Chichén Itzá. Despite the chronicles, archaeology would seem to support a drive inland from the west coast. (Perhaps both are possible?)

The arrival of the Itzá created a whole new power structure. There was an overlap of at least 50 years in the ninth century when Cobá and the Puuc communities found themselves with an unwelcome Itzá intrusion. We know these Itzá to have been aggressive warrior-merchants who surely came looking for a territorial base in northern Yucatán, knowing the value of salt exploitation and maritime trade. They were probably not well received, intruding in a region already well populated by competing communities. Uxmal, for example, enclosed 50 ha with fortifications, and smaller sites, Cuca, Chunchucmil, Ake, Muna, and Chacchob fortified from 15 to 30 ha (Kurjack and Garza, 1981). Monumental structures were often built outside the defenses, suggesting little central control. Communities were probably politically unstable, a situation that must have benefited the incoming Itzá.

The date of their arrival has been difficult to determine but the traditional date of A.D. 918 is now seen as too late. Ball and Taschek (1989) prefer A.D. 771. Schele and Freidel suggest a ninth century date and believe Izamal may have been an early Itzá capital (1990: 498). The time of arrival is problematical but their rise to power is well established. In A.D. 850 we find their bellicose successes celebrated at Chichén Itzá by a military Itzá leader of the Chontal Maya named Kakupacal. This person is mentioned in the famous Books of Chilam Balam. In these fragmented texts we read of competing communities and political struggles of prominent families from the terminal Classic into the Colonial Period. There are also conflicting opinions of the Itzá, the descriptions ranging from talented and brilliant administrators to rogues of the worst order.

The Itzá takeover of Chichén Itzá was in no way an accident or haphazard event, but represents careful forward planning and calculation. The goal in mind was to gain control and make Chichén a leading base for the import/export trade and to acquire management of any resources, such as salt, for commercial exploitation. The Itzá were successful but in the process were abrasive, creating friction and rousing the enmity of competitors. Understandably, they were challenged in frequent confrontations.

Kakupacal is the only major leader named in the inscriptions, who reputedly was related dynastically to the rulers of Palenque. The major buildings of Chichén Itzá erected from A.D. 869 to 881 honored him as well as his family and probably his prowess in war. It was during his reign that some Itzá groups led expansionist programs south where they continued to offer transport and distribution of goods from coastal communities. Comalcalco may have been one participant in this enterprise, replacing Matacapan. Kakupacal is credited with the conquest of Champotón (Chakan-putún), an important port on the west coast of Yucatán (see Map 8.1). The date of this seizure is a matter of debate (Ball and Taschek, 1989), but there is no doubt that the Itzá were highly successful in their political and economic adventures during the ninth to twelfth centuries.

The Western Highlands of Chiapas and Guatemala

The two basic routes from the southern Maya lowlands to the highlands were the Usumacinta-Chixoy River combination and the Motagua River drainage. Other Chontalapa groups farther west followed the Grijalva River to reach highland Chiapas. The Pasión region at the headwaters of the Usumacinta was a hub for traffic coming from all directions and would have served as a starting point for groups heading into the highlands of Chiapas and Guatemala.

One of the earliest dates in the highlands is at Chinkultic, Chiapas, where a stela dated A.D. 810 may reflect the beginning of a diaspora of Maya to the highlands. Earlier there were no dated monuments in this part of Chiapas (Kowalski, 1989).

Kowalski (1989) believes that some members of the Itzá in Yucatán moved south after A.D. 849 into the Pasión drainage and continued on into the Comitán Valley in highland Chiapas and the Chacula district in Guatemala. A stela at Comitán records a date of A.D. 874 and another at Quen Santo, Guatemala, is dated at A.D. 879. Cycle 10 stelae at Quen Santo and Uaxac Canal in highland Guatemala (Terminal Classic/ Early Postclassic) suggest a trade network that funtioned from these sites (A.D. 770/ 900–1200) by way of Chinkultic in the Comitán Valley to the Usumacinta River centers and from there continued west to the Gulf coast.

Although some settlers had come earlier, the most dramatic incursions were those at the end of the ninth century. These were Chontal Maya, belonging to the same Itzá family of warriors who established the new lineage at Chichén Itzá. Kowalski (1989) has identified two names on the stelae at Quen Santo as being common ones at Chichén Itzá. One is "Jawbone-Legbone," father of Kakupacal. Either they refer to northern Yucatecans who went to Seibal and continued on up to Chiapas after A.D.

849, or both Chiapas and Yucatán share family ties and political connections with new rulers in the south.

These ninth century intruders were wary of settling in open valleys and chose to locate in defensible positions such as hilltops or high locations on the brink of a ravine. They often felt the need of further protection and added ditch-and-wall fortifications (Morley *et al.*, 1983).

East   An eastern intrusion into the southern lowlands from northern Yucatán seems to have taken place around A.D. 810. The postulated route headed east from Chichén Itzá to reach Cozumel and then turned south along the coast of Quintana Roo and Belize. Reaching the Bay of Chetumal, there are two settlements that testify to an Itzá presence at this time. The Itzá may have come here to arrange a trading facility to serve as a terminus for an overland corridor to the Gulf of Mexico. The chronicles speak of Champotón on the Campeche coast being seized by Itzá of Kakupacal. Such a corridor might have run west from Aventura, 6 km from Chetumal Bay across the peninsula passing through Becán. A spur may have branched off to the south to El Tigre on the Candelaria River and followed it to the Laguna de Términos ending at Guarixes (See Map 6.5). Such a route would have served the dual purpose of an overland all-weather route for trans-shipment of goods, as well as further isolating Cobá and effectively strangling its economic activity (Andrews and Robles, 1985; Ball and Taschek, 1989). Future excavations in this area will be of interest to see if this route is confirmed. It surely would have had many advantages for the Itzá.

The other Itzá-related site is Nohmul, a major settlement only 20 km southwest of Aventura on the Río Hondo. Nohmul is a site with a long history of continuous occupation surviving the southern collapse to receive a new influx of elites from the north about this time. New buildings were constructed over and alongside Late Classic ones. Structure 20 is a particular type of residence called a patio-quad seldom found in the Maya area outside of Chichén Itzá. Another structure (circular) is also compared to Chichén's Caracol (Chase and Chase, 1982). Ceramics, however, include both Sotuta and Cehpech spheres along with some terminal Classic wares of the southern lowlands. That both areas would have been in contact with Nohmul is natural since it is situated to deal with both north and south and could have controlled the river routes to the interior as well as having access to the maritime trade along the east coast.

If some travelers branched off for Aventura or Nohmul, others continued on south, choosing to go inland to Caracol and Machaquilá, eventually reaching Seibal, or continuing up the Motagua River to Quiriguá (Chase, 1985a). The latter was a key route for movement of jade, obsidian, and quetzal feathers to the coastal plain from the Guatemalan highlands. We have noted that the Postclassic inhabitants of Quiriguá were in touch with Chichén Itzá and the east coast cultures in late times. It is possible that the Itzá controlled this river route to the highlands as well as east coast trade.

At this point we can speak of western Itzá on the Gulf Coast and an eastern contingent around the Petén lakes and southern Belize, and still another on the

Motagua River at Quiriguá. Eventually these groups were destined to become competitors, but prior to the tenth century, the easterners were simply participants in the ongoing Itzá trade monopoly based at Chichén Itzá.

Seibal   Returning now to the Pasión region laid waste by the Petexbatún wars (see page 307), Seibal had survived only to find newcomers arriving from downstream. These were the Chontal Putún who had pushed up the river past Piedras Negras and Yaxchilán that were already carving their final monuments about ten years after Palenque laid down its tools. A direct effect of these intruders was to cause the cessation of stela erection in the southwestern lowlands and parts of the Petén (Chase, 1985a).

At Seibal, after a break in carving stela from A.D. 800 to 849, stelae were again erected but this time by a new group of Mexicanized Maya believed to have come in from the east (Figure 6.75). This intrusion took place around A.D. 810, only slightly after the arrival of the western Putún. At Seibal east met west.

The resumption of stela erection in A.D. 849 was fostered by an interesting figure, Ah-Bolon-Tun. He was a foreigner with an undeformed head and wore his hair long

FIGURE 6.75   A non-Maya stela at Seibal, Guatemala. Evidence of late ninth century intruders. (Photographed by Lorraine Matys.)

(Schele and Freidel, 1990). Despite his non-Maya appearance, he adhered to the Classic Maya way of life and commissioned Temple A-3 to celebrate an important baktun period-ending date in A.D. 849 (Figure 6.76).

This temple was placed in the center of the south plaza with stairs leading up all four sides, a radial plan modeled perhaps on the High Priest's Grave at Chichén Itzá (Schele and Freidel, 1990). The style was Puuc with veneer masonry and new iconographic symbols of northern Yucatán. But it was in Classic Maya attire that Ah-Bolon-Tun appears in the stucco reliefs over each of the four entrances to his temple. A stela was erected inside the temple and four more at the base of each stairway, creating a quincunz pattern of 5, a Venus number (see Coggins, 1990, for the related significance of baktun endings at Seibal and Tikal). On these stelae depicting 5 rulers, the northern one notes that lords from Tikal, Calakmul, and Motul de San José gathered at Seibal to celebrate the period-ending rites. So we know that as late as the ninth century these centers were still making an effort to maintain the old traditions of the Classic Maya.

Motul de San José, mentioned on the stela above, was a village on the north shore of Lake Petén Itzá. This was one of the last capitals of the southern lowlands but has never been systematically investigated. The IK-sign may have been its emblem. Unfortunately, all mounds were trenched and looted in the 1980s (Mexicon, 1988).

Central Mexican elements that were introduced at this time to the Pasión region

FIGURE 6.76 Seibal. Temple A-3, commissioned to celebrate a period-ending date in A.D. 849. The structure has many Puuc features of the north, and was built in a radial pattern. A stela was placed at the base of each of the four stairways, and a fifth at the entrance to the temple. (Photographed by Lorraine Matys.)

are Ehécatl figures, darts, *atlatls*, and Mexican day-signs. The "knife-wing" bird headdress (Graham, 1973) worn by a figure on Stela 1 that was erected by Ah-Bolon-Tun in A.D. 860 bears a striking resemblance to that on the Temple of the Four Lintels at Chichén Itzá. The Seibal figure, together with other elements shared with Chichén, led Kowalski (1989) to suggest that the Chichén texts refer to the same person depicted on Seibal's Stela 1. Further evidence from carvings, ball courts, ceramics, and detail of costume linking Seibal with the Itzá in northern Yucatán support an ethnic affiliation.

Seibal was deteriorating and no effort by the last rulers could revitalize the old city. Inscriptions were confused, poorly executed, and would not have been understood by a learned scribe. The last monument erected at Seibal, Stela 17 in A.D. 889, depicts two figures that face each other. The one on the left is dressed as a Classic Mayan, holding the manikin scepter in his left hand while he raises his right hand and arm in a "traditional gesture of friendship or submission." A non-Maya foreigner on the right receives this gesture (Chase, 1985a).

Thus evidence of foreign intrusions from east and west is present at the base of the peninsula along the river sites. Signs of the Itzás' passing are recorded on monuments along the way, an example being the prowling jaguar at Atasta near Xicalango. Meanwhile, another Chontal group had settled around the Petén lakes and became intermediaries between the central Maya lowlands and the eastern riverine Caribbean region.

Northeast of Seibal, the sites of Yaxhá, Ucanal, Ixlú, and Jimbal exhibit a new sky-figure, possibly Itzá related, that appears in their ninth century monuments. The figure in the upper register is a sky deity that peers down from a sun disk (Chase, 1985a; Hellmuth, 1986). Related versions exist at Naranjo, Flores, and Seibal. This would logically fall in the path of the eastern intrusion, yet the Itzá presence at these sites may be derived instead from westerners at Seibal who moved in after the collapse of the Petexbatún state (Freidel, 1985; Chase, 1985a).

Although a number of sites inscribed their final date at A.D. 810, this does not necessarily mean immediate abandonment. These include Piedras Negras, Chinkultic, Calakmul, Naranjo, and Quiriguá. Seibal, Uaxactún and, Jimbal stopped at A.D. 889. The last-known long Count date is from Toniná, that site off the major trade routes that captured and beheaded a Palenque king. This final date, January 20, 909, was effected in the traditional style of the southern lowlands.

Jaina

Returning to the north via the west coast of Yucatán, one passes by the extraordinary island of Jaina, "House on the Water." Jaina is located 32 km north of Campeche and is separated from the mainland at low tide by mangrove swamps and palms. This site has two small ceremonial centers, Zayosal and El Zacpool, and a small ball court. The buildings were all constructed of an earth nucleus faced with irregular stones that were stuccoed and painted.

Some of the most beautiful clay figurines in the New World were placed in Jaina graves and the island is famous as a cemetery. We do not know if elites from mainland areas were buried at Jaina or if the graves are those of the local inhabitants only. The island was used for more than 700 years as a major coastal port for fishing and trading (Piña Chan, 1968; Andrews 1990a).

The figures display both the idealized Maya beauty and realistic old men, invalids, hunchbacks, or dwarfs; animals and abstract objects are also represented. The finest figures are solid and were hand modeled prior to A.D. 650, while more standardized, hollow examples were produced by molds thereafter. Both techniques might be combined in one figurine—a mold-made body with a hand-modeled head. Details of faces and headdresses were given great attention; hands and feet were less well done. Molded figures concentrate on religious themes such as the Sun God or Moon Goddess (Fonserrada de Molina and Cárdos de Méndez, 1988). Some examples are whistles and others rattles (Figure 6.77), but all were manufactured primarily as grave offerings (Piña Chan, 1968).

Cobá

Northeastern Yucatán had developed in a different tradition from the west, retaining close ties to the Petén and the southern lowlands. A corridor of Petén-like centers are known to have existed from Quintana Roo up the Río Hondo, and Cobá was the most northern related site. At the same time, Cobá shared certain pottery styles (the Cehpech Ceramic Sphere) with Uxmal and adopted the northern penchant for constructing masonry causeways, the *sacbeob*. Architecture, however, clung to the more conservative tradition of the southern lowlands. The Classic stela cult that celebrated kingship and commemorated personal events was a practice begun at Cobá in A.D. 618. Stela 1, dated at A.D. 682, shows Cobá's ruler dressed as a Holmul dancer, standing atop two bound captives flanked by two others (Schele and Freidel, 1990). Recall that Ruler 1 of Dos Pilas sent his daughter off to marry into the royalty of Naranjo (see page 426). Her name is inscribed on this stela at Cobá, so the event must have been of some importance to these northerners who may have attended the festivities.

In the shift of focus to northern Yucatán in the tenth century, Cobá not only survived, but increased in power to become the dominant polity on the northeastern plains (Freidel, 1985). It is believed to have controlled the area from Yaxuná to the Caribbean coast, having Xelhá as its port. It was a natural role for Cobá because the fairly uniform environment tended to facilitate communication and centralization of settlements. Cobá was well linked to the south by rivers, to the east with the Bay of Honduras, and with the Puuc centers in the west. It had occupied the role of middle-man in the north–south trade since the Late Preclassic (Robles and Andrews, 1986).

Cobá was set among five shallow lakes. Here it built its largest pyramid Nohoch Mul (Structure 1) (Figure 6.78), amidst an architectural complex at the beginning of the Cobá-Yaxuná causeway. The main group of structures to the southwest was dominated by an equally high pyramid of 24 m. Two ball courts were added, both in the style of the Copán region with short playing walls and large, sloping benches. Rather than using serpent or bird heads, however, the Cobá courts have tenoned stone

a   b   c   d

FIGURE 6.77   Jaina figurines.
a. A hand-modeled, standing figure of a dignitary, perhaps a warrior. Traces of painted decoration. Height: 11.5 cm. (Courtesy of the Museum of the American Indian, Heye Foundation, N.Y. [22/6348].)
b. Delicate figure; a woman in a pod. A water-lily spirit? Late Classic. Height: 8.25 cm. (The Metropolitan Museum of Art. The Michael C. Rockefeller Memorial Collection, bequest of Nelson A. Rockefeller, 1979 [1979.206.728].)
c. Standing figure of a warrior holding a rectangular shield in his left hand. The paint or tatooing on the face symbolizes rulership. Height: 21.5 cm. (The Denver Art Museum. Photographed by Justin Kerr [No. 2818].)
d. Hollow human figure, a redware rattle. Greatest attention was focused on the head and headdress. Height: 17.5 cm. (Courtesy of the Museum of the American Indian, Heye Foundation, N.Y. [21/4632].)

rings as goals. At its peak, Cobá is estimated to have occupied about 30 km plus satellite cummunities.

Communication was facilitated by a system of masonry causeways providing easy and direct access between centers. These are one of the most characteristic features of northern Yucatán. Road building was extremely labor intensive and an expensive enterprise. The *sacbé* acted as a cohesive factor and may have symbolized alliances between high-status families. In all, Cobá boasts 16 limestone roads. These were raised as much as 2.5 m above ground level, were 4.5 m wide, and topped with a natural lime cement packed down using huge rollers. One giant roller was found to weigh 5 tons; it would have needed 15 men to push it along (Morley *et al.*, 1983). Of the 43 roads that intersected at Cobá (Kurjack and Garza, 1981), the most notable was

FIGURE 6.78 Nohoch Mul pyramid (Structure 1) at Cobá. (Photographed by Lorraine Matys.)

a 100-km *sacbé* that connected Cobá with Yaxuná. But there were many more. From Izamal, two causeways of 13 km and 32 km radiated to outlying areas. Uxmal and Kabah were connected by an 18-km causeway 4 m wide and 30 cm high. An 8-m-wide causeway ran out from Ucí for 18 km and changed directions to reach another center.

It is not clear if the Cobá-Yaxuná causeway was constructed before the Itzá arrived, or in response to their coming. Robles and Andrews (1986) suggest the year A.D. 800 for its construction.

Yaxuná had been prominent early in Preclassic and Early Classic years when massive pyramids were raised. Nothing much happened in the Late Classic, but now it sprang to life as a rich urban center in the ninth century. It not only formed the border between Cobá's domain and the Puuc cities to the west, but it also set the stage for the economic and political struggles that were to ensue between Cobá and Chichén Itzá. Yaxuná was revitalized and rebuilt, adding a ball court with its associated temples and platforms. The Puuc cities must have lent a hand, as the new structures are done in their style, whereas nothing suggests participation by Cobá.

Schele and Freidel (1990) believe that war was under way between Cobá and

Chichén Itzá by A.D. 850. Apparently this conflict went on for years. A final battle took place on the fields of Yaxuná and its war reliefs were "cast down from its temples." This was a blow that lessened Cobá's ability to compete commercially, but there is no sign that it was ever occupied by the Itzá. The only battle scars are found at Yaxuná, which seems to have borne the brunt of the competition. At Cobá only the public works program halted and outlying communities abandoned their homes, many moving coser to the center.

The Puuc communities did not prosper after Chichén Itzá attained great power, eventually dominating northern Yucatán. Gradually they declined one by one. Cobá retained its indigenous flavor and independence but was further weakened after the battle when commercial ties were cut by Chichén's expansion to the east coast, cutting off Cobá's maritime trade. The Sotuta Ceramic Sphere (a pottery complex associated with the Itzá) spread from coast to coast across northern Yucatán, but few examples are found in Cobá's terrain, where people adhered to the Cehpech style. In border areas, the ceramics may be mixed. Life must have been difficult, but Cobá hung on. It was probably reaching the capacity of its resource base in the twelfth century and there was no way of increasing agricultural production with the technology available.

By A.D. 1000 an irreversible decline set in and the communities at the terminals of the *sacbeob* were abandoned. People still lived around the lakes and old city core until A.D. 1200. Then Cobá failed about the same time as her powerful Itzá neighbor.

Chichén Itzá

It is time to examine the well-known center of northern Yucatán, Chichén Itzá, located on the flat plain 124 km east of Tihoo, today's Mérida. This is a site with so many historical references in the early chronicles that one of the main difficulties in using them has been their correlation with archaeological remains.

Chichén Itzá captured headlines long ago as the result of the 20-year excavations of the Carnegie Institution of Washington, D.C. that began in 1924 under Sylvanus Morley and have been continued under INAH in recent years. When one thinks of Chichén Itzá, the names of the following scholars come to mind: Oliver Ricketson, Harry Pollock, Eric Thompson, Tatiana Proskouriakoff, Alfred V. Kidder, Alberto Ruz, and Jorge Acosta.

Archaeological work has concentrated on clearing, consolidating, and restoring the major buildings. To date, despite its fame, there is little we know of population estimates, settlement patterns, and housing. Warfare is a prominent iconographic theme, but did any battles take place at Chichén? Ruz Lhuillier (1951) tells us that the large structures on the North Terrace were enclosed by a high wall forming an irregular polygon with entrances at the four cardinal points, the sides of which were faced with dressed stone. The wall is now entirely destroyed, so it is not known if it had a parapet, nor can its dimensions be determined. Although not visible today, Ruz assured me in the 1970s that Chichén Itzá's central area had been thus fortified.

The early history of Chichén Itzá begins in the late 800s when Puuc and early Maya structures were built. Some of the earliest remains are out of sight, to be seen only via tunnels buried beneath the later structures we see today. Most of the major Maya buildings were erected between A.D. 866 and 884, with a few others to follow. Chichén Itzá remained a vibrant, busy capital until its demise around A.D. 1200.

There was no crowded nucleated core or acropolis here. On the contrary, buildings on the North Terrace were widely dispersed along a consistent 17° east of magnetic north, the common arrangement in central Mexico. Of the many *cenotes* that once existed, two were particularly important. The Sacred Cenote (Well of Sacrifice) is reached by a causeway nearly 300 m long that links it to the heart of the northern ruins. The most imposing of all *cenotes*, with very steep sides, it was used primarily for receiving ritual offerings. Water for practical purposes was available from the Xtoloc Cenote in the center of Chichén Itzá where one could descend to the water level by two masonry staircases. (See Figure 6.80.) In addition, *chultuns* that caught rainwater are found throughout the site.

The early structures and those constructed in Puuc style with veneer masonry are located south of the centrally placed Xtoloc Cenote. This group includes the terrace of the circular Caracol or Observatory, the House of the Deer, and the Casa Colorada (Red House). The Casa Colorada contains an inscribed frieze with two dates (A.D. 869 and A.D. 870). Several lords are named in relation to some kind of fire creation and bloodletting ceremony that took place at these times. The finest Puuc examples are those comprising the Nunnery or Monjas group (Monjas, the Annex, and the Iglesia) (Figure 6.79), nearby Akab-Tzib, and several others, one of these Puuc-style buildings, the Temple of the Four Lintels, graphically illustrates another ritual involving fire and bloodletting. The inscription includes the names of a number of people and the date A.D. 881 is recorded three times. We are told nothing about the people themselves, but from the iconography, the theme is a similar ritual. Both the Casa Colorada and the Monjas are associated with ball courts with bench reliefs depicting ball-players like those to be seen in the Great Ball Court.

Continuing north on the *sacbé* leading to the main center, one immediately comes upon the Caracol. This is a curious cylindrical tower perched on two rectangular terraces, the upper one bearing a date of A.D. 840 (Figure 6.81). The interior spiral staircase (*caracol* in Spanish) leads to a small observation chamber. Square openings in the walls might have been used to sight movements of the heavenly bodies. Architecturally it contains Puuc features with mosaic-sky-serpent-mask panels and moldings, as well as elements of Toltec design. Here, corbeled vaulted construction is combined with Mexican ornamentation.

The North Terrace group of structures is located on an enormous artificial platform near the Xtoloc Cenote that supports the Great Ball Court, the Castillo or Temple of Kukulcán (Feathered Serpent), the Temple of the Warriors and group of a Thousand Columns, and smaller buildings (Figure 6.81).

The Temple of Kukulcán (Figure 6.82) forms the center of the so-called Toltec Chichén. Greatly contributing to its grandeur is the fact that it rises in lonely splendor from an immense clearing. Thousands could have gathered on every side to share in the pageantry of religious celebrations. Nearly square, with steep staircases leading up all four sides, this radial temple commands one of the best views of the entire site.

FIGURE 6.79   Las Monjas (the Nunnery), at Chichén Itzá. A building in Puuc-style architecture. (Photographed by the author.)

This was Chichén's most revered temple, dedicated to Kukulcán, in which serpents wind down the balustrades with heads flanking the bottom steps. Maya corbeled vaulting is found in the temple along with carved reliefs to Toltec warriors on the door jambs. The pyramidal base is decorated in a series of alternating recessed and projecting panels recalling Monte Albán (Kubler, 1984). This is a "highly cosmological structure" with steps totalling 365, panels or niches numbering 52 to a side, and a pyramidal base of 9 tiers (Coggins, 1980).

This pyramid encases an earlier one, the inner Temple of Kukulcán that can be seen via a tunnel. This smaller building was also formed with 9 tiers but has a single staircase. Its profile resembles that of Puuc structures and the temple of the summit has twin chambers. This is decorated in relief with a procession of jaguars prowling beneath a row of round Mexican-style shields. The temple houses a famous Red Jaguar Throne, carved in the shape of a jaguar with flat back to serve as a seat or place of offerings. This gorgeous animal is painted bright red with incrustations of 73 green jade disks, jade eyes, and shell fangs.

From the height of the Temple of Kukulcán, one can look across at the Temple of the Warriors and observe that the plan is basically the same as the reconstructed

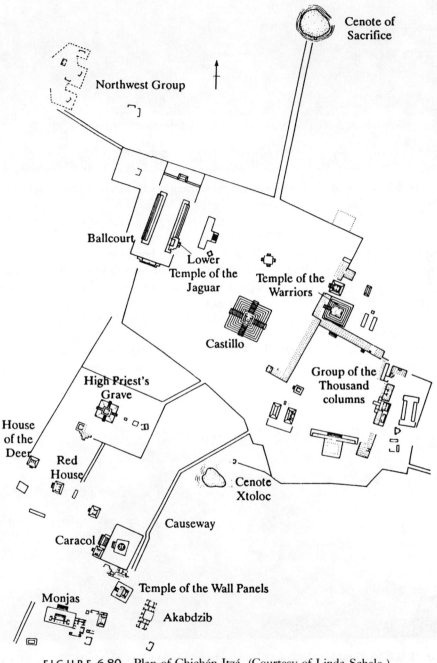

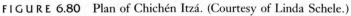

FIGURE 6.80 Plan of Chichén Itzá. (Courtesy of Linda Schele.)

FIGURE 6.81   Round structure known as the Caracol at Chichén Itzá. (Photgraphed by the author.)

Temple of Quetzalcoatl (Building B) at Tula. Here, however, it is much larger and more skillfully executed. Maximum spaciousness, light, and air were admitted through great colonnaded courts that perhaps served as meeting places or council halls, as suggested by the dais or thrones. The Group of the Thousand Columns, a huge, open plaza of 4.5 acres, is completely surrounded by colonnades. This great plaza may well have served as the marketplace.

One enters the Temple of the Warriors by passing through one of the great colonnaded courts of square columns, that are carved on all four sides with typical

FIGURE 6.82   Temple to Kukulcán, the feathered serpent, at Chichén Itzá. A radial temple with four staircases containing an earlier structure with the famous red jaguar throne. (Photographed by the author.)

Toltec-style warriors (Figure 6.83). This structure was built in 4 tiers resembling the architecture of Teotihuacan. Climbing the wide staircase, one encounters a fine *chacmool* at the entrance to the temple. The entry is again framed by feathered rattlesnake columns (Figure 6.84). At the back of the temple is the main sanctuary with an altar supported by small Atlantean figures such as those found at Tula. The walls had once been frescoed with battle scenes between the Putún and groups of Maya. The frescoes are now in such a deteriorated state that they are best viewed in the literature.

The Temple of the Warriors also contains an interior structure known as the Temple of the Chacmool with carved columns still brightly painted. The profile of the pyramid of this inner temple is virtually identical to the outer one of the Castillo in which Kubler (1984) finds resemblances to both Monte Albán and the Petén. Under a throne of this temple in a bundle of sacred objects was a mosaic pyrite mirror framed by a turquoise mosaic in the design of four serpents. This was set below the throne to transmit power and authority to the occupant (Schele and Freidel, 1990). Paintings on the two benches of this structure depict two protagonists: Toltecs or Chontal elites (?) seated on jaguar skins thrown over stools. The latter may not be Yucatec Maya, judging from their dress, ornamentation, and paraphernalia.

FIGURE 6.83   Group of the Thousand Columns adjacent to the Temple of the Warriors, Chichén Itzá. (Photographed by the author.)

FIGURE 6.84   The Temple of the Warriors, containing the interior Temple of the Chacmool, murals, and Atlantean figures. The entrance to the temple is framed by huge feathered-serpent columns behind a large *chacmool* figure at the top of the stairs. (Photographed by the author.)

Minor structures such as two dance platforms in the Great Plaza out in front are completely Mexican in flavor (Figure 6.85). Their sloping talud and vertical tablero are not unlike the profile of Xochicalco and are covered with themes of eagles and jaguars devouring human hearts. These low platforms had an important integrative role in the religious life. Here, according to Bishop Landa, dances and public spectacles were held, affording vicarious participation by the public.

FIGURE 6.85   A low dance platform located in front of the Temple of the Warriors. (Photographed by the author.)

On the far side of the Great Plaza beyond the Temple of Kukulcán is the largest of seven ball courts at Chichén Itzá. This huge I-shaped court has been the subject of study and controversy for many years, as it embraces Puuc, Petén, Usumacinta, and central Mexican architectural styles and motifs, making the dating of its various structures difficult. The playing alley is 146 m long and 37 m wide—the giant of all Mesoamerican courts (Figure 6.86). The most dramatic features are the great vertical walls rising 8 m in height with stone rings still set in place. Six carved reliefs show the decapitation of a participant. Fourteen players are shown decked out as ball-players. Each has a skull hanging from his belt, signaling that these figures represent "Lords of the Underworld." Again the myth of the Hero Twins is reenacted.

A small temple is located at either end of the court. The one at the north has some remarkable reliefs, only recently interpreted (Wren and Schmidt, 1991). The wall reliefs illustrate accession ceremonies at Chichén Itzá. Actually they tell us a great deal, a kind of substitute for comparable hieroglyphic texts. The lengthy events depicted here correspond to the heir-designation rites at Bonampak and Palenque (see page 325) and also resemble the investiture ceremony of a Mexican ruler as described for Tenochtitlán (Durán, 1967).

The narrative scene begins on the south vault following the death of one ruler and the selection of a new one. The north vault shows the new ruler visiting sacred shrines after his investiture ceremony, letting blood, and sacrificing birds and animals. In the final scene on the east wall we see the end of a ball game. The new ruler stands behind a kneeling ball-player holding one end of a rope around the neck of the athlete just decapitated. Blood flows freely from his neck in the form of serpents.

In the absence of later hieroglyphic texts, the murals portray ritual and ceremonies

FIGURE 6.86 The giant of all Mesoamerican ball courts, with dramatic vertical walls, in which rings were set. Its bas-reliefs in the court and the murals in the two temples overlooking the playing alley provide rich iconographic information. (Courtesy of the Instituto Nacional de Antropología e Historia, Mexico.)

that combine native Maya with central Mexican and non-Maya traditions. These give us a rare example of interaction among the various elite groups.

The most imposing structure dominating the playing alley is the Upper Temple of the Jaguars above the east wall (Figure 6.87). Feathered-serpent columns again support the lintels of its entryway, while above on the exterior façade is a procession of jaguars carved in relief similar to those prowling on Building B at Tula. Frescoes decorating the inner walls portray the gory details of a battle scene. Thompson (1970) has pointed out that while the attackers' attire have some elements of Toltec dress, their shields and feathers denote another group he believes to be Putún Itzá. The people they are attacking are a different ethnic group. Two settings are depicted. The first could have taken place in the flat, forested lowlands of the Chontalapa, while the second in some arid upland. It could be hill country of Acalán, around the Río Negro, or even in Oaxaca, Xochicalco, or Cacaxtla. Finally, there is a scene of reconciliation under two Toltec leaders showing the duality that was a feature of state offices under the Itzá (Fox, 1987). Landa also referred to two captains for each military group. (See Tozzer, 1941.)

Of considerable interest is the identification of the Great Ball-Court Stone, a hemispherical sacrificial stone that was retrieved in 1920 from the ball court and was "rediscovered" in the Mérida museum in 1983. Around the rim of the stone are 24 hieroglyphs in three panels in Chichén-Toltec style showing a decapitation scene. It bears a Calendar Round date of A.D. 864, belonging to the period of partial overlap of Toltec and tenth century Maya occupation (Wren and Schmidt, 1991).

Out in the plaza near the ball court is a macabre *tzompantli*, or skull rack, covered with carved human skulls. After seeing decapitation scenes on the playing walls of the ball court, the *tzompantli* is self-explanatory.

FIGURE 6.87   View out the ball court toward the Temple of the Warriors in the distance and the Temple of Kukulcán at the right. Towering over the court is the Temple of the Jaguars with an entrance framed by feathered-serpents, above which prowl a row of jaguars in bas-relief. (Courtesy of the Instituto Nacional de Antropología e Historia, Mexico.)

The Sacred Cenote   This sheer-sided sinkhole was described by Landa (see Tozzer, 1941) as a sacred place where live humans and "a great many other things were thrown in" (Figure 6.88). The "other things" were not trash, but objects the Maya prized such as precious stones, idols, copper and gold, fine, wooden objects, and cloth. The history of "exploring" the cenote (diving and dredging) and the recovery of its treasures (Coggins and Shane III, 1984) reveals that from A.D. 800 to 1200 valuables were often crushed, broken, and burned before being cast into the water. Many were special imports and like the ruins, reflect Toltec taste. The gold disks with Maya-Toltec scenes are of local manufacture (Bray, 1989). After the fall of Chichén Itzá the offerings were poorer and often consisted of simple deity idols and tripod bowls containing copal incense.

Eventually the Sacred Cenote became more of a pilgrimage center, enhanced by colorful tales such as the experience of Hunac Ceel. Archaeologically nothing is known of the ceremonies that must have taken place. The human bones were poorly preserved, but adults and children of both sexes were offered to the gods.

Pilgrimages often took place in groups to honor a deity on a special day. Sacrifices and offerings were made to ward off possible disasters and to ensure the continuation of this unstable world (Kubler, 1985). Sites chosen were usually close at hand as travel was considered dangerous. Mountains, caves, or near a spring or water were appropriate locations for shrines and none were more famous than the Sacred Cenote

FIGURE 6.88   The Sacred Cenote of Chichén Itzá, a short walk from the center of Chichén. This was Yucatán's most famous pilgrimage shrine. (Courtesy of Curt Muser.)

at Chichén Itzá. It was still in use at the time of the Conquest and continued attracting the public in the Colonial Period, never losing its aura of a sacred place.

Housing   Associated with the Temple of Hieroglyphic Jambs (Structure 6E-3) are some elite residences called Patio-Quad or Gallery-Patio structures. These usually consist of colonnaded buildings around a sunken patio. It is a type of residence typical of Chichén Itzá but has a limited distribution in Mesoamerica. Aside from Chichén Itzá, it is known at Nohmul in Belize and on Cozumel Island. It is also reported from highland central Mexico in the Coxcatlán area during the same tenth to eleventh centuries (Freidel, 1981; Chase and Chase, 1982; Schele and Freidel, 1990; Sisson, 1973; Wilk and Ashmore, 1988).

The High Priest's Grave   South of the North Terrace on the way to the Casa Colorada (Figure 6.80) is a funerary temple. It was possibly designed as a proto-type or replica (?) for the Temple of Kukulcán, having a radial plan with feathered-rattlesnakes descending the balustrades and tails framing the doorway of the temple above to support the lintel.

Several burials were found in a shaft beneath the floor leading to a natural 7-lobed cave, with remains of a high-status individual, perhaps a ruler. This temple-cave combination recalls a parallel one at Teotihuacan and perhaps in a similar way could symbolize the origin of the cosmos at Chichén Itzá.

The inscriptions on a column here have for many years been read as A.D. 998. Now, a revised reckoning places it earlier at A.D. 842 (Schele and Freidel, 1990). This revision would make the High Priest's Grave the earliest structure known at Chichén, and allow more time for the written history of the site.

Chacmool   The *chacmool* figure was associated with the New Fire Ceremony and the end of the 52-year cyle (see page 145) (Figure 6.89). This ritual in Mesoamerica was marked by the crossing of the zenith by the seven stars of the Pleiades that divide the solar year in half, signaling the beginnings of the rainy season and the end of the dry. In Yucatán the Pleiades were called *tzab* (rattlesnake rattles), thus the pairs of feathered rattlesnakes flanking balustrades and doorways symbolize the transition from rainy to dry seasons (Coggins, 1987).

The sculptured stone figured called a *chacmool* probably represented a noble captive warrior. He always rests on his back, knees and elbows bent, looking uncomfortable as he strains to sit upright. He looks sharply to one side, not for the view, but in order to turn his head away from the fire burning on his chest or belly, for this served as a platform for drilling the new fire.

These figures, found *in situ*, are invariably placed at the entrance to a temple, often flanked by serpent columns, as at the Temple of the Warriors at Chichén Itzá. Because of this location, they are sometimes thought to have served as sacrificial stones. Their function may have changed with time, but initially they were an important feature of the New Fire Ceremony.

Chacmool figures have been found in Postclassic contexts from central Mexico to

FIGURE 6.89 One of the numerous *chacmool* figures of Chichén Itzá. (Photographed by the author.)

Costa Rica (at Tula, Hidalgo; Tlaxcala; Michoacán; Cempoala; and Quiriguá) but none are known from the major Classic centers such as Teotihuacan or Tikal. With 14 examples from Chichén Itzá alone, Mary Miller (1985b) credits the Maya with the origin of this sculpture, pointing convincingly to their similarities to traditional Classic Maya representations of captives crouching under the feet of rulers on stelae. Coggins (1987) noted that earlier non-Maya examples might be expected and, in effect, a primitive, perhaps proto-*chacmool* of Classic date has been found at Cerro de Huistle, Jalisco, by Marie-Areti Hers (1989) (see page 193). The *chacmool* figure may prove to be a feature derived from northwestern Mesoamerica.

Inscriptions Inscriptions at Chichén Itzá are found on lintels and jambs of doorways, on columns or piers, and on friezes in buildings, areas that elsewhere were reserved for royal texts. The earliest secure date at Chichén Itzá of A.D. 867 is recorded on a monument found on the ground called the Watering Trough Lintel. The new revised date for the High Priest's Grave, if accepted, will begin inscriptions 25 years earlier.

As mentioned, these differed from the southern lowland inscriptions by using an abbreviated Short Count (a series of 13 katuns, approximately 256 years) and yet they are not as well understood as those of the southern lowlands. They contain a higher percentage of phonetic signs and the glyphs are more difficult to read. The inscriptions give some dynastic information as to names of rulers and parentage statements but do not follow the format of birth, accession, and death information seen in the south. Here, texts recount elite group activity, emblem glyphs, and stress commemoration of ritual honoring ancestors. The system of recording dates is also somewhat different but is definitely Maya and can be deciphered (Kowalski, 1985a).

Only a few figures have been identified, Kakupacal being the most prominent. His name appears 14 times. We still know relatively little about him, but he seems to have shared power with one of his brothers, Kim-Cimi. Their mother is named Lady Bone, but it is difficult to distinguish generations. In sharp contrast to the southern lowlands, the government in the north was in the hands of a group, or confederation. Celebrations were not personal but group affairs. In this case we look to public art and iconography for history and the structure of society.

The Itzá

Although the early history of Chichén Itzá is still a little murky we believe it became the capital of the Itzá by mid-ninth century. These were intruders said to speak a Maya tongue who readily assimilated the local Maya traditions. The greatest change took place in the realm of government; instead of relying on a single ruler or king, power was now in the hands of a group of lords or relatives.

It is during the tenth century that the flight of a Toltec contingent led by Quetzalcoatl (the Feathered Serpent) from Tula to the Gulf Coast is supposed to have taken place. Legend has it that thereafter, a figure called Kukulcán, feathered serpent in Maya, made his way to Yucatán with the help of the Mexicanized Putún (Thompson, 1970). A kind of Toltec empire developed, centered at Chichén Itzá, accounting for its foreign or Mexican influence. This Toltec intrusion gave rise to the asserted claims of Toltec descent from lineages of the Itzá, Xiu, and Cocom (Fox, 1987).

However, there are contradictions. Earlier Toltec influence in northern Yucatán is yet to be accounted for. Some of this predates the Tollan phase at Tula (see page 344) and there are inconsistencies and inaccuracies that suggest this is more myth than history. Some early features erroneously called "Toltec" are better termed Mexican and may be derived from Teotihuacan, Oaxaca, the Gulf Coast region, or other as yet unidentified areas. Groups bearing these traits could have channeled influences from the Chontalapa both to central highland Mexico as well as to Chichén Itzá (Andrews V and Sabloff, 1986). As we observed in the southern Maya region, there had already been considerable interaction with central Mexico in earlier periods, perhaps more direct than with eighth and ninth century Yucatán. The Mexicans were not total strangers.

The Maya chronicles tell of a Toltec invasion, a takeover of Chichén Itzá, but by Maya speakers. Legends of Kukulcán pervade the folklore and the claims of dynastic descent throughout the Maya realm match in quantity those of Quetzalcoatl in the rest of Mesoamerica. Leaving aside the historic documents, the archaeological record fully supports ninth to eleventh century contact between central highland Mexico and the Maya region. Its greatest manifestation is at Chichén Itzá, in architecture, art styles, pottery, and special elements such as *tzompantlis*, *chacmools*, and smoking pipes. The source of some features is yet to be determined; some have antecedents in both areas.

Some scholars support an outright conquest of Chichén Itzá by invading Toltecs, while others envision a gradual collaboration as an outgrowth of initial commercial activities (Andrews and Robles, 1985; Freidel, 1985). Although the "foreignness" is so startling it has been the focus of much attention, Chichén Itzá was still very Maya of local derivation. It is difficult to see how a band of Toltecs could manage a hostile takeover of such a powerful city with the military experience of the Itzá. However it happened, foreign features and indigenous architecture, ceramics, settlement patterns, and an elite symbolism were incorporated into a new hybrid culture.

Wren and Schmidt (1991) see the new political order as the result of merging elite elements that freed the populace from the restrictions of royalty and granted greater flexibility and social mobility. The success of the city may well have been due to a multi-ethnic collaboration.

The idea of an "old Chichén" with Puuc architecture being superseded by a "new Toltec Chichén" is no longer viable. Archaeology has now confirmed that there are Toltec features in the so-called Puuc center and an eclectric nature is reflected in the art and architecture of the city in general. Several contemporaneous styles produced the hybrid result of an uninterrupted Late Classic Period.

The Working Capital

This was a cosmopolitan capital with buildings representing the ethnic blend of northern Yucatán, the southern Maya, Guatemala, Oaxaca, and highland Mexico. Curiously this new style did not spread (or was not permitted to spread) to other nearby centers. Many aspects of administration are poorly understood, but under the Itzá, authority resided in a group or several leaders instead of a single ruler or king.

The wealth of Chichén Itzá was probably derived from a tributary system that poured commodities into the capital. Inland cities including the Puuc supplied agricultural foodstuffs and possibly labor as tribute. From the coastal communities came fish and marine products. Attention probably centered on the economy securing trade routes and control over exploitation of the salt resources.

Yucatán salt beds produced the finest quality known. As salt is heavy and bulky to transport, sea trade was preferable. The Petén region imported thousands of tons of salt annually, requiring great fleets of canoes (Andrews, 1983). There were other salt sources such as Salinas de los Nueve Cerros (see page 286), coastal Belize (see page 272), and Amatitlán in the Guatemala Valley. But these could not meet the demand and the quality was not as fine as that of northern Yucatán. Producing and marketing salt became a major industry, organized and administered by wealthy elite merchants. We know this to be true in the sixteenth century (Roys, 1943) and believe the evidence is there for the Classic Period as well.

Isla Cerritos

As Chichén was located 90 km from the north coast, a good port was essential for control of the maritime trade. A high priority was the improvement of existing port facilities on Isla Cerritos. This was an island 500 m off the north coast that had been occupied as a fishing village since Preclassic times (Andrews *et al.*, 1988). Now, in the tenth century the port was enlarged and provided with proper docks, piers, and a large seawall 330 m long. Passing through one of several entrances a voyager was guaranteed calm water with much needed protection. Both riverine and coastal trade must have used canoes, as there is no evidence that the Maya had sails. (A possible "sail" in Tikal graffiti is the only archaeological hint; Epstein, 1990). Paddling commodities around by canoe would have been a sporty exercise in the open Caribbean currents and Isla Cerritos was a welcome port.

Trade was carried on with Mexico (obsidian), Guatemala and the Gulf Coast (ceramics), Belize (basalt), and Central America (a gold frog pendant). Excavations on Isla Cerritos (test-pitting, structural remains, and 10 burials) have left little doubt that this was an Itzá operation. One of the most surprising results was the provenance of obsidian. Sources turned out to be identical to those used by Tula: Cerro de las Navajas, Otumba, and Zinapécuaro. This represents a clean break by Isla Cerritos with the sources in highland Guatemala, but one that lasted only as long as Chichén Itzá. When it fell, the obsidian network with central Mexico collapsed, and the Yucatec Maya renewed their ties to the highlands.

The Itzá State

The exact domain of Chichén Itzá is difficult to determine because many towns, once conquered, were permitted to keep their own leaders and only sent in tributary remittances to the capital. Itzá pottery, that of the Sotuta Ceramic Sphere, is found in a vast area from the Usumacinta drainage basin to Cozumel. This may mean it was simply a profitable commodity, but could also signify certain influence. Only the Cobá region seems to have remained aloof and with its satellites continued to produce the Cehpech ceramics of the Puuc tradition.

As much of the coast of Quintana Roo was swampy, the island of Cozumel was nicely positioned to accommodate the growing maritime commerce. Did the Itzá control trade at Cozumel? We know that Itzá traders reached as far south as Nito and Naco on the coast of Honduras but the extent of control along the way is not known (see Andrews and Robles, 1985).

This was a new kind of international Maya state based on military conquest and warfare. If this was an attempt to consolidate many different groups into an international Mesoamerican culture, it was never realized. There were inherent problems present from the start.

The economy relied heavily on tribute and the wealth of imported goods from the long-distance trade networks. Power was based on maintaining and administering control of these systems. Military and commercial control was probably more effective than political. The chronicles give mixed reports on the Itzá as people, suggesting that others grew to despise them for their mannerisms and behavior (see notes in Andrews, 1990b).

The traditional fall of Chichén Itzá is traced to trickery and deception. This is the oft-told tale of Hunac Ceel, a Tabascan mercenary imported by the Cocoms, an Itzá-related group who rose to leadership nearby at Mayapán. This colorful figure had become something of a hero by surviving the sacrificial ordeal of the Sacred Cenote at Chichén Itzá. Being still alive the following morning, he was able to bring back the prophecy of the Rain God concerning prospects for crops in the forthcoming year. Once he became chief of Mayapán, he schemed to rid himself of his rivals at Chichén Itzá. Aided by sorcery, he persuaded the ruler of Chichén Itzá to abduct the bride of the chief of Izamal during the wedding feast. Then, with feigned indignation, Hunac Ceel and some Mexicans drove the Itzá from their capital city.

However exaggerated or embellished with time this account may be, the Itzá had outlived their welcome. Between corruption and debauchery, it sounds as if they had lost control. Again, as in the southern lowlands, maintenance of the capital and the elite may have become too great a burden. There are also several references to drought and famine about this time. Perhaps the Itzá had become too dependent on long-distance trade. These are a few possible causes underlying the end of Chichén Itzá put forth by Andrews (1990b). In essence, perhaps the Itzá had attempted to create a multi-ethnic state on an international level beyond their abilities. After all, they were intruders who could not reconcile a new order that they were unable or unwilling to give up with the pervading ancient Maya traditions.

SUMMARY

The Early Classic Period viewed from the perspective of Teotihuacan involves her relationships with Matacapan, Monte Albán, Kaminaljuyú and Tikal. She only went north for her mining enterprises at Alta Vista, Zacatecas and paid scant attention to the west where the Teuchitlán Valley was filled with monumental circular architecture of unprecedented complexity. Interested in building a great commercial network, Teotihuacan established an enclave at Matacapan, well positioned to serve as a distant outpost. The relationship with Monte Albán was apparently a peaceful, political one and there was a long-standing Zapotec community resident at Teotihuacan with no signs of discontent. The glyphic texts on stone-carvings at Monte Albán graphically record visits of Teotihuacanos.

The relationship with the Guatemala Valley is still unclear. The presence of talud-tablero architecture could be derived from the Mundo Perdido compound at Tikal, a much closer source. The Teotihuacan-style vessels, green obsidian, and Thin Orange pots at Kaminaljuyú, being portable objects, do not necessarily indicate a direct contact. However, it is possible that Teotihuacan merchants were residents at Kaminaljuyú for some time, stayed on after the fall of Teotihuacan, and were integrated into the local society.

A trading network may have initiated the contact between Tikal and Teotihuacan that grew into something more substantial. The apparent appeal of the Mexicans may have been their "foreignness," their special war-sacrifice ritual concepts, for after Tikal's successful war against Uaxactún, the Teotihuacan-style warrior costume with all its symbolism was summarily adopted by the Maya. Henceforth, the Teotihuacan symbols were incorporated into Maya iconography and their wars were programmed to coincide with the movements of Venus.

Tikal, after decorating façades of temple/pyramids with giant monster masks, replaced this format with stelae for displaying royal portraits, commemorating period-endings, important dedications, recording accessions, births, parentage statements, and victories. The institution of kingship first seen in the northeast Petén, had spread through the southern lowlands by the fourth century. With the decipherment of hieroglyphs, we now have emblem glyphs for major centers and dynastic histories of Tikal, Dos Pilas, Calakmul, Naranjo, and the Usumacinta sites, as well as for Copán and Quiriguá in the southeast.

Tikal was the most powerful polity in the Early Classic. A hiatus in inscriptions in the sixth century is at least partially blamed on Caracol, a Belize site whose aggressive ruler and son waged war in the Petén for over 100 years, counting Tikal among its conquests.

After some disruption, Late Classic Maya civilization underwent a realignment of political power, with new centers emerging in peripheral areas where trade was brisk and prosperous. Tikal was forced to share leadership with Palenque, Calakmul, and Copán. Maya civilization now reached its brilliant cultural climax in artistic and intellectual levels. Tikal recovered to enjoy a brilliant renaissance by remodeling, adding causeways and twin-temple complexes and the giant funerary temples of Ruler Ah Cacau and his descendants. Eventually ball courts reached a total of five.

In the Basin of Mexico, Teotihuacan's competitors closed the Teotihuacan Corridor, effectively severing important commercial ties. There may also have been additional internal problems (?). The city withdrew into central Mexico and managed to prosper for another 100–150 years. During the Metepec phase (A.D. 650–750), the Techinantitla murals were painted, a landmark in Teotihuacan's mural art exhibiting a wealth of glyphs and insignias. About A.D. 750 a great fire was deliberately set to destroy the religious and political center of the city. The result was a catastrophic destruction of 2 km of the Street of the Dead, most likely the work of rebellious local residents.

Only the main center was abandoned, however, and Teotihuacan continued to be the largest urban center in the Basin for another 100 years. Activity in this period (Coyotlatelco or Epi-Classic), centered around settlements but without any central authority. The Great Goddess was seen no more.

In the Maya area, Copán became the greatest polity on the southeastern frontier. It has always been closely allied to the southern periphery, Chalchuapa, and the southern Guatemalan highlands and this relationship continued throughout its history, even during the years of close ties to the Petén. The beautiful monumental art and stone carving can be viewed as an elite Maya overlay. Inscriptions and recent excavations have revealed Copán's dynastic history and shed light on residential compounds in the Sepulturas area and other outlying groups. The architectural arrangement at Copán conformed to Maya cosmology. The east and west causeways led out from the main plaza, set with stelae, to complete a quadripartite plan. By A.D. 750 Copán was starting to decline but a reduced population lived on in the valley until A.D. 1200.

Neighboring Quiriguá on the Motagua River grew wealthy on the highland/lowland and north–south trade that passed by its portals and its own agricultural exports. It is famous for its unusually tall sandstone stelae erected by Ruler Cauac Sky and his capture and decapitation of one of Copán's most illustrious kings, XVIII-Jog.

Belize, fairly bristling with archaeological remains, started early. The ninth century "collapse" in the southern lowlands affected this area least of all and activity continued at centers such as Lamanai, Caracol, Santa Rita Corozal, and most sites with advantageous riverine or coastal locations.

To the west, events leading to the "collapse" of the Petexbatún area are now well documented. The shift in the rules of warfare from raids and skirmishes to territorial conquest resulted in the devastation of agricultural lands, the economy, and eventual abandonment by A.D. 820. The affairs of Dos Pilas show how fragile is the ecology of the tropical forest. It also furnishes a good example of the role of warfare to Maya kingship.

The Usumacinta regions of Bonampak, Yaxchilán, Piedras Negras, and Palenque were among the first cities to decline. How much is due to the incursions of the merchant-minded Putún, or an effect of Teotihuacan's withdrawal from the exchange networks, we do not know. Among the inhabitants of the Usumacinta sites were expert builders and artisans who carved beautiful scenes on long wall panels at Piedras Negras and decorated the walls of Palenque with exquisite stucco sculptures. Kingship had its day on the Usumacinta, enjoying royal visits, forming alliances, and faithfully observing calendrical cycles and period-endings. It also had its share of competition, raids, local victories, and defeats.

In the ninth century Putún and Itzá-related groups appeared at Seibal from both east and west. A non-Maya ruler celebrated an important period-ending date in A.D. 849. His new radial temple was modeled much like one at Chichén Itzá and decorated with Puuc veneer masonry, a strong hint of the coming new order. The last date at Seibal is A.D. 889, close to the final Long Count date at Toniná in A.D. 909.

The next segment of Maya history deals with the politically complex events of northern Yucatán. From A.D. 800 to 1200 the main centers were Uxmal, the giant of the Puuc cities in the west, and Chichén Itzá, the capital of the intrusive Itzá. The Puuc cities with beautiful buildings with façades decorated with small cut stones set in masonry are impressive. Puuc sites are located close together, many linked by *sacbeob* (Labná, Kabah, Sayil).

To the east, Cobá retained close ties to the Petén and in the tenth century was the dominant polity on the northeastern plains. One of its many *sacbeob* was 100 km in length, connecting Cobá with Yaxuná. In the Postclassic struggles with the Itzá, Cobá was encircled and cut off from her east coast trading port at Xelhá, but managed to retain her independence.

The Itzá are seen as astute, aggressive intruders from the Chontalapa. Taking over Chichén Itzá, probably about A.D. 850, they continued some of the Maya traditions, but in their capital we see a blend of multi-ethnic tastes. There are elements of the southern Maya lowlands, the Gulf Coast, Oaxaca, and strong Toltec features. A

Toltec relationship is traditionally explained by the Quetzalcoatl/Kukulcán legend, but archaeology and the "historic" documents seem to be irreconcilable. There is presently little support for an actual invasion by Tula Toltecs, but the similarities of the two sites are yet to be clarified. The ruling Itzá ran a successful mercantile operation with an expanded port facility at Isla Cerritos. Trade was brisk between central Mexico and the entire coastline around Yucatán to Nito and Naco in Honduras.

The Itzá attempted to form a unified Mesoamerican international state, but it never materialized. Around A.D. 1200 the Maya finally rose up in revolt and drove the Itzá from northern Yucatán. Some groups went south to settle around the Petén lake area.

CHAPTER 7

Tula and the Toltecs

The period following the fall of Teotihuacan is very confusing and one of the least well known archaeologically. In the 300 years following A.D. 900, Mesoamerica had to readjust to many changes that resulted from the crises suffered by some centers at the close of the Classic Period. It is now time to see what was happening in central highland Mexico as we enter its Postclassic Period. Tula rose to assume the role of leadership formerly held by Teotihuacan and emerges as the next great power around A.D. 900. This was a geographical shift of about 60 km in central highland Mexico, but one that placed the new capital closer to the northern limits of agriculture.

TOLLAN, TULA, AND THE TOLTECS

The geographical location of Tula in the state of Hidalgo is vitally important in that it was situated close to the northern boundary of Mesoamerica, which from A.D. 900 to 1200 reached its northernmost limits and thereafter began to recede. An advantage of being on the Tula River, a tributary of the Pánuco, was easy communication with people in northern Veracruz, the Huasteca. To the west contact was facilitated by the great Lerma River, which flowed out of the nearby Valley of Toluca. These were the areas of greatest Toltec impact.

It is often said that the historical record begins with Tula, but fact and fiction are so confused and distorted that no one has been able to combine the data into a logical sequence. Somehow a tale began that grew over several centuries with continual adjustments. It seems that Toltec history was manipulated and embellished with great imagination by the Aztecs, the Spaniards, and early chroniclers such as Sahagún, Muñoz Camargo, Motolinía, and anonymous sources such as La Historia de los Mexicanos por sus Pinturas (1941), Anales de Cuauhtitlán (1945), and the Historia Tolteca-Chichimeca (1947). Torquemada (1943) and Ixtlilxóchitl (1952) also participated.

The Quetzalcoatl Legend

The historic sources recount a popular legend or myth dealing with a personage named Ce Acatl Topiltzin (Quetzalcoatl), son of a famous leader of northern Chichimecs, Ce Técpatl Mixcoatl, who settled in Culhuacán in the Valley of Mexico. After his father's death, Topiltzin went to Tula and assumed leadership of a group whose head claimed the name or title of Quetzalcoatl, and took over as the political-religious ruler. Under his leadership the arts were stimulated, and metallurgists, feather-workers, sculptors, and craftspersons of every type were assembled from other regions and encouraged to produce their finest work. The Toltecs excelled in all arts and sciences; hunger and misery were unknown, everything was plentiful, and all were rich and happy.

Trouble arose from Huémac, the head of a traditional Toltec dynasty who resented the intrusion of this outsider. Huémac seems to have had the support of the evil Tezcatlipoca, God of the Night and Darkness. Duality, a common theme in Mesoamerica, is portrayed here between the forces of good (Quetzalcoatl) and evil (Tezcatlipoca). The elaborate tricks and evil deeds of Tezcatlipoca eventually humiliated Quetzalcoatl who was forced to flee from Tula. A.D. 1170 is the most accepted date for Tula's collapse.

Quetzalcoatl then went east to the Gulf of Mexico where he set fire to himself and rose to the heavens to become Venus, the Morning Star. In another version he set sail on a raft of serpents, prophesying that in another year Ce Acatl, the anniversary of his birth, he would return to conquer his people.

Huémac was also forced to leave. He supposedly went to Chapultepec where he met a violent death by hanging (suicide?), or lived out the rest of his life in a cave, depending on your source.

History and Archaeology

There are no pre-Conquest central Mexican texts. Topiltzin Quetzalcoatl appears in the earliest documents (La Historia de los Mexicanos por sus Pinturas, 1941), as a migration leader, a great warrior and ruler. With the passing of time this secular image became transformed into a pacific, penitential figure, and finally emerges Christianized, a priest and culture hero, dressed as a deity (Keber, 1988). Archaeologically there are no stone carvings or representations of a ruler or warrior that can be identified with this famous Toltec leader. The only pre-Conquest image of Quetzalcoatl is the carving on the Cerro de la Malinche, a rocky hill near Tula, dated to the Aztec period (Nicholson, cited in Keber, 1988).

Is it any wonder that later groups all over Mesoamerica claimed descent from these people? By the late sixteenth century, the Toltecs had become mythical heroes. To identify oneself with them was to claim a superior birthright (Armillas, 1950).

The history of the Toltecs as reconstructed by the archaeological record (Acosta, 1956–1957) portrays them as a multi-ethnic group that introduced changes in public and religious architecture and new styles of stone carving and ceramics. Toltec pottery and figurines, with their characteristic stiffness and monotony are a far cry from the imaginative elegance achieved by their Preclassic and Classic ancestors. The remains at the site of Tula give the impression of having been put together by both skilled and unskilled labor. The Toltecs portrayed themselves as warriors, a claim not yet documented (Benfer, 1974).

Who were these people we call Toltecs and from where did they come? Actually the builders of the Tula ruins in the state of Hidalgo did not call themselves Toltecs although we do not know what name they used. The Aztecs used the word "toltec" to refer to a skilled craftsperson or artisan. It may be derived from the same root as Tollan, meaning place of rushes and/or metropolis. The people we call "Toltecs" were composed of many different ethnic groups and spoke Náhuatl, Otomí, and various other tongues. The Nonoalca, originally a lowland people, may have come in from Teotihuacan (Jiménez Moreno, 1941). We have already noted that Teotihuacan was not suddenly abandoned but that many residents continued to live there around the ruins of the great metropolis. Some of these were Olmeca-Xicalanca people who came from the area of Puebla-Tlaxcala but originated in the Gulf coast region. Other Toltecs were Chichimec peoples (Tolteca-Chichimecas), who came down to Tula from the northwest via the Bajío (Mastache and Cobean, 1989).

Tollan or metropolis eventually had the connotation of a place where craftspersons, that is, skilled or knowledgeable people, gathered (Davies, 1977) and eventually symbolized power. It was thus possible to speak of Tollan Teotihuacan, or Tollan Cholula for example.

The first excavations we know of at Tula were carried out in the late 1800s by a Frenchman named Désiré Charnay. He explored various regions of Central America and Mexico, but it was Tula that caught his eye. He believed he had found Tollan, the legendary capital of the Toltecs. His work was clumsy and typical of early explorers and his ideas were not taken seriously since these ruins seemed entirely too modest to be the magnificent capital of the Toltecs lauded in the chronicles.

No further attention was given to Tula until the Carnegie Institution of Washington working at Chichén Itzá in Yucatán revealed architecture and sculpture similar to that at Tula. The archaeologists' problems were just beginning. Was Charnay right? Feathered serpents, jaguars, and the goggle-eyed Tlaloc had just come to light at the Temple of Quetzalcoatl at Teotihuacan but the prowling jaguars, feathered serpents, and colonnaded hall in Yucatán more closely resembled the ruins at Tula. Finally, at a celebrated Mexican Round Table Conference in 1941, the historian Wigberto Jiménez

Moreno (1941) settled the question by convincingly arguing that Tula, Hidalgo was the Tula (Tollan) of the chronicles. His premise was based largely on writings of Sahagún (1946) and on place-names in the area identified with the geographic setting spelled out in historical sources.

Excavations

Following the 1941 conference, enthusiasm mounted for renewed excavations at Tula, Hidalgo. The INAH excavations at Tula in the 1940s and 1950s under the direction of Jorge Acosta left little doubt of the Tula–Chichén Itzá connection. More recently in the decade following 1966, two groups, the University of Missouri, Columbia (UMC) under direction of Richard A. Diehl, together with the INAH Proyecto Tula led by Eduardo Matos Moctezuma, worked simultaneously at Tula conducting surveys and excavations. This collaborative effort proved tremendously productive, a most rewarding demonstration of cooperation. Whereas our knowledge of Tula was formerly based on the ruined core of Tula Grande and an inventory of recovered artifacts, now Tula is emerging as the vibrant city it was, and for a brief span the leading power in Mesoamerica. The following account of the Toltecs and Tula is culled largely from writings by Acosta (1941, 1945, 1956, 1956–1957), Diehl (1981, 1983), Healan (1989), Matos Moctezuma (1974), and their assistants.

Tula lies about 65 km northwest of Teotihuacan and can be reached by road or train from Mexico City in less than two hours. The area today is arid and dotted with cactus and scrub vegetation due to effects of overgrazing and subsequent erosion. But it was not always like this. Two thousand years ago, farmers settled here because of water for irrigation, forests, game, and availability of lime. The Tula River flows northeast from here to eventually join the great Pánuco River and empty into the Gulf of Mexico. The rolling terrain is marked by sharp ridges and escarpments. The modern town of Tula de Allende is located at the base of one of these ridges, at the confluence of the Tula and Rosa rivers (Map 7.1). Farmers irrigate the valley today as their predecessors have done for generations, in the process covering over the earliest archaeological remains which lie underneath the town. Above the town to the north extends a ridge, lumpy with mounds of the ancient capital.

Before these were built however, we now know of earlier developments that led to the formation of historic Tula.

In the Tula region chronology has been based largely on ceramics. Pottery is the most common artifact and can be correlated with the carefully established cultural sequence for the Basin of Mexico (Sanders *et al.*, 1979). The importance of the Tula region begins with Early Classic settlements from A.D. 300 to 750, years coeval with Teotihuacan's major Classic phases.

Early Regional Settlements in the Classic Period

Prior to 400 the Tula region was integrated into Teotihuacan's orbit. Teotihuacan's interest was strictly aimed at extracting lime for use in its great building program and a number of settlements were installed. To handle this enterprise and probably

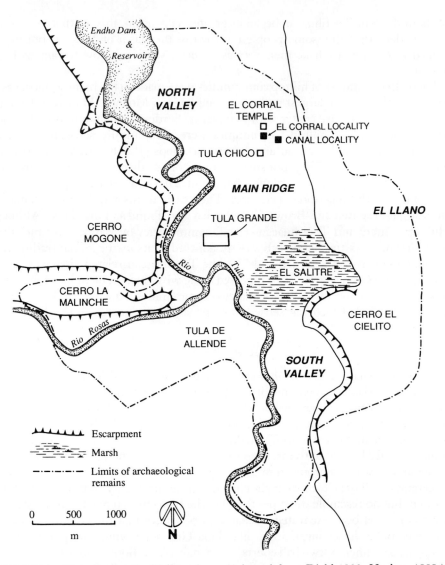

MAP 7.1   Tula during the Tollan phase. (Adapted from Diehl 1983; Healan, 1989.)

administer and operate a large irrigation system as well, the settlement of Chingú was founded 10 km east of Tula. This was the provincial political and administrative center for the whole region and was composed of a large Ciudadela-like plaza and numerous groups of apartment compounds. The Teotihuacanos would have felt comfortable with buildings oriented as at home, living with talud-tablero architecture, and having their own figurines and ceramics. Oaxaca-type pottery at Chingú and Tepejí del Río suggests that at least several settlements were associated with the Zapotecs from Teotihuacan's Oaxaca Barrio.

About the time Teotihuacan began its greatest expansion, this northern economic venture ended. Probably some people returned to the Basin of Mexico, but others remained in the area to make their way as farmers, settling in low terrain with the best soil.

Thereafter a number of hilltop communities were made in the highest, most easily defended locations. The largest and most complex was Mogone (Map 7.1), having a ceremonial-administrative center with two plazas, bordered by pyramids and palace-type structures. These hilltop communities were economically self-sufficient with their own terraces and ceramic and lithic workshops. Basalt, chert, and rhyolite predominated for tool-making, but small amounts of obsidian were found of the gray opaque Zinapécuaro variety. Ceramics of these sites have Coyotlatelco pottery similar to that of the northern peripheral cultures. Their early forms and decorations may be prototypes, for the Red-and-Brown Coyotlatelco ware found at Tula Chico. Although the hilltop centers and Teotihuacan-related communities overlapped in time, there was no sharing of pottery and each strictly adhered to its own ceramic tradition.

Sometime between A.D. 650 and 750, the Teotihuacan-related sites were abandoned and Thin Orange pottery disappeared along with them. The hilltop folk moved to lower levels and set up new Coyotlatelco communities. During the Prado Phase (A.D. 700–800) Tula Chico was settled, the first significant center on the Tula ridge.

Tula Chico

There is a sharp break from Early to Late Classic at this time. Tula Chico represents a marked change from its earlier predecessors in the region. Its ruins, oriented north–south, are perched on a low hill overlooking the Tula River, occupying between 3 and 5 km^2 about 1.5 km northeast of Tula Grande (See Map 7.1). The founders and inhabitants of Tula Chico do not seem to have been of local origin. Their ceramics, strictly limited to the area around a new civic-ceremonial center, suggest an intrusion of a new elitist group from the northern frontier. For example, the Coyotlatelco ceramics at Tula Chico were simple and of inferior quality to those of the Basin of Mexico, but do resemble the types found in the Bajío and up north. Although Tula Chico has not yet been excavated, archaeologists believe that the layout of its civic-religious complex looks surprisingly like Tula Grande, having two pyramids, the counterpart of Edificio 3, two ball courts, and a main plaza. Both plans are so strikingly similar that Tula Chico could have served as a prototype for the larger, later center. Logically this intrusive pattern would carry with it the same deity and cult complexes. However, if Tula Chico proves to have the same basic attributes of the Tollan Phase, then this Coyotlatelco settlement would be equally Toltec (Healan, 1989).

Elsewhere in the region, Late Classic ceramics are similar to the Coyotlatelco wares of the Basin of Mexico. It is only the Tula Chico settlement that displays disjunction and introduces northern features. The arrival of foreigners at this time would support Jiménez Moreno's premise that an influx of Tolteca-Chichimeca from the north founded Tula. Life on the Tula ridge was profoundly affected by the arrival of these outsiders.

One prominent group was the Nonoalca from the southern Veracruz-Tabasco region. Some may have come via Cholula and Teotihuacan to become some of the residents of Chingú and later valley farmers with their Thin Orange ceramics. Other Nonoalca could have made their way north to the Huasteca and arrived at Tula via Tulancingo. Of diverse ethnic backgrounds, these people are said to have been highly skilled in all the arts. Eventually Mixtecs also may have come.

According to tradition, other Toltecs were Chichimec peoples (Tolteca-Chichimeca) who came down to Tula from the northwest. These were people of the Chalchihuites region (See page 193). Prior to A.D. 600, Alta Vista, under Teotihuacan control, already looked like a model for Tula with colonnaded halls, feathered serpents, and *tzompantli*. These Tolteca-Chichimeca pushed on south, bringing with them the "new" features first seen at Tula Chico that would reach their full development in the Tollan Phase at Tula Grande. These northerners had developed a strong cohesion in regional isolation and were extremely miltaristic. The overall cast of Tula looks startlingly different from its immediate predecessors in the Basin of Mexico, but it had deep-rooted Mesoamerican antecedents in the far north (Hers, 1989). We do not know when these peoples began making their way to Tula but no one envisions a mass migration.

Remember that when Teotihuacan's fortunes waned and its commercial markets dried up, the expensive mining and trading enterprises in the north could no longer be maintained. We know that many mines closed down. A severe drought is documented for the American Southwest and is believed to have affected northern Mexico as well, causing the frontier of Mesoamerica (farming limits) to recede. Farmers would have certainly drifted south in search of arable land and such conditions would have increased pressure from the nomadic Teo-Chichimecas in the semiarid desert to the east. Tula with two rivers and springs would have been the first well-watered area encountered. What was the result of this influx of intruders? Somehow the mix of these ethnic groups of such diverse backgrounds and languages led to Tula's greatest years: the Tollan Phase.

Just what triggered the events leading up to it during the first half of the tenth century is still not known, but during these critical years Tula experienced a sudden leap into urbanism. We can only speculate on the impact of foreigners and what the changes were.

The role of Mazapa pottery is interesting (See Figure 7.11c). It has been used for years as a diagnostic market of Tula. Excavations show that it reached its peak prior to the Tollan Phase and occupied a relatively minor role in the sequence. It should no longer be considered a horizon marker for Tula's apogee. Its greatest concentration was in an outlying settlement in the south valley associated with an early obsidian industry. This area maintained a separate identity until the beginning of the Tollan Phase. Other settlements were made off the Tula ridge in nearby lowlands, particularly to the north.

A notable change was the closing down of Tula Chico and the shift of the main ceremonial precinct to a more central position on the ridge at Tula Grande. Only the central plaza of Tula Chico was abandoned, but construction ceased and activity trickled to a halt. There must have been a compelling reason to take this momentous decision to relocate. It may have been more convenient; perhaps there was more room to expand, or was it a display of power?

Tula in Its Prime: Tollan Phase A.D. 950–1150

The city of Tula embraced 13 km with a resident population estimated at anywhere from 30,000–60,000. These city dwellers were craftspersons, tradespersons, and religious personnel, but non-food producers.

There is no agreement on Tula's maximum population, as this is particularly difficult to estimate. Densities are uncertain within the urban zone and many homes underlie modern developments off the ridge. The rural population consisted of more than farmers who lived in outlying villages where water from local springs made permanent irrigation possible. These outlying areas also had resident industrial workers such as those producing *manos* and *metates* who settled near basalt outcrops, and toolmakers near their chert deposits. There were also irrigation operators and administrators and those involved in lime extraction. Obsidian workshops were initially located outside the urban zone in outlying areas. In the Tollan Phase this industry expanded into clusters of workshops within the urban zone on the east flank of El Salitre. Tula was a large urban city, perhaps the largest in Mesoamerica during the Tollan Phase.

Much is yet to be excavated and only Tula Grande suggests its exciting role in history. The site today is rather deceiving as the city has been thoroughly looted and mistreated. But excavations show that it was laid out on a carefully planned orientation at 18° east of magnetic north.

The center was a huge double-plaza complex with two pyramids, council halls, united by a colonnaded vestibule. Close by were two ball courts (Figure 7.1). Much of this was built on a large, single platform, reinforced by stone-faced retaining walls 10–15 m in height.

To the east of the large central plaza is Building C, the largest and most important structure in the city. Unfortunately it was nearly destroyed by the Aztecs, who helped themselves to the original stone facings and temple, leaving us only the exposed core of rock and earth and fragments of stone carvings. Tula pyramids were built with a single staircase leading up one side to the temple. None of the temples are preserved, but it is likely that they were small stone buildings with two rooms, an antechamber, and a special sanctuary to house an idol.

The smaller but more impressive structure is Building B, (Temple of Quetzalcoatl), the pyramid north of the plaza (Figure 7.2). It once supported a temple of which nothing remains but the stone-carved roof supports. Some of these are square-sided carved pillars. Others are great figures of warriors sculpted in the round and portions of giant columns in the form of feathered serpents, believed to have supported the lintel at the entrance to the temple as at Chichén Itzá. All of these are made in sections that are doweled together. A complete figure measures over 3.5 m high and represents a warrior richly attired, wearing a feathered headdress, rectangular ear

FIGURE 7.1 Aerial view of Tula Grande in 1957 prior to reconstruction of the colonnades and placement of Atlantean figures atop Building B, center. Building C is to the right, the Palacio Quemado at the left, all facing the Main Plaza. One ball court is at upper left. (Courtesy of Compañía. Mexicana Aerofoto, S.A.)

FIGURE 7.2 South side of the Pyramid or Building B, dedicated to Quetzalcoatl. (Photographed by the author after reconstruction.)

pieces, a butterfly pectoral, a belt that clasps in the rear with a great mirror (*tezcacuitlapi-lli*, associated with a shield), necklace, bracelets, anklets, and sandals decorated with plumed serpents. The smooth elliptical mouth and eye sockets were probably inlaid with shell or obsidian. One hand holds an *atlatl*. There are still traces of the red and white pigment with which the warriors were painted. Similar figures adorn the pillars of the same height that supported the roof beams in the rear chamber of the temple where small Atlantean figures raise their arms to hold an altar or shrine (Figure 7.3). The plumed serpents, small Atlantean figures, and pillars carved with warriors, are already familiar from Chichén Itzá (see page 369 and Figure 7.17). *Chacmools* also are found at Tula, (see Figure 7.7) but as yet only one *in situ* in the Palacio Quemado. Another surely lay at the entrance to the temple atop Building B.

When excavating Tula in the 1940s, Jorge Acosta found sections of these carvings where they had been toppled into a deep trench cut into the northern side of the pyramid. Diehl (1983) believes this destruction was the work of looters who may have been interrupted or found the stones too heavy to haul away. Now, after many seasons of excavation and reconstruction, a number of the great warrior figures and pillars

FIGURE 7.3 Atlantean figures in four sections doweled together. Representing warriors, they wear a butterfly breastplate, feathered headdress, and carry *atlatls* in their hands. Height: 4.6 m. (Photographed by the author.)

have been reassembled and returned to their original setting on top of Building B (Figures 7.3 and 7.4).

The five tiers of this pyramid were once completely faced with carved panels of which only those on the east and north sides have survived. These depict prowling jaguars, coyotes, and eagles devouring human hearts (Figure 7.5d), suggesting to Acosta (1956–1957) military orders comparable to the Eagle and Jaguar Knights of the Aztecs. Berlo thinks it is more likely that they are all single logograms naming the individual they depict (Berlo, 1989). The lower panels depict a human face protruding from a monster mouth with elements of bird, serpent, and jaguar. This figure is thought to represent Quetzalcoatl in his aspect of Venus or the Morning Star, *Tlahuiz-calpantecuhtli*.

Stone sculpture is largely concerned with architecture: columns, Atlantids, pillars, or relief panels. Several carved Maya-like stelae are exceptional pieces of art (Figure 7.5b). Artisans at Tula may have been plentiful, but the quality of their workmanship is not extraordinary despite later claims of Toltec superiority. The panels offer a good example of the uneven quality of workmanship. Nevertheless, this Pyramid of Quetzalcoatl (Building B), faced with brightly colored carved panels, *chacmool* at the

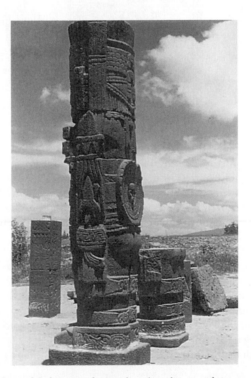

FIGURE 7.4 Side view of Atlantean figure showing the round *tezcacuitlapilli* mirror fastened on the back. (Photographed by the author.)

a   b   c

FIGURE 7.5 Toltec stone carving.
a. Small Atlantean warrior figure carved from a single block of stone. Exact provenance at Tula unknown. Height: 1.15 m. (Courtesy of the Museo Nacional de Antropología, Mexico.)
b. Early Toltec stela depicting a warrior wearing the Storm God headdress with the trapeze-and-ray year-sign. Height: 1.22 m. Tula. (Photographed by the author.)
c. Carved stela depicting a standing jaguar. Tula. Height: approximately 1.22 m. (Courtesy of the Museo Nacional de Antropología, Mexico.)
d. East wall, Building B. Jaguars and coyotes march across top rows; below are eagles eating human hearts, and the head of the deity *Tlahuizacalpantecuhtli* (Quetzalcoatl in his aspect of Venus, the Morning Star). (Photographed by the author.)
e. The *Coatepantli* (serpent wall) limiting access along the north side of Building B. Tula. (Photographed by the author.)
f. Polychromed bench of the Palacio Quemado with procession of figures below the cornice of undulating serpents. (Photographed by the author.)
g. Tula ball court north of Building B. (Photographed by the author.)

d

e

FIGURE 7.5—Continued

f

g

FIGURE 7.5—Continued

entrance to the temple on the summit, framed by columns of feathered serpents, must have been quite impressive.

Against Building B to the east is the Palace of Quetzalcoatl (Edificio 1). Only remnants remain of a colonnaded terrace divided into 3 rooms. It was this construction that protected and ensured the survival of the paneled facing mentioned above. This palace was largely destroyed, but the walls were made of adobe faced with stone, then stuccoed and painted. Acosta defined 7 stages of construction that never exceeded a height of 4.5 m. In one phase the façade was built in talud-tablero style with a projecting cornice.

A new architectural feature makes its appearance in this Tollan Phase called a *coatepantli* or serpent wall (a different wall from one of the same name of later Aztec design). The Tula *coatepantli* is a free-standing wall which does not surround the Pyramid of Quetzalcoatl, but simply extends along its northern side, limiting access to the main precinct. This was damaged in antiquity but has been restored except for a center section. Between two friezes of geometric design a serpent devours a human skull while dismembered arms and legs are enmeshed with the serpent's body. The central theme of the frieze was surely Quetzalcoatl.

Feathered serpents have been around in Mesoamerican iconography since Preclassic times. Although Quetzalcoatl is a good translation (*quetzal* referring to the gorgeous bird with long tail feathers, and *coatl* meaning serpent in Náhuatl), we cannot assume that every feathered serpent we find refers to Quetzalcoatl, the Postclassic deity. At Tula, however, feathered serpents are associated with the morning star or the east (*Tlahuizcalpantecuhtli*) and with the wind god, Ehécatl, (intimately related to round temples and the Huasteca). At Tula there are far more representations of Quetzalcoatl as the morning star than as the feathered serpent. By the sixteenth century some sources identify Quetzalcoatl as a god, while others refer to him as a priest-king. Among the Aztecs, Quetzalcoatl was known as a dignitary or the holder of a titled position in the priesthood. He was still represented as Ehécatl and as the morning star, with his twin Xólotl, the evening star or the planet Venus.

West of Pyramid B is the so-called Palacio Quemado (Burnt Palace, or Edificio 3). Burned it was in a major conflagration although we cannot be sure when or how it happened. This is an enormous 91 m × 59 m building. It was laid out with 3 large colonnaded halls facing south onto a long colonnaded gallery or vestibule with several smaller rooms in the rear (Figure 7.6). Each of these halls has a sunken central patio flanked by columns like the layout of rooms in Edificio 1. The small rooms at the back opened out to a wider colonnaded gallery. Each of the large halls contained remains of offerings, altars, and *tlecuils*, but no household debris. Room 1 contained a Tollan phase cache of more than 200 vessels including censers, dishes, bowls, large *incensarios*, and tobacco pipes arranged in sized groupings. This arrangement is suggestive of storage, close to a possible marketplace out front. Around the walls of Room 2 are low masonry benches carved with small warriors wearing plumed headdresses, jewelry, short skirts, and carrying darts and shields. Although the colors in which they were originaly painted (red, blue, yellow, white, and black) are not as vivid as when first uncovered, they are still remarkably well preserved. Rattlesnakes adorn the

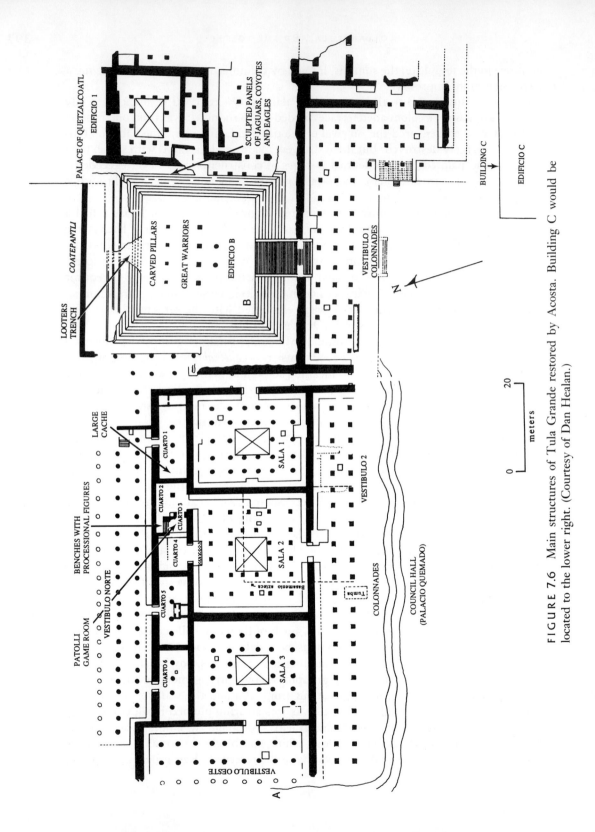

FIGURE 7.6 Main structures of Tula Grande restored by Acosta. Building C would be located to the lower right. (Courtesy of Dan Healan.)

cornice above these processional figures (See Figures 7.5f; Figure 7.18) that appear to march toward the front exits. The long colonnaded vestibule or gallery in front of the Palacio Quemado that continues eastward to connect Building B with C (see Figure 7.6) is a reconstruction that has been questioned (Molina-Montes, 1982).

The Palacio Quemado was once thought to be a residence, but after further excavations this seems unlikely. Sunken patios, altars, caches, and ritual objects, together with the absence of household features suggest use of the building for governmental purposes: meetings, reception of dignitaries, or special events, hence its designation as a Council Hall (Diehl, 1983). It was also where a gambler went to place his bets.

Patolli

Room 3 was the scene of *patolli* playing, a welcome hint of recreation (gambling?) for all the possible religious overtones it may have had. Patterns of 3 game boards are scratched in the plastered floor, the same game the Aztecs played at Conquest time.

A slight digression is in order here, for this game has a significance beyond the Toltecs or highland Mexico. So similar is it to our modern game of *pachisi* that spread to the western world from India, that the striking resemblances caught the attention of one of the early anthropologists, Edward B. Tyler. This set off a lively discussion of the principles of diffusion as a cultural process. Students are still fascinated by the *pachisi-patolli* game without ever having settled its history of histories.

Both games are played on a cross-shaped board with safety zones and progression of counters according to the throw of dice. Durán (1971) gives a detailed description of the game as played by the Aztecs. Their "dice" were marked beans and the game was played on a painted mat. Durán adds that bets were taken and gambling was lively among the crowd of onlookers. Apparently prior to the simple Aztec cross pattern, a more elaborate shape of cruciform and squares was used (Mountjoy and Smith, 1985). This pattern is found at pre-Aztec sites and is illustrated in several central Mexican *códices*.

Until recently, there was never any hint of the playing pieces, but on the central coast of Jalisco in a habitation site of the Tomatlán River valley, what might well be a *patolli* pattern was found along with markers and dice. A pattern pecked on a rock greatly resembles the early cruciform-square game depicted in the códices, not the cross-form of the Aztecs described by Durán. Pottery disks with a gouged indentation on one side and an excised cross on the other might well have served as dice. Associated cone-shaped pieces of pottery (markers?) would complete the set. Mountjoy and Smith (1985) estimate these objects might be dated at A.D. 1000–1525 or possibly A.D. 600–1000. Either choice is compatible with other Mesoamerican *patolli* remains.

The Teotihuacan pattern in the Zacuala residence may date to the seventh or eighth century. Other playing patterns are known at El Tajín, Chiapa de Corzo, and among the Maya who were avid gamblers, the list is long. Best-known sites are Uaxactún, Tikal, Palenque, Piedras Negras, El Cayo, Chichén Itzá, Dzibilchaltún, Stann Creek, and Benque Viejo. Dating is not precise, as a pattern could be placed on a floor at any time (Smith, 1977), but we know the game was popular from the Late Classic Period to the Conquest.

Returning to Tula, two ball courts have been excavated. One, cleared and restored, is similar to a court at Xochicalco, being of the same size and shape. This Tula court lies across the north plaza from Building B and possesses a fine drainage system (see Figure 7.5g). It was once faced with panels and friezes but these were carried off by the later Aztecs. Originally stone rings, a feature of Postclassic courts, protruded from the walls, but today only the empty holes for their insertion are visible. Apparently Charnay saw one still *in situ* (Acosta, 1956). We are not certain of the purpose of niches located diagonally at the ends of the court, but these are also found in Oaxaca at Monte Albán and Atzompa.

A city of this size would surely have had a marketplace located in a central and prominent position. In many sites the marketplace was situated in proximity to a ball court and Tula was probably no exception. The most logical location for it would have been in the area between the main plaza and the large western ball court. Here the public could have come to buy goods, exchange news, attend parades and special events, and have a chance to watch a ball game.

A shrine or altar of some sort was located in the center of the main plaza, but not much was left after Charnay put a trench through it (Healan, 1989). His trench missed fragments of a large *chacmool* that were eventually recovered by Acosta. The altar once had a stairway on each of its four sides and was originally built in talud-tablero style. Height is estimated at 1.7 m. Its restoration by Acosta might have been influenced by his reconstruction of the Platform of the Eagles at Chichén Itzá, (Molina-Montes, 1982) but Healan (1989) feels the restoration is scientifically accurate. An unexcavated long structure on the south side of the plaza completes the civic-religious center of Tula Grande.

FIGURE 7.7   *Chacmool*, Tula. Exact provenance unknown. Height: 63.5 cm (Courtesy of the Museo Nacional de Antropología, Mexico.)

Later evidence of the Aztecs at Tula Grande can be found in debris, offerings, and burials. The Aztecs held the Toltecs in great esteem, but they did nothing to enhance or restore this land they claimed as home of their ancestors.

Northern Structures on the Ridge

Other buildings belonging to the Tollan Phase are located in the northern part of the ridge above the old area of Tula Chico (See Map 7.1). Near the El Corral Locality is a most unusual structure called El Corral Temple excavated many years ago by Jorge Acosta (Figure 7.8). This is a temple-platform that faces east, oriented 17° west of magnetic north. A broad staircase leads to a wide rectangular platform joined by a circular unit. The west side has a short rectangular extension. The whole thing is constructed of cobble-and-mud faced with stone veneer and plastered. The profile has two tiers of talud-tableros. A small altar to the right of the staircase is also built in talud-tablero style with some friezes carved with skulls and crossed long bones; others are carved with reclining warriors. There is no clue as to when this curious structure was erected. The general combination of a round and rectangular form bears some resemblance to the fifteenth century Tarascan *yácatas* of Tzintzuntzan, Michoacán, but nothing else comes to mind. Immediately in front of the pyramid in an adoratorio (shrine), a famous Tohil Plumbate jar lid decorated with a marine shell mosaic was recovered. This extraordinary vessel takes the form of a bearded face emerging from a coyote's mouth (Diehl, 1983). The only structures associated with this pyramid 10 m away were remains of several rooms, one with four columns and a central *tlecuil*, and a shrine. As yet, these buildings have not been accommodated among the Toltec remains.

FIGURE 7.8   El Corral Temple. (Photographed by the author.)

Housing   It often happens that pyramids, temples, and tombs capture the head-lines and monopolize the funds to investigate. But in the 1970s, further work at Tula Grande was put on hold, and INAH and the University of Missouri concentrated on surveying and investigating housing. In doing so they have greatly enlarged our knowledge of Toltec living conditions, the economy, and the origins of the city. We now know that aside from palaces for the elite such as the Palace of Quetzalcoatl in Tula Grande, homes for lesser nobility and non-elite were not separate individual structures, but were placed in groups around interior courtyards (Healan, 1989).

El Corral Locality

A curious structure at El Corral Locality north of Tula Chico (see Map 7.1) was probably part of a larger complex that housed high-status individuals as well as serving political and ritual needs. The structures here were all oriented on a nearly perfect north–south axis following the trend of the Coyotlatelco communities. Only a few rooms were excavated but the well-cut stone, use of lime-plastered walls, and the presence of some U-shaped drain stones, otherwise found only at the Palace of Quet-zalcoatl, were indications that this was special construction. The most distinctive feature in this special settlement was the presence of large rooms with central, col-umned enclosures. Columns were a prominent feature of public areas in Tula Grande, but none had been previously found in residential areas.

El Corral is notorious for the peculiar human remains found scattered about on the floor of two large rooms and a passageway. Bones of children and adults had been smashed or split and with some difficulty it was ascertained that they belonged to 7 individuals (1 adult male, 3 adult females, 2 children, and 1 infant). The frag-mented state of the bones, associated with fire, stone tools, and pottery raised the spector of cannibalism, but this was ruled out when no tell-tale cut marks were found. Perhaps a massacre of an entire family? It is believed that the individuals had been intact when buried on the floor and the scattering may have been done by animals.

The Canal Locality

Non-elite Toltecs lived in "house groups" exemplified by the complex known as the Canal Locality, 1.5 km northeast of Tula Chico. This housing was probably erected after the El Corral structures late in the Tollan Phase and was occupied for no more than 100–200 years. All these structures were oriented 18° west of magnetic north.

A house here might consist of 4–8 rooms. More than one family could have lived in one of these houses and alterations such as partitions are not uncommon. The relationship of 10 houses can be seen in Figure 7.9, that illustrates the L-shaped or baffled entryway to each dwelling with connecting passageways and narrow alleys between them. A cobblestone paved street ran on the south side along the Central and West Groups. Stone, *tepetate*, adobe, and mud were used in various combinations for walls; floors were either of packed earth or plastered. Roofs were presumably flat,

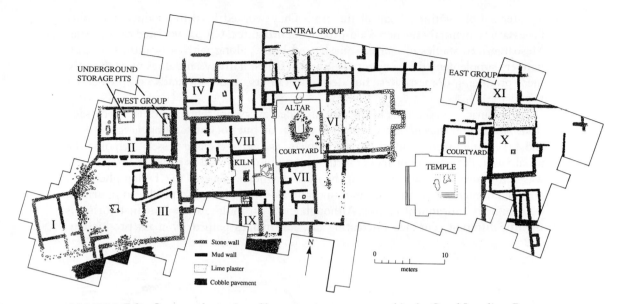

CENTRAL GROUP

UNDERGROUND
STORAGE PITS

WEST GROUP

EAST GROUP

IV

XI

ALTAR

V

VI

VIII

X

II

KILN

COURTYARD

COURTYARD

VII

TEMPLE

I

III

IX

N

Stone wall
Mud wall
Lime plaster
Cobble pavement

0   10

meters

FIGURE 7.9 Structural remains of house groups encountered in the Canal Locality. Roman numerals designate individual houses. (Courtesy of Dan Healan.)

covered with poles overlaid with soil, clay, or plaster. Houses differed as to size, use of lime plaster, and decoration that might consist of varying the façade, doorway, or the use of paint. Kitchen areas were identified by the presence of hearths and/or cooking utensils. No doubt many household activities took place in the patios. Families had their privacy at home while the common courtyard provided an area for companionship, joint projects, and a focus for ritual activities around the altar.

A drainage system was well engineered both to store water and to remove the excess from the rooftop or house. The production of clay tubes for drains was a local industry at Tula. The residents of House VIII fired ceramic tubes in a kiln placed directly in the floor of their open patio at the time the house was built. This was a rather sophisticated arrangement in which air was forced from a furnace to a firing chamber to be baked. These drain tubes were cleverly formed with a flare at one end for easy connection, and turning corners were facilitated by inserting one tube in a slotted opening in another.

Similar multi-room structures have been identified at other sites such as Tenochtilán, Monte Albán, and Tikal.

Economy

Tula's economy was based on irrigated agriculture since rainfall alone was insufficient and undependable. Local springs were utilized for water distributed via canals, ditches, and simple brush and earth dams. Farmers lived in small villages located near a water supply within 15 km of the city. They worked hard to produce a surplus necessary to maintain the non-food-producing urbanites. Crops consisted of the usual Mesoamerican staples of maize, squash, and beans, along with amaranth, and chili peppers supplemented by a variety of seasonal fruits. Turkeys and dogs were the only meat-producing domesticates, but deer, jackrabbits, and cottontails complemented the diet.

In return, craftspersons in the city provided every household with the necessary stone *metates* and *manos*. Toltec pottery is utilitarian but not outstanding. (Figures 7.10 and 11). Potters turned out water jars, goblets, *molcajetes*, cooking vessels including the usual *comal* (flat griddle for frying tortillas), and braziers used as stoves. Mazapa ware was still in use in a few sectors but the most diagnostic ware of the Tollan phase is a polished orange. Aside from utilitarian ceramics, the Toltecs also produced figurines, both human and animal forms. Although made in molds, each human figurine is slightly different, curiously defeating any advantages gained by mass production.

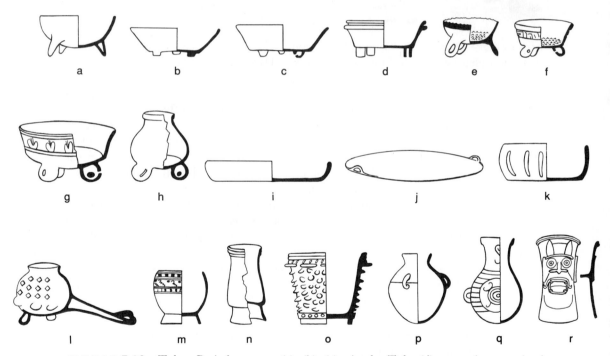

FIGURE 7.10   Toltec Period pottery. (a), (b), (c) tripods, Tula; (d) coarse brown tripod, Tula; (e), (f) *molcajetes*, Tula; (g), (h) Z Fine Orange ware, Chichén Itzá; (i) brown-ware bowl, Tula; (j) *comal*, Tula; (k) gadrooned plain ware, Tula; (l) handled censer, Tula; (m) black-on-orange ring stand, Aztec I; (n) X Fine Orange, incised and painted in black, Chichén Itzá; (o) hobnail-decorated coarse ware, Tula; (p) red-on-brown jug, Tula; (q) black-on-orange jar, Aztec II; (r) Tlaloc incense burner, Tula. (From the following sources: a, k, q, Acosta 1945; b, c, d, e, f, i, j, l, o, p, r, Acosta 1956-1957; g, h, n, Brainerd 1941; m, Piná Chán 1960.)

Animal forms depict birds, dogs, and cats. Of particular interest are the wheeled figures (Stocker *et al.*, 1986) measuring up to 12 in. in length. The legs have holes for the attachment of axles and wheels. Over the years these have been called wheeled "toys," as they resemble a child's toy in our society, but there is no indication of how or who used them in Mesoamerica (see page 229). Although never common, several dozen of these objects have now been found in sites from Tula to El Salvador, dating largely to the Postclassic Period.

The Toltecs could have been quite self-sufficient, needing only to import salt, obsidian, and any freshwater lake products they might want (Sanders and Santley, 1983).

Obsidian was the best medium for cutting instruments and an industry began in pre-Tollan phases with the manufacture of biface tools in outlying areas. Most of this early obsidian was imported from Zinapécuaro, Michoacán.

In the Tollan Phase, the obsidian industry became a far more prestigious and prosperous occupation. Extensive clusters of workshops organized as "cottage industries" were concentrated east of El Salitre and Cerro el Cielito within the urban zone. These workers specialized in the exclusive production of fine prismatic blades struck from green obsidian cores, the finest on the market, that came from Pachuca only 70 km to the east.

The location of the obsidian industry that eventually constituted 80% of the production corresponds to that of Mazapa pottery production. This ware was much more common in the Basin of Mexico and at Teotihuacan. A group from that area may have moved to the south valley at Tula, bringing with them their taste for Mazapa pottery and stimulating the very lucrative core/blade industry in the Tollan Phase. Success resulted in their eventual incorporation into Tula's urban society and the eclipse of their earlier background. By this time the Toltecs had probably gained control over the Pachuca mines. At the very least they had a fine organization reflecting efficient procurement, production, and trash disposal techniques (Healan, 1986).

A minor industry was work in *tecalli*, a white sedimentary stone available locally. This may have been a small-scale elite craft. Beads, ornaments, and bowls of *tecalli* were special, luxury items in demand for export and for the wealthy.

The Toltecs could have lived well off their own resources, growing much of their food, taking fish from the rivers, eating meat from local animals, making mats and baskets from reeds of El Salitre swamp, and procuring specialized products from the Basin of Mexico only 60 km away. But to meet the demands of ritual and to satisfy the tastes of the elite, certain imports were deemed necessary such as cacao, semiprecious stones, feathers, peyote, marine shells, cotton, jewelry, fancy pottery, and metal, which was just beginning to make its appearance in this area.

The Toltec Sphere of Influence

It is best to think of a Toltec sphere of influence rather than an empire, for there was never an integrated territory with well-defined boundaries and nothing to indicate centralized control. The Toltecs were a dominant power for perhaps 250 years, during which time they built Tula Grande and established far-flung contacts. The extent of their domain was not comparable to that of the Teotihuacanos, the Aztecs, or what we have seen among the Maya. But the Toltecs filled a leadership and power gap after the collapse of Teotihuacan with a stunning and lasting impact on Mesoamerican peoples.

How was this accomplished? Trade may have initiated the early contacts but the driving force was probably wealth acquired by tribute. Just how they set up the organization and management of their activities we do not know. The Toltecs made a great display of being warriors, portraying militaristic themes in their art. Perhaps a show of strength was enough to enlist cooperation and ensure allegiance. But no coercion or conquest is apparent archaeologically.

Toltec artifacts have a wide but uneven distribution in Mesoamerica that may indicate nothing more than down-the-line movement or sporadic exchange. But the distribution is noteworthy for revealing sizeable areas lacking any sign of the Toltecs.

To the north, an area of ancient roots, Toltec goods are recovered at Casas Grandes, which became a major trading center around A.D. 1050. It is not clear if direct contact was made with the Toltecs, or if their artifacts were passed along via the west coast cultures.

Links to west Mexico are found in the pottery called *blanco levantado* or Tula Watercolored, present at Tula although not common. The same can be said of cloisonné. These wares are found across Guanajuato and in parts of the Bajío. Mazapa pottery and Tula-type figurines are scattered through Michoacán, Jalisco, and Nayarit and a crude *chacmool* occurs in the Lake Pátzcuaro area at a later time.

Metallurgy may have a western source. It made an entrance into central Mexico after A.D. 900 (?) from Central or South America (see page 200; Hosler, 1990). Few articles of metal have been found at Tula itself, but gold ornaments began to appear at Maya sites following the earliest gold trinket at Altun Há in A.D. 550 (Bray, 1989). Either the Maya or west Mexico could have been the source of metallurgy for the central Mexicans and the Tula Toltecs.

Tula retained a relationship with the Huasteca throughout its history, seen in imported pottery from central Veracruz and the northern Gulf Coast. This was one original home of some Toltecs and Teotihuacanos and it is logical that elements of ritual and religion from the Gulf would be reflected in Toltec art. More southern Gulf Coast contacts may have been somewhat hampered by competitors. El Tajín and Cempoala were potential rivals and could have blocked any attempt by Tula at communication with the southern lowlands. This might explain the paucity of Toltec remains in these regions. We are not sure what was happening at Cholula, but there are no indications that the Toltec were in the area to any great extent.

Immediately south of Tula, archaeology indicates that the Toltecs controlled only the northern part of the Basin of Mexico. The southern portion was closely allied to the area of Puebla. Eastern Morelos would have been a valuable region for Tula to acquire with its cultivation and spinning of cotton fibers. The area of the Amatzinac Valley had been under Teotihuacan domination in Late Classic times, but Toltec control is doubtful. By A.D. 900 Xochicalco in western Morelos had passed its prime and there is little in this area to indicate contact with Tula.

FIGURE 7.11 Toltec Period pottery.
a. Vessel with ringstand and handle representing Tlaloc, painted blue. Height: 13 cm. (Courtesy of the Museo Nacional de Antropología, Mexico.)
b. Clay spindle whorls (*malacates*), incised decoration. Central Mexico. Diameter largest 6 cm. (Courtesy of the Museum of the American Indian, Heye Foundation, N.Y [22/8559].
c. Mazapan red-on-buff bowl. Design has been painted with a multiple-brush technique. Height: 13 cm. (Courtesy of the Museo Nacional de Antropología, Mexico.)
d. Large orange-ware tripod with stamped decoration. Height: 28 cm. (Courtesy of the Museo Nacional de Antropología, Mexico.)
e. Resist-painted olla. Tlacotepec, State of Mexico. Early Postclassic Period. Height: 14 cm. (Courtesy of the Museum of the American Indian, Heye Foundation, N.Y. [8/7873].
f. Plumbate effigy vessel from San Antonio Suchitepequez, Guatemala. Height: 12.5 cm. (Courtesy of the Museum of the American Indian, Heye Foundation, N.Y. [16/3463].

Bypassing Morelos, good communication southwest could have taken place from Tula through the Toluca Valley where the great site of Teotenango is sometimes mentioned as another "Tollan." It was visited by some Nonoalca on the way to Tula, Hidalgo, and may have received Toltecs after the fall of Tula. Toluca Valley can be included in a Toltec domain (Sanders and Santley, 1983).

Passing on south to Ixtapan and Tonatico in the State of Mexico, to northern Guerrero, a route then leads to the Middle Balsas and the Pacific Coast. The trip in reverse would have been a possible route for the entry into central Mexico of Tohil Plumbate that is found in the Tollan Phase in surprising quantities. Plumbate is an exotic ceramic manufactured in coastal Guatemala (Neff and Bishop, 1988) and was Tula's most common import. An even longer trip north was made by some Maya polychromes and other wares attributed to Yucatán and Quintana Roo (but Fine Orange and the fine paste wares of the southern Gulf Coast and northern Yucatán are entirely absent at Tula). Amazingly, four trade vessels of Papagayo Polychrome from even farther south in Central America were found with Plumbate in a storage bin of a house at Tula where precious items had been stored (Figure 7.9) (Diehl et al., 1974). Distance was seemingly of little concern. Time and manpower were in unlimited supply.

What about the Oaxaca area? The Zapotecs had close relations of some sort with the Teotihuacanos, and from the Oaxaca Barrio at Teotihuacan, they had aided the lime exploitation in early settlements near Tula. Monte Albán prospered during the Classic Period but had declined by the time of Tula's affluence. During Tula's prominence, the Oaxaca folk to deal with were the Mixtecs living in the western highlands of Oaxaca (Mixteca Alta), best known for their fine talents in crafting ceramics and jewelry. Their códices speak of a ruler Eight Deer and of his traveling to Tula. Despite this, there is little archaeologically to show contact between the Mixtecs and Toltecs.

East of the Isthmus are the dramatic similarities between Chichén Itzá and Tula, yet to be accounted for (see below).

In summary, what then comprised a Toltec "empire" or sphere of influence? The heartland of the Toltecs was the Tula-to-Tulancingo area, with strongest influences exerted in an east–west band from the Huasteca across Guanajuato and Querétaro (the Bajío) to Jalisco. The Toltec domain seems to have integrated no more than the northern Basin of Mexico, the State of Hidalgo, perhaps the Tulancingo area, Toluca Valley, parts of the Bajío, and closer areas of the Lerma River drainage.

This does not begin to represent the role of the Toltecs in Mesoamerican history. If one were to judge their influence or trace their foreign relationships according to the distribution and imports of material goods (Casas Grandes to Central America), one would include the major part of Mesoamerica.

Final Days at Tula

The Toltecs at A.D. 1100 were a talented and multi-ethnic group, living well, dominating its nearest neighbors and participating in the greater world of the Maya. What would have brought on its destruction in A.D. 1200?

Signals are mixed. There seems to be little doubt that Tula Grande was sacked and burned amidst Aztec II pottery around A.D. 1150–1200. But there is little Aztec II pottery found in the area outside of the ceremonial center. Were the "sackers" satisfied to just demolish the ceremonial heart of Tula and leave?

Rubbish carelessly dumped all around the Canal Locality may be some indication of a weakening of community spirit and the general morale. The killings or massacre (?) at El Corral are not a healthy sign. There was some looting of altars and courtyards, although we are not sure just when this happened. These are indications of disturbances, or of an angry, demoralized populace to whom the future looked bleak. At present, there is no clear explanation of the final days.

The record shows that the first major reoccupation of the Tula region occurred about 150 years later around A.D. 1350–1400 with the appearance of Aztec III pottery. This leaves a gap after the fall of Tula both in time and continuity, but does not complete the story of the Toltecs. These were a people whose fame and prestige increased with time assisted by the Aztecs.

The Northwest

The Chalchihuites mining operations did not close down completely. As their markets with Mesoamerica dried up, they looked north and continued their search for turquoise and strengthened their association with the North American Southwest. Although the collapse of Teotihuacan may have slowed down some mining operations, Chalchihuites found there was increasing demand in Mesoamerican cities for turquoise. At Guasave and at La Quemada, representing coastal and inland routes respectively, turquoise is found that originated at various sources, mostly from the American Southwest. Was it more available, easier to work than jade? Or was the bright blue color a sudden attraction? Whatever the reason, by Late Postclassic times the demand for turquoise had surpassed that for the traditional jade (Weigand and Harbottle, 1987).

The miners were also in contact with coastal cultures over the mountains to the west. Just over the Sierra Madre Occidental lay the present-day state of Sinaloa on the coastal corridor to the North American Southwest. Archaeological remains there are known largely from surface collections and burials excavated by Gordon Ekholm and Isabel Kelly in the 1930s which produced some of the most elaborate pottery in the Americas. This ware forms part of the Aztatlán complex or horizon which extended along the coast from Sinaloa south to Nayarit and part of Jalisco. The greatest development took place in the Early Postclassic in the area of Guasave, at the mouth of the Sinaloa River. This is known largely from a pottery style with engraved and 4- to 6-color polychrome vessels, resist painting, and paint cloisonné techniques.

The rich Guasave phase also yielded abundant metal: copper (awls, rings, and bells) and some gold and silver ornaments, iron-pyrite beads, onyx and alabaster vases, and turquoise mosaics and elbow pipes. This exotic inventory of artifacts is unaccompanied by stone architecture or monumental sculpture and Guasave has remained a kind of unexplained pocket of wealth on the very frontier of Mesoamerica.

The Aztatlán horizon was once thought to represent an actual migration of people out of central Mexico because certain designs are shared with the Mixteca-Puebla culture. But Meighan (1974) points out that this was a cultural complex in Postclassic years that is found all along the west coast, spreading through Jalisco, Nayarit, and Sinaloa around A.D. 1000–1350. It did not arrive suddenly but its development can be traced through the earlier Sinaloa phases of Culiacán and Chametla.

The Smiths (Smith and Heath-Smith, 1980) point out that the most elaborate pottery of Guasave resembles that of Nicoya, Costa Rica, more than that of the Mixteca-Puebla culture. Specific designs such as the stepped-fret or greca, feathered serpent, and sunburst are shared themes.

We have already observed that metallurgy, and probably shaft-and-chamber tombs as well, reached west Mexico via the coast from South America. The fancy polychromes of the Aztatlán horizon could have been influenced by Nicoya. It has always been difficult to imagine a westward migration of people from Puebla to the west coast that traveled so rapidly that no trace of its passage has been found and influence is limited to polychrome ceramics. The resemblances between the Mixteca-Puebla art style and the Aztatlán polychromes could be due to a diffusion of tastes out of central Mexico south to the Nicoya peninsula where they were absorbed and eventually passed north via the Pacific coast. This was the time of great coastal trade in Mesoamerica with ancient roots. This eclectic art style could have moved in the same trading network that brought Plumbate and Fine Orange north. After A.D. 1250 far west Mexico went its own way with little central Mexican influence apparent thereafter.

In the Bolaños Canyon, located in a northern tongue of the state of Jalisco, are the sites of Cerro de Colotlán and La Ventanas. Cerro de Colotlán near Juchipila has circular architecture derived from earlier and more complex examples near Totoate. These sites may well represent the last remnants of the old Teuchitlán Tradition so prominent in much of west Mexico during the Classic Period. There are still some few Tepecanos who visit the shrine in Cerro de Colotlán circle (Weigand, 1985b).

Another ethnic group of particular interest is the Caxcanes. These were people from northwest Mesoamerica who played an oft-mentioned role in the uncertain times of the northern frontier. Weigand (1985b) believes that their original home lay in the Chalchihuites area with a possible relation to the early history of the Mexica. At least their language is more closely related to Náhuatl than to any of the western Uto-Aztecan languages. The Caxcanes figure prominently in history as highly competitive warriors, well organized into military brotherhoods, who pressed south over a long period following A.D. 900/1000 into the Juchipila Valley occupied by the Texcuexes. Weigand (1985b) speculates that the belligerent Caxcanes may have pushed these people farther west and, combined with their central Mexican tradition, caused the end of the Teuchitlán Tradition (see page 195).

The Caxcanes no longer exist as an ethnic group but they distinguished themselves in the Colonial Period by nearly exterminating the Spaniards in west Mexico. Helping to lead this revolt was a Caxcan king, Siutecutli, whose palace was the citadel of Las Ventanas.

Las Ventanas, near Juchipila, Jalisco, is an impressive cliff dwelling on top of a mesa, a highly fortified citadel, with a single narrow stairway providing the only easy access. Courts, rooms, terraces, and a huge tightly packed building complex at the top is dominated on one edge by a 25-m pyramid, 8 m in height. This is a major site, and its various types of ceramics include bichromes, elaborate polychromes, and resist painting, with certain ties to the Chalchihuites and Malpaso Valley ceramics.

History of the large important settlements of the Juchipila Valley undoubtedly predates the Caxcanes incursion, probably extending as far back as Preclassic times. There are tales of shallow, boot-shaped shaft tombs, and although none have been excavated, Weigand (1985b) has seen many artifacts that would support their presence. Later tombs are clearly Postclassic containing copper objects. Las Ventanas is but one of many sites in the large zone of habitation.

Puebla-Tlaxcala

This is a particularly good area for further research, as somehow the key to many questions lies in this region just east of the highland volcanoes in the Valley of Puebla. A modern map of Mexico shows highways radiating from the Valley of Puebla in four directions. The valley has always been strategically situated to attract travelers, merchants, and pilgrims from the earliest pre-Conquest days to the present. The control of the Puebla-Tlaxcala region may have been necessary to maintain major stability in the central highlands for any length of time. After reestablishing Cholula in the Early Postclassic, the old pyramid was gradually enlarged four times until it eventually covered 16 ha^2 and reached a height of 55 m, rivaled only by El Mirador in the Petén (see page 131). Today it is easily mistaken for a hill, as the pyramid is covered with soil and grass, and crowned by a Catholic church, an effort by the Spaniards to substitute their religion for the old (Figure 7.12).

Excavations at Cholula have revealed a veritable maze of superimposed platforms, walls, patios, and open and covered stone drains. Chronology is based largely on ceramic correlations with other areas (Noguera, 1965). The early Postclassic phases are characterized by *molcajetes*, resist painting, handled censers, griddles with high walls, and Coyotlatelco ware, introduced in the last days of Teotihuacan. Mazapan, with parallel, wavy, red lines on buff, is found in small quantities. Plumbate and Culhuacán wares, the latter from the Basin of Mexico, are more common. Fine Orange vessels from the Isla de Sacrificios are proof of continuing ties with the eastern lowlands. In these years one of the great art styles of Mesoamerica (the Mixteca-Puebla) makes its appearance. It will be seen to exert a strong influence on many aspects of Mesoamerican art in the Late Postclassic Period.

The site of Cholula lay outside the survey limits of the Basin of Mexico Project of Sanders *et al.* (1979), but was only 40 km east of the Chalco region, and they found it to be closely allied to the history of the southern Basin. After the fall of Teotihuacan, some of its inhabitants may have drifted over to the Puebla Valley, as we know the population in the Basin of Mexico was somewhat reduced. It seems that Cholula controlled, or at least was in close contact with, the southern part of the Basin, while Tula dominated the north.

FIGURE 7.12   Excavations on the south side of the great pyramid at Cholula on which the church is built. (Photographed by the author.)

How strong was Cholula? Could Tula and Cholula have been political and economic rivals? Was the Teotihuacan Corridor still closed? Certainly there is little evidence of contact between the two centers. It is also possible that Cholula, while regaining its strength, might not yet have been able to assume a prominent role in interregional trade. It was about the time Tula collapsed that Cholula entered its greatest period of prosperity.

The Huasteca

The close bond that had existed between the Huasteca and southern Veracruz, Tabasco, and the lowland Maya region in earlier times had been abruptly severed, perhaps by the intrusion of Náhuatl-speaking peoples into central Veracruz during the Classic Period. The Huasteca was, however, strongly influenced by Teotihuacan, as seen in the "portrait"-type figure and resist painting. The most significant Huastec development took place after A.D. 900, the Las Flores phase in the local sequence (Ekholm, 1944).

We do not know the nature of the relationship of the Huastecs with the Toltecs, but they probably shared early ethnic roots, and during these years shared many material goods. For the first time, objects of copper, clay smoking pipes, stamps, *malacates*, engraved shells, and wheeled figures are found. These all have parallels at Tula as well as in the far western cultures of coastal Sinaloa. Although Plumbate has not been reported from the Huasteca, the lines of communication were well established across northern Mesoamerica at this time.

Huastec pottery and figurines followed local styles of development. Basically the clay was fired well, and has a characteristic cream or pinkish color. In Late Postclassic times, a distinctive black-on-white decoration became extremely popular (see Figure 8.25m). Styles incorporating teapot forms, flat ribbonlike handles, and spouts were common. This new pottery has no counterpart elsewhere and does not have a long tradition in the Huasteca, simply appearing fully developed.

In addition, the use of alphalt as paint or glue is shared with the Classic Veracruz cultures. Thin layers of asphalt were used to cover floors and even to surface mounds after the Late Classic Period. The application of asphalt depended entirely on natural seepages, so the technique was geographically limited.

Stone-carving reflects a totally new artistic expression (Figures 7.13 and 7.14), the style of which is flat and slablike. Figures often wear a conical-shaped headdress backed by a fanlike shield, and a cavity in the chest may have held an inlay of some kind.

Perhaps the Huasteca is most famous for its round structures that are found here in greater number than in any other region of Mesoamerica and were the prevalent form of architecture. At the sites of Las Flores, Pavón, and Tancol, round structures predominate. Numerous others have been reported from the mountains as well and from as far west as Buenavista Huaxcama in San Luis Potosí. Round structures are generally associated with Quetzalcoatl in his aspect as the wind god, Ehécatl, and also closely linked to the east as a cardinal point. Ekholm (1944) felt that the great concentration of round structures made this east coast region a likely center of origin.

The geographical position of the Huasteca makes it the best potential link between Mesoamerica and the southeastern cultures of the United States. But in sharp contrast to the northwestern frontier of Mesoamerica that shows a blending into the American Southwest, the northeastern seaboard seems to have had but sporadic contact with its northern neighbors.

THE POSTCLASSIC IN OAXACA

The Zapotecs

In the Early Postclassic the Zapotecs were living in separate communities throughout the Oaxaca valleys. The higher elevations at Monte Albán had been abandoned as people moved down around the base of the hill closer to roads and commercial activity. The population dropped from 30,000 in Monte Albán IIIb, to 4000-8000 in Monte Albán V, but workshops continued to produce obsidian tools and *manos* and

FIGURE 7.13   Huastec stone stela with attributes of Quetzalcoatl. Castillo de Teayo, Vera-cruz. Height: approximately 12 ft. (Courtesy of the Museo Nacional de Antropología, Mexico.)

metates (Blanton, 1983a,b). A colony of Mixtecs moved in on the southern flanks of the mountain and there are increasing signs of their presence. Some Mixtec royalty married into the Zapotec nobility. Other Mixtecs came in as laborers, but no longer were pyramids and major constructions built.

Times had changed and a new political system of small city-states replaced the old capital at Monte Albán. Some of the earlier administrative centers of Monte Albán IV (Cuilapan, Zaachila, Macuilxóchitl, Mitla, and Matatlań) became centers of political control after A.D. 900.

The earlier alluvium-based communities disappeared perhaps as the result of importing Mixteca labor (Blanton and Kowalewski, 1981). With this influx of people, craft specialization and trade intensified. By the Late Postclassic Period, a greatly expanded commercial network was in place. Obsidian blades could be found even in isolated residences and scattered hamlets, reflecting a much more integrated and flexible economic system than the tight control exerted by the older Monte Albán capital. The new political organization (*cacicazgos*) was much like that of the Mixtecs,

FIGURE 7.14 Priest (?) performing autosacrifice by running a stick of thorns through his tongue. Height: approximately 6.5 ft. Huastec culture. Huilocintla, Veracruz. (Courtesy of the Museo Nacional de Antropología, Mexico.)

in which a series of rural communities were subject to a hereditary lord. This was a major Postclassic change (Marcus, 1983c).

Another change was an emphasis on increased social stratification. Monte Albán tombs after A.D. 600 had often contained small carved stones with information of births, parents and ancestral data. These are called genealogical registers (Marcus, 1980). Now, this record assumed greater importance. The Zapotec elite began to stress status and seek out marriage alliances with an eye to some political advantage. A ruler or lord would arrange to have his genealogical record included in the antechamber of his tomb for consultation by future generations.

In 1985 an unusually fine example was found in an elaborate tomb (9 m × 4 m) in the Etla Valley in the jurisdiction of two towns: Huijazoo and Suchiquitongo. Eight steps led 5 m underground to Tomb 5 beneath a platform in a large series of mounds. The north–south cruciform antechamber had east–west side-niches as did the large burial chamber. Remarkably there are 40 m of painted murals and 11 stones carved with human figures and glyphs all in a fine state of preservation (Méndez Martínez, 1988).

This Zapotec tomb was constructed around A.D. 700 (Monte Albán IIIb) and had been reused several times. In Period IV (A.D. 850?) it was opened to add a beautifully carved register or stela documenting the detailed ancestry of a lord, tracing his descent to a venerated ancestor. Graphic scenes complement the written text that provides names, dates, and events in the lives of descendants and in-laws (Miller, 1991).

Mitla   The well-known site of Mitla in the Tlacolula Valley is unusual, for it was one of the few such construction projects undertaken. Mitla had been settled since 1200 B.C. but was of little importance until the Postclassic Period of Monte Albán V. The ruins straddle the Río Grande de Mitla with rocky slopes and hills on the north side. Here the ceremonial-civic center of an urban zone of 1–2 km^2 was constructed of groups that consisted of long, narrow buildings around three sides of a rectangular patio. To the south were the famous cruciform tombs for burial of nobility that extended beneath another patio and structures. The core of the construction was mud and stone, covered with plaster or well-cut trachyte. The façades and door frames were decorated with mosaics of small stones combined to form a wide variety of geometric patterns such as the stepped fret (Figure 7.15). Beams from wall to wall supported the roofs. These were covered first with small slabs, then gravel, and finally plastered over. The roofs were made with a gentle slope to direct rainwater toward the patio. The *greca* motif is especially prominent at Mitla. It was first painted on walls or pottery, but eventually was made in stone mosaics and decorated façades of

FIGURE 7.15   Interior of palace structure at Mitla, Oaxaca. Construction technique is mosaic veneer masonry. Note variety of greca motifs. (Photographed by the author.)

buildings, residences, and tombs. Only the availability of local stone made this distinctive architecture possible. Mitla's architecture is Zapotec, but the Mixtecs decorated some palace rooms with paintings done in their codex-style (Flannery and Marcus, 1983c).

Extending up and down the river was a suburban sector with housemounds, while 5 kms of surrounding hinterland was occupied by farmers and their visible terracing. A 2-chambered pottery kiln in this area demonstrates the presence of some craft specialization outside the urban zone. Finally, four hilltop fortresses protected the valley. Mitla may have exercised considerable independence but was apparently subject to the Zapotec lord of Zaachila (Flannery and Marcus, 1983c). By the Late Postclassic there was considerable mingling of Zapotec and Mixtec cultures.

The Mixtecs

The Mixtec religion, often called simply the Mixteca, consists of three subareas (see Map 6.3). The Mixteca Baja (land of the Ñuíñe), is centered in western and northwestern Oaxaca. To the east and south lies the Mixteca Alta, an area of high, cold, fertile valleys surrounded by mountains. This region borders on and is most intimately related to the Zapotecs. Finally, there is the Mixteca de la Costa or the coastal lowlands of Oaxaca (Spores, 1967).

Despite being tucked away in mountain valleys with some areas difficult to reach and many yet unexplored, the Mixtecs are outstanding among Mesoamericans as metallurgists and craftspersons of many kinds. Their códices are among Mexico's most beautiful.

Native Kingdoms (*cacicazgos*) They also excelled in the organization of their native kingdoms called *cacicazgos*, formed at least 500 years prior to the Conquest (Spores, 1967, 1984). This was a territory usually small enough to be crossed by foot in a day, controlled by a privileged aristocracy with royal lineages. A class structure was based on an intricate ranking system. At the top was a privileged kin group, headed by a ruler who was an absolute monarch. Marriages were contracted to strengthen alliances and to preserve and limit prerogatives. The Mixtecs developed one of the most highly stratified systems in Mesoamerica. Even the nobility and royalty were tightly ranked. So important was status and descent that rulers might marry full siblings. The ruler was responsible for the welfare and protection of the populace, including their religious needs handled by trained practitioners. The ruler also saw to external affairs. In return he demanded unquestioned allegiance from his people, exacted tribute, and could call on both nobility and commoners in time of war. It was a carefully organized system whose success depended on the effectiveness of the ruler and his personal abilities. The office was naturally inherited by the ruler's closest direct descendant.

There were a number of such *cacicazgos* and the same type of system is thought to have operated among the Zapotecs after the demise of Monte Albán. Each of these headed a tributary territory but no one great center ever emerged and there was never a unified Mixtec empire. Of the five major kingdoms in the Nochixtlán Valley, Yanhuitlán was the largest and wealthiest, controlling at least 20 settlements. One of these was Yucuita that had had very early beginnings (see page 106) and had eventually grown into a huge site. Coixtlahuaca was another large site that stretched along a high ridge with public buildings, private dwellings, and rich tombs. Special burial vaults were cut into a slope where the deceased was placed after being wrapped in his *petate*.

I have singled out a few other sites for special mention. Tilantongo (Mixteca Alta) and Tututepec (Mixteca de la Costa) were both important kingdoms (see Map 8.4). Tilantongo was famous as the seat of a prestigious royal lineage at the time of the Conquest. It is curiously very small (300 m^2) and although it yielded abundant elite ceramics, its archaeological remains hardly support the prominence attributed to it in the historical records.

A somewhat parallel situation was found upon investigating Tututepec on the Oaxaca Coast. This, also, is a well-known name among the Mixtecs associated with a famous Mixtec leader, 8 Deer "Tiger Claw." At the age of 15 he inherited the kingdom of Tilantongo upon the death of his father. Politics with threats and challenges are the consuming theme of his life. His five marriages and numerous children are scarcely mentioned. Eight Deer "Tiger Claw" went to Tula to receive his turquoise nose ornament, a distinct honor awarded to the nobility. He thereupon attempted to set up a bureaucratic state at Tututepec and may have briefly united the Mixteca Alta and Baja (Marcus, 1983c). His efforts to create an empire finally ended in his being sacrificed. Versions of this story are known from the Codex Nuttall, Codex Colombino-Becker, and the Bodley Codex. Archaeologically Tututepec is unimpressive and exhibits no signs of an expansionist state. In fact, there is little evidence in Oaxaca of contact with the Toltecs, whether in art, architecture, or artifacts. There seems to be an unexplained lack of correspondence between the historical pictographs and archaeology. At the time of the Conquest, however, the Mixtec dynasties were among those that claimed Toltec ancestry.

The best known of Mixtec northern sites is Tepexi el Viejo, a fortress at 1700 m elevation in the Mixteca Baja (see Map 8.4; Gorenstein, 1973). A series of massive walls enclosed the main precinct, perched on a hill with deep canyons on three sides. Gates, probably two, were located so the attacker had to expose his right (unshielded) side to the defenders. Walls were 3–5 m high, straight, smooth, and plastered, to discourage any potential climber.

Tepexi marks the frontier between Mixtec and Náhuatl-speaking peoples and where polychrome ceramics of both the Mixtecs and Cholula are found together. Early in its history Tepexi was allied to Tlatelolco in the Basin of Mexico through marriage. It was the center of a small community of 10,000–11,000 inhabitants, whose lord exercised jurisdiction over nearby hamlets. It seems to have fought constantly with its neighbors. The early marriage alliance with the Aztecs did not deter Moctezuma II from attacking and conquering Tepexi el Viejo in 1503. Thereafter Tepexi was required to send tribute to the Aztecs at Tepeaca in the Tehuacán Valley. Seventeen years later it fell to Cortés.

Mixteca-Puebla culture refers to the development around Cholula and Tlaxcala in Toltec and Aztec times and the pottery is valuable as a chronological marker for the Epi-Classic and Postclassic years. The sumptuous wares manufactured in the Mixteca Alta (see Figure 8.28c,h,i) share the same colors, styles, and forms of the Puebla region. They are also seen in the style of the Oaxaca palace murals.

Writing   Instead of keeping records in stone, Zapotec style, the Mixtecs used códices as a media for recording their genealogical records. Códices Vindobonensis, Nuttall, Bodley, Colombino, Seldens, and Beckers are all beautiful examples of picture writing from this area in pre-Conquest style, with precise, clear figures in bright, vivid colors. These deal primarily with genealogies and historical data but divinatory manuals are also included that have a wealth of symbols and representations of deities. Elements of writing are found on stone monuments, wall paintings, carved bones, pottery, and ornaments, but the only texts that can be clearly identified with the Mixtec language are those of the painted manuscripts. Lacking the specific language represented has been a primary difficulty in understanding other early writing systems.

Mixtec signs give names of people and places. People usually have two names: a calendrical birth date, and a personal name (Figure 7.16). Sometimes a person may take a deity name as his personal name. Favorite choices were the Rain God, Fire Serpent, and an "Earth Man" believed to represent the original Mixteca. Signs are also pictorial to represent a word that is hard to otherwise portray, or as a phonetic indicator to clarify another word or sound. Smith (1983) has been successful in identifying toponyms in the códices with today's archaeological sites. Symbols sometimes called pictographs are easiest to understand, as they do not depend on the language, and some are familiar from their wide distribution in Mesoamerica, such as the well-known symbol for speech (a volute emitted from the mouth of a figure or animal), or a footprint to denote a route. Gestures and postures of codex figures were

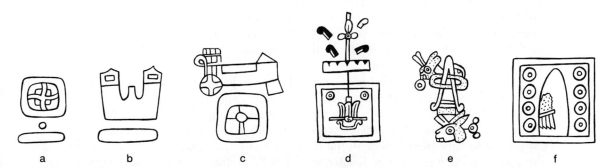

a   b   c   d   e   f

FIGURE 7.16   Various calendrical glyphs. a. Zapotec day-sign. (From Caso, 1965b.) b. Zapotec month-sign. (From Caso, 1965b.) c. Year-sign, Monte Albán II. (From Caso, 1965b.) d. Fire-drilling glyph over sign of Ome Acatl (2 reed), 1351. Completion of the 52-year-cycle. (From Codex Mendoza, 1830–1848.) e. Mixtec year-glyph. (From Caso, 1965c.) f. Aztec day-sign (8 Tecpatl). (From Acosta, 1956–1957.)

used to communicate such ideas as request, acceptance, or hostility. The body postures are the most difficult and were probably only understood by trained personnel. But by combining signs it was possible to communicate war, travel, or even indicate a sacred mission (Troike, 1987).

Craft Specialization   Mixtec craft specialization was highly prized and greatly sought out by others, and this area was a great center for the production of small, fine, luxury items such as gold objects, jade and turquoise mosaics, small carvings in hard stone, and beautiful polychrome ceramics. In the Late Postclassic, turquoise was favored by Mixtec jewelers to replace the earlier taste for jade.

A fabulous treasure in Tomb 7 was discovered in Monte Albán by the Mexican archaeologist Alfonso Caso in 1932 (Caso, 1965a). The tomb was built in the typical style of Period IIIb Zapotec tombs. There are two east–west chambers with a large antechamber, funerary urns, and a carved stone with Zapotec hieroglyphs. In the Late Postclassic, the tomb was reopened to inter nine skeletons, probably secondary "bundle" burials (Marcus, 1983d). It is difficult to say if the second interment was made by Zapotecs or Mixtecs, as by this time the elite of both groups were becoming more compatible and internal divisions were disappearing.

Left with the deceased were 24 silver objects, 121 gold objects, and 8 vessels of *tecalli* as well as necklaces formed of beads of jet, jade, pearl, amber, coral, and shell. Other finds including rock crystal jewels and vases, disks, rings, ear and nose ornaments, obsidian earspools less than 1 mm thick, and beautifully carved jaguar bones demonstrate beauty, precision, and superb attention to craft by these artists.

CHICHÉN ITZÁ AND THE TOLTECS

There is good evidence of Toltec influence at Chichén Itzá as well as increasing signs of Maya presence in highland Mexico. To substantiate the Quetzalcoatl-Kukulcán legend, however, the Toltecs must have left Tula before the Tollan Phase, which seems unlikely. Nonetheless, Mastache and Cobean (1989) suggest that the abandonment of the Tula Chico plaza might have been caused by the conflict between the followers of Quetzalcoatl and Tezcatlipoca, leading to the subsequent building of the new center at Tula Grande.

Leaving aside the historical accounts until more archaeological data are available, the iconography and architecture at both sites share very specific resemblances (Figures 7.17 and 7.18). The fine details in sculpture, smoking pipes, use of simple name glyphs, and the role of the feathered serpent are only a few of the features that seem too precise to have passed through the hands of many craftspersons with inevitable alterations on the way. George Kubler, after careful architectural analyses, has long held the belief that Tula was a colonial outpost of Chichén Itzá, rather than the reverse, or, at the very least, Chichén Itzá was the major contributor to this relationship. His support is growing and although not everyone agrees, there are a number of Maya precedents for what we see at Tula (Kubler, 1984; Cohodas, 1978, 1989).

FIGURE 7.17   Comparative features: Tula and Chichén Itzá. a. Atlantean figures (Bacabs ?) Left, Tula. Right, Chichén Itzá. (From Tozzer, 1957. Courtesy of the Peabody Museum of Archaeology and Ethnology, Harvard University.) b. Eagles with human heart from sculptured panels. Left, Tula. (From Marquina, 1951.) Right, Chichén Itzá. (From Morris *et al.*, 1931). c. Pottery pipes. Upper, Tula. (From Acosta, 1945.) Lower, Chichén Itzá. (From Morris *et al.*, 1931.) d. Jaguar in relief. Top, Tula. (From Acosta, 1941.) Bottom, Chichén Itzá. (From Tozzer, 1957. Courtesy of the Peabody Museum of Archaeology and Ethnology, Harvard University.) e. Figures from sculptured columns. Left, Tula. Right, Chichén Itzá. (From Acosta, 1941.)

Just how the contact took place and the relationship materialized is still unanswered. Any emigrants from Tula left no visible trail that we have seen. The central Mexicans and the Maya had been in contact for many years during the Classic Period, and archaeology confirms that foreigners had some part in establishing the hybrid capital at Chichén Itzá.

Chichén Itzá

Tula

FIGURE 7.18 A comparison of benches carved in relief from Tula and Chichén Itzá. Each shows a procession of richly attired figures. Snakes adorn the cornice above. Top, Chichén Itzá. (From Marquina, 1951.) Bottom, Tula. (From Acosta, 1945.)

That the Maya were in central highland Mexico is also not in doubt. We know that they had been in contact with the Teotihuacanos for many years. Recall the Maya pottery in the Merchants' Barrio, some Maya features in the murals, and the use of Maya signs among Teotihuacan's notational glyphs. Evidence of the Maya physical presence in central highland Mexico has been strengthened with the discovery of the Cacaxtla murals. Maya features are also recognized in the architecture, sculpture, and writing at Xochicalco.

At Tula itself, Maya influence is not easily isolated, as there are northern precedents for colonnaded halls, *tzompantlis*, and perhaps also for the *chacmool* figure.

Mexicanized Maya is an appropriate descriptive term often used for the inhabitants of Chichén Itzá. Many of this center's features can be found in the Chontalapa. Groups in this area could have been the source of political, military, and economic successes of both Chichén Itzá and Tula. An amalgamation of some elite from central highland

Mexico and various Maya polities somehow produced a new Maya society that emerged from the changing political and economic environment. This leaves many questions unanswered, but may lead us closer to the eventual clarification that will surely emerge.

What we see in the murals of Chichén Itzá is the result of artists dealing with this complex blend of ethnic, linguistic, and culturally elite people that formed a new brief cultural tradition in northern Yucatán (Wren and Schmidt, 1991). Out of this fusion came the success it enjoyed until the thirteenth century.

CHAPTER 8

Final Scenes: The Maya, the Tarascans, and the Aztecs

As we approach the sixteenth century, archaeological and "historical" documents are much more abundant. Many cities had been abandoned but were not built over by the next generations. Traditions, myths, and native accounts, however embellished or biased, provide much valuable information. Out of such a wealth of material I will center attention on three groups: the Maya, the Tarascans, and the Aztecs, people living in different environments, with different cultural orientations and style, but sharing long traditions that unite them as Mesoamericans.

We will see the Maya in the Yucatán Peninsula and the highlands of the south readjusting to a new order; the Tarascans of west Mexico with a great heritage of independence; and the Aztecs expanding an empire that had not yet reached its apogee when interrupted by the Spanish.

THE MAYA

Mayapán

We left the Maya as Chichén Itzá fell around 1200. The rather minor center of Mayapán that had been founded about A.D. 1100 now attempted to take over the prestige, power, and domain of Chichén. Its first structure was a small-scale replica of the Temple to Kukulcán at Chichén Itzá. A number of nearby buildings tried to emulate the design and layout of the former capital. The inner core of the settlement was eventually densely packed with a small ceremonial center of 100 structures, including a round one. This core was separated from the residential area by a low boundary wall and all were enclosed by an outside masonry wall with two entrances and stairs leading up to the parapet. The construction is shoddy and inferior compared to the fine architecture at Uxmal and Chichén Itzá. There are no ball courts, *tzompantlis*, corbeled arches, or sweat baths. There are also fewer religious edifices, but as we will see, the elite now seem to be more interested in commercial activities than in a public display of wealth, power, and ancestry. This change, however, should not be taken as a sign of decadence; religion was probably as strong as before but is manifested in less ostentatious ways. (Figure 8.1).

Population is estimated at 11,000–12,000 with local lineage heads brought in to reside in the city. A joint rule (The League of Mayapán) was set up to which most of the western provinces sent a lord to live at Mayapán as the central authority (Pollock *et al.*, 1962). Although representation was equal, the most powerful lineages were the Cocom dynasty at Mayapán and the Xiu who claimed Uxmal as their ancestral home (the Xiu were actually migrants from the Chontalapa).

Ecab, the largest eastern province along with Cobá's old territory and northern Quintana Roo, remained aloof from the western group at Mayapán, yet never formed any political entity of their own. This eastern area was one of the most densely populated areas of the Maya lowlands, equalled only by the Chontalapa and southwest Campeche (Robles and Andrews, 1986). Cozumel dealt with everyone.

Cozumel

Until A.D. 1200 the Putún Itzá based at Chichén Itzá had exercised great control over the Yucatán waters. Now Mayapán took over this lucrative trade and worked closely with Cozumel (Map 8.1). Work on the island has led Freidel and Sabloff (1984) to interpret the role of Cozumel as a local administrative center of port facilities for

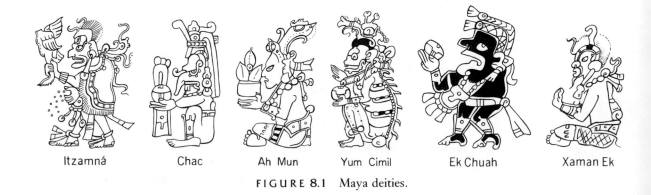

Itzamná   Chac   Ah Mun   Yum Cimil   Ek Chuah   Xaman Ek

FIGURE 8.1   Maya deities.

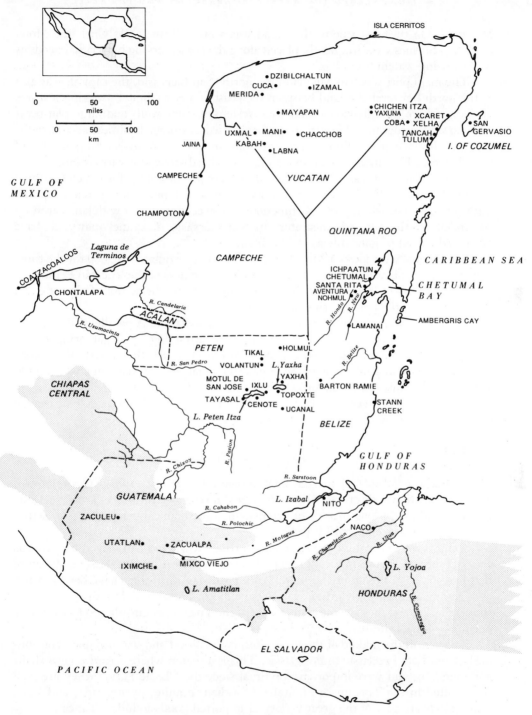

MAP 8.1 The Postclassic Maya.

Mayapán. On the west side of the island was a great shrine to Ix Chel, the Moon Goddess. Shrines were frequently placed along the coast, serving both ritual needs as well as being watchtowers.

The main port was San Miguel in the north. San Gervasio, the capital, was also in the north but located inland between the coast and San Miguel. Striking features of Cozumel are the extensive island-wide system of stone walls and large platforms with no superstructures. These were probably used as storage facilities, necessary for the long-distance trade. Similar constructions are known from nearby Xcaret and from Naco in Honduras. Trade in obsidian and hard stone was carried on all year, but such seasonal items as salt, honey, and cacao required storage for which Cozumel was ideally suited. The walls and platforms are dispersed, not forming areas of special trading zones. The island probably functioned as an economic unit with land carefully controlled by the elite administrators in San Gervasio. Cozumel may well have instigated a kind of joint rule as at Mayapán.

Settlements were located 2 to 3 km from the coast, estimated at 3000 for the three major towns. This was one of the major pilgrimage centers of the Yucatán Peninsula. The Sacred Cenote at Chichén Itzá was the most famous shrine but of almost equal importance was the oracle-shrine of Ix Chel.

Commerce and religion seem to form a strong association. A parallel situation was that of Cholula in highland Mexico, famous for attracting great gatherings to its marketplace and pilgrimages to the Temple of Quetzalcoatl. But in Late Postclassic Yucatán, instead of public worship in large ceremonial centers, religion now centered around smaller dispersed religious edifices and some household shrines.

Commercial ties were strong with Mayapán but also with the people of nearby coastal sites such as Tulum, who also were traders and shrine-keepers.

East Coast Sites

Xcaret, the Polé of Colonial days, on the central coast just opposite Cozumel, had a large population at this time. Although there is no early architecture, Late Preclassic ceramics indicate a long history of occupation. Like many other late coastal settlements, Xcaret was enclosed by walls.

Xelhá, north of Tulum, was a smaller fortified town and had served for years as the port for Cobá. A causeway leading inland from the main plaza passes a structure that has both a vaulted roof and mural paintings. Many paintings have been lost but enough remain to show that these are related to both Tancah and Tulum. These three sites are located on the extreme eastern edge of the Yucatán Peninsula and face directly out to the Caribbean sea.

Tancah, in the middle of the three sites, is the oldest and was occupied continuously from Late Preclassic to Postclassic. This is a region where *Strombus gigas* shells are abundant, and were important for ritual since the Classic Period (they are well represented in the Teotihuacan murals). Obsidian, granite, pyrite, jade, and Puuc slate vessels are part of the great variety of imported goods found at Tancah.

This whole area became a prominent regional cult center for this was the "east," that land where the gods of the moon, Ix Chel, and Kukulcán as the Planet Venus were reborn. The Tancah Cenote has a special sacred cave oriented east–west, with murals that depict fear of the sea. The combination of directions, the watery Underworld, darkness, and glyphs dealing with death even the local Maya today find forbidding (Miller, 1982).

Tulum, founded in 1200, has the most dramatic setting of all, perched on a cliff overlooking the blue waters of the open sea (Figure 8.2). This was a fortress protected by a massive wall (800 m long by 2 m high) with five gates. In contrast to Mayapán, Tulum looks like a planned city. It is organized around a main-street axis, bordered by both civic and residential buildings and includes a marketplace. The earliest structure has Puuc traits with roof combs, pecked masonry, and colonnades. Later shrinelike structures are set on rocky points.

The murals at Tulum are some of the most interesting and complex of all pre-Columbian examples. These, along with Xelhá and Tancah, form a series. The finest murals, temple of the Frescoes (Structure 16) and the Temple of the Diving God (Structure 5), are monochrome and date from 1450 to 1500. They are artistically complex, illustrating great technical ability and control by the artist. On the west façade of Structure 5 the Diving God can be seen in a niche over the doorway (Figure 8.3). Many interpretations have been made of this descending deity (Miller, 1982; Coggins, 1988b).

Santa Rita Corozal near the modern town of Corozal in northern Belize is a very old settlement that reached its greatest prominence and prosperity during these late Postclassic years. Much continuity can be found between Classic and Postclassic in this area, for during the Late Classic Period the Itzá had had a close relationship with Nohmul and Aventura just down the Río Hondo (See Map 8.1). The architectural tradition at Santa Rita is also closely related to northern Yucatán, but lacks the use of columns. The settlement pattern, as at Caracol and the Lake Petén area, is rather

FIGURE 8.2   View of Tulum, Quintana Roo, Mexico. (Photographed by Lorraine Matys.)

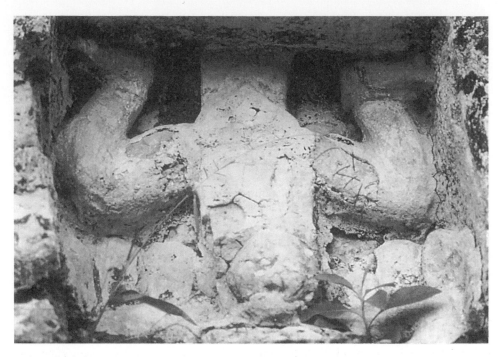

FIGURE 8.3   Diving God, Tulum. (Photographed by Lorraine Matys.)

dispersed with the most elaborate residences and burials located away from the central core (Chase and Chase, 1988).

Santa Rita also has murals whose origins have been puzzling because of some resemblances to central Mexican art, although the themes are typically Maya. The figures in the murals are quite different from the Mixteca-Puebla region and may simply represent the cosmopolitan nature of Postclassic Mesoamerica. There is no architectural evidence for the presence of a non-Maya population. Sadly, the only mural with a glyphic text from the area has deteriorated beyond recovery (Quirarte, 1982).

An outstanding feature of Santa Rita is the caching of *incensarios*. Found in pairs, this practice seems to be associated with the Uayeb rituals that have parallels at Caracol. The effigy censers were apparently a standardized item found among the general population, excluding the elite. This suggests that religion was an important element in the integration of the society.

The Fall of Mayapán and the Rise of City-States

During the joint rule at Mayapán (A.D. 1250–1441) the capital enjoyed a wonderful period of prosperity. Tribute flowed in, in the form of cotton, turkeys, cacao, honey, and copal. It has been described as a time of unprecedented renaissance. But the

Cocoms became overbearing, and had brought in Mexican mercenaries from Tabasco, fostering jealousy, competition, and dissension. The Xiu, with enthustiastic support from other lineages, fell upon the Cocoms and massacred all but one member of the family who was away hunting. Mayapán was burned, sacked, and abandoned; the lords all returned to their hometowns. The Xiu now moved away from Uxmal and founded Mani, a well-populated area south of Mayapán with more water than Uxmal could offer. After this, Uxmal remained an important Xiu shrine (Kowalski, 1987).

The collapse and destruction of Mayapán in A.D. 1441 marks the end of the last centralized government in Yucatán. Thereafter a system of city-states divided northern Yucatán into 16 provinces (Roys, 1965). In some cases a single lord reigned as the authority over his town and was recognized by a few others. He could call warriors to battle, exact tribute, and check on boundaries (a major concern). Other territories were combined into a lineage rule based on kinship whereby the towns of the same name would unite to help each other if need arose. Still other city-states might simply join temporarily to aid one another if threatened by an outside force. Mérida was of the latter type.

This political situation endured for almost 100 years from the fall of Mayapán to the conquest of the northern end of the peninsula. These years are filled with accounts of petty quarrels, local competitions, and struggles. Chichén Itzá continued to be the object of pilgrimages but supported no concentrated population. Mayapán was in shambles and no one chose to live there. The Puuc cities had been abandoned for many years. Dzibilchaltún managed to maintain itself, though with no particular distinction. These were hard years for the Maya, as in 1464 they weathered a devastating hurricane, followed in 1480 by a plague. Worse still was the smallpox epidemic that swept through Yucatán in 1514, 3 years after some shipwrecked Spaniards had been cast ashore. Is it any wonder that, with the exception of a few bloody uprisings, the Spanish Conquest of Yucatán met with little resistance?

By the time the Spanish religious personnel arrived and Landa (See Tozzer, 1941) wrote his account of the Yucatán Indians, the greatest period of Maya development had passed. He found the Maya leading a simple village life, competing with neighbors for prestige, and constantly warring over any trivial dispute.

Southern Lowlands

When the Itzá unceremoniously departed from Chichén Itzá in one of the dreaded Katun 8 Ahaus (either 1201 or 1458 ?), they wandered south to Lake Petén Itzá where they took over whatever resident population they found. According to most accounts they set up a capital on the lake shore at Tayasal, an area off any major trade route. Little is known of their arrival and it is debatable if the capital was on the island (Flores today), or on the lake shore (Figure 8.4).

Lake Petén Itzá was part of a chain of lakes in the central Petén that was the scene of the greatest Postclassic activity in the southern lowlands. The great Classic development had seemingly bypassed this region, but when the "collapse" came, some people moving away from their homes may have come to this area that did not

FIGURE 8.4   View of Flores (Tayasal), Petén, Guatemala. (Photographed by Lorraine Matys.)

experience any great change. The area had a long occupation reaching back through the Classic period to 300 B.C. at Cenote, but it had never played a major role in Maya history.

The most interesting material comes from the other Petén lakes: Macanche, Yaxhá, and Salpetén (Rice and Rice, 1984). At Lake Macanche a sizeable fortress (Muralla de León) had been constructed on a high spur of land in the Late Preclassic. In the Postclassic it was reoccupied and ceremonial structures were added within the walls. At Topoxte (See Map 8.1), an island in Lake Yaxhá, one can still see one of the few temples of this period left standing, built in the tradition of Mayapán. Zacpetén was a lake-shore site on Lake Salpetén with 190 structures built on hills and terraces. Two damaged stelae of Classic date have survived that resemble those of Ixlú at the west end of the lake.

The prevailing feature at all these sites is the so-called "open hall," a 3-walled building with a central staircase on the open front and a row of columns along the axis. This is a strong link to Mayapán-style buildings and to those of eastern Yucatán. Another close tie uniting these regions is a common unslipped effigy censer, and skull burials at Topoxte and Flores.

This area can boast of no large urban centers, but it did produce a resident population that continued many earlier traditions with idols, sacrifices, and incense burning. And even as the Spaniards arrived, several local groups were engaged in hostilities.

In 1524 Cortés came through with his army on the way to Honduras to put down a rebellion against Spaniards at Nito. He was well received by the local king, Ahau Canek, on his island city of Noh Petén. Ahau Canek shared his inherited power with a high priest. Fortunately, Cortés was probably seeking information rather than a confrontation and it was not until 1697 that a full-scale army came in for the one-day final victory over the Maya.

To the northeast in Belize at Ambergris Cay and Lamanai, the Late Postclassic was a busy time for entrepreneurs. Marco González, out on the barrier reef, experienced a boom in construction, exploitation, and trade. A close trading relationship with Lamanai was most likely related to their respective positions on water routes. For Lamanai, it was a rich period and the southern part of the site developed a new interest in ceramic production. Although there was some drop in population, as late as the sixteenth century Lamanai was involved in a trade of copper artifacts. This site adapted to changing times, made its own choices, and survived with its own style until the end of the seventeenth century (Pendergast, 1990).

Southern Highlands

Farther south in the Terminal Classic Period, the highlanders had given up their open valley sites and sought out areas more easily defended. These people were Mexicanized Maya warriors, the Chontal Putún, who had penetrated the lowlands using the major rivers and then followed lesser tributaries to their highland sources. Recall that there were Itzá intrusions from both east and west from northern Yucatán that had settled at the base of the peninsula.

The Putún Maya had probably come in around 1200 bringing news of Toltecs and a new ideology. Some of these warring groups became the Quiché who entered the Guatemalan highlands from the eastern lowlands after the abandonment of Chichén Itzá in Yucatán (Fox, 1978). They took up settlements in remote but defensible positions.

After a long gradual development sudden changes occurred in the fourteenth century, bringing in a Mexican flavor. Ceramic styles became standardized, twin temples were built on a single pyramidal base, ball courts were enclosed, metallurgy was now a specialized occupation, and the annals record a new social structure based on segmentary lineages. In this type of organization the "basic unit is the lineage, with its brotherhood of men occupying the same territory, sharing obligations of wife-giving, collective labor, mutual defense, ritual and honor" (Carmack, 1981:61–62) (see also Fox, 1987).

Gradually the Quiché acquired more productive land and in the early 1400s they conquered much of the Guatemalan highlands expanding their kingdom north and west to reach the Pacific Coast. A capital was first established at Jakawitz (Chitinamit) and eventually at Utatlán, chosen for its protective ravines. The city was divided into quarters, each with its own temple-mounds, ball court, and house platforms. A round temple was dedicated to the Feathered-Serpent deity.

Revolts were not long in coming. Of those offering the greatest resistance to the yoke of the Quiché were the Cakchiquels who, after an uprising, established their own kingdom with a capital southeast of Utatlán, called Iximché. This happened around 1486(?). A typical fortress of the period, Iximché was in fact a huge center well protected by deep ravines on three sides. The central ruins, Mexican style, had a ceremonial center and among the 10 temples was one with twin shrines and double stairways, and 2 ball courts. Residential areas extended far beyond the protective ravines, and in case of serious conflict the populace could take refuge within the city. Two of the four main groups are especially imposing and accommodated the resident-ial, administrative, ceremonial, and religious facilities for the two ruling families who shared the supreme power.

Battles raged constantly between the Quiché and Cakchiquels, followed by the usual sacrifice of leaders and slaughter of many warriors.

Utatlán and Iximché were capitals of the largest city-states, but there were others such as the Pokomam with their capital of Mixco Viejo, the Mam at Zaculeu, and the Zutzughil nations. When the old center of Zacualpa was conquered by the early Quiché king, Quicab, it was not destroyed, but simply reoccupied. Warfare was a way to acquire slaves and to increase wealth and prestige. Tribute was imposed as among the Aztecs, but unlike the latter, the Quiché put conquered leaders to death and their wives were taken into the local ruling lineages.

The Aztecs traded with all these groups and may have had a friendship treaty with the Cakchiquels. There is some disagreement as to the language spoken, but probably the bulk of the population spoke a Maya tongue. The calendar in operation at the time of the Conquest was synchronized with that of Tenochtitlán and all groups claimed Toltec ancestry and honored the Feathered Serpent. There are indications that power was becoming increasingly centralized (Fox, 1978, 1987).

The great Utatlán and Iximché capitals were finally burned to the ground by Alvarado after the Conquest in 1526. According to sources, this was the punishment meted out to the Cakchiquels for not wanting to join the Spanish on their march to Honduras.

THE TARASCANS

We know most about the culture and empire of the Tarascans because they were thriving at the time of the Spanish Conquest. They have also attracted attention because they never succumbed to the yoke of the Triple Alliance. Source material for this region is not as extensive as that for the Aztec but fortunately the Spanish monarchs requested geographical and historical information about New Spain, and these records, called the *Relaciones*, provide the best data we have. Other early sources are the traditions recorded by members of the religious orders, sixteenth century *códices*, and references to the Tarascans in the Mexican manuscripts. We know of no Precolumbian Tarascan codex. The basic work on the Tarascans is the *Relación de Michoacán*, believed to have been written by a Franciscan friar around 1538 (Brand, 1943; León, 1904).

The heart of the late Postclassic development was centered in the Lake Pátzcuaro region where by A.D. 1200 four autonomous lake shore centers had emerged: Ihuatzio, Pátzcuaro, Pacanda (an island), and Tzintzuntzan (Map 8.2). During the Classic period scattered centers in Michoacán had exhibited a number of central Mexican features. Some of these such as bloodletting, sky deities, divinatory elements of the calendar system, the ball game, and astronomical site orientation were associated with the patron deity of Ihuatzio (Pollard, 1991). None of these are found at Tzintzuntzan, for its background probably lay with outsiders who migrated to the area following their Chichimec leader, Tariácuri. He succeeded in unifying the local polities under his control and in doing so, dropped or diminished any central Mexican features of the region. There is no ball court at Tzintzuntzan.

A conscious decision was made to create a new empire and Tariácuri planned it methodically and successfully. It was up to his sons and nephews to create the Tarascan empire. This was not easily accomplished in view of competing towns and conflicts over rights of succession, but Tzintzuntzan prevailed. The king was the only legitimate authority. Dissenting elites were either absorbed or "removed" (Pollard, 1991). All resources such as land and water rights were declared property of the state.

A new state religion was formed with Tzintzuntzan's patron deity Curicaueri

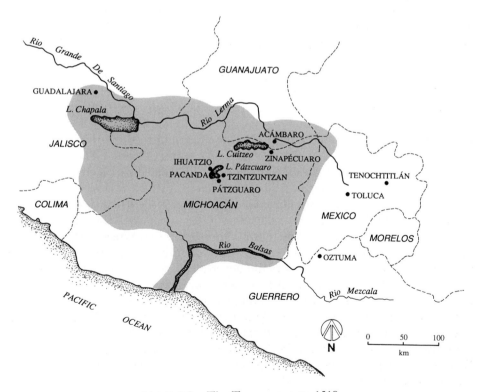

MAP 8.2   The Tarascans, A.D. 1519.

occupying the prime position in the sky. Patron deities of conquered towns held lesser posts such as the cardinal directions and the central position. If an elite were found to be worshiping a local patron deity, it was punishable by death, for this was tantamount to legitimizing an independent power. In effect, a new cosmos was created.

In warfare, credit was given to the gods for success, but they did not justify a conflict or cause expansion. Victims were sacrificed as a result of the battle, but were not the reason for its inception (Pollard, 1991).

The "Empire"

The Tarascan "empire" is rather loosely defined. A favorite eastern raid of the Tarascans was to reach the fine salt deposits of Ixtapan, probably within the Aztec domain. They were also interested in deposits of copper, gold, silver, cinnabar and all the products of the *tierra caliente* in the Balsas and Tepalcatepec River basins. It is uncertain how far south the Tarascans reached. To the north their frontier fluctuated from time to time as they endeavored to push back Chichimecs and Otomís. One frontier settlement was Acámbaro on the Lerma River. Raids reached as far west as Guadalajara, Jalisco, but the "empire" itself probably included only the lands in modern Michoacán (Brand, 1943).

The expansion of the Aztec empire was initiated by Itzcóatl who extended warfare into northern Guerrero. This area was expanded further south by Moctezuma I but it was Axayácatl who tried hardest to penetrate the west. His armies reached Lake Cuitzeo where they were decisively beaten. This was the last full-scale campaign ever attempted into Michoacán. Both Aztecs and Tarascans maintained forts in a north–south line that extended more or less just west of Toluca. Otzuma on the northern Guerrero border was the scene of numerous battles under Ahuítzotl but he gained no western land. Thereafter the Aztecs concentrated on the southeast but were ever conscious of a large, independent kingdom located directly at their backs.

Wherein lay the power or the weakness of the great Aztecs? There were real cultural differences between the two protagonists. The Aztecs conducted warfare for economic reasons. Their tributary regions were loosely held with weak control. After a conquest many local administrators were often left in place. Aztec military leaders might also be heads of *calpullis* with obligations to the social elite. As a result military operations were often inept and inefficient. In warfare the Aztecs were not out to expand the administration but to support their economy and gain prestige.

In contrast, the Tarascan dynasty did not share power with any other polities or local rulers. The population and authority was concentrated in the Pátzcuaro basin, easily controlled under the king's tight administration. Large quantities of foodstuffs were imported and turned over directly to the ruling dynasty at Tzintzuntzan who handled the distribution and supplied the army. The military was an arm of the government, a full-time occupation, extending the political control throughout the territory. The Aztecs never understood the Tarascans. They were "playing a different game" (Gorenstein and Pollard, 1983).

Archaeology at Tzintzuntzan

The five pyramids known as *yácatas* at Tzintzuntzan are set in a single row on a gigantic terrace (260 m wide by 440 m long) facing east overlooking the lake and today's mestizo pottery-making village (Figure 8.5). The odd-shaped *yácata* with a single steep staircase, has a round section linked to a rectangular body forming a kind of T-formation. The first tier is common to all five. Short excavations by INAH began in the 1930s and have continued intermittently into the 1980s (Piña Chan, 1960; Cabrera Castro, 1987).

A number of graves have been recovered close to the *yácatas*, and others to the north, associated with groups of multi-room structures. Building B, called El Palacio, was built with a central patio, a narrow gallery with a roof supported by rectangular pillars (Cabrera Castro, 1987).

In 1944 a series of multiple graves were excavated in the patios of Yácata V (where the round and rectangular parts join). On the southwest side were five female secondary graves with many miniature vessels of ritual use and copper ornaments decorated with animal heads, bells, and needles. The nine skeletons to the north were interred at one time with arms interlocked, placed on *petates*, and covered with stones. They were accompanied by the finest objects yet found at Tzintzuntzan: an axe, copper bells and bracelets, silver tweezers, long-stemmed clay smoking pipes, obsidian lip and earplugs with turquoise mosaic, and gold earrings (Rubín de la Borbolla, 1944). (See Figure 6.12).Pottery included much resist decoration, stirrup-handles, and teapot spouts (Figure 8.6).

From the *Relación de Michoacán* (León, 1904), it seems clear that these deceased were retainers buried to accompany the king at the time of his death. We are told they were spontaneous volunteers and were buried "behind the temple with all their adornments and instruments." The king's tomb is described in great detail except for

FIGURE 8.5 The five *yácatas* of Tzintzuntzan. These five structures rest on a huge terrace and look north over Lake Pátzcuaro. (Courtesy of Román Piña Chan.)

FIGURE 8.6   Red "teapot" vessel with stirrup-spout handle and spout. Michoacán, Tarascan culture. Height: 20 cm. (Courtesy of the Museum of the American Indian, Heye Foundation, N.Y. [24/3025].)

its location, yet to be determined. Of the copper tools and ornaments, bells were the most common and all are typical of late west Mexican metallurgy (Hosler, 1990).

When the Spaniards were making their way up to Tenochtitlán, the Aztecs sent some emissaries to the Tarascans to ask for aid. The latter, not knowing what to do, solved this dilemma by sacrificing the visitors. Later when Tenochtitlán lay in ruins, they belatedly questioned their hasty actions. When their own turn came to face the Spaniards in 1522, the last Tarascan king, Tangaxoan II, offered little resistance.

THE AZTECS

The Chichimec Period

From the fall of Tula, roughly A.D. 1200 until A.D. 1370, marked by the accession of Tezozomoc as ruler of the Tepanecs at Azcapotzalco, the Basin of Mexico was occupied by various central Mexican peoples and groups of Chichimecs who had come in at various times. It was a troubled period of conflict between these seminomads of the north and the sedentary farmers who had been in residence over a longer period of time.

The Basin of Mexico Survey (Sanders *et al.*, 1979) concedes that this is one of the most difficult periods to assess archaeologically. The difficulty is partly because of an identity problem with the later material, and partly because modern Mexico City chose to inhabit the same terrain. In general, the northern end of the valley was dominated by Azcapotzalco and Tenayuca to the west of Lake Texcoco, and Huexotla and Coatlichan on the east, each with a population estimate at 10,000 to 15,000 people. The southern part was the most densely populated of all with regional centers of Culhuacán, Xochimilco, Cuitláhuac, Mixquic, Chalco, Xico, and Amecameca. Chalco was probably the largest. This area is the best watered and most desirable for living and had been the first choice of settlers back in Preclassic days. At this time, people were beginning to settle down near the lake shore and to experiment with *chinampa* cultivation.

The historical record that follows deals mainly with the Aztecs, but there is a wealth of source material for the entire region (Nicholson, 1978).

The early history of the Aztecs is sketchy, and until the reign of Nezahuacoyotl in Texcoco in the fifteenth century, we trace events in the Valley of Mexico through oral traditions. Later history is pieced together from the Spanish chronicles and the pre-Hispanic and Colonial códices. Excellent ethnogaphic data and genealogic and chronologic information abound in the writings of Conquest witnesses such as Cortés (1908), Sahagún (1946), and Díaz del Castillo (1944), and later authors such as Torquemada (1943) and Durán (1967). Best of the native sources are the Tira de la Peregrinación, Historia de los Mexicanos por sus Pinturas, Codex Xólotl, the Tlotzin and Quinatzin maps, and the interpretations of Ixtlilxóchitl (1952), for despite exaggerations and confusions, valuable information is contained as to how the Aztecs conceived of their past and present world. For other works dealing with this period see Barlow (1949), Bray (1972, 1977b), Carrasco (1971), Caso (1958), Davies (1973), Gillespie (1989), Hassig (1988), Jiménez Moreno (1962), Kirchhoff (1954-1955), Matos Moctezuma (1987, 1988), Nicholson (1982), Pasztory (1983), Soustelle (1964), Townsend (1987), Umberger (1987, 1988), van Zantwijk (1985), and Wolf (1959).

Sources vary as do interpretations, but what follows is a generally accepted view of the main outlines of a complex Aztec history. The word Aztec is derived from Aztlán, "place of the seven legendary caves" where these warriors of the sun were spawned. They did not call themselves Aztecs, but the word properly refers to related Náhuatl-speaking groups who inhabited central Mexico in the Late Postclassic Period (Umberger, 1987). The group of Aztecs that inhabited Tenochtitlán-Tlatelolco are specifically called the Mexica, the name they used. In the discussion here I will sometimes refer to the Mexica as Aztecs.

After the destruction of Tula, a great Chichimec leader, Xólotl, settled first at Tenayuca and later moved his capital to Texcoco, which was to play a vital role in the history of the Basin of Mexico. But of the several Toltec groups, the lineage at Culhuacán was the most prestigious. Before long, the best land for cultivation was in use, and the lake shore was settled by Náhuat and Otomí-speaking peoples and by descendants of refugees from the old centers of Teotihuacan and Tula.

With the choice areas already taken, no one welcomed an additional band of immigrant Chichimecs with the unpleasant habits of stealing women and practicing human sacrifice. These were *tamimes*, or semicivilized Chichimecs, not as barbaric as the Teochichimecs such as Xólotl and his followers. The *tamimes* had a knowledge of the 52-year cycle and the ball game; they cultivated a few crops with irrigation, constructed with stone, and dressed in maguey fiber clothing. They also had a *calpulli*-type organization (See page 468). These early Aztecs followed their tribal leader, Ténoch, under whom they straggled into the Valley of Mexico as unwanted squatters and for whom they later named their city Tenochtitlán. Stressing an association with the Toltec lineage at Culhuacán, they eventually became known as the Culhua-Mexica.

But they are frequently called simply the Mexica, a name that came to be known and dreaded from coast to coast. Today the term Aztec is more common.

The story (or legend) of the Aztecs' or Mexica's rise to power is a dramatic rags-to-riches tale. This miserable band, despised by all, was driven from one location to another around the western lake shore. There they lived as best they could on fly eggs, snakes, and other vermin. Between A.D. 1250 and 1298 they served as vassals to the Tepanecs at Azcapotzalco but they later pushed on farther south. Eventually, the Aztecs took refuge in the tall reeds of the lake shore and finally moved to some swampy islands in the lake.

According to legends, their tribal war god, Huitzilopochtli, led them to this place. Here an eagle, sitting on a cactus with a serpent in its beak, told them to build their temples and nourish the sun with the sacrifice of human victims. To sustain the sun and other deities with sacrificial blood became the purpose and mission of the Aztecs in this world, and here the prophecy was to be fulfilled. The legend is depicted on the Mexican flag today.

Another version of Aztec beginning is less colorful but perhaps more accurate (van Zantwijk, 1985). In this tale the Mexica were civilized, urban farmers who had probably been around for several centuries. Their way to power and rulership was by acquiring agricultural land.

Accounts vary as to the date of the founding of Tenochtitlán, but it probably occurred close to A.D. 1345, the date given by Jiménez Moreno and Davies (see Nicholson, 1978). Other Aztecs went over to a nearby island in A.D. 1358 and founded another settlement, Tlatelolco. These two cities were to thrive side by side for many years, the former becoming a great mercantile center, the latter growing steadily in military strength. Rivalry between the twin cities was unavoidable, and Tlatelolco was finally taken over by Tenochtitlán under Axayácatl in A.D. 1473, after 128 years of jealous, competitive coexistence.

The rise of Aztec power and events in the Basin of Mexico can be followed by tracing the succession of kings and outstanding personalities of the times.

In the Chichimec period the Aztecs were led by Acamapichtli, the first king, his son Huitzilíhuitl, and his grandson Chimalpopoca (Figure 8.7). During this time the Aztecs served as mercenaries to the Tepanecs, the people of Azcapotzalco, who were led by a ruthless but extraordinarily gifted ruler, Tezozomoc. Undoubtedly the Aztecs benefited greatly under this master warrior and administrator, but at the same time they seethed under the yoke of tribute and subjugation. Tensions were eased temporarily by intermarriage with the Tepanecs, only to worsen in the reign of Chimalpopoca, when the Aztecs were accused of becoming arrogant and demanding. Accounts vary as to whether Chimalpopoca was poisoned, strangled, starved in a cage, or committed suicide, but in all likelihood the Tepanecs were responsible (Ixtlilxóchitl, 1952).

Emergence as a Political Power

The subsequent election of Itzcóatl in Tenochtitlán took place after the tyrant Tezozomoc had died in Azcapotzalco, and with the rule of Itzcóatl a new phase was

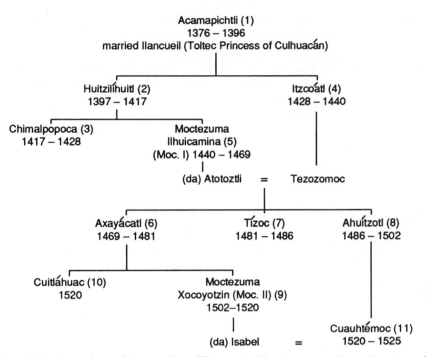

FIGURE 8.7 Genealogy of Aztec rulers. This geneaology is not complete, showing only the probable relationship between rulers. There are often conflicting accounts in the chronicles. For example, some sources list Chimalpopoca rather than Huitzilíhuitl as the father of Moctezuma Ilhuicamina, and Itzcóatl as the son of Huitzilíhuitl rather than his brother. Numbers refer to order of succession; dates to reigns. (Based on Carrasco, 1971, and Gillespie, 1989.)

initiated. Aided by Texcoco and Huexotzingo, Azcapotzalco was finally conquered, ruthlessly sacked, and its people brutally massacred. All the pent-up vengeance of years gone by was unleashed on the defeated Tepanecs. The surviving Tepanec town of Tlacopan, today's Tacuba, had been sufficiently neutral to be selected as the weakest member of a Triple Alliance formed with Tenochtitlán and Texcoco. Henceforth, all three cities were to receive part of the tribute exacted from subservient towns; Tenochtitlán and Texcoco were entitled to two-fifths each, and Tlacopan received the remaining fifth.

The defeat of Azcapotzalco in A.D. 1428 established the Aztecs as the dominant power in the Basin of Mexico, a position they were to maintain until struck down by the Spaniards. The victory over Azcapotzalco not only gave them independence and political power, but a foothold on the mainland as they confiscated the rich *chinampas*, increasing their wealth and prestige and strengthening their class structure. The year A.D. 1428 launched the Aztecs on their way to statehood and empire.

Itzcóatl, Obsidian Snake, was a strong ruler himself and his reign is intimately associated with two of the most important figures in the history of the Valley of Mexico:

Tlacaélel and Nezahuacóyotl. Tlacaélel, a half brother of Moctezuma Ilhuicamina (Moctezuma I), occupied a position of power, an office known as the *cihuacóatl*, or Snake Woman. In early times this office included some priestly duties along with acting as advisors to the king, but eventually the religious aspect seems to have been discarded. Tlacaélel was a famous *cihuacóatl* who served under three successive kings. He emerges in history as an able administrator who exercised great influence. But he is probably to blame for the book burning that took place during Itzcóatl's reign. At the time the Aztecs gained their freedom from the Tepanecs, it was decided to wipe out their inglorious and degrading past and to rewrite history to their liking. Thus every available record of the Aztecs as conquered peoples was destroyed and a new indoctrination began, extolling the glories of the Warriors of the Sun.

Nezahuacóyotl of Texcoco is linked with both Itzcóatl and his successor in Tenochtitlán, Moctezuma Ilhuicamina. With Itzcóatl he took part in the destruction of Azcapotzalco, which effectively ended Tepanec power in the valley. One by one other cities fell around the lake shore: Culhuacan, Xochimilco, Huexotla, Coatlichan, and Coatepec.

The reign of Nezahuacóyotl was unparalleled in cultural achievements and learning. He codified Texcocan law, which was more severe than that of the Aztecs, and constructed a great dike across Lake Texcoco to hold back the brackish water of this lake from the sweetwater of Lake Chalco. He initiated an intricate system of canals and dams to increase agricultural production; he helped Moctezuma Ilhuicamina build the aqueduct that carried sweetwater to Tenochtitlán from Chapultepec; and he stimulated arts and crafts, offering prizes for the finest achievements in gold and feather-working, music, and poetry. His summer residence at Texcotzingo, in ruins today, still retains elements of the former beauty of its stairways, temples, fountains, aqueducts, and baths, that were either cut out of bedrock or constructed of mortar. While Texcoco under his administration became famous as a center of learning, Tenochtitlán grew in military strength and eventually prevailed as a political power.

The Triple Alliance provided Tenochtitlán with a base for its scramble to power. Under Moctezuma Ilhuicamina, Archer of the Sky, the Aztecs began their great expansion. Their domain was extended to the Gulf Coast, an area of special commercial interest. Influenced and aided by his friend and ally Nezahuacóyotl, Moctezuma built botanical and zoological gardens. Every known plant, bird, and animal was collected and brought to Huastepec, Morelos. It was also during his reign. about A.D. 1451 that Tenochtitlán suffered privation under a great 4-year drought. Hunger was so great that in a final spasm of desperation, the Aztecs appealed to their powerful gods through mass human sacrifice. From this time on, large-scale human sacrifice formed part of the Aztec pattern of life.

The two great leaders, Moctezuma Ilhuicamina and Nezahuacóyotl, died within a few years of each other, and the stage was set for the final thrust of Aztec militarism. The great urban center was by now made up of diverse groups. The growing population of Tenochtitlán-Tlatelolco was composed of full-time occupational specialists, not peasant farmers.

Axayácatl, the first of Moctezuma Ilhuicamina's grandsons to succeed him, spent much time reconquering territory and suppressing rebellions. He attempted western expansion, only to be met with firm resistance from the Tarascans (Map 8.4). But he finally took Tlatelolco, which from A.D. 1473 on was governed from Tenochitlán, and he also managed to take over central Veracruz. Upon his death his brother Tízoc reigned, but only for a short time. Tízoc has been branded in history as a coward because his love of battle did not match that of his brothers. However, the third brother, Ahuítzotl, thrived on war. Under him Aztec influence was extended from coast to coast to include the Balsas basin and coastal Guerrero, and he pressed his claims to the Isthmus. At home he managed to complete the Great Temple of Tenochtitlán (see Figure 8.9), celebrated by a great dedication ceremony in December, 1478. For this 4-day event, 20,000 victims were stretched over the sacrificial blocks to have their hearts removed while the multitudes watched and approved. Thereafter Ahuítzotl added Tehuantepec to his victories.

MAP 8.3 The Basin of Mexico, A.D. 1519.

The Aztecs in 1519

Moctezuma Xocoyotzin (Moctezuma II) is remembered largely for his tragic fate and forced surrender of Tenochitlán to the Spanish. Usually unnoticed is the fact that he was a powerful, well-educated, and able ruler who continued military expeditions in the area of Oaxaca and adjacent regions and dealt with his share of uprisings. In 1510–1511 he took over rich Mixtec holdings and expanded the Aztec domain to include Chiapas and Soconusco to the border of Guatemala. In his day about 20% of the Basin of Mexico was clustered in Tenochtitlán-Tlatelolco and its urbanized lakeshore towns with a combined total of 200,000 inhabitants (Sanders *et al.*, 1979). Tenochtitlán was a beautiful city that embraced hereditary nobles, priests, specialized artisans in a variety of crafts, merchants, and an enormous peasantry.

Arrival of the Spaniards

The first city the Spaniards saw was Cempoala on the Veracruz coastal plain where they were amiably received by the Totonac ruler. This was a large, urban center with five temple/pyramids and a round temple dedicated to Quetzalcoatl-Ehécatl. The city was neatly walled in and raised above the ground level, which served both for defense and for protection from floods. The Spanish must have felt some surprise at finding fresh water provided to dwellings and marveled at the gorgeous multicolored pottery in Mixteca-Puebla or Isla de Sacrificios style. But this in no way prepared them for what lay ahead.

After making the ascent to the altiplano, they were dazzled by the sight of the great metropolis that could be seen as they passed between the snow-covered volcanoes of Popocatépetl and Iztaccíhuatl. There, spread beneath them, stretched the vast sweep of the Basin of Mexico, some 7700 km^2, enclosed by forested mountains embracing in the center a chain of five lakes. Coming closer, they saw an island city with towering temple/pyramids connected to the mainland by three great causeways a city of canals rather than streets.

Banding the island were *chinampas*, some of the most fertile gardens in the Americas (see Figure 8.27). At the center of Tenochtitlán was a great court enclosed by a *coatepantli*, or serpent wall, within which were the main religious structures, 78 according to Sahagún's count (see Figure 8.8 and Map 8.3). The main temples of Huitzilopochtli and Tlaloc and those dedicated to Tezcatlipoca, Xipe Totec, and Quetzalcoatl, together with the ball courts, grisley *tzompantlis*, altars, houses of retreat, and minor structures, were all located within the walls. Outside this main center were the sumptuous palaces of the nobility, lay buildings, humble dwellings, plazas and marketplaces, all interlaced by canals. The latter separated the different private holdings in the city. Sweetwater was carried to the Great Temple by an aqueduct from Chapultepec. What a magnificent spectacle it must have been, this island-city with its painted temples and whitewashed houses gleaming in the bright valley sun.

In the 90-day siege against the Spaniards, many buildings were destroyed to fill in the canals. The Mexica hurled stones and debris from temples, houses, and bridges in a desperate attempt to save their city. The battle was heroic but futile. The centralized government of Tenochtitlán did not extend throughout the Aztec "empire." There were groups that were happy to join ranks against the oppressive Aztecs. A decisive impetus was given by the Tlaxcalans, who joined the Spaniards and contributed both manpower and knowledge of native warfare.

It is not clear exactly how Moctezuma Xocoyotzin met his death in the year 1520, but surely he must have felt that his gods had failed him. Having welcomed the Spanish into the city, he soon found himself their prisoner. During the absence of Cortés, who made a trip back to Veracruz, Pedro de Alvarado, left in charge of Moctezuma, became nervous as he heard dancing in front of the Great Temple. Fearing an uprising, he massacred a number of young Aztec nobles. By the time Cortés returned, the Mexica were beyond pacifying. A bad omen was the disastrous prophecy of doom issued by the ruler of Tlacopan after consulting his divinatory device, a polished obsidian mirror. Bloody battles ensued inflicting serious damage on the Great Temple. Sadly, Moctezuma died as he saw his shrines destroyed. It is not known what happened to the idols. Some accounts maintain they were carefully lifted down and hidden. Cortés was finally victorious after hand-to-hand battles and then he burned and blew up the temple shrines (Nicholson, 1982).

Moctezuma was succeeded by his brother Cuitláhuac, who ruled only 4 months and died of illness the same year. Their nephew Cuauhtémoc, the last of the Aztec kings, fought savagely in the defense of Tenochtitlán and is regarded today as a national hero. In the final death throes of Tenochtitlán, every Aztec fought valiantly, persistently but in vain. The city lost heart and was shattered in the struggle, and after the battle ended, the Spaniards completed the destruction of its temples. Still not feeling completely secure, rather than leaving him behind, Cortés took Cuauhtémoc along on an expedition to Honduras. In the jungle country of Chiapas the last Aztec king was cruelly hanged in A.D. 1524.

The Great Temple of Tenochtitlán (Templo Mayor)

In February 1978, INAH was notified that an unusual stone had been discovered by workmen of the Mexico City Light and Power Company in Mexico City (this was the great Coyolxauhqui stone; see Figure 8.11). An investigation led to the excavations that exposed the entire twin-pyramid complex that was the Great Temple of Tenochtitlán. It stood in the center of the sacred precinct of the city built to represent the landscape of Mexica myths. The decision to excavate was not made lightly in view of the necessity to tear down buildings, divert traffic, and cause considerable inconvenience in the busy heart of Mexico City, a block north of the Zócalo. With great enthusiasm and public interest, however, a massive excavation was undertaken that continued for 10 years, guided by Eduardo Matos Moctezuma and a large staff of specialists.

The Spaniards had seen the latest structure and severely damaged it, along with many sculptures, paintings, and reliefs. But beneath lay earlier structures, all believed to have been basically similar. The Great Temple, representing the Hill of Coatepec where Huitzilopochtli was born, was a twin pyramid with two staircases leading to two shrines or temples. The southern shrine was dedicated to Huitzilopochtli, the Mexica tribal and war god. Adjacent to it on the north was the shrine of Tlaloc, God of Fertility and Rain of great antiquity. Both faced west across the great ceremonial precinct (Figure 8.8).

The construction of the Great Temple is a visual chart of Mexica history just related. Each ruler is accounted for through some alteration in this gigantic structure, and some of them placed a dated plaque in the platform of his construction (Figure 8.9). The Stage II template was miraculously well preserved and although much damage ensued thereafter, enough of the basic pattern is present to know it was followed throughout. Stages IV through VI were years of military expansion and reflect periods of stress (drought and flood) as well as a time when great offerings were made of extraordinary objects. The surprising quantity of faunal and marine remains emphasizes their special significance to the Aztecs.

In the course of exposing the buildings, 86 offerings totalling more than 6000 objects were found. Some were placed in stuccoed, stone-lined cists, in stone boxes with lids, or placed directly in the rubble fill (Figure 8.10). Tlaloc received far more offerings than Huitzilopochtli.

The variety of material is extraordinary. Most of it comes from Guerrero, Oaxaca, the Gulf Coast region, and Puebla, areas under Mexica control, none from the Maya or the Tarascans. Among the contents are stone figures, stone vessels with lids, and beautifully polished objects of obsidian. Well over half of the small stone figures and carvings come from Guerrero, in a style called Mezcala. There is a gorgeous green

FIGURE 8.8   Model of the ceremonial precinct of Tenochtitlán. Top center is the Great Temple surmounted by two shrines; the one on the right is dedicated to Huitzilopochtli, the Aztecs' patron deity, and the other to Tlaloc, the fertility-rain god. Recent excavations have revealed the temple was about 2/3 the height of this restoration. (Courtesy of the Instituto Nacional de Antropología, Mexico.)

jade jaguar; many representations of Xiuhtecuhtli, the Fire God, and innumerable Tlalocs with inlaid eyes of shell and obsidian. There are flint sacrificial knives decorated with shell; human skulls, some with lateral openings for the insertion of *tzompantli* poles; all manner of ornaments: beads of stone, shell and turquoise; earspools of shell decorated with turquoise. There is surprisingly little metal: copper is scant and gold is extremely rare. Pottery vessels number less than 100, but these are of the finest quality (Heyden, 1987).

The sculpture of Coyolxauhqui, the Moon Goddess, representing the malevolent sister of Huitzilopochtli, is one of the most sensational discoveries (García Cook and Araña, 1978) (Figure 8.11). According to Aztec mythology, Coyolxauhqui conspired with her brothers to kill their mother, Coatlícue, when she was about to give birth.

a

FIGURE 8.9   Details of the Great Temple precinct, Tenochtitlán.
a. View overlooking excavations of the Great Temple toward the cathedral of Mexico City.
b. Colossal undulating stone and stucco serpent flanking western edge of the great platform. Length: approximately 6 m.
c. Ancient model of a *tzompantli*, decorated on three sides with panels of stone skulls, numbering 240.
d. Serpent head and two stone braziers on the landings of the platform. Huitzilopochtli braseros seen here are characterized by a knot or bow, symbol of this deity. They were stuccoed. (Photographed by the author.)

b

c

FIGURE 8.9—Continued

d

FIGURE 8.9—Continued

At just the right moment, out of her womb sprang Huitzilopochtli fully armed, who promptly slew his sister who led the assault. On this Great Temple sculpture Coyolxauhqui appears decapitated and dismembered, and lies at the base of the stairway to Huitzilopochtli's shrine as if she had been thrown down from above.

The life-size eagle warrior (see Figure 8.10d) is one of two such figures that flanked an entryway to rooms in the northern complex. This is an extraordinary ceramic piece made in 4 sections. It represents a figure dressed as a member of the Eagle Knights, one of the leading military orders of the Aztecs (the eagle was the sun symbol). Their roster included the bravest and the boldest in battle; those that came home with the greatest number of captives. This was an old institution in Mesoamerica, present among the Toltecs and probably the Teotihuacanos.

These excavations uncovered not only great tributary offerings but Mexica structures in ancient styles (Umberger, 1987). Two small talud-tablero buildings with Teotihuacan symbols and carved figures of Huehuéteotl were tributes to that sacred city as the home of the gods and the birthplace of the sun. A Tula-style stone bench with reliefs of warriors in procession was viewed by the Mexica as a link to dynastic legitimacy. One of the most appealing finds in Toltec form is the little *chacmool* with contorted face from the earliest stage of construction (Figure 8.12). Reportedly, Xochicalco also was represented. One cache contained a small stone mask, Olmec in design, perhaps treasured for many years before being contributed to the Great

a

b

c

d

FIGURE 8.10   Aztec Treasures.
a. A human stone figure from Mezcala, Guerrero, typical of many objects found as offerings at the Great Temple. Height: 35 cm. (Courtesy of the Metropolitan Museum of Art, the Michael C. Rockefeller Memorial Collection. Gift of Luis de Hoyos, 1959 [1979.412.42].)
b. Stone model of a temple, typical of Mezcala-type offerings at the Great Temple. (Courtesy of the Metropolitan Museum of Art, the Michael C. Rockefeller Memorial Collection. Bequest of Nelson A. Rockefeller, 1979 [1979.206.525].)
c. One of the many Tlaloc vessels found as offerings to the fertility-rain deity. A spectacular find, part of Offering 31 on Tlaloc's side of the Great Temple. Painted in blue and white and outlined by incisions, it contained snail shells. Height: 30.4 cm (Courtesy of Arqlgo. Eduardo Matos Moctezuma.)
d. Life-size Aztec dressed as an Eagle Knight, one of the prestigious warrior societies. Ceramic, made in 4 sections. Dated A.D. 1485. Discovered standing on bench in the northern sector of the Great Temple. (Courtesy of Arqlgo. Eduardo Matos Moctezuma.)

Temple. It could have come from any part of central Mexico or Guerrero. These were valued links with antiquity.

Once again the Great Temple of Tenochtitlán has become the center of pilgrimages of sorts, attracting Mexicans and foreigners alike to see the ancient pyramids, the great Coyolxauhqui, and visit the stunning on-site museum that relates Tenochtitlán history and exhibits the discoveries of this remarkable excavation (see Matos Moctezuma, 1988).

FIGURE 8.11   Sculptured monolith representing a dismembered Coyolxauhqui, moon goddess. Found *in situ* at the base of the stairs leading to the Temple of Huitzilopochtli. Diameter: 3.26 m. (Courtesy of the Museo Nacional de Antropología, Mexico.)

Related Sites

There are numerous remains of the Aztecs' ancient contemporaries from Tenochtitlán's twin city, Tlatelolco, and from surrounding sites such as Tenayuca, Tezcotzingo, Calixtlahuaca, Teotenango, Malinalco, Teopanzolco, Tepozteco, and Cholula. These give an excellent idea of the final Mesoamerican construction, and are easily accessible today from Mexico City.

Tlatelolco   Across the city, the ruins of Tlatelolco can still be seen, but they have been badly damaged by the modern city. Tlatelolco originally occupied an island to the north of Tenochtitlán but lost its independence when taken over by Axayácatl around A.D. 1473. Thereafter it became a fifth ward of Tenochtitlán. It resembled Tenochtitlán in having a central ceremonial precinct from which four major causeways led to surrounding areas. Its Great Temple was similar in size and shape to its sister city and likewise dedicated to Tlaloc and Huitzilopochtli. Distinguishing features are a great wall or platform along the north side of the central precinct and an unusual structure south of the Great Temple. This structure, known as the Temple of the

FIGURE 8.12   A unique *chacmool* figure from the earliest construction level of the Great Temple. Dates approximately A.D. 1350. (Courtesy of Arqlgo. Eduardo Matos Moctezuma.)

Numerals, is lavishly paneled with sculpted numerals and glyphs of Aztec gods (Matos Moctezuma, 1989). Tlatelolco is most famous for the huge daily market that was held in an open-air plaza. Today, the whole area constantly yields sculptured stones, pottery, and artifacts of all kinds when digging for foundations or constructions.

Tenayuca   Tenayuca, that old settlement of Xólotl near the modern town of Tlalnepantla, was enlarged many times (Figure 8.13) and its construction with a double staircase may have preceded that of the Great Temple at Tenochtitlán. Three sides of this pyramid are encircled by a *coatepantli* consisting of once brightly colored, coiled serpents made of mortar with great, carved heads. Two large fire serpents with crested heads are coiled on either side of the stairways. Three km away is the small pyramid of Santa Cecilia (Figure 8.14).

Calixtlahuaca   Calixtlahuaca, in the Valley of Toluca, home of the Matlatzinca, was a center closely allied first to the Tepanecs and then to the Aztecs. Particularly outstanding is a round structure believed to have been dedicated to Quetzalcoatl as the Wind God, Ehécatl. Axayácatl swept through the area in A.D. 1474 and 2 years later had added Calixtlahuaca, Teotenango, and Malinalco to the Aztec tribute rolls.

Teotenango   Teotenango could not have been an easy prey, located as it is high above the valley. This huge site was restored under the direction of Román Piña Chan (1975) and crowns the end of a steep hill overlooking the southern part of the Valley of Toluca (Figure 8.15). An enormous wall on the north makes that side impenetrable, while the other three sides fall off sharply to the valley below. From A.D. 750–

FIGURE 8.13 Pyramid of Tenayuca, Tlalnepantla, D. F. (Courtesy of the Instituto Nacional de Antropología e Historia, Mexico.)

FIGURE 8.14 Restored pyramid and temple of Santa Cecilia at Tenayuca. (Courtesy of the Instituto Nacional de Antropología e Historia, Mexico.)

FIGURE 8.15   General view of Teotenango, State of Mexico. (Courtesy of Román Piña Chan.)

1162 it grew to an imposing civic-ceremonial center with spacious plazas and temple-platforms with talud and cornices somewhat like Teotihuacan. Altars, a Tula-Xochicalco-like ball court, streets, residences, markets, and Coyotlatelco pottery are typical of the Epi-Classic Period. By the Postclassic Period, great rivalry existed between the Toluca Valley towns, and any idea of unification was solved by its conquest by Axayácatl in 1476.

Malinalco   Southeast of Toluca near the modern town of Tenancingo is Malinalco, one of the most picturesque sites in central highland Mexico. Its unique main temple was hewn out of the mountainside bedrock. Jaguar sculptures flank the main staircase that leads to a circular chamber by way of a doorway shaped like jaws of a serpent. The inner chamber has several features of the *kiva* or ceremonial room of the southwestern United States. A low bench built into the circular wall bears eagle skins and a central jaguar pelt sculptured in stone. In the center of the floor is another eagle with outspread wings facing the door.

This was a sacred symbolic cave where Mexica overlords could perform ceremonies and ritual to certify their government. It corresponds to a similar place in the Basin of Mexico where the final accession ceremonies of a new ruler were held as described by Durán and Tezozomoc. The center jaguar pelt was the seat of the *tlatoani*. The buildings were commissioned around A.D. 1500 by Ahuítzotl and executed by masons and sculptors sent out from Tenochtitlán (Townsend, 1987).

Morelos   In the state of Morelos, another twin pyramid can be seen at Teopan-zolco, across the tracks from the railroad station at Cuernavaca. More spectacular because of its setting is the simple pyramid of Tepozteco that clings to the cliffs overlooking the village of Tepoztlán.

Writing

The fact that Náhuatl was the language spoken at the time of the Conquest, and being a living language today, has greatly facilitated the study of Aztec writing (Dibble, 1971). The painting of códices was an important craft and artists occupied a special status in society. The painted manuscripts are a major source of calendrical information but other writing is found on low-relief stone sculptures and plaques on some objects of wood and stone (Figures 8.16, 17, and 18).

At the Great Temple of Tenochtitlán, there are some date glyphs placed in the base of the platform. It is not always easy to know if these refer to days, years, or which 52-year cycle. Some are dedication dates that were laid for certain stages of the construction (Umberger, 1988). Many years ago a greenstone plaque was found to mark the dedication date of the last major innovation of the temple in A.D. 1487. It contains both the portraits and name-signs of the ruler who began the enlargement (Tízoc) and the one who completed it (Ahuítzotl).

A great *cuauhxicalli* (2.22 m diameter) was discovered in 1988 in Moneda Street near the Great Temple. It was found *in situ* where a temple once stood dedicated to Tezcatlipoca (Solís, 1989). The stone, in beautiful condition, is similar to the well-

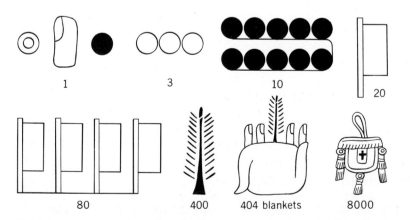

FIGURE 8.16   Aztec numerals. A dot was used for each unit through 19; a flag represented 20; a feather (?) 400; a bag of copal incense 8000. (From Codex Mendoza.)

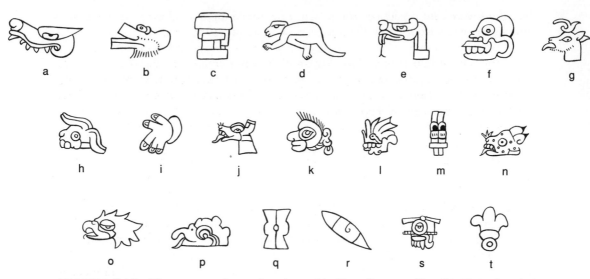

FIGURE 8.17   The twenty Aztec day-signs: (a) Cipactli, crocodile; (b) Ehécatl, wind; (c) Calli, house; (d) Cuetzpallin, lizard; (e) Coatl, serpent; (f) Miquiztli, death; (g) Mazatl, deer; (h) Tochtli, rabbit; (i) Atl, water; (j) Itzcuintli, dog; (k) Ozomatli, monkey; (l) Malinalli, herb; (m) Acatl, reed; (n) Ocelotl, jaguar; (o) Quauhtli, eagle; (p) Cozcaquauhtli, vulture; (q) Ollin, movement or earthquake; (r) Técpatl, flint knife; (s) Quiauitl, rain; (t) Xóchitl, flower. (From Codex Laud, 1966.)

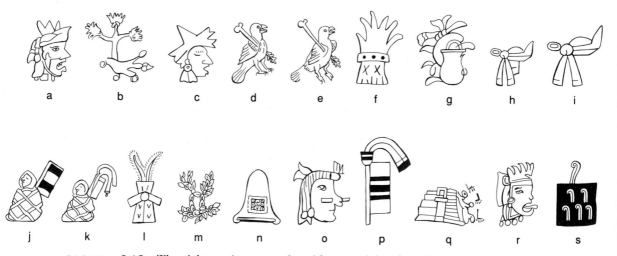

FIGURE 8.18   The eighteen Aztec months with 5 remaining days (Nemontemi): (a) Izcalli; (b) Atecahuallo; (c) Tlacaxipehualiztli; (d) Tozoztontli; (e) Hueytozoztli; (f) Tozcatl; (g) Etzalcua-lizli; (h) Tecuilhuitontli; (i) Huey tecuilhueitl; (j) Miccailhuitontli; (k) Huey micaeilhuitl; (l) Ochpaniztli; (m) Pachtli; (n) Huey pachtli; (o) Quecholli; (p) Panquetzaliztli; (q) Atemoxtli; (r) Tititl; (s) Nemontemi. (From Caso, 1967.)

known Stone of Tízoc. As on that stone, signs accompany a band of prisoners held by the hair, and each glyph identifies one of eleven towns captured by Axayácatl.

Among the most important códices are the Tira de la Peregrinacion that relates the migrations of the Aztecs until they settled in the Basin of Mexico, the Tonalamatl of Aubin gives calendrical cycles, and the Codex Mendoza or Mendocino was drawn up on orders of the Viceroy Antonio de Mendoza. It deals with Aztec conquests, tribute exacted from various towns, and some aspects of Aztec daily life. Sahagún (1946) tells us that there were instruction books on court proceedings, land ownership, inheritance, and boundaries.

The writing system of the Aztecs followed the same tradition of central Mexico that had its roots in Teotihuacan. Text and image were very closely related. The Aztecs combined a pictograph with ideographs to convey a meaning or action. For example a bundle of reeds meant the tying (or end) of the 52-year cycle. Except for calendrical dates, glyphs usually give personal or place names. Some phoneticism occurs aided by the use of homonyms. The reader decided which meaning was intended (Berlo, 1989). For example, to represent Tenochtitlán they combined a picture of a stone (*tena*) with a picture of a nopal cactus (*nochtli*); similarly Chapultepec was represented by a grasshopper (*chapullin*) sitting atop the glyph for hill (*tepec*) (Figure 8.19). People are shown in profile; no perspective was attempted and depth of field was indicated by placing the object higher on the page.

Most of the códices are probably post-Conquest, but painted in the sixteenth century with style and glyphs corresponding to pre-Conquest stone carvings. Unfortunately, many early documents were burned by the Aztecs themselves (see page 442).

Art

The greatest artistic expression of the Aztecs was achieved in stone carving, not to function as decoration but as a way to communicate ideas. It could serve political purposes, as propaganda, or to illustrate relationships between the Aztecs and their universe. A sculpture can also be viewed as a form of wealth. Gold ornaments and fine garments were signs of personal wealth, whereas the state invested in buildings and monuments (Pasztory, 1983).

The free-standing figures of Aztec deities are true idols (Figure 8.20). Many of the deities can be identified by the face, headdress, clothing, or posture. Facial painting seems to be diagnostic, for example: blue with horizontal and yellow stripes identifies Huitzilopochtli; black with horizontal lines indicates Tezcatlipoca (Nicholson, 1973). Ear and nose ornaments, pectorals, and objects held such as shields, all help identification. Female figures are shown kneeling (Figure 8.21), whereas male figures, often with ankles crossed, sit on stools. Stone sculpture falls into two very distinct groups: (1) colossal sculptures made for sacred precincts; and (2) smaller deity images that personified nature, spirits, and objects of all kinds. These were very popular, less well crafted, and possibly mass produced. Little was purely decorative but everything was meaningful.

The Aztecs were anxious to leave a fine permanent record of their achievements

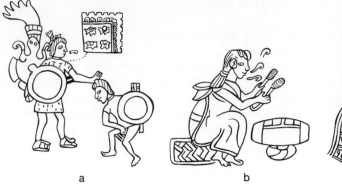

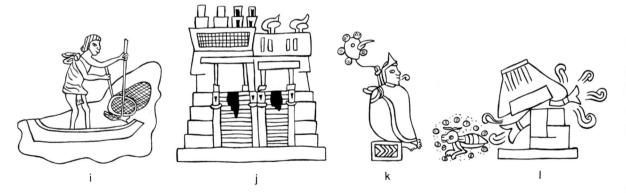

FIGURE 8.19 Aztec picture writing: (a) Warrior receiving insignia for having taken three prisioners of war; (b) priest playing *teponaztli* drum; (c) symbol for song (speech scroll adorned with a flower); (d) glyphs for Chapultepec from Náhuatl *chapulín* (grasshopper) and *tepec* (hill); (e) glyph for Coatepec, from *coatl* (serpent) and *tepec* (hill); (f) glyph for Cuernavaca (near a tree); (g) goldsmith at work; (h) priest observing the stars; (i) boy fishing; (j) temples of Huitzilopochtli and Tlaloc in Tenochtitlán; (k) King Huitzilíhuitl (glyph is a hummingbird's head and five white down feathers); (l) the conquest of Azcapotzalco (*azcatl* means ant, and *putzalli*, sand heap. *Co* means in. Thus the translation of Azcapotzalco is "in the ant heap" or the place of dense population. The temple toppled by flames is a sign of conquest). (Sources: a, b, d, e, f, g, h, i, j, k, l, Codex Mendoza, 1830–1848; c, Codex Borbónico, 1899).

FIGURE 8.20 Stone statue of Xipe Totec, Tlalpan, Valley of Mexico. Height: 76 cm. (Courtesy of the Museum of the American Indian, Heye Foundation, N.Y. [16/3621].)

FIGURE 8.21 Aztec water goddess, Chalchihuítlicue. Height: 66 cm. (Courtesy of the Trustees of the British Museum.)

in stone. Moctezuma I may have been the first king of Tenochtitlán to conceive the idea of having his portrait carved on the stone cliffs at Chapultepec. Later, Moctezuma II added his image to the Chapultepec cliffs, but unfortunately these are now barely visible.

Eventually, huge stone sculptures were commissioned to place in religious precincts to commemorate great victories such as the defeat of Azcapotzalco, or the inauguration of a new ruler. Examples of these are the famous Calendar Stone, Coatlicue, the Stone of Tízoc, and Coyolxauhqui.

The famous Aztec Calendar Stone, a relief carving nearly 4 m wide, is in fact a representation of the Sun God who emerges from the Underworld out of the central symbol for 4 Earthquake, the date on which, according to legend, an earthquake will end this world. Former worlds were destroyed by 4 Jaguar, 4 Wind, 4 Rain, and 4 Water. All this information is enclosed by a band of the 20 day-signs, solar symbols, and 2 fire serpents. Unnoticed by most observers in the complex relief are the dates 13 Reed and 1 Flint, along with a noncalendrical glyph identified as the name of Moctezuma II. Emily Umberger tells us that the dates 13 Reed and 1 Flint refer to the ceremonial day of the tribal god, Huitzilopochtli, "the day the sun was born." After the sun was created, it could not move until the gods sacrificed themselves to provide it with sustenance. Probably carved in the reign of Moctezuma II, this monument may have been a sacrificial stone, placed horizontally somewhere in the main ceremonial precinct of Tenochtitlán (Umberger, 1988).

Another notable stone is that of Tízoc, carved to validate his rule (Townsend, 1979). Around the edge of the wheel-like stone is Tízoc himself, identified by his name glyph as he leans toward another figure that he grabs by the hair, signifying capture. There are 15 nearly identical scenes of paired figures that in effect publicize Aztec conquests up to this time (Wicke, 1976). This stone was found in 1791 when repaving the Zócalo of Mexico City. A more recent discovery of a similar stone (cuauhxicalli), names 11 towns conquered by Axayácatl (Solís, 1989).

Atlantean figures and chacmools, a survival of Toltec art forms, continued to be carved. Although pre-Aztec chacmools had no deity association, the Aztecs often gave them a Tlaloc insignia and made them more elaborate than the known Toltec examples. The Aztecs probably had no idea of the meaning of the figure. To them, Tlaloc was a Toltec deity who represented the glorious past they wanted to perpetuate. They did not distinguish between Tula and Teotihuacan, referring to both as Toltec (Pasztory, 1983, 1988b). The importance given to Tlaloc by the Aztec may have been not for his role as a rain and fertility god, but because of his antiquity as an early dynastic deity. He was elevated to the highest rank of Aztec deities and shared honors with Huitzilopochtli in the Great Temple. At the top of the stairs of Tlaloc's temple, a gorgeous chacmool reclines in situ. Perfectly preserved, and painted in red, blue, white, and black (with a nose of black bitumen), this chacmool belongs to Stage II construction and is rather crudely executed. He gazes today out over the excavations that replace his earlier view of the great ceremonial precinct of Tenochtitlán (Figure 8.22).

Although most sculptures are life size or even larger, there are a series of smaller outstanding carvings of coyotes, serpents, grasshoppers, and plant forms. All have a

FIGURE 8.22   Colorful *chacmool* (black, white, yellow, blue, red) at entrance to the shrine of Tlaloc, Great Temple of Tenochtitlán. Length: 118 cm. (Photographed by the author.)

religious connotation and were probably cult objects placed in sacred areas, for Aztec art was highly symbolic and the gods often assumed animal forms. There are also stone blocks, perhaps used as pedestals, and stone boxes. Even wooden drums (*huehuetl*) and the *xiuhmolpilli* or year bundle (representing the completion of a 52-year cycle) were copied in stone. As Nicholson (1973) has pointed out, friezes and panels popular among earlier peoples were rare. Aztec art was characterized by symbolism and free-standing sculpture.

   Metallurgy   The art of metallurgy was acquired from the Maya who had picked up the technology in the Late Classic Period from the Isthmus region further south. It did not become widespread in central and southern Mesoamerica until the Late Postclassic. There was only a single jewelry style from the Basin of Mexico south to the Maya border known as the South Mexican International Style (SMIS) (Bray, 1989).

   Work was largely in gold, tumbaga, and a little silver. It had three characteristic traits that Bray tells us assures instant recognition: (1) close stylistic links with the codex painting of the Mixteca-Puebla códices (Figure 8.23), and the polychrome pottery; (2) technical superiority especially in lost-wax casting (*cire-perdue*) with particular liking for false wirework, for example, in headdresses; and (3) a fondness for composite jewelry either in metal alone or combined with stone. In this regard they liked to attach danglers to finger rings, necklaces, and ornaments. The style of the jewelry is distinctly Mesoamerican, using motifs of humans and animals of the real world, designed to appeal to the Mexican elite (Figure 8.24e–h).

   Distribution coincides almost exactly with the presence of Mixteca-Puebla pottery, whether manufactured or traded, so the centers of production were likely the

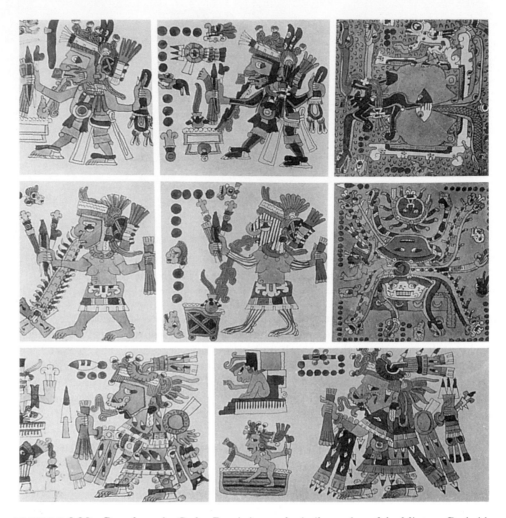

FIGURE 8.23   Page from the Codex Borgia in a style similar to that of the Mixtecs. Probably of Puebla origin. (Courtesy of the Instituto Nacional de Antropología e Historia, Mexico.)

FIGURE 8.24   Postclassic adornments.
a. Ground obsidian earspool associated with a grave. Tzintzuntzan, Michoacán. Maximum diameter: 5.7 cm. (Courtesy of the Museo Nacional de Antropología, Mexico.)
b. Pair of obsidian earplugs. Aztec culture. Height: 1 3/8 in. (Courtesy of the Metropolitan Museum of Art, The Michael C. Rockefeller Memorial Collection. Bequest of Nelson A. Rockefeller, 1979 [1979.206.1088;1089].)
c. Obsidian lip plugs or labrets, showing front, lateral, and interior surfaces. Aztec culture. Sizes: .1090, Height: 1.2 cm; .1091, length: 4.1 cm; .1092, length: 3.1 cm. (Courtesy of the Metropolitan Museum of Art, The Michael C. Rockefeller Memorial Collection. Bequest of Nelson A. Rockefeller, 1979 [1979.206.1090-1092].)
d. Copper bells from the Ulua River Valley, Honduras. Length of largest: 9 cm. (Courtesy of the Museum of the American Indian, Heye Foundation, N.Y. [18/4724].)

e. Gold necklace, Oaxaca. Mixteca culture. Length: 51 cm. (Courtesy of the Museum of the American Indian, Heye Foundation, N.Y. [16/3451].)

f. Gold-filigree ring representing an eagle. Oaxaca, Mixteca culture. (Courtesy of the Museum of the American Indian, Heye Foundation, N.Y. [16/3447].)

g. Gold ring, Monte Albán, Oaxaca (?). Mixtec culture. Good example of the SMIS metallurgy. (Courtesy of Museo Nacional de Antropología, Mexico.)

h. Gold labret representing a jaguar head with flexible tongue, Ejutla, Oaxaca. Mixtec culture. Length: 6 cm. (Courtesy of the Museum of the American Indian, Heye Foundation, N.Y. [18/756].)

i. Necklace of rock crystal beads. Mixteca culture. Maximum bead diameter: 1.8 cm. (Courtesy of the Museo Nacional de Antropología, Mexico.)

j. Necklace of pink shell beads, Oaxaca. Bead diameter: 3 mm. (Courtesy of the Museo Nacional de Antropología, Mexico.)

same. The Aztecs were adherents to the SMIS and there is no distinct Aztec style in metallurgy as was seen in the fields of architecture and sculpture. This led me to erroneously presume that the fine gold jewelry from the Basin of Mexico was produced by imported Mixteca craftspersons. It was likely made by Mexica in the Basin of Mexico at Azcapotzalco or other nearby centers (Nicholson, 1982). Gold dust was readily available in the great Tlatelolco market as well as finished products.

The Tarascan region was outside of this SMIS tradition, as it had a different background, its own technology, style, and forms. Moreover, it dealt mostly with copper and silver alloys (see page 201). The frontier between the Aztecs and Tarascans was real and apparently there was little peaceful contact between them.

Minor Arts   Small objects used in daily living as well as a vast array of ceremonial paraphernalia have been unearthed in great quantities (see Figures 8.24 and 8.25f). Diaz del Castillo (1944) mentions that multicolored pottery vessels were especially

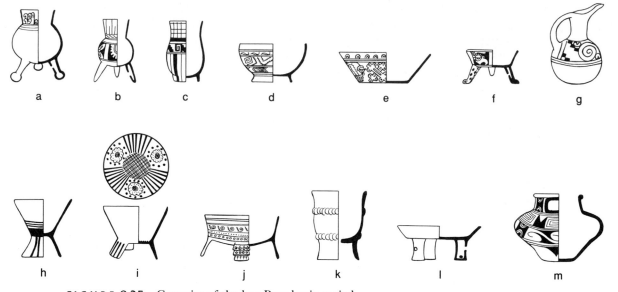

FIGURE 8.25   Ceramics of the late Postclassic period.
(a), (b), (c), (d), (f) Cholula polychrome; (e) red-on-white bowl, skull-and-crossbones motif; (g) polished black-on-red pitcher; (h) black-on-red goblet; (i) black-on-orange *molcajete*; (j) black-on-orange tripod; (k) monochrome unslipped censer with a circular central vent in the base, Burial 5, Tikal; (l) Ixpop polychrome tripod vessel, rattle supports, surface debris, Temple II, Tikal; (m) black-on-white vessel, Huasteca culture. Sources: (a) Piña Chan, 1960; (b,d) Noguera, 1965; (c) Noguera, 1950; (e) Covarrubias, 1957, redrawn from *Indian Art and Central America*, by Miguel Covarrubias, copyright 1957 by Alfred A. Knopf, Inc. Reprinted by permission of the publisher; (f,g) Toscano, 1952; (h,j,m) Marquina, 1951; (i) Museum of the American Indian, Heye Foundation, N.Y. [8/8694]; (k,l) Adams and Trik, 1961, The Tikal Project. The University Museum, University of Pennsylvania.

favored by the rulers, a probable reference to the famous Cholula polychrome or Mixteca-Puebla ware (see Figure 8.25h). The Aztecs' traditional pottery was well fired, decorated in black-on-orange (Figure 8.25i). Early forms were continued but supports now were either thin slabs or sharp spikes. *Molcajetes* are common (Figure 8.25i). A fine, highly polished, red ware sometimes decorated in black is characteristic. Elaborate long-handled censers were designed strictly for ceremonial use. Stamps, smoking pipes, *malacates,* and figurines representing deities were all standardized and produced in great quantities.

With the exception of some work in copper, especially by the Tarascans, tools changed but slightly after Preclassic days. The digging stick, *manos* and *metates,* bark-beaters, pounders and obsidian blades, knives and scrapers remained standard equipment.

Religion

Because all aspects of a functioning society are interrelated and integrated, it is impossible to discuss one feature as an isolated entity. For example, warfare was both a privilege and duty of every able-bodied man, carefully reinforced by religious beliefs. After important battles, honors and titles were handed out for bravery or for capturing 4 or 5 prisoners. In this way nobility could be achieved. Every young man was considered to be a potential warrior dedicated to providing prisoners for sacrifice. The sacrifice of human hearts was the "food" necessary to sustain the sun (Huitzilopochtli) in his daily flight across the sky, and was not the sun necessary to life itself?

Aztec religion with over 200 deities, each with multiple forms, seems an exaggerated polytheism (Caso, 1958). Full of fear, dread, and apprehension, the Aztecs mirrored in their gods their own preoccupation with magic, divination, and forces of good and evil. All Aztecs believed they were living under a constant threat of doomsday, which they tried to ward off as long as possible by human sacrifices. Most gods were represented in human form and were felt to have human problems and weaknesses.

In general, Aztec religion had great flexibility and a unique capacity to embrace deities of both ancestral peoples and contemporaries. Thus the ancient Gods of Fire (Huehuéteotl), Rain and Water (Tlaloc), Springtime (Xipe Totec), and the Feathered Serpent (Quetzalcoatl) still occupied important roles, although their meaning and symbolism may well have undergone reinterpretations (Figure 8.26).

Tezcatlipoca (Smoking Mirror) is familiar from Toltec days as the adversary of Quetzalcoatl. His talisman was the smoking mirror that often takes the place of a foot in his representations (Figure 8.26). By gazing into this mirror he could predict events (note the parallel with the Maya God K). Tezcatlipoca had perhaps the greatest variety of attributes and prerogatives of any god and appears in many different overlapping roles.

Much confusion arises because one god could appear in different forms. Quetzalcoatl, for example, might be the Wind God, God of Life, God of the Morning, the Planet Venus, or God of Twins and Monsters, and he could only be recognized

Tlaloc   Xipe Totec   Quetzalcóatl   Tezcatlipoca

FIGURE 8.26   Aztec deities. *Tlaloc*, the god of rain and lightning (Storm God), probably one of the oldest gods; known as Chac among the Maya, Tzahui among the Mixtecs, and Cocijo among the Zapotecs. *Xipe Totec*, the Flayed One, god of planting, springtime, and jewelers; in his honor victims were flayed and their skins worn by a priest. He is also the red Tezcatlipoca. *Quetzalcoatl*, the feathered-serpent deity, god of learning and the priesthood. He is also god of life, the morning, the planet Venus, and twins and monsters. In his various aspects he may be called Ehécatl, Tlahuizcalpantecuhtli, Ce Acatl, or Xólotl. *Tezcatlipoca*, the Smoking Mirror, appears in many forms. He is associated with the nocturnal sky, the moon, and the forces of evil, death, and destruction. Sources: *Tlaloc*, Codex Telleriano-Remensis, 1889; *Xipe Totec*, Codex Borbónico, 1899; *Quetzalcoatl*, Codex Féjévary-Mayer, 1830–1848; *Tezcatlipoca:* Stone of Tízoc, drawn after Tozzer, 1957, courtesy of the Peabody Museum of Archaeology and Ethnology, Harvard University. Copyright 1957 by the President and Fellows of Harvard College.

by particular attributes that distinguished his various roles. Aztec deities were not conceived as distinct entities. The concept of duality, the forces of good and evil being represented by different aspects of the same deity, was a common feature of this religion.

Every child from birth was taught that humans' very existence depended on the gods, and to ensure their well-being, they must be provided with the magic substance of life found only in blood and human hearts. Children learned that their mission on earth was to prepare for the sacred war, and to provide the necessary victims for sacrifice.

Several types of sacrifices were performed. Most common was that of stretching a captive over a convex sacrificial stone and removing the heart. This was then placed in a special stone eagle vase (*cuauhxicalli*) where it was burned for the god's consumption. Flaying the victim was a sacrifice performed in honor of *Xipe Totec*. Another form was a "gladiatorial combat" in which the prisoner, tied to a gigantic stone, was forced to defend himself with a wooden club against Aztec warriors armed with obsidian-edged swords. Whatever form was chosen, the sacrifice was always carried out to nourish the gods and for the eternal glorification of the Aztecs.

Religion touched almost every aspect of Aztec society. Art, of course, was almost exclusively of a religious and symbolic nature, and religious instruction was an integral part of education for both sexes. Even games were played under divine guidance. Sahagún (1946) tells us that the two ball courts in Tenochtitlán were dedicated to the sun and the moon. This game (*tlachtli*), had been known in some form for probably 2000 years, and a match always met with enthusiastic anticipation. All knew that the final outcome was decided in the heavens.

Social Structure

When one king died, the next was elected from the royal lineage by a council composed of nobles, titled warriors, and important priests. Although the council gathered to "elect" a new king, the genealogical chart (see page 441) illustrates how tightly the reins of succession were held. It looks as if the rulership passed from brother to brother before descending to the following generation, but relationships are not well defined. Reckoning descent from the Toltecs was of primary importance.

Knowing the anxiety and uncertainty with which Mesoamericans viewed their world, dynastic succession was one additional worry. A cyclical nature may have been in operation for it is possible that three wives bound the male rulers to each other in one descent line. (The first wife was the Toltec princess Ilancueitl, and the other two were the daughters of Moctezuma I and II. Each one married her grandfather's brother's son after a cycle of four kings, thus regenerating the dynasty (see Figure 8.7). (For a detailed discussion and implications of Mexica rulership, see Gillespie, 1989).

The hereditary nobility, from which the king was chosen, reckoned its descent from the Toltecs and enjoyed certain privileges not shared by others. The king claimed that he was selected by the god Tezcatlipoca and was the god's representative on earth. He also claimed descent from deified ancestors, not real ones. As expected, the king had special insignia and the finest clothing. His official cape was tie-dyed in an allover pattern of blue-and-white squares with a central dot, the prestigious marker of the Toltec lineage (Anawalt, 1990). He, as well as his own court, was permitted to have many wives and to send his male children to the *calmecac*, a strict, elite school for sons of the nobility. Here, formal education was given in the arts and sciences, with emphasis placed on basic religious instruction. There were six such institutions in Tenochtitlán. At these schools much time was devoted to sacrifice, prayers, ritual purification, bloodletting, and autosacrifice, wherein the students pierced their ears and tongues with the sharp spines of the maguey.

These young boys became the *pilpiltin* (descended from the *tlatoanis*), and *tectecuhtin* (professional warrior group), forming a privileged ruling class that included the king (*tlatoani*), from which people were chosen to occupy posts as governors, ministers of justice, and coordinators. This group owned land but did not work it themselves. Although they formed a hereditary nobility, another group of nobility was eventually created.

A warrior who distinguished himself in battle might be singled out for honors and thus be elevated to a special nobility, freed from his *calpulli* and the requirement to work its lands. This neonobility was somewhat in conflict with the hereditary one

(Monzón, 1949). The crucial step that provided the *pipiltin* with economic as well as political power was the resounding defeat of the Tepanecs, thus gaining mainland acreage.

Commoners (*macehualtin*) and laborers who made up 80% of the population were extremely poor. They were free peasant farmers, merchants, and craftspersons with direct access to land of the state which they could use but not own, for they could not pass it on to their heirs. They could improve their social position by distinguishing themselves in commercial enterprises or on the battlefield and be given the right to dedicate a captive for sacrifice, or add an insignia to their clothes. A *macehaul* had only one wife, meager belongings, and his male children attended the *telpochcalli* school. These schools did not produce leaders. They turned out Aztec citizens who learned what their place was in society and how to be good citizens and warriors (Bray, 1977b). This school was less severe than the *calmecac*. Boys were instructed in the arts of warfare and were given religious training. Girls were educated in separate schools receiving instruction in domestic arts as well as religion.

Another social group was the *mayeques*, or bondsmen, often called slaves that made up about 10% of the population. They worked the land of others but could neither own nor inherit land. There were different categories and for some the status was only temporary. A person might voluntarily go into slavery or temporarily place his children in bondage to pay off a debt. Women and children captured in war were treated as slaves, as were criminals, who were sometimes forced to work for the family they had offended. The *mayeques* were used as beasts of burden, but their children were free. This was a special fluctuating social category. As a servile group, they worked the lands of the *pilpiltin*.

Much has been written about the *calpulli*, which originally was a kind of tribal organization, but came to mean a barrio or territorial division (Carrasco, 1971). A member of the *calpulli* could farm an individual plot of land and transmit it to his heirs. But if he failed to cultivate it for 2 years, it reverted back to the barrio. Not all *calpullis* had equal status; some owned more land than others and some were associated with certain craft specializations. According to van Zantwijk (1985), changes took place in which kinship and class distinctions had a lesser role and the corporate professional groups gained strength. This resulted from the formation of the neonobility mentioned above. The *calpulli* functioned as a corporate body, owning land and paying taxes.

Law and Justice

At the time of the Conquest, the highest authority was the king himself, who was considered to be semidivine and so supreme that only those of the highest rank were permitted to look at him directly. When approaching the king, one had first to touch the ground and then his mouth with his hand, a sign of humility and reverence. The king ate alone and received visitors and foreign dignitaries only after they had removed their sandals and covered their fine clothes with a humble maguey fiber cape. The king was carried about in a litter and did not touch his foot to the earth.

A complex juridical system grew out of early customs and was probably influenced by Nezahuacóyotl, king of nearby Texcoco, whose far-reaching code of law has been preserved (Ixtlilxóchitl, 1952). Aztec law dealt with all aspects of human relations—civil, criminal, and legal matters as well as foreign affairs of the state. The entire structure of the legal system was taught at the *calmecac*.

The advisory position of *cihuacóatl* was originally one of considerable power with administrative and juridical authority. Probably the most famous *cihuacóatl* was Tlacaélel who served as advisor to Moctezuma Ilhuicamina, and participated in all major decisions. One of his chief duties was to preside over a supreme court that was composed of four judges. He was aided by 13 wise men who formed a special high court that met about every 12 days. Their verdict was passed on to the king, the ultimate authority, who then pronounced judgment. There were also lower courts of justice, provincial courts, and a kind of local judge in each town. Sahagún (1946) stresses that these offices were filled from the ranks of well-qualified nobles who had been educated in the *calmecac*.

Because of the nature of Aztec law, there was little need for jails or prisons. Most crimes were punished by some kind of death: flogging, sacrifice, decapitation, or being placed in slavery either temporarily or for life, depending on the nature of the offense. Small wooden cages housed those who committed minor crimes. If Aztec law seems brutal today, it was clearly understood by society that the law-abiding citizen was protected and could feel secure under the justice of the land.

The law was harsh, yet it contained certain rather surprising exceptions. For example, stealing corn was punishable by death, but a person in need was permitted to help himself to 4 ears from those rows planted along the road for his immediate use without castigation. An interesting concept of Aztec law was that the severity of punishment was measured in accordance with the offender's station in life. A man of high office assumed greater moral responsibilities and his conduct was expected to be beyond reproach. A high priest would be put to death for a crime that might be tolerated if committed by a bondsman. Laws were designed to preserve the family, the society, and the state. Nobles had the right to defend themselves and be heard in private, but they were duly punished if found guilty. Under no circumstance was the individual permitted to take action or settle a dispute on his own. The state only was authorized to make decisions and mete out punishment.

A good law-abiding Aztec was careful about his conduct and was anxious to do what was right and appropriate as well as gain approval of others. He wanted to be highly regarded, but his conduct on earth was in no way connected with a belief in reward or punishment after death (León-Portilla, 1963).

Trade and Tribute

It was not until after the defeat of the Tepanecs that the real transition was made from a rural to an urban economy. This event in 1428 marked the beginning of the rapid increase in private wealth among the elite, that in turn led to class differentiation, desire for more foreign and exotic goods, and the emergence of a complex statehood.

The large nucleated settlements of Tenochtitlán-Tlatelolco were composed of full-time occupational specialists rather than farmers. By 1519 the population is estimated at 150,000–200,000 people in an area of 12 km (Calnek, 1976). But prior to 1428, with no arable land in the immediate vicinity, the island habitat presented a difficult problem of provisioning. Under Itzcóatl they began to extend *chinampas* (Figure 8.27).

The ingenious system of *chinampa* cultivation was initially begun by digging ditches in swampy lakeshore areas or on natural islands (Armillas, 1971). The ditches drained off water to reveal plots of soil where planting could be done. Aerial photographs show a carefully laid out grid network of canals. From canoes they renewed the soil by scooping up and spreading mud from the lake bottom, extremely rich in organic matter. Eventually the *chinampas* became more elevated, which reduced the danger of flooding, always a threat with the arrival of summer rains. This system was ideally suited for the island dwellers of Tenochtitlán, for it provided tillable land and easy transport of produce by canoe. Owing to the constant renewing of the soil, *chinampas* never wore out. Here the Aztecs grew corn, squash, beans, chili, *chia*, amaranth, innumerable vegetables, and flowers.

Chinampas were cultivated from Tenochtitlán and Tlatelolco south to the shore of

FIGURE 8.27   *Chinampa* at Mixquic, Valley of Mexico. (Courtesy of Victoria Bach.)

Lake Xochimilco and then east to Lake Chalco. The Aztecs worked hard to protect these valuable lands. The greatest threat to their existence was the possibility of infiltration of nitrous salts from the eastern part of Lake Texcoco. Eventually they constructed a network of dikes built of stone, earth, poles, and branches, with sluice gates to protect the western part of Lake Texcoco from the salty waters of the east.

Large-scale development was continued under Moctezuma Ilhuicamina. Great attention was devoted to procuring new markets, controlling sources of raw materials, and expanding trade and commerce. Sanders believes that the subsistence base of Tenochtitlán could have been met by the Basin of Mexico itself.

The urban dwellers were the ruling class, full-time professionals, artisans, and merchants. About half of the people in the surrounding area of 400 km^2 were non-food producers engaged in cottage industries such as making mats or maguey cloth. Beyond this were farmers and others who brought in lime, firewood, and construction materials. Obsidian came from Otumba and salt from Ecatepec. Fishing was less important but was an occupation that mattered.

Taxes were collected within 150 km. Areas beyond were listed on the tribute rolls (Sanders and Santley, 1983). Once an area was conquered, trade became tribute. Conquered territory was given quotas to be filled annually, semiannually, or every 80 days, depending on goods and distance. The Aztec economy relied on revenue raised through taxes on state farmlands, rent, markets, and tribute.

There were different levels and types of trade. The professional merchants were the *pochteca*, who formed a well-organized, state-sponsored guild and worked beyond the borders of the Aztec domain. Theirs was a hereditary occupation. They had their special gods, their own rites, feasts, courts, hierarchy, and insignia. Although carried out under the auspices of particular gods, trade was primarily a secular business operation. The *pochteca* traveled armed, in long caravans and sought out high-level, low-bulk items such as precious stones, feathers, copal, jewelry, that is, special elite and ceremonial items (Acosta Saignes, 1945). The *pochteca* also took advantage of local markets to do a little personal trading of their own on the side (Berdan, 1988).

The main route south from highland Mexico led to Tuxtepec (see Map 8.4). Here, groups might split, some going east toward the Gulf of Mexico, and others heading south to meet other traders, or pick their counterparts in special places called ports-of-trade, neutral areas traditionally removed from political conflict. Such areas were Xicalango in Tabasco and probably Acalán on the lower Usumacinta River. A port-of-trade was ideally located near lagoons or rivers for convenient access by canoe. In Xicalango, the *pochteca* would have met traders (Postclassic Putún) who handled commerce to the east, traveling around Yucatán by sea to the Bay of Chetumal. These sea-going traders along the coasts of Yucatán and Honduras reportedly used large canoes 2 m wide by 15 m long in which the heaviest cargo could be carried. Remember that on land all goods were transported by tumpline by porters. The maximum load permitted was 50 pounds per person.

The highly desirable cacao-producing area of Soconusco, often erroneously considered a port-of-trade, was far from being neutral, and was finally conquered by Ahuítzotl in 1486 after 4 years of battles. It then became a prize tributary province that paid in cacao, jaguar pelts, feathers, and jewelry (Voorhies, 1989a; Codex Mendoza 1830–1848).

By the thirteenth century, Mesoamericans clamored for more turquoise. It reached Central Mexico from the Southwest by way of the eastern fringes of the Sierra Madre Occidental, apparently already processed. A west coast route was also used, overcoming Tarascan attempts to block the trade. The Codex Mendoza illustrates turquoise as tribute passing to the Mexica by way of the Veracruz coast. Now it was viewed not only as extravagant jewelry, a symbol of noble status, but adorned religious paraphernalia, shields, masks and mirrors, outstripping the traditional use of jade (Harbottle and Weigand, 1992).

Other trading systems have received less attention. Regional and local business was transacted in the indigenous marketplaces. Here, middlemen merchants and farmers dealt as independents. Control of obsidian was not the key factor in Aztec economy as it may have been to the Teotihuacanos, and obsidian workers were not high status members of society. Obsidian was just one of a number of items carried by itinerant merchants. The *pochteca* might take along a few earspools or knives for the "common folk" (Hirth, 1984). Nonetheless, obsidian production increased dramatically in the late Postclassic and was present in every household (Smith, 1990). Always in demand were salt and cacao, for which some individuals might travel a distance of some 200 km. People looked to make a profit and might move marketable items across ecological boundaries for a high rate of exchange.

Miahuatlán in the Mixteca area was a famous market center where one could buy or sell "anything." The giant of all markets was the one at Tlatelolco that dazzled even the Spanish. It was held in the wide paved area that stretched in front of the great Temple of Huitzilopochtli where boats could draw up in the canal at one side to unload their merchandise. Every imaginable product was available here and occupied a designated place; vendors of vegetables, fish, and fruit products squatted in orderly rows with their goods in neat piles before them on *petates*. For sale were not only finished products such as mantles, baskets, pottery, tools, jewelry, and feather work, but also slaves and raw materials such as unrefined gold ore, stone, untanned hides and skins, lime, and wood (Acosta Saignes, 1945; Sahagún, 1946; Torquemada, 1943) (Figure 8.28).

The goods were taxed as they were brought in and sales were carefully regulated by special courts and judges, and for this reason transactions were forbidden outside the marketplace. Misdemeanors were severely punished; anyone caught pilfering was immediately stoned to death. Accordingly, business was orderly and the marketplace respected. It also functioned as a social and religious gathering place for gossip and worship.

The medium of exchange was cacao or chocolate, a favorite drink of the nobility. The control of its areas of production was of great concern. These lands lay in Tabasco and northern Oaxaca, central and southern Veracruz, Soconusco, and Honduras. Other types of money were cotton cloaks, quills filled with gold dust, and small copper axes. Known as money axes, these were used in parts of Oaxaca and northern Guerrero as a form of negotiable wealth. As many as 377 were found in one cache and dozens have been recovered in pots (Bray, 1989).

What was done with this constant flow of incoming commodities? Little trickled down to the populace at large. Most was stored in warehouses for emergencies (a poor harvest, war) or was saved to hand out as political gifts, rewards, or as special favors. Raw materials (cotton, gold, precious stones) went to the appropriate craftspersons to produce fine articles for export. No doubt the administration and elite received a share (van Zantwijk, 1985). The economy did not depend wholly on tribute, as the basic subsistence needs were met largely by the local farmers, fishermen, and natural resources, but tribute raised the standard of living, helped maintain a high morale, and diverted thoughts from doomsday.

The Aztec rulers took care of their people and in return demanded their allegiance and respect. Van Zantwijk (1985) believes that this Aztec "arrangement" could take care of 20 million people in central Mexico by 1520.

The "Aztec Empire"

The Aztec "empire" was a strange entity. A coordinated, centralized political empire never emerged, but the strong state power of Tenochtitlán maintained its domain through force and threat of force. Military expeditions were twofold in purpose. The first and foremost goal was to exact heavy tribute to meet the increasing demands in Tenochtitlán for all the food, cloth, feathers, raw materials, and slaves necessary to maintain the highly structured urban society of the island city. Another goal was to maintain an ever-ready supply of sacrificial victims to satisfy the gods.

The *pochteca* doubled as government spies, and often the Mexica war council would act on their information. When the order went out for war, every able-bodied man received his weapons and paraphernalia from the local storehouse, as no standing army was maintained. The weapons were obsidian-edged wooden swords, *atlatls*, spears, bows and arrows, slings, and blowguns. Shields were made of reeds and feathers and were sometimes jeweled. A warrior's initial costume was cotton-quilted armor. In addition, there were ten higher-ranking feathered outfits that included a variety of fantastic headdresses, jewelry, ornaments and devices attached to the back with protective and supernatural power and symbolism (Anawalt and Berdan, 1992). The outfits of the nobility were dazzling. Thus geared for war, *pipiltin* and *macehualtin* alike plunged into battle to the music of trumpets and drums and noise makers (Figure 8.29).

A conquest was planned in advance. Tactics included ambushes, feints, trickery, attacks at narrow mountain passes, at strategic locations, or at an unsuspected hour. The "flower war" (*xochiyaotl* in Náhuatl. *Xóchitl* means flower) was a different exercise with the same number of people on each side, meeting at a specified time, fighting according to rules and no trickery. It was a show of martial skills, a way to distinguish oneself, and could be followed by a full-scale war. To lose one's life in this war was viewed as a blissful, fortunate, or flowery death. (Hassig, 1988).

a

b

d

e

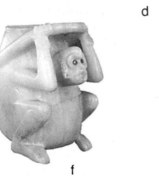

f

g

i

j

k

c

h

The lack of any true, cohesive, political empire is seen in the fact that many towns were constantly reconquered. Alliances and personal ties might be used to hold the empire together. Once a town was taken, the Aztecs might or might not retain its ruler and the same local administration. Often a marriage might be arranged with a prominent member of Tenochtitlán's ruling family. Tribute arrangements were quickly set up but could be complicated. Some towns received tribute from others, while they in turn were forced to send contributions to the Triple Alliance (this led to another distributive arrangement). If the *pochteca* reported signs of unrest, or were themselves captured or put to death, immediate retribution would follow in the form of a sweeping attack by the dreaded Mexica, to which resistance was usually useless (Kelly and Paleron 1952).

Defensive sites and fortifications were built on strategic hilltops, and walls and moats were constructed with defense in mind. There is nothing in the record to indicate a professional army but there are reports of garrisons at Oztuma, Tututepec, Xicalango, and about 20 other settlements (Gibson, 1971). These were manned by only a few troops or for short periods of time. Tenochtitlán itself was not a fortified

---

FIGURE 8.28   Prominent commercial goods.

a. Clay seals or stamps. Dimensions of specimen on the right: 5 cm × 6 cm. (Courtesy of the Museum of the American Indian, Heye Foundation, N.Y. Left [23/5490]; right [23/5489].)

b. Mold-made clay figurine, perforated for suspension. Height: 15 cm. (Courtesy of the Museum of the American Indian, Heye Foundation, N.Y. [22/1025].)

c. Beautiful example of Mixtec ceramics. Polychrome with blue hummingbird on the rim. Tomb 2, Zaachila, Oaxaca. Height: 9 cm. (Courtesy of the Museo Nacional de Antropología, Mexico.)

d. Carved jaguar bone. Mixtec culture. Length: 13 cm. (Courtesy of the Museo Nacional de Antropología, Mexico.)

e. Highly prized onyx vessel. Isla de Sacrificios, Veracruz Height: 22 cm. (Courtesy of the Museo Nacional de Antropología, Mexico.)

f. Onyx monkey/effigy vessel with inlaid obsidian eyes. Isla de Sacrificios, Veracruz. Height: 13 cm. (Courtesy of the Museo Nacional de Antropología, Mexico.)

g. Black-and-white spouted vessel of Huasteca origin, Veracruz. Height: 19.5 cm. (Courtesy of the Metropolitan Museum of Art, the Michael C. Rockefeller Memorial Collection. Purchase, anonymous gift, 1966. [1978.412.155].)

h. Cholula polychrome vessel with ring stand. Height: 24 cm. (Courtesy of the Museum of the American Indian, Heye Foundation, N.Y. [16/3394].)

i. Mixteca-Puebla polychrome tripod. Outstanding example. (Courtesy of the Museo Nacional de Antropología, Mexico.)

j. Conch-shell pendant of great prestigious value with three holes for suspension. Design: a warrior holds a feathered standard and shield. Behind him are 3 human skulls and a serpent. Veracruz. Height: 16 cm. (Courtesy of the Museum of the American Indian, Heye Foundation, N.Y. [23/9573].)

k. Aztec polished red clay smoking pipe. Basin of Mexico. Height: 6.7 cm. (Courtesy of the Metropolitan Museum of Art, the Michael C. Rockefeller Memorial Collection. Bequest of Nelson A. Rockefeller, 1979 [1979.206.1016].)

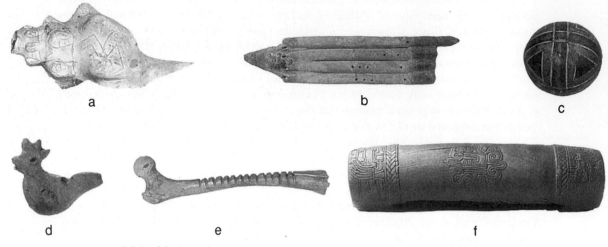

FIGURE 8.29 Music makers.
a. Incised conch shell trumpet. Oaxaca. Mixteca culture. Length: 24 cm. (Courtesy of the Museum of the American Indian, Heye Foundation, N.Y. [22/6377].)
b. Pottery pan pipes from Tabasco, Mexico. Length: 57 cm. (Courtesy of the Museum of the American Indian, Heye Foundation, N.Y. [23/902].)
c. Pottery rattle resembling a game ball. Painted orange and incised. Tlacotepec, Toluca Valley. Diameter: 9 cm. (Courtesy of the Museum of the American Indian, Heye Foundation, N.Y. [8/8752].)
d. Clay whistle in the form of a bird. Tlatilco. Length: 10 cm. (Purchased by the author.)
e. *Omechicahuaztli* (bone rasp) made of a human femur. Basin of Mexico. (Courtesy of the Museum of the American Indian, Heye Foundation, N.Y. [2/6719].)
f. Carved wooden *teponaztli* drum. Azotla, Puebla. The base is hollowed out and the top is slitted to form two tongues that were struck with a beater of some sort. Length: 44 cm. (Courtesy of the Museum of the American Indian, Heye Foundation, N.Y. [16/3373].)

city. Its best means of defense was its natural position in the lake but it possessed no special military structures. In the battle for its life, fighting raged from housetops, temples, aqueducts, and bridges (Diaz del Castillo, 1944; Sahagún, 1946)

Aztec expansion began under Itzcóatl after 1430, and the first area brought into the fold outside the Basin of Mexico was the region around Tula and the old Toltec empire. Moctezuma Ilhuicamina expanded the domain into southern Guerrero below Oztuma and struggled in vain with the Tlaxcalans. He added some territory to the northeast, in Veracruz and upland Puebla. Axayácatl ran into difficulties in the west and was turned back by the Tarascans but helped define the western frontier (see page 436). Close to home Tlatelolco was taken over. The greatest territorial gains were made under Ahuítzotl and Moctezuma Xocoyotzin in the southeast (see Map 8.4).

Oaxaca, Tehuantepec, and Soconusco were the greatest goals to be conquered. The Zapotecs, Chiapanecs, and Tehuantepecs were all belligerent and had to be either taken by force or subdued in certain regions to be able to reach Soconusco. This was achieved in 1486 by Ahuítzotl. Soconusco was an area thriving with eight inland polities close to the foothills and secondary centers along the coast. Its conquest was a major prize. Thereafter its biannual payment to tribute collectors included 200 loads of cacao; drinking containers (gourds?); spotted cat pelts; bird feathers and skins; fine greenstone jewelry and amber (Gasco and Voorhies, 1989). The Aztecs probably kept the commercial system and existing hierarchy intact and superimposed their own political structure (Voorhies, 1989a,b). This makes for a smooth takeover although control may be weak and difficult to maintain. It must have been after acquiring Soconusco that the most famous battle of Zapotec history was fought for the great fortress of Guiengola just west of the town of Tehuantepec. The mountain there rises 1000 m above the river; defense was afforded by a thorny forest and walls. It was originally built as a Zapotec administrative center for the Isthmus with a huge civic-ceremonial complex of 54,000 m at 400 m elevation, a kind of Postclassic imitation of Monte Albán (Flannery, 1983d). In 1497 Zapotecs and Mixtecs united to successfully rout the forces of Ahuítzotl after a long siege. However, the Spanish required only one month to take it 24 years later.

Independent Kingdoms

Although the Aztec and Tarascan states were the largest and most powerful at the time of the Conquest, smaller, less well-defined kingdoms were located east and south of the Valley of Mexico (see Map 8.4). It is not clear how much autonomy or political unity these areas enjoyed, but they do not appear to have paid tribute to Tenochtitlán.

Tlaxcala was a rather traditional enemy that always maintained its independence. It was well prepared for war. The Tlaxcalans possessed fortifications as well as a good mercenary army of Otomís and refugees from the Basin of Mexico eager for revenge (Davies, 1986, 1973). Tlaxcala represented no great economic prize. From the time that Moctezuma Ilhuicamina extended the Aztec empire to the Gulf Coast, cutting off the Tlaxcalans' communications and supplies with this eastern region, they became notoriously poorly clothed and suffered from lack of salt. These economic problems created by its isolation did not greatly alter its effectiveness in warfare because few imports were needed. It is also possible that the Aztec encirclement was not as effective on the eastern side as on the west. In the final showdown, the Tlaxcalans threw in their lot with the Spanish and participated in the battle for Tenochtitlán, which could have been a deciding factor.

Two other kingdoms lay north and south of Tlaxcala (Davies, 1986). To the north lay Meztitlán, embracing parts of the modern states of Puebla, Tlaxcala, Hidalgo, and Veracruz. It was a region rich in agricultural land but poor in salt. To the south lay Yopotzingo that was more like a confederation of tribes with no true urban settlements, located in the harsh mountainous environment of Oaxaca and Guerrero. This is believed to be the homeland of the famous deity Xipe Totec (Caso and Bernal, 1952; see Figure 6.3j, 8.20, and 8.26). Perhaps the region had some special religious and traditional significance for the Aztecs, for they left it alone.

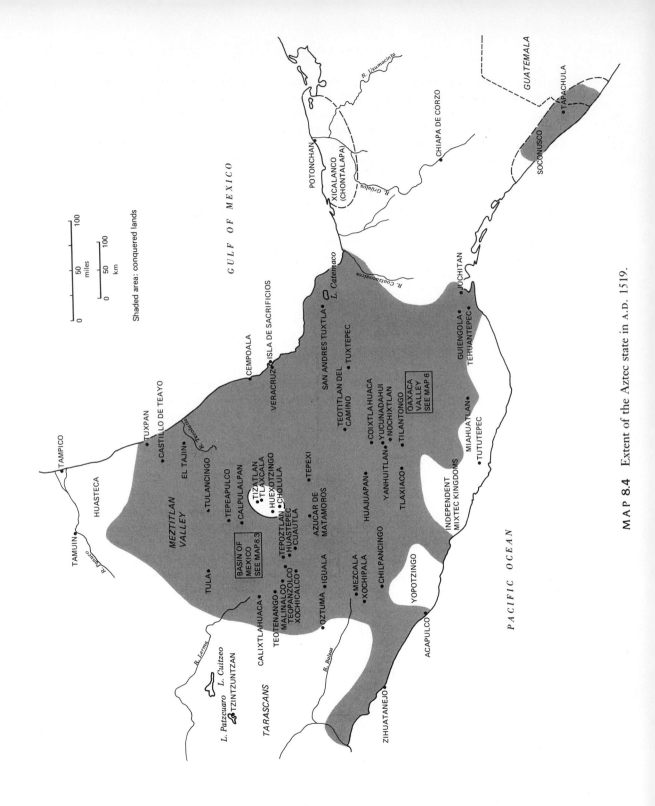

MAP 8.4 Extent of the Aztec state in A.D. 1519.

In contrast, Tututepec del Sur, with well-defined borders and a single capital, had greater cohesion as an independent kingdom. This was the legendary domain of the famous Mixtec king, 8 Deer "Tiger Claw." Apparently in the years prior to the Aztec supremacy, Tututepec established itself as a separate kingdom. A cotton- and cacao-producing area, self-sufficient in salt, it was rich and prosperous. Tribute was rendered to it in gold dust, jewels, and copper. Eventually its boundaries were reduced as a result of Aztec expansion, but it retained its independence.

The political status of Teotitlán del Camino, an area lying between Oaxaca and Tlaxcala, is not clear. It may have been subject to the Aztecs at the time of the Conquest. Support for this belief comes from the Aztecs themselves, who traditionally invited their enemies to Tenochtitlán on special occasions to witness great sacrifices. As Teotitlán del Camino was not included in the invitations, it already may have been subservient to the Mexica (Davies, 1968).

SUMMARY

The maximum extent of the Aztec empire is shown on Map 8.4. It includes central Mexico as far west as the western edge of the Toluca Valley where a line of forts extended south through Guerrero to mark the line of demarcation with the Tarascans. To the north, the boundary was Mesoamerica itself, which did not extend far north of Tula and northeast to Tamuin in the Huasteca. To the east and south, all regions fell to the Triple Alliance, including Oaxaca and the Gulf Coast region. At times the Aztecs reached the modern boundaries of Guatemala. There were a few pockets of independence such as Tlaxcala, the Mixtec kingdoms, and the Tarascans. Although few had kind words for these Warriors of the Sun, they were nonetheless highly respected for their power.

The role of religion in war is not clearly defined. Aztec warfare may seem like a senseless exercise in which military campaigns were fought only to be fought again. This is not the whole picture. Warfare, in addition to providing tribute in staples and luxury goods, was a social mechanism that helped reinforce the stringent class stratification as well as offer some mobility, contributing to the redistribution of wealth.

CHAPTER 9

Mesoamerica in Perspective

For archaeologists the long history of cultural evolution in Mesoamerica is complex, due in part to understanding the influence of geographical and ecological factors, the importance of resources (their distribution and access), and the diversity and interaction of ethnic groups. The history of research has not contributed to its clarity. Over the years, sites have not been dug in an orderly, planned scheme, but randomly selected on the basis of accessibility, tourism, pressure of salvage operations (bulldozers, dams, erosion), available funding, and permits to dig, among other factors.

History has been pieced together along the way in a lopsided fashion as opportunity arose. How differently we might have viewed the early Tlatilco graves had San Lorenzo been dug first, or had the C-14 dating method been discovered sooner. Suppose the Carnegie Institution had excavated Dos Pilas in the 1930s!

Eventually the pieces fit together; this has happened at a rapid pace in the last ten years. First, I would like to take a brief backward glance at the early time frames and highlight salient features.

It has been taken as a "given" that humans entered the New World by way of the Bering Strait, spreading out and populating North America and eventually South America. Although possible, this route has now been challenged by (1) the paucity of evidence of humans' passage south to Mexico, while (2) early discoveries of humans and artifacts appear in South America. It is hard to plot humans' course of entry but boats have been seriously proposed. It is difficult to otherwise justify dates appearing earlier in South America than in Mesoamerica. The possibility of very early peoples in South America is no longer viewed as preposterous, nor are later Preclassic incursions from Southeast Asia direct to the Guatemalan or Chiapas coasts.

Sedentary life, the presence of pottery, and domestication of maize and other crops are documented for 23,000 B.C. in some areas, and they had spread from the Pacific to the Gulf Coast and to Belize by 2500/2000 B.C. As Mesoamerica's maize spread north to what is now the United States and south to South America, manioc and probably cacao made their way north via Central America. Maize constituted a minor part of the Mesoamerican diet until its size increased, since people had a wealth of food from the forest, estuaries, and rivers in the meantime. As maize grew larger so did farming communities.

These early years are usually characterized as a period of egalitarian living in villages with no centralized authority or large public works. This is true for some regions, but there are notable exceptions. The development in Guerrero is a reminder that the Balsas drainage region may be the hearth of maize domestication; a central ceremonial patio of Teopantecuanitlán has given us two C-14 dates around 1400 B.C. Its greatest years of construction (1000–700 B.C.) were the same as those at San Lorenzo, and we find hollow ceramic dolls, iron ore mirrors, a huge (not colossal) head, Olmec vessel forms and decorations, and a Pacific Coast marine shell that traveled in long-distance trade networks. We call this Olmec, but only in the sense of similarities to San Lorenzo—not suggesting origins, for these are still an enigma.

The Gulf Coast Olmec are now seen as being cosmopolitan, perhaps the first mestizo civilization of Mesoamerica, containing a Mixe-Zoque/Mokaya ingredient from the Chiapas Pacific Coast. La Venta had a long early occupation on levees along an ancient Río Barí from 23,000 B.C. By 900 B.C. the central core of La Venta had a resident population and functioned as an urban community until 600 B.C. Thus it overlaps with and outlasts San Lorenzo, carving colossal heads and monumental sculptures. After 700 B.C., ties to peoples east of the Isthmus increased (site layout, imported goods) and toward the end, an elaborate depiction of the Maya watery Underworld is portrayed by Complex A.

From the first indication of the Sacred Round (260-day cycle) in Oaxaca, there is a surge of early glyphic signs and texts yet to be read, many badly eroded, others only rudimentary beginnings. These are found in the Gulf Coast area, the Pacific piedmont, and highland regions of Guatemala. In the first century B.C. the Long Count system was in use.

The Maya lowlands encoded their first messages of kingship in stucco and plastered architecture; in the highlands stelae were carved with dates accompanying hieroglyphic texts. Teotihuacan had become a large urban city and Monte Albán the capital of a Zapotec state. By 300 B.C. in some areas and A.D. 300 in others, the flowering of Mesoamerican civilization was in progress.

This roughly completes Mesoamerican linear evolution from egalitarian societies to stratified kingdoms and states. (Metallurgy came in during the Postclassic but, being used largely for jewelry, had little effect on the culture as a whole.) History from this time forward is a matter of variation, adaptations, movements of peoples, politics, competition, warfare, and struggle for survival. Mesoamericans had their basic design for living, now what did they do with it?

THE SOUTHERN CLASSIC LOWLAND MAYA

Problems of food, clothing, and shelter had been solved. Trade routes and contacts were carefully nurtured. The economy seemed well balanced with farmers in rural surroundings supporting the professional urbanites that maintained the elite nobility. Actually, it was a fragile scheme.

All activity was ultimately tied into an ideology designed to continue the functioning of the cosmos. A Maya king was an "absolute" monarch only as long as his personal abilities and performances were convincing, for he had no other power. There was no legal body for sanctions, no military. He lived and ruled by prescribed ancestral behavior and by his wits. It was important that he be recognized and sanctified as the divine, legitimate dynastic heir. This might be established in a number of ways; witness the manipulations of Pacal of Palenque to establish his legitimacy, and Bird Jaguar of Yaxchilán who had to overcome competition from those of purer blood, for his mother was an outsider. Once on the throne, power had to be maintained and reinforced through public demonstrations of bloodletting rituals, making and receiving royal visits, observance of calendrical cycles, presiding over period-ending ceremonies, inaugurations, sacrifices, warfare, and all manner of public events. Much would have depended on the ruler himself, his personality, charisma, and power of persuasion.

Bearing this in mind, most other aspects of society fall into place. Exotic goods (brilliant feathers, carved jade and greenstones, marine products, amber, fine polychrome pottery, eccentric flints or obsidian) were important for ostentatious display and propaganda.

Furthermore, it carries through to the social, economic, and political fields: marriages, alliances, ritual, warfare. All public events were essentially political. A weak leader would not be effective and a good one may have worn himself out constantly rebuilding, letting blood, warring, and engaging in ritual. (There were two exceptionally long reigns: Ah Cacau of Tikal who ruled for 60 years, and Pacal of Palenque, 68 years.) The situation at Dos Pilas demonstrates how fragile a kingdom could be, for despite its apparent success overtaking neighboring towns and widely publicizing victories on inscribed monuments, warfare led to devastation of the agricultural fields and, with their continued exploitation, the economy was ruined. The city was thus doomed (Demarest, n.d.b.). Ruler 2 was lucky to die a natural death, if true. Given many scenes like this, we can see how people would begin to relocate, and kingship as an institution would collapse.

Copán

Fragility of this system at Copán is illustrated by the efforts of Yax-Pac to increase his power as he saw Copán falling on hard times. His efforts are rather pathetic as he first attended a ceremony in a private home and permitted the occasion of his presence to be mentioned in a bench inscription. This was unheard-of behavior for a king! He also tried sharing rulership with his half brother. Neither brought him acclaim or renewed status, for it was unrealistic to try to share divinity. The failure of kingship at Copán was accelerated.

TEOTIHUACAN

In sharp contrast to the Maya region where there was a proliferation of centers, there was only one major Classic power west of the Isthmus until A.D. 900: Teotihuacan. Here too cosmological planning went into the choice of its location, having an orientation of 15° 25' east of north, and a quadripartite layout. This was a highly organized, centralized polity of some 125,000 inhabitants living in standardized apartment compounds in the city.

Differences with the Classic lowland Maya are startling, for these cultures were contemporary and in contact with one another. Yet at Teotihuacan, one finds no monuments with dates, news of births, accession, ancestors, parentage statements, events, or even portraits. Everyone was anonymous and life is breathed into the ruins through its painted murals. The massive city surely required a strong governing power concentrated in a single ruler or an elite group (?), but we have no way of knowing how it was handled since there are no hieroglyphic texts and people were not depicted in the remote, impersonal art.

Although warfare is a prominent theme and warriors were sacrificed at the temple of Quetzalcoatl, there is no evidence of conflicts or of an enemy close by or abroad. Nonetheless, Teotihuacan dominated all the Basin of Mexico, some outlying areas and enclaves, and exerted influence far beyond central Mexico. Its fine quality products were carried by merchants (or copied) to distant corners of Mesoamerica, and objects from Oaxaca, the Gulf Coast, and the Maya region are found at Teotihuacan. This was a commercial enterprise, not based on tribute or empire-building. Teotihuacanos must have inspired more than just admiration, as they carried abroad their imagery and associated ritual. Their iconography was copied by the Classic Zapotec and the Maya elite decked themselves out wearing Teotihuacan warrior-style costumes, insignias, and headdresses. They surely understood the underlying concepts of war and sacrifice ritual that these symbolized.

Religion must have been the unifying and driving force behind a powerful centralized authority. For 700 years the Teotihuacan arrangement was tremendously successful before being willfully destroyed. Perhaps it was a conscious experiment in government as Pasztory (n.d.a) has suggested. Its roots stemmed from the Basin of Mexico's earlier cultures and continued in much of the non-elite artifacts and customs. It was very much a local product. The sociopolitical scheme, whatever it was, did not survive the final burning of the city, nor was it ever copied or repeated elsewhere.

However, Teotihuacan remained the sacred place "where the sun was born" for all succeeding generations, and much of its imagery was passed along.

THE MAYA OF NORTHERN YUCATÁN

The kingship of the south did not transfer to northern Yucatán. This area went through a period of turmoil with warfare, invasions, and an influx of foreigners from the Chontalapa with new ideas. The aggressive, enterprising Itzá established their capital at Chichén Itzá and set up a new system of government headed by a group of lords or relatives. At first it enjoyed some success but their efforts to unite all northern Yucatán into a state never materialized. Cobá and the eastern provinces never participated in attempts at unification.

The commercial interests of the multi-ethnic elite focused on coastal trade, leaving internal affairs to languish unattended. The same ideology continued but was less pervasive and economic interests were the dominating force. A restructuring of the social and economic order of the region was needed, which the Itzá were not able or were unwilling to accomplish (A.P. Andrews, 1990b).

Under the leadership of Mayapán, which followed in the thirteenth century, a set of local leaders tried a joint rulership. With the Itzá gone, the lineage heads wanted to restore the old prestigious Maya pattern emulating Chichén Itzá with its grand ceremonial center—a kind of renaissance, but it was not possible. Raids and warfare continued; walls and fortifications increased. Religion was important but took a different turn. Large ceremonial precincts were replaced by pilgrimage centers such as the Sacred Well at Chichén Itzá and the shrine of Ix Chel at Cozumel. A period of intense trade and prosperity lasted until 1441 but competition, jealousy, and fighting among the lineages of the western provinces prevented any hope of political consolidation and ended in disaster. Religion was not to blame. There was no longer a strong authority and the rule of the elite was diminished (Sabloff, 1990). The small quarreling city-states that fell to the Spaniards were but a sad trace of the Maya civilization.

THE MEXICA

The Mexica and Tarascans offer our final examples of state organizations. The first shared with the Classic Maya the yearning for prestige, status, and an elite, ancestral history. The Maya worked to preserve what they had; however, the background of the Mexica was far from elite, so they stressed a tenuous linkage by marriage with Culhuacán to claim a prestigious Toltec ancestry.

Government was in the hands of a hereditary ruler, but succession was not necessarily by primogeniture. It might pass among brothers before the next generation, and keeping the Toltec bloodline was an important consideration in which some women may have had an important role (Gillespie, 1989). The Mexica ruler had a power advisor (the *tlacaélel*), a court of nobles, administrators, and a law code. The power of the king may have varied according to the personal acumen of each one in handling his elite personnel. Hassig (1988) tells us that support for the king was not entirely automatic. Succession was a stressful and worrisome time for there was no guarantee of continuity. Among the Mexica, selection was made by consensus among qualified contenders and the system was more stable than in other Aztec communities, but what happened in Tenochtitlán was of concern to all the empire.

We can recognize the ancient ideology in Mexica religion, with many gods, or rather, concepts of deities with various aspects. They also embraced all sorts of ethnic deities as these were assimilated from other peoples upon their incorporation into the Aztec empire. Period-endings, elaborate inauguration ceremonies, accession, victories, and conquests were all grand public displays of power accompanied by sacrifices of different kinds. Foreign visitors were invited to Tenochtitlán on these occasions to be impressed by the demonstration of power, and to return home with increased fear, realizing the futility of resisting a future attack by the Triple Alliance.

Religion had a role in warfare but was manipulated by state politics and practical necessities. The Aztecs had Military Orders as did Teotihuacan and Tula, but not a professional standing army. Many warriors were *calpulli* heads in charge of their commoners. The empire was loosely held, often leaving the same local ruler in place. It was a tributary empire that entailed few administrative or control costs, but with greatly increased trade. The power of the state fluctuated as it depended on flexible alliances between other peoples and city-states. It seems less fragile than the Maya system but was weakly integrated. The Spanish Conquest was successful not so much because of their superior weapons but due to groups such as the Tlaxcalans who threw in their lot and their expertise with the Spaniards.

THE TARASCANS

The Tarascans on Lake Pátzcuaro managed to create a quite efficient and powerful government. It got off to a good start under Tariácuri and his son by unifying the four independent polities that were on the lake, instituting a state religion and demanding allegiance. This was a no-nonsense, able, and astute government.

The king shared his power with no one. In Tzintzuntzan decisions were made concerning war, the territory, religious activities, the collection of tribute, and the operation of governmental agencies (Gorenstein and Pollard, 1983). The military was an important branch of the government and constituted a full-time profession. The battles with the Aztecs are well known, resulting in a hard frontier between them. The Aztecs were skilled fighters but the Tarascans who chose to go into battle with the bow and arrow managed to hold the frontier. Warfare was conducted for territorial gain and local leaders were replaced from the capital.

Religion was state mandated, so was not the sociopolitical force seen elsewhere. The Tarascans consciously diminished traditional Mesoamerican customs and one had to go to Ihuatzio for a ball game. Crude *chacmools* are found at this time, but not at Tzintzuntzan. These newcomers with Chichimec roots were very independent-minded, and came closest to establishing a true political empire. Unfortunately we will never know the extent of their potential, for the Conquest interfered. By the time the Spaniards went west to Michoacán in 1522, the well-informed Tarascans wisely offered little resistance.

In the end, the ideology may have been the best unifying element of Mesoamerican cultures. Sharing the same worldview made contact easy over great distances. Even so, the nature of the system did not provide stability or a long-lasting political arrangement. Later examples did not fare much better in their variety of experimental schemes. We have yet to hear evidence from Teotihuacan, which lasted longest of all.

We feel we know much about these ancients, but each excavation poses more questions and opens up a new field of research. One might well ask, if ideology was the bond that held these cultures together, did it also act as a deterrent for forming strong centralized political states? Answers will be forthcoming as the linguists, epigraphers, ethnohistorians, and artists continue working with archaeologists to tell us more of these Aztecs, Maya, and their predecessors.

GLOSSARY

adosadas A frontal platform of a pyramid.

aguadas Seasonal water holes in lowland Maya region. Some may have been cultivated.

amate Paper made from the inner bark of the wild fig tree for making códices.

Atlantean figures Figures of men used as columns to support roofs or low table-top altars.

atlatl Spear-thrower. A short, grooved stick with finger loops at one end used to propel a dart or lance. Weapon of great antiquity.

Aztecs Late inhabitants of the Basin of Mexico who created the largest empire in Mesoamerica. Conquered by the Spaniards in 1521.

Bacabs See Pauahtuns.

Bajío Lerma River drainage from Guanajuato to Jalisco.

Bajos Broad, swampy depressions in Petén area that fill with water in the rainy seasons. Some were cultivated by the Maya.

baktun Period of 144,000 days in the Maya calendar. (See also Long Count.)

bigotera A cover for mustaches. Spanish.

blanco levantado An unburnished painted decoration of white transparent streaky lines, usually rectilinear. Also known as Tula Watercolored. Widespread in Bajío region and central highlands during Classic and Early Postclassic Periods.

cacao Beans of the cacao tree (*Theobroma cacao*) used to make chocolate.

cacicazgo A small territorial Mixtec kingdom under strict control of a royal lineage. Early Postclassic, Oaxaca.

cahals Regional governors or military captains. Term used in the Usumacinta drainage region.

calendar round Cycle of 52 years produced by the permutation of the 260-day cycle and the 365-day true year.

calmecac Strict Aztec school for the children of the king and nobility.

calpulli A territorial division or ward into which an Aztec was born. A powerful social and land-owning group. Head of *calpulli* was intermediary between its members and the ruler. Each *calpulli* had its own patron deity and temple.

candelero   Small clay incense burner, probably for domestic use. Typical of Teotihuacan.

cenote   Natural underground well or sinkhole in northern Yucatán. A major source of water for drinking and bathing.

Chac   The Rain God of the Maya. (See also Tlaloc.)

chacmool   Life-size stone figure in reclining position, legs flexed, head turned to one side, arms flexed to hold receptacle on chest. Usually placed at entrance to temples as sacrificial stone or to receive offerings.

chía   Plant (*Salvia chian*) cultivated for food, drink, and oil.

Chichimecs   A generic term loosely applied to a multitude of peoples considered to be uncivilized barbarians, living beyond the northern limits of Mesoamerica. They were nonfarming nomads. The Teochichimecas were the least civilized of all.

chinampa   Productive system of agriculture created by ditches made in swamps, and built up by repeated resurfacing with muck from the lake bottom. Popularly called "floating gardens" in the Basin of Mexico.

Chontalapa   Coastal region of southern Veracruz and western Campeche. Homeland of the Putún and many cultural currents.

chultun   Bottle-shaped underground cistern hollowed out of limestone bedrock in northern Yucatán and used for water storage. In the southern Maya lowlands, smaller lateral chambered *chultuns* were dug for food storage, particularly of the ramon nuts of the breadnut tree. They were sometimes lined with stones to make them impermeable.

cihuacóatl   Prestigious position as advisor to the king among Aztecs.

cloisonné   Method of decorating pottery, wood, or gourds in which a layer of paint is applied to the surface. A design is marked off and the paint cut out within the design area. The hollow spaces are then filled in with another color and the surface remains smooth. Several layers of paint can be worked in this way. Northern and western Mexican cultures.

coatepantli   Serpent wall, forming limit of sacred precincts in Postclassic highland Mexico.

Coatlícue   Aztec Earth Goddess and mother of Huitzilopochtli, typically shown wearing a skirt made of entwined serpents.

codex (plural: **códices**)   Painted book made from amate paper or deerskin that folds like a screen.

comal   Flat clay griddle for cooking tortillas among the Mexicans.

Copador   Late Classic polychrome ceramic produced in great quantities at Copán. Widely traded in the southeast periphery.

cord-making   Decorative technique in which a fine cord was wrapped around a paddle and pressed against an unfired clay vessel, leaving a characteristic imprint.

Coyolxauhqui   Aztec Moon Goddess and sister of Huitzilopochtli accused of plotting to kill their mother, Coatlícue. Her dismembered body is depicted on monumental slab at foot of Temple to Huitzilopochtli at Great Temple of Tenochtitlán.

Coyotlatelco ware   Distinctive red-on-buff pottery tradition of Epi-Classic or Early Postclassic central Mexico.

cuauhxicalli   So-called "eagle cup." Stone receptacle for burning or storing sacrificed human hearts. Aztec.

Curicaueri   Tarascan Fire and Sun God. Postclassic, western Mexico.

"Danzantes"   Life-size carvings of sacrificed victims on bas-relief stone slabs at Monte Albán. Preclassic.

double-line-break   Incised parallel lines on interior rim of pottery vessel in which the lower line turns to join the upper one. Early-Middle Preclassic.

E-group   An astronomical arrangement of structures designed to observe the sun at the time of the soltices and equinoxes. Lake Petén zone, Uaxactún, Mundo Perdido.

Ehécatl   Quetzalcoatl in his aspect as the Wind God. Associated with round temples.

Fine Orange ware   Fine-grained, untempered pottery with several distinct varieties. Produced in Gulf Coast plains and lower Usumacinta region.

florero   Pottery jar with tall restricted neck and flaring rim.

greca   Step fret design.

Haab   Maya calendar year of 365 days, corresponding to the Aztec Xíhuitl.

hacha "thin stone head." Beautifully carved stone, associated with the ball-game cult. There is often a notch or projecting tenon at the back for attachment. Especially common in Classic Veracruz and highland Guatemala.

Huehuéteotl The Old Fire God also known as Xiuhtecuhtli. One of the most ancient of Mesoamerican deities.

huéhuetl Vertical drum with skin head, played with palms and fingers.

Huitzilopochtli War and Sun God of the Aztecs, chief deity of Tenochtitlán. Identified by his special weapon, the fire serpent.

ílhuitl Decorative motif of two reversed scrolls.

incensario A pottery vessel made for ceremonial purposes to hold coal and incense. A special lidded stone box known from Palenque and Copán.

Ix Chel Important goddess and oracle shrine on Cozumel. Associated with lakes, wells, and underground water. Moon Goddess and also goddess of childbirth, procreation, and medicine.

Jester God Identified by a 3-pointed headband of Late Preclassic kings. Became the personified version of the *ahau* glyph for "lord" in the Classic Period. Maya.

katun 7200-Day period of the Maya calendar. (See also Long Count.)

kin 1 Day on the Maya calendar. (See also Long Count)

Kinich Ahau Important Maya Sun God, represented with a square eye and prominent aquiline nose. His head glyph personifies the number 4. As a young man, he may personify the day *ahau*.

Kukulcán Feathered-serpent deity (Quetzalcoatl) of the Maya.

Long Count Total number of days elapsed from a mythical starting point in the past (3113 B.C. in the GMT correlation) recorded by the Maya in number of baktun (144,000 days or 20 katuns), katun (7200 days or 20 tuns), tun (360 days or 20 uinals), uinal (20 days or 20 kins), and kin (1 day). Classic lowland Maya.

"lost wax" (cire perdue) Method of casting metals; the desired form was carved in wax, coated with charcoal and clay, and the whole encased in an outer pottery form leaving ducts. The wax melted and ran out one duct as molten metal was poured in another, replacing the wax model. After cooling, the clay casting was broken, and the finished product extracted, each one an original. Used to produce magnificent gold jewelry in the SMIS Postclassic. Central and southern Mesoamerica.

macehualtin Commoner or laborer. Aztec.

malacate Spindle whorl usually of pottery; a perforated round disk used as a weight in spinning thread.

manikin scepter A ceremonial bar often held by Maya reelers against the chest; a badge of honor.

mano (See *metate*.)

mat design Woven design, symbol of royalty.

mayeque Bondsman or slave. Aztec.

Mazapa ware Pottery decorated by wavy parallel lines on buff-colored vessel. Early Postclassic, but a minor ware at Tula.

metate Stone basin (quern) for grinding maize, often troughlike, accompanied by a hand stone, *mano*.

Mexica The Aztecs of Tenochtitlán-Tlatelolco.

Mokaya Early proto-Mixe-Zoque speakers that lived in the Mazatán region of Soconusco. Makers of Barra pottery.

molcajete Bowl, usually tripod, with interior scoring or roughening for grinding fruits and vegetables.

Náhua Language of Uto-Aztecan group; also applied to people.

Náhuatl Language derived from Náhua that became the *lingua franca* of the Aztecs.

nemontemi Five unlucky days at year-end of the Aztec calendar corresponding to the Maya Uayeb.

Nonoalca Inhabitants of Tula who came from the southeast (Tabasco) neighbors of the Chontal Putún. These were people of high skills and culture who coexisted with the Tolteca-Chichimeca at Tula, Hidalgo.

olla Pottery jar with flaring neck. Usually used for cooking.

Olmeca-Xicalanca People of probably Gulf Coast origin, particularly southern Veracruz-Tabasco region. Believed to have occupied Cholula and Cacaxtla and were driven out of the central highlands at the end of the seventh century (?).

palma Carved, fan-shaped stone with smooth dorsal surface, associated with ball-game cult. Classic Veracruz culture.

patolli Widespread game of chance played by Aztecs, Toltecs, Teotihuacanos, west Mexicans, and the Maya, on cross-shaped board, much like modern game of Parcheesi.™

pauahtuns (also known as bacabs, and God N). Maya deities, brothers, who held up the four corners of the sky. Often associated with scribes and artisans.

petate Woven straw mat.

pipiltin Privileged class in Tenochtitlán.

Pipil Term applied rather loosely to the speech and culture of migratory Náhua-speaking groups in Central America.

Plumbate Fine texture ware with a high percentage of iron compounds; upon firing the surface acquires a hard, lustrous, vitrified finish often with a metalic iridescence. Two varieties: San Juan (Classic Maya); Tohil (Postclassic Maya). Manufactured in western Guatemala and widely traded.

pochteca Professional merchants, sometimes serving as intelligence agents for the Aztecs. Specialized in long-distance trade, but operated at times within the empire.

Pox pottery A ware pitted by lack of control in the firing process. One of earliest ceramics; reported only from Acapulco area.

Puuc Hilly region of northwestern Yucatán. Name given to Classic architecture style using veneer masonry decorated with mosaic façades.

Putún Chontal Maya inhabiting western Campeche (Xicalango) and delta regions of the Usumacinta and Grijalva Rivers of Tabasco. Aggressive merchants who extended their commercial interests inland via rivers and around the coast of Yucatán.

Quetzalcoatl The Feathered-Serpent deity. His many different aspects include: the Wind God (Ehécatl), the Morning Star (Tlahuizcalpantecuhtli), and the Evening Star (Xólotl, his twin). Counterparts: Kukulcán and Gucumatz among the Maya. A feathered serpent is prominent throughout Mesoamerican art. In Postclassic central Mexico, the name was given to a ruler and a religious office.

Quincunx A square or rectangular glyph with a dot in each corner and one in the center. It often forms part of the Primary Standard Sequence on Maya bowls and cylindrical cups and has a possessive function.

resist painting (negative painting). Technique of pottery decoration in which the design may be covered before firing with some substance, probably wax, and paint applied. The wax is subsequently removed, revealing the design in base color.

rocker-stamping Decorative technique in which a curved sharp edge, probably a shell, is "walked" back and forth on a pottery vessel creating a curved, zigzag, incised line. Preclassic.

roof comb (or crest). A tall stone superstructure built on the roof of lowland Maya temples, adding height and grandeur to the temple pyramid. They were often elaborately stuccoed, carved, and painted with human figures and hieroglyphic texts. Classic lowland Maya.

sacbé (plural: **sacbeob**) Maya causeway, constructed of huge blocks of stone, leveled with gravel and paved with plaster. Typical of northern Yucatán, La Quemada, and Xochicalco.

Short Count Abbreviated date-recording system utilized by the Maya in Postclassic Yucatán. Based on a 13-katun count that equalled 256 1/4 years.

slash-and-burn agriculture Swidden agriculture, in which fields are cleared, burned, and planted until yield decreases, then allowed to lie fallow for several years to regain fertility.

slip A wash of clay applied to vessel before firing that adds color.

SMIS The metallurgy style in jewelry called South Mexican International Style, closely resembling Mixteca-Puebla iconography. Postclassic.

Soconusco Fertile geographic province of Pacific coastal plain of Chiapas and Guatemala. Important cacao-growing region and eventually conquered by the Aztecs in 1486.

stela (plural: **stelae**) Stone shaft that may be carved with figures, scenes, and hieroglyphic texts.

stirrup-spouted jar Distinctive ceramic form with two hollow tubes that rise from the body of the vessel to form a single spout. Preclassic. A form more common in northwest South America.

talud-tablero Architectural feature consisting of a sloping apron (talud) surmounted by a horizontal, rectangular panel (tablero). Either portion may at times be carved or painted. Many variations are known. Particularly characteristic of Teotihuacan.

Tamemes Bearers or porters. Central Mexico.

Tamimes Semicivilized Chichimecs of Late Postclassic Period, of which the Aztecs are an example. They spoke Náhuatl, had a knowledge of the 52-year cycle, the ball game, dressed in maguey-fiber clothes, and practiced some agriculture.

tecalli Mexican onyx, either a banded calcite, travertine, or alabaster.

tecomate Spherical pottery vessel with restricted opening and no collar. A very early form believed to be derived from a gourd.

tecuhtli An Aztec of privileged class or nobility in Tenochtitlán. Also used as an honorary title.

telpochcalli Aztec schools for *macehaltin*, standard training, instruction in warfare.

temescal Sweat bath, often used for ritual purification and located near a ball court.

Teotihuacan Corridor A Classic period trade route from Teotihuacan across Tlaxcala (via Calpulalpan and Huemantla) to Veracruz and the Gulf Coast region.

tepetate (talpetate) A fine-grained compact yellowish sterile layer of volcanic origin.

Tezcatlipoca A god of creation possessing many diverse forms, often identified by a smoking mirror that replaces his foot which was wrenched off by the earth monster. God of Night, closely associated with deities of death, evil, and destruction. Patron deity of sorcerers and robbers. Important because of his direct intervention in the affairs of humans. Tezcatlipoca has some parallels with the Maya God K.

tezontle A porous volcanic stone, red, gray, or black, common in the Basin of Mexico.

Thin Orange ware Fine paste, thin-walled pottery produced in Tepexi, in the State of Puebla, and brought to Teotihuacan for distribution. Carried widely to many parts of Mesoamerica during the Classic Period.

tlachtli Aztec name for the ancient ritual ball game.

tlacolol agriculture A variant of slash-and-burn system in which cultivable land is divided into sectors, some of which are planted for 2 to 3 years, then left to fallow for 3 to 4 years. Usually practiced on slopes.

Tlahuizcalpantecuhtli Quetzalcoatl, the planet Venus as the Morning Star. (See also Quetzalcoatl.)

Tlaloc The Rain God of the Aztecs. Associated with serpents, mountains, flooding, drought, hail, ice, and lightning. A better term for many of these aspects is Storm God. Probably one of the most ancient Mesoamerican deities. In the Great Temple of Tenochtitlán, Tlaloc occupied one of the twin temples and received the bulk of the offerings. Counterparts among other Mesoamerican cultures: Chac (lowland Maya); Tajín (Totonacs); Tzahui (Mixtecs); Cocijo (Zapotecs).

tlatoani The Aztec king.

tlecuil Mud-packed basin sunk in the earth, filled with ash where funerary or ritual fires had been lit.

Tolteca-Chichimeca People who came to Tula from the "northwest" and spoke Náhuatl (derived from Náhua). They were more civilized than the Chichimecas and brought many new features to Tula.

Tonalpohualli Cycle of 260 days. Aztec. Composed of 20 days combined with 13 numbers, corresponding to the Maya Tzolkin.

Tripsacum Wild grass that ranged from Texas to South America.

tumpline Carrying strap passed over either the chest or forehead, facilitating transportation of a burden packed on the back.

tun 360-Day period of Maya calendar. (See also Long Count.)

Tzolkin Cycle of 260 days. Maya. Composed of 20 days combined with 13 numbers, corresponding to Aztec Tonalpohualli.

tzompantli Skull rack, usually located near a temple, to which skulls of sacrificial victims were skewered. Postclassic.

Uayeb Remaining 5 unlucky days at year-end of Maya calendar; known as Nemontemi among the Aztecs.

uinal 20-Day period in Maya calendar. (See also Long Count.)

Usulután ware Pottery decorated with a resist technique producing groups of yellowish lines on a dark orange or brown background. Produced in great quantities in western El Salvador and marketed over wide area in southern Mesoamerica.

white-rimmed black ware (differentially fired black

and white). Called a variety of similar names, a ware with a contrast in surface color produced by the firing technique.

Xicalango Gulf Coast region of Campeche, inhabited by the Putún. Important port-of-trade in the Late Postclassic Period.

Xíhuitl Aztec calendar year of 365 days, corresponding to the Maya Haab.

Xipe Totec Aztec God of Springtime, seeding, and planting; believed to have come to central Mexico from the Oaxaca-Guerrero border. A victim was flayed in honor of Xipe Totec, a ritual signifying the renewal of vegetation in the spring.

Xiuhmopilli The binding of the years, completion of a 52-year cycle.

Xólotl Aztec god of the planet Venus as the evening star, twin brother of Quetzalcoatl. Represented as having the head of a dog. Postclassic central Mexico. Also the name of a Chichimec leader who established his capital at Texcoco in the Early Postclassic.

yácata Tarascan pyramid with a form combining a round with a rectangular structure.

yoke U-shaped stone, often elaborately carved, believed to be an imitation of the protective belt worn by ballplayers. Classic Veracruz cultures.

I. GUIDE TO ABBREVIATIONS

AA	American Antiquity
APS	American Philosophical Society
BAR	British Archaeological Report
FLAAR	Foundation for Latin American Anthropological Research
HMAI	Handbook of Middle American Indians
INAH	Instituto Nacional de Antropología e Historia (Mexico)
JFA	Journal of Field Archaeology
LAA	Latin American Antiquity
MNA	Museo Nacional de Antropología (Mexico)
PNWAF	Papers of the New World Archaeological Foundation
RMEA	Revista Mexicana de Estudios Antropológicos
UNAM	Universidad Nacional Autónoma de Mexico

II. SELECTED VOLUMES OF ARTICLES LISTED BY EDITORS

Adams, R. E. W.
    1977   *The origins of Maya civilization*. A School of American Research Book. Albuquerque:
            University of New Mexico Press.

Ashmore, W.
1981   *Lowland Maya settlement patterns.* Albuquerque: University of New Mexico Press.

Benson, E. P.
1981   *The Olmec and their neighbors.* Dumbarton Oaks Research Library and Collections. Washington, D.C.

Benson, E. P., and G. G. Griffin.
1988   *Maya iconography.* Princeton: Princeton University Press.

Berrin, K.
1988   *Feathered serpents and flowering trees: reconstructing the murals of Teotihuacan.* San Francisco, California: Fine Arts Museums of San Francisco; Seattle: University of Washington Press.

Boone, E. H.
1987   *The Aztec Templo Mayor: A symposium at Dumbarton Oaks 1983.* Dumbarton Oaks Research Library and Collections. Washington, D.C.

Boone, E. H., and G. R. Willey
1988   *The southeast Classic Maya zone.* A symposium at Dumbarton Oaks, 1984. Dumbarton Oaks Research Library and Collections. Washington, D.C.

Cárdos de Méndez, A.
1990   *La epoca Clasica; Nuevos hallazqos, nuevas ideas.* Museo Nacional de Antropología, Instituto Nacional de Antropología e Historia, Mexico.

Chase, A. F., and P. M. Rice
1985   *The lowland Maya Postclassic.* Austin: University of Texas Press.

Clancy, F. S., and P. D. Harrison
1990   *Vision and revision in Maya studies.* Albuquerque: University of New Mexico Press.

Culbert, T. P.
1973   *The Classic Maya collapse.* Albuquerque: The University of New Mexico Press.
1990   *Classic Maya political history: Hieroglyphic and archaeological evidence.* School of American Research Advanced Seminar Series. Cambridge University Press.

Culbert, T. P., and D. S. Rice
1990   *Precolumbian population history in the Maya lowlands.* Albuquerque: University of New Mexico Press.

Diehl, R. A., and J. C. Berlo
1989   *Mesoamerica after the decline of Teotihuacan* A.D. 700–900. Dumbarton Oaks Research Library and Collections. Washington, D.C.

Flannery, K. V., and J. Marcus
1983   *The cloud people: Divergent evolution of the Zapotec and Mixtec civilizations.* New York: Academic Press.

Folan, Jr., W. J.
1985   *Contributions to the archaeology and ethnohistory of greater Mesoamerica.* Carbondale, Illinois: Southern Illinois University Press.

Foster, M. S., and P. C. Weigand
1985   *The archaeology of west and northwest Mesoamerica.* Boulder, Colorado and London: Westview Press.

Fowler, Jr., W. R.
1991   *The formation of complex society in southeastern Mesoamerica.* Boca Raton, Florida: CRC Press.

Hammond, N.
  1977 *Social process in Maya prehistory: Studies in memory of Sir Eric Thompson.* London: Academic Press.
Hammond, N., and G. R. Willey
  1979 *Maya archaeology and ethnohistory.* Austin, Texas: University of Texas Press.
Hirth, K. G.
  1984 *Trade and exchange in early Mesoamerica.* Albuquerque: University of New Mexico Press.
Miller, A. G.
  1983 *Highland-lowland interaction in Mesoamerica: Interdisciplinary approaches.* Dumbarton Oaks Research Library and Collections. Washington, D.C.
Pahl, G. W.
  1987 *The periphery of the southeastern Classic Maya realm.* UCLA American Center Publication. UCLA Latin American Studies, Vol. 61.
Sabloff, J. A., and E. W. Andrews V.
  1986 *Late lowland Maya civilization: Classic to Postclassic.* A School of American Research Book. Albuquerque: University of New Mexico Press.
Sanders, W. T., and J. W. Michels
  1977 *Teotihuacan and Kaminaljuyú: A study in prehistoric cultures contact.* University Park: The Pennsylvania State University Press.
Sharer, R. J., and D. C. Grove
  1989 *Regional perspectives on the Olmec.* School of American Research Advanced Seminar Series. Cambridge University Press.
Urban, P. A., and E. M. Schortman,
  1986 *The prehistoric southeast Maya periphery: Problems and prospects.* Austin: University of Texas Press.
Voorhies, B.
  1989 *Ancient trade and tribute: Economics of the Soconusco region of Mesoamerica.* Salt Lake City: University of Utah Press.

III. REFERENCES[1]

Acosta, J. R.
  1941 Los ultimos descubrimientos arqueológicos en Tula, Hgo. 1941. *RMEA 5:*239–248.
  1945 La cuarta y quinta temporada de excavaciones en Tula, Hgo. 1943–1944. *RMEA 7:*23–64.
  1956 Resumen de las exploraciones arqueológicas en Tula Hgo. durante los VI, VII, y VIII Temporadas 1946–1950. *Anales 8:*37–116.
  1956– Interpretation de algunos de los datos obtenidos en Tula relativos a la época Tolteca.
  1957 *RMEA 14:*75–110.
  1964 El Palacio de Quetzalpapálotl. *INAH. Memorias 10.*
Acosta Saignes, M.
  1945 Los Pochteca. *Acta Antroplógica 1*(1).

---

[1] Full references for edited volumes may be found in II. Selected Volumes of Articles Listed by Editors, pp. 495–497

Adams, R. E. W.
  1977a   *Prehistoric Mesoamerica*. Boston: Little Brown and Co.
  1977b   Comments on the glyphic texts of the "Altar Vase." In Hammond, 409–420.
  1978   Routes of Communication in Mesoamerica: The northern Guatemalan highlands and the Peten. In *Mesoamerican communication routes and cultural contacts*, edited by T. A. Lee, Jr. and C. Navarrete. *PNWAF 40*:27–35.
  1981   Settlement patterns of the central Yucatán and southern regions. In Ashmore, 211–257.
  1986   Río Azul: Lost city of the Maya. *National Geographic Magazine 169*:420–451.
  1990   Archaeological research at the lowland Maya city of Río Azul. *LAA 1*(1): 23–41.
Adams, R. E. W., and A. S. Trik.
  1961   Temple 1 (Str. 5-D-1): Post-constructional activities. *Tikal Reports* No 7 Philadelphia, Pennsylvania: The University Museum.
Adams, R. M.
  1961   Changing patterns of territorial organization in the central highlands of Chiapas, Mexico. *AA 26*(3):54–63.
Agurcia F., R.
  1986   Late Classic settlements in the Comayagua Valley. In Urban and Schortman, 262–274.
Agurcia Fasquelle, R., and W. L. Fash, Jr.
  1991   Maya artistry unearthed. *National Geographic Magazine 180*(3):94–105.
Anales de Cuauhtitlán
  1945   Edited by P. F. Velasquez, *UNAM*, Instituto de Historia, 1st series:1.
Anawalt, P. R.
  1990   The emperor's cloak: Aztec pomp, Toltec circumstances: *AA 55*(2):291–307.
Anawalt, P. R., and F. F. Berdan
  1992   The Codex Mendoza. *Scientific American 266*(6):70–79.
Andrews, A. P.
  1983   *Maya salt production and trade*. Tucson: University of Arizona Press.
  1990a   The role of trading ports in Maya civilization. In F. S. Clancy and Harrison, 160–167.
  1990b   The fall of Chichén Itzá: A preliminary hypothesis. *LAA 1*(3):258–267.
Andrews A. P., T. Gallareta N., F. Robles C., R. Cobos P., and P. Cervera R.
  1988   "Isla Cerritos: An Itzá trading post on the north coast of Yucatán, Mexico." *National Geographic Research 4*(2):196–207.
Andrews, A. P., and F. Robles C.
  1985   Chichén Itzá and Cobá: An Itzá-Maya standoff in Early Postclassic Yucatán. In Chase and Rice, 62–72.
Andrews IV, E. W.
  1965   Archaeology and prehistory in the northern Maya lowlands. *HMAI 2*:288–330.
Andrews IV, E. W., and E. W. Andrews V
  1980   Excavations at Dzibilchaltún, Yucatán, Mexico. *Middle American Research Institute Publication* 48. New Orleans: Tulane University.
Andrews V, E. W.
  1977   The southeastern periphery of Mesoamerica: A view from eastern El Salvador. In Hammond, 115–134.
  1981   Dzibilchaltún. *HMAI, Supplement I: Archaeology*:313–341
  1990   Early ceramic history of the lowland Maya. In Clancy and Harrison, 1–19.
Andrews V., E. W., W. M. Ringle III, P. J. Barnes, A. Barrera R., and T. Gallareta M.

1984   Komchén: An early Maya community in northwest Yucatán. Investigaciones recientes en el area maya. *XVII Mesa Redonda 1*:73–92. Mexico: Sociedad Mexicana de Antropología.

Andrews V., E. W., and J. A. Sabloff
1986   Classic to Postclassic: A summary discussion. In Sabloff and Andrews V, 433–456.

Andrews, G. F.
1984   Edzná, Campeche, Mexico. Settlement patterns and Monumental architecture. Culver City, California. (1–149) *FLAAR*.

Andrews V., E. W., and B. W. Fash
1992   Continuity and change in a royal Maya residential complex at Copán. *Ancient Mesoamerica 3*(1):63–88.

Angulo V, J.
1987   The Chalcatzingo reliefs: an iconographic analysis. In *Ancient Chalcatzingo*, edited by D. C. Grove. Austin: University of Texas Press. 145–158.

Armillas, P.
1944   Exploraciones recientes en Teotihuacan, Mexico. *Cuadernos Americanos 16* (4):121–158.
1950   Teotihuacan, Tula, y los Tolteca. *Runa 3*:37–70.
1969   The arid frontier of Mexican civilization. *Transactions of the New York Academy of Sciences*, Series II, 31:697–704.
1971.   Gardens in swamps. *Science 174*:653–661.

Ashmore, W.
1984   Quiriguá archaeology and history revisited. *JFA 11*:365–386.
1986   Petén cosmology in the Maya southeast: An analysis of architecture and settlement patterns at Classic Quiriguá. In P. A. Urban and E. M. Schortman, 35–49.
1987   Cobble crossroads: Gualjoquito architecture and external elite ties. In *Interaction on the southeast Mesoamerican frontier*, edited by E. J. Robinson. *B.A.R.* International, Oxford, England. Series 327:28–48.
1991   Site-planning principles and concepts of directionality among the ancient Maya. *AA 2*(3):199–226.

Ashmore, W., E. M. Schortman, P. A. Urban, J. C. Benjo, J. M. Weeks, and S. M. Smith
1987   Ancient society in Santa Barbara, Honduras. *National Geographic Research 3* (2):232–254.

Ashmore, W., and R. Sharer
1987   Excavations at Quiriguá, Guatemala: The ascent of a Maya elite center. *Archaeology 31*(6):10–19.

Aufdermauer, J.
1973   Aspectos de la cronología del preclásico en la cuenca de Puebla-Tlaxcala. *Comunicaciones Projecto Puebla-Tlaxcala 9*.

Aveleyra, L.
1950   *Prehistoria de México*. Ediciones Mexicanas.
1956   The second mammoth and associated artifacts at Santa Isabel Iztapan, Mexico. *AA 22*:12–28
1963   *La estela teotihuacana de la Ventilla, Mexico*. Mexico, D.F.MNA.
1964   The primitive hunters. In *HMAI 1*:384–412.

Aveni, A. F., and H. Hartung
1986   Maya city planning and the calendar. *APS* Transactions Vol. 76, Part 7. Philadelphia, Pennsylvania.

Aveni, A. F., H. Hartung, and B. Buckingham
    1978   The pecked cross symbol in ancient America. *Science 202*:267–279
Aveni, A. F., H. Hartung, and J. C. Kelley
    1982   Alta Vista (Chalchihuites) astronomical implications of a Mesoamerican outpost at
            the Tropic of Cancer. *AA 47*(2):316–335.
Baird, E. T.
    1989   Stars and war at Cacaxtla. In Diehl and Berlo, 105–122.
Ball, J. W.
    1977a   The archaeological ceramics of Becán, Campeche, Mexico. *Middle American Research
            Institute Publication* No. 43.
    1977b   The rise of the northern Maya chiefdoms. A socioprocessual analysis. In R.E.W.
            Adams, 101–132.
    1983   Teotihuacan, the Maya, and ceramic interchange: A contextual perspective. In A.
            Miller, 125–145.
Ball, J. W., and J. T. Taschek
    1989   Teotihuacan's fall and the rise of the Itzá: Realignments and role changes in the
            Terminal Classic Maya lowlands. In Diehl and Berlo, 187–200.
Barba, P., L. A. Manzanilla, R. Chavez, and L. Flores
    1990   Caves and tunnels at Teotihuacan, Mexico: A geological phenomenon of archaeologi-
            cal interest. *Geological Society of America*. Centennial special volume *4*:431–438.
Barlow, R. H.
    1949   The extent of the empire of the Colhua-Mexica. *Ibero-Americana*, No. 48.
Barthel, T. S., and H. von Winning
    1989   Some observations of Stela 1, La Mojarra, Veracruz. In *Tribus*, No.*38*:91–120.
Baudez, C. F.
    1986   Iconography and history at Copán. In Urban and Schortman, 17–26.
    1991   The cross pattern at Copán: forms, ritual and meanings. In *Sixth Palenque round table,
            1986*, Merle Greene Robertson (general editor) and Virginia M. Fields (volume
            editor). Norman and London: University of Oklahoma Press. Pp.81–88.
Baudez, C. F., and P. Becquelin
    1973   Archéologie de Los Naranjos, Honduras. *Etudes Mesoamericaines*, Vol. II. Mission
            archaeologique et étnologique Française au Mexique, Mexico.
Baus, C., C.
    1990   El Culto de Venus en Cacaxtla. In Cárdos de Méndez *MNA, INAH*:351–369.
Beadle, G. W.
    1977   The origin of *Zea Mays*. In *Origins of agriculture*, edited by C. A. Reed. Mouton: The
            Hague. 615–635.
Bell, B.
    1972   Archaeological excavations in Jalisco, Mexico. *Science 175*:1238–1239.
Benfer, R. A.
    1974   The human skeletal remains from Tula. In *Studies of ancient Tollan: A report of the
            University of Missouri Tula archaeological project*, edited by R. A. Diehl. *University of
            Missouri Monographs in Anthropology*, No. 1. Columbia, Missouri: Department of
            Anthropology, University of Missouri:105–116.
Berdan, F. F.
    1988   Principles of regional and long distance trade in the Aztec empire. In *Smoke and mist:
            Mesoamerican studies in honor of Thelma S. Sullivan*, edited by J. K. Josserand and K.
            Daken. *B.A.R. International Series* 402(2):639–658.

Berlin, H.
  1958   El glifo "emblema" en las inscripciones mayas. *Journal de la Société des Americanistes*
          47:111–119.
Berlo, J. C.
  1983   Text and image in Pre-Columbian Art. *BAR International Series* 180, Oxford.
  1989   Early writing in central Mexico; In Tlilli, In Tlapalli. In Diehl and Berlo, 19–47.
Bernal, I.
  1973   Stone reliefs in the Dainzú area. In *The iconography of Middle American sculpture*. New
          York: Metropolitan Museum of Art. Pp.13–23.
Blake, M.
  1991   An emerging early formative chiefdom at Paso de la Amada Chiapas, Mexico. In
          Fowler, Jr., 27–46.
Blanton, R. E.
  1978   *Monte Albán: Settlement patterns at the ancient Zapotec capital*. New York: Academic
          Press.
  1983a   The founding of Monte Albán. In Flannery and Marcus, 83–87.
  1983b   Monte Albán in Period V. In Flannery and Marcus, 281–282.
Blanton, R. E., and S. A. Kowalewski
  1981   Monte Albán and after in the Valley of Oaxaca. In *HMAI, Supplement 1, Archae-
          ology*:94–116.
Blanton, R. E., S. A. Kowalewski, G. Feinman, and J. Appel
  1981   *Ancient Mesoamerica: A comparison of change in three regions*. Cambridge University
          Press.
Boksenbaum, M. W., P. Tolstoy, G. Harbottle, J. Kimberlin, and M. Neivens
  1987   Obsidian industries and cultural evolution in the Basin of Mexico before 500 B.C.
          *JFA 14:*65–75
Bove, F.
  1991   The Teotihuacan-Kaminaljuyú-Tikal connection: A view from the south coast of
          Guatemala. In *Sixth Palenque round table 1986*, Merle Greene Robertson (general
          editor) and Virginia M. Fields (volume editor). Norman: University of Oklahoma
          Press. Pp.135–142.
Brainerd, G. W.
  1941   Fine Orange pottery in Yucatán. *RMEA 5:*163–183.
Brand, D. D.
  1943   An historical sketch of geography and anthropology in the Tarascan region. Part 1.
          *New Mexico Anthropologist 6:*37–108.
Braniff, B.
  1974   Oscilación de la frontera septentrional mesoamericana In *The archaeology of West
          Mexico*, edited by Betty Bell. Ajijíc; Jalisco, Mexico: West Mexico Society for Ad-
          vanced Study. Pp.40–50.
Bray, W.
  1972   The city state in central Mexico at the time of the Spanish conquest. *Journal of Latin
          American Studies 4*(2):161–185.
  1977a   Maya metalwork and its external connections. In Hammond, 365–403.
  1977b   Civilizing the Aztecs. In *The evolution of social systems*, edited by J. Friedman and
          M. J. Rowlands. London: Duckworth. Pp.373–398.
  1978   Gold-working in ancient America. *Gold Bulletin 11*(4):136–143.

1989   Fine metal jewelry from southern Mexico. In *Homenaje a José Luis Lorenzo*. Lorena Mirambell, Coordinadora. *INAH*:244–280.

Bronson, B.
1966   Roots and the subsistence of the ancient Maya. *Southwestern Journal of Anthropology* *22*(3):251–279.

Brown, K. L.
1977a   The Valley of Guatemala: A highland port-of-trade. In Sanders and Michels, 205–395.
1977b   Toward a systematic explanation of culture change within the middle Classic Period of the Valley of Guatemala. In Sanders and Michels, 411–440.

Brueggemann, J., and R. Ortega G.
1989   El Projecto Tajín. *Arqueología* 5, *INAH*, 153–174.

Burger, R. L., and N. J. van der Merwe
1990   Maize and the origin of Chavin civilizations. *American Anthropologist* *92*(1):85–95.

Brush, E. S.
1968   The archaeological significance of ceramic figurines from Guerrero, Mexico. Ph.D dissertation. 1968 New York: Columbia University.

Brush, C. F.
1965   Pox pottery, earliest indentified Mexican ceramic. *Science 149*:194–195
1969   A contribution to the archaeology of coastal Guerrero, Mexico. Ph.D. dissertation. 1965 New York: Columbia University.

Cabrera Castro, Rubén
1987   Tzintzuntzan: Décima temporada de excavaciones. In *Homenaje a Román Piña Chan*. Instituto de Investigaciones Antropológicas. *UNAM* Mexico:531–565.
1990a   Proyecto Templo de Quetzalcoatl. In Cárdos de Méndez, 123–146.
1990b   Los nuevos resultados del Proyecto Arqueológico Teotihuacan 80–82. Resumen general de sus resultados en la Ciudadela. In Cárdos de Méndez, 73–80.

Cabrera Castro, R., S. Sugiyama, and G. L. Cowgill
1991   The Templo de Quetzalcoatl Project at Teotihuacan. *Ancient Mesoamerica 2*:77–92.

Calnek, E. E.
1976   The internal structure of Tenochtitlán. In *The valley of Mexico*, edited by E. R. Wolf. Albuquerque: University of New Mexico Press. Pp.287–302.

Carlson, J. B.
1976   Astronomical investigations and site orientation at Palenque. In *Segunda mesa redonda de Palenque*, edited by Merle Greene Robertson. Pebble Beach, California: The Robert Louis Stevenson School. Pp.107–122.
1981   Olmec concave iron-ore mirrors: the aesthetic of a lithic technology and the Lord of the Mirror. In Benson, 117–147.

Carmack, R. M.
1981   *The Quiché Maya of Utatlán*. Norman, Oklahoma: University of Oklahoma Press.

Carneiro, R. L.
1960   Slash and burn agriculture: a closer look at its implications for settlement patterns. In *Men and cultures*, edited by F. C. Wallace. Philadelphia, University of Pennsylvania: 229–234.
1970   A theory of the origin of the state. *Science: 169*:733–738.

Carr, R. F., and J. E. Hazard
1961   Map of the ruins of Tikal, El Petén, Guatemala. Tikal Report No. 11. *Museum Monographs, The University Museum*. Philadelphia, Pennsylvania.

Carrasco, P.
1971   Social organization of ancient Mexico. In *HMAI* 10:349–375.

Caso, A.
1958   *The Aztecs, people of the sun.* Norman: University of Oklahoma Press.
1965a Lapidary work, goldwork and copperwork from Oaxaca. In *HMAI* 3:896–930.
1965b Zapotec writing and calendar. In *HMAI* 3:931–947
1965c. Mixtec writing and the calendar. In *HMAI* 3:948–961.
1967   *Los calendarios prehispanicos.* Mexico, D. F. *UNAM* Instituto de Investigaciones Historicas.

Caso, A., and I. Bernal,
1952   Urnas de Oaxaca. *INAH Memorias 2.*
1965   Ceramics of Oaxaca. In *HMAI*(3):871–895.

Cepeda, C. G.
1970   Estela del Cerro de los Monos, Tlalchapa, Guerrero. *Boletin* 40, *INAH:*15–20.

Charlton, T. H.
1978   Teotihuacan, Tepeapulco and obsidian exploitation. *Science 200:*1227–1236.

Chase, A. F.
1985a Troubled times: The archaeology and iconography of the Terminal Classic southern lowlands Maya. *Fifth Palenque round table*, Merle Green Robertson (general editor) and Virginia M. Fields (volume editor). San Francisco: The Pre-Columbian Art Research Institute. Pp.103–114.
1985b Archaeology in the Maya heartland. *Archaeology 38:*32–39.
1991   Cycles of time: Caracol in the Maya realm. In *Sixth Palenque round table*, Merle Greene Robertson (general editor) and Virginia M. Fields (volume editor). San Francisco: The Pre-Columbian Art Research Institute. Pp.32–42.

Chase, A., and D. L. Chase
1987   Investigations at the Classic Maya city of Caracol, Belize 1985–1987. San Francisco: *Precolumbian Art Research Institute Monograph* 3.
1988   A Postclassic perspective: Excavations at the Maya site of Santa Rita Corozal, Belize. San Francisco: *Pre-Columbian Art Research Institute Monograph* 4.

Chase, D., and A. Chase
1982   Yucatec influence in terminal Classic northern Belize. *AA 47:*596–614.
1989   Routes of trade and communication and the integration of Maya society: The vista from Santa Rita Corozal, Belize. In *Coastal Maya Trade. Occasional Papers in Anthropology* No. 8. edited by H. McKillop and P. F. Healy. Trent University, Peterborough, Ontario. Pp.19–32.

Cheek, C. D.
1977a Excavations at the Palangana and the Acropolis, Kaminaljuyú. In Sanders and Michels, 1–204.
1977b Teotihuacan influence at Kaminaljuyú. In Sanders and Michels, 441–452.

Clancy, F. S.
1983   A comparison of highland Zapotec and lowland Maya graphic styles. In A. Miller, 223–240.

Clark, J. E.
1991   The beginnings of Mesoamerica: Apologia for the Soconusco Early Formative. In Fowler, Jr., 13–26.

Clark, J. E., and M. Blake
1989   El origen de la civilizacion en Mesoamerica: Los Olmecas y Mokaya del Soconusco

de Chiapas, Mexico. In *El Preclásico o Formative. Advances y perspectivas.* Martha Carmona, Coordinadora. *MNA, INAH:* 385–403.

Clark, J. E., T. A. Lee, Jr., and T. Salcedo
    1989   The distribution of obsidian. In *Voorhies:* 268–284.

Cliff, M. A.
    1988   Domestic architecture and origins of complex society at Cerros. In *Household and community in the Mesoamerican past*, edited by R. R. Wilk and W. Ashmore. Albuquerque: University of New Mexico Press. Pp. 199–225.

Cobean, R. H., J. R. Vogt, M. Glascock, and T. L. Stocker
    1991   High precision trace-element characterization of major Mesoamerican obsidian sources and further analyses of artifacts from San Lorenzo, Tenocthitlán, Mexico. *LAA 2*(1):69–91.

Codex Borbonico
    1899   In *Manuscrit Mexicain de la Biblioteque de Palais Bourbon*, edited by M. E. T. Hamy. Paris.

Codex Borgia
    1898   *Il manoscritto Messicano Borgiano del Museo Etnografico.* Loubat ed. Rome.

Codex Dresden
    1930   In *Códices Maya*, edited by J. A. Villacorta and C. A. Villacorta. Guatemala City: Tipografía Nacional.

Codex Féjévary Mayer
    1830–   In *Antiquities of Mexico*, Vol. III, edited by Lord E. K. Kingsborough. London:
    1848   Robert Havel & Calnaglie Son & Co.

Codex Florentino (see Sahagún, 1950–1982)

Codex Laud
    1966   (Ms. Laud Misc. 678) Bodleian Library. Oxford, England.

Codex Magliabecchiano
    1904   *Manuscrit Mexicain* Post-Colombian de la Bibliothèque National de Florence, Rome: Duke of Loubat.

Codex Mendoza
    1830–   In *Antiquities of Mexico*, Vol. 1, edited by Lord E. K. Kingsborough London: Robert
    1848   Havel & Calnaglie Son & Co.

Codex Telleriano-Remensis
    1889   In Facsimile Edition, Commentary by E. T. Hamy, Paris: Duke of Loubat.

Codex Tro-Cortesiano
    1930   In *Códices Maya*, edited by J. A. Villacorta and C. A. Villacorta. Guatemala City: Tipografía Nacional.

Codex Vaticanus A
    1900   Il manoscritto Messicano Vaticano 3738, detto il codice Ríos, Rome: Loubat reproduction.

Coe, M. D.
    1960   Archaeological linkages with North and South America at La Victoria, Guatemala. *American Anthropologist 62*:363–393.
    1965a   Archaeological synthesis of southern Veracruz and Tabasco. In *HMAI 3*:679–715.
    1965b   The Olmec style and its distribution. In *HMAI 3*:739–775.
    1968   *America's first civilization: Discovering the Olmec.* New York: American Heritage.
    1973   *The Maya scribe and his world.* New York: Grolier Club.
    1977   Olmec and Maya: A study in relationships. In R. E. W. Adams, 183–195.

1981   San Lorenzo Tenochtitlán. In *HMAI Supplement 1* Archaeology:117–146.

1988   *The Maya*. 4th Edition. Thames and Hudson, Ltd. London.

1989   The Hero Twins: myth and image. In J. Kerr, *The Vase Book, Vol. 1*. New York: Kerr Associates Inc. Pp. 161–184.

Coe, M. D., and R. A. Diehl

1980a   *In the land of the Olmec. Vol 1 :The archaeology of San Lorenzo Tenochtitlán*. Austin: University of Texas Press.

1980b   *In the land of the Olmec. Vol. 2 The people of the river*. Austin: University of Texas Press.

Coe, W. R.

1959   Piedras Negras archaeology: Artifacts, caches, and burials *Museum Monographs*. The University Museum. The University of Pennsylvania.

1965a   Tikal, Guatemala and emergent Maya civilization. *Science 147*:1401–1419.

1965b   Tikal: Ten years of study of a Maya ruin in the lowlands of Guatemala. *Expedition Bulletin of the University of Pennsylvania*, 8:5–56.

Coe, W. R.

1975   Resurrecting the grandeur of Tikal. National Geographic Magazine 148(6):792–811.

1988   *Tikal: A handbook of the ancient Maya ruins*. Philadelphia, The University Museum, University of Pennsylvania. Fourteenth printing.

1990   Excavations in the Great Plaza, North Terrace and North Acropolis of Tikal. *Tikal Report No. 14*, Philadelphia, The University Museum. University of Pennsylvania.

Coe, W. R., and J. J. McGinn

1963   The North Acropolis of Tikal and an early tomb. *Expedition. Bulletin of the University of Pennsylvania* 5(2):24–32.

Coggins, C. C.

1979a   A new order and the role of the calendar. Some characteristics of the Middle Classic period at Tikal. In Hammond and Willey, 38–50.

1979b   Teotihuacan at Tikal in the Early Classic Period. *Actes de XLII Congrés International des Americanistes 8*:251–269, Paris.

1980   The shape of time. Some political implications of a four-part figure. *AA 45*:727–739.

1983   An instrument of expansion: Monte Albán, Teotihuacan, and Tikal. In A. Miller, 49–68.

1987   New Fire at Chichén Itzá. *Memorias del Primer Coloquio Internacional de Mayistas 5–10 de agosto de 1985. Instituto de Investigaciones Filologicas. UNAM*, Mexico. Part 1:427–484.

1988a   On the historical significance of decorated ceramics at Copán and Quiriguá and related Maya sites. In Boone and Willèy, 95–123.

1988b   The manikin scepter; Emblem of lineage. *Estudios de Cultura Maya. Vol. XVII UNAM*, Mexico:123–158.

1990   The birth of the baktun at Tikal and Seibal. In Clancy and Harrison, 79–97.

Coggins, C. C., and O. Shane III.

1984   *Cenote of Sacrifice: Maya treasures from the Sacred Well, Chichén Itzá*. Austin: University of Texas Press.

Cohodas, M.

1978   Diverse architectural styles and the ball game cult: The Late Middle Classic Period in Yucatán. In *Middle Classic Mesoamerica*. A.D. 400–700, edited by E. Pasztory. New York: Columbia University Press. Pp. 86–107.

1989   The Epiclassic problem: A review and alternative model. In Diehl and Berlo, 219–240.

Cortés, H.
 1908   *The letters of Cortés to Charles V*. (F. A. MacNutt, translator). New York and London: Oxford University Press. 2 vols.
Covarrubias, M.
 1946a El arte Olmeca: o de la Venta. *Cuadernos Americanos 28*(4): 153–179.
 1946b *Mexico South: the Isthmus of Tehuantepec*. New York: Alfred A. Knopf.
 1957   *Indian art of Mexico and Central America*. New York: Alfred A. Knopf.
Cowgill, G. L.
 1962   An agricultural study of the southern Maya lowland. *American Anthropologist* 64:(2): 273–286.
 1979   Teotihuacan, internal militaristic competition, and the fall of the Classic Maya. In Hammond and Willey, 51–62.
 1983   Rulership and the Ciudadela; political inferences from Teotihuacan architecture. In *Civilization in the Ancient Americas: Essays in honor of Gordon R. Willey*, edited by R. M. Leventhal and A. L. Kolata, University of New Mexico Press and Peabody Museum of Archaeology and Ethnology. Pp. 313–343.
Culbert, T. P.
 1988a Political history and the decipherment of Maya glyphs. *Antiquity 62*:135–152,
 1988b The collapse of Classic Maya civilization. In *The collapse of ancient states and civilizations*, edited by N. Yoffee and G. L. Cowgill. Tucson: University of Arizona Press. Pp. 69–101.
 1991a Politics in the northeast Petén, Guatemala. In Culbert, 128–146.
 1991b Maya political history and elite interaction: a summary. In Culbert, 311–346.
Culbert, T. P., L. J. Kosakowsky, R. E. Fry, and W. A. Haviland
 1990   The population of Tikal, Guatemala. In Culbert and Rice, 103–121.
Dahlin, B. H.
 1979   Cropping cash in the Proto-Classic: a cultural impact statement. In Hammond and Willey: 21–37.
 1984   A colossus in Guatemala: The Preclassic city of El Mirador. *Archaeology 37*(3):18–25.
Davies, C. N.
 1968   Los senorios independientes del imperio azteca. *Serie Historia* 19: *INAH*.
 1973   *The Aztecs: a history*. New York, Macmillan.
 1977   *The Toltecs until the fall of Tula*. Norman, Oklahoma. University of Oklahoma Press.
Demarest, A. A.
 1984a Projecto el Mirador de la Harvard University 1982–1983. In *Mesoamerica*, No. 7, 1–13.
 1984b Conclusiones y especulaciones acerca de El Mirador. In *Mesoamerica*, No. 7, 138–150.
 1984c La ceramica preclásica de El Mirador. In *Mesoamerica*, No. 7, 53–92.
 1986   The archaeology of Santa Leticia and the rise of Maya civilization. *Middle American Research Institute Publication* 25, Tulane University, New Orleans.
 1988   Political evolution in the Maya borderlands: The Salvadoran frontier. In Boone and Willey, 335–394.
 1989   The Olmec and the rise of civilization in eastern Mesoamerica. In Sharer and Grove: 303–344.
 n.d.a Ideology in ancient Maya cultural evolution: In *Ideology and the evolution of PreColumbian civilizations*, edited by A. A. Demarest and G. Conrad. A School of American Research Advanced Seminar.
 n.d.b. The Vanderbilt University Petexbatun regional archaeological project. Findings of the 1990 season. A progress report to the National Geographic Society.

Demarest, A. D., and A. E. Foias
n.d.b. Mesoamerican horizons and the cultural transformations of Maya civilization. A symposium at Dumbarton Oaks on Latin American horizons in 1986, edited by D. Rice and S. Boone. Dumbarton Oaks Research Library and Collections, Washington, D.C. (In Press.)

Demarest, A. D., and S. D. Houston (editors)
1989 Informe preliminar de la primera temporada (1989) del Projecto Arqueológico Regional Petexbatún, Guatemala. Report submitted to the Instituto de Antropología e Historia de Guatemala.

Demarest, A. D., and R. J. Sharer
1982 The origins and evolution of the Usulután ceramic style. *AA 47*(4):810–822.

1986 Late Preclassic ceramic spheres, culture areas and cultural evolution in the southeastern highlands of Mesoamerica. In Urban and Schortman, 194–223.

Díaz del Castillo, B.
1944 *História verdadera de la conquista de la Nueva Expaña*. Mexico. Editorial Pedro Robredo. 3 vols.

Dibble, C. E.
1971 Writing in central Mexico. In *HMAI 10*:322–331.

Diehl, R. A.
1974 Studies of ancient Tollan: A report of the University of Missouri Tula archaeological project, edited by R. A. Diehl. *University of Missouri Monographs in Anthropology* Columbia, Missouri: Department of Anthropology. 1:1–220.

1981 Tula. In *HMAI Supplement 1: Archaeology* 277–295.

1983 *Tula: The Toltec capital of ancient Mexico*. New York: Thames and Hudson.

1989 A shadow of its former self: Teotihuacan during the Coyolatelco Period. In Diehl and Berlo, 9–18.

Diehl, R. A., R. Lomas, and J. T. Wynn
1974 Toltec trade with Central America: New light and evidence *Archaeology 26*(3):182–187.

Diehl, R. A., and M. D. Mandeville
1987 Tula and wheeled animal effigies in Mesoamerica. *Antiquity 61*:239–246.

Dillon, B. D.
1975 Notes on trade in ancient Mesoamerica. *University of California Archaeological Research Facility Contribution No.24*: 80–135.

1987 The highland-lowland Maya frontier: Archaeological evidence from Alta Verapaz, Guatemala. In Pahl: 137–143.

Dixon, E. J.
1985 The origins of the first Americans. *Archaeology 38*(2):22–27.

Drucker, P.
1943a Ceramic sequences at Tres Zapotes, Veracruz, Mexico. *Bureau of American Ethnology, Bulletin* 140.

1943b Ceramic stratigraphy at Cerro de las Mesas, Veracruz Mexico. *Bureau of American Ethnology, Bulletin, 141*.

1952 La Venta, Tabasco: A study of Olmec ceramics and art. *Bureau of American Ethnology, Bulletin* 153.

1981 On the nature of Olmec polity. In Benson, 29–47.

Drucker, P., R. F. Heizer, and R. J. Squier
1959 Excavations at La Venta, Tabasco, 1955. *Bureau of American Ethnology, Bulletin* 170.

Dumond, D. E.
   1974   Swidden agriculture and the rise of Maya civilization. *Southwestern Journal of Anthro-pology* 4:301–316.
Dumond, D. E., and F. Muller
   1972   Classic to Post Classic in highland central Mexico. *Science 175*: 1208–1215.
Duran, Fray D.
   1967   *Historia de las indias de Nueva España e islas de las Tierra Firme* (2 vols), edited by A. M. Garibay K. Mexico: Porrúa.
   1971   *Book of the gods and rites and the ancient calendar.* Translated by Fernando Horcasitas and Doris Heyden. Norman: University of Oklahoma Press.
Eaton, J. D.
   1974   Chicanná: An elite center in the Río Bec region. In *Archaeological investigations on the Yucatecan Peninsula. Middle American Research Institute Publication.* 31:33–138. New Orleans, Louisiana.
   1975   Ancient agricultural Maya farmsteads in the Río Bec area. *University of California Archaeological Research Facility.* Contributions No. 27:56–82.
Edwards, C.
   1969   Possibilities of Pre-Columbian maritime contacts among New World civilizations. In *Precolumbian contact within Nuclear America*, edited by J. C. Kelley and C. Riley. Carbondale, Illinois: Southern Illinois University Museum, No. 4:3–10
Ekholm, G. F.
   1944   Excavations at Tampico and Pánuco in the Huasteca, Mexico. *American Museum of Natural History. Anthropological Papers 38*:321–509.
   1948   Ceramic stratigraphy at Acapulco, Guerrero. In *El Occidente de Mexico, Mesa Redonda, Mexico.* Sociedad Mexicana de Antropología. 95–104.
Ekholm, S.
   1990   Una ceremonia de fin-de-siglo: El gran basurero de Lagartero, Chiapas. In Cárdos de Méndez, 455–467.
Epstein, J. F.
   1990   Sails in aboriginal Mesoamerica: Revaluating Thompson's argument. *American An-thropologist.* 92:187–192.
Fagan, B. M.
   1987   *The great journey: The peopling of ancient America.* London: Thames and Hudson.
Fash, B. W.
   1992   Late Classic architectural sculpture themes in Copán. *Ancient Mesoamerica: 3(1)*:89–104
Fash, W. L.
   1985   La sequencia de ocupacion del Grupo 9N-8, Las Sepulturas Copán, y sus implicaciones teoricas. *Yaxkin 8*:135–149.
   1986   History and characteristics of settlement in the Copán Valley, and some comparisons with Quiriguá. In Urban and Schortman, 72–93.
   1988   A new look at Maya statecraft from Copán, Honduras. *Antiquity 62*:157–169.
   1991a   Lineage patrons and ancestor worship among the Classic Maya nobility: The case of Copán Structure 9N-82. In *Sixth Palenque round table 1986.* Merle Green Robertson (general editor) and Virginia M. Fields (volume editor). Norman: University of Oklahoma Press. Pp. 68–80.
   1991b   *Scribes, warriors and kings The city of Copan and the ancient Maya.* London: Thames and Hudson, Ltd.

Fash, W. L., and R. J. Sharer
  1991   Sociopolitical developments and methodological issues at Copán, Honduras: A conjunctive perspective. *LAA 2(2):* 166–187.
Fash, W. L., and D. S. Stuart
  1991   Dynastic history and cultural evolution at Copán, Honduras. In Culbert, 147–179.
Fash, W. L., R. V. Williamson, C. R. Larios, and J. Palka
  1992   The hieroglyphic stairway and its ancestors: Investigations of Copán Structure 10L-26. *Ancient Mesoamerica 3(1):*105–116.
Feinman, G., R. Blanton, and S. Kowalewski
  1984   Market system development in the Prehispanic Valley of Oaxaca. In Hirth, 157–178.
Fialko C., V.
  1987   El marcador de juego de pelota de Tikal: Nuevas referencias epigráficas para el clásico temprano. In *Primer Simpósio Mundial Sobre Epigrafía Maya.* Guatemala: Associación Tikal. Pp. 61–80.
Flannery, K. V.
  1976   The early Formative household cluster on the Guatemalan Pacific Coast. In *The early Mesoamerican village,* edited by K. V. Flannery. New York: Acadamic Press. Pp. 31–34.
  1982   *Maya subsistence: Studies in memory of Dennis E. Puleston,* edited by K. V. Flannery. New York: Academic Press.
  1983a   Tentative chronological phases for the Oaxaca preceramic. In Flannery and Marcus, 26–29.
  1983b   The Tierras Largas Phase and the analytical units of the early Oaxacan village. In Flannery and Marcus, 43–46.
  1983c   Monte Negro: A reinterpretation. In Flannery and Marcus, 99–102.
  1983d   The development of Monte Albán's main plaza in Period II In Flannery and Marcus, 102–104.
Flannery, K. V, and J. Marcus
  1983a   The growth of site hierarchies in the valley of Oaxaca. In Flannery and Marcus, 53–64.
  1983b   The origins of the state in Oaxaca: Editors' Introduction. In Flannery and Marcus, 79–83.
  1983c   Urban Mitla and its rural hinterland. In Flannery and Marcus, 295–300.
  1983d   Zapotec Warfare: Archaeological evidence for the battles of Huitzo and guiengola. In Flannery and Marcus: 318–322.
Flannery, K. V., J. Marcus, and S. A. Kowalewski
  1981   The preceramic and formative of the Valley of Oaxaca. In *HMAI Supplement 1: Archaeology,* 48–93.
Flannery, K. V., and R. Spores
  1983   Excavated sites of the Oaxaca preceramic. In Flannery and Marcus, 20–26.
Florance, C. A.
  1985   Recent work in the Chupícuaro region. In *The archaeology of western and northwestern Mesoamerica,* edited by M. Foster and P. C. Weigand. Boulder, Colorado Westview Press. Pp. 9–45.
Folan, Jr., W. J.
  1990   Calakmul, Campeche: El auge del preclásico Maya. In *El preclásico o formativo.:Avances y perspectivas.* Marta Carmona Macías, Coordinadora. *MNA, INAH:*353–362.

Folan, Jr., W. J., E. R. Kintz, and L. A. Fletcher
    1983   *Cobá, a Classic Maya metropolis*. New York: Academic Press.
Folan, Jr., W. J.
    1989   *The cultural evolution of ancient Náhua civilizations: The Pipil-Nacarao of Central America*.
            Norman: University of Oklahoma Press.
Fonserrada de Molina, M., and A. Cárdos de Méndez
    1988   *Las figurillas de Jaina, Campeche en el Museo Nacional de Antropología*. Instituto de
            Investigaciones Estéticas de UNAM, INAH. Mexico.
Fowler, Jr., W. J., A. Demarest, F. Asaro, H. Michel, and F. Stross
    1989   Obsidian from El Mirador, Guatemala: New evidence on Preclassic Maya interac-
            tion. *American Anthropologist 91*(1): 158–168
Fox, J. W.
    1978   *Quiché conquest:Centralism and regionalism in highland Guatemalan state development*.
            Albuquerque, New Mexico: University of New Mexico Press.
    1987   *Maya Postclassic state formation*. Cambridge University Press.
Freidel, D. A.
    1978   Maritime adaptation and the rise of Maya civilization: the view from Cerros, Belize.
            In Prehistoric Coastal Adaptations, edited by B. Stark and B. Voorhies, New York:
            Acadamic Press. 239–265.
    1981   Continuity and disjunction. late Postclassic settlement patterns in northern Yucatán.
            In Ashmore: 311–332.
    1985   A new light on the dark age: A summary of major themes. In Chase and Rice,
            287–309.
    1986   Terminal Classic lowland Maya: Successes, failures and aftermaths. In Sabloff and
            Andrews V.: 409–430.
Freidel, D. A., and J. A. Sabloff
    1984   *Cozumel: Late Maya settlement patterns*. New York: Academic Press.
Freidel, D. A., and L. Schele
    1988a   Symbol and power: a history of the lowland Maya cosmogram. In Benson
            and Griffin: 44–93.
    1988b   Kingship in the late Preclassic Maya lowlands: the instruments and places of ritual
            power. *American Anthropologist: 90*: 547–567.
Furst, P.
    1965   West Mexican tomb sculpture as evidence for shamanism in Prehispanic Mesoamer-
            ica. *Antropolóqica 15*:29–60
García Cook, A.
    1981   The historical importance of Tlaxcala in the cultural development of the central
            highlands. *HMAI: Supplement 1 Archaeology*: 244–276.
García Cook, A., and R. M. Araña A.
    1978   *Rescate arqueológico del monolito Coyolxauhqui, INAH*.
García Cook, A., and B. L. Merino C.
    1977   Nota sobra caminos y rutas de intercambio al este de la cuenca de México. *Comunica-
            ciones Projecto Puebla-Tlaxcala 14*:71–92.
Gasco, J., and B. Voorhies
    1989   The ultimate tribute: The role of Soconusco as an Aztec tributary. In Voorhies,
            48–94.
Gay, C. T.
    1972   *Xochipala: the beginnings of Olmec art*. Princeton, New Jersey: University Press.

Gibson, C.
1971   Structure of the Aztec empire. In *HMAI 10*(1):376–394.

Gillespie, S.
1989   *The Aztec kings: The construction of rulership in Mexica history*. Tucson: University of Arizona Press.

Gómez-Pompa, A., J. S. Salvador F., and M. A. Fernández
1990   The sacred cacao groves of the Maya. *LAA 1*(3): 247–257.

González, L., R.
1988   Proyecto Arqueológico La Venta. *Arqueología* 4. *INAH:* 121–165.

González Licon, E.
1987   Tipología cerámica de la gruta de Loltún, Yucatán. *Memorias del primer coloquio internacional de Mayistas 5–10 de agosto de 1985*. Part 1:165–174 Instituto de Investigaciones Filológicas, *UNAM*, Mexico.

Gorenstein, S.
1973   Tepexi el Viejo: a Post-Classic fortified site in the Mixteca-Puebla region of Mexico. *APS Transactions 63*(1).

Gorenstein, S., and H. P. Pollard
1983   The Tarascan civilization: a late Prehispanic cultural system. *Vanderbilt Publications in Anthropology* No. 28. Nashville, Tennessee.

Graham, J. A.
1973   Aspects of non-Classic presences in the inscriptions and sculptural art of Seibal. In Culbert, 207–219.
1979   Maya, Olmecs and Izapans at Abaj Takalik. *Actes du XVII Congres International des Americanistes*, Paris. 8:179–188
1989   Olmec diffusion, a sculptural view from Pacific Guatemala. In Sharer and Grove, 227–246.

Graham, J. A., and L. Benson
1990   Maya civilization of cycles 6 and 7: Classic Maya in the Preclassic Period. Conference 1990. University of California, Berkeley.

Graham, J. A., R. R. Hester, and R. N. Jack
1972   Sources for the obsidian at the ruins of Seibal, Petén, Guatemala. *University of California Archaeological Research Facility* Contribution No. 16:111–116.

Green, D. F., and G. W. Lowe
1967   Altamira and Padre Piedra, early Preclassic sites in Chiapas, Mexico. *PNWAF 20*: 1–133.

Greengo, R. E., and C. W. Meighan
1976   Additional perspectives on the Capacha complex of western Mexico. *Journal of New World Archaeology 1*(5):15–23.

Griffin, G. G.
1972   Xochipala, the earliest great art style in Mexico. *APS Proceedings 116:* 301–309.
1976   Portraiture in Palenque. *Segunda mesa redonda de Palenque*, edited by Merle Greene Robertson. Pebble Beach, California: The Robert Louis Stevenson School. Pp. 137–147.

Grove, D. C.
1971   The Mesoamerican Formative and South American influences. *Primer simpósio de correlaciones antropológicas Andino-Mesoamericano.*, Salinas, Ecuador. Manuscript.
1981   The formative period and the evolution of complex culture. In *HMAI Supplement 1: Archaeology:* 373–391.

1987   *Ancient Chalcatzingo*, edited by D. C. Grove. Austin: University of Texas Press.

1989   Chalcatzingo and its Olmec connection. In Sharer and Grove, 122–147

Grove, D. C., and S. Gillespie

1984   Chalcatzingo's portrait figurines and the cult of the ruler. *Archaeology 37*(4):27–33.

Guderjan, T. H., J. F. Garber, and H. H. Smith

1989   Maritime trade on Ambergris Cay, Belize. In *Coastal Maya trade: Occasional papers in anthrolpology* No. 8, edited by H. McKillop and P. F. Healy. Trent University, Peterborough, Ontario. Pp. 123–133.

Guillén, A. C., and D. C. Grove

1987   Chronology and cultural phases at Chalcatzingo. In *Ancient Chalcatzingo*, edited by D. C. Grove. Austin: University of Texas Press. Pp. 56–62.

Hammond, N.

1975   Preclassic to Postclassic in northern Belize. Actos del XLI Congreso Internacional de Americanistos 1:442–448.

1987   The sun also rises: Iconographic syntax of the Pomona flare. *Center for Maya research. Research papers on ancient Maya writing.* No. 7. Washington, D.C.

1988   *Ancient Maya civilization*. New Brunswick, New Jersey: Rutgers University Press.

1991   Cuello considered: Summary and conclusions: In *Cuello, an early Maya community in Belize*, edited by N. Hammond. Cambridge University Press. Pp. 235–248.

Hammond, N., and W. Ashmore

1981   Lowland Maya settlement: Geographical and chronological frameworks. In Ashmore, 19–36.

Hammond, N., and C. Miksicek

1981   Ecology and economy of a Formative Maya site at Cuello, Belize. *JFA 8:259–270.*

Hansen, R. D.

1991   The road to Nakbé. *Natural History Magazine May:8–14.*

Harbottle, G., and P. C. Weigand

1992   Turquoise in Pre-Columbian America. *Scientific American 226* (2):78–85.

Harrison, P. D.

1990   The revolution in ancient Maya subsistence. In Clancy and Harrison, 99–113.

Harrison P. D., and B. L. Turner II (editors)

1974   *Prehistoric Maya agriculture*. Albuquerque, New Mexico: University of New Mexico Press.

Hassig, R.

1988   *Aztec warfare: Imperial expansions and political control.* Civilization of the American Indian Series. Vol. 188. Norman: University of Oklahoma Press.

Haviland, W. A.

1967   Stature at Tikal, Guatemala: Implications for ancient Maya demography and social organization. *AA 32:* 316–325

1985   Population and social dynamics: The dynasties and social structure of Tikal. *Expedition, Bulletin of the University of Pennsylvania* 27(3):34–41

Healan, C. M.

1986   Technological and nontechnological aspects of an obsidian workshop; excavated at Tula, Hidalgo. In *Economic aspects of prehispanic highland Mexico*, edited by B. L. Isaac. Research in Economic Anthropology, Supplement 2. Greenwich: JAI Press. Pp. 133–152.

1989   *Tula and the Toltecs*, edited by D. M. Healan. Iowa City: University of Iowa Press.

Healy, P. F.

1974   The Cuyamel caves: Preclassic sites in northeast Honduras. *AA, 30:* 435–447.

Heizer, R. F., and J. Bennyhoff
  1972   Archaeological investigations at Cuicuilco, Mexico, 1957. *National Geographic Society Research Reports* 1955–1960. Projects: 93–104.
Hellmuth, N.
  1972   Report on first season explorations and excavations at Yaxhá, El Petén, Guatemala. *Katunob 7*(4):24–49; 92–97.
  1978   Teotihuacan art in the Escuintla, Guatemala region. In *Middle Classic Mesoamerica* A.D.400-700, edited by E. Pasztory, New York: Columbia University Press: 71–85.
  1986   Yaxhá. *Mexicon 8*(2):36–37.
Hers, M. A.
  1985   Los Tolteca-Chichimecas y el concepto de Mesoamerica. *XIX Mesa Redonda Sociedad Mexicana de Antropología*, Querétaro.
  1989   *Los Toltecas en tierras Chichimecas.* Instituto de Investigaciones Estéticas. *UNAM*, Mexico.
Heyden, D.
  1970   Nueva interpretacion de las figuras sonrientes, señalada por las fuentes históricas. *Tlalocan 6*(2): 159–162.
  1981   Caves, gods, myths: World view and planning at Teotihuacan. In *Mesoamerican sites and world views. A conference 1976.* Dumbarton Oaks Research Library and Collections. Washington, D.C. Pp. 1–39.
  1987   Symbolism of ceramics from the Templo Mayor. In Boone, 109–130.
Hirth, K. G.
  1978   Interregional trade and the formation of prehistoric gateway communities. *AA 43:*35–45.
  1984   Trade and Society in Late Formative Morelos. In *Hirth:* 125–146.
  1987   Formative Period settlement patterns in the Rio Amatzinac Valley. In *Ancient Chalcatzingo*, edited by D. C. Grove. Austin: University of Texas Press. Pp. 343–367.
  1988   Beyond the Maya frontier: Cultural interaction and syncretism along the central Honduran corridor. In Boone and Willey, 297–334.
  1989   Militarism and social organization at Xochicalco, Morelos. In Diehl and Berlo, 69–81.
Hirth, K. G., and J. Angulo V.
  1981   Early state expansion in central Mexico: Teotihuacan in Morelos. *JFA 8:*135–150.
Historia de los mexicanos por sus pinturas.
  1941   In *Nueva colección de documentos para la historia de México: 1988–1892.* J. García Icazbalceta, editor. Vol. 3:207–240.
Historia Tolteca-Chichimeca
  1947   *Anales de Quauhtinchan (prologue by P. Kirchhoff)*, Mexico, D. F. Antigua Librería Robredo de José Porrúa e Hijos.
Hosler, D.
  1988   Ancient west Mexican metallurgy: South and Central American origins and west Mexican transformations. *American Anthropologist 90*(4):832–855.
  1990   The development of ancient Mesoamerican metallurgy. *The Journal of the Minerals, Metals and Materials Society 42*(5):44–46.
Houston, S. D., and P. Mathews
  1985   The dynastic sequence of Dos Pilas, Guatemala. *Pre-Columbian Art Research Institute. Monograph* 1. San Francisco, California.
Ixtlilxôchitl, F. de A.
  1952   *Obras históricas* (2 vols.) Editoria Nacional, Mexico, D. F.

Jack, R. N., T. E. Hester, and R. F. Heizer
  1972   Geologic sources of archaeological obsidian from sites in northern and central Vera-
          cruz. *University of California Archaeological Research Facility Contribution No. 16:*
          117–122.
Jennings, J. D.
  1968   *Prehistory of North America.* New York: McGraw-Hill.
Jiménez Moreno, W.
  1941   Tula y los Toltecas según las fuentes históricas. *RMEA 5:*79–83.
  1942   El enigma de los Olmecas. *Cuadernos Americanos 1:*113–145.
  1962   La historiografía Tetzocana y sus problemas. *RMEA 18:*81 85.
Johnson, F., and R. S. MacNeish
  1972   Chronometric dating. In *The prehistory of the Tehuacán Valley*, Vol 4, edited by R. S.
          MacNeish. Austin, Texas: University of Texas Press. Pp. 3–55.
Johnson, I. W.
  1967   Textiles, Vol. 2, edited by R. S. MacNeish, S. A. Nelken-Terner, and I. W.
          Johnson, *The Prehistory of the Tehuacán Valley*. Austin, Texas: University of Texas
          Press. Pp. 191–226.
Johnston, K.
  1985   Maya dynastic territorial expansion: Glyphic evidence from Classic centers of the
          Pasión River, Guatemala. *Fifth Palenque round table, 1983, Vol. VII*, Merle Greene
          Robertson (general editor) and Virginia M. Fields (volume editor). San Francisco,
          California: Pre-Columbian Art Research Institute. Pp. 49–56.
Jones, C.
  1984   *Deciphering Maya hieroglyphs.* The University Museum of the University of Pennsyl-
          vania.
  1985   The rubber ball game: A Universal Mesoamerican sport. *Expedition, Bulletin of the
          University of Pennsylvania 27*(2):44–52.
  1989   Builders of Tikal: Archaeology and history. In Hanks and Rice, 255–259.
  1991   Cycles of growth at Tikal. In Culbert, 102–127.
Jones, C., and I. Satterthwaite
  1982   The monuments and inscriptions of Tikal: The carved monuments *Tikal Report 33A*.
          Philadelphia, The University Museum, University of Pennsylvania.
Jones, C. and R. J. Sharer
  1986   Archaeological investigations in the site-core of Quiriguá, Guatemala. In Urban and
          Schortman, 27–34.
Joralemon, P. D.
  1976   The Olmec dragon: a study in Pre-Columbian iconography. In *Origins of Religious
          Art and Iconography in Preclassic Mesoamerica.*, edited by H. B. Nicholson. Latin
          American Studies Series 31. Los Angeles: UCLA Latin American Center.
Joyce, R. A.
  1988   The Ulua Valley and the coastal Maya lowlands: The view from Cerro Palenque.
          In Boone and Willey, 269–295.
Justeson, J. E.
  1986   The origin of writing systems: Preclassic Mesoamerica *World Archaeology.*
          17(3):437–458.
Justeson, J. S., W. M. Norman, and N. Hammond
  1988   The Pomona flare: A Preclassic Maya hieroglyphic text. In Benson and Griffin,
          95–151.

Kaufman, T.
1976   Archaeological and linguistic correlations in Mayaland and associated areas of Meso-
        america. *World Archaeology 8*(1):101–118.
Keber, E. Q.
1988   The Aztec image of Topilzin Quetzalcoatl. In *Smoke and mist: Mesoamerican studies in
        honor of Thelma S. Sullivan*, edited by J. K. Josserand and K. Daken. *BAR International
        Series (1):329–343.*
Kelley, D. H.
1962   Glyphic evidence for a dynastic sequence at Quiriguá, Guatemala. *AA 27*:323–335.
1976   *Deciphering the Maya Script*. Austin: University of Texas Press.
Kelley, E. A.
1978   The Temple of the Skulls at Alta Vista, Chalchihuites. In *Across the Chichimec
        sea*, edited by C. L. Riley and B. C. Hedrick. Carbondale: Southern Illinois Press.
        Pp. 101–126.
Kelley, J. C.
1990a   The Classic epoch in the Chalchihuites culture of the state of Zacatecas. In Cárdos
        de Méndez, 11–14.
1990b   The Early Postclassic in northern Zacatecas and Durango IX to IXX centuries. In
        Mesoamerica y Norte de Mexico, Siglo IX-XII. Federica Sodi Miranda, Coordinadora.
        MNA, INAH, Vol. 2:487–519.
Kelly, I.
1974   Stirrup pots from Colima: Some implications. In *The archaeology of west Mexico*, ed-
        ited by B. Bell. Ajijíc, Jalisco, Mexico: West Mexican Society for Advanced Study.
        Pp. 206–211.
1978   Seven Colima tombs: An interpretation of ceramic content. *University of California
        Archaeological Research Facility Contribution* No. 36:1–26.
1980   Ceramic sequence in Colima: Capacha, an early phase. *Anthropological Papers of the
        University of Arizona* No. 37. Tucson, Arizona: University of Arizona Press.
Kelly, I., and A. Palerm
1952   The Mexican conquests. In *The Tajín Totonac*, Part 1, *Publication 13*. Washington,
        D.C. Smithsonian Institution Institute of Social Antropology. Pp. 264–317.
Kerr, J.
1989   *The vase book: Vol. 1*. New York: Kerr Associates, Inc.
1990   *The Maya vase book: A corpus of rollout photographs of Maya vases. Vol. 2*. New York:
        Kerr Associates, Inc.
1992   *The Maya vase book. Vol. 3*. New York: Kerr Associates, Inc.
Kerr, J., and J. Spero
1989   Glyphic names of animals and supernaturals. *Seventh Palenque Round Table* ab-
        stracts:37–39.
Kidder, A. V., J. D. Jennings, and E. M. Shook
1946   Excavations at Kaminaljuyú, Guatemala. *Carnegie Institution of Washington*. Publica-
        tion 576.
Kirchhoff, P.
1943   Mesoamerica. *Acta Americana 1*:92–107.
1954-   Land tenure in ancient Mexico. *RMEA 14*(1):351–362.
1955
Knorosov, Y. V.
1958   The problem of the study of the Maya hieroglyphic writing. *AA* (3):284–291.

1967   The writing of the Maya Indians (selected chapters), translated by Sophie D. Coe. *Russian Translation Series* Vol. 4. *PMAE*. Cambridge: Harvard University.

Kolb, C. C.
1986   Commercial aspects of Classic Teotihuacan Period "Thin Orange" wares. In *Economic aspects of prehispanic highland Mexico: Research in economic anthropology Supplement 2*, edited by B. L. Isaac. Greenwich, Connecticut: JAI Press. Pp. 155–205.

Kowalski, J. K.
1985a   Lords of the northern Maya: Dynastic history in the inscriptions of Uxmal and Chichén Itzá. *Expedition, Bulletin of the University of Pennsylvania, 27*(3):50–60.

1985b   An historical interpretation of the inscriptions of Uxmal. In *Fourth Palenque round table 1980 Vol. 6*, edited by Merle Greene Robertson and Elizabeth P. Benson. San Francisco: Pre-Columbian Art Research Institute. Pp. 235–248.

1987   *The house of the governor: A Maya palace at Uxmal, Yucatán Mexico*. Norman: University of Oklahoma Press.

1989   Who am I among the Itzá?: Links between northern Yucatán and the western Maya lowlands and highlands. In Diehl and Berlo, 173–185.

Kowalski, J. K., and W. L. Fash
1991   Symbolism of the Maya ball game at Copán: Synthesis and new aspects. In *Sixth Palenque round table 1986*, Merle Greene Robertson (general editor) and Virginia M. Fields (volume editor). Norman: University of Oklahoma Press. Pp. 59–67.

Kowalewski, S. A.
1980   Population balances in Period I of Oaxaca. *AA. 45*(1):151–165.

Kroster, P. H., and G. R. Krotser
1973   The life style of Tajín. *AA 38*:199–205.

Kubler, G. A.
1967   The iconography of the art of Teotihuacan. *Dumbarton Oaks, Studies in Pre-Columbian Art and Archaeology for Harvard University*. Washington, D.C. No. 4.

1984   *The art and architecture of ancient America. The Mexican, Maya and Andean peoples*, Third Edition. New York: Penquin Books.

1985   Pre-Columbian pilgrimages in Mesoamerica. In *Fourth Palenque round table 1980 Vol. 6*, Merle Greene Robertson (general editor) and Elizabeth P. Benson (volume editor). San Francisco: Precolumbian Art Research Institute. Pp. 313–316.

Kurjack, E.
1974   Prehistoric lowland Maya community and social organization: A case study at Dzibilchaltún, Yucatán,. Mexico. *Middle American Research Institute*. Tulane University. Vol. 38.

Kurjack, E. B., and S. Garza, T.
1981   Pre-Columbian community form and distribution in the northern Maya area. In Ashmore, 287–309.

Lackey, L. M.
1986   "Thick" Thin Orange amphorae: Problems of provenience and usage. In *Economic aspects of prehispanic highland Mexico research in economic anthropology*, Supplement 2, edited by B. L. Isaac. Greenwich, Connecticut: JAI Press, Inc. Pp. 207–219.

Landa See Tozzer, 1941.

Lange, F. W., and D. Z. Stone (editors)
1984   *The archaeology of lower Central America*. Albuquerque: University of New Mexico Press.

Langenscheidt, A., and C. Tang Lay

1982   La minería prehispánica en la Sierra Gorda. In *Mining and mining techniques in ancient Mesoamerica*, edited by P. C. Weigand and G. Gywnne. *Antropology VI*:135–148.

Langley, J. C.

n.d.   Teotihuacan warriors and the mural paintings of Teopancaxco. Paper delivered at the 44th International Congress of Americanists, Manchester, England, 1982.

1986   *Symbolic notation of Teotihuacan elements of writing in a Mesoamerican culture of the Classic period. BAR* International Series 313. Oxford.

1991   The forms and usage of notation at Teotihuacan. *Ancient Mesoamerica* 2(2):285 298.

Laporte, J. P.

1987a   El "talud-tablero" en Tikal, Petén: Nuevos datos. In *Homenaje a Román Piña Chan*, Instituto de Investigaciones Antropológicas, *UNAM*, Mexico: 265–316.

1987b   El Grupo 6C-XVI, Tikal, Petén: Un centro habitacional del clásico temprano. *Memorias del primer coloquio internacional de mayistas, 5–10 de agosto de 1985. UNAM*, Mexico. Part 1:221–244.

Laporte, J. P., and V. Fialko C.

1990   New perspectives on old problems: Dynastic references for the Early Classic at Tikal. In Clancy and Harrison, 33–66.

Laporte, J. P., and L. Vega de Zea

1988   Aspectos dinásticos para el clásico temprano en Mundo Perdido, Tikal. In *Primer Simposio Mundial sobre Epigrafía Maya*, Guatemala, Associación Tikal: 127–141.

Lathrap, D. W.

1973   The antiquity and importance of long-distance trade relationships in the moist tropics of pre-Columbian South America. *World Archaeology 5:*170–186.

1975   *Ancient Ecuador: Culture, clay and creativity*. Chicago: Field Museum of Natural History.

Lee, Jr., T. A.

1985   Los códices Maya, edited by T. A. Lee, Jr. Chiapas, Mexico: Universidad Autónoma de Chiapas.

1989   Chiapas and the Olmec. In Sharer and Grove, 198–226.

León, N.

1904   *Los Tarascos*. Mexico, D. F: *MNA*.

León-Portilla, M.

1963   Aztec thought and culture, a study of the ancient Náhuatl mind. Norman, Oklahoma: University of Oklahoma Press.

Leventhal, R. M.

1986   A reexamination of stela caches at Copán: New data for Copador. In Urban and Schortman, 138–142.

1990   Southern Belize: An ancient Maya region. In Clancy and Harrison, 125–141.

Leventhal, R. M., A. A. Demarest, and G. R. Willey

1987   The cultural and social components of Copán. In *Human boundaries and the growth of complex societies*, edited by K. M. Trinkaus. Arizona State University, Tempe, Arizona. *Anthropological Research Papers*. No. 37:179–206.

Longyear, III, J. M.

1952   Copán ceramics: A study of southeastern Maya pottery. *Carnegie Institution of Washington, Publication* 597.

López Austín, A., L. López L., and S. Sugiyama

1991   The Temple of Quetzalcoatl at Teotihuacan: Its possible ideological significance. *Ancient Mesoamerica* 2(1):93–105.

Love, M. W.

1991   Style and social complexity in Formative Mesoamerica. In Fowler, Jr., 47–76.

Lowe, G. W.

1977   The Mixe-Zoque as competing neighbors of the lowlands Maya. In R. E. W. Adams, 197–288.

1978   Eastern Mesoamerica. In *Chronologies in New World archeology*, edited by R. E. Taylor and C. W. Meighan. New York: Academic Press. Pp. 331–393.

1989   The heartland Olmec: evolution of material culture. In Sharer and Grove. 33–67.

Lowe, G. W., and J. A. Mason

1965   Archaeological survey of the Chiapas and highlands and Upper Grijalva Basin. In *HMAI* (2):195–236.

Lowe, G. W., T. A. Lee, Jr., and E. M. Espinosa

1982   Izapa: An introduction to the ruins and monuments. *PNWAF* No. 31. Provo, Utah.

MacKinnon, J. J., and S. M. Kepecs

1989   Prehispanic saltmaking in Belize: New evidence. *AA 54*(3):522–533.

MacNeish, R. S.

1958   Preliminary archaeological investigations in the Sierra de Tamaulipas, Mexico. *APS Transactions 44* (Part 5):543–646.

1962   Second annual report of the Tehuacán archaeological botanical project, Project Reports, No. 2. R. S. Peabody Foundation for Archaeology. Andover, Massachusetts.

1967   *The prehistory of the Tehuacán Valley: Nonceramic artifacts*, edited by D. S. Byers. Austin and London: University of Texas Press.

1970   Megafauna and man from Ayacucho, highland Peru. *Science 168*:975–977.

1981   Tehuacán's accomplishments. In *HMAI: Supplement 1: Archaeology* 31–47.

MacNeish, R. S., and F. A. Peterson

1962   The Santa Marta rock shelter, Ocozocoautla, Chiapas, Mexico. *PNWAF* No. 14, Publication 10.

Maler, T.

1908   Explorations in the Department of eten, Guatemala and adjacent region. *Memoirs of the Peabody Museum of Archeology and Ethnology*, Harvard University, Cambridge: (4):1.

Mangelsdorf, P. C., R. S. MacNeish, and W. C. Galinat

1967   Prehistoric wild and cultivated maize. In *prehistory of the Tehuacan valley*, Vol. 1, edited by D. S. Byers. Austin, Texas: University of Texas Press. Pp.178–200.

Marcus, J.

1976   *Emblem and state in the Classic Maya lowlands*. Dumbarton Oaks Research Library and Collections. Washington, D.C.

1980   Zapotec writing. *Scientific American 242*(2):46–60.

1983a   The Espiridión Complex and the origins of the Oaxaca Formative. In Flannery and Marcus, 42–43.

1983b   The first appearance of Zapotec writing and calendrics. In Flannery and Marcus, 91–96.

1983c   Summary and conclusions. In Flannery and Marcus, 355–360.

1983d   Monte Albán's Tomb 7. In Flannery and Marcus, 282–285.

1987   The inscriptions of Calakmul: Royal marriage at a Maya city in Campeche, Mexico. Ann Arbor. *University of Michigan Museum of Anthropology Technical Report* 21.

1989   Zapotec chiefdoms and the nature of Formative religions. In Sharer and Grove, 148–197.

Marquina, I.
  1951   Arquitecturea prehispanica. *INAH*, Memorias 1.
Martínez Donjuan, G.
  1986   Teopantecuanitlán. In *Arqueología e etnohistoria del estado de Guerrero*. edited by
          C. Vega Sosa and R. Cervantes Delgado. Mexico, D.F. *INAH:* Gobierno del Estado
          de Guerreró. 55–80.
Mastache, A. G., and R. H. Cobean
  1989   The Coyotlatelco culture and the origins of the Toltec state. In Diehl and Berlo,
          49–67.
Matheny, R.
  1987   El Mirador: An early Maya metropolis uncovered. *National Geographic Magazine*
          172(3):316–339.
Matheny, R., D. Gurr, D. Forsyth, and F. R. Hauck
  1983   Investigations at Edzná, Campeche, Mexico. Vol. 1: The hydraulic system. Vol. 2:
          Ceramics. *PNWAF* No. 46. Provo, Utah.
Mathews, P.
  1983   Corpus of Maya hieroglyphic inscriptions. Vol. 6 Part 1. *PMAE* Cambridge, Massa-
          chusetts: Harvard University.
Mathews, P., and M. G. Robertson
  1985   Notes on the Olvidado, Palenque, Chiapas. *Fifth Palenque round table*, Vol. VII,
          Merle Green Robertson (general editor) and V. M. Fields (volume editor). San
          Francisco: The Pre-Columbian Art Research Institute. Pp. 7–18.
Mathews, P., and L. Schele
  1974   Lords of Palenque. The glyphic evidence. *Primera mesa redonda de Palenque*, Part 1,
          edited by Merle Greene Robertson. Pebble Beach, California: The Robert Louis
          Stevenson School. Pp. 63–76.
Mathews, P., and G. R. Willey
  1991   Prehistoric polities of the Pasion region: Hieroglyphic texts and their archaeological
          settings. In Culbert: 30–71.
Matos Moctezuma, E.
  1974   Proyecto Tula, primera parte. Colección Científica 15. edited by E. Matos Mocte-
          zuma. *INAH*. Mexico, D. F.
  1987   Symbolism of the Templo Mayor. In Boone: 185–209.
  1988   *The Great Temple of the Aztecs*. Translated by Doris Heyden. London, Thames and
          Hudson. Ltd.
  1989   *The Aztecs*, New York. Rizzoli International Publications, Inc.
Maudslay, A. P.
  1889   Archaeology: Biologia Centrali-Americana. Vol. 1
  1902   London: Dulau and Co.
McKillop, H., and P. F. Healy (editors)
  1989   *Coastal Maya trade. Occasional Papers in Anthropology* No. 8. Peterborough, Ontario:
          Trent University.
McKillop, H., and L. Jackson
  1989   Maya obsidian sources and trade routes. In *Coastal Maya trade*, edited by H. McKillop
          and P. F. Healy. Trent University. Petersborough, Ontario: *Occasional Papers in
          Anthropology* No. 8:59–77.
McVicker, D.
  1985   The "Mayanized" Mexicans. *AA 50*(1):82–101.

Meggers, B. J., C. Evans, and E. Estrada
    1965   Early Formative period of coastal Ecuador: The Valdivia and Machalilla phases. *Smithsonian Contributions to Anthropology* 1.

Meighan, C. W.
    1969   Cultural similarities between western Mexico and Andean regions. Research Records of the University Museum, Southern Illinois University, Carbondale, Illinois. *Meso-american Studies 4*:11–25.
    1972   Morett site. *University of California Publications in Anthropology*, Vol. 7.
    1974   Prehistory of west Mexico. *Science 184*:1254–1261.
    1976   The archaeology of Amapa, Nayarit. In *The archaeology of Amapa, Nayarit. Monumenta archaeologica*, Vol. 2:1–162, edited by C. W. Meighan. Los Angeles, California: The Institute of Archaeology, University of California.

Mendez Martinez, E.
    1988   Tumba 5 de Huijazoo. Dirección de Monumentos Prehispánicos *INAH*, Mexico *Arqueologia:*27–16.

Mexicon
    1987   *Edzná*, Vol. IX(4):74.
    1988   *Motul de San José*, Vol. X(4):66–67.

Michels, J. W.
    1977   Political organization at Kaminaljuyú: Its implications for interpreting Teotihuacan influence. In Sanders and Michels, 223–240.
    1979   *The Kaminaljuyú chiefdom*. University Park: The Pennsylvania State University Press.

Miles, S. W.
    1965   Sculpture of the Guatemala-Chiapas highlands and Pacific slopes, and associated hieroglphs. *HMAI 2*:237–275.

Miller, A. G.
    1973   *The mural painting of Teotihuacan*. Dumbarton Oaks Research Library and Collections. Washington, D.C.
    1982   *On the edge of the sea. Mural painting at Tancah-Tulum, Quintana Roo, Mexico*. Dumbarton Oaks Research Library and Collections. Washington, D.C.
    1991   The carved stela in Tomb 5, Suchiquitongo, Oaxaca, Mexico. *Ancient Mesoamerica 2*(2):215–224.

Miller, M. E.
    1985a   Tikal, Guatemala: A rationale for the placement of the funerary pyramids. *Expedition, Bulletin of the University of Pennsylvania 27*(3)6–15.
    1985b   A re-examination of Mesoamerican Chacmool. *The Art Bulletin* LXVII:7–17.
    1986   *The murals of Bonampak*. Princeton, New Jersey: Princeton University Press.
    1988a   The meaning and function of the main acropolis, Copán. In Boone and Willey, 149–194.
    1988b   The boys in the Bonampak band. In Benson and Griffin, 318–330.

Millon, C.
    1966   The history of mural art at Teotihuacan. Paper presented at 11th Mesa Redonda, Mexico, D.F.
    1973   Painting, writing and polity at Teotihuacan. *AA 8*:294–314.
    1988   A re-examination of the Teotihuacan tassel headdress insignia. In Berrin, 114–134.

Millon, R.
    1955   When money grew on trees. Ph.D. dissertation. Department of Anthropology, Columbia University, New York.

1973   The Teotihuacan map. In *Urbanization at Teotihuacan, Mexico*, Vol. 1, part 1, Text edited by R. Millon. Austin, Texas: University of Texas Press.

1981   Teotihuacan: city, state and civilization. In *HMAI Supplement 1: Archaeology:*198–243.

1988a   The last years of Teotihuacan. In *The collapse of ancient states and civilization*, edited by N. Yoffee and G. L. Cowgill. Tucscon: University of Arizona Press. 102–175.

1988b   Where do they all come from? The provenance of the Wagner murals from Teotihuacan. In Berrin, 78–113.

Millon, R., R. B. Drewitt, and G. L. Cowgill

1973   The Teotihuacan map. In *Urbanization at Teotihuacan, Mexico*, Vol. 1, Part 2, edited by R. Millon. Austin: University of Texas Press. *Maps*

Moholy-Nagy, H.

1978   The utilization of Pomacea snails at Tikal, Guatemala. *AA 43:*66–73.

Moholy-Nagy, H., and F. W. Nelson

1990   New data on sources of obsidian artifacts from Tikal, Guatemala. *Ancient Mesoamerica. 1:*71–80.

Molina-Montes, A.

1982   Archaeological buildings: Restoration or misrepresentation. In *Falsifications and misreconstructions of Pre-Columbian art*, edited by E. H. Boone. Dumbarton Oaks Research Library and Collections. Washington, D.C. 125–141.

Monzón, A.

1949   *El calpulli en la organizacion social de los Tenochca*. Mexico, D.F. *UNAM*, Instituto de Historia.

Morley, S. G.

1915   An introduction to the study of Maya hieroglyphs. *Bureau of American Ethnology, Bulletin 57.*

Morley, S. G.

1937-   *The Inscriptions of Petén*. Carnegie Institution of Washington. Publication 437. 5 vols.
1938

Morley, S. G., G. W. Brainerd, and R. J. Sharer

1983   *The ancient Maya*, Fourth Edition. Stanford, California: Stanford University Press.

Morris, E. H., G. Charlot, and A. A. Morris

1931   The Temple of the Warriors at Chichén Itzá, Yucatán. *Carnegie Institution of Washington, Publication 406.* (2 Vols.)

Moser, C. L.

1973   Human decapitation in ancient Mesoamerica. Dumbarton Oaks Research Library and Collections. Washington, D.C. *Studies in Pre-Columbian art and archaeology* No. 11.

1977   The head effigies of the Mixteca Baja. *Katunob 10*(2):1–118.

1983   The Middle Classic Ñuíñe style of the Mixteca Baja, Oaxaca. In Flannery and Marcus, 211–213.

Mountjoy, J. B.

1978   Prehispanic cultural contact on the south-central coast of Nayarit. In *Mesoamerican communication routes and cultural contacts*, edited by T. A. Lee and C. Navarrete. *PNWAF* 40:127–139.

Mountjoy, J. B., and D. Peterson

1973   Man and land at prehispanic Cholula. *Vanderbilt University Publications in Anthropology* No. 4.

Mountjoy, J. B., and J. P. Smith

1985   An archaeological patolli from Tomatlán, Jalisco, Mexico. In Folan, Jr. 240–262.

Munera, B. C.
1989   Una forma de lenguaje en Teotihuacan expresado en la ceramica ritual. In *Proceedings of the 46th International Congress of Americanists, Amsterdam, 1988*, edited by J. Galarza. *BAR International Series 518*(2):273–278.

Nagao, D.
1989   Public proclamation in the art of Cacaxtla and Xochicalco. In Diehl and Berlo, 63–104.

Nations, J. D.
1979   Snail shells and maize preparation: A Lacandón Maya analogy. *AA 44*:568–571.

Navarrete, C.
1974   The Olmec rock carvings at Pijijiapan, Chiapas, Mexico and other Olmec pieces from Chiapas and Guatemala. *PNWAF* No. 3.

Neal, L. A., and P. C. Weigand
n.d.   The salt procurement industry of the Atoyac Basin, Jalisco. Paper presented at American Anthropological Association meeting, New Orleans, Louisiana, 1991.

Neff, H., and R. L. Bishop
1988   Plumbate origins and development. *AA 53*(3):505–522.

Nelson, B. A.
1990   Observaciones acerca de la presencia tolteca en La Quemada, Zacatecas. In *Mesoamerica y el norte de Mexico, siglo, IX-XII*. Federica Sodi Miranda, Coordinadora. *MNA, INAH 2*:521–540.
n.d.   Outposts of Mesoamerican empire and domestic patterning a La Quemada, Zacatecas, Mexico. In *Culture and contact: Essays in honor of Charles C. Dipeso*, edited by A. I. Woosley and J. C. Ravesloot. Albuquerque: University of New Mexico Press. (In press.)

Nelson, F. W., Jr.
1973   Archaeological investigations at Dzibilnocać, Campeche, Mexico. *PNWAF* No. 33.

Nichols, D. L., M. W. Spence, and M. D. Borland
1991   Watering the fields of Teotihuacan: Early irrigation at the ancient city. *Ancient Mesoamerica 2*(1):119–129.

Nicholson, H. B.
1973   The late prehispanic central Mexican (Aztec) iconographic system. In *The iconography of Middle American sculpture*. New York: The Metropolitan Museum of Art. Pp. 72–97.
1978   Western Mesoamerica A.D. 900–1520. In *Chronologies in New World archaeology*, edited by R. E. Taylor and C. W. Meighan. New York: Academic Press. Pp. 285–329.
1982   Revelation of the Great Temple. *Natural History 91*(7):48–58.
1987   The Mixteca-Puebla concept revisited. In Boone, 227–254.

Niederberger, C.
1976   Zohapilco, cinco milenios de ocupación humana en un sitio lacustre de la cuenca de México. *Departamento de Prehistoria. Colección Científica* No. 30 *INAH*.
1986   Excavación de una area de habitación doméstica en la capital "Olmeca": de Tlacozotitlán. Reporte preliminar. In *Arqueología e etnohistoria del estado de Guerrero*. Mexico, D.F. *INAH*:83–103.
1987   Paleopaysages et archeologie pre-urbaine du bassin de Mexico. *Collection Etudes Mesoamericaines* 1–11. CEMCA, Mexico (2 Vols.)

Noguera, E.

1942 Exploraciones en El Opeño, Michoacán. *Proceedings 27th International Congress of Americanists:* 574–586.

1950 El horizonte Tolteca-Chichimeca. Enciclopedia Mexicana de Artes. No. 4. Mexico, D.F. Ediciones Mexicana.

1965 La cerámica arqueológica de Mesoamerica. *UNAM Instituto de Investigaciones Historicas* No. 86.

Oliveros, J. A.

1974 Nuevas exploraciones en El Opeño, Michoacán. In *The archaeology of west Mexico*, edited by B. Bell. Ajijíc, Jalisco, Mexico: West Mexican Society for Advanced Study. Pp. 182–201.

Paddock, J.

1966 Oaxaca in ancient Mesoamerica. In *Ancient Oaxaca, discoveries in Mexican archaeology and history*, edited by J. Paddock. Stanford, California: Stanford University Press. Pp. 83–242.

1972 Distribución de rasqos teotihuacanos en Mesoamerica. In *Teotihuacan: XI Mesa Redonda de la Sociedad Mexicana de Antropología*. Mexico. Pp. 223–239.

1978 The Middle Classic Period in Oaxaca. In *Middle Classic Mesoamerica* A.D. 400–700, edited by E. Pasztory. New York: Columbia University Press. Pp. 45–62.

1983a Monte Albán II in the Yagul-Caballito Blanco area. In Flannery and Marcus, 115–117.

1983b The Oaxaca barrio at Teotihuacan. In Flannery and Marcus, 170–175.

Parsons, L. A.

1969 Bilbao, Guatemala: An archaeological study of the Pacific Coast Cotzumalhuapa region, Vol.2. Milwaukee: Milwaukee Public Museum. *Publications in Anthropology*, 12.

1981 Post-Olmec stone sculpture: the Olmec-Izapan transition on the Pacific Coast and highlands. In Benson: 257–288.

1986 The origins of Maya art: Monumental stone sculpture of Kaminaljuyú, Guatemala, and the southern Pacific coast. Dumbarton Oaks Research Library and Collections. Washington, D.C. *Studies in Pre-Columbian Art and Archaeology* 28.

1988 Proto-Maya aspects of Miraflores-Arenal monumental sculpture from Kaminaljuyu and the southern Pacific Coast. In Benson and Griffin: 6–43.

Pasztory, E.

1972 The historical and religious significance of the Middle Classic ball game. In *XII Mesa Redonda, Mexico*. Sociedad Mexicana de Antropología: 441–455.

1976a *The murals of Tepantitla, Teotihuacan*. New York and London: Garland Publishing, Inc.

1976b The Xochicalco stelae and a Middle Classic deity triad in Mesoamerica. *XXIII International Congress of the History of Art 1:*185–215. Granada, 1973.

1983 *Aztec art*. New York: H. N. Abrams, Inc.

1988a A reinterpretation of Teotihuacan and its mural painting tradition. In Berrin, 45–47.

1988b Feathered serpents and flowering trees with glyphs. In Berrin, 136–161.

1988c The Aztec Tlaloc: God of antiquity. In *Smoke and mist: Mesoamerican studies in honor of Thelma S. Sullivan*, edited by J. K. Josserand and K. Daken. *BAR International Series* Oxford, England 402(1):289–327.

1990 El poder militar como realidad y restorica en Teotihuacan. In Caŕdos de Méndez: 18–201.

n.d.a   Abstraction and the rise of a utopian state at Teotihuacan. Paper presented at "The Art and Polity of Teotihuacan," a conference at Dumbarton Oaks, Washington, D.C. in 1988. (In Press.)

n.d.b   The natural world as a civic metaphor at Teotihuacan. (In Press.)

Paulsen, A.

1977   Patterns of maritime trade between south coastal Ecuador and western Mesoamerica, 1500 B.C.–A.D. 600. In *The sea in the Pre-Columbian world*, edited by E. P. Benson. Dumbarton Oaks Research Library and Collections. Washington, D.C. Pp. 41–160.

Pearsall, D. M., and D. R. Piperno

1990   Antiquity of maize cultivation in Ecuador: Summary and reevaluation of the evidence. *AA* 55(2):324–337.

Pendergast, D. M.

1969   Altun Há, British Honduras (Belize): The sun god's tomb. *Royal Ontario Museum of Art and Archaeology, Occasional Paper* No. 19.

1979–   *Excavations at Altun Há, Belize, 1964–1970*, Vol. 1. Toronto: Royal Ontario Museum.
1982

1981   Lamanai, Belize: summary of excavation results 1977–1980. *JFA* 8(1):29–53.

1982   Ancient Maya mercury. *Science 217:533–535*.

1985   Stability through change: Lamanai, Belize, from the ninth to the seventeenth century. In Sabloff and E. W. Andrews V, 223–250.

1990   Up from the dust: The central lowlands Postclassic as seen from Lamanai and Marco González, Belize. In Clancy and Harrison, 169–179.

Peterson, K. A.

1985   Observations on the IK windows at Palenque. *Fifth Palenque round table*, Merle Greene Robertson (general editor) and Virginia M. Fields (volume editor). San Francisco: The Pre-Columbian Art Research Institute. Pp. 19–27.

Piña Chan, R.

1955a   Chalcatcingo, Morelos. *Informes* 4. Mexico, D.F.: *INAH*.

1955b   Las culturas preclásicas de la cuenca de México. Mexico, D.F: Fondo de Cultura Económica.

1958   *Tlatilco*. Mexico, D.F: *INAH* Serie Investigaciones 1, Part 1.

1960   Mesoamerica. *INAH Memorias* 6.

1968   *Jaina*. Mexico, D.F: *INAH*.

1975   *Teotenango: El antiquo lugar de la muralla*. Gobierno del Estado de Mexico. Dirección de Turismo. (2 Vols.)

1990   Inicios de la escritera zapoteca. In Cárdos de Méndez: 71.

Pollard, H. P.

1991   The construction of ideology in the emergence of the prehispanic Tarascan state. *Ancient Mesoamerica* 2(2):167–179.

Pollock, H. E. D., R. L. Roys, and A. L. Smith

1962   Mayapán, Yucatán, Mexico. *Carnegie Institution of Washington*, Publication 619.

Porter, M. N.

1953   Tlatilco and the Pre-Classic cultures of the New World. *Viking Fund Publications in Anthropology* No. 19.

1956   Excavations at Chupícuaro, Guanajuato, Mexico. *APS* Transactions 46, Part 5.

Porter Weaver, M. N.

1967   Tlapacoya pottery in the museum collection. *Indian Notes and Monographs, Miscellaneous Series* No. 56. New York: Museum of the American Indian, Heye Foundation.

1969   A reappraisal of Chupícuaro. In *The Natalie Wood collection of Pre-Columbian ceramics from Chupícuaro, Guanajuato, Mexico*, edited by J. R. Frierman. Los Angeles, California: University of California: Pp. 3–15; 81–92.

Proskouriakoff, T.

1946   An album of Maya architecture. *Carnegie Institution of Washington, Publication 558.*

1950   A study of Classic Maya sculpture. *Carnegie Institution of Washington*, Publication 593.

1960   Historical implications of a pattern of dates at Piedras Negras, Guatemala. *AA 25:*454–475.

1961   The lords of the Maya realm. *Expedition: Bulletin of the University of Pennsylvania 4*(1):14–21.

Puleston, D. E.

1971   An experimental approach to the function of Maya *chultuns*. *AA36:*322–335.

1977   The art and archaeology of hydraulic agriculture in the Maya lowlands. In Hammond: 449–467.

1979   An epistemological pathology and the collapse, or why the Maya kept the Short Count. In Hammond and Willey, 63–71.

Puleston, D. E., and D. W. Callendar, Jr.

1967   Defensive earthworks at Tikal. *Expedition: Bulletin of the University of Pennsylvania 9*(3):40–48.

Pye, M. E., and A. A. Demarest

1991   The evolution of complex societies in southeastern Mesoamerica: New evidence from El Mesak, Guatemala. In Fowler, Jr., 77–100.

Quirarte, J.

1973   Izapan style art: a study of its form and meaning - *Studies in Pre-Columbian Art and Archaeology No. 10* Washington, D.C. Dumbarton Oaks.

1982   The Santa Rita murals: A review. In *Aspects of the Mixteca-Puebla style and Mixtec and central Mexican culture in southern Mesoamerica*. New Orleans, Louisiana: *Tulane University Occasional Paper 4:*43–55.

Rands, R.

1977   The rise of Classic Maya civilization in the northwestern zone: Isolation and integration. In R. E. W. Adams, 159–180.

Rands, R. L., and R. E. Smith

1965   Pottery of the Guatemalan highlands. In *HMAI 2:*95–145.

Rathje, W. L.

1971   The origin and development of lowland Classic Maya civilization. *AA 36:*275–285.

Rattray, E. C.

1987a   Introduction. In *Teotihuacan: Nuevos datos, nuevas síntesis, nuevos problemas*, edited by E. McClung de Tapia and E. C. Rattray. *UNAM:*9–55.

1987b   Los barrios foraneos de Teotihuacan. In *Teotihuacan: Nuevos datos, nuevas síntesis, nuevos problemas*, edited by E. McClung de Tapia and E. C. Rattray. *UNAM:* 243–273.

1989   El barrio de los comerciantes y el conjunto Tlamimilolpa, un estudio comparativo. *INAH: Arqueología* 5:105–129.

1990   Nuevos hallazgos sobre los orígenes de la cerámica anaranjado delgado. In Cárdos de Méndez, 59–106.

Recinos, A.

1950   *Popol Vuh: The sacred book of the ancient quiché Maya.* Norman, Oklahoma: University of Oklahoma Press.

Redmond, E. M.

1983   A fuego y sangre: Early Zapotec imperialism in the Cuicatlán Cañada, Oaxaca. Ann Arbor: University of Michigan. *Museum of Antropology, Memoirs* No. 16.

Reilly III, F. K.

1990   Cosmos and rulership: The function of Olmec-style symbols in Formative Mesoamerica. In *Visible language*, special edition, *The emergence of writing in Mesoamerica*. Providence: Rhode Island School of Design. Vol. XXIX, No. 1

n.d.   Enclosed ritual spaces and the watery underworld in Formative Period architecture: New observations on the function of La Venta Complex A. Manuscript.

Reyna Robles, R. M., and F. Rodríguez B.

1990   La época clásica en el estado de Guerrero. In Cárdos de Méndez, 221–236.

Rice, D. S., and P. M. Rice

1984   Collapse to contact: Postclassic archaeology of the Petén Maya. *Archaeology 37*(2):46–51.

Richardson, F. B.

1940   Non-Maya monumental sculpture of Central America. In *The Maya and their neighbors*, edited by C. Hay. New York: Appleton. Pp. 395–416.

Riese, B.

1986   Late Classic relationship between Copán and Quiriguá: Some epigraphic evidence. In Urban and Schortman, 94–101.

1988   Epigraphy of the southeast zone in relation to other parts of Mesoamerica. In Boone and Willey, 67–94.

Robertson, M. G.

1975   Stucco techniques employed by ancient sculptors of the Palenque piers. *Actas del XLI Congreso Internacional de Americanistas, México 1*:449–472.

1977   Painting practices of the Palenque stucco sculptors. In Hammond, 297–326.

1983   *The Temple of the Inscriptions. The Sculpture of Palenque.* Vol. 1. Princeton: Princeton University Press.

1991   The Pre-Columbian Art Research Institute Newsletter (San Francisco):13.

Robertson, M. G., M. S. R. Scandizzo, M. D., and J. R. Scandizzo, M. D.

1976   Physical deformities in the ruling lineage of Palenque and the dynastic implications. *Segunda mesa redonda de Palenque*, edited by Merle Greene Robertson. Pebble Beach, California: The Robert Louis Stevenson School. Pp. 59–86.

Robles, C. F., and A. P. Andrews

1986   A review and synthesis of recent Postclassic archaeology in northern Yucatán. In Sabloff and Andrews V, 53–98.

Roys, R. L.

1933   The book of Chilam Balam of Chumayel. *Carnegie Institution of Washington*, Publication 438.

1965   Lowland Maya native society at Spanish contact. *HMAI 3*:659–678.

Rubín de la Borbolla, D. F.

1944   Orfebrería tarasca. *Cuadernos Americanos 3*:127–138.

Rue, D. J.

1989   Archaic Middle American agriculture and settlement: Recent pollen data from Honduras. *JFA 16*(2):177–184.

Rust III, W. F., and B. W. Leyden

n.d.   Evidence of maize use at early and middle Preclassic La Venta Olmec sites. In *Corn and culture in the prehistoric New World*, edited by C. Hastorf and S. Johannessen. Minneapolis, Minnesota: Westview Press. (In Press.)

Rust III, W. F., and R. J. Sharer
    1988   Olmec settlement data from La Venta, Tabasco, Mexico. *Science 242:* 102–104.
Ruz Lhuillier, A.
    1951   Chichén Itzá y Palenque, ciudades fortificadas. In *Homenaje al doctor Alfonso Caso.*
            Mexico, D. F. Imprenta Nuevo Mundo, S. A:331–342.
    1960   *Palénque, official guide,* Mexico, D. F. *INAH.*
    1963   *Uxmal, official guide.,* Mexico, D. F. *INAH.*
Sabloff, J. H.
    1990   *The new archaeology and the ancient Maya.* New York: Scientific American Library.
Sáenz, C. A.
    1961   Tres estelas en Xochicalco. *RMEA 17:*39–65.
Sahagún, Fray B. de
    1946   *Historia General de las Cosas de Nueva Espana.* Mexico, D.F. Editorial Nueva España.
            3 vols.
    1950–   *Florentine Codex: General history of the things of New Spain,* translated by C. H. Dibble
        1982 and A. J. O. Anderson. Santa Fé: School of American Research and the University
            of Utah. (12 Vols.)
Salazar, P.
    1966   Maqueta prehispánica teotihuacana. *INAH Bulletin 23:*4–11.
Sanders, W. T.
    1973   The cultural ecology of the lowland Maya: A reevaluation. In Culbert, 325–365.
    1977   Ethnographic analogy and the Teotihuacan horizon style. In Sanders and Michels,
            397–410.
    1981   Ecological adaptations in the Basin of Mexico: 23,000 B.C. to the present. In *HMAI
            Supplement 1: Archaeology:*147–97.
Sanders, W. T., and J. W. Michels
    1969   *The Pennsylvania State University Kaminaljuyú Project 1968 Season, Part 1. The Ex-
            cavations.* Pennsylvania State University, Occasional Papers in Anthropology
            No.2.
Sanders, W. T., and C. N. Murdy
    1982   Cultural evolution and ecological succession in the Valley of Guatemala: 1500 B.C.–
            A.D. 1524. In *Maya subsistence: Studies in memory of Dennis E. Puleston,* edited by
            K. V. Flannery. New York: Academic Press. Pp.19–63.
Sanders, W. T., and D. L. Nichols
    1988   Ecological theory and cultural evolution in the Valley of Oaxaca. *Current Anthropology
            2:*33–80.
Sanders. W. T., J. R. Parsons, and R. S. Santley
    1979   *The Basin of Mexico: Ecological processes in the evolution of a civilization.* New York:
            Academic Press.
Sanders, W. T., and B. J. Price
    1968   *Mesoamerica: the evolution of a civilization.* New York: Random House.
Sanders, W. T., and R. Santley
    1983   A tale of three cities: Energetics and urbanization in prehispanic central Mexico. In
            Prehistoric settlement patterns: Essays in honor of Gordon R. Willey, edited by E. Vogt
            and R. Leventhal. Albuquerque, New Mexico: University of New Mexico Press.
            Pp.243–291.
Santley, R. S.
    1983   Obsidian trade and Teotihuacan influence in Mesoamerica. In Miller, 69–124.

1989   Obsidian working, long-distance exchange and the Teotihuacan presence on the
          south Gulf Coast. In Diehl and Berlo, 131–152.

Santley, R. S., J. M. Kerley, and R. R. Kneebone
1986   Obsidian working, long-distance exchange, and the politico-economic organization
          of early states in central Mexico. In *Economic aspects of prehispanic highland Mexico*,
          edited by B. L. Isaac. Research in Economic Anthropology, Supplement 2. Green-
          wich: JAI Press. Pp.101–132.

Scarborough, V. L., B. Mitchem, H. S. Carr, and D. A. Freidel
1982   Two late Preclassic ball courts at the lowland Maya center of Cerros, northern
          Belize. *JFA* 9:21–34.

Schele, L.
1976   Accession iconography of Chan-Bahlum in the Group of the Cross at Palenque.
          Segunda mesa redonda de Palenque, edited by Merle Greene Robertson. Pebble Beach,
          California: The Robert Louis Stevenson School. 9–34.
1987   Stela I and the founding of the city of Copán. *Copán note 30*. Copán, Honduras:
          Copán Mosaics Project and the Instituto Hondureño de Antropología e Historia.
1988   The Xibalbá shuffle: A dance after death. In Benson and Griffin, 294–317.

Schele, L., and D. Freidel
1990   *A forest of kings: The untold story of the ancient Maya*. New York: William Morrow and
          Co., Inc.

Schele L., and M. E. Miller
1986   *The blood of kings: Dynasty and ritual in Maya art*. Fort Worth, Texas: Kimbell Art
          Museum.

Schmidt S., P.
1986   Sequencia arqueológica de Xochipala. In *Arqueología e ethnohistoria del estado de Guer-
          rero*. Mexico, D. F. *INAH*:107–115.
1990   *Arqueología de Xochipala, Guerrero. UNAM*.

Schortman, E. M., and P. Urban
1991   Patterns of late Preclassic interaction and the formation of complex society in the
          southeast Maya periphery. In Fowler, Jr., 121–142.

Séjourné, L.
1966   *Arqueología y pintura en Teotihuacan*. Mexico, D. F.: Siglo Veintiuno.

Serra Puche, M. C.
1988   Los recursos lacustres de la cuenca de Mexico durante el Formativo. *UNAM* Instituto
          de Investigaciones Antropológicas.

Sharer, R. J., J. C. Miller, and L. P. Traxler
1992   Evolution of Classic Period architecture in the eastern Acropolis, Copán. *Ancient
          Mesoamerica* 3(1):145–159.

Sharer, R. J.
1978a   Archaeology and history at Quiriguá, Guatemala. *JFA* 5(1):51–70.
1978b   *The prehistory of Chalchuapa, El Salvador*. Philadelphia: University of Pennsylvania.
          (3 Vols.)
1983   Interdisciplinary approaches to the study of Mesoamerican highland-lowland interac-
          tion: A summary view. In Miller, 241–263.
1985   Archaeology and epigraphy revisited. An archaeological enigma and the origins of
          Maya writing. *Expedition: Bulletin of the University of Pennsylvania* 27(3):16–19.
1989a   The Preclassic origins of Maya writing: A highland perspective. In Hanks and Rice,
          165–175.

1989b   The Olmec and the southeast periphery of Mesoamerica. In Sharer and Grove, 247–271.

1990   *Quiriguá: A Classic Maya center and its sculptures*. Durham, North Carolina: Academic Press.

1992   The Preclassic origin of lowland Maya states. In *New theories on the ancient Maya*, edited by E. C. Danien and R. J. Sharer. Philadelphia, University of Pennsylvania. University Museum Symposium Series (3):132–136.

Sharer, R. J., and D. W. Sedat

1987   *Archaeological investigations in the northern Maya highlands Guatemala: Interaction and the development of Maya civilization*. Philadelphia: University Museum, University of Pennsylvania.

Sheehy, J. J.

1991   Structure and change in a late Classic domestic group at Copán, Honduras. *Ancient Mesoamerica* 2(1):1–19.

Sheets, P. D.

1982   Prehistoric agricultural systems in El Salvador. In *Maya subsistence: Studies in memory of Dennis E. Puleston*, edited by K. V. Flannery. New York: Academic Press. Pp.99–118.

Sheets, P. D.

1984   *Archaeology and vulcanism in Central America: The Zapotitán Valley of El Salvador*, edited by P. D. Sheets, Austin: University of Texas Press.

Shook, E. M.

1957   The Tikal Project. Philadelphia, Pennsylvania. *The University Museum Bulletin*, 21(3):36–52.

1958   The Temple of the Red Stela. *Expedition: Bulletin of the University of Pennsylvania* 1(1):26–33.

Shook, E. M., and A. V. Kidder

1952   Mound E-III-3, Kaminaljuyú, Guatemala. *Carnegie Institution of Washington, Contribution* 53.

Siller, J. A.

1984   Presencia de elementos arquitectónicos teotihuacanoides en occidente: Tingambato, Michoacán. In *Cuadernos de arquitectura mesoamericana*. *UNAM*, Facultad de arquitectura (2):60–65.

Sisson, E. B.

1973   *First annual report of the Coxcatlán Project. Tehuacán Project Report* No. 3. Andover, Massachusetts: R. S. Peabody Foundation for Archaeology, Philips Academy.

Smith, A. L.

1977   Patolli at the ruins of Seibal, Petén, Guatemala. In Hammond, 349–363.

Smith, A. L., and A. V. Kidder

1951   Excavations at Nebaj, Guatemala. *Carnegie Institution of Washington, Publication* 594.

Smith, Mary E.

1983   The Mixtec writing system. In Flannery and Marcus, 238–245.

Smith, Michael E.

1990   Long-distance trade under the Aztec empire: The archaeological evidence. *Ancient Mesoamerica* 1:153–169.

Smith, Michael E., and C. M. Heath-Smith

1980   Waves of influence in Postclassic Mesoamerica? A critique of the Mixteca-Puebla concept. *Anthropology* 4(2):15–50.

Smith, R. E., and J. C. Gifford
    1965   Pottery of the Maya lowlands. In *HMAI 2*:498–534.
Solís O., F.
    1989   Un nuevo *cuauhxicalli* descubierto en la ciudad de México. *MNA Boletín informativo* No. 4:10–11.
Soustelle, J.
    1964   *The daily life of the Aztecs*. London: Pelican Books.
Spence, M. W.
    1989   Excavaciones recientes en Tlailotlaca, el barrio oaxáqueño de Teotihuacan. *INAH, Arqueología 5*:82–104.
Spencer, C. S.
    1982   The Cuicatlán Cañada and Monte Albán. New York: Academic Press.
Spores, R.
    1967   *The Mixtec kings and their people*. Norman: University of Oklahoma Press.
    1984   *The Mixtecs in ancient and colonial times*. Norman: University of Oklahoma Press.
Stark, B. L., and V. Voorhies (editors)
    1978   *Prehistoric coastal adaptations: The economy and ecology or maritime Middle America*. New York: Academic Press.
Stern, T.
    1948   The rubber-ball game of the Americas. New York: J. J. Augustin. *American Ethnological Society Monograph* 17.
Stirling, M. W.
    1943   Stone Monuments of Southern Mexico. *Bureau of American Ethnology, Bulletin 138*.
Stocker, T., B. Jackson, and H. Riffell
    1986   Wheeled figurines from Tula, Hidalgo, Mexico. *Mexicon, 8*(4):69–73.
Stromsvik, G.
    1947   Guide book to the ruins of Copán. *Carnegie Institution of Washington, Publication* 577.
Stuart, D.
    1988   The Río Azul cacao pot: Epigraphic observations on the function of a Maya ceramic vessel. *Antiquity 62*:153–157.
    1989   Hieroglyphs on Maya vessels. in *The Maya Vase Book*, by J. Kerr. New York; Kerr Associates, Inc. Vol. 1:149–160.
    1992   Hieroglyphs and archaeology at Copán. *Ancient Mesoamerica 3*(1):169–184.
Stuart, D., and S. D. Houston
    1989   Maya writing. *Scientific American* August:82–89.
Sugiyama, S.
    1989a   Iconographic interpretation of the Temple of Quetzalcoatl at Teotihacan, *Mexicon 11*(4):68–74.
    1989b   Burials dedicated to the old temple of Quetzalcoatl, Mexico. *AA 54*(1):85–106.
Tate, C.
    1985   Summer solstice ceremonies performed by Bird Jaguar III of Yaxchilán, Chiapas, Mexico. *UNAM Estudios de cultura Maya 16*:85–112.
    1989   Scribes, artists and workshops at Yaxchilán. *Seventh Palenque round table*, abstracts:66–68.
Taube, K. A.
    1989   The maize tamale in Classic Maya diet: Epigraphy and Art *AA 54*(1):31–51.
    1992   The Temple of Quetzalcoatl and the cult of sacred war at Teotihuacan. *RES 21*:53–87.

Tedlock, D.
1985   *Popol Vuh*. New York: Simon and Schuster.

Thompson, J. E. S.
1942   The civilization of the Mayas. Leaflet 25. Chicago, Illinois: Field Museum of Natural History, Anthropology.
1970   *Maya history and religion*. Norman: University of Oklahoma Press.
1974   Canals of the Rió Candelaria Basin, Campeche, Mexico. In Mesoamerican Archaeology: New approaches, edited by N.N. Hammond. Austin, Texas. University of Texas Press. 297–302.

Tolstoy, P.
1975   Settlement and population trends in the Basin of Mexico: Ixtapaluca and Zacatenco phases. *JFA 2*:331–349.
1980   Western Mesoamerica before A.D. 900. Manuscript.
1986   Trans-Pacific contacts: What, where and when? *The Quarterly Review of Archaeology* Vol. 7 No. 3:1–9.
1989a   Coapexco and Tlatilco sites with Olmec materials in the Basin of Mexico. In Sharer and Grove, 85–121.
1989b   Western Mesoamerica and the Olmec. In Sharer and Grove, 275–302.
1991   Paper route. *Natural History* June:6–14.

Tolstoy, P., and S. K. Fish
1975   Surface and subsurface evidence for community size at Coapexco, Mexico. *JFA 2*:97–104.

Tolstoy, P., S. K. Fish, M. W. Boksenbaum, K. B. Vaughn, and C. E. Smith
1977   Early sedentary communities of the Basin of Mexico. *JFA 4*:91–106.

Tolstoy, P., and L. I. Paradis
1971   Early and middle Preclassic culture in the Basin of Mexico. In *Observations on the emergence of civilization in Mesoamerica, Contributions of the University of California archaeological research facility*, edited by R. F. Heizer and J. A. Graham, No. 11:2–28.

Torquemada, J. de
1943   *Monarquía Indiana* (facsimile edition). Mexico, D. F: Editorial Chavez Hayhoe. (3 Vols.)

Toscano, S.
1952   *Arte Precolombino de México*, Mexico, D.F. *UNAM*.

Townsend, R. F.
1979   State and cosmos in the art of Tenochtitlán. Dubarton Oaks Research Library and Collections. Washington, D.C. *Studies in Pre-Columbian Art and Archaeology* No. 20.
1987   Malinalco and the lords of Tenochtitlán. In Boone, 111–140.

Tozzer, A. M.
1941   Landa's Relacion de las cosas de Yucatán, a translation. *Peabody Museum. Harvard University, Archaeological and Ethnological Papers* 18.
1957   Chickén Itzá and its cenote of sacrifice: A comparative study of contemporaveues Maya and Toltac. Peabody Museum of Archaeology and Ethnology. Harvard University, Cambridge, Massachusetts. Memories 11–12.

Troike, N. P.
1987   The interpretation of postures and gestures in the Mixtec códices. In Boone, 175–206.

Trombold, C. D.
1985   Conceptual innovations in settement pattern methodology on the northern Mesoamerican frontier. In Folan, Jr., 204–239.

1990   A reconsideration of chronology for the La Quemada portion of the northern Mes-
        oamerican frontier. *AA 55*(2):308–324.

Turner II, B. L.
1974   Prehistoric intensive agriculture in the Maya lowlands. *Science 185:*118–124.
1979   Prehispanic terracing in the central Maya lowlands. Problems of agricultural intensi-
        fication. In Hammond and Willey, 103–115.
1990   Population reconstruction for the central Maya lowlands; 1000 B.C.–A.D. 1500. In
        Culbert and Rice, 301–323.

Umberger, E.
1987   Events commemorated by date plaques at the Templo Mayor: Further thoughts on
        the solar metaphor. In Boone, 411–449.
1988   A reconsideration of some hieroglyphs on the Mexica Calendar Stone. In *Smoke and
        mist: Mesoamerican studies in honor of Thelma S. Sullivan*, edited by J. K. Josserand and
        K. Daken. *BAR International Series 402*(1):345–388.

Urban, P. A.
1986   Precolumbian settlement in the Naco Valley, northwestern Honduras. In Urban
        and Schortman, 275–295.

Urban, P. A., and E. M. Schortman
1988   The southeast zone viewed from the east: The Naco and lower Motagua valleys. In
        Boone and Willey, 223–267.

Vaillant, G. C.
1930   Excavations at Zacatenco. *American Museum of Natural History, Anthropological Papers*
        32:1–197.
1931   Excavations at Ticomán. *American Museum of Natural History, Anthropological Papers*
        32:199–439.
1935   Excavations at El Arbolillo. American Museum of Natural History, Anthropological
        Papers 35:137–379.

Valdés, J. A.
1988   Los mascarones preclásicos de Uaxactún: el caso del Grupo H. In *Primer simpósio
        mundial sobre epigrafía maya*. Guatemala City: Asociación Tikal. Pp.165–181.

Valdez, F., Jr., and S. B. Mock
1991   Additional considerations for prehispanic saltmaking in Belize. *AA 56*(3):520–525.

van Zantwijk, R. A. M.
1985   The Aztec arrangement: The social history of pre-Spanish Mexico. Norman: Univer-
        sity of Oklahoma Press.

Vlcek, D. T., and W. L. Fash
1986   Survey in the outlying areas of the Copán region and the Copán-Quiriguá "connec-
        tion." In Urban and Schortman, 102–113.

von Winning, H.
1987   La iconografía de Teotihuacan: los dioses y los signos. Mexico, D. F: *UNAM*.

Voorhies, B.
1976   The Chantuto people: An archaic period society of the Chiapas littoral, Mexico.
        PNWAF No. 41.
1989a   An introduction to the Soconusco and its prehistory. In Voorhies, 1–18.
1989b   Whither the king's traders? Reevaluating fifteenth century Soconusco as a port-of-
        trade. In Voorhies, 21–47.

Weaver, M. P. See Porter Weaver, M.
Webster, D.

1976   Lowland Maya fortifications. *Proceedings of the American Philosophical Society*, *120:*361–371.

1988   Copán as a Classic Maya center: In Boone and Willey, 5–30.

1990   The House of the Bacabs, Copán, Honduras, edited by D. Webster. Dumbarton Oaks Research Library and Collections. Washington, D.C. *Studies in Precolumbian Art and Archaeology* No. 29.

Weigand, P. C.

1974   The Ahualulco site and the shaft tomb complex of the Etzatlán area. In *The archaeology of west Mexico*, edited by B. Bell. Ajijic, Jalisco, Mexico: West Mexican Society for Advanced Study: 120–131.

1982   Mining and mineral trade in prehispanic Zacatecas. In *Mining and mining techniques in ancient Mesoamerica*, edited by P. C. Weigand and G. Gwynne. *Anthropology* 6(1–2): (special issue).

1985a   Evidence for complex societies during the western Mesoamerican Classic period. In Foster and Weigand, 47–91.

1985b   Considerations on the archaeology and ethnohistory of the Mexicaneros, Tequales, Coras, Huicholes, and Caxcanes of Nayarit, Jalisco, and Zacatecas. In Folan, Jr. 126–187.

1990   The Teuchitlán tradition of western Mesoamerica. In Cárdos de Méndez, 25–54,

1992   Los códices prehispánicos de la zona de Teuchitlán, Jalisco. *El Occidental* No. 352:3 Guadalajara, Jalisco, Mexico.

Weigand, P. C., and G. Harbottle

1987   The role of turquoises in the ancient Mesoamerican trade structure. Paper presented at the Society for American Archaeology, Toronto, 1987.

Weigand, P. C., G. Harbottle, and E. V. Sayre

1977   Turquoise sources and source analysis: Mesoamerica and the southwestern U.S.A. In *Exchange systems in prehistory*, edited by T. K. Earle and J. E. Ericson, New York: Academic Press: 15–34.

West, R. C.

1961   Aboriginal sea navigation between Middle and South America. *American Anthropologist 63:*133–135.

1964   The natural regions of Middle America. *HMAI 1:*363–383.

Wicke, C.

1976   Once more around the Tízoc stone: A reconsideration. *Actas del XLI Congreso Internacional de Americanistas*, Mexico. II:210–221.

Widmer, R. J.

1987   The evolution of form and function in a Teotihuacan apartment compound: The case of Tlajinga 33. In *Teotihuacan: Nuevos datos, nuevas síntesis, nuevos problemas*, edited by E. McClung and E. C. Rattray. *UNAM:*317–368.

Wilk, R. R., and W. Ashmore

1988   Household and community in the Mesoamerican past. In *Household and community in the Mesoamerican past*, edited by R. R. Wilk and W. Ashmore. Albuquerque, New Mexico: University of New Mexico Press. Pp.1–27.

Wilkerson, S. J.

1975   Pre-agricultural village life. The late preceramic period in Veracruz. *University of California Archaeological Research Facility Contribution* No. 27:111–122.

1980   Man's eighty centuries in Veracruz. *National Geographic Magazine 158*(2):203–231.

1984   In search of the Mountain of Foam: Human sacrifice in eastern Mesoamerica. In

Ritual human sacrifice in Mesoamerica, edited by E. Boone. Dumbarton Oaks Research Library and Collections. Washington D.C. 101–132.

Wilkinson, R. G., and M. C. Winter
1975   Cirugía craneal en Monte Albán. *INAH Boletín época* II(12):21–26.

Willey, G.R.
1973   The Altar de Sacrificios excavations: General summary and conclusions. Papers of the Peabody Museum of Archaeology and Ethnology, Harvard University, Cambridge, Massachusetts 64(3).

1974   The Classic Maya hiatus: A rehearsal for the collapse? In *Mesoamerican archaeology: New approaches*, edited by N. Hammond. Austin: University of Texas Press. Pp.313–334.

1977a   The rise of Classic Maya civilization: A Pasión Valley perspective. In R. E. W. Adams, 133–157.

1977b   The rise of Maya civilization: A summary view. In R. E. W. Adams, 383–423.

1980   Towards an holistic view of ancient Maya civilization. *Man 15*(2):249–266.

1986a   The Postclassic of the Maya lowlands: A preliminary overview. In Sabloff and Andrews V, 3–16.

1986b   The Classic Maya sociopolitical order: A study in coherence and instability. In *Research and reflections in archaeology and history: Essays in honor of Doris Stone*, edited by E. W. Andrews V. Tulane University, New Orleans: Middle American Research Institute Publication 57. Pp. 289–198.

Willey, G. R., W. R. Bullard, Jr., J. B. Glass, and J. C. Gifford
1965   Prehistoric Maya settlements in the Belize Valley. *Peabody Museum, Harvard University, Archaeological and Ethnological Papers* 54.

Willey, G. R., and D. B. Shimkin
1973   The Maya collapse: A summary view. In Culbert, 457–503.

Willey, G. R., and A. L. Smith
1969   The ruins of Altar de Sacrificios, Department of Petén, Guatemala, an introduction. *Peabody Museum, Harvard University, Archaeological and Ethnological Papers 62*(1).

Willey, G. R., A. L. Smith, G. Tourtellot III, and I. Graham
1975   Excavations at Seibal, Department of Petén, Guatemala. Introduction. The site and setting. *Memoirs of the Peabody Museum of Archaelogy and Ethnology*, Harvard University, Cambridge, Massachusetts. 13(1).

Winfield Capitaine, F.
1988   La Estela 1 de La Mojarra, Veracruz, Mexico. Center for Maya Research, Washington. *Research reports on ancient Maya writing* 16.

Winter, M.
1982   *Guia zona arqueológica de Yucuita*. Centro regional de Oaxaca. *INAH*.

1989   From Classic to Postclassic in prehispanic Oaxaca. In Diehl and Berlo, 123–130.

1990   El clásico en Oaxaca. In Cárdos de Méndez, 55–59.

Wolf, E. R.
1959   *Sons of the shaking earth*. Chicago, Illinois: University of Chicago Press.

Wonderley, A.
1991   The late Preclassic Sula Plain, Honduras; Regional antecedents to social complexity and interregional convergences in ceramic style. In Fowler, Jr., 143–170.

Wren, L. H., and P. Schmidt
1991   Elite interaction during the terminal Classic period.: New evidence from Chichén Itzá. In Culbert, 199–225.

Zeitlin, R. N.

1978 Long-distance exchange and the growth of a regional center. An example from the southern isthmus of Tehuantepec. In *Prehistoric coastal adaptations: The economy and ecology of maritime Middle America*, edited by B. L. Stark and B. Voorhies. New York: Academic Press. Pp.163–210.

1982 Toward a more comprehensive model of interregional commodity distribution: Political variables and prehistoric obsidian precurement in Mesoamerica. *AA* 47:260–275.

1990 The Isthmus and the Valley of Oaxaca: Questions about Zapotec imperialism in Formative Period Mesoamerica. *AA* 55(2):250–261.

AUTHOR INDEX

Numbers in italics refer to pages on which the complete reference appears.

A

Acosta, J. R., 86 (Fig. 4.7), 165, 385, 386, 393, 400, 404 (Fig. 7.10), 419 (Fig. 7.16), 421 (Fig. 7.17), 422 (Fig. 7.18), *497*

Acosta Saignes, M., 404, 471, 472, *497*

Adams, R. E. W., 134, 246, 253, 265, 266, 309, 337, 342, 464 (Fig. 8.25), *495, 497, 498*

Adams, R. M., 237, *495, 498*

Agurcia F. R., 279, 300, *498*

Anales de Cuauhtitlán 384, *498*

Anawalt, P. R., 467, 473, *498*

Andrews, A. P., 244, 334, 353, 357, 361, 363, 376, 377, 378, 379, 426, 485, *498, 526*

Andrews IV, E. W., 345, 350, *498*

Andrews V, E. W., 72, 112, 113, 115, 138, 232, 274, 290, 334, 344, 350, 351, 355, *497, 498, 499*

Andrews G. F., 135, 343, *499*

Angulo V. J., 43, 216, *499, 513*

Appel, J., 98, *501*

Araña A. R. M., 477, *510*

Armillas, P., 166, 187, 385, 470, *499*

Asaro, F., 131, *510*

Ashmore, W., 114, 238, 272, 274, 276, 291, 292, 293, 297, 301, 374, *499, 512, 533*

Aufdermauer, J., 42, *499*

Aveleyra, L., 8, 9 (Fig. 1.6), 10, 118, *499*

Aveni, A. F., 82, 191, 345, *499, 500*

B

Baird, E. T., 207, 209, 210, *500*

Ball, J. W., 138, 185, 236, 334, 342, 343, 344, 353, 355, 356, 357, *500*

Barba, P., 81, 83, *500*

Barlow, R. H., 439, *500*

Barnes, P. J., 138, *498*

Barrera A. J., 138, *498*

Barthel, T. S., 157, 160, *500*

Baudez, C. F., 112, 113, 274, 279, 280, *500*

Baus C. C., 210, *500*

Beadle, G. W., 14, *500*

Becquelin, P., 112, *500*

Bell, B., 96, *500*

Benfer, R. A., 385, *500*

Benjo, J. C., 301, *499*

Bennyhoff, J. A., 30, *512*

Benson, E. P., *496*

Benson, L., 53, 110, 111, *511*

Berdan, F. F., 471, 473, *498*, *500*

Berlin, H., 153, 158, 163, *501*

Berlo, J. C., 176, 177, 210, 215, 217, 218, 225, 334, 393, 457, *496*, *501*

Bernal, I., 33 (Fig. 3.4), 107, 118, 235 (Fig. 6.27), 477, *501*, *502*

Berrin, K., 80, 163 (Map 6.1), 172, 174, *496*

Bishop, R. L., 237, 408, *522*

Blake, M., 55, 56, 61, 68, *501*, *503*

Blanton, R. E., 98, 102, 218, 219, 220, 222, 223, 414, *501*, *509*

Boksenbaum, M. W., 30, 33, *501*, *531*

Boone, E. H., 209 (Fig. 6.14), *496*, *521*, *534*

Borland, M. D., 83, *522*

Bove, F. J., 231, *501*

Brainerd, G. W., 133, 150 (Fig. 5.6), 272, 275 (Fig. 6.37), 333, 345, 346, 351, 357, 362, 404 (Fig. 7.10), *501*, *521*

Brand, D. D., 434, 436, *501*

Braniff, B., 97, *501*

Bray, W., 200, 271, 303, 373, 406, 439, 461, 468, 473, *501*, *502*

Bronson, B., 243, *502*

Brown, K. L., 233, 234, *502*

Brueggemann, J., 225, *502*

Brush, C. F., 29, 202, *502*

Brush, E. S., 202, *502*

Buckingham, B., 82, *500*

Bullard, Jr., W. R., 135, *534*

Burger, R. L., 14, *502*

C

Cabrera Castro, R., 80, 89, 90, 91, 92, 234, 437, *502*

Callender, Jr., D. W., 252. *525*

Calnek, E. E., 470, *502*

Cárdos de Méndez, A., 361, *496*, *510*

Carlson, J. B., 60, 330, *502*

Carmack, R. M., 353, 433, *502*

Carneiro, R. L., 55, 241, *502*

Carr, H. S., 137, *502*

Carr, R. F., 264 (Fig. 6.36) *528*

Carrasco, P., 439, 441 (Fig. 8.7), 468, *503*

Caso, A., 33 (Fig. 3.4), 235 (Fig. 6.27), 419 (Fig. 7.16), 420, 439, 456 (Fig. 8.18), 465, 477, *503*

Cepeda, C. G., 118, *503*

Cervera, R. P., 377, *498*

Charlot, J., 421 (Fig. 7.17) *521*

Charlton, T. H., 83, 183, *502*

Chase, A. F., 122, 135, 238, 252, 255, 259, 266, 270, 334, 353, 357, 358, 360, 374, 430, *496*, *503*

Chase, D., 270, 357, 374, 430, *503*

Chávez, R., 81, 83, *500*

Cheek, C. D., 233, *503*

Clancy, F. S., 219, *496*, *503*

Clark, J. E., 55, 56, 61, 68, 243, *503*, *504*

Cliff, M. A., 135, *504*

Cobean, R. H., 182, 385, 420, *504*, *519*

Cobos, C., 377, *498*

Codex Borbónico, 458 (Fig. 8.19), 466 (Fig. 8.26), *504*

Codex Borgia, 462 (Fig. 8.23), *504*

Codex Dresden, 142, 143 (Fig. 5.1), 146 (Fig. 5.2), 426 (Fig. 8.1), *504*

Codex Féjévary Mayer, 466 (Fig. 8.26), *504*

Codex Florentino, 13 (Chapter heading), Sahagún *527*

Codex Grolier, 144, *see* M. D. Coe, 1973, *504*

Codex Laud, 456 (Fig. 8.17) *504*

Codex Magliabecchiano, 487 (end of text), *504*

Codex Matritense, 425 (Chapter heading), *see* Sahagún *527*

Codex Mendoza, 1 (Chapter heading), 77 (Chapter heading), 419 (Fig. 7.16), 455 (Fig. 8.16), 457, 458 (Fig. 8.19) 472, *504*

Codex Telleriano-Remensis, 141 (Chapter heading), 144, 466 (Fig. 8.26), *504*

Codex Tro-Cortesiano, 426 (Fig. 8.1), *504*

Codex Vaticanus A, 481 (Chapter heading), *504*

Coe, M. D., 10, 33 (3.4), 48, 53, 55, 58, 59, 60, 61, 66, 67, 118, 144, 155, 227, 323, 333, *504*, *505*

Coe, W. R., 11, 33, 123, 124, 126, 128, 257 (Fig. 6.31), 319, *505*

Coggins, C. C., 124, 128, 219, 250, 252, 283, 314, 359, 366, 373, 374, 375, 429, *505*

Cohodas, M., 344, 420, *505*

Cortés, H., 439, *506*

Covarrubias, M., 53, 464 (Fig. 8.25), *506*

Cowgill, G. L., 80, 83, 85, 86, 87, 89, 90, 91, 92, 163 (Map 6.1), 166, 182, 234, 241, 334, *506*, *521*

Culbert, T. P., 134, 240, 252, 259, 265, 266, 320, 333, 334, *496*, *506*

D

Dahlin, B. H., 242, *506*

Davies, C. N., 207, 217, 353, 385, 439, 477, 479, *506*

Demarest, A. A., 53, 69, 73, 111, 112, 115, 116, 120,

131, 133, 231, 232, 236, 244, 249, 250, 274, 276, 291, 303, 304, 307, 334, 483, *506, 507, 510, 517, 525*

Díaz del Castillo, B., 439, 464, 476, *507*

Dibble, C. E., 455, *507*

Diehl, R. A., 53, 56, 60, 61, 203, 227, 229, 334, 386, 387 (Map 7.1), 392, 399, 401, 408, *496, 505, 507*

Dillon, B. D., 246, 286, *507*

Dixon, E. J., 8, *507*

Drewitt, R. B., 80, 163 (Map 6.1), 182, *521*

Drucker, P., 33 (Fig. 3.4), 53, 58, 63, 66, 120, 299, 235 (Fig. 6.27), *507*

Dumond, D., 206, 241, *507, 508*

Durán, Fray D., 208, 266, 371, 399, 439, *508*

E

Eaton, J. D., 243, 337, *508*

Edwards, C., 201, 202, *508*

Ekholm, G. F., 202, 412, 413, *508*

Ekholm, S., 332, *508*

Epstein, J. F., 378, *508*

Espinosa, E. M., 109, *518*

Estrada, E., 55, *520*

Evans, C., 55, *520*

F

Fagan, B. M., 8, *508*

Fash, B. W., 274, 288, *499, 508*

Fash, W. L., 71, 113, 228, 274, 278, 279, 285, 287, 288, 289, 290, 293, *508, 509, 532*

Feinman, G., 98, 218, *501, 509*

Fernández, M. A., 245, *511*

Fialko C. V., 118, 128, 129, 236, 250, 251, *509, 517*

Fish, S. K., 30, 34, *531*

Flannery, K. V., 14, 15, 21, 49, 68, 98, 102, 103, 106, 107, 417, 477, *496, 509*

Fletcher, L. A., 355, *509*

Florance, C. A., 96, *509*

Flores, L., 81, 83, *500*

Foias, A. E., 244, *507*

Folan, Jr., W. J., 133, 134, 268, 355, *496, 510*

Fonserrada de Molina, M., 361, *510*

Forsyth, D., 138, *519*

Foster, M. S., 509, 533, *496*

Fowler, Jr., W. R., 131, 133, *496, 510*

Fox, J. W., 207, 213, 353, 354, 372, 376, 433, 434, *510*

Friedel, D. A., 109, 122, 123, 124, 128, 129, 133, 134, 135, 136, 137, 139, 250, 252, 255, 259, 266, 274, 279, 286, 290, 293, 303, 312, 313, 321, 322, 326, 332, 334, 344, 355, 359, 360, 361, 363, 369, 374, 376, 426, *510, 528*

Fry, R. E., 265, *506*

Furst, P. T., 96, *510*

G

Gallareta, N. F., 138, 377, *498*

Galinat, W. C., 14 (Fig. 2.1), *518*

Garber, J. F., 270, *512*

García Cook, A., 42, 80, 97, 205, 206, 207, 477, 510

Garza, T. S., 351, 355, 362, *516*

Gasco, J., 477, *510*

Gay, C., 48, *510*

Gibson, C., 475, *510*

Gifford, J. C., 33 (Fig. 33.4), 235 (Fig. 6.27), *530, 534*

Gillespie, S., 45, 439, 441 (Fig. 8.7), 467, 485, *511, 512*

Glascock, M., 182, *504*

Glass, J. B., 135, *534*

Gómez-Pompa, A., 245, *511*

González L., R., 53, 54, 62, 69, *511*

González Licón, E., 71, 139, *511*

Gorenstein, S., 418, 436, 486, *511*

Graham, I., 305, *534*

Graham, J. A., 69, 110, 111, 244, 318, 360, *511*

Green, D. F., 44, 201, *511*

Greengo, R. E., 28, *511*

Griffin, G. G., 48, 321, 326, *496, 511*

Grove, D. C., 43, 44, 45, 46, 47, 53, 245, *497, 511, 512*

Guderjan, T. H., 270, *512*

Guillén, A., 43, *512*

Gurr, D., 138, *519*

H

Hammond, N., 48, 137, 242, 243, 246, 270, 272, 273, 309, *496, 497, 512, 514*

Hansen, R. D., 73, *512*

Harbottle, G., 33, 191, 192, 409, 472, 501, *512, 533*

Harrison, P. D., 242, *496, 512*

Hassig, R., 439, 473, 485, *512*

Hartung, H., 82, 191, 345, *499, 500*

Hauck, F. R., 138, *519*

Haviland, W. A., 124, 127, 248, 265, *506, 512*

Hazard, J. E., 264, *502*

Healan, D. M., 386, 387 (Map 7.1), 388, 398 (Fig. 7.6), 400, 402, 403, (Fig. 7.9), 405, *512*

Healy, P. F., 70, *512, 519*

Heath-Smith, C. M., 410, *529*

Heizer, R. F., 30, 53, 63, 120, 244, *507, 512, 514*

Hellmuth, N. M., 265, 333, 360, *513*
Hers, M. A., 189, 193, 375, 389, *513*
Hester, T. R., 244, *511*, *514*
Heyden, D., 82, 299, 447, *513*
Hirth, K. G., 43, 45, 46, 80, 213, 216, 217, 300, 301,
    472, *497*, *513*
Historia de los mexicanos por sus pinturas, 384, 439, *513*
Historia Tolteca-Chichimeca, 384, 513
Hosler, D., 200, 201, 406, 438, *513*
Houston, S. D., 154, 303, 304, 305, *507*, *513*, *530*

I

Ixtlilxóchitl, F. de A., 384, 439, 440, 469, *513*

J

Jack, R. N., 244, *511*, *514*
Jackson, B., 405, *530*
Jackson, L., 258, *519*
Jennings, J. D., 7, 9 (Fig. 1.5), 11, 233, 235 (Fig. 6.27),
    514, *515*
Jiménez Moreno, W., 56, 385, 386, 439, *514*
Johnson, F., 9, *514*
Johnson, I. W., 245, *514*
Johnston, K., 305, *514*
Jones, C., 124, 125, 126, 127, 128, 129, 148, 154 (Fig.
    5.7), 254, 256, 258, 259, 263, 274, 291, 292, *514*
Joralemon, P. D., 66, *514*
Joyce, R. A., 302, *514*
Justeson, J. E., 56, 137, *514*

K

Kaufman, T., 179, *515*
Keber, E. Q., 384, 385, *515*
Kelley, D. H., 154, *515*
Kelley, E. A., 190, 193, *515*
Kelley, J. C., 82, 189, 191, 193, 292, *500*, *515*
Kelly, I., 26, 27, 34, 44, 75, 94, 201, 475, *515*
Kepecs, S. M., 272, *518*
Kerley, J. M., 182, *528*
Kerr, J., 154, 156, *515*
Kidder, A. V., 33 (Fig. 3.4), 117 (Fig. 4.17), 233, 235
    (Fig. 6.27). *515*, *529*
Kimberlin, J., 33, *501*
Kintz, E. R., 355, *509*
Kirchhoff, P., 1, 439, *515*
Kneebone, R. R., 182, *528*
Knorozov, Y. V., 153, *515*, *516*

Kolb, C. C., 182, *516*
Kosakowsky, L. J., 265, *506*
Kowalewski, S. A., 21, 98, 99, 102, 218, 219, 220, 222,
    414, *501*, *509*, *516*
Kowaleski, J. K., 227, 334, 345, 346, 347, 349, 353, 356,
    360, 376, 431, *516*
Krotser, G. R., 223, *516*
Krotser, P. H., 223, *516*
Kubler, G., 166, 170, 174, 176, 246, 320, 343, 366, 369,
    373, 420, *516*
Kurjack, E. B., 350, 351, 355, 362, *516*

L

Lackey, L. M., 181, *516*
Landa, *see* Tozzer, 1941, *531*
Lange, F. W., 232, *516*
Langenscheidt, A., 194, *516*
Langley, J. C., 80, 87, 172, 174, 176, 179, *517*
Laporte, J. P., 128, 129, 236, 250, 251, *517*
Larios, C. R., 285, *509*
Lathrap, D. W., 55, 243, *517*
Lee Jr., T. A., 53, 58, 60, 64, 109, 144, 243, *504*,
    517, *518*
León, N., 434, 437, *517*
León-Portilla, M., 469, *517*
Leventhal, R. M., 273, 274, 276, 283, 291, *517*
Leyden, B. W., 14, 54, 62, *526*
Lomas, R., 408, *507*
Longyear III, J. M., 235 (Fig. 6.27), *517*
López Austin, A., 88, *517*
López L. L., 88, *517*
Love, M. W., 69, *518*
Lowe, G. W., 33 (Fig. 3.4), 44, 53, 68, 72, 109, 201,
    511, *518*

M

MacKinnon, J. J., 272, *518*
MacNeish, R. S., 8, 9, 14, 16, 21, 23, 33 (Fig. 3.4),
    514, *518*
Maler, T., 123, *518*
Mandeville, M. D., 14 (Fig. 2.1), 229, *507*
Mangelsdorf, P. C., 14 (Fig. 2.1), *518*
Manzanilla, L. A., 80, 81, 83, *500*
Marcus, J., 21, 49, 50, 51, 98, 99, 100, 102, 104, 105
    (Fig. 4.14), 106, 222, 268, 414, 417, 418, 420, *496*,
    509, *518*

Marquina, I., 33 (Fig. 3.4), 251 (Fig. 6.29), 336 (Fig. 6.66), 421 (Fig. 7.17), 422 (Fig. 7.18), 464 (Fig. 8.25), *519*

Martínez Donjuan, G., 46, *519*

Mason, J. A., 33 (Fig. 3.4), *518*

Mastache, A. G., 385, 420, *519*

Matheny, R. T., 131, 138, *519*

Mathews, P., 303, 305, 321, 323, 332, *513*, *519*

Matos Moctezume, E., 386, 439, 450 (Fig. 5.10), 452 (Fig. 8.12), *519*

Maudslay, A. P., 123, 161 (Chapter heading), *519*

McGinn, J. J., 124, *505*

McKillop, H., 268, *519*

McVicker, D., 209, *520*

Meggers, B. J., 55, *520*

Meighan, C. W., 26, 28, 93, 201, 202, 410, *511*, *520*

Méndez M. E., 416, *520*

Merino C. B. L., 205, *510*

Mexicon 1987, 344, *520*

Mexicon 1988, 359, *520*

Michel, H., 131, *512*

Michels, J. W., 116, 233, *497*, *500*, *527*

Miksicek, C., 243, *510*

Miles, S. W., 111, *520*

Miller, A. G., 164, 170, 416, 429, *497*, *520*

Miller, J. C., 274, *528*

Miller, M. E., 64, 66, 124, 130, 148, 152, 209, 213, 215, 227, 248, 262, 274, 279, 280, 286, 288, 311, 312, 375, *520*, *528*

Millon, C., 170, 172, 174, 176, 177, 234, *520*

Millon, R., 80, 81, 82, 83, 87, 91, 92, 163 (Map 6.1), 168, 170, 175, 180, 182, 183, 184, 185, 204, 205, 219, 223, 244, *520*

Mitchum, B., 137, *528*

Mock, S. B., 272, *532*

Moholy-Nagy, H., 242, 244, *521*

Molina-Montes, A., 399, 400, *521*

Monzón, A., 468, *520*

Morley, S. G., 123, 133, 147 (Fig. 5.3), 150 (Fig. 5.6), 272, 275 (Fig. 6.37), 333, 345, 346, 351, 357, 362, *521*

Morris, A. A., 420 (Fig. 7.17), *521*

Morris, E. H., 420 (Fig. 7.17), *521*

Moser, C. L., 96, 217, 218, *521*

Mountjoy, J. B., 26, 206, 399, *521*, *522*

Muller, F., 206, *508*

Munera, B. C., 180, 181, *522*

Murdy, C. N., 233, *527*

N

Nagao, D., 210, 212, 215, 218, *522*

Nations, J. D., 242, *522*

Navarrete, C., 61, 68, *522*

Neal, L. A., 199, *522*

Neff, H., 237, 408, *522*

Neivens, M., 33, *501*

Nelson, B. A., 139, 189, 190, *521*

Nelson, Jr., F. W., 244, *522*

Nichols, D. L., 83, 102, *522*, *527*

Nicholson, H. B., 385, 439, 440, 445, 457, 461, 464, *522*

Niederberger, C., 20, 21, 29, 30 (Fig. 3.3), 37, 47, *522*

Noguera, E., 26, 28 (Fig. 3.1), 411, 464 (Fig. 8.25), *523*

Norman, W. M., 137, *514*

O

Oliveros, J. A., 26 (Fig. 3.1), *523*

Ortega G. R., 225, *502*

P

Paddock, J., 108, 217, 218, 222, *523*

Pahl, G. W., *497*

Palerm, A., 475, *515*

Palka, P., 285, *509*

Paradis, L. L., 30, 46, *531*

Parsons, J. R., 39, 40, 80, 109, 117, 118, 167, 180, 204, 205, 386, 411, 438, 444, *527*

Parsons, L. A., 133, 320, 333, *521*, *523*

Pasztory, E., 80, 81, 87, 168, 170, 171, 172, 173 (Fig. 6.5), 176, 204, 215, 227, 439, 457, 460, 484, *523*, *524*

Paulsen, A., 201, *524*

Pearsall, D. M., 14, *524*

Pendergast, D. M., 137, 244, 270, 271, 272, 433, *524*

Peterson, D. A., 206, *521*

Peterson, F. A., 23, *518*

Peterson, K. A., 330, *524*

Piña Chan, R., 19 (Fig. 2.4), 25 (Chapter heading), 29, 30, 33 (Fig. 3.4), 37, 100, 101, 194, 235 (Fig. 6.27), 361, 404 (Fig. 7.10), 437, 452, 464 (Fig. 8.25), *524*

Piperno, D. R., 14, *524*

Pollard, H. P., 194, 435, 436, 486, *511*, *524*

Pollock, H. E. D., 124 (Fig. 4.19), 426, *524*

Popul Vuh, 145; *See* Recinos, *525*; Tedlock, *531*

Porter, M. N., 33 (Fig. 3.4), 37, 96, *524*

Porter Weaver, M. N., 97, *524*

Price, B. J., 135, *527*

Proskouriakoff, T., 153, 318, 320, 338 (Fig. 6.67), 344, 354, *525*

Puleston, D. E., 124, 238, 241, 242, 252, 334, *525*

Pye, M. E., 69, *525*

Q

Quirarte, J., 109, 430, *525*

R

Rands, R. L., 33 (Fig. 3.4), 235 (Fig. 6.27), 331, *525*

Rathje, W. L., 135, *525*

Rattray, E. C., 80, 181, 184, 185, 230, *525*

Recinos, A., 145, *525*

Redmond, E. M., 104, *525*

Reilly III, F. K., 44, 48, 53, 64, 135, *526*

Relación de Michoacán, see León

Reyna Robles, R. M., 202, 203, *526*

Rice, D. S., 240, 353, 432, *496, 526*

Rice, P. M., 240, 353, 432, *496, 526*

Richardson, F. B., 296, *526*

Riese, B., 274, 279, 284, 286, *526*

Riffell, H., 405, *530*

Ringle III, W. M., 138, *498*

Robertson, M. G., 321, 322, 323, 326, 330, 332, *519, 526*

Robles C. F., 334, 353, 361, 363, 377, 378, 426, *498, 526*

Rodríquez B. F., 202, 203, *526*

Roys, R. L., 144, 377, 426, 431, *524, 526*

Rubín de la Borbolla, D. F., 437, *526*

Rue, D. J., 14, *526*

Rust III, W. F., 14, 53, 54, 62, *526, 527*

Ruz Lhuillier, A., 235 (Fig. 6.27), 325, 364, *527*

S

Sabloff, J. A., 334, 344, 349, 353, 355, 376, 426, 485, *497, 499, 510, 527*

Sáenz, C. A., 215, *527*

Sahagún, Fray B. de, 82, 208, 226, 386, 439, 457, 467, 469, 472, 476, *527*

Salazar, P., 86 (Fig. 4.7), *527*

Salcedo, T., 243, *504*

Salvador, F. J. S., 245, *511*

Sanders, W. T., 39, 40, 78, 80, 102, 116, 117, 135, 167, 180, 182, 204, 205, 233, 234, 334, 386, 408, 411, 438, 444, 471, *497, 527*

Santley, R. S., 39, 40, 80, 167, 180, 182, 204, 205, 221, 226, 231, 386, 408, 411, 438, 444, 471, *527, 528*

Satterthwaite, L., 124, 259, *514*

Sayre, E. V., 191, *533*

Scandizzo, J. R., 321, 322, *526*

Scandizzo, M. S. R., 321, 322, *526*

Scarborough, V. L., 137, *528*

Schele, L., 64, 66, 109, 122, 123, 124, 128, 129, 130, 133, 134, 135, 136, 137, 139, 148, 152, 209, 213, 215, 226, 227, 248, 250, 252, 255, 259, 266, 274, 279, 286, 290, 293, 303, 309, 312, 313, 321, 322, 326, 330, 332, 344, 355, 359, 361, 363, 368 (Fig. 6.81), 374, *510, 519, 528*

Schmidt, P. J., 371, 372, 377, 423, *534*

Schmidt, S. P., 48, 203, *528*

Schortman, E. M., 113, 297, 301, 302, *497, 528, 532*

Sedat, D. W., 72, 108, 119, 120, *529*

Séjourné, L., 80, 170, 176, 235 (Fig. 6.27), *528*

Serra Puche, M. C., 34, *528*

Shane III, O., 373, *505*

Sharer, R. J., 53, 54, 62, 72, 73, 108, 112, 113, 114, 115, 118, 119, 120, 131, 133, 150 (Fig. 5.6), 245, 272, 274, 275 (Fig. 6.37), 278, 285, 290, 291, 292, 293, 297, 333, 334, 345, 346, 351, 353, 357, 362, *499, 507, 509, 514, 521, 527, 528, 529*

Sheehy, J. J., 276, *529*

Sheets, P. D., 232, *529*

Shimkin, D. B., 334, *534*

Shook, E. M., 33 (Fig. 3.4), 117 (Fig. 4.17), 123, 233, 235 (Fig. 6.27), 259, *515, 529*

Siller, J. A., 194, *529*

Sisson, E. B., 374, *529*

Smith, A. L., 235 (Fig. 6.27), 305, 309, 400, 426, *524, 529, 534*

Smith, C. E., 30, *531*

Smith, H. H., 270, *512*

Smith, J. P., 399, *522*

Smith, Mary E., 410, 419, *529*

Smith, Michael E., 410, 472, *529*

Smith, R. E., 33 (Fig. 3.4), 235 (Fig. 6.27), *525, 530*

Smith, S. M., 301, *499*

Solís O. F., 455, 460, *530*

Soustelle, J., 439, *530*

Spence, M. W., 83, 185, 186, *522, 530*

Spencer, C. S., 104, 106, *530*

Spero, J., 156, 189, *515*

Spores, R., 21, 417, *509, 530*

Squier, R. J., 53, 63, 120, *507*

Stark, B. L., 23, *530*

Stern, T., 226, *530*

Stirling, M. W., 53, 62, *530*

Stocker, T. B., 182, 405, *504*, *530*
Stone, D., 232, *516*
Stross, F., 131, *510*
Stuart, D., 154, 156, 189, 245, 267, 274, 276, 278, 285, 286, *509*, *530*
Sugiyama, S., 87, 88, 89, 90, 91, 92, 234, *502*, *517*, *530*

T

Tang Lay, C., 194, *516*
Taschek, J. T., 334, 344, 353, 355, 356, 357, *500*
Tate, C., 314, 318, *530*
Taube, K. A., 80, 87, 89, 241, *530*
Tedlock, D., 145, *531*
Thompson, J. E. S., 146 (Fig. 5.2), 149 (Fig. 5.4), 150 (Fig. 5.6), 241, 310, 318, 334, 343, 354, 372, 376, *531*
Tolstoy, P., 10, 11, 30, 33, 34, 45, 53, 75, 102, 142, 501, *531*
Torquemada, J. de, 384, 439, 472, *531*
Toscano, S., 464 (Fig. 8.25), *531*
Tourtellot III, G., 305, *534*
Townsend, R. F., 439, 455, 460, *531*
Tozzer, A. M., 332, 372, 373, 421 (Fig. 7.7), 431, 466 (Fig. 8.26), *531*
Traxler, L. P., 274, *528*
Trik, A. S., 464 (Fig. 8.25), *498*
Troike, N. P., 420, *531*
Trombold, C. D., 189, *531*
Turner II, B. L., 240, 241, 242, *512*, *532*

U

Umberger, E., 439, 449, 455, 460, *532*
Urban, P. A., 112, 114, 297, 301, 302, *497*, *499*, *528*, *532*

V

Vaillant, G. C., 30, 33 (Fig. 3.4), *532*
Valdés, J. A., 123, *532*
Valdéz, Jr. F., 272, *532*
Van der Merwe, N. J., 14, *502*
van Zantwijk, R. A. M., 439, 440, 468, 473, *532*
Vaughn, K. B., 30, *531*
Vega de Zea, L., 128, 251, *517*
Vlcek, D. T., 279, *532*
Vogt, J. R., 182, *504*
von Winning, H., 157, 160, 176, *500*, *532*
Voorhies, B., 23, 472, 477, *497*, *510*, *530*, *532*

W

Weaver, M. P., *see* Porter Weaver
Webster, D., 138, 274, 289, *533*
Weeks, J. M., 301, *499*
Weigand, P. C., 93, 189, 191, 192, 195, 196, 197 (Fig. 6.11), 199, 409, 410, 411, 472, *496*, *512*, *522*, *533*
West, R. C., 6, 201, 202, *533*
Wicke, C., 460, *533*
Widmer, R. J., 163 (Map 6.1), 166, 170, *533*
Wilk, R. R., 374, *533*
Wilkerson, S. J. K., 23, 224, *533*
Wilkinson, R. G., 221, *534*
Willey, G. R., 133, 135, 240, 248, 274, 276, 291, 305, 309, 334, 344, *496*, *497*, *517*, *519*, *534*
Williamson, R. V., 285, *509*
Winfield Capitaine, F., 157, 160, *534*
Winter, M. C., 106, 219, 221, 222, *534*
Wolf, 439, *534*
Wonderley, A., 113, *534*
Wren, L. H., 371, 372, 377, 423, *534*
Wynn, J. T., 408, *507*

Z

Zeitlin, R. N., 51, 104, 106, 115, 226, *535*

SUBJECT INDEX

Numbers in italics refer to entries in the Glossary.

A

Abaj Takalik, 68, 69–70, 110–111, 133, 160
Acalán, 354, 471
Acamapichtli (ruler, Aztecs), 440
Acanceh, 139
Acosta, Jorge, 80, 364, 386, 392, 393, 400, 401
Acula River, 160
Adams, R. E. W. 134, 246, 266
Adosada, 83, 87, 88, 92, *489*
Agave, *see* Maguey
Agriculture
  incipient, 11, 12, 23, 24
  raised fields, 135, 241, 270, 307
  slash-and-burn (swidden), 234, 241, 307
  see also Bajos; Chinampa; Water management
Aguateca, 305, 307
Aguadas, 239, *489*
Ah-Bolon-Tun (ruler, Seibal), 558–559, 360
Ahau (glyph) (Lord), 133, 136
Ah Cacau (ruler, Tikal), 259–262, 483
Ah Canek (ruler, Petén), 433

Ah Mun, *see* Deities, corn god
Ahuízotl (ruler, Aztecs), 443, 455, 471, 476, 477
Ajalpan, 29, 49
Alabaster, *see Tecalli*
Alliances, 155, *see also* Marriage
Alphabet, 153, *see also* Writing systems
Altar, 40, 48, 111, 112, 141, 185, 234, 258, 265, 267, 285, 290, 320, 351, 399, 400, 401, 454
  Olmec "altar" (throne), 45, 58, 66
  paired with stelae, 108, 109, 258, 259, 290
  Q (Copán), 277, 278
Altar de Sacrificios
  Classic Period at, 302, 309–310, 343, 354
  Preclassic remains at, 73
  vase, 309
Alta Verapaz, 4, 246, 283, 286
Alta Vista, 82, 191, *see also* Chalchihuites
Altotongo, 33, *see also* Obsidian, sources
Altun Há, 137, 244, 271
Alvarado, Pedro de, 434, 445
Amanalco, 174, 175
Amapa, 199–200, 202
Amaranth, 17, 23, 29, 470

Amate, 489, see also Paper
Amate phase, 43, 44
Amatitlán (Frutal), 234, 377
  Lake, 232, 233, 272
Amatzinac Valley, 43, 45, 213
Amber, 420, 477
Ambergris Cay, 269–270, 433
Ancestor, 64, 129, 134, 253, 261, 285, 286, 289, 376, 467,
  see also Lineage
Andesite, 4, 21, 31, 203, 213
Andrew, Anthony, 379
Animal Skull (ruler, Tikal), 256
Aqueduct, *see* Water management
Architecture, 124, 125, 397
  block masonry, 138, 345, 352
  circular, 93–94
  doorways (monster), 280, 337, 343, 454
  style
    Chenes, 343
    Puuc, 345
    Río Bec, 337
    see also Ball court; Corbeled arch; Round structure;
      Talud-tablero construction
Arizona, *see* United States, southwestern
Armadillo, 50, 242
Armillas, Pedro, 187
Arroyo de Piedra, 305
Ash
  temper, 119, 133, 244
  traded, 133, 236, 244
Ashmore, W., 242, 293
Asia, 8, 12, 75, 142
Asphalt (bitumen), 229, 413
Atemajac Valley, 194, 195, 198
Atlantean figure, 369, 385, 392, 460, *489*
Atlatl, 18, 19, 21, 100, 174, 307, 349, 360, 393, 473, *489*
Aveni, Anthony, 82
Aventura, 357, 429
Avocado, 15, 16, 17, 23
Awl, 10, 21, 200, 202
Axe, 19, 63, 200, 437, 472
Axayácatl (ruler, Aztecs), 442, 451, 452, 460, 471, 476
Ayotla (subphase), 31
Azcapotzalco, 205, 438, 440, 460, 464
Aztatlán, 409, 410, *see also* Mixteca Puebla art style
Aztecs, *489*
  art, 457–461
  crafts, 446, 464–465
    economy, 470–471, 472, 473
    empire, 473–477, 479
    government, 450, 457
    history, 440, 442, 450, 457
    ideology, 465–467
    kingship, 467, *see also* rulers: Acamapichtli, Ahuízotl;
      Axayácatl; Chimalpopoca; Cuauhtémoc;
      Cuitláhuac; Huitzilíhuitl; Itzcóatl; Moctezuma
      Ilhuicamina; Moctezuma Xocoyotzin; Ténoch
      (leader), Tízoc
    law, 468–469
    role of women, 485
    social organization, 467–468
    stone sculpture
      monumental, 457, 460
      small scale, 457–458, 460–461
    Toltecs and 439, 449, 457, 473–477, 479
    warfare, 466, 479
    warrior, 467
    writing, 455, *see also* Mexica; Tenochitlán; Great
      Temple; Triple Alliance

B

Bacabs, House of the, 289, *see also* Deitiies, God N
Bac T'ul, (ruler, Petén) *see* Hauberg stela
Bajío
  phase, 57
  region, 204, 385, 388, 406, *489*
Bajos, 132, 134, 137, 239, 242, 243, 268, *489*
Baktun, *489, see* Long Count, system
Balankanché Cave, 344
Balberta, 231
Ball court
  Belize, 136, 271, 273, 326
  Central Mexico, 46, 136, 206, 215, 273, 400, 434
  Gulf Coast, 61, 224, 226, 229
  highland Maya, 332
  imitation, 286, 287
  in north Mexico, 190, 193
  in Oaxaca, 51, 107, 220
  in west Mexico, 194, 196
  lowland Maya, 238, 258, 263, 271, 273, 277, 280, 286,
    287, 295, 301, 305, 307, 309, 314, 319, 321, 344,
    346–347, 360, 361, 363, 365, 388
  marker, 118, 172, 250
  Southern periphery, 300, 301
  styles, 226–227

see also Ball game, Ball player; Chichén Itzá; Great Ball Court Stone; named sites

Ball game, 12, 239, 251, 276, 315, 316, 333, 371, 435, 467, *see also* Ball court; Ball player; *Hacha; Palma; Yoke*

Ball player
    figures, 26, 227, 288
    sculpture of, 61, 191, 305
    stone relief, 107, 118, 333, 347, 350, 371
    see also Ball court; Ball game

Balsas, 14, 24
    depression, 4, 7
    River basin, 4, 47, 48, 202, 436, 443

Bark beater, 233, 465, *see also* Paper, manufacture of

Barnard Site, 202

Barranca de los Estetes, *see* Otumba

Barranca phase, 44–45

Barra phase, 55, 56

Barthel, Thomas, 153, 160

Barton Ramie 137, 272

Basalt, 4
    columns, 62
    in building, 81, 64
    monuments, 58
    tools, 21, 29, 54

Basin of Mexico
    Classic Period, 162–176, 179–187, 203–205
    Postclassic Period, 388, 405, 406, 408, 411, 438, 444, 471, 484
    Preceramic remains, 8–10, 18–21
    Preclassic Period, 29–40, 77–93, 97
    Basin of Mexico Project, 80, 411

Basketry, 11, 12, 17, 21, 34, 180, 211, 405, 472

Bat, 6, 103, 221, 283
    House of, 288

Batres, Leopoldo, 79, 187

Bay Islands, Honduras, 302

Bean, 13, 15, 18, 21, 22, 23, 232, 241, 399, 470

Becán, 137–138, 342–343, 357

Belize, 72
    Classic period in, 268–273
    Postclassic period in, 429–430
    Preceramic remains, 11–12
    Preclassic remains, 72–73, 135–137

Bell, 200, 432, 439, *see also* Copper; Metallurgy

Benque Viejo, *see* Xunantunich

Bering (Berengia) land bridge, 7, 12

Berlin, Heinrich, 153

Berlo, Janet, 176, 177, 215, 393

Bernal, Ignacio, 80

Beyer, Herman, 153, 176

Big Game Hunting Tradition, 12

Bigotera, 489

Bilbao, *see* Cotzumalhuapa, Santa Lucía

Bird, 6, 18, 19, 24, 29, 45, 54, 393
    celestial, 64, 211
    dressed as, 48, 209, 360
    enormous, 76

Bird Jaguar (ruler, Yaxchilán), 154, 309, 315–316, 483

Bison, 7

Bitumen, *see* Asphalt

Blanco levantado, 489, *see* Pottery, decorative techniques

Blow gun, 473

Bloodletting, 50, 64, 116, 125, 126, 127, 130, 135, 136, 155, 270, 288, 307, 312, 315, 365, 435, 467, 483

Boas, Franz, 30

Bonampak
    site, 310–313
    band, 311
    murals, 307, 311–312

Bone, carved, 260, *see also* Tools

Bottle (ceramic form), 31, 34, 44, 57, 75, *see also* Storage pits, bottle-shaped

Bottle gourd (*Lagenaria siceraria*), 17, 21, 23, 49

Bow and arrow, 18, 473

Brazier, 3-pronged (stove), 45, 120, 164

Bray, Warwick, 461

Breadnut tree (ramon), 241, 337

British Honduras, *see* Belize

Bronze, 202, *see also* Metallurgy

Brush, Charles, 202

Brush, Ellen, 202

Burial, 33, 35, 71, 88–91, 96, 103, 125, 185, 200, 231, 240, 267, 278, 300, 309, 360–361, 374, 401, 432
    massacre (?), 190, 402
    retainer, 91, 116–117, 119, 129, 233, 323, 437–438
    secondary, 70, 71, 72, 208, 420
    urn, 221
    see also Cremation; Tombs

Butterfly, 89, 166, 181, 392

Butz Chan (ruler, Copán), 279

C

Caballito Blanco, 107–108

Cabrera Castro, Rubén, 88, 89

Telleriano Remensis, 141
Tro-Cortesiano, 144
Vidobonensis, 419
Wright, 144
Xólotl, 439
Códices, 1, 12, 142–144, 389, 419, 434, 439, 455
  manufacture of, 142
  see also Writing systems
Codz Poop, Kabah, 339
Coe, Michael, 53
Coe, William, 123, 292
Coggins, Clemency, 375
Colhá, 72, 270
Colima, see Capacha; West Mexico
Colonnades, 189–190, 219, 224, 265, 272, 368, 397, 422,
  432
Colson Point, 137
Comal, 39, 45, 113, 185, 241, 404, 411, 464, 490
Comalcalco, 331, 356
Comayagua, see Ulua-Comayagua drainage basin
Comitán, 23, 356
Compass, 60
Conquest, see Spanish Conquest
Copador, (pottery), 232, 283, 291, 297, 301, 302, 490
Copal, 219, 373, 430, 471
Copán
  Acropolis, 274, 290
  altars, 278, 285, 290
  Altar Q, 276, 278, 279, 285, 287
  buildings
    ball court, 276, 280, 286, 287
    Council House (Str.10L-22a), 284–285, 290
    House of the Bacabs (9N-82), 289
    House of the Bats (Str.20), 288
    Papagayo, 276, 279
    Rosalila, 279, 287
    structures, 278, 279, 280, 285, 287, 288
    Temple #11: 274, 286–287, #16: 278–279, 287,
      #18: 290, #20: 288, #22: 287
  caches and offerings, 278, 279, 280, 285, 287
  Classic period at, 273–291
  decline of, 286, 290, 291
  Hieroglyphic Stairway, 284, 285
  hiatus at, 291
  housing, 71, 274, 276, 288, 291
  outside relationships, 276, 278, 279, 283, 284,
    285–286, 291, 301
  population, 113, 231, 283

  pottery, 113, 278, 283, 291
  Preclassic period at, 20, 21, 70–71, 113, 276, 278
  rulers, 228, 278, see also Butz Chan; Cu-Ix; Eighteen
    Jog; Moon Jaguar; Smoke Jaguar; Smoke Monkey;
    Smoke Shell; U Cit-Tok Waterlily Jaguar; Yax
    K'uk Mo'; Yax Pac
  Sepulturas compound, 156, 278, 283, 288, 289
  site, 273–275, 276
    layout, 74, 291
  stelae, 159, 276, 278, 279, (Stela A) 280, 282
  warrior imagery, 279, 290, 295
  see also Classic period, Maya civilization; Southeast
    Periphery
Copper
  artifacts, 200, 202, 296, 373, 413, 433, 436, 437
    source of, 71, 195, 202
  see also Metallurgy; Tumbaga
Corbeled arch (vault), 124, 125, 129, 137, 140, 161–162,
  202, 203, 224, 225, 267, 280, 297, 305, 319, 320,
  323, 325, 335, 346, 365, 366, 426
Cord marking, 490, see also Pottery, decorative techniques
Corn, see Maize
Cortés, Hernán, 418, 433, 445
Cosmology, 483
  Maya, 238–239, 267, 274
  Mexican, 238
Costa Rica, 1, 112, 302, 303, see also Nicoya
Cotton, 17
  armor, 473
  clothing, 245
  early appearance of, 245
  production, 186–187, 236, 242, 245, 246, 269, 279, 297
Cotzumalhuapa, Santa Lucia, 279, 320, 332-333
Counting, see Numeral systems
Covarrubias, Miguel, 46
Cowgill, George, 83, 90
Coxcatlán phase, 17–18, 22
Coyolxauhqui, 445, 447, 449, 450, 490
Coyote, 6, 18, 177, 178, 393, 401, 460
Coyotlatelco
  period, 204–205, 380
  ware, 187, 216, 388, 411, 454, 490
Cozumel, 378, 426–428
Cremation, 17, 208, 267
  see also Burial; Tomb
Cross-circles, 82, 192
  see also Cosmology
Crocodile, 6, 54, 64, 278

Cuadros phase, 60
Cuanalán, 81
Cuauhtémoc (ruler, Aztecs), 445
Cuauhtitlán, 39, 180
Cuahxicalli, 455, 460, 466, *490*
Cuca, 355
Cuello, 72–73, 242, 243
Cueva Blanca, 22
Cuicatlán Cañada, 104–106
Cuicuilco, 30, 40, 45, 78, 79, 80, 97, *see also* Basin of
    Mexico, Preclassic Period
Cuitláhuac (ruler, Aztecs), 445
Cu Ix, (ruler, Copán), 278
Culbert, Patrick, 259
Culhuacán, 411, 438, 439, 442
Curiaueri, 435, *490*
Curl Nose (ruler, Tikal), 250, 251, 253, 266
Cuyamel caves, Honduras, 70

D

Dahlin, Bruce, 131, 242
Dainzú, 107, 118
Dam, *see* Water management
Danzantes, 99–101, *490*
Dart, 21, 174, 397
Decapitation, 61, 96, 284, 312, 332, 333, 371, 372, 469
Deer, 1, 18, 21, 242
Deities, 204
    Coatlícue, 447, 460
    Cocijo, 50, 221
    corn (Ah Mun), 66, 227, 241
    Creator (Maya) Itzamná, 279
    Curicaueri, 435
    Diving God, 429
    Earth Man, 419
    Ehécatl, 199, 397, 413, 444, 452, *490*, *see also*
        Quetzalcoatl
    Fire-serpent (Xiúhcoatl), 50, 87, 419, 452, 465
    God K, 280, 322, 323, 465
    God N (pauahtuns, bacabs), 239, 280, 289
    Jester God (3-pointed headband; royalty), 109, 127,
        136, 137, 139, *491*
    Great Goddess, 172
    Lords of the Underworld, 239, 276
    Moon goddess, 239, (Maya: Ix Chel), 428, 429, *491*
    Nine Lords of the Night, 259, 323
    Old Man God (Huehuéteotl/Xiutecuhtli), 174, 176,
        259, 323, 333, 447, 449, 465, *491*

Palenque Triad, 326
Sky, 109, 118, 265, 295, 360, 435
Springtime (Xipe Totec), 333, 465, 466, 472
Storm God, 172, 174, 175, 177, 179, 266 *see also* Tlaloc
Sun, 136, 215, 227, 239, 271, 280, (Maya: Kinich
    Ahau), 295, 460, *491*
War serpent, 87–88
Witz Monster, 123, 280, 286,
    See also Huitzilopochtli; Quetzalcoatl; Tezcatlipoca;
        Tlaloc; Venus
Del Monte Corporation, 292
Demarest, Arthur, 53, 131, 283, 303
Desert Tradition, 11, 12
De Young Museum, 174
Diehl, Richard, 386, 392
Dike, *see* Water management
Ditch, *see* Fortifications
Dog, 18, 54, 94, 167, 179, 208, 404, 405
Domestication of plants, 13–21, 23–24
Dos Pilas, 249, 256, 304–307, 483
Double Bird (ruler, Tikal), 253, 255
Double-line-break, *490*, *see also* Pottery, decorative
    techniques
Drains, *see* Water management
Drewitt, Bruce, 80
Drought, 133, 389, 442, 446
Drucker, Philip, 229
Drum, 311, 473
    huéhuetl, 461, *491*
Dualism, 290, 372, 384
Dumbarton, Oaks of Washington, 274
Durán, Fray Diego de, 226, 399, 454
Durango, 187, 189
Dwarf, 39, 300
Dzibilchaltún
    architecture, 138, 351
    Classic Period at, 350–352
    Postclassic Period at, 352, 399
    Preclassic Period at, 138
    Temple of the Seven Dolls, 351
Dzibilnocác, 139, 343

E

Eagle, 100, 370, 393, 449, 454
Earspool (earplug), 89, 90, 103, 126, (Pomona) 137, 208,
    244, 253, 437, 447, 457, 472
Ecab, 426

Eaton, J. D., 243
Ecatepec, 180, 471
Ecuador, 14, 55, 200, 202, *see also* Trade, maritime
Edzná, 138, 343–344
E-Group layout, 121, 140, *490*
Eight Deer "Tiger Claw" (ruler, Tututepec), 408, 418, 479
Eighteen Jog (Eighteen Rabbit, ruler Copán), 280–284, 285, 291, 294
Ekholm, Gordon, 202, 409
Ekholm, Susanna, 332
El Baúl, 111, 157
El Chayal, 52, 58, 108, 116, 133, 236, 243, 244, 270, 273, *see also* Obsidian, sources
El Jobo, 68
El Mesak, 68, 69
El Mirador, 76, 115, 131–133
El Opeño, 26
El Palmar, 337
El Portón, 118, 119, 160, 246
El Salvador, 1, 4, 12, 111–112, 160, 231–232, 283, *see also* Chalchuapa; Quelepa; Santa Leticia
El Tabasqueño, 343
El Tajín, 203, 206, 213, 223–226, 399
El Terremote, 33, 40
Equinox, 82, 192
Esperanza phase, 49
Etla Valley, 49, *see also* Oaxaca, Preclassic Period
Etzatlán, 93–94
Exchange
  media of, 50, 472
  networks of, 47, 53, 234, 243, 244, 270, 283, 285, 302, 304, 356
Excising, *see* Pottery, decorative techniques

F

Fash, Barbara, 285
Fash, William, 228, 274
Faulhaber, Johanna, 35
Feathers, 120, 234, 236, 246, 283, 357, 385, 392, 405, 442, 471, 472
Feathered Serpent, 66, 90, 213, 346, 353, 385, 392, 397, 420, 433, 434
  Columns, 390, 397
  see also Deity, Feathered-Serpent; Quetzalcoatl
Fifty-two year cycle, *see* Calendar Round
Figures, hollow ceramic, 35
  baby (doll), 35, 37, 42, 47, 58, 67

Figurines, 56, 413
  burial of, 26, 39, 94, 360–361
  in central highland Mexico, 30, 38, 39, 215, 404
  moldmade, 168, 204, 230, 361, 404
Fine Gray ware, 310, 331
Fine Orange ware, 207, 215, 310, 331, 410, 411, *490*
Fire, 96, 190, 209, 213, 374, 397, *see also* Ceremony, fire
Fire serpent, *see* Deity, Fire Serpent
Fish
  breeding of, 241, 242
  as food, 18, 20, 23, 242
  see also, Marine material
Flannery, Kent, 49
Flint, 208, 234, 285, 447
  eccentric, 234, 270, 279, 287, 320
  source of, 72, 133, 191, 239
  see also Tools
Flood, 206, 292, 293, 446, 470
Florance, Charles, 96
Florero, 221, 234, *490*
Flute, 94, 311
Folan Jr., William, 355
Folsom point, 8, 9
Formative Period, *see* Preclassic Period
Forstemann, Ernst, 152
Fortification, 133, 138, 189, 231, 289, 337, 352, 355, 357, 475–476, 477
  ditch/moat, 73, 137–138, 213, 242–243, 252
  fortress, 207, 300, 307, 337, 429
  hilltop, 78, 97, 187, 191, 237, 357
  wall, 134, 202, 213, 252, 267, 307, 364, 444
Freidel, David, 279
French Archaeological Mission, 331
Frog, 291, 234, *see also* Toad
Frutal, *see* Amatitlán
Furst, Peter, 96

G

Gamio, Manuel, 30, 187
García Cook, Angel, 80
Gateway Community, *see* Chalcatzingo, Calpulalpan; Cerros; Sakajut
German Foundation of Scientific Investigations, 206
Gheo Shih, 22
Glyphs, *see* Hieroglyphs
Gold, 437, 461, 464, 472, 473
  Cire-perdue (lost wax method of casting), 200, 461, *491*
  ornaments, 97, 195, 200, 373, 409, 420, 437
  source of, 195, 202, *see also* Metallurgy

Goldstein, Marilyn, 144
Goodman-Martínez-Thompson correlation, *see* Calendar, correlation
Governor's Palace, (Uxmal), 347–349
Graham, John, 69
Graham, Ian, 131
Greater Isthmian Tradition, 56, 71, 72
Great Temple (Tenochtitlán), 444, 445–451, 455, 460
    offerings, 446, 447, 449
Greca (step-fret), 229, 302, 416, *490*
Grijalva River, 54
Grove, David, 34, 53
Gualjoquito, Honduras, 300, 301
Guadalupe Victoria, 52, 182, *see also* Obsidian, sources
Guasave, 409, 410
Guatemala Government, 123, 233, 292
Guerrero, 14, 24, 26, 203, 443, 476
    Preclassic Period, 46–48
    resources, 47
Guggenheim Foundation, 303
Guiengola, 477
Guilá Naquitz cave, 22
Guiñope, 300
Gulf Coast region, 4, 24, 52, 53, 54, 56, 353, *see also*
    Campeche; Chontalapa; Veracruz; Tabasco

H

Haab, 145, *490*
Hacha (thin stone head), 227, 232, *491, see also* Ball game
Hallucinogens, 54, 229
Hammond, Norman, 72, 270
Harbottle, Garman, 192
Harvard University Project, 131
Hauberg stela, 130, 160
Hellmuth, Nicholas, 265
Hematite, 31, (cubes) 60, 65, 191, 195, 236, 271
    mirror, 33, 60, 63, 136, *see also* Cinnabar
Hero Twins, 73, 155, 228, 239, 371
Hers, Marie-Areti, 189
Hershey Food Corporation Technical Center, 267
Heyden, Doris, 82
Hieroglyphs, 73, 141
    decipherment, 152–154
    emblem, 153, 250, 263–265, 266, 304, 375
    historical, 154–155
    ideographic, 153
    notational signs, 177–179
    pictographs, 419

sources of, 141, 155, 305, 455
    see also Alphabet; Calendar; Códices; Writing systems
Holmul, 137, 343
Honduras, 1, 12, 24, 70–71, 112, 297–302
    Bay of, 309, 310
    see also Copán; Southeast Periphery
Honduras Government, 274
Honey, 310, 428, 430
Hosler, Dorothy, 201
Housing
    construction, 31–32, 39, 49, 68, 107, 167, 225, 272, 318, 320
    elite, 117, 131, 164–166, 240, 288, 290, 294, 295, 319, 320, 444
    modest, 164, 167, 243, 402–403
Huasteca, 56, 406, 412–413, 479
Huastepec, 442
Huauhtli, see Amaranth
Huéhueteotl, *see* Deity, Old Man God
Huéhuetl, 491, see also Drum
Huémac, 384
Huexotzingo, 441
Huijazoo, 415–416
Huistle, 193
Huitzilíhuitl (ruler, Aztecs), 440
Huitzilopochtli
    deity, 444, 446, 447, 449, 451, 457, 460, 465, *491*
    Temples of, 446, 449, 451, 472
    see also Tenochtitlán, Great Temple
Huitzo, 51
Hunac Ceel, 373, 378–379
Hunting and gathering, 11, 12, 16

I

Ihuatzio, 435
Ilancueitl (Toltec princess), 467
Ilhuitl, 67, 491
Ilmenite, 60, 65
Imix Dog (ruler, Quiriguá), 295
Incense burner, 56, 167, 180, 181, 186, 220, 344, 432, 465
    3-pronged censer, 120, 234
    see also Brazier, Copal
Incensario, 286, 397, 430, 491
Independent kingdoms, 477–479
Initial Series, *see* Long Count
Inscriptions, *see* Hieroglyphs

Instituto Hondureño de Antropología e Historia
  (IHAH), 274
Instituto Nacional de Antropología e Historia
  (Guatemala), 132, 303
Instituto Nacional de Antropología e Historia (INAH,
  Mexico), 53, 59, 89, 364
Iron ore, *see* Hematite
Irrigation, *see* Water management
Isla Cerritos, 377–378
Itzá
  economy, 378
  expulsion of, 379
  incursions
    east, 357–358
    north, 355–356
    west, 353–355
  state, 376, 378–379
Itzcóatl (ruler, Aztecs), 440, 441, 471, 476
Ix Chel, *see* Deities, Moon Goddess
Iximché, 434
Ixlú, 360
Ixtlilxóchitl, 384
Ixtapalapa, 180
Ixtapaluca phase, 31–39, 44
Ixtepete, 194
Ixtepeque, 232, 243, 283, 297, 301
Izamal, 351, 352
Izapa, 65, 68, 70, 109–110, 121
Iztapan, Santa Isabel, 8, 12

J

Jade, 103, 116, 126, 136, 185, 215, 219, 229, 233, 236,
  244, 253, 259, 271, 280, 285, 293, 297, 300, 303,
  304, 366
  see also named site, burial; named site, caches and
    offerings
Jadeite, 72, 191, 203
Jade Sky (ruler, Quiriguá), 295–296
Jaguar, 5, 6, 211, 225, 280, 454
  altar (throne), 112, 348
  cache, 287
  at Chichén Itzá, 366, 370, 372
  at Tula, 385, 393
  iconography, 48, 66, 109, 111, 126, 211
  military order, 343
  sculpted, 287, 360, 454

skins, 246, 369, 434, 477
throne, 348, 366
tribute, 472
were-jaguar, 47, 50, 109
Jaguar Paw I (ruler, Tikal) (Scroll-Ahau-Jaguar), 125
Jaguar Paw II (ruler, Tikal) (Moon Zero Bird), 129
Jaguar Paw III (ruler, Tikal) (Jaguar Paw Skull I), 129,
  250, 252
Jaguar Paw Jaguar (ruler, Calakmul), 259, 268
Jaguar Paw Skull (ruler, Tikal), 253, 259
Jaina, 360–361
Jalisco, 31, 93–94, 195, 196
Jester God, *491*, *see also* Deities
Jeweled Skull (personage), 154, 317
Jilotepeque, San Martin, 67, *see also* Obsidian, sources
Jimbal, 360
Jiménez Moreno, Wigberto, 385
Jones, Christopher, 226
Joralemon, David, 66
Juxtlahuaca cave, 48

K

Kabah, 349
Kakupacal (ruler, Chichén Itzá), 355, 356, 376
Kaminaljuyú, 108
  Classic Period, 233–237
  Mound E-III-3, 117
  population estimates, 233
  port-of-trade, 234
  Preclassic Period, 116–118
  stelae, 160
  stone carving
    sculpture, 117–118, 133
  Teotihuacan and, 234, 236
  tombs, 233–234
Kan Boar (ruler, Tikal), 253
Kan Xul (ruler, Palenque), 322
Katun, *491*, *see also* Long Count system; Short Count;
  Twin Pyramid Complex
Kelley, Charles, 189, 191
Kelley, Ellen, 191
Kelly, Isabel, 409
Kidder, Alfred, 364
Kin, *491*, *see also* Long Count system
Kingship, 66, 109, 121, 135–137, 140, 213, 247–248,
  291, 323, 335, 380, 381, 482–483, 484

Knorosov, Yuri, 153
Komchén, 73, 138
Kowalski, Jeff Karl, 356, 360
Kubler, George, 176, 369
Kuhunlich, 137
Kuk (ruler, Palenque), 330
Kukulcán
 Legend, 376
 Temple of, 365–366, 426, *491*
 see also Quetzalcoatl

L

La Amelia, 305
La Blanca, 68
Labná, 350
Lady Bone (Uxmal), 348, 376
Lady Zac-Kuk, (Palenque), 321–322
Lady Xoc (Yaxchilán), 315
La Esperanza, 300, *see also* Obsidian sources
La Florida, 279
Lagartero, 332
Laguna de los Cerros, 61
Laguna de Términos, 138, 357
Laguna Zope, 51–52, 115
La Hormiguera, 337
Lake Macanché, 432
Lake Pátzcuaro region, 435
Lake Petén-Itzá, 256, 431
Lake Xochimilco, 421
Lake Yojoa, 112, 297, 301
Lake Zacpetén, 432
La Lagunita, 120
Lamanai, 137, 270, 271–272, 433
Lambityeco, 222
La Mojarra, 157, 160
Landa, Bishop Diego de, 153, 370, 372
Langenscheidt, Adolfo, 194
Langley, James, 176, 179
Language
 Chol, 4, 152, 153
 Mayan, 4, 144, 353
 Mixe, 55, 56
 Náhua, 333, *491*
 Náhuatl, 3, 179, 353, 410, 439, 455, *491*
 Old Yucatec, 14, 152, 153
 Otomanguean, 98

 Uto-Aztecan, 3, 56
 Zoque, 55, 56, 353
La Organera, Guerrero, 263
La Quemada, 189–191, 409
Las Bocas, 29, 42, 43
Las Ventanas, 410–411
La Venta
 architecture, 54, 62
 art and iconography, 66, 482
 caches and offerings, 63, 64
 Complex A, 62–65
 see also Olmec; Río Barí; San Lorenzo Tenochtitlán
La Victoria, 68
Law
 Aztec, 468–469
 Texcocan, 442
Legend, *see* Myths
Lerma-Santiago River system, 193, 195
Lime, 180, 181, 186, 187, 234, 471
 in building, 181, 311
 in paper-making, 142
Limestone, 23, 234
Lineage, 40, 166, 248, 251, 278, 285, 289, 353, 431, 485
 Copán, 278, 290
 Culhuacán, 439, 443
 Mayapán, 425
 Oaxaca, 50, 417
 Segmentary, 433
 Tikal, 251
  Ma-Cuch, 250
 Toltec, 439, 467
Lip plug, 208, 437
Loltún Cave, 71, 139
Locona phase, 55–57
Loma Terremote, 40
Long Count system, 108, 109, 111, 148–152, 229, 482, *491*
 see also Calendar; Hieroglyphs
Lord Chac (ruler, Uxmal), 347, 348
Lord Kan II (ruler, Caracol), 256
Los Angeles County Museum, 94
Los Higos, 279
Los Mangales, 119, 160
Los Naranjos, 112, 297, 300, 301
Lost Wax casting, *491*, *see also* Gold, *cire-perdue*
Lounsbury, Floyd, 154
Lowe, Gareth, 53
Lubaantún, 273

M

Macehualtin, 468, 473, *491*
MacNeish, Richard, 15, 21
Magnetite, 50, 60, 65
Maguey (agave), 21, 22, 167, 180
  clothing, 439, 471
Maize (*teosinte*), 21, 54, 71, 229, 241, 470
  diffusion of, 14, 482
  domestication of, 13–15, 17, 18, 23–24
  representations of, 28, 280
  Zea Mays, 13, 18, 54
Malacate, 202, 208, 413, 465, *491*
Malachite, 191, 195
Maler, Teobert, 123, 152
Malinalco, 451, 452, 454–455
Malpaso Valley, 189, 191, 411
Mam, 434
Mammoth, 7, 8, 9, 10, 182
Mamom, 73, 121, 133
Manantial subphase, 34–39
Mani, 431
Manikin Scepter, 360, *491*
Manioc, 13, 54, 243, 269
Mano, see *Metate* and *mano*
Manzanal, 236
Marble, 295, 300, 302
Marco González, 270, 433
Marcus, Joyce, 49, 53, 222, 268
Marine material, 47, 50, 65, 103, 124, 125, 126, 127, 135, 136, 203, 253, 259, 260, 271, 278, 285, 405
Marketplace, 92–93, 182, 259, 267, 397, 400, 429, 444, 472
  see also Exchange networks; Trade
Marriage, 248, 250, 268, 285–286, 304, 305, 309, 312, 317, 361, 417, 475
Martinez Donjuan, Guadalupe, 46
Mask
  clay, 56
  in paintings, 210, 211
  on buildings, 73, 76, 122, 126, 136, 254, 270, 279, 295, 320, 323, 351
  relief sculpture, 139
  stone, 63, 170, 203, 323, 449
Mastache, Alba Guadalupe, 420
Matacapan, 229–231
Matanchén, 23, 26
Mat design, 295, 347, *491*
Matos Moctezuma, Eduardo, 386, 445

Maudslay, Alfred, 123, 152, 161, 313
Maya
  agriculture, 241, 242, 243
  architecture, 335, 343, 345
  concepts, 237–239, 258, 314
  daily life, 64, 65
  diet, 241–243
  housing, 239, 240
  political organization, 246–249
  population estimates, 240
  society, 246–249
  trade, 243–244
Maya civilization
  Classic Period, 231–297, 303–379
  "collapse," 238, 249, 307, 333–335, 431, 432
  Postclassic Period, 425–434, 483–484, 485
  Preclassic remains, 67–74, 108–139
Mayapán, 425–428, 430–431, 485
  destruction of, 431
  League of, 426
Mayeque, 468, *491*
Mazapa ware, 389, 404, 405, 406, 411, *491*
Mazatán, 55, 61, 68
Media of exchange
  axe money, 437
  cacao, 244
  cotton cloaks, 472
  gold dust, 472
Meighan, Clement, 193
Mendoza, Viceroy Antonio de, 457
Merchants, *see also Pochteca;* Putún
Mercury, 194, 272
Mérida (Tihoo), 351, 352
Mesoamerica, 6, 8
  boundaries, 1, 2, 12
  characteristics of, 1
  fauna and flora, 6
  geography, 4
  languages, 3, 4
Metallurgy, 201, 202, 282, 443
  introduction of, 200, 406
  see also Bronze; Copper; Gold; Silver; SMIS, Tin
Metate and *mano*, 11, 18, 31, 35, 56, 57, 72, 119, 283, 290, 291, 390, 404, 413, 465, *491*
Metepec phase, 92, 175, 177, 183, 204
Mexica, 439, 440, 444, 445, 446, 454, 475, 464, 472, 285–486, *491*, see also Aztecs; Tenochtitlán
Mezcala, 48, 202, 402

Meztitlán, 477
Miahuatlán, 104, 472
Mica, 58, 85, 116, 166
Miccaotli phase, 83, 90
Michoacán, 26, *see also* Tarascans
Migration, 4, 231, 283, 333, 353, 354
Military orders, 393, 449
Miller, Arthur, 164
Miller, Mary, 226, 279, 375
Millon, Clara, 172, 176, 177
Millon, René, 80, 82, 83, 92, 175, 185
Milpa, *see* Agriculture, slash-and-burn
Mining, 191, 193, 449, *see also* Chalchihuities culture
Mirador, 58, 60, 68
Miramar, 60
Miraflores phase, 116–118, 233
Mirror, 33, 50, 56, 57, 60, 63, 136, 282, 292, 472
    smoking, 465
Mitla, 21, 22, 416–417, *see also* Mixtecs; Zapotecs
Mixcóatl, Ce Técpatl (ruler, Chichimec), 384
Mixco Viejo (Pokomam), 434
Mixe-Zoque
    language, 56, 179
    people, 482
Mixteca region, 98, 417
Mixteca-Puebla
    art style, 410, 411, 444, 461
Mixtecs
    códices, 417, 418, 419
    crafts, 420
    independent kingdoms, 417–418, 477, 479
    social stratification, 417
    writing, 419–420
Moat, *see* Fortifications
Moctezuma Ilhuicamina (Moctezuma I; ruler, Aztecs), 442, 460, 469, 471, 476
Moctezuma Xocoyotzin (Moctezuma II; ruler, Aztecs), 418, 444, 445, 460, 476
Moho Cay, 137
Mokaya, 55–57, 61, 74, 482, *491*
Molcajete, 189, 404, 411, 465, *491*
Mollusk, *see* Shellfish
Money, *see* Media of exchange
Monte Albán
    capital, 98–104
    Classic period at, 218–223
    murals, 221
    Preclassic period at, 98–106

statehood, 102–104
stelae, 100–101
Teotihuacan and, 219, 221, 223
tombs, 415, *see also* Huijazoo
Monte Alto, 111
Monte Negro, 106–107
Moon Jaguar (ruler, Copán), 279
Morelos, 186, 406, *see also* Chalcatzingo; Cotton; Xochicalco
Morett, 93
Morley, Sylvanus, 123, 152, 364
Motagua River, 69, 72, 292, 297, 357
Moser, Christopher, 217, 218
Motul de San José, 316, 317, 359
Mountain Cow, 137
Mountain systems, 4
Mount Ilopango, 114–115, 231, 232
Moyotzingo, 42
Mundo Perdido, 128–129, 236
Muralla de León, 432
Mural paintings
    east coast, 428, 429, 430
    Guerrero, 48
    highland Mexico, 170–176, 206, 209–213
    Maya, 369, 372, 428–430
    Oaxaco, 221, 415–416
Museum of the American Indian, Heye Foundation, 296
Music, 442, 473, *see also* Bonampak, band
Musician, 39, 248, 311
Myth
    Hero Twins, 239
    Creation of the World (sun), 82

N

Nabanché phase, 73
Nacaste phase, 61
Naco, 112, 297, 303, 353, 378, 382
Nagao, Debra, 218
Náhua, *491*, *see also* Language
Náhuatl, *491*, *see also* Language
Nakbé, 71, 73, 76, 132, 140
Naranjo, 256, 265, 304–305
National Endowment for the Humanities, 303
National Geographic Society, 52, 131, 274, 303
National Science Foundation, 131
Nayarit, 24, 26, 196
Nebaj, 234

Needle, 21, 200, 202
Negative painting, *see* Pottery, decorative techniques, resist painting
Nelson, Ben, 145, 189–191
Nemontemi, 54, *491*
Nevada subphase, 31
New Mexico, *see* United States, southwestern
New World Archaeological Foundation, 131
Nezahuacoyotl (ruler, Texcoco), 442, 469
Nicaragua, 1, 12, 115
Nicholson, Henry, 461
Nicoya Peninsula, 115, 302, 410
Niederberger, Christine, 30, 46
Nim Li Punit, 273
Nine Lords of the Night, *see* Deities
Nito, 353, 378, 382, 432
Nochixtlán Valley, 98, 106
Nohmul, 270, 357, 429
Noh Petén, 433
Nonoalca, 385, 389, *491*, *see also* Toltecs
Nopal cactus, *see* Prickly pear
Notational signs, *see* Teotihuacan, "writing"
Ñuíñe, 217, 218
Numbers, 148, 149, 150, 215, 177, 333, *see also* Writing systems

O

Oaxaca
  Classic period in, 218–223
  Postclassic Period, 413–420, 476
  Preceramic remains, 21–23, 24
  Preclassic remains, 48–52
  see also Mixtecs, Zapotecs
Observatory, 68, 192, 330, 348, 365
  see also E-Group layout
Obsidian, 23, 233, 253, 300, 445, 471, 472
  blades, 9, 18, 21, 133, 182, 185, 405, 414
  eccentric, 90, 215, 271
  industries, 82, 83, 182, 183, 196, 221, 390, 405
  sources, *see* Altotongo, Cerro de las Navajas, El Chayal; Guadalupe Victoria; Guiñope; Ixtepeque; La Esperanza; Otumba; Oyameles; San Martín Jilotepeque; Zaragoza; Zinapécuaro
Ocós, 55, 57, 65, 68
Old Man God, *see* Deities
Old World, 13
Oliveros, Arturo, 26

Olla, 28, 31, 33, 39, 49, 218, *491*
Olmeca-Xicalanca, 207, 353, 385, *491*
Olmec, Gulf Coast, 52–54, 57–65
  civilization, 53, 65–67, 74–76, 482
  language, 56
  outside relationships of, 31, 33, 35, 37, 39, 42, 45–49, 67–71, 74–76, 449
  see also La Venta, San Lorenzo Tenochtitlán; Tres Zapotes
Onyx, *see Tecalli*
Oxpemul, 337
Opossum, 6
Otomís, 385, 436, 439, 477
Otumba, 21, 33, 183, 231, 378, 471, *see also* Obsidian sources
Owl, 6, 165, 210, 280, 322, 343
Oxkintok, 345
Oxtotitlán Cave, 48, 202
Oyameles, 226, 231, *see also* Obsidian sources
Oztoyahualco (Old City), 80, 81
Oztuma, 436, 475, 476

P

Pacanda, 435
Pachuca, *see* Cerro de las Navajas
Paddock, John, 217, 218
Painting, *see* Mural painting; Pottery, decorative techniques
Palace, *see* Housing, elite; named sites
Palangana phase, 61
Palenque, 255, 285–286, 321–331, 351, 399
  architecture, 321, 322, 323, 325, 331
  building
    ball court, 61
    Group of the Cross temples, 326–330
    Palace Complex, 323, 326, 330
    Temple XIV, 330
    Temple Olvidado, 322, 325
    Temple of Inscriptions, 323, 325
  dynastic history, 321–330
  see also Chaacal; Chac Zutz; Chan Bahlum; Kan Bahlum Mo' Kan Xul; Kuk; Lady Zac Kuk; Pacal
Palenque Triad, *see* Deities
Paleo-Indian, 8
Palma (palmate stone), 227, 229, 232, *491*
Palo Hueco, 23, 54
Pánuco River, 4

Papaloapan River, 53, 54
Paper
    amate, 1, 142, 233, 489
    manufacture of, 142
Paredón, 183
Parsons, Jeffrey, 80
Paso de la Amada, 68
Pasión
    region, 72, 209, 302, 303, 356
    River, 354
Pasztory, Esther, 172, 176, 215, 484
Patlachique phase, 79, 82
Patolli, 164, 399, 492
Pauahtún 492, see Deities, God N
Paxcaman, 122
Peabody Museum of Archaeology and Ethnology,
    Harvard University, 123, 274, 309
Pearl, 103, 260, 272, 420
Peccary, 6, 18
Pechal, 342
Pendergast, David, 271
Pennsylvania State University, 233
Peor es Nada, 342
Period ending rite, 252, 254, 258, 359
Petate, 33, 437, 472, 492
Peru, 8, 18, 202
Petén, 4, 6, 120, 135
    hiatus, 253–255
    lakes, 382, 431–433
    settlement of, 72
    wars, 256
Petexbatún, 249, 303, 304, 309
Peyote, 405
Piedras Negras, 318–320, 399
Pilgrimage, 373, 428, 450
Piña Chan, Román, 30, 100
Pipe, smoking, 187, 397, 409, 413, 437, 465
Pipipiapan, 61, 68
Pipil, 333, 492
Pipiltin, 467, 468, 492
Pleistocene Period, 11, 12
Plumajillo, 58
Plumbate ware, 207, 237, 401, 408, 410, 411, 413,
    492
Pochteca, 471, 472, 473, 475, 492
Pokomam, 434
Polé, see Xcaret
Pollack, Harry, 349, 364

Pomona, 137, 160
Popocatépetl, 207, 444
Population, 239–241
    estimating, 233, 240
Popul Vuh, 109, 145, 155, 288
Port-of-Trade, see Kaminaljuyú; Pochteca; Xicalango
Portraiture, 45, 58, 69, 252, 285, 312, 321
Postclassic Period
    early, 383–423
    late, 425–479
Pot belly boulder sculpture, 110–111, 112, 113, 117, 118,
    120, 231
Potrero Nuevo, 61
Pottery
    appearance of, 28
    decorative techniques
        blanco levantado, 93, 187, 406, 489
        cloisonné, 406, 409, 490
        cord-marking, 35, 55, 72, 490
        double-line-break, 34, 39, 44, 47, 48, 50, 490
        differential firing, 31, 42, 50, 57, 65, 72
        excising (carved), 31, 42, 44, 50, 56, 58, 66, 67,
            74
        iridescent painting, 55
        polychrome, 45, 97, 121, 246, 252, 302, 305, 309,
            409, 461
        resist (negative) painting, 26, 31, 68, 93, 97, 168,
            221, 409, 411, 412, 436
        rocker-stamping, 31, 49, 50, 55, 57, 72
    forms, see Bottle; Molcajete; Olla; Stirrup-spout;
        Tecomate; Trifid
    motifs,
        cleft-head, 31, 47
        figures (animal, human, scenes), 155, 309
        fire-serpent, 67
        flame-eyebrow, 31, 47, 66, (in stone), 67
        greca (step-fret), 302, 416, 490
        ílhuitl, 67
        paw-wing, 31, 42, 66, 67
        St. Andrews Cross, 26, 31, 66, 109
    origin, 55–56
    see also Ceramic sphere; Fine Gray ware; Fine Orange;
        Thin Orange, Plumbate; Usulután
Pox pottery, 29, 492
Preclassic Period, 13, 21, 51
    Summary, 74–76, 139–140
Prickly pear, 21
Priest, see Shaman

Primary Standard Sequence (PSS), 155, 156, 364, *see also* Writing system, Maya
Proskouriakoff, Tatiana, 153, 320, 344
Puebla, *see* Cholula; Puebla-Tlaxcala
Puebla-Tlaxcala
    Classic Period, 205–207
    Postclassic Period, 411–412
    Preclassic remains, 40–42
Puleston, Dennis, 241
Pulque, 167, 206
Pumpkin, 18, 21, 23
Punta Chimino, 305, 307
Purrón phase, 28, 49
Pusilhá, 255, 273, 297
Putún (Chontal Maya), 310, 331, 343, 354, 358, 372, 433, 471, *492, see also* Itzá; Trade
Puuc, *492*
    region, 345
    style, 280, 429
    see also Chenes, Río Bec
Pyrite, 37, 50, 60, 63, 95, 233, 292, 428
    mirror, 233, 278, 369

Q

Quebrada Sesemil (Copán), 70
Quartz, 195, 203
Quelepa, 112, 232
Querétaro, 23, 193
Quetzal (bird), 120, 236, 246, *see also* Feathers
Quetzalcoatl, *492*
    Ce Acatl Topiltzin, 384
    deity, 333, 393, 397, 444, 465
    legendary history of, 384–385, 420
Quetzalpapálotl Palace, 45, 174
Quiché, 145, 353, 433–434
Quicab, (ruler, Quiché), 434
Quincunz, 359, *492*
Quiriguá
    Acropolis, 293–295
    Classic Period, 292–296
    Copán and, 293, 294, 295, 296
    housing, 294, 295
    monumental, art, 292, 294–295
    Petén and, 292, 293
    rulers, *see* Cauac Sky; Imix Dog; Jade Sky; Scroll Sky
    site layout, 293
    trade, 293, 297

R

Rabbit, 18, 21
Raccoon, 6
Ramon tree, *see* Breadnut tree
Rattle, 278, 311
Rattray, Evelyn, 80, 181
Redmond, Else, 104
Relación de las Cosas de Yucatán, 153
Relación de Michoacán, 434, 437
Remojadas, 229
Resist painting, *492, see also* Pottery, decorative techniques
Reyna Robles, Rosa Maria, 203
Ricketson, Oliver, 340
Richmond Hill, 11
Ridged field, *see* Agriculture
Río Azul, 134, 253, 255, 266–267
Río Barí, 54, 482
Río Bec region, 280, 337–343, *see also* Chenes, Puuc
Río Grande de Santiago, *see* Lerma-Santiago River system
Río Pelo, 113
Rocker-stamping, *492, see also* Pottery, decorative techniques
Rodriquez Betancourt, Felipe, 203
Roof comb (crest), 224, 234, 261, 279, 287, 314, 322, 325, 337, 350, 424, *492*
Root crop, *see* Manioc
Rosario phase, 51
Round structure, 40, 194, 196, 270, 397, 401, 413, 426, 433, 437, 444, 452, 454
Rubber, 12, 226, 256
Ruler, 246–247, *see also* Kingship
Ruler X (ruler, Río Azul), 253, 267
Rust III, William, 54
Ruz Lhuillier, Alberto, 325, 364

S

Sabloff, Jeremy, 349
Sacbé, 492, see also Causeway
Sacred Round, *see* Calendar Round
Sacrifice, 192–193, 233, 256, 262, 312, 316, 323, 331, 442, 466–467
    children, 208, 233, 373, 402
Sahagún, Fray Bernardino de, 384, 386, 457, 469
Salamá Valley, 108, 118–119
Sakajut, 120, 246
Salinas de los Nueve Cerros, 286, 377

Salinas la Blanca, 68
Salinas River, 304
Salt, 50, 66, 310, 477
    production, 138, 199
    sources, 119, 180, 230, 233, 272, 350, 352, 377, 436,
        471, 479
    trade, 244, 377, 472
Salitrón Viejo, 300
Salpetén (site), 432
    Lake, 432
Sanders, William, 80, 471
San Gervasio, 270, 428
San Isidro, 60, 68
San Juan, Ambergris Cay, 270
San Juan River, 85, 180
San José Mogote, 49–51, 98–99, 157, see also Oaxaca,
    Preclassic
San Lorenzo Tenochtitlan, 31, 35, 50, 53, 57–61,
    65–67, 74
    phases, 57, 61
    monumental art, 58
    outside relationships of, 58–61
    pottery, 57–58
    site, 57
    see also La Venta; Olmec
San Martín Jilotepeque, 244, see also Obsidian, sources
San Miguel Amuco, 34, 46
Sandstone, 309
Santa Barbara, 301
Santa Leticia, 111–112
Santa Luisa, 23, 24
Santa Marta rock shelter, 23, 24
Santa Rita Corozal, 137, 270, 429–430
Santley, Robert, 80, 226
Sapote, 18, 336
Sarcophagus, 120, 323
Sayil, 349–350
Schele, Linda, 154, 226, 279
Schelhas, Paul, 152
Schmidt, Paul, 48, 203
Schroeder site, 193
Scroll Sky (ruler, Quiriguá), 295
Scorpion, 210
Scribe, 156, 248
    burial of (Copán), 280
    lineage compound (Copán), 288, 289
    Yaxchilán, 317–318
    see also Bacabs, House of the

Seibal, 72, 305, 354, 358–360, see also Dos Pilas
Séjourné, Laurette, 176
Serpent, 6, 130, 295, 300, 374
    doorways, 369, 372
    feathered, 90, 213, 353, 385, 392, 397, 433, see also
        Quetzalcoatl
    in sculpture and relief, 213, 366, 460
Serpentine, 46, 58, 62, 63, 64, 65, 203
Settlement pattern
    Belize, 268, 271, 273
    Central Mexico, 40, 97, 185, 388, 390, 444
    Kaminaljuyú, 234
    northern Yucatán (patio-quad), 374
    Oaxaca, 98–99, 107, 215, 417
    Southeast periphery, 300, 302
    Southern Maya lowlands, 121, 139, 239–240, 248,
        274–275
Shaft-and-chamber tomb, 26, 28
Shaman, 119, 278
Shamanism, 96
Sharer, Robert, 131, 278, 292
Shell
    offerings, 89, 90, 94, 103, 185, 447
    ornamental, 126, 136
    Pachychilus, 241–242
    Pinctada mazatlanico, 46, 50
    Pomacea, 241
    Spondylus, 202, 301
    Strombus gigas, 73, 428
Shellfish, 6, 23, 26, 54, 68, see also Marine material
Shield, 89, 192, 285, 366, 372, 392, 397, 457, 472, 473
Shield Jaguar, (ruler, Yaxchilán), 315
Shield Skull, (ruler, Tikal), 259
Shook, Edwin, 123, 126, 349
Short Count, 375, 492, see also Calendar; Long Count
Sierra Madre del Sur, 4
Sierra Madre Occidental, 46, 187, 472
Siller, J. A., 194
Silver, 47, 195, 200, 409, 420, 436, 437
Site layout, see Cosmology; Twin Temple Complex
Siutecutli (ruler, Las Ventanas), 410–411
Sky Xul (ruler, Quiriguá), 295
Slash-and-burn agriculture, 492, see also Agriculture
Slave, 310, 434, 472, 473, see also Mayegue
Slip, 31, 48, 57, 68, 139, 492
SMIS (South Mexican International Style), 461, 464,
    492, see also Metallurgy
Smith, Mary, 419

Smith, Michael, 410
Smithsonian Institution of Washington, 52
Smoke Jaguar (ruler, Copán), 279–280, 284
Smoke Monkey (ruler, Copán), 285
Smoke Shell (ruler, Copán), 285
Smoking Frog (ruler, Uaxactún), 251, 252
Smoking Squirrel (ruler, Naranjo), 305
Snake, *see* Serpent
Soconusco, 4, 54, 55–57, 67–69, 444, 471, 476, *492*
Solonos, 232, 234
Solstice, 82, 192, 267, 314, 330, *see also* Observatory; E-
    Group layout
Sotuta ceramic sphere, 357, 364, 378
South America, 8, 12, 18, 24, 76, 94, 200, 202, 226, 244,
    481, 482
Southeast Periphery
    Classic Period, 297–303
    Preclassic Period, 112–114
Southwest, *see* United States, southwestern
Spanish Conquest, 1, 3, 12
    of Aztecs, 444–445, 455, 486
    of Maya, 144, 145, 434
    of Tarascans, 486
Spears, 8, 473
Spearthrower, *see* Atlatl
Spence, Michael, 186
Spencer, Charles S., 104
Spinden, Herbert, 153
Spindle whorl, *see* Malacate
Squash, 13, 15, 18, 22, 23, 241, 470
Stamps, 33, 58
State, 109, 110, 111, 141, 378–379, 382
    Aztec, 473–477
    Dos Philas, 249, 305
    Monte Albán, 102–104
    Tarascan, 436
    see also Independent kingdoms
Stela (pl. stelae), 141, *492*
    hiatus (erection), 254, 305
    mutilation of, 215, 255, 259, 292
    see also Tikal; Copán; Quiriguá
Stephens, John Lloyd, 321
Stern, Theodore, 226
Sting-ray spines, *see* Marine material
Stirling, Mathew, 52, 65
Stirrup-spout vessel, 31, 34, 44, 75, 76, 96, *492*
Storage, 240
    pits, 31, 33, 49, 97, 111

rooms, 243, 288, 397, 408, 428, 473
    see also Chultuns; Water management
Storm God, *see* Deities
Stormy Sky (ruler, Tikal), 253, 259, 266
Stove, *see* Brazier (3-pronged)
Stuart, David, 267
Sugiyama, Saburo, 88, 89, 90
Sula Plain, 113, 297
Sula-Ulua-Comayagua Corridor, 112, 297, 301, 302
Sun, *see* Cosmology, Deities, Myths
Supernaturals, 47, 50, 66, 89, 156, 238, 248
Swasey phase, 72–73
Sweat house, *493, see also* Temescal
Swidden, *see* Agriculture, slash-and-burn
Sword, 466, 473

                    T

Tabasco, 246, 331, 471
Tacuba, 441
Talud-tablero construction, 224, 231, *492*
    in central Mexico, 80, 86, 92, 97, 186, 205, 213, 401,
        449
    in Maya region, 140, 236, 250, 258, 267, 303, 350, 370
    in west Mexico, 202
Tamale, 241
Tamarindito, 305
Tamaulipas, 21, 23
Tamemes, 181, 246, *493*
Tamimes, *439*, 493, *see also* Chichimecs
Tancah, 424, 428, 429
Tancol, 413
Tapir, 6
Tangaxoan II (ruler, Tzintzuntzan), 438
Tang Lay, C., 194
Tarascans, 434–438, 476
Tariácuri (leader, Chichimecs), 435
Tassel headdress, 174, 175, 177, 219, *see also* Tlaloc; War
    sacrifice imagery
Taube, Karl, 87
Tayasal (Flores), 431
Tecalli, 46, 219, 405, 420, *493*
Techinantitla, 170, 172, 174–175, 177, 204, *see also*
    Teotihuacan, murals; Teotihuacan, "writing"
Tecoluta River, 23
Tecomate, 27, 28, 31, 47, 49, 57, 113, *493*
Tectecuhtin, 467
Tecuhtli, 493

Tehuacán Valley, 21, 28, 15–18, 105, 205
Tehuantepec, 477
  Isthmus, 4, 5, 476–477
Telpochcalli, 468, 493
Temescal (sweat bath), 92 (?), 263, 319, *493*
Tenampua, 300
Tenayuca, 251, 452
Tencoa, 301
Ténoch (leader, Aztecs), 439
Tenochtitlán, 439, 440, 444, 471, 447
  archaeology, 445–451
  Great Temple of, 445–451, 455, 460
  offerings, 446, 447, 449
  see also Calixtlahuaca; Malinalco; Morelos; Tenayuca;
      Teotenango; Tlatelolco
Teopancaxco, 171, 177, *see also* Teotihuacan, murals
Teopanzolco, 451, 455
Teosinte, 13, 14, 15, 18, 23, 24, *see also* Maize
Teotenango, 215, 408, 451, 452
Teotihuacan, 79–93, 454, 457, 484
  abroad, 343, 379–380
  Amanalco, 174–175
  art, 170–172
  ball game, 172
  burials, 185
  Calle de los Muertos Complex, 84–85, 166
  caves, 81, 82
  Ciudadela, 85–87, 91–92
  founding of, 80–82
  decline/collapse, 203, 204–205
  deities and ideology, 168, 172, 176
  domain, 186
  economy, 179–183
  exchange networks, 181, 182–183
  Great Compound, 92–93, 180, 206
  housing, 162–166
    compounds, 164
    elite, 83–84, 91, 164–166
  La Ventilla, 165
  Merchants' Barrio, 183–185
  murals, 170–176
  Oaxaca Barrio, 185–186, 387
  Temple/pyramid of the Moon, 83, 204
  Temple/pyramid of Quetzalcoatl, 85, 87–91
  Temple/pyramid of the Sun, 81, 82, 83, 84, 91
  Tlajinga, 33
  Viking Group, 85, 166
  warfare, 175

  water management, 83, 92, 164, 180
  "writing" (notational signs), 176–179
Teotihuacan Corridor, 203, 205–207, *493*
Teotihuacan Mapping project, 80
Teotitlán del Camino, 479
Tepanecs, 438, 440, 452, 468, 469, *see also* Aztecs; Triple
    Alliance
Tepantitla, 172, 173, 174–176, 177, *see also* Teotihuacan,
    murals
Tepeapulco, 183, 205
Tepetate, 27, 37, 39, 90, 237, 402, *493*
Tepeu phase, 237
Tepexí el Viejo, 418
Tepexpan "man", 9–10
Tequixquiac, 10
Tetitla, 172, *see also* Teotihuacan murals
Teuchitlán tradition, 195–199, 410
Texcoco, 39, 439, 441, 442, *see also* Triple Alliance
    Lake, 9, 10, 438, 442, 471
Texcotzingo, 442, 451
Tezcatlipoca, 187, 192, 323, 384, 420, 444, 455, 465, 467,
    493
Tezcacuitlapilli, 89, 392
Tezontle, *493*
Tezoyuca, 78
Tezozomoc (ruler, Azcapotzalco), 440, 454
Thin Orange ware, 170, 181–182, 198, 221, 278, 388,
    389, *493*
Thirteen Rabbit (ruler, El Tajin), 224–225
Thompson, J. Eric, 153, 310, 364, 372
Throne, 48, 65, 112, 204, 290, 320, 348, 368, 369
Ticomán, 40
Tierras Largas, 44, 49
Tihoo, *see* Mérida
Tikal, 123–131, 249–255, 256–265, 293, 399
  architecture, 124, 254, 321
  ball courts, 263
    marker, 250–251
  burials, 126, 253, 256, 260
  caches and offerings, *see* Tikal, burials; Tikal stelae,
      26, 31
  conflict, 252–256
  Early Classic Period, 249–253
  fortification, 252
  Group 6C-XVI, 250–251, 359
  Late Classic Period, 253–265
  Mundo Perdido, 128
  North Acropolis, 125–127, 131, 254, 258

Preclassic remains, 123–131
realm, 263–265
rulers, *see* Ah Cacau; Animal Skull; Chitam; Curl Nose;
    Double Bird; Jaguar Paw I (Scroll Ahau Jaguar);
    Jaguar Paw II (Moon Zero Bird); Jaguar Paw III;
    Jaguar Paw Skull; Kan Boar; Shield Skull; Stormy
    Sky; Yax Kin; Yax Moh-Xoc
Stelae
    26: 259
    29: 128, 160, 253
    31: 253, 259
    39: 129, 252
Temples, (funerary), 260–262
Twin Pyramid Complex, 239, 258–259, 260, 263, 265
Tikal Project, 123
Tilantongo, 418
Tin, 300, 302, *see also* Metallurgy
Tingambato, 194
Tira de la Peregrinación, 457
Tízoc (ruler, Aztecs), 443, 455, 457, 460
Tlacaélel, 442, 469, 485
Tlachtli, 417, *493*
Tlacolol, *493*, *see* Agriculture, slash and burn
Tlacopan (Tacuba), 441, *see also* Triple Alliance
Tlacozotitlán, *see* Teopantecuanitlán
Tlahuizcalpantecuhtli, 393, 397, *493*, *see also* Quetzalcoatl,
Tlailotlacan, *see* Teotihuacan, Oaxaca Barrio
Tlaloc, 172, 210, 215, 220, 231, 234, 236, 279, 285, 300,
    320, 333, 346, 385, 444, 446, 465, *493*, *see also* Chac;
    Cocijo; Storm God; War sacrifice imagery
Tlalpan phase, 30
Tlamimilolpa,
    Compound, 164, 185
    phase, 90, 92, 170
Tlapacoya, 18, 19, 20, 21, 24, *see also* Basin of Mexico,
    Preclassic Period; Zohapilco
Tlatelolco, 418, 440, 452, 476, *see also* Tenochtitlán
Tlatilco, 26, 33–39
Tlatoani, 454, 467, *493*
Tlaxcala, 15, 17, 97, 477, *see also* Puebla-Tlaxcala
Tlaxcalans, 97, 445, 476, 477
Tlecuil, 96, 397, 401, *493*
Toad, 54, 117, 225, *see also* Frog; Hallucinogens
Tolteca-Chichimeca, 193, 385, 388 *493*
Toltecs
    Chichén Itzá and, 420–423
    history, 385–385, 389
    identification of, 385, 389

sphere of influence, 405–408
Teotihuacan and, 386–388
see also Chichén Itzá; Tula
Tolstoy, Paul, 30, 35, 53
Tombs, 64, 162;
    Belize, 136, 255, 270, 271, 275
    Guerrero, 202
    Gulf Coast Olmec, 64, 224
    highland Maya, 116–117, 119, 120, 232, 233–234
    lowland Maya, 126–127, 129, 137, 353, 259, 260, 261,
        266, 267
    Oaxaca, 102, 107, 221, 415–417, 418, 420 (Tomb 7)
    west Mexico, 194, 196, 411, 437
Tonalá River, 53, 54
Tonalamatl of Aubin, 457
Tonalpohualli, 45, 225, *493*, *see also* Calendar
Toniná, 255, 313, 331–332, 360
Tools, 9, 21, 26, 33, 37, 50, 201, 332, 465
    bone, 19, 21, 23, 116
    copper, 200, 202, 437
    flint, 9, 285
    obsidian, 4, 9, 10, 18, 21, 26
    stone, 8, 10, 11, 12, 16, 17, 18, 21, 23, 28
    see also Clovis; Folsom; *Metates* and *manos*; Obsidian;
        blades
Topoxte, 432
Torquemada, 384
Tourtellot, Gair, 349
Tower, 288, 330, 337, 351, 365
Trade,
    long-distance, 378, 410, 428, 472
    maritime, 76, 200, 355, 361, 378, 410
    port-of, 471
    routes, 47, 69, 120, 246, 356, 357, 471, 472
    see also Teotihuacan Corridor
Trans-Pacific contact, 12, 142, 482
Travel, 246
Travesía, 300, 302
Trepanation, 221
Tres Zapotes, 65, 109
Tribute, 104, 215, 217, 418, 430, 434, 471, 477,
    479
Trifid vessel, 28
Triple Alliance, 434, 441, 442, 475, 479, 486
Tripsacum, 13, *493*, *see also* Maize
Trombold, Charles, 189
Tropical forest, 6, 242
Tropic of Cancer, 192

Tula, 186, 189, 193, 397–399, 401
  Aztecs at, 400, 401, 409, 449, 476
  ball court, 400
  Building B (*Tlahuizcalpantecuhtli*), 368, 372, 390, 393, 397
  destruction of, 409
  economy, 403–405
  El Corral Temple, 401
  housing, 397, 402–403
  population, 390
  pottery, 386, 388, 389, 404, 406, 408
  stone carving, 390–394
  Tollan phase, 390–408, 420
  Tula Chico, 388–390
  Tula Grande, 390–399, 401–403
  see also Toltecs
Tulancingo, 183, 206
Tulum, 424, 428, 429
Tumbaga, 200, 271, 303, *see also* Metallurgy
Tumpline (chapter heading), 1, 182, 471, *493*
Tun, 278, *493*, *see also* Long Count
Turkey, 167, 179, 404, 430
Turquoise,
  mosaic, 369, 420, 437
  ornaments, 215, 472
  sources of, 191, 192
  trade, 191, 409, 472
turtle, 18, 242, 278, 311
Tututepec, 418, 475, 477, 478
Tuxtla statuette, 157
Tuxtepec, 471
Twin Pyramid Complex, *see* Tikal, Twin Pyramid Complex
Tyler, Edward, 399
Tzacualli phase, 82, 83
Tzakol phase, 234, 235, 237, 331
Tzintzuntzan, 437, 486, *see also* Tarascans
Tzolkin, 145, *493*
Tzompantli, 187, 192, 372, 389, 422, 444, 447, *493*
Tzutzuculi, 68

U

Uaxactún, 82, 121–123, 399, *see also* Cross-circles; E-Group; Tikal
Uayeb, 145, 332, 430, *493*
Ucanal, 360
U-Cit-Tok (ruler? Copán), 290

Uinal, 114, *493*, *see also* Long Count
Ulua Comayagua, *see* Sula-Ulua-Comayagua Corridor
Ulua Fine Orange, 302
Ulua Polychrome, 302
Umberger, Emily, 460
Underworld (Xibalbá), 44, 48, 64, 66, 73, 135, 155, 211, 212, 228, 238, 280, 309, 323, 330, 429, *see also* Cosmology; Hero Twins
United States, 8, 26
  southeastern, 413
  southwestern, 191, 192, 226, 409, 472
United States Agency for International Development, 303
Universidad Veracruzana, 224
University of California, 53
University Museum of the University of Pennsylvania, 123, 131, 233, 274, 278
University of Missouri, 402
University of Texas, 274
Uolantún, 129
Usulután ware, 52, 73, 112, 113, 121, 133, 283, *493*
  production of, 115
Usumacinta regional sites, 309–331
Usumacinta River basin, 54, 209
Utatlán, 433, 434
Uxmal, 267, 345–349, 255, 431, *see also* Architecture style, Puuc; Xiu

V

Vaillant, George, 30
Valley of Mexico, *see* Basin of Mexico
Valsequillo, 11
Vanderbuilt University, 303
Van Zantwijk, Rudolf, 468, 473
Vault, *see* Corbeled arch
Venus (planet), 397
  birth of, 429
  in códices, 142–144
  cycle, 150, 312, 359
  symbol, 177, 280, 288, 348–349
  warfare, 252, 256, 305
  see also Cacaxtla; Quetzalcoatl; *Tlahuizcalpantecuhtli*
Veracruz, 209, 472
  Classic Period in, 223–231
  Postclassic period in, 406, 412–413
  Preceramic remains, 23
  Preclassic remains, 54, 57–67

Vision Serpent, 123, 130, 136, 315, 326
Von Winning, 160, 176
Vulcanism, 4, 114, 115, 232, 283

W

Walls, *see* Fortification, walls
Warfare
   "Flower," 473
   purpose of, 109, 213, 252, 307
   representations of, 209, 213, 320
   see also Aztecs, "empire," Cuicatlán Cañada; Dos Pilas;
      Guiengola; Tarascans
Warriors, 1, 192, 215
   Aztec, 473
   Maya, 252, 262, 320
   Teotihuacan, 88–89, 166, 174, 175
   Toltec, 390–392, 397, 401, 406
War sacrifice imagery, 209, 252, 253, 279, 285, 305, 321
Water management, 135, 206
   aqueduct, 46, 321, 442, 444
   canal, 43, 180, 225, 242, 269
   dam, 44, 46, 196
   dike, 47, 471
   ditch/moat, 112, 137–138, 139, 206, 213, 231, 252,
      307, 342
   drain, 46, 58, 61, 73, 225, 233
   storage, 131, 180, 225, 255–256, 403
   see also Aquadas; Bajos; Chultun
Waterlily Jaguar (ruler, Copán), 278
Weapons, 473, *see also* Armor; *Atlatl;* Warriors
Weigand, Phil, 93, 189, 192, 195, 199, 440, 411
West Mexico
   Classic Period remains in, 194–202
   external relationships of, 194
   Postclassic remains in, 434–438
   Preclassic remains in, 26–29, 93–97
Wheeled figures, 229, 232, 405, 413
Whistle, 117, 311
White-rimmed black ware (differentially fired), *493, see*
      Pottery, decorative techniques
Window, 132, 359
Winter, Marcus, 219
Women,
   marriage, 256, 285, 376, 485
   remains of, 10, 35, 233, 437
   representations of, 45, 210, 268, 309, 315, 321, 322,
      457
   status of, 248, 434

Writing systems, 215
   Aztec, 455–457
   hieroglyphic, 1, 12, 297
   incipient, 119, 140
   Maya, 130
   Mixtec, 419–420
   see also Cacaxtla, Ñuíñe; Teotihuacan, "writing"

X

Xcaret, 428
Xe complex, 71, 72, 73, 120, 309
Xelhá, 361, 425
Xibalbá, *see* Underworld
Xicalango region, 471, 475, 477, *494*
Xíhuitl, 145, 225, *494*
Xipe Totec, 221, 333, 444, 465, 477, *494*
Xiu, 353, 426, 431
Xiúhcoatl, *see* Deities, Fire-serpent
Xiuhmolpilli, 46, 457, 461, *494*
Xiuhtecuhtli, *see* Deities, Old Man God
Xochicalco, 213–217, 320, 406, 449
Xochimilco, 180, 442, 471
Xochipala, 48, 216
Xolalpan
   compound, 164, 165
   phase, 170, 175, 183, 185
Xólotl, *494*
   deity, 397
   leader, 439, 452
Xpuhil, 337, 342
Xunantunich (Benque Viejo), 244, 272, 399

Y

Yácata, 401, 437, *494*
Yagul, 107–108
Yanhuitlán, 418
Yarumela, 297, 300, 301
Yaxchilán, 155, 313–318, 343
   kingship, 314–316
   outside relationships, 305, 312, 317, 318, 354
   see also Bird Jaguar (ruler); Jeweled Skull; Lady Xoc;
      Shield Jaguar (ruler)
Yaxhá, 255, 256, 265
Yax K'uk Mo' (ruler, Copán), 276, 278, 287
Yax Kin (ruler, Tikal), 261–262, 309
Yax Moh-Xoc (ruler, Tikal), 127
Yax Pac (ruler, Copán), 286–290, 483
Yaxuná, 139, 363–364

Yoke, 107, 120, 194, 227, 229, 232, 256, *494*, *see also* Ball game
Yojoa-Comayagua drainage, 297
Yopotzingo, 477
Yucatán Peninsula, 4, 12, 34, 335–344, 345
Yucuita, 106, 418

Z

Zaachila, 218
Zacatenco phase, 39–40

Zacualpa, 434
Zaculeu (Mam), 234, 434
Zapotecs, 98, 106, 219–223
    Teotihuacan and, 185–186
    see also Mixtecs; Monte Albán; Oaxaca; Preclassic,
        Classic and Postclassic Periods
Zea Mays, *see* Maize
Zinapécuaro, 33, 276, 376, 388, 405
Zohapilco, 19–21, *see also* Tlapacoya
Zutzughil, 434

		WEST MEXICO	NORTHWEST MEXICO	BASIN OF MEXICO AND TULA	TLAXCALA	PUEBLA	MORELOS	GUERRERO	OAXACA
POSTCLASSIC	1521	(STELAE) TARASCANS / AMAPA / GUASAYE / AZTATLÁN TRADITION	CASAS GRANDES	AZTEC / TENOCHTITLÁN-TLATELOLCO / TULA GRANDE (TOLLAN)	INDEPENDENT KINGDOMS / TLAXCALA / TEXCALAC	AZTEC / MIXTECA PUEBLA ART STYLE	AZTEC / LOCAL REGIONAL CENTERS	AZTEC	AZTEC / SOME NATIVE KINGDOMS / MONTE ALBÁN V MITLA / CACICAZGOS / MONTE ALBÁN IV
	1200								
	1100					CHOLULA			
	900								
CLASSIC	700	TEUCHITLÁN TRADITION	ALTA VISTA / LA QUEMADA / QUE-RETARO MINING / CANUTILLO	COYOTLA-TELCO FIRE? / METEPEC / XOLALPAN / TLAMIMI-LOLPA	TULA CHICO / CACAXTLA / TENANYECAC		XOCHICALCO / TEOTIHUACAN DOMINATION OF AMATZINAC VALLEY	LA ORGANERA / TEOTIHUACAN AND MAYA TRAITS / MEZCALA	ÑUIÑE / MONTE ALBÁN III B / MONTE ALBÁN III A
	500				TEOTIHUACAN	LATE PALO BLANCO			
	300					CHOLULA			
LATE PRECLASSIC OR PROTO-CLASSIC	100 A.D. B.C. 100	AHUA-LULCO / GAVILÁN / MORETT / AMAPA	CHUPÍCUARO GRAVES ON LERMA RIVER / SHAFT AND CHAMBER TOMBS	MICCAOTLI / TZACUALLI / PATLACHIQUE	TEZOQUIPAN	EARLY PALO BLANCO		XOCHIPALA / ?	MONTE ALBÁN II / MONTE NEGRO / MONTE ALBÁN I
	300			TICOMÁN / CUICUILCO		LATE SANTA MARIA			
MIDDLE PRECLASSIC	500	SAN BLAS			TEXOLOC	EARLY SANTA MARÍA	CANTERA / BARRANCA	OXTOTI-TLÁN CAVES / JUXTLA-HUACA CAVES	ROSARIO / GUADALUPE / SAN JOSÉ
	700			ZACATENCO					
	900			TLAPACOYA	TLATEMPA				
	1000						CHALCATZINGO	TEOPANTECUANITLÁN III / II / I	LAGUNA ZOPE
	1100			MANANTIAL / AYOTLA / TLATILCO / COAPEXCO		AJALPAN			
	1300	EL OPEÑO CAPACHA		NEVADA	TZOMPAN-TEPEC	PURRÓN	AMATE		TIERRAS LARGAS
	1500								ESPIRIDIÓN
EARLY PRECLASSIC	1700			TLAPACOYA / TLALPAN?					
	1900	MATANCHÉN							
	2100					?			
	2300			ZOHAPILCO		ABEJAS		POX	
	2500								

IXTAPALUCA (West Mexico / Basin of Mexico column)

TEHUACÁN VALLEY (Tlaxcala/Puebla column)

YUCUITA (Oaxaca column)